HANDBOOK *of* SERVICES MARKETING & MANAGEMENT

Teresa A. Swartz
Dawn Iacobucci

Editors

Sage Publications, Inc.
International Educational and Professional Publisher
Thousand Oaks ▪ London ▪ New Delhi

For information:

Sage Publications, Inc.
2455 Teller Road
Thousand Oaks, California 91320
E-mail: order@sagepub.com

Sage Publications Ltd.
6 Bonhill Street
London EC2A 4PU
United Kingdom

Sage Publications India Pvt. Ltd.
M-32 Market
Greater Kailash I
New Delhi 110 048 India

Printed in the United States of America

Library of Congress Cataloging-in-Publication Data

Main entry under title:

Handbook of services marketing and management / by Teresa A. Swartz and Dawn Iacobucci, editors.
    p. cm.
  Includes bibliographical references and index.
  ISBN 0-7619-1611-3 (cloth: acid-free paper)
  ISBN 0-7619-1612-1 (pbk.: acid-free paper)
  1. Service industries—Marketing. 2. Service industries—Management.
3. Customer services—Marketing. 4. Customer services—Management. I.
Swartz, Teresa A. II. Iacobucci, Dawn. III. Title.
HD9980.5 .H36 2000
658—dc21   99-006902

00 01 02 03 04 05 06 7 6 5 4 3 2 1

Acquiring Editor:	Harry Briggs
Editorial Assistant:	Mary Ann Vail
Production Editor:	Sanford Robinson
Production Assistant:	Karen Wiley
Designer/Typesetter:	Danielle Dillahunt
Indexer:	Will Ragsdale
Cover Designer:	Candice Harman

Contents

Preface and Acknowledgments

Our goal in developing the *Handbook of Services Marketing and Management* is to present the latest critical thinking in the foundations of services, while simultaneously challenging and expanding current services practices. Although to some this might seem like an ambitious undertaking, it really wasn't, thanks to the generous work and support of our friends and colleagues in the services arena. We were very fortunate to obtain the enthusiastic participation of our contributing authors. Without their work and the work of countless others, services would still be in their infancy. To them and all those who have embraced the study of services with the same joy and enthusiasm that we have in undertaking this project, we say "thank you."

A volume such as this could not succeed without the support and foresight of a wonderful editor and publishing company. We, and the entire services community, owe a debt of gratitude to Harry Briggs and Sage Publications. Harry's efforts through Sage have had a tremendous impact in marketing in general, and in services in particular, as it relates to spreading the "news."

Finally, we would like to acknowledge the support and encouragement of our colleagues at our respective institutions.

Terri Swartz
California Polytechnic State University, San Luis Obispo

Dawn Iacobucci
Northwestern University

Introduction

TERESA A. SWARTZ
DAWN IACOBUCCI

Services dominate most developed economies, representing significantly more than half of these countries' gross domestic product (GDP). For example, in the United States, 75% of the GDP is attributed to services. Countries such as Germany, the United Kingdom, and Japan also have a significant proportion of their GDP represented by services. Conversely, many lesser developed nations have turned to services as a way to expand and stimulate their economic growth and development without the significant cash infusion often associated with a manufacturing-based economy.

Consistent with the economic growth has been a growth in services employment. Currently, more than 75% of the workforce in the United States is employed in services jobs, and the projected job growth for the rest of the 1990s and into the 21st century is overwhelmingly dominated by services. It is no wonder that the study of services has enjoyed the same growth and development.

Over the last three decades, services marketing and management (also known as services marketing and/or services management) has blossomed into a thriving field of inquiry and academic investigation, cutting across the broader disciplines of marketing and management, including human resources and operations. Much of the initial discussion and attention in the 1970s and early 1980s centered around the questions of "if" and "how" services differed from goods. From this work came some of the classic distinctions between goods and services, most notably inseparability (simultaneous production and consumption), intangibility, perishability, and heterogeneity (in product) (Shostack 1977). This line of inquiry was followed by questions regarding the marketing and managerial implications of these differences. Over the years, these implications have been and continue to be refined as scholars and practitioners alike moved from more broad gener-

1

alizations and propositions to testable hypotheses and theories. (For more information on the evolution of services thought, please see Swartz, Bowen, and Brown 1992; Berry and Parasuraman 1993; Brown, Fisk, and Bitner 1994; and Fisk, Brown, and Bitner 1995).

Further evidence of mushrooming in the area of services is reported by Iacobucci (1998). Her electronic search under just two keywords, "services marketing," resulted in approximately 1,000 references for the time period between 1986 and 1997. This is *without* the inclusion of articles from "services management" or articles from sources not represented in the electronic databases employed.

Given the growth in services research, along with the dominance of services in the economy, the time seems ripe for a "handbook" on services marketing and management. There was no one book that could serve as a guide for researchers and practitioners, highlighting the latest in theory and turning it into the latest in practice. Such is the goal of the *Handbook of Services Marketing and Management*: to present the latest critical thinking in the foundations of services, while simultaneously challenging and expanding current services practices.

To this end, we invited contributed chapters from a stellar cast—the premier academics studying any aspect of services marketing and management. Readers familiar with the area will recognize that we were enormously successful in doing so: Our list of contributing authors is a most impressive group, an extraordinary and eclectic bunch. We expect that readers will be informed and challenged by the authors' presentations and impressed with the variety of issues tackled within these pages. The majority of our contributors are U.S. scholars, but we attempted to include some of our international colleagues. In addition, the majority of authors are also highly experienced, having contributed to the field of services marketing for extended careers. We also attempted to include some of the up-and-coming scholars who will carry on the traditions of strong research in the field. We are grateful to all of our contributing authors for their superb efforts.

The primary target markets for the *Handbook* are academics and graduate and executive students desiring a strong foundation in the critical areas of services. A key secondary market is the informed practitioner who is seeking the latest thinking in order to turn it into practice. These practitioners may be lifelong careerists in service sectors seeking new paradigms and tools with which to approach daily management needs, or their roles within their organizations or even their organizations may be changing. For example, numerous middle-level managers seek new career challenges by moving up the corporate ladder, but they may be confronting services marketing issues more frequently than they had previously. Higher-level managers increasingly find themselves overseeing new divisions as their responsibilities cumulate, and they may find their supervision of customer service departments bewildering. Top-level management in many industries not traditionally thought of as service providers are finding their customers expecting better service, and they see their competitors beginning to rise to the occasion. As a result, senior management also seeks to understand services marketing and management with greater acuity in an effort to provide greater added value to the customer, and in an attempt to develop competitive advantages. Our contributing authors were informed of these intended target audiences and asked to write accordingly. We think they have been successful in doing so, and we hope the reader will find the *Handbook* useful in providing chapters that are conceptual but not esoteric.

One unique structural feature of this *Handbook* is the inclusion of both the usual, in-depth chapters as well as shorter, more focused "mini" chapters. This variation enables the book to provide a broader coverage of an area through the inclusion of more topics. Usually, these mini-chapters were somewhat shorter simply because, to date, not much research has been done in the area, so there are fewer definitive statements to be made or fewer concepts and conjectures to offer. Sometimes the mini-chapters were shorter because, although the topic treated in the chapter might not be thought of as a mainstream services management issue, we felt that the topic was sufficiently relevant to be included, to at least highlight the basic issues for the reader's awareness. Thus, in either scenario—again, toward the goal of providing a thorough reference source, a *Handbook*—we thought that mini-chapters would prove more useful than the exclusion of topics that either were not yet as fully developed or were somewhat more tangential.

To achieve the goal of breadth of coverage, the *Handbook* is organized into six major sections. Each section focuses on a broad component of services marketing and management, with specific topics addressed by chapters within the section. The reader may want to focus on a particular section of interest or seek out topics by chapter title. Taken in total, the sections and their chapters provide extensive coverage of services marketing and management. Now for an overview of the handbook.

The *Handbook* begins with two mini-chapters that we label "Service Reflections," provided by a few of the early pioneers of the field, Pierre Eiglier with the late Eric Langeard, and Christian Grönroos. These reflections provide differing perspectives on the field, reminding us all of early issues in the study of services and some views on where the field is headed. Their views seemed a fitting beginning and appear immediately following this introduction.

The first section, "Services: The Setting," examines the environment in which service occurs, including the well-known paradigmatic orientations of Grove, Fisk, and John in "Services as Theater: Guidelines and Implications" and Bitner's "The Servicescape." Aspects of the performance that occurs within that environment are captured in Grayson and Shulman's "Impression Management in Services Marketing" and in Wagner's "A Model of Aesthetic Value in the Servicescape." Services settings increasingly involve technology, which in turn requires more initiative on the part of the customer (i.e., self-service). These themes are explored in the chapters by Barnes, Dunne, and Glynn and by Dabholkar on the confluence of self-service and technology; Risch Rodie and Kleine's explicit discussion of customer participation; and Bateson's chapter on perceived control.

"Services: Demand Management," the second section, examines issues related to the perishability of services. Shugan and Radas describe how services are seasonal in demand. When customer demand exceeds a provider's supply, the analogy to inventories in services is the experience of customers waiting for service, as considered in the chapter by Taylor and Fullerton. Kraus explores a classic marketing tool, pricing, that has been used as a means of managing demand, signaling certain positions regarding issues such as quality.

Next, "Services: Excellence and Profitability" addresses issues that have provided a popular arena for academic study—the critical issues of service quality and customer satisfaction. The chapter by Hallowell and Schlesinger summarizes a good deal of the Harvard research on the service profit chain, providing the reader with a critical road map for service success. Zahorik, Rust, and Keiningham require the sensible criterion that a corporate quality initiative pay for itself (i.e., providing a return on quality). Oliver offers a nice overview of the extensive work on customer satisfaction, and Anderson and Fornell demonstrate the importance of their customer satisfaction index in predicting economic and financial performance figures.

Services are said to be heterogeneous: They do not come off an assembly line in a standardized manner, but rather are created by human service providers and are consumed by human customers. The human interactions can be somewhat less than optimal. Hence, we asked another group of researchers to write on the area of "Service Recovery," the subject of the fourth section. Tax and Brown offer suggestions from research regarding service recovery, Stephens explores the phenomenon of customer complaining, and Ostrom and Hart present the increasingly popular choice among high-quality service providers of offering a service guarantee.

One of the fast-growing areas in research and practice in services is "Service Relationships," the next section. Patterson and Ward offer an extensive overview of "Relationship Marketing and Management" issues. Wetzels, de Ruyter, and Lemmink examine these concepts in a popular setting, that of "Business-to-Business Services." Johnson and Grayson look at models of the interpersonal aspect of trust in service relationships, and Gutek offers a perspective on what she calls pseudo-relationships in services. Dubé and Shoemaker examine "Brand Switching and Loyalty for Services," Deighton discusses loyalty and frequency programs, and Glazer explores the emerging arena of smart services.

The last section of the *Handbook* addresses "Services: The Firm." This section takes the broadest look at services, under the umbrella of "services management," by Lovelock. This section also considers the roles of human resource management (Bowen, Schneider, and Kim), service operations management (Chase and Haynes), and franchising (Cross and Walker).

We close with a few observations on services marketing and management. Specifically, we have tried to step back and identify future directions as well as challenges for practitioners and researchers alike.

Given that our goal was to create a useful reference in this *Handbook*, we realize that different sections will appeal to different readers. We attempted to provide a useful ordering of chapters, but this book is not intended to be a linear, textlike introduction. For the novice, we would suggest beginning with the first chapter, "Services as Theater," because it provides an excellent overview on services marketing and management.

Another framework for examining services that researchers and practitioners have found useful is the "7 Ps" (Product, Price, Place of Distribution, Promotion, People, Process, and Physical Evidence), also referred to as the expanding marketing mix (given that classic goods marketing was characterized by the tools of the 4 Ps; Booms and Bitner 1981). Readers to whom a 7 Ps framework is intuitively appealing (e.g., because it works off the expanded marketing mix and acknowledges the interrelationship among the components) should initially read chapters 1, 2, 7, 11, 27, and 28 for more of a foundation before exploring the rest of the handbook.

REFERENCES

Berry, Leonard L. and A. Parasuraman (1993), "Building a New Academic Field: The Case of Services Marketing," *Journal of Retailing*, 69(1), 13-60.

Booms, Bernard and Mary Jo Bitner (1981), "Marketing Strategies and Organizational Structures for Service Firms," in *Marketing of Services,* James H. Donnelly and William R. George, eds. Chicago: American Marketing Association, 47-51.

Brown, Stephen W., Raymond Fisk, and Mary Jo Bitner (1994), "The Development and Emergence of Services Marketing Thought," *International Journal of Service Industry Management*, 5(1), 21-48.

Fisk, Raymond P., Stephen W. Brown, and Mary Jo Bitner (1995), "Services Management Literature Overview: A Rationale for Interdisciplinary Study," in *Understanding Services Management*, William J. Glynn and James G. Barnes, eds. Chichester, UK: Wiley, 1-32.

Iacobucci, Dawn (1998), "Services: What Do We Know and Where Shall We Go? A View From Marketing," in *Advances in Services Marketing and Management*, Vol. 7, Teresa A. Swartz, David E. Bowen, and Stephen W. Brown, eds. Greenwich, CT: JAI, 1-96.

Shostack, G. Lynn (1977), "Breaking Free From Product Marketing," *Journal of Marketing*, 41 (April), 73-80.

Swartz, Teresa A., David E. Bowen, and Stephen W. Brown (1992), "Fifteen Years After Breaking Free: Services Then, Now and Beyond," in *Advances in Services Marketing and Management*, Vol. 1, Teresa A. Swartz, David E. Bowen, and Stephen W. Brown, eds. Greenwich, CT: JAI, 1-21.

Service Reflections:
Services in the Village

PIERRE EIGLIER
ERIC LANGEARD

The new century is tomorrow, and it certainly will be the century of services. Two sets of elements will challenge survival and efficiency of service companies: market challenges and management challenges. It is interesting to note that these two sets of elements are independent, their conjunction in time is due to chance, and this coincidence reinforces the strength of each one.

MARKET CHALLENGES

The world is a village. This means economic interdependence of emerging markets and developed economies. It benefits from instant information on any event, sees the same TV and films, shares similar experiences, and develops many different points of view, like a village. This village consumes more and more services.

The globalization of the economy is the consequence of a political will. For several decades, the General Agreement on Tariffs and Trade (GATT) has been the framework for a gradual decrease of tariffs on manufacturing goods. A new international organization, the World Trade Organization, has been set up, after 8 years of bargaining of the Uruguay Round of the GATT. Its goal is mainly the liberalization of services all over the world. The growth of services without frontiers is an important part of the so-called global economy. As a result, agreements on deregulation have taken place industry by industry (e.g., financial services and telecommunications).

The market scope of service firms is exploding. For example, a French company won a water distribution contract in Atlanta but lost a French city contract against a foreign competitor. It is more and more difficult to be an industry leader for firms that only provide domestic services in their home country. Atlanta is next door to France; the world is a village. Is it any wonder the global development of service networks is already big business? In 1996, according to statistics from the Organization for Economic Cooperation and Development (OECD), services accounted for 60% of total direct investments abroad. Clearly, services, far above manufacturing, are the most dynamic component of the global economy.

A regional event shows the sensitivity of European service managers to the various facets of a global economy. Specifically, 11 countries of Europe have made the decision to share the same currency, the Euro. At the same time, there is the new experience of a domestic market the size of a continent, along with the challenge of a multicultural environment that has the flavor of a global service economy. European service companies urgently need to develop an ability to deal with different tax, labor, and environmental regulations. Truly, it is a good training ground before investing in the world village.

Villages are known for their quiet life. The world-village is shaken by crises, some of which involve key service industries. Public opinion questions the soundness of their management and their sensitivity to social, political, and ethical issues. For example, the financial services industry is strongly associated with the negative consequences of the Asian crisis in 1997 and the Russian crisis in 1998. This industry has been heavily regulated in most countries from the 1930s to the early 1980s. Since then, financial markets have exploded, with less than 5% of worldwide transactions related to exchange of goods and services, rather than financial instruments. As a result, a growing number of countries have challenged the freedom of action given recently to financial institutions. Or consider retailing, where large stores and shopping malls are criticized for their ugliness. Laws have been passed in several countries against openings of such new enterprises. The entertainment industry is a last example of services under attack for their lack of sensitivity to the diversity of cultural identities. Complaints about banking, retail, and entertainment are a sign of the new power of services in a worldwide economy, yet most services managers have no idea of the growing power of their industry. Their geopolitical and macromarketing skills are limited; they are spending their time and energy increasing the size and the market power of their service firms.

Concentration, mergers, and alliances are buzzwords of the late 1990s. For the first time, service mergers are surpassing manufacturing mergers in number and size of deals. No service industry is left aside. WPP, a London-based communication group, has had two strategic goals since its creation: to be a major actor in the worldwide communication market and to integrate all communication skills—not just advertising—to fill the needs of clients. Many of WPP's competitors have followed the same track of external growth. An American, Sandy Weil, is a hero of mergers. After acquiring a credit company and an insurance company, he went on with a broker, another insurance company (Travelers), and a well-known investment bank (Salomon); finally, he made a deal with John Reed and merged with Citicorp to become a global financial leader. Many North American and European banks have done the same, with the explicit goal of increasing market share, brand visibility, and economies of scale. Two large Swiss banks have merged. Together, they want to be the world leader of private banking.

Retail firms are easing their entry into emerging markets by acquiring domestic networks. Other retailers expand in developed countries by taking over existing local leaders. Kingfisher, a British home equipment retailer, has bought Darty and But, two large French retail networks for home equipment and furniture. The buying spree is not over. Hotel groups have slowed down their construction of new hotels and are investing through acquisitions, buying hotels one by one or taking over a well-known brand and network.

Among knowledge-based companies, the trend is the same. Large accounting firms want to combine their skills, and engineering firms take participants or make alliances to get access to new sites. The airline industry is suspected by several experts—among them the Antitrust Commission in the United States and the Brussels Commission in Europe—of attempting to thwart competition.

The concentration trend is very strong in services. Behind this phenomenon are two strategic scenarios. A leadership scenario attempts the addition of complementary skills and network sites. This strategy recognizes the impact of market share on a worldwide basis for most services. Until recently, market share was defined primarily on a domestic basis in Western Europe and on a regional-state basis in North America. Now the question is a company's share of the market on the American and European continents or the main cities of the world.

Texaco had a reasonable gas station market share in the United Kingdom and the Netherlands; however, it did not exist as a network in other European countries. Hence, it decided to sell to Shell. Shell was eager to buy because external growth was the only opportunity to become number one again in Europe. This ranking had been lost with the BP-Mobil gas stations merger.

The second scenario is defensive. There is excess capacity in most service industries because they are at a maturity stage (fast food, airlines, hotels, retail) or are an easy target for the developers of virtual networks (banking, insurance, travel agencies). We have known for a long time the strategic weakness of the medium-sized service company, squeezed between the very small and the very big. In the new international environment, it makes sense to merge medium-sized service companies and to benefit from economies of scale.

More than ever, competition will involve global leaders, large specialists, and niche players. Concentration is a popular game because many service managers want to change category. Globalization and new technologies are quickly changing the rules of competition, and at the moment, internal growth is perceived as too slow a strategy.

MANAGEMENT CHALLENGES

Despite appearances, we, as inhabitants of the village, have just entered the era of services, and in terms of marketing and management, we do not yet possess the necessary frameworks or the mentalities to face most of the business problems of services. An indicator is the fact that most management disciplines—except for marketing, operations, and organizational behavior—deliberately fail to recognize service businesses as being specific. Where are the scholars of strategy, finance, control, and other disciplines who think and work on businesses of the service sector as being different from industries producing tangible products?

Among the numerous reasons for this phenomenon is the fact that economic reality moves much faster than psychology and mentalities. We live in economies where more than 70% of annual wealth is produced by services, but the vast majority of people still think that only "hard stuff" industries are wealth producers. Hence, the only important objects of study remain tangible goods; in these conditions, why develop management models specific to services?

Services marketing and management challenges lie precisely there, and they present several facets. The first one is how to escape from the traditional, dominant model of management thought, which is the manufacturing-based model. The Harvard school, represented by James L. Heskett and Leonard A. Schlesinger (Schlesinger and Heskett 1991), is the pioneer of this idea. Schlesinger and Heskett demonstrate the inefficiency and even the failure of the manufacturing model applied to service businesses, and they identify, through examples, some key orientations of a new service management model. This kind of model, based on the very nature of services and its specificity, has yet to be developed, tested, and widely accepted, with all its implications and ramifications in the diverse disciplines of management. Development of such a model probably is the most difficult challenge facing services, because it deals with the framework of management thinking, reflexes, and decision making. This framework was set up at the turn of the century by people like Fayolle and Ford, among the most prominent names, who themselves were heirs of more than a century of industrial revolution. The new service model will integrate both the traditional thinking under certainty, impregnated by engineers and mechanization, and the world of thinking under uncertainty, dominated by human relations problems and impregnated by psychologists.

The second challenge, closely related to the first, is the management of contact staff, and more generally human resources (HR) management in service businesses. Here also, the traditional model fails: It is not possible anymore to recruit, train, and promote employees and organize work along the lines used in manufacturing. The pioneering work of Benjamin Schneider and David Bowen (Schneider and Bowen 1995) is paramount. They draw conclusions and original recommendations from the analysis of psychology and behavior of both customer and staff (contact staff as well as back office staff) in service situations. Also challenging is the fact that employees should look at themselves in an innovative way. Traditional labor relations techniques fail, and unions should reconsider their organization and their normal means of pressure. Contrary to the manufacturing world, a strike in a service business is more harmful for customers than for management.

The third challenge is closely related to the previous one: the impact of new technologies on the way service businesses will handle their relations with their customers. In the village, every shop owner knows each of his or her customers, their names, their social situations, their stories. In the near future, miniaturization and the power of electronic devices will allow service providers to record and recognize personally, on the spot, each customer who is in contact with the service company; this will drastically transform contact staff as well as customers' expectations and behavior in the service encounters, toward a greater personalization of these kind of relations. In fact, technically, this is already possible, but service companies lag behind technology and the conception and setup of new information systems.

A fourth challenge is the emerging policy of numerous manufacturing companies to mix products and services. More and more industrial companies sell services associated with their products, not only the traditional after-sales services but also much more elaborate services, from financial to training and distance maintenance. The reason for this is clear: Opportunities for profit are higher for services than for products. The challenge also is clear: Will these companies be able to balance a true service culture with their present manufacturing culture?

Our village is small, but contrary to the normality of villages, it is not particularly quiet, and the road ahead will be difficult. Turbulence will arise from disequilibrium of financial markets, from interdependence of economies, and from unsolved problems and drawbacks in service management.

REFERENCES

Schlesinger, Leonard A. and James L. Heskett (1992), "De-Industrializing the Service Sector: A New Model for Service Firms," in *Advances in Services Marketing and Management*, Vol. 1, Teresa A. Swartz, David E. Bowen, and Stephen W. Brown, eds. Greenwich, CT: JAI, 159-176.

Schneider, Benjamin and David E. Bowen (1995), *Winning the Service Game*. Boston: Harvard Business School Press.

Service Reflections:
Service Marketing Comes of Age

CHRISTIAN GRÖNROOS

In the service marketing literature, services are frequently described by characteristics such as intangibility, heterogeneity, inseparability of production from consumption, and the impossibility of keeping services in stock. In services, customers participate in the production process and therefore also influence the flow and outcome of the process. It is also often said that customers have difficulty evaluating a service before buying it and that such is not the case for physical goods. Many of these characteristics, however, may not be particularly discriminating between physical goods and services. In the mind of a customer, a car can be as intangible as a restaurant service, and it easily may be as difficult to evaluate a pound of tomatoes before eating them as it is to evaluate the service of a bank. Nevertheless, the more or less standardized list of service characteristics is still presented in most publications on services.

Critics of service marketing research have frequently argued that services are not that different from goods and that identified "service" characteristics are not in fact unique to services. The most conservative conclusion from this argument has been that the marketing of goods and services is not that different. Following the development of modular production and mass customization of goods and of customer influence on the design and manufacturing of physical products in various stages of the production process, the criticism of the uniqueness of services has grown louder. Indeed, to an increasing extent, customers are participating in the production of physical goods, and they influence the flow of at least parts of this process. As a result, for example, the heterogeneity of goods increases.

GOODS AND SERVICES
ARE BECOMING SIMILAR

All of this leads to the conclusion that services and physical goods are becoming more and more similar in nature, and it seems as if this observation cannot be denied. What is important, though, is that the correct and, for the sake of marketing, the most productive conclusions are drawn from this observation. Service marketing research has defended its existence by arguing that service marketing is different and has earned a position as a separate subfield of marketing because of the unique characteristics of services. If the key differences between services and goods are vanishing, what is left? One answer to this question could be that service marketing has played its role in the development of marketing and will perhaps leave some concepts that can be assimilated into mainstream marketing, with its foundation in consumer goods. Then, the special chapters on service marketing in standard textbooks of marketing can finally be omitted, and some of the concepts, such as perceived quality and internal marketing, can be included in the rest of the text.

It is also possible to draw a totally different conclusion. As characteristics of services and physical goods merge, the fundamental basis for mainstream marketing may be changing. It is not a matter of services returning to the mainstream of goods-based marketing; rather, it is physical goods that are becoming "service-fied." Following that argument, the very foundation of mainstream marketing is changing from a goods focus toward a service focus. Two decades ago, the cochair of the very first special conference on the marketing of services in North America, William R. George, said in a plenary speech that he waited for the day when standard marketing textbooks would be based on a service perspective, with a chapter about the special characteristics of goods marketing toward the end of the book.

This day is not far away; however, there may not be a special chapter on physical goods, because from a marketing point of view, the differences between goods and services are disappearing and the service perspective is becoming dominant. Hence, services are becoming the focus of mainstream marketing.

CHARACTERISTICS OF
THE SERVICE PERSPECTIVE

As previously suggested, the normally offered list of service characteristics is misleading because it focuses on aspects that to varying degrees have always been of relevance for physical goods as well. Thus, critics of service marketing get the impression that services do not offer anything fundamentally new to mainstream marketing. This, however, is not the case. The focus on services introduces a new perspective that changes the fundamentals of marketing altogether.

The most basic characteristic of services is their process nature. Services are produced in a process wherein consumers interact with the production resources of the service firm. Some parts of the service may be prepared in a back office before the customer enters the process, but from the service quality perception, the crucial part of the service process takes place in interaction with customers and in their presence. What the customer consumes in a service context is, therefore, fundamentally different from what traditionally has been the focus of consumption in the context of physical goods.

The consumption of services can be characterized as *process consumption* (Grönroos 1998), where the consumer perceives the production process as part of the service consumption, not just the outcome of a production process as in traditional marketing of physical goods. Heterogeneity and customer participation in service production follow from these basic notions of services as processes and the consumption of services as process consumption.

In traditional mainstream marketing, the role of marketing is to bridge the gap between production and consumption by making distribution, marketing communication, pricing, and product decisions. Marketing mix management is a logical perspective, and the marketing department becomes a logical organizational structure for effectively and efficiently bridging this gap. In a service context, however, *no such gap exists*; hence, the very basis for mainstream marketing is gone. Marketing becomes part of the service production process, because in a service context that is where the gap exists between producer and consumer. Of course, elements of traditional gap-bridging activities such as marketing communication and pricing are still needed; however, instead of being in the center of the marketing activities as in traditional goods-based marketing, these activities become supportive. The heart of marketing of services is how the service production process and service consumption process match each other, so that consumers perceive good service quality and are persuaded to continue patronizing the same service firm. This is what has been called *interactive marketing* (Grönroos 1998), where *part-time marketers* (Gummesson 1991) are instrumental, to use concepts originally developed in the Nordic School of services research tradition. This is also why the *internal marketing* concept emerged in service marketing research and not in other fields of marketing.

SERVICE MARKETING BECOMES THE MAINSTREAM

In the traditional goods context, the consumption of physical goods can be described as *outcome consumption*, where only the outcome of a production process is consumed and influences the quality perception of customers. As the very foundation for the production and consumption of physical goods is changing, the basis for marketing also is changing. With mass customization and modular production, the customer is brought into the production process. Some parts of goods production processes (in most cases, major parts) still occur in a factory, similar to a back office; however, the part of the process intended to influence the customer's purchasing and consumption behavior is recreated so that the customer is brought into the production process. In this new production logic, the process becomes part of the offering to the market. In other words, the physical goods are *servicefied*, or turned into service offerings: The goods components take the same role as, for example, the beef in a restaurant service or the seat in an airline service.

When this logic is introduced into a business that traditionally has been defined as a goods-producing business and where traditional goods-oriented marketing logic has been useful, the basis for doing business and for marketing changes. The consumption becomes *process consumption*, and the central area of marketing is no longer bridging the gap between the outcome of a production process and consumption but instead balancing the production and consumption processes. Interactive marketing takes a dominant position.

In conclusion, service marketing truly is coming of age. It is becoming a marketing perspective valuable not only for service firms but also for any situation where consumption can be characterized as process consumption. The importance of service marketing already has been extended far beyond what traditionally is called the service sector or service industries. The development of *relationship marketing* has also emphasized the role of services for manufacturers and service firms alike. Every business is a service business (Webster 1994), and the competitive environment in more and more situations can be characterized as *service competition*, again regardless of whether the core of the offering to the market is services or physical goods (Grönroos 1997). The marketing of services is becoming mainstream marketing.

REFERENCES

Grönroos, Christian (1997), "Value-Driven Relational Marketing: From Products to Resources and Competencies," *Journal of Marketing Management, 13*(5), 407-19.

Grönroos, Christian (1998), "Marketing Services: The Case of a Missing Product," *Journal of Business & Industrial Marketing, 13*(4/5), 322-38.

Gummesson, Evert (1991), "Marketing Revisited: The Crucial Role of the Part-Time Marketers," *European Journal of Marketing, 25*(2), 60-67.

Webster, Frederick E., Jr. (1994), "Executing the New Marketing Concept," *Marketing Management, 3*(1), 9-18.

SECTION 1

Services: The Setting

PART 1

Environment/Performance

1

Services as Theater

Guidelines and Implications

STEPHEN J. GROVE
RAYMOND P. FISK
JOBY JOHN

Yogi Berra, philosopher and baseball great, once said "you can observe a lot just by watching." When customers enter a service organization, they are likely to *observe* a number of things: service workers scurrying about creating the service product, the ambience of the service establishment, the other customers sharing the service setting, and the acumen with which the service is enacted. In Yogi Berra's terms, by simply *watching*, service customers observe a theatrical performance. The dimensions of actors, audience, setting, and performance create the customer's service experience, just as at a theater play.

Services *are* theater. Services provided by restaurants, banks, airlines, hospitals, hotels, and many other service providers are easily characterized as theater. Whether the customer realizes it or not is immaterial; all the components of a stage production are present in most service experiences. What is more important is that service organizations recognize the theatrical nature of their service product. This chapter develops the proposition that service firms may benefit by considering theatrical aspects of their offering.

Much of the reasoning behind the observation that services are theater rests on the fact that the service, which a service customer receives, is essentially a *performance*. It cannot be held or stored—only experienced. Like its theatrical counterpart, both the manner and the execution of a service performance affect the customer's experience. In other words, *how* the service is performed (e.g., the courtesy and care that are displayed) is just as important as *what* is performed (e.g., the specific tasks that are completed). As with a stage production, a service exists only during the time of its enactment—a circumstance that makes ensuring its excellence an arduous task. Every service manager struggles with the difficulty of providing a service product of consistently high quality. For example, take a bank manager's situation. The service performed by a bank varies from one teller to the next, across customers, and for the same teller-customer combination over time. Planning, organizing, and delivering a service product that minimizes the variability of service quality is critical for customer satisfaction. Hence, any tool that helps a bank manager design and implement a consistently satisfying service performance is likely to be welcome. The consideration of a bank's offering as theater may provide insights to help accomplish that end.

This chapter presents the metaphor of services as theater as a framework for describing and analyzing the service experience, which is synthesized from a series of articles (Fisk and Grove 1996; Grove and Fisk 1983, 1989, 1991, 1992, 1995; Grove, Fisk, and Bitner 1992; Grove, Fisk, and Dorsch 1998). The theater framework combines the elements of actors (service workers), setting (the venue for the service experience), audience (service customers), and performance (the service process) to create the customer's experience. Any service experience can be described in theatrical terms, and the principles that apply to a stage production may be used to enhance the effectiveness of services marketing. First, we establish the rationale for the theater metaphor as a communication device for business purposes. Next, we examine the service theater metaphor by attending to its applicability across each of the elements of the services marketing mix. We also discuss several ways the theater metaphor may be adapted to accommodate the unique character of various services. Finally, we suggest some managerial guidelines derived from the services theater metaphor that may be helpful to service organizations in their effort to create a favorable impression with their customers.

THE UTILITY OF METAPHOR AND
ITS PLACE IN THE BUSINESS LITERATURE

Poets, philosophers, and sociolinguists have long recognized the power of the metaphor as a descriptive and analytical tool. In its essence, the metaphor is a way of "seeing something from the viewpoint of something else" (Brown 1977, p. 77)—a means of comprehending the unknown. It accomplishes this by invoking the transfer of qualities from a familiar phenomenon to one that is less understood (Leary 1990; Ortony 1975). A good metaphor has the power to create vivid mental images by presenting a symbolically rich message. These mental images elicit from the receiver details or "chunks" of information that are lacking in a literal translation of the message. As such, a metaphor often succeeds at capturing the unique, experiential, and/or procedural characteristics of phenomena that resist comprehension through logic or words alone. These features establish the metaphor as an important device in making sense of the world about us. In fact, some have argued that metaphors can serve as the basis for entire schools of thought (Arndt 1985; Morgan 1980) and that metaphors are capable of generating hypotheses and analysis regarding the implicit comparisons they engender (Zikmund 1982).

The metaphor has a rich tradition across the various business disciplines. Indeed, the metaphor's presence in the business literature is so pervasive that metaphors are often overlooked (Clancy 1989; Stern 1988). For example, metaphors can be seen in the application of the concept of "war" to competition among competing businesses (e.g., the burger wars, cola wars, or fare wars), the categorization of stock market investors as bulls or bears, and the depiction of a business organization as a machine. In each case, the metaphor moves beyond the literal to capture "in an instantaneous, almost unconscious, flash of insight" (Nisbet 1969, p. 4) the essence of a complex or remote phenomenon.

The metaphor has earned a lofty place in marketing as a pedagogical tool. Few areas of inquiry rely on the metaphor to the degree that marketing does (Goodwin, Grove, and Fisk 1996; Zaltman, LeMasters, and Heffring 1982; Zikmund 1982). Consider the enhanced understanding offered through the metaphors of "the wheel of retailing," the "product life cycle," the "channel of distribution," or the "marketing mix." In each of these examples, the use of a metaphor conjures up a relationship that prompts the audience to infer new meaning regarding the unknown phenomenon. Metaphors such as these encourage the exploration of an implied relationship between two phenomena and are sometimes referred to as *theoretical* metaphors. If considered in conjunction with *literary* metaphors—those metaphors whose "sole task is to vividly, colorfully, and dramatically convey" (Hunt and Menon 1995, p. 82), such as "scrambled merchandising" or "full and empty nests"—it is easy to see that the marketing literature is indeed metaphor rich. In summary, metaphors help scholars, practitioners, and the general public communicate and comprehend marketing principles and concepts in a lively, interesting manner.

THEATER AS A METAPHOR FOR SERVICES

Theater is a theoretical metaphor that generates many analytical observations regarding the nature of services marketing. Framing services as theater is a logical extension of the metaphor that human behavior is drama—a school of thought found in the sociology literature called "dramaturgy" (cf. Brissett and Edgley 1975; Burke 1968; Goffman 1959; Perinbanayagam 1974; Stone 1962). Because services involve interaction between the service organization and the customer and, hence, are behavioral, the application of the behavior-as-drama metaphor to services seems reasonable. Based on that rationale, services are theater.

Conceiving human behavior as drama depicts the service experience as a theatrical "performance" among "actors" who present themselves in such a way as to create a desired impression before an "audience," or in what might be termed "front stage." Though the "rehearsal" of performances is away from the audience's view "backstage," aspects of the actors' presentation can be worked out. Here, too, much of the planning, design, and implementation of the frontstage action occurs. Dramaturgy argues that the development and maintenance of any definition of social interaction relies on the audience's input as well as the actors'

Services as Theater

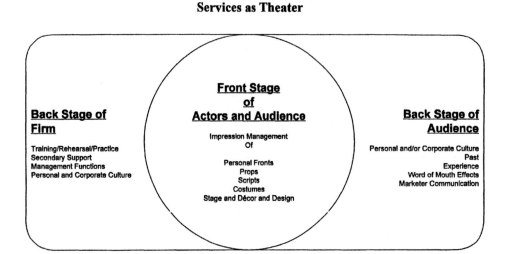

Figure 1.1 Services as Theater

presentation. Similarly, a service experience often requires customer participation in the process of service assembly. Theatrical performances can be tenuous, fragile processes that can be disrupted by minor mishaps such as unintended gestures or behavioral slips. In like fashion, unattended details or slight miscues can undermine the aura of service excellence. Several parallels can easily be drawn between the concerns of a services marketing manager and the proposition that drama is a metaphor for human behavior. Both service marketing and drama employ strategies and tactics by participants to create and maintain a desirable impression before an audience. Figure 1.1 presents a diagram showing the frontstage and backstage aspects of services as theater.

The general aim of any service organization is to create a positive response to its offering. Conceiving service as theater may help accomplish that goal. Overall, applying the theater metaphor to services is a cogent way to capture the nature of service experiences. Services, by definition, require a measure of interaction between the service provider and the service customer. Whether that interaction is face to face or at arm's length (as in the case of broadcast or securities investment services, for example), the service organization's goal is the same as that of a theatrical performance—to create a favorable impression before an audience. The character of theater may be more obvious in some types of services than in others, yet it is always there to some degree. For instance, *people processing* services (Lovelock 1994)—such as those delivered by airlines or hotels—involve considerable provider-customer interaction, and the theatrical aspects of such service are apparent. Yet even among *possession processing*, *mental stimulus processing*, or *information processing* services—such as auto repair, education, or accounting— theater is present. Each of these service types involves a "performance" by the service organization before an audience. The only difference is the theatrical devices that are used.

The proposition that services are theater, then, rests on the observation that comprehension of, evaluation of, and response to a service emerges over time, just as understanding of a motion picture or a theatrical production develops as the plot unfolds. Meanings are assigned to the many signs, symbols, and actions that are part of any service experience. Hence, services are not simply *like* theater, they *are* theater. As Shakespeare (1600/1954) put it, "All the world's a stage, and all the men and women merely players." Viewed in this context, services are simply a particular type of stage upon which players perform.

THE SERVICES MARKETING MIX

Over the years, there has been a realization that the traditional marketing mix (McCarthy 1960)—the tools or activities that are essential to organizations' marketing efforts—does not adequately capture the special circumstances that are present when marketing a service product. Hence, the well-known "4 Ps" of marketing have been expanded within the services literature to include such elements as the service's *participants, physical evidence,* and *process of service assembly* (Booms and Bitner 1981). In addition to the product, price, place, and promotion considerations that are part of any marketing effort, a service firm needs to manage the personnel and customers who are involved in the service experience, the physical aspects of the service, and the process by which the service is created and delivered. These "three new Ps" are analogous to major components of a theatrical production. The participants element of the services marketing mix parallels a theatrical production's actors and audience, the physical evidence corresponds to the setting, and the process of service assembly is comparable to the staged performance.

Four strategic theatrical elements, derived from the services marketing mix, constitute the service experience:

1. The *actors* (service personnel) whose presence and actions define the service,
2. The *audience* (customers) to whom the service is directed,
3. The *setting* (the venue) in which the service process occurs, and
4. The service *performance* itself (the actions that shape the customers' experience).

The overall theatrical production (or the service that is delivered) is the product of the actors and the enactment of their roles, the scenery and the staging of the action, and the audience and its involvement. Just as the unique combination of these elements can create and distinguish any stage production, a particular combination of service personnel and customers, physical evidence, and process of service assembly defines any service experience. For example, a premium-priced, upscale restaurant strives to create a distinctively luxurious service experience with careful attention to the facility's design, decor, and ambience; the actors' roles and costumes; the service script development and the rehearsal of its enactment; and the careful selection and education of an appreciative audience.

In contrast, a low-priced, no-frills restaurant reduces its emphasis on these various elements to reduce costs. The goal of that effort, nevertheless, is a theatrical performance intended for a distinctly different audience. For any service organization, managers may stress different theatrical elements to establish a particular impression. For example, until recently, hospitals delivered babies with the physician in complete control of the delivery and without the father present. Today, a woman is more likely to deliver her baby by natural childbirth methods in a hospital's "birthing" room that is adorned with reminders of home, and with the father assisting in the process.

The Actors

The appearance, skill level, and dedication of the service personnel are crucial for forming the appropriate service impression for the customer, just as a theatrical production is greatly affected by the expertise of those on stage. The skills displayed by the actors in fulfilling their service roles refer to myriad considerations such as competence, courtesy, knowledge, reliability, and communicative abilities, all of which have been identified as important determinants of service quality (Parasuraman, Zeithaml, and Berry 1985). The dedication of the actor may be seen in commitment to sustaining the service's impression even under conditions of personal stress and in ability to recognize and respond to the audience's particular needs or wants. In high-contact services, such as hair styling salons or dentist practices, the appearance and manner of service personnel form the image of the employees and, ultimately, the organization that is conveyed to the customer. In services where the personnel exercise a high degree of discretion in their roles, such as in education or medical services, the audience more closely scrutinizes visage, skill level, and commitment. In these cases, the actors *are* the service to the customer. In industries where the importance of the actors is not as obvious—for example, the possession or information processing services discussed earlier—service firms may distance themselves from competition by emphasizing the role of the actors in the service production.

The Audience

In many cases, the customer must be physically present during the service enactment for the service to occur (e.g., hair styling). In others, the customer needs to provide information to help an organization create the service desired (e.g., catalog retailing). In addition, it is not unusual for an organization to deliver its service to numerous customers sharing the service setting simultaneously. Such a circumstance is similar to theater in that the customers are in one another's presence, much like the audience attending a stage production. Just as one theater attendee may influence another's enjoyment of the performance, one customer's actions may affect another customer's service experience. Disorderly or unruly behavior on the part of some customers can destroy a service performance for all involved. To guard against such occurrences, it is important that customers are educated regarding the expectations of service participants. Whether it is learning how to use an information kiosk correctly, giving the lawyer an accurate account of circumstances, or respecting the rights and privileges of others who are present in the service setting, the audience plays a vital role in the service production. The significance of the audience's role is especially evident in services requiring a high degree of personalization, such as medical care, insurance, and financial advice.

Firms that are skillful in their management of customer participation and customer-to-customer interaction can improve the value of the service from the patron's point of view. In theater, an appreciative audience comprising the right mix of people who are well-informed about the nature of the performance increases the likelihood of a successful production. The same is true with service delivery. Hence, service patrons must be taught their role in the service script and what is required of them as customers. Furthermore, in services where customers share the setting, such as the case of a hotel, incompatible customer groups (e.g., families on a vacation vs. businesspersons at a conference) should probably be segregated. Such a move is likely to enhance the enjoyment of both parties and protect each from the unwelcome influence of unwanted others. Obviously, this circumstance increases in complexity as the number of potentially incompatible groups increases among the service audience.

The Setting

A service's physical environment can be likened to the setting of a theatrical production. In theater, the setting helps to frame the story that the audience views. A service setting performs a similar function. In general, the service setting includes the various features that surround the service interaction between the actors and the audience. Its design can substantially color the consumer's perception of a service as well as influence the nature of the service performance itself. As in the staging of a theatrical production that relies on scenery, props, and other physical cues to create desired impressions, a service may employ a variety of devices to do likewise. The devices' appearance and placement may affect the stage action as well. Among a setting's features that may influence the character of a service are the colors or brightness of the surroundings and the volume and pitch of sounds present within the setting. Also at play are the scents, movement, freshness, and temperature of air; the use of space; the style and comfort of the furnishings; the setting's design and cleanliness; and a host of other "atmospherics" (cf. Bitner 1992). All of these represent evidence or tangible cues that help shape a service's reality. Organizations that carefully consider the various setting devices can effectively communicate important information about the service to those in the audience. Questions such as whether the service is formal or informal, fun or serious, upscale or budget, or personal or communal can be answered by the setting's design. The setting can also impede or enhance the performance of the service through its layout, furnishings, or equipment. Thoughtful attention to this consideration by a service organization can strengthen the actors' and the audience's experience by increasing the speed and effectiveness of service delivery.

The setting increases in importance when the service environment distinguishes the nature of the service, as is the case of hospitality services or restaurants. Elements of the setting may assume increased importance depending on the venue of the service experience. It is, of course, important to think of the service setting in broader terms than simply "a place." Many services are delivered at arm's length; that is, the setting is remote (Bitner 1992) or takes on a different complexion. Nevertheless, it is likely that there are aspects of the setting that may be designed to stage the service performance effectively. For example, in the case of interactions with the customer over the telephone, such elements as the digital menu, the waiting time, the script of the service person, and the tone and courtesy of voice determine the setting. Similarly, when delivering a service over the Internet, the website features such as the webpage content, the design of text and graphics, the ease of use, and the links assume the role and features of the setting. Rather than configuring the setting based solely on a professional designer's point of view or on operational efficiencies, the audience to whom the site is targeted should also be consulted. Physical evidence can be used effectively to accomplish a variety of marketing goals, including communicating a new concept, repositioning an organization in the eyes of its target market, or attracting new market segments.

The Performance

In the quest to present a credible service performance, it is critical to coordinate the evidence provided by the actors and the setting and involve the audience adequately in the staging of the action. Because services are processes, a service's definition emerges over time as a result of the blending of the various service features. Each feature contributes in its own way to a gestalt impression that becomes the service performance. If they work together, a seamless flow of action occurs. If they lack compatibility or consistency, an uneven performance ensues. A theatrical production that is adorned by magnificent scenery is likely to fail if the actors' skills are poor, just as the artful enactment of actors' roles may be in vain if the production's staging is remiss. Maintaining congruity among the actors' manner, actions, and appearance and the cues from the service's physical evidence in the performance can establish a clear definition of a service. Furthermore, to ensure a credible performance, a strong customer orientation is needed. Actors must actively monitor and adapt to the audience's responses to the unfolding service drama. This includes the willingness and ability of service actors to recognize even the subtle cues of the audience's satisfaction with various aspects of the emerging service action and to adjust the enactment of their roles accordingly. Whether it is altering the script or adjusting the physical evidence or undertaking some other action in response to perceived audience desires, such changes reflect the adaptive character of a service performance and the necessity of coordination among its components.

ADAPTATIONS FOR
DIFFERENT TYPES OF SERVICES

Not all services are alike. Some services are delivered by people (e.g., hair styling or financial advice), others by equipment (e.g., freight transportation or telecommunications), and others by a combination of the two (e.g., airline service or restaurants). Furthermore, some services involve a good deal of interaction between the service provider and the customer (e.g., dental care or physical therapy), whereas others involve very little interplay (e.g., utilities or telecommunications). The former are often referred to as high-contact services while the latter are identified as low-contact services. In addition, some services are delivered on the customer's premises (e.g., lawn care or maintenance), whereas others occur at the service organization's site (e.g., hotels or auto repair). Although it is possible to make other distinctions among services (cf. Lovelock 1983), it is important to recognize that each distinction results in a unique set of requirements for staging the service performance. For instance, high-contact services necessitate careful attention to casting and training the service actors, whereas services delivered at the firm's location require thoughtful design and implementation of the service setting.

A commonly used classification of services focuses on the tangibility of the service act and the nature of the service recipient (Lovelock 1983, 1994). Specifically, services can be depicted as *tangible* processes—much like manufacturing—or as *intangible* ones. The recipient of the service act may be a *person* or a *possession*. By combining these two distinctions, four different groupings of services emerge. *People processing services* occur where the service provider and the service customer are in close contact and involve tangible acts on people's bodies (e.g., lodging or medical care). In such services, there are many features and elements of the setting, the actors' behaviors, and the performance that combine to create the service. Hence, there are many opportunities for managing the audience's (i.e., the customer's) impressions. Because many people processing services are performed for multiple customers (e.g., airline service or restaurants), the presence of other patrons may affect the delivery and outcome of the service performance through their sheer numbers, behaviors, and demeanor.

A second category, *mental stimulus processing services*, involves intangible acts performed on or for people's minds (e.g., broadcast entertainment or education). Such services commonly require significantly less contact with the audience than people processing services. Consequently, there are often fewer elements with respect to the setting, the actors, and, sometimes, even the other customers that need to be managed. For example, in management consulting or market research, the customer may not even have to interact with the service provider directly, which renders the importance of these theatrical elements less relevant. This is not, however, always the case. In service settings such as cinema theaters or classroom education, the situation is similar to that of people processing services, where there are numerous features of the setting, actors' roles, and audience characteristics to consider.

In the third category, *possession processing services*, tangible acts are performed on physical possessions (e.g., furniture moving or appliance repair). In these types of services, the setting can be either the customer's premises (e.g., landscaping services) or the service provider's premises (e.g., automotive services). However, in either case, the customer is not likely to spend a good deal of time observing the service performance—only its outcome. Interaction with those who actually produce the service may be limited as well. The relatively few setting and actor cues ultimately may increase the potential significance of each because it must carry a heavier load in helping the audience form impressions. For instance, the audience may have little more than the appearance and condition of the equipment used to produce the service, or perhaps only a snippet of social exchange, upon which to base their assessment of service excellence. Because possession processing services are seldom delivered to large audiences, the impact of the audience aspect of service theater is reduced greatly across such services.

The fourth and final category produced by the tangibility of the service act versus nature of the service recipient classification is *information processing services*. These services involve intangible acts performed on intangible possessions (e.g., banking or data processing). In general, information processing services involve the least amount of contact with the service provider. In fact, in some cases, following an initial exchange, no direct contact at all between the customer and service provider is necessary. As with the discussion earlier, the lack of contact may increase the importance of the limited opportunities for the service actors or setting to impress the audience. In the effort to discern the nature and the quality of the service being received, even very small or seemingly unimportant aspects of the theatrical performance can carry significance. Hence, a misspelled name in written communications, inaccuracies of any kind, or unintentional discourteous behavior can destroy the service performance. Obviously, information processing services cannot afford to overlook the tiniest detail in managing customer impressions. See Table 1.1 for a brief summary of each of these service categories and their theatrical aspects.

MANAGERIAL GUIDELINES

The services as theater approach offers managers a holistic framework that combines all the interactive aspects of services. Much like the original metaphor of the marketing "mix," the drama model suggests a combination of ingredients that can be blended optimally to achieve different goals. Furthermore, the services as theater metaphor can serve as a tool for planning, coordinating, and implementing specific service designs. Used in conjunction with blueprinting (Kingman-Brundage 1989; Shostack 1984a, 1984b, 1987), the drama metaphor offers managers directions for (a) the different emphases to place on service components (e.g., low-contact services should stress "setting" to increase perceptions of service quality); (b) the amount of attention to devote to recruiting, selecting, training, and controlling service workers (e.g., high-contact services need actors with

TABLE 1.1 Theatrical Considerations for Different Types of Services

Service Characteristic	Services Examples	Drama Implications
People processing: Tangible action directed at people's bodies	Airlines Hotels Restaurants/bars Hair styling services Fitness centers	Actors and audience are in close contact. The setting and frontstage performances have significant influence on customer evaluations of quality. This includes design, décor, and ambience of the setting and the appearance and demeanor of the actor(s). Props, costumes, and scripts become important. There may be others in the audience who share the setting and can influence one another's service experience and overall evaluations of the service performance.
Mental stimulus processing: Intangible action directed at people's minds	Management consulting Medical consulting Education Entertainment Telephone services (voice)	When actors and audience are in physical proximity, some of the implications of the *people processing services* are applicable here. If the service is conducted at arm's length, such as medical or management advice given over the telephone, members of the audience do not interact with one another and the physical appearance/actions of the actors is less important. Overall, it is harder to make this type of service tangible; that is, there are fewer cues to manage impressions on the customer.
Possession processing: Tangible action directed at tangible possessions	Janitorial services Retailing services Auto and appliance repair Home contracting services Landscaping services	The setting can be either the organization's premises or the audience's premises. Contact between actor and audience can be limited to the start and the end of the service, and the service need not be performed in the audience's presence. Because both the service act and the service recipient are tangible, the outcome of the performance is usually more evident and may be used as a proxy to evaluate the performance itself.
Information processing: Intangible action directed at intangible assets	Accounting services Banking and financial services Insurance services Legal services Computer software services	There can be minimal contact between actor and audience. Because both the act and the recipient are intangible, the process is a less important source of evaluation. In most cases, the service occurs in the absence of the customer. In such circumstances, the outcome is more important than the process, yet even it may be difficult to assess.

SOURCE: Adapted from Lovelock (1994).

strong dramatic skills); and (c) the influence that customer expectations have on service quality levels (e.g., patrons demanding high quality dictate a greater attention to detail in service delivery).

Several specific managerial guidelines can be developed from the services as theater approach for actors and audience, setting, and performance. Table 1.2 provides a template for an audit of these elements and the impressions they create.

Actors and Audience

Selection of both actors and audience and determining which actors are best suited for which audience are critical. Some service firms such as Disney and the

TABLE 1.2 Worksheet for a Marketing Audit of Services as Theater

Theater Elements	Features of Each Element	Impression Effects (What impressions do each of the features of each element and the interplay among the features give?)
Participants: Actors and audience	What is the profile of participants? What are the roles of participants? What interaction is there between and among participants? What are the scripts of actors? What are the roles of backstage members?	
Physical evidence: Setting	What props are necessary? What should the costumes look like?	
Process of service assembly: Performance	What are the scenes or acts? What are the outcomes of the scenes or acts? What is the nature of the intermissions?	

Ritz Carlton have constructed a detailed profile of the type of person they hire for customer-contact roles. Just as cast members are auditioned for plays, so also frontstage service personnel need to have certain characteristics. Similarly, target market selection should take into account the type of audience that would be appropriate for the service. In other words, both actors and the audience need to be selected so that they are compatible with each other. Routine service performances can be carefully scripted and, where there is a significant amount of customization of service, several different scripts could be crafted for the different audience situations and requirements. Training and rehearsing are as important as in theatrical productions. Synchronization of the various actors and their respective roles and scripts is critical in services where there is more than one actor in a scene, or when there is a significant dependence between frontstage and backstage activities. On-the-job training might be best utilized without hurting the service performance by matching experienced actors with apprentices.

Setting

Frontstage and backstage decisions should be made carefully to determine what aspects of the setting need to be visible to the audience. A balance needs to be maintained between what physical cues need to be shown to the audience on the front stage to create the necessary impression and which cues should be kept backstage. These cues can be evaluated along the five senses of sight, hearing, touch, smell, or taste. Costumes of actors (e.g., uniforms of service personnel) and props (e.g., company vehicles and equipment or music, furnishings, and magazines in waiting areas) create an image for the service. The appropriate combination of the various elements that constitute the setting can be tested in concept and as an experiment for customer reactions before large-scale investments are made.

Performance

The actors, audiences, and setting, and the interplay of their respective roles, combine to create the performance. Performances need to be rehearsed, tested, and continually improved. To do this, performances have to be documented and audience reactions measured. Elements of the settings, actors, and audiences that have been poorly received need to be revised, and those that have been well received need to be rewarded. This might necessitate recasting the actors, reconfiguring the elements of the setting, or even targeting a new group within the audience depending on reviews and attendance levels.

CONCLUSION

The theater metaphor and the application of its theatrical constructs to service experiences unites the "three new Ps" of Booms and Bitner (1981). The term "participants" is analogous to the theatrical terms of actors and audience, "physical evidence" is analogous to the setting, and "process of service assembly" is analogous to the performance. Viewing services as theater addresses many services marketing issues by demonstrating the implicit and explicit relationships among the service organization, its customers, its employees, and its physical properties. As with any metaphor, the description of services in dramatic terms facilitates communication and analysis of the phenomena at hand and can be used to generate researchable propositions.

To many people, the drama metaphor may carry the dangerous connotation of superficial "just acting" behaviors. The "Have a Nice Day" phrase so dutifully mouthed by the employees of many service businesses is woefully insincere. It is imperative that the customer believe in the performance. If the public believes that a service business is presenting a "false front," they may quickly take their patronage elsewhere. Service marketers should recognize the importance of honest actors and authentic performances.

A second hazardous connotation of the services as theater metaphor is that of "canned" performances. Many dramas are rigidly scripted and may convey the image of a fixed product. Managers should recognize the need for adaptability and should pursue strategies that maximize the adaptability of the service experience. Service organizations should strive to maintain the adaptability of an "ethic of service" rather than the precision of an "ethic of efficiency" (Schneider and Bowen 1984). Where possible, rather than follow a fixed script, the service worker should adapt the performance to the needs of the audience. Services managers should recognize the need for appropriateness. Grotesque or vulgar performances are likely to yield very negative consumer reviews and may "close early." Attractive, soothing, or refined performances are likely to be "held over by popular demand." In short, service performances must be tailored to the tastes of the service audience.

REFERENCES

Arndt, Johan (1985), "On Making Marketing Science More Scientific: Role of Orientations, Paradigms, Metaphors and Puzzle Solving," *Journal of Marketing*, 49 (Summer), 11-23.

Bitner, Mary Jo (1992), "Servicescapes: The Impact of Physical Surroundings on Consumers and Employees," *Journal of Marketing*, 56 (April), 57-71.

Booms, Bernard H. and Mary Jo Bitner (1981), "Marketing Strategies and Organizational Structures for Service Firms," in *Marketing of Services*, James H. Donnelly and William R. George, eds. Chicago: American Marketing Association, 47-51.

Brissett, Dennis and Charles Edgley (1975), *Life as Theatre: A Dramaturgical Sourcebook*. Chicago: Aldine.

Brown, Richard H. (1977), *A Poetic for Sociology*. Cambridge, UK: Cambridge University Press.

Burke, Kenneth (1968), "Dramatism," in *International Encyclopedia of the Social Sciences*, Vol. 7. New York: Macmillan, 445-52.

Clancy, John J. (1989), *The Invisible Powers: The Language of Business*. Lexington, MA: Lexington Books.

Fisk, Raymond P. and Stephen J. Grove (1996), "Applications of Impression Management and the Drama Metaphor in Marketing," *European Journal of Marketing*, 30(9), 6-12.

Goffman, Erving (1959), *The Presentation of Self in Everyday Life*. New York: Doubleday and Co.

Goodwin, Cathy, Stephen J. Grove, and Raymond P. Fisk (1996), "Collaring the Cheshire Cat: Evaluating Service Experience Through Metaphor," *Services Industries Journal*, 16 (October), 421-42.

Grove, Stephen J. and Raymond P. Fisk (1983), "The Dramaturgy of Services Exchanges: An Analytical Framework for Services Marketing," in *Emerging Perspectives on Services Marketing*, Leonard L. Berry, G. Lynn Shostack, and Gregory D. Upah, eds. Chicago: American Marketing Association, 45-49.

——— and ——— (1989), "Impression Management in Services Marketing: A Dramaturgical Perspective," in *Impression Management in the Organization*, Robert A. Giacalone and Paul Rosenfeld, eds. Hillsdale, NJ: Lawrence Erlbaum Associates, 427-38.

——— and ——— (1991), "The Theatrical Framework of Service Encounters: A Metaphorical Analysis," in *1991 AMA Educators' Conference Proceedings*, Mary C. Gilly et al., eds. Chicago: American Marketing Association, 315-17.

——— and ——— (1992), "The Service Experience as Theater," in *Advances in Consumer Research*, John E. Sherry, Jr. and Brian Sternthal, eds. Provo, UT: Association for Consumer Research, 455-61.

——— and ——— (1995), "Service Performances as Drama: Quality Implications and Measurement," in *Managing Service Quality*, Paul Kunst and Jos Lemmink, eds. Maastricht, The Netherlands: Van Gorcum, Assen/Maastricht, 107-19.

———, ———, and Mary Jo Bitner (1992), "Dramatizing the Service Experience: A Managerial Approach," in *Advances in Services Marketing and Management: Research and Practice*, Teresa A. Swartz, Stephen W. Brown, and David E. Bowen, eds. Greenwich, CT: JAI, 91-121.

———, ———, and Michael J. Dorsch (1998), "Assessing the Theatrical Components of the Service Encounter: A Cluster Analysis Examination," *Services Industries Journal*, 18 (July), 116-34.

Hunt, Shelby D. and Anil Menon (1995), "Metaphors and Competitive Advantage: Evaluating the Use of Metaphors in Theories of Competitive Strategy," *Journal of Business Research*, 33 (June), 81-90.

Kingman-Brundage, Jane (1989), "The ABC's of Service System Blueprinting," in *Designing a Winning Service Strategy*, Mary Jo Bitner and Lawrence A. Crosby, eds. Chicago: American Marketing Association, 30-33.

Leary, David E. (1990), "Psyche's Muse: The Role of Metaphor in the History of Psychology," in *Metaphors in the History of Psychology* (Cambridge Studies in the History of Psychology), David E. Leary, ed. Cambridge, UK: Cambridge University Press, 1-78.

Lovelock, Christopher H. (1983), "Classifying Services to Gain Strategic Insights," *Journal of Marketing*, 47 (Summer), 9-20.

——— (1994), *Product Plus: How Product+Service=Competitive Advantage*. New York: McGraw-Hill.

McCarthy, E. Jerome (1960), *Basic Marketing: A Managerial Approach*. Homewood, IL: Richard D. Irwin.

Morgan, Gareth (1980), "Paradigms, Metaphors, and Puzzle Solving in Organizational Theory," *Administrative Science Quarterly*, 25 (December), 605-22.

Nisbet, Robert A. (1969), *Social Change and History*. London: Oxford University Press.

Ortony, Andrew (1975), "Why Metaphors Are Necessary and Not Just Nice," *Educational Theory*, 25(1), 45-53.

Parasuraman, A., Valarie A. Zeithaml, and Leonard L. Berry (1985), "A Conceptual Model of Service Quality and Its Implications for Future Research," *Journal of Marketing*, 49 (Fall), 41-50.

Perinbanayagam, R. S. (1974), "The Definition of the Situation: An Analysis of the Ethnomethodological and Dramaturgical View," *The Sociological Quarterly*, 15 (Autumn), 521-41.

Schneider, Benjamin and David E. Bowen (1984), "New Services Design, Development and Implementation and the Employee," in *Developing New Services*, William R. George and Claudia E. Marshall, eds. Chicago: American Marketing Association, 82-101.

Shakespeare, William [1600] (1954), *As You Like It*. S. C. Burchell, ed. New Haven, CT: Yale University Press.

Shostack, G. Lynn (1984a), "Designing Services That Deliver," *Harvard Business Review*, 62 (January-February), 133-39.

——— (1984b), "A Framework for Services Marketing," in *Marketing Theory: Distinguished Contributions*, Stephen W. Brown and Raymond P. Fisk, eds. New York: John Wiley and Sons, 250-61.

——— (1987), "Service Positioning Through Structural Change," *Journal of Marketing*, 51 (January), 34-43.

Stern, Barbara (1988), "Medieval Allegory: Roots of Advertising Strategy for the Mass Market," *Journal of Marketing*, 52 (July), 84-94.

Stone, Gregory P. (1962), "Appearance and the Self," in *Human Behavior and Social Process*, Arnold Rose, ed. Boston: Houghton-Mifflin, 86-117.

Zaltman, Gerald, Karen LeMasters, and Michael Heffring (1982), *Theory Construction in Marketing: Some Thoughts on Thinking*. New York: John Wiley & Sons.

Zikmund, William G. (1982), "Metaphors as Methodology," in *Proceedings of the 1982 Winter Educators' Conference*, Ronald F. Busch and Shelby D. Hunt, eds. Chicago: American Marketing Association, 75-77.

The servicescape, or service setting, plays a critical role in shaping expectations, differentiating service firms, facilitating customer and em_r goals, and influencing the nature of customer experiences (Bitner 1992; She.. 1998a). The servicescape can influence critical customer relationship goals from the initial attraction of the customer through to retention and even enhancement of the relationship. Its marketing impact cannot be understated, yet theoretical and practical knowledge of the servicescape is relatively meager when compared to knowledge of other marketing variables.

The objectives of this chapter are to (a) define and delimit the servicescape concept, (b) illustrate the ties between key marketing issues and the servicescape, (c) provide an overview of recent theoretical and marketing contributions to our understanding of servicescape effects, and (d) propose an integrated framework for managers to facilitate marketing practice with respect to the servicescape.

WHAT IS THE SERVICESCAPE?

The servicescape has been defined as the built environment surrounding the service (Bitner 1992). This definition and the servicescape framework flowing from it focus exclusively on dimensions of the *physical* environment; however, because people within the built environment can shape and influence the physical space and its impact, the *social environment* is included here in an expanded definition of the servicescape (Baker, Grewal, and Parasuraman 1994; Baker, Levy, and Grewal 1992). Although we could expand the notion of servicescape or setting even further to include the natural, cultural, temporal, or political environment, these definitions of environment are beyond the scope of the current effort. The focus here is on marketing practice. Thus, we confine the notion of

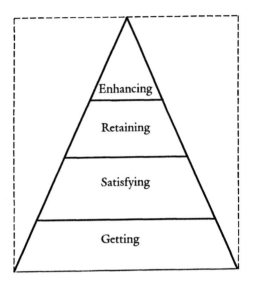

Figure 2.1 The New Marketing Concept: Customer Goals

servicescapes to *the immediate physical and social environments surrounding a service experience, transaction, or event.*

THE SERVICESCAPE AND MARKETING PRACTICE

In this section we draw linkages between the servicescape and key substantive issues and concepts within the practice of marketing, including the servicescape's influence on customer goals; its marketing roles as a package, a differentiator, a socializer, and a facilitator; and its effects on employees as well as customers.

Influence on Customer Goals

The new marketing concept extends beyond the traditional marketing focus of customer attraction to include customer satisfaction, relationship building, and even the enhancement of customers to increase their value to the firm (Webster 1992). These expanded goals with respect to customers are shown in the customer goals pyramid (Figure 2.1). Under the new marketing concept, the goal is to move customers up this pyramid, by first attracting the right customers and then developing the relationship through all levels.

The servicescape influences goals at all levels of the pyramid. Clearly the design and presentation of the servicescape can serve to attract customers into the service facility. Signage, colors, attractive design, music, or scents can be used to draw customers into a place. Once inside, the servicescape will help to shape the

TABLE 2.1 Servicescape Examples

	Built Environment	*Social Environment*
Hospital	Building exterior Parking Signs Waiting area Admissions area Patient care room Medical equipment Recovery room	Nurses Doctors Volunteer staff Other patients Family members
Airline	Airline gate area Airplane exterior Airplane seats, decor, air Quality Baggage area	Pilots Ticket agents Flight attendants Baggage handlers Other passengers
Sporting event	Parking Stadium exterior Ticketing area Entrance Seating Restrooms Concession areas Playing field	Ticketing people Ushers Concession attendants Players Other fans
Child care center	Building exterior Parking Signs and layout Hallways and rooms Equipment Decor, air quality	Teacher Staff Parents Other children

customer's experience and influence his or her satisfaction with the service delivery. In some cases, the servicescape may even be a determining factor in whether the customer returns or gives more of his or her business to the firm. Table 2.1 shows examples of built and social environment factors that would be relevant in particular service and marketing contexts.

The importance of servicescape is acknowledged in our inclusion of this marketing variable in the expanded marketing mix for services (Booms and Bitner 1981). The complexity of the notion of space and place is further captured in conceptual work drawing on dramaturgical theory (Grove, Fisk, and Bitner 1992). In this work, theoretical parallels are drawn between the setting in dramaturgy theory and the physical environment, as a marketing concept. In a recent book (Sherry 1998a), the concept of servicescapes is broadened even further through a collection of chapters that address such diverse concepts as themed environments (Gottdiener 1998), the wilderness servicescape (Arnould, Price, and Tierney 1998), cybermarketscapes (Venkatesh 1998), and private servicescapes (Grayson 1998).

Roles of the Servicescape

In achieving the customer goals highlighted above, it is clear that the servicescape plays a number of different roles, often simultaneously (Zeithaml and Bitner 1996, chap. 18).

Package. Similar to a tangible product's *package*, the servicescape essentially "wraps" the service and conveys an external image of what is "inside" to consumers. Product packages are designed to portray a particular image to the consumer as well as to evoke a particular sensory or emotional reaction in the consumer. The physical setting of a service does the same thing through the interaction of many complex stimuli. The servicescape is the outward appearance of the organization and thus can be critical in forming initial impressions or setting up customer expectations—it is a visual metaphor for the intangible service. This packaging role extends to the appearance of contact employees through their uniforms or dress and other elements of their outward appearance (e.g., Rafaeli 1993; Solomon 1998).

Facilitator. The servicescape can also serve as a *facilitator*. How the setting is designed can enhance or inhibit the efficient flow of activities in the service setting, making it easier or harder for customers and employees to accomplish their goals (e.g., Titus and Everett 1996). A well-designed, functional facility can make the service a pleasure to experience from the customer's point of view and a pleasure to perform from the employee's viewpoint. On the other hand, poor and inefficient design may frustrate both the employees and customers. For example, an international air traveler who finds himself in a poorly designed airport with few signs, poor ventilation, and few places to sit or eat will find the experience quite dissatisfying, and employees who work there will be unmotivated as well.

Socializer. The design of the servicescape aids in the *socialization* of both employees and customers in the sense that it helps to convey expected roles, behaviors, and relationships. For example, consider a Club Med vacation environment that is set up to encourage customer-customer interactions as well as to facilitate guest interactions with Club Med staff. The organization also recognizes the need for privacy, providing areas that facilitate solitary activities as well. The design of the facility can also suggest to customers what their role is relative to employees, what parts of the servicescape they are welcome in and which are for employees only, how they should behave while in the environment, and what types of interactions are encouraged. In these ways the servicescape plays a part in conveying the organizational culture and purpose, socializing both customers and employees.

Differentiator. The design of the physical facility can differentiate a firm from its competitors and signal who the intended market segment is. Given its power as a *differentiator*, changes in the environment can be used to reposition a firm and/or to attract new market segments. In shopping malls, the signage, colors used in decor and displays, and the type of music wafting from different stores signal the intended market segments. In another context, the servicescape of a storefront legal services clinic located in a strip development differentiates it from corporate law firms located in downtown high-rises. The design of a physical setting can also differentiate one area of a service organization from another. This is commonly the case in the hotel industry, where one large hotel may have several levels of dining possibilities, each signaled by differences in design. Price differentiation is often partially achieved through variations in physical setting. Bigger rooms with more physical amenities cost more, just as larger seats with more legroom (generally in first class) are more expensive on an airplane. A recent development in movie theaters is the addition of luxury screening rooms with club chairs and waiters ("The New VIP Rooms" 1998). Taking advantage of this alternative, customers who wish to pay a higher price to see the same film can experience the service in an entirely different physical and social environment.

Employees, Not Just Customers

Service employees also will be influenced by dimensions of the servicescape, as will the interactions between and among employees and customers. The environmental conditions that work best for one group (employees), however, may not be the best for the other (customers), and vice versa. Servicescape design thus takes on added complexity when effects on both groups are considered simultaneously (Bitner 1992). In addition to being influenced by it, customers and employees will affect the environment simply by their passive presence. They can also actively change the environment by moving things, removing things, redesigning, and adding to or destroying it.

THEORETICAL GROUNDING AND RECENT RESEARCH

The preceding section confirms the importance of the servicescape in marketing practice by illustrating its relationship to marketing goals, concepts, and issues. Here, attention is shifted to recent theoretical and empirical work that sheds light on these relationships. (For coverage of prior environment and behavior research in marketing, see Bitner 1992.) The combination of substantive issues and theory provides the grounding for the revised servicescapes framework presented in the final section of the chapter.

Environmental Psychology Perspectives

Our current understanding of servicescapes is grounded in environmental psychology—a very broad theoretical domain built on work in psychology, sociology, architecture and design, social geography, and urban studies (Bonnes and Secchiaroli 1995; Cassidy 1997). Recent reviews of the literature illuminate the diversity of the field in terms of theoretical paradigms and applications (Saegert and Winkel 1990; Sundstrom et al. 1996). Paradigms for understanding person-environment relations include traditional stimulus-organism-response frameworks in psychology as well as sociocultural frameworks in sociology and geography. Applications range from large-scale urban and natural environments, to institutional environments such as prisons and schools, to residential and consumption environments. To a limited degree, recent research in marketing—described next—reflects this diversity of theoretical approaches and methodologies.

Research in Marketing

This section overviews recent marketing literature related to servicescape concepts. It is based primarily on work published in the last 6 years, since the term servicescapes was coined and introduced to the marketing literature (Bitner 1992). The servicescapes framework presented in Bitner (1992) inspired the title of the 1998 collection *Servicescapes*, edited by John Sherry (1998a). This book is a major contribution to the field in that it gathers in one place current, innovative thinking using a diverse set of methodologies to examine the servicescapes topic. A number of the chapters in that volume are referenced throughout this chapter.

In addition to the chapters in *Servicescapes*, other papers appeared in marketing, management, and service journals between 1992 and 1998. The published works fall into two broad categories: (a) research that tests the effects of environmental dimensions on marketing and consumer outcomes, and (b) theory building and methods research that expands our basic understanding of servicescapes. None of the recent work in marketing explicitly incorporates servicescape effects on employees or on employee/customer interactions.

Effects of Environmental Dimensions

A number of primarily experimental studies published between 1992 and 1998 examine how individual or multiple environmental dimensions affect consumer outcomes such as satisfaction, perceived quality, perceptions of waiting time, and emotional responses.

Music. Several experimental studies examine the effects of music on customer responses. Dubé, Chebat, and Morin (1995) studied the effects of music-induced pleasure and arousal on consumers' desire to affiliate in buyer-seller interactions, and Chebat, Gelinas-Chebat, and Filliatrault (1993) examined the interactive effects of music and visual cues on time perception in banks. Hui, Dubé, and Chebat (1997) looked at the impact of music on consumers' reactions to waiting. Another study found that manipulated variations in music did not affect amount of time and money spent; however, customers' *attitudes* toward the music did affect time and money expenditures (Herrington and Capella 1996). Herrington and Capella (1994) provide a practical, nonempirical piece looking at the use of background music in retail settings—what is known and its implications.

Scent. Other experimental studies manipulated scent in service and retail environments and tested the effects on consumer responses. Mitchell, Kahn, and Knasko (1995) showed how scents affect consumer decision making depending on whether the scents are congruent or incongruent with the target product class. In another study, Spangenberg, Crowley, and Henderson (1996) examined the effects of scents versus no scents and the intensity of scent on consumer perceptions of time spent and other shopping behaviors.

Facilities/layout. Facilities and store layout have also been studied in terms of their impact on customer responses. Sulek, Lind, and Marucheck (1995) conducted an experimental field study showing the effects of three different types of retail food store design on customer satisfaction and store performance. Titus and Everett (1996) report an exploratory study within a large supermarket aimed at understanding customer search behaviors in a complex retail environment. Results suggest that the layout of the store environment will affect wayfinding behaviors and other consumer outcomes. In a study conducted in two large department stores in Korea, Yoo, Park, and MacInnis (1998) found that store facilities significantly affected consumers' emotional responses.

Multiple dimensions. Most of the studies cited above examine the effects of one particular dimension of the physical environment (e.g., music, scent, layout) on customer perceptions and/or behaviors. Others simultaneously propose or test the effects of multiple dimensions. For example, Baker and Cameron (1996) propose a model and propositions linking variations in lighting, temperature, music, color, furnishings, layout, employee visibility, and other customers to customer affect and perceptions of waiting time. Their specific propositions are not tested. In an earlier experimental study, Baker, Grewal, and Parasuraman (1994) examine the effects of ambient factors, design factors, and social factors on perceptions of merchandise quality, service quality, and store image in a retail context. Within each of the manipulated factors, multiple environmental cues were used to create a prestige versus discount retail setting. Results showed that the ambient and social factors significantly affected perceptions of quality, while the design factor had no statistically significant impact. In another experimental study, Baker, Levy, and Grewal (1992) found that both ambient and social factors (and their interactions) influenced subjects' perceptions of pleasure and arousal in response to the videotaped retail environments. Sherman, Mathur, and Smith (1997) also examine the effects of multiple store environment dimensions (social, design, and ambience) on pleasure and arousal responses.

In a study of leisure service settings (college football, minor league baseball, and casinos), Wakefield and Blodgett (1996) examine the effects of specific layout and design dimensions on perceptions of servicescape quality. In turn, they test the effects of perceptions of servicescape quality on satisfaction and repatronage intentions. They found positive and significant effects of all dimensions on perceptions of servicescape quality, along with a significant effect of servicescape quality on overall satisfaction, leading to increased repatronage intentions. In an earlier study, these same authors (Wakefield and Blodgett 1994) examined somewhat more general servicescape questions in football and baseball sports venues.

Theory Building, Methodologies, and Measurement

The papers discussed in the preceding section deal with effects of environmental dimensions on consumer behaviors and outcomes, using experimental methodologies almost exclusively. Other research in recent years expands our basic understanding of the servicescape by extending and developing servicescapes theory, proposing and using alternative methodologies, and developing appropriate servicescape measures.

Drawing on the broader theory base of environmental psychology, combined with an underlying postmodern view, Aubert-Gamet (1997, 1999) proposes that we consider the environment not as a given, but as something that is co-constructed by its inhabitants. She views customers as active molders of their own experience—within this view, customers are affected by the environment, but at the same time they change, interpret, mold, and construct the environment, perhaps in ways unanticipated. Her view is consistent with the "transactional-contextual," "ecological," or "socio-systemic" perspectives in environmental psychology.

"The transactional perspective basically aims at re-composing the subject-object dichotomy and more particularly the dichotomy between the person and the environment; it suggests a dynamic relationship between the two, no longer considered as independent units but as interdependent aspects of the same unit" (Bonnes and Secchiaroli 1995, p. 153). It is pointed out that this perspective is followed more in programmatic intentions than in actual research practice within environmental psychology (Bonnes and Secchiaroli 1995).

The ecological or transactional view of the servicescape is reflected in Bloch, Ridgway, and Dawson (1994). In that study, the authors draw on the ecological sciences' notion of habitat as a foundation for examining consumer behavior within shopping malls. They adopt concepts and terminology from ecological theory to better understand the "shopping mall as consumer habitat." They examine patterns of activities and related benefits within the mall setting.

The transactional-contextual view is reflected in a number of studies reported in *Servicescapes* (Sherry 1998a). These studies use phenomenological methods to understand more fully the reciprocal, dynamic, holistic aspects of person-environment interactions in consumption venues. For example, in her study of "Seed," a retail environment in Japan, Creighton (1998) illustrates how the servicescape creates a setting for behavior that is culturally embedded and reflective of norms and values of the time. On one hand, the Seed's environment wraps the space and molds behavior in it; on the other hand, it allows consumers to reflect and create their own contemporary realities. In a similar way, Sherry (1998b) explores Nike Town Chicago, a retail phenomenon that shapes consumer behaviors but at the same time allows consumers to interpret and create their own realities and experiences. "Nike Town, like the ancient city, is a symbol of the cosmos. Perhaps more vividly than many buildings, it condenses culture in one place" (Sherry 1998b, p. 136). Nike Town is an example of "entertainment retail" that is as culturally embedded within the United States as the Seed is within Japanese culture. In another study, Otnes (1998) reflects on the variety of roles played by the bridal salon servicescape in assisting women as they prepare for their weddings. Again, the bridal salon servicescape is a setting that encourages certain consumer behaviors; it is also a setting that allows customers to create their own realities, supporting enactment of their own personal wedding shopping rituals. Other chapters in *Servicescapes* reflect on consumer-environment interplay in art galleries (Joy 1998), in toy stores (Wallendorf, Lindsey-Mullikin, and Pimentel 1998), at brandfests (McAlexander and Schouten 1998), in wilderness servicescapes (Arnould, Price, and Tierney 1998), and in cybermarketspaces (Venkatesh 1998).

From a more deterministic view, the social dimension of the environment has also been emphasized by a number of authors, most notably Baker and her colleagues (Baker, Levy, and Grewal 1992; Baker, Grewal, and Parasuraman 1994). Although this research does not focus on the constructive, reciprocal, or transactional aspects of the social dimension, it does extend the concept of "servicescape" beyond the physical or built environment. Although our understanding of servicescape effects and multimethod approaches to understanding consumer-environment transactions is growing, little has been published to date on the measurement of the servicescape construct. Promising exceptions are a recent working paper and dissertation testing (across 10 industries) a measure of perceived servicescape quality based on a three-dimensional servicescapes model (Cronin, Hightower, and Hult 1998; Hightower 1997). The resulting parsimonious 11-item measure includes an ambient factor, a design factor, and a social factor that exhibit good reliability and predictive validity.

AN INTEGRATED SERVICESCAPES FRAMEWORK FOR MANAGERS

From a marketing management perspective, key servicescape questions naturally emanate from the appreciation of its effects: How can the servicescape be designed to aid in attraction of profitable customer segments? How can the servicescape be designed to enhance customer satisfaction and retention? How much should be invested in the servicescape versus other marketing investments (e.g., promotion, employee training)? Drawing on the issues presented earlier and recent research contributions, the following sections describe an integrated framework for marketing practice to aid in answering questions such as these (see Figure 2.2). This framework builds from Bitner (1992) but provides a simplified version of that framework (for more detailed descriptions of some of the constructs and relationships, see Bitner 1992). The revised framework also integrates the social environment as a dimension of the servicescape and explicitly acknowledges the reciprocal or transactional relationship between environmental influences and human behaviors. The latter was an underlying assumption of the early framework and is made more explicit here.

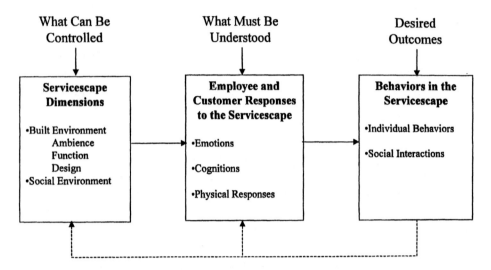

Figure 2.2 The Servicescape: An Integrated Framework for Managers

The brief discussion below and the framework are organized around three key servicescape management questions: What can be controlled? What must be understood? What are the desired outcomes?

What Can Be Controlled?

The framework suggests that servicescape dimensions, including the physical and social environments, will affect customers and employees, and thus must be planned and controlled for their marketing impact just as any marketing mix variable would be. Controlling the physical environment means designing the ambience, the functional layout, and elements of the decor and design of the physical space to encourage particular responses and behaviors. Much of the empirical, experimental research reported earlier is aimed at understanding the effects of particular elements of the physical environment (e.g., music, scent, layout) on consumers' responses and behaviors. Managers who recognize the impact of the servicescape can use this knowledge and their own research to design effective physical spaces.

The social environment also will have an impact on consumers and employees. To some extent the social environment and its effects can be controlled, although perhaps less easily than the physical environment. Managing which customers have access to the servicescape through careful segmentation is one approach to controlling the social environment. The appearance and behavior of employees can also be managed through training and dress codes to engender the appropriate social environment. Cues in the environment can also provide indirect guidance to both customers and employees regarding the behaviors expected of them in the servicescape.

What Must Be Understood?

To effectively manage the physical and social dimensions of the servicescape, employee and customer responses to the servicescape must be understood. These responses fall into three basic categories: cognitive, emotional, and physiological. From a cognitive perspective, we know that the servicescape can have an effect on people's beliefs about a place and their beliefs about the products and services found in that place. In a sense the servicescape can be viewed as a form of nonverbal communication, imparting meaning through the objects in the environment. Therefore, understanding the meaning customers and employees attach to elements of environmental design will be critical to fully appreciating the marketing impact of the servicescape (Baker 1998; Gottdiener 1998).

Research also tells us that customers and employees will have purely emotional responses to the servicescape that can greatly affect their behaviors. Just being in a particular place can engender feelings of happiness, lightheartedness, and relaxation, while another place may bring out feelings of sadness, anxiety, or gloom. Elements of the physical and social environment can have unexplainable and sometimes very subconscious effects on behaviors of both customers and employees.

Finally, it is clear that dimensions of the servicescape can directly affect physiological responses of customers and employees. Noise that is too loud may cause physical discomfort, the temperature of a room may cause people to shiver or perspire, the air quality may make it difficult to breathe, and the glare of lighting may decrease ability to see or even cause physical pain. All these examples illustrate the importance of understanding the actual physical or ergonomic implications of servicescape design.

What Are the Desired Behaviors?

Before actually designing or attempting to control the servicescape, managers will want to clearly articulate the behaviors they desire from both employees and customers. Environmental psychologists suggest that individuals react to places with two general, and opposite, forms of behavior: approach and avoidance. Approach behaviors include all positive behaviors that might be directed at a particular place, such as desire to stay, explore, and affiliate. Avoidance behaviors reflect the opposite.

The servicescape can also affect the ability of customers and employees to carry out goal-directed behaviors. For customers this may translate into their ability to find what they need, purchase or consume the service in a manner they desire, and complete the transaction in a timely manner. For employees this may mean that the servicescape is designed to facilitate their work tasks and productivity.

Clearly the servicescape also influences the nature of social interactions that take place within the physical space. The space may affect the nature of inter-actions in terms of duration and the actual progression of events. Environmental variables such as physical proximity, seating arrangements, size, and flexibility can define the possibilities and limits of social episodes and even define the sequencing of interactions.

Reciprocal Effects

The framework in Figure 2.2 suggests that not only will the servicescape affect customer and employee responses and behaviors, but these behaviors can in turn impact the environment. By being in the environment, acting and interacting, customers and employees will have a reciprocal influence on the space itself. They can change, alter, destroy, or rearrange the servicescape dimensions in ways that may affect its meaning and effects. This reciprocal or feedback loop in the framework reinforces the notion that the servicescape is dynamic, and that it is continually construed and constructed by its inhabitants.

CONCLUSION

One purpose of this chapter was to convey the critical marketing impact of the servicescape. The chapter has defined and delimited the servicescape construct from a managerial perspective as *the immediate physical and social environments surrounding a service experience, transaction, or event*. In looking at the servicescape in this way we can immediately see its relevance to marketing issues and the many marketing roles it can play, often simultaneously.

A second purpose of the chapter is to update our understanding of the servicescape through reviewing recent research on the topic. It is clear from this review that although much has been learned, there are still many unanswered questions, particularly from a managerial perspective. Despite the tremendous and obvious importance to marketing, there is still relatively little published research on servicescape effects when compared to other marketing variables.

A final purpose of this chapter was to present a simplified and updated servicescape framework for managers. Using the framework, managers can begin to plan and implement servicescape designs that can achieve important marketing and organizational goals.

REFERENCES

Arnould, Eric J., Linda L. Price, and Patrick Tierney (1998), "The Wilderness Servicescape: An Ironic Commercial Landscape," in *Servicescapes: The Concept of Place in Contemporary Markets*, John F. Sherry, Jr., ed. Chicago: NTC/Contemporary Publishing Company, 403-38.

Aubert-Gamet, Veronique (1997), "Twisting Servicescapes: Diversion of the Physical Environment in a Re-appropriation Process," *International Journal of Service Industry Management*, 8(1), 26-41.

———— and Bernard Cova (1999), "Servicescapes: From Modern Non-Places to Postmodern Common Places," *Journal of Business Research*, 44, 37-45.

Baker, Julie (1998), "Examining the Informational Value of Store Environments," in *Servicescapes: The Concept of Place in Contemporary Markets*, John F. Sherry, Jr., ed. Chicago: NTC/Contemporary Publishing Company, 55-80.

——— and Michaelle Cameron (1996), "The Effects of the Service Environment on Affect and Consumer Perception of Waiting Time: An Integrative Review and Research Propositions," *Journal of the Academy of Marketing Science*, 24(4), 338-49.

———, Dhruv Grewal, and A. Parasuraman (1994), "The Influence of Store Environment on Quality Inferences and Store Image," *Journal of the Academy of Marketing Science*, 22(4), 328-39.

———, Michael Levy, and Dhruv Grewal (1992), "An Experimental Approach to Making Retail Store Environment Decisions," *Journal of Retailing*, 68(4), 445-60.

Bitner, Mary Jo (1992), "Servicescapes: The Impact of Physical Surroundings on Customers and Employees," *Journal of Marketing*, 56(2), 57-71.

Bloch, Peter H., Nancy M. Ridgway, and Scott A. Dawson (1994), "The Shopping Mall as Consumer Habitat," *Journal of Retailing*, 70(1), 23-42.

Bonnes, Mirilia and Gianfranco Secchiaroli (1995), *Environmental Psychology: A Psycho-social Introduction*. London: Sage.

Booms, Bernard H. and Mary Jo Bitner (1981), "Marketing Strategies and Organization Structures for Service Firms," in *Marketing of Services*, James H. Donnelly and William R. George, eds. Chicago: American Marketing Association, 47-51.

Cassidy, Tony (1997), *Environmental Psychology: Behaviour and Experience in Context*. East Sussex, UK: Psychology Press.

Chebat, Jean-Charles, Claire Gelinas-Chebat, and Pierre Filliatrault (1993), "Interactive Effects of Musical and Visual Cues on Time Perception: An Application to Waiting Lines in Banks," *Perceptual and Motor Skills*, 77, 995-1020.

Creighton, Millie (1998), "The Seed of Creative Lifestyle Shopping: Wrapping Consumerism in Japanese Store Layouts," in *Servicescapes: The Concept of Place in Contemporary Markets*, John F. Sherry, Jr., ed. Chicago: NTC/Contemporary Publishing Company, 199-228.

Cronin, J. Joseph, Jr., Roscoe Hightower, Jr., and G. Tomas M. Hult (1998), "PSSQ: Measuring Consumer Perceptions of the Servicescape," unpublished working paper, Florida State University.

Dubé, Laurette, Jean-Charles Chebat, and Sylvie Morin (1995), "The Effects of Background Music on Consumers' Desire to Affiliate in Buyer-Seller Interactions," *Psychology and Marketing*, 12(4), 305-19.

Gottdiener, M. (1998), "The Semiotics of Consumer Spaces: The Growing Importance of Themed Environments," in *Servicescapes: The Concept of Place in Contemporary Markets*, John F. Sherry, Jr., ed. Chicago: NTC/Contemporary Publishing Company, 29-54.

Grayson, Kent (1998), "Commercial Activity at Home: Managing the Private Servicescape," in *Servicescapes: The Concept of Place in Contemporary Markets*, John F. Sherry, Jr., ed. Chicago: NTC/Contemporary Publishing Company, 455-82.

Grove, Stephen J., Raymond P. Fisk, and Mary Jo Bitner (1992), "Dramatizing the Service Experience: A Managerial Approach," in *Advances in Services Marketing and Management: Research and Practice*, Vol. 1, Teresa A. Swartz, David E. Bowen, and Stephen W. Brown, eds. Greenwich, CT: JAI, 91-122.

Herrington, J. Duncan and Louis M. Capella (1994), "Practical Applications of Music in Service Settings," *Journal of Services Marketing*, 8(3), 50-65.

——— and ——— (1996), "Effects of Music in Service Environments: A Field Study," *The Journal of Services Marketing*, 10(2), 26-41.

Hightower, Roscoe (1997), "Conceptualizing and Measuring the Impact of Servicescape on Service Encounter Outcomes," doctoral dissertation, Florida State University, Tallahassee, FL.

Hui, Michael K., Laurette Dubé, and Jean-Charles Chebat (1997), "The Impact of Music on Consumers' Reactions to Waiting for Services," *Journal of Retailing*, 73(1), 87-104.

Joy, Annamma (1998), "Framing Art: The Role of Galleries in the Circulation of Art," in *Servicescapes: The Concept of Place in Contemporary Markets*, John F. Sherry, Jr., ed. Chicago: NTC/Contemporary Publishing Company, 259-304.

McAlexander, James H. and John W. Schouten (1998), "Brandfests: Servicescapes for the Cultivation of Brand Equity," in *Servicescapes: The Concept of Place in Contemporary Markets*, John F. Sherry, Jr., ed. Chicago: NTC/Contemporary Publishing Company, 377-402.

Mitchell, Deborah J., Barbara E. Kahn, and Susan C. Knasko (1995), "There's Something in the Air: Effects of Congruent or Incongruent Ambient Odor on Consumer Decision Making," *Journal of Consumer Research*, 22 (September), 229-38.

"The New VIP Rooms" (1998), *The Wall Street Journal* (1998), December 11, W1.

Otnes, Cele (1998), " 'Friend of the Bride'—and Then Some: Roles of the Bridal Salon During Wedding Planning," in *Servicescapes: The Concept of Place in Contemporary Markets*, John F. Sherry, Jr., ed. Chicago: NTC/Contemporary Publishing Company, 229-58.

Rafaeli, Anat (1993), "Dress and Behavior of Customer Contact Employees: A Framework for Analysis," in *Advances in Services Marketing and Management*, Vol. 2, Teresa A. Swartz, David E. Bowen, and Stephen W. Brown, eds. Greenwich, CT: JAI, 175-212.

Saegert, Susan and Gary H. Winkel (1990), "Environmental Psychology," *Annual Review of Psychology*, 41, 441-77.

Sherman, Elaine, Anil Mathur, and Ruth Belk Smith (1997), "Store Environment and Consumer Purchase Behavior: Mediating Role of Consumer Emotions," *Psychology and Marketing*, 14(4), 361-78.

Sherry, John F., Jr. (1998a), *Servicescapes: The Concept of Place in Contemporary Markets*. Chicago: NTC/Contemporary Publishing Company.

———— (1998b), "The Soul of the Company Store: Nike Town Chicago and the Emplaced Brandscape," in *Servicescapes: The Concept of Place in Contemporary Markets*, John F. Sherry, Jr., ed. Chicago: NTC/Contemporary Publishing Company, 109-46.

Solomon, Michael R. (1998), "Dressing for the Part: The Role of Costume in the Staging of the Servicescape," in *Servicescapes: The Concept of Place in Contemporary Markets*, John F. Sherry, Jr., ed. Chicago: NTC/Contemporary Publishing Company, 81-108.

Spangenberg, Eric R., Ayn E. Crowley, and Pamela W. Henderson (1996), "Improving the Store Environment: Do Olfactory Cues Affect Evaluations and Behaviors," *Journal of Marketing*, 60 (April), 67-80.

Sulek, Joanne M., Mary R. Lind, and Ann S. Marucheck (1995), "The Impact of a Customer Service Intervention and Facility Design on Firm Performance," *Management Science*, 41(11), 1763-73.

Sundstrom, Eric, Paul A. Bell, Paul L. Busby, and Cheryl Asmus (1996), "Environmental Psychology 1989-1994," *Annual Review of Psychology*, 47, 485-512.

Titus, Philip A. and Peter B. Everett (1996), "Consumer Wayfinding Tasks, Strategies, and Errors: An Exploratory Field Study," *Psychology and Marketing*, 13(3), 265-90.

Venkatesh, Alladi (1998), "Cyberculture: Consumers and Cybermarketscapes," in *Servicescapes: The Concept of Place in Contemporary Markets*, John F. Sherry, Jr., ed. Chicago: NTC/Contemporary Publishing Company, 343-76.

Wakefield, Kirk L. and Jeffrey G. Blodgett (1994), "The Importance of Servicescapes in Leisure Service Settings," *Journal of Services Marketing*, 8(3), 66-76.

———— and ———— (1996), "The Effect of the Servicescape on Customers' Behavioral Intentions in Leisure Service Settings," *Journal of Services Marketing*, 10(6), 45-61.

Wallendorf, Melanie, Joan Lindsey-Mullikin, and Ron Pimentel (1998), "Gorilla Marketing: Customer Animation and Regional Embeddedness of a Toy Store Servicescape," in *Servicescapes: The Concept of Place in Contemporary Markets*, John F. Sherry, Jr., ed. Chicago: NTC/Contemporary Publishing Company, 151-98.

Webster, Frederick (1992), "The Changing Role of Marketing in the Corporation," *Journal of Marketing*, 56 (October), 1-17.

Yoo, Changjo, Jonghee Park, and Deborah J. MacInnis (1998), "Effects of Store Characteristics and In-Store Emotional Experiences on Store Attitude," *Journal of Business Research*, 42, 253-63.

Zeithaml, Valarie and Mary Jo Bitner (1996), *Services Marketing*. New York: McGraw-Hill.

3

Impression Management in Services Marketing

KENT GRAYSON
DAVID SHULMAN

Comparisons between theatrical performances and everyday life are embedded in our language. A person doing a good job is said to be "well-suited for the role." When someone's behavior is stilted, it seems "scripted." A person behaving in unexpected ways is "acting out of character." In the academic literature, drawing links between theater and life is more formally called the "dramaturgical metaphor," and it is a cornerstone of impression management theory. Just as Shakespeare wrote that "all the world's a stage and all the men and women merely players," impression management theorists propose that people enact "roles" and "scripts" on the "stages" of life.

Despite this metaphor's common use, some researchers have argued that it provides a shaky foundation for academic progress. For example, based on their work with psychiatric patients, Messinger, Sampson, and Towne (1962) suggest that people rarely feel like actors on a stage and that such feelings are more indicative of mental illness than everyday experience. Both Wilshire (1982) and Dewey (1969) argue that there are so many differences between theater and life that the dramaturgical metaphor is misleading and inappropriate for scientific inquiry. Dewey (1969) goes so far as to conclude with the hope that "dramaturgical analysis and description . . . will follow the mechanistic and organic models into the pages of histories of social thought, bereft of all but historical relevance for sociology and social psychology" (p. 310).

We concur with the spirit of these criticisms. A research paper or program that stops solely at proposing that life is like theater is unlikely to produce useful empirical and theoretical generalizations. The observation that one domain's

AUTHORS' NOTE: The authors thank Amy Ostrom for her suggestions regarding consumer impression management.

terminology is applicable to another may prompt creative metaphorical thinking (Polanyi 1964) and help with everyday understanding (Burke 1945; Fernandez 1986) but can be vulnerable to the criticism of being purely descriptive rather than explanatory, prescriptive, or predictive. While recognizing the limits to simply drawing comparisons between life and theater, however, it is important to note that most impression management scholars seek a more substantive goal in their research: to offer an analytic framework for exploring, testing, and understanding how people manage contradictions between appearance and reality in social interaction. Given this emphasis, impression management theory has considerable potential for the study and management of services marketing.

Service companies depend on front-line service workers to control and communicate the image that consumers will have of their product or service. Because image control often demands that service workers act according to scripts that diverge from their actual inherent preferences and capacities, a number of conflicts arise regarding the truthfulness or sincerity of service performances. For example, many service employees want to do a good job for their employers and yet sometimes find that performing well means being deceptive with customers. Service employees commonly must smile when they are frustrated, promise what may not be delivered, and treat seemingly mundane customer concerns with due earnestness and deference.

On the other side of the service relationship, customers often want to be served by a "real person," and yet they are also aware that service employees are paid for performing certain service scripts. When a hotel desk clerk tells a frequent customer that "It's nice to see you're staying here again," will the customer interpret this as a genuine expression of feeling or as a programmed response to a notation in the hotel's customer database? Which interpretation will result in higher satisfaction? To complicate matters further, consumers themselves are often trying to create impressions, so service workers must also try to gauge consumers' true intentions. Such scrutiny is particularly relevant, for example, when customers are applying for loans, making comments in a classroom, or describing an embarrassing illness to a medical professional.

Theatrical metaphors are useful for describing conflicts between appearance and reality because theatrical personnel explicitly tackle these conflicts in crafting their performances. Thus, the language of their profession provides researchers with a useful set of commonly accepted terms for exploring sincerity and deception. It is important, however, not to assume that scholars use dramaturgical terms only for metaphorical comparisons. Such an assumption misses the great promise and applicability of impression management research—a promise that, as we now shall show, has been only partially fulfilled in services marketing research.

THEORETICAL BACKGROUND

As Victor Turner's anthropological works have suggested (e.g., Turner 1988), the act of playing a role is one of human society's earliest rituals, beginning with the ancient hunters who "transformed" themselves into the spirits of their prey. Ever since, the dynamics and pitfalls of pretense have been central to culture, literature, and philosophizing, ranging from Plato's Dialogues and Shakespearean plays through the 19th-century works of William James and Charles Peirce to the present-day works of Jean Baudrillard and Umberto Eco. Because we do not know what others are truly thinking or intending when they act, we must determine their intentions based on the symbols and signs they offer to us (such as the clothes they wear or the gestures they use). Building from this basic social fact, George Herbert Mead (1934) and Herbert Blumer (1986) emphasized the symbolic nature of all society and founded a theoretical perspective called symbolic interactionism. Impression management research is an offshoot of symbolic interaction theory and can be thought of as an applied, empirical arm of this theoretical tradition.

Erving Goffman, a sociologist, is widely recognized as the founder of modern impression management theory. In *The Presentation of Self in Everyday Life*, Goffman (1959/1973) observed that people's behaviors in social situations are strongly guided by the norms that exist for that situation. Goffman (1959/1973) calls these norms the "definition of the situation." His term emphasizes that people actively—although often implicitly—develop a definitional consensus about each interaction, particularly concerning how people are to perform in it. This consensus can apply generally to many social situations or narrowly to a specific type of interaction. For example, in most social situations, people are prohibited from hitting one another, but contestants in a boxing ring are supposed to do so.

The expected sets of behaviors associated with each definition of the situation are called "roles" (Goffman 1959/1973; Solomon et al. 1985). "Role expectations" are sets of beliefs and subjective assumptions that people have about the appropriate conduct for individuals occupying a particular status in a social situation (Sarbin and Allen 1968, p. 498). In each situation, people are influenced by different role expectations, so each definition has a "role set" associated with it, which is a group of complementary behavioral expectations (Merton 1957).

Despite an endless variety of social situations and rules, most people from the same cultural background have a remarkable ability to determine quickly—based on environmental cues, socialization, and nonverbal signals from others—what the appropriate definition of a situation is. Alfred Schutz, a phenomenologist whose writings also influenced impression management theory, observes that this ability is due to the "stock of knowledge" that people have about social situations. This knowledge is developed via socialization and comprises social "recipes" that dictate appropriate behaviors in different situations (e.g., Schutz and Luckmann 1973, pp. 99-116). For example, experience dictates that waiters and waitresses who affect a helpful, deferential demeanor and deliver prompt service should receive tips. Both customers and service personnel depend on this "social recipe" to facilitate a smooth service encounter that satisfies both parties to the exchange.

Roles equate metaphorically to the sense of direction that an actor's lines offer in a play—they are bundles of "social scripts" that dictate the type of impression that an individual must present. In both the theater and in everyday life, actors have some latitude in their individual performance of a role, but just as an actor's behaviors are constrained by a script, a director, and the motivations of the "character" or role she or he is playing, social norms and personal goals usually limit an individual's everyday behaviors. For example, if a guest wishes to make a good impression at a dinner party, social norms are likely to keep him from saying that he does not like the food being served. If a job applicant wants to make a good impression at an interview, social expectations will encourage her to hide any nervousness she feels.

Although impression management theory does attend to how definitions of the situation govern frontstage behavior, it does not posit that people are completely bound by preset social recipes. Although most social activity will run smoothly because actors have a shared definition of the situation, there are occasions when people will disagree, and these require more explicit negotiation among actors (Grayson 1998a; Rafaeli 1989). For example, a graphic designer who runs her business from home may find that her clients fall into a more casual set of role behaviors (because of the home environment) despite her personal signals that they maintain a more professional role. Some consumers also gain value by purposefully breaking situational rules (Bitner, Booms, and Mohr 1994; Grayson 1999). For instance, a customer may enjoy the fun of driving a rental car in off-road environments despite the car rental company's restrictions against such behavior.

As these examples indicate, and as we have emphasized from the outset, individuals may often be required to act in ways that contradict their personal feelings and attitudes. Researching those occasions when a person's actual feelings diverge from his or her performed attitudes and emotions is a central concern for impression management theorists. To represent the potential divergence between appearance and reality, impression management scholars classify social interaction as occurring in two "regions" or, metaphorically, two theatrical stages (Goffman 1959/1973; Scheier and Carver 1983; Schlenker 1980). Members of the "audience" generally see one of these regions, called the "front stage," while the other region, called the "back stage," is generally hidden. Thus, in the back stage, people can take actions that, if seen, would contradict a desired impression. For example, a waiter who behaves abjectly at a diner's table can pass through kitchen doors and then, safely out of view, enter a backstage region where his show of deference can be dropped (Goffman 1959/1973). The back stage is also a region where people may, out of an audience's sight, prepare for frontstage performances, such as when amusement park workers put their costumes on in dressing rooms and when chefs prepare meals in kitchens beyond the view of patrons.

How people manage the borders between front- and backstage performances is a significant question to impression management theorists. In fact, a prominent stream of research in impression management scholarship addresses the scripts individuals use when they believe that their backstage "reality" has discredited their frontstage appearance and their ability to adhere to acceptable social norms. Goffman (e.g., 1967) referred to these scripts as attempts by the norm-breaker to "save face"—that is, to maintain his or her positive image. Accounts (Scott and Lyman 1968) and techniques of neutralization (Sykes and Matza 1957) are among the rationalizing scripts that impression management scholars have examined, and these have been expanded and enriched by additional researchers (e.g., Gardner and Martinko 1988; Jones and Pittman 1982; Schlenker 1980).

Because impression management is conceived as an inherently social activity, marketing researchers have applied impression management theory primarily to services marketing activities, which are inherently more social than product marketing activities (Lovelock 1991, p. 7). Although we will emphasize services marketing issues in this chapter, it is important to note that the impression management framework can be applied to a wider range of business-related social phenomena, including product marketing (e.g., Folkes 1984) and intraorganizational behavior (e.g., Giacalone and Payne 1995). Even within services marketing, impression management can be applied in a number of ways. Grove and Fisk (e.g., 1989, 1991, 1992) have been among the strongest proponents for the benefits of applying a dramaturgical metaphor to services marketing. Their work (represented in Chapter 1 of this handbook) has been particularly useful in highlighting how impression management offers a useful framework for the development and implementation of new approaches to service management. However, as Grove and Fisk (1989, p. 427) point out, their approach is just one of many ways that impression management can be applied to services marketing, and in this chapter we emphasize some of the alternatives.

To do so, we examine four general issues that highlight additional ways in which impression management theory and research have been, and can be, applied in services marketing. First we describe the different "actors" in services marketing who can engage in impression management: service employees, service organizations, and service customers. We then address issues related to authentic and deceptive impression management and follow with a section on the relative influence of front- and backstage actions on consumer perceptions. We conclude with a discussion of how other academic literatures in marketing offer points of contact with impression management theory.

THE ACTORS: SERVICE PROVIDERS, ORGANIZATIONS, AND CUSTOMERS

Because the dramaturgical terms "front stage" and "back stage" denote physical spaces, they imply that impression management theory applies primarily to service environments. Indeed, impression management is useful for analyzing the design and management of service environments because it highlights the potential impact of making some areas visible to consumers and some areas hidden (e.g., Shostack 1981, 1987). Impression management theory was initially conceived, however, for application to human social action, and therefore can also be applied more metaphorically to people and even to organizations.

Scholars have frequently applied impression management theory to understand how service employees manage the expectations of service roles. There is a rich literature on the rigors of service performance and on the assessment of service

workers as actors. One of the most influential books in this tradition is
Hochschild's (1983) *The Managed Heart*, which examines how students, flight
attendants, and bill collectors handle social expectations for enacting required
emotions and demeanor. There is a great dependency and pressure on service
workers, who are often lowest on the organizational hierarchy, to fulfill the needs
and implement the strategies of the service organizations that employ them. In
particular, as the "front person," a service worker carries much of the responsibility for organizational representation. This is particularly true when the service
worker's behaviors are a large part of what the service organization is offering to
customers. For example, nearly every action and emotional display of a tour guide
during the several days of a river-rafting trip shapes the very interpretation of the
consumption experience of that extended service encounter (Price, Arnould, and
Tierney 1995).

When considering the emotional demands placed on service workers,
Hochschild (1983) coined the term "emotional labor"—labor that "requires one
to induce or suppress feeling in order to sustain the outward countenance that
produces the proper state of mind in others" (p. 7). For example, Hochschild
observes that, regardless of their personal feelings, flight attendants must often
"manufacture smiles" for hundreds of passengers because airline managers view
a flight attendant's pleasant demeanor as crucial to their product. Thus, emotional
labor occurs when a waitress smiles even when she is angry, when a teacher is
stern even when he prefers to be lenient, and when an attorney appears to remain
neutral even when she is biased. Using Goffman's terms, emotional labor occurs
when social requirements demand frontstage emotional displays that belie divergent backstage feelings.

Hochschild's (1983) book documents many ways that human beings in general
and service providers in particular are asked to perform emotional labor, and how
people manage these demands. Building from this work, Leidner (1993) further
delineates the training process of emotional labor, examining how fast food
organizations and large insurance companies teach and routinize emotional labor
and impression management in their employees' service work. Together, these
works identify a number of ethical and cultural implications associated with the
growing emotional demands placed on service providers. The impact of emotional labor (and the associated influence of role conflict and role ambiguity) on
service providers has promoted considerable additional research. For more detailed conceptual coverage, refer to Rafaeli and Sutton (1987, 1989) and Morris
and Feldman (1996). Empirical studies include Boles and Babin (1996); Gaines
and Jermier (1983); Hartline and Ferrell (1996); Staw, Sutton, and Pelled
(1994); Sutton (1991); and Wharton and Erickson (1993). These studies and
others paint a complex picture of emotional labor's antecedents and consequences, with mixed benefits for employees and employers.

A further issue relevant to impression management in service employees is
what can be called the "casting" requirements of varied service roles. How does
an individual's outward (frontstage) appearance affect the audience's willingness
to accept him or her in a particular role? For example, men and women who
perform jobs that are traditionally undertaken by the other gender (for example,

male nurses or female construction workers) report that audiences have difficulties accepting them as legitimate performers of those roles (Williams 1995). Audiences look for particular "legitimating" characteristics, even though these characteristics sometimes do not tangibly affect the ability of the performer to perform the role. For example, male and female nurses are equally able to administer doses of medication, and male and female construction workers are equally able to maneuver a bulldozer. Gender stereotypes nevertheless can invade the audience's evaluation of these occupations to the extent that the physical characteristics of a service performer legitimate (or not) the performer's ability to play the role successfully. Audiences also use ethnicity and race as evaluative characteristics of performances, such as when people recommend ethnic restaurants based on observing members of that ethnic group eating there. Research by Neckerman and Kirschenman (1991), for example, has found that some employers will not hire minority candidates for certain jobs because of the employers' perceptions that audiences will not accept those candidates as legitimate performers of those roles (see also Ginsberg 1996). Employer concern for how audiences will interpret an actor's capacity for a role also may lead to subterfuge by employers and employees. For example, a legal or consulting intern might perform more important work backstage than can be revealed to a client in the front stage.

Just as people have front and back stages, so too do organizations. Managers, employees, and customers view organizations as entities with identities that are managed and controlled (Olins 1994). Organizational identity is crucial for attracting and sustaining consumers, for distinguishing an organization from competitors, and for maintaining employee morale. The potential impact of organizational identity is illustrated in research by Dutton and Dukerich (1991), who examine how perceptions of organizational identity affected employee and customer reactions to the management of a transportation service. Elsbach and Kramer (1996) have also documented how a threat to organizational identity can affect the behavior of employees in educational service organizations.

Other research has documented impression management strategies that companies use to influence perceptions of company image. Elsbach and Sutton (1992) examine how organizations involved with illegitimate activities (such as the "spiking" of trees by environmental activists) manage their front stages in ways that may be divergent from those employed at the back—depending on the audience. Similarly, Elsbach, Sutton, and Principe (1998) document how a hospital used "anticipatory impression management" techniques to minimize the potential impact of a change in policy on customers. Some researchers (e.g., Staw, McKechnie, and Puffer 1983) have even examined how organizational documents, such as annual reports, are crafted with varied impression management goals in mind. For example, Lutz (1983) has collected examples of "doublespeak," which is frontstage terminology that individuals and organizations use to diminish potential negative reactions to controversial backstage activities—such as referring to firing workers as providing them with a "new career alternative enhancement" program.

Surprisingly, the impression management actor studied least of all in services marketing research is the customer. Although scholars have documented deceptions by service workers (Maiken 1979; Mars 1982), much less attention has been paid to understanding how customers manage their own impressions in service environments, such as when homeowners misrepresent a home's condition to real estate agents or pretend to be surprised by the "high price" quoted by a merchant. When research does examine customers' impressions, it tends to study how they do or do not meet the role requirements of a particular service activity (e.g., Bitner, Booms, and Mohr 1994; Grove, Fisk, and Bitner 1992, pp. 102-4). This is a focus on the customer's front stage, but customers have back stages as well, which they will reveal or hide depending on the situation (Grove and Fisk 1992).

Some service professions are dedicated to assisting consumers with frontstage management, while other service workers specialize in penetrating peoples' backstage secrets. For example, plastic surgeons, beauticians, and personal trainers all provide frontstage "identity work" for their clients (e.g., Schouten 1991). Even the service workers themselves can become part of the client's front stage, such as in situations where "anybody who is anybody" has to have a particular professional working for them. Conversely, consumers may hire service workers who specialize in working in the back stage, such as psychologists, who help consumers understand their own back stages, or private detectives, who work clandestinely to reveal the backstage secrets of others (e.g., Shulman 1994).

In this section we have examined three "actors" in the service environment who can manage impressions: the service employee, the service organization, and the service customer. Although we have considered each of these social actors independently, they interact with one another in the service environment, and few researchers have made progress in understanding these interactions. For example, it is useful to consider the relative influence that service workers, employers, and customers have in determining the operating definition of the situation. The definition of the situation may be elastic to the degree that a customer, employer, or service worker has the relative power to influence it. For example, a customer may use the threat of a complaint to management or the reward of a monetary tip to convince a hotel worker to deliver room service after hours. Similarly, an aerobics instructor may manipulate peer pressure to encourage clients to "loosen up" and behave in unaccustomed ways. Furthermore, service firms, via employee regulation manuals, may demand that both customers and employees dress in particular clothing. The malleability of definitions of the situation in service work, and the relative power of each service actor to define the situation, should be better understood, given its consequence to all the involved parties.

MANIPULATING FRONT AND BACK STAGES: AUTHENTICITY, SINCERITY, AND DECEPTIVE IMPRESSION MANAGEMENT

Much impression management research has focused on how people construct an attractive or appropriate front stage in situations where the back stage is disagreeable or undesirable to the target audience (Goffman 1959/1973; Schlenker 1980,

p. 8). A deceptive construction may exist, however in another frontstage/backstage combination: an individual may construct a negative front stage in situations where the back stage is positive. Becker and Martin (1995), for example, found that some employees purposefully perform poorly at work to avoid workplace competition or challenging tasks.

Another possible front/backstage combination is having a front stage that accurately reflects the back. This has been called "authentic self-presentation" (Leary 1993, p. 146), "deep acting" (Hochshild 1983, p. 33), and "self projection" (Schlenker 1980, p. 8). It may initially seem as if "authentic self-presentation" should come naturally and is therefore not as worthy of study as more misleading impression management; however, the impression management framework emphasizes that all successful self-presentations, even the most authentic, do not "just happen" and require a keen understanding of the social rules in which the presentation occurs. Actors must communicate to audiences that what appears to be an honest performance actually is an honest performance. As Goffman (1959/1973) observes, a

> *Vogue* model, by her clothing, stance, and facial expression, is able expressively to portray a cultivated understanding of the book she poses in her hand; but those who trouble to express themselves so appropriately will have very little time left over for reading. . . . Those who have the time and talent to perform a task well may not . . . have the time or talent to make it apparent that they are performing well. (pp. 32-33)

To be perceived as sincere, one must enact social behaviors according to accepted recipes of sincerity. This necessity presents a paradox: The behaviors dictated by the recipe might not be those that one would "sincerely" enact in the absence of social rules—a philosophical dilemma that attracted Sartre's (1956) attention on several occasions (cf. Trilling 1972). From a practical perspective, the implication is that being perceived as authentic does require strategic effort and is therefore an area that could benefit from inquiry.

Goffman (1959/1973) points out that "some organizations resolve this dilemma by officially delegating the dramatic function to a specialist who will spend his time expressing the meaning of the task and spend no time actually doing it" (p. 33). He is, of course, referring to marketing practitioners. Organizational theorists as well have written of the increasing "decoupling" of production and legitimation functions in contemporary organizations (Meyer and Rowan 1977).

Besides arising from unintentionally poor or amorally motivated performers, fraudulent impression management may also result from benevolent intentions. For example, doctors sometimes give anxious patients placebos to help them feel better, teachers sometimes give undeserved praise to encourage students, and shoe salespeople sometimes secretly bring a larger shoe size to customers because the size requested would have been too small (e.g., Goffman 1959/1973, p. 18). Regardless of whether the deception is intentional or benevolent, people are often interested in the extent to which the front stage matches the back. Impression management scholarship has developed a thorough capacity for researching and conceptualizing these issues. Goffman (1969), for example, has categorized processes of "strategic interaction," where actors engage in "moves" and "countermoves" to expose inauthentic performances. There also is a rich literature on how individuals and organizations attempt to repair their images when they are caught "out of character," such as when an expert makes a discrediting mistake or when a person is caught betraying a friend's secret. Impression management theorists have inventoried specific tactics and excuses people use to smooth out the "strained interactions" that result either from actors having to manage physical and social stigmas or from actors having to compensate for failing to perform as they are expected (see Goffman 1963 and Scott and Lyman 1968 for classic examples).

THE IMPACT OF THE FRONT STAGE AND BACK STAGE ON CONSUMER PERCEPTIONS

The scope of impression management research need not be limited only to visual elements of services marketing. Some researchers do emphasize this element: Front stage is the area that can be seen by the consumer, and back stage is the area that cannot (Gummesson 1990, p. 44; Lovelock 1991, p. 14; Shostack 1987). The front stage, however, may also include aural, olfactory, and tactile elements. In fact, when a "talking Yellow Pages" service gives restaurant advice by phone, this service's front stage is wholly aural.

More important, by defining the back stage as what consumers cannot see, marketers often conclude that the back stage cannot influence consumer perceptions. In Lovelock's (1991) words, the back stage "is of little interest to customers. Like any audience, [customers] evaluate the production with reference to those elements that they actually experience" (p. 14). The managerial utility of this perspective is illustrated by Matteis (1979) in his analysis of Citibank's customer satisfaction efforts in the 1970s. By streamlining account processing activities, Citibank managers increased efficiency, reduced costs, and improved employee morale, but the impact on customer evaluations was weak. Matteis (1979) concluded that Citibank's efforts were ineffective at the consumer level because the changes were entirely backstage and were not directly communicated using frontstage activity. Similarly, Mangold and Babakus (1991) found that service employees' perceptions of a service are often different from those of their customers because the employees are exposed to backstage areas of which customers are not aware.

Although observations like these are useful, they overlook some important contributions that an impression management orientation can make in researching services marketing. Although front and back stage are often physically separated, the distinction between front and back stage is socially, not physically, determined (MacCannell 1976, p. 92). Consumer judgments of the marketer's intention, not physical barriers, create the critical dividing line between front and back stage. Consumers examine the cues presented by the marketer and make a decision about whether this is frontstage or backstage information. In the language of impression management, this means that the consumer makes a judgment about whether or not the marketer has successfully "performed" a particular "social reality" (Goffman 1959/1973, pp. 65-66; Sarbin and Allen 1968; Schlenker 1980, pp. 98-105). If the consumer believes that the marketer is primarily trying to make a certain consumer impression, the marketer has successfully enacted a frontstage performance. If the consumer believes that the marketer is not altering things so as to make such an impression, then the marketer has enacted a backstage performance.

The idea that consumers might be influenced by what they believe to be the back stage is widely mentioned by scholars, although not often emphasized (Goffman 1959/1973, p. 209; Grove and Fisk 1989, p. 436; Price, Arnould, and Tierney 1995, p. 90; Schlenker 1980; Tedeschi and Riess 1981; Thomas 1937, p. 137). The managerial benefits of managing the back stage are illustrated in Grayson's (1998b) study of consumer responses to a hotel scenario. Here, customer exposure to the "perceived back stage" did, under certain conditions, affect consumer attitudes toward the service.

ACADEMIC LITERATURES WITH RELEVANCE TO IMPRESSION MANAGEMENT

Given that impression management addresses the ubiquitous activity of controlling one's image, it has relevance to a wide range of human activities and academic literature. For example, persuasion research is also concerned with how people influence other people's perceptions and opinions (Keller and Block 1996; Petty, Cacioppo, and Schuman 1983). Whereas persuasion research tends to examine the manipulation and perception of factual information (such as the quality of a camera or the performance of an automobile), however, impression management research tends to examine the manipulation and perception of more social information (such as the integrity of an attorney or the politeness of a waiter). As a result, persuasion research tends to invoke cognitive explanations for its phenomena, whereas impression management research tends to invoke social or social-psychological explanations.

The flip side of impression management—and therefore its close ally—is attribution theory. Whereas the former examines strategies that people use to influence other people's impressions, the latter examines how people respond (i.e., make attributions) to impression management activities. Accordingly, it is natural that research in one theoretical domain will lead to observations that are relevant to the other: Response tendencies will affect the strategies designed to influence these responses. For example, although Staw, McKechnie, and Puffer (1983) examine the strategies that companies use to justify their performance, they use attribution theory as a way of examining these strategies. When Bitner (1990) examines how consumers respond to different accounts for service failure, she is inherently exploring the different accounts that service providers use to manage their images. Attribution theory, however, is not the only theoretical base for understanding customer responses to impression management activity. For example, a pair of studies by Rafaeli and Sutton (Rafaeli and Sutton 1990; Sutton and Rafaeli 1988) point to the potential impact of the service context (e.g., busy stores versus quiet ones) on perceptions of emotional display in convenience stores. In addition, Grayson (1998b) suggests that social-psychological theories relating to trust and self-disclosure offer a foundation for predicting customer responses to emotional display in hotels.

Another related academic literature is that focusing on "interpersonal deception theory" (Buller and Burgoon 1996). Researchers pursuing this type of research do not invoke the dramaturgical metaphor; however, they are interested in the strategies that actors use when trying to deceive one another and the skills required to know whether or not someone is being deceptive. What is perhaps most interesting about this literature is the finding that individuals generally do not make accurate assessments of other people's deceptiveness or sincerity (Ekman and O'Sullivan 1991; Fleming et al. 1990; Poole and Craig 1992). Certain facial cues, however, have been shown to indicate deceptive communication (Ekman, Freisen, and O'Sullivan 1988), and increased suspicion has been shown (in some circumstances) to increase one's ability to detect deception (McCornack and Levine 1990). Alternatively, there has been little research exploring the skills and resources actors require to sustain and conceal deceptive back- and frontstage performances. Hence, when a service must be marketed or an issue negotiated, the ability to bluff and camouflage one's true feelings draws on performance resources and skills that are not well understood. Although there is a burgeoning literature on how to detect deception, there is a clear need to understand better the architecture and performance of successful deceptions.

CONCLUSION: IMPRESSION MANAGEMENT AND IDENTITY

Impression management is just one of many potential perspectives on social life. Although it has proven useful to researchers seeking to understand social inter-action, alternative perspectives have been raised. One potential criticism of impression management theory is that it presents an overly simplistic and binary view of the self (Wilshire 1982). Some researchers view impression management theory as proposing that the self comprises a "real" self in the back stage and a performed self (one that is to some extent "unreal") in the front. The roles that people play, however, have been shown to have an influence on the self (Thoits 1983), which suggests that an individual's front stage is as much a "real" part of the self as his or her back stage. In fact, Silver and Sabini (1985) go so far as to argue that the impression management framework has no room for a "real" self because it depends so heavily on social rules and restrictions.

Goffman himself supported this latter view. Those who advocate the Western view of an authentic self worry about the effects of displaying contradictory pretenses to the world; their concern is not to let "their masks become their face."

Goffman, however, argued that there is no authentic self behind the masks. In Goffman's view, individual identity exists only as layers of different external self-presentations. From his perspective, there are only masks, and each mask comes with an accompanying identity that people "wear" until switching to a different mask. Goffman's view is consistent at a basic level with the postmodern perspective that there is no unitary (or authentic) identity, and that one's self is fragmented by the many social demands placed on each individual as he or she moves from one interactional relationship to another (Lyotard 1979, p. 15).

Is there an authentic individual identity, or is it just an individual image that appears authentic to others? Do people possess an intrinsic individuality, or are they simply able to express an image that appears individual to others? One reading of impression management theorizing suggests that a real self exists in the back stage and that one's performed self can accurately or inaccurately reflect this self via social interaction. This view of the self may oversimplify the real complexity of managing identity in our current social climate, but it does reflect an everyday view held by many people as they go through their everyday interactions throughout the world. Although different cultures place different emphases on the balance that should be placed on front stage and back stage, the idea that everyone has a "real self" is a common assumption in daily life throughout the world (e.g., Abiodun, Drewal, and Pemberton 1990; Cheek and Hogan 1983; Drewal 1977; Fenigstein, Scheier, and Buss 1975; Hamaguchi 1985; Scheier and Carver 1983). Thus, it is useful to study how this view of the self affects human interaction in general and service interactions in particular.

Furthermore, as Goffman's own writings indicate, this simplistic view of the self is not the only way to use impression management theory as a basis for research and management insight. Impression management research is more generally concerned with how people manage contradictions between appearance and reality in social interaction; thus, it offers a number of perspectives and tools for tackling these often difficult social issues. The issue of human identity is so complex that one perspective will never offer a complete picture of its inner workings, but impression management theory is uniquely positioned to prompt questions about identity that not only are important to both research and management, but also are not prompted by other theoretical perspectives.

REFERENCES

Abiodun, Rowland, Henry J. Drewal, and John Pemberton II (1990), *Yoruba Art and Aesthetics.* Zurich: Center for African Art and the Rietberg Museum.

Becker, Thomas E. and Scott L. Martin (1995), "Trying to Look Bad at Work: Methods and Motives for Managing Poor Impressions in Organizations," *Academy of Management Journal*, 38, 174-99.

Bitner, Mary Jo (1990), "Evaluating Service Encounters: The Effects of Physical Surroundings and Employee Responses," *Journal of Marketing*, 54 (April), 69-82.

———, Bernard Booms, and Lois A. Mohr (1994), "Critical Service Encounters: The Employee's Viewpoint," *Journal of Marketing*, 58 (October), 95-106.

Blumer, Herbert (1986), *Symbolic Interactionism: Perspective and Method.* Berkeley: University of California Press.

Boles, James S. and Barry J. Babin (1996), "On the Front Lines: Stress, Conflict, and the Customer Service Provider," *Journal of Business Research*, 37, 41-50.

Buller, David B. and Judee K. Burgoon (1996), "Interpersonal Deception Theory," *Communication Theory*, 6 (August), 203-42.

Burke, Kenneth (1945), *A Grammar of Motives*. Berkeley: University of California Press.

Cheek, Jonathan M. and Robert Hogan (1983), "Self-Concepts, Self-Presentations, and Moral Judgments," in *Psychological Perspectives on the Self*, Vol. 2, Jerry Suls and Anthony G. Greenwald, eds. Hillsdale, NJ: Lawrence Erlbaum, 249-73.

Dewey, Richard (1969), "The Theatrical Analogy Reconsidered," *The American Sociologist*, 5 (November), 307-11.

Drewal, Henry J. (1977), *Traditional Art of the Nigerian Peoples*. Washington, DC: Museum of African Art.

Dutton, Jane E. and Janet M. Dukerich (1991), "Keeping an Eye on the Mirror: Image and Identity in Organizational Adaptation," *Academy of Management Review*, 34, 517-54.

Ekman, Paul, Wallace V. Freisen, and Maureen O'Sullivan (1988), "Smiles When Lying," *Journal of Personality and Social Psychology*, 54, 414-20.

——— and Maureen O'Sullivan (1991), "Who Can Catch a Liar?" *American Psychologist*, 49, 913-19.

Elsbach, Kimberly D. and Roderick M. Kramer (1996), "Members' Responses to Organizational Identity Threats: Encountering and Countering the *Business Week* Rankings," *Administrative Science Quarterly*, 41, 442-76.

———, and Robert I. Sutton (1992), "Acquitting Organizational Legitimacy Through Illegitimate Actions: A Marriage of Institutional and Impression Management Theories," *Academy of Management Journal*, 35, 699-738.

———, ———, and Kristine E. Principe (1998), "Averting Expected Challenges Through Anticipatory Impression Management: A Study of Hospital Billing," *Organization Science*, 9 (January-February), 68-86.

Fenigstein, A., M. F. Scheier, and Arnold H. Buss (1975), "Public and Private Self-Consciousness: Assessment and Theory," *Journal of Consulting and Clinical Psychology*, 43, 522-27.

Fernandez, James W. (1986), "The Mission of Metaphor in Everyday Culture," in *Persuasions and Performances*. Bloomington: University of Indiana Press.

Fleming, John H., John M. Darley, James L. Hilton, and Brian A. Kojetin (1990), "Multiple Audience Problem: A Strategic Communication Perspective on Social Perception," *Journal of Personality and Social Psychology*, 58, 593-609.

Folkes, Valerie (1984), "Consumer Responses to Product Failure: An Attributional Approach," *Journal of Consumer Research*, 10, 398-409.

Gaines, Jeannie and John M. Jermier (1983), "Emotional Exhaustion in a High Stress Organization," *Academy of Management Journal*, 26, 567-86.

Gardner, William L. and Mark J. Martinko (1988), "Impression Management in Organizations," *Journal of Management*, 14(2), 321-38.

Giacalone, J. and J. Payne (1995), "Evaluation of Employee Rule Violations: The Impact of Impression Management Effects in Historical Context," *Journal of Business Ethics*, 14, 477-87.

Ginsberg, Elaine K., ed. (1996), *Passing and the Fictions of Identity*. Durham, NC: Duke University Press.

Goffman, Erving (1963), *Stigma: Notes on the Management of Spoiled Identity*. Englewood Cliffs, NJ: Prentice Hall.

——— (1967), "On Face Work: An Analysis of Ritual Elements in Social Interaction," in *Interaction Ritual: Essays on Face-to-Face Behavior*. Middlesex, UK: Penguin Books, 5-46.

——— (1969), *Strategic Interaction*. Philadelphia: University of Pennsylvania Press.

——— [1959] (1973), *The Presentation of Self in Everyday Life*. Woodstock, NY: Overlook.

Grayson, Kent (1998a), "Commercial Activity at Home: Managing the Private Servicescape," in *Servicescapes: The Concept of Place in Contemporary Markets*, John F. Sherry, Jr., ed. Chicago: NTC/Contemporary Publishing Company, 455-82.

——— (1998b), "Customer Responses to Emotional Labor in Discrete and Relational Service Exchange," *International Journal of Service Industry Management*, 9, 103-25.

——— (1999), "The Dangers and Opportunities of Playful Consumption," in *Consumer Value*, Morris B. Holbrook, ed. New York: Routledge, 105-25.

Grove, Stephen J. and Raymond P. Fisk (1989), "Impression Management in Services Marketing: A Dramaturgical Perspective," in *Impression Management in the Organization*. Hillsdale, NJ: Lawrence Erlbaum, 427-38.

———— and ———— (1991), "The Dramaturgy of Services Exchange: An Analytical Framework for Services Marketing," in *Services Marketing: Text Cases and Readings*, 2nd ed., Christopher Lovelock, ed. Englewood Cliffs, NJ: Prentice-Hall, 59-68.

———— and ———— (1992), "The Service Experience as Theater," in *Advances in Consumer Research*, Vol. 19, Brian Sternthal and John F. Sherry, Jr., eds. Provo, UT: Association for Consumer Research, 455-61.

————, ————, and Mary Jo Bitner (1992), "Dramatizing the Service Experience: A Managerial Approach," in *Advances in Service Marketing and Management*, Vol. 1, Teresa A. Swartz, David E. Bowen, and Stephen W. Brown, eds. Greenwich, CT: JAI, 91-121.

Gummesson, Evert (1990), "Marketing Organization in Services Businesses: The Role of the Part-Time Marketer," in *Managing Marketing Services in the 1990s*, Richard Teare, Luiz Moutinho, and Neil Morgan, eds. London, UK: Cassell Educational, 35-48.

Hamaguchi, E. (1985), "A Contextual Model of the Japanese: Toward a Methodological Innovation in Japan Studies," *Journal of Japanese Studies*, 11, 289-321.

Hartline, Michael D. and O. C. Ferrell (1996), "The Management of Customer-Contact Service Employees: An Empirical Investigation," *Journal of Marketing*, 60 (October), 52-70.

Hochschild, Arlie Russell (1983), *The Managed Heart*. Berkeley: University of California Press.

Jones, E. E. and T. S. Pittman (1982), "Toward a General Theory of Self-Presentation," in *Psychological Perspectives on the Self*, Jerry Suls, ed. Hillsdale, NJ: Erlbaum, 231-62.

Keller, Punam Anand and Lauren Goldberg Block (1996), "Increasing the Persuasiveness of Fear Appeals: The Effect of Arousal and Elaboration," *Journal of Consumer Research*, 22 (March), 448-59.

Leary, Mark R. (1993), "The Interplay of Private Self-Processes and Interpersonal Factors in Self-Presentation," in *Psychological Perspectives on the Self*, Vol. 4, Jerry Suls, ed. Hillsdale, NJ: Lawrence Erlbaum, 127-55.

Leidner, Robin (1993), *Fast Food, Fast Talk: Service Work and the Routinization of Everyday Life*. Berkeley: University of California Press.

Lovelock, Christopher H. (1991), *Services Marketing: Text Cases and Readings*, 2nd ed. Englewood Cliffs, NJ: Prentice-Hall.

Lutz, William (1983), *DoubleSpeak*. New York: HarperCollins.

Lyotard, Jean-Franois (1979), *The Postmodern Condition: A Report on Knowledge*, Geoff Bennington and Brian Massumi, trans. Minneapolis: University of Minnesota Press.

MacCannell, Dean (1976), *The Tourist: A New Theory of the Leisure Class*. New York: Schocken.

Maiken, Peter T. (1979), *Ripoff: How to Spot It, How to Avoid It*. Kansas City, MO: Andrews and McNeel.

Mangold, W. Glynn and Emin Babakus (1991), "Service Quality: The Front-Stage vs. the Back-Stage Perspective," *The Journal of Services Marketing*, 5 (Fall), 59-70.

Mars, Gerald (1982), *Cheats at Work: An Anthropology of Workplace Crime*. Boston: Allen and Unwin.

Matteis, Richard J. (1979), "The New Back Office Focuses on Customer Service," *Harvard Business Review*, 57, (March-April), 146-59.

McCornack, Steven A. and Timothy R. Levine (1990), "When Lovers Become Leery: The Relationship Between Suspicion and Accuracy in Detecting Deception," *Communication Monographs*, 57 (September), 219-30.

Mead, George H. (1934), *Mind, Self and Society*. Chicago: University of Chicago Press.

Merton, Robert K. (1957), "The Role-Set: Problems in Sociological Theory," *British Journal of Sociology*, 8, 106-20.

Messinger, Sheldon L., Harold Sampson, and Robert D. Towne (1962), "Life as Theater: Some Notes on the Dramaturgic Approach to Social Reality," *Sociometry*, (March), 98-110.

Meyer, John W. and Brian Rowan (1977), "Institutionalized Organizations: Formal Structure as Myth and Ceremony," *American Journal of Sociology*, 83, 340-63.

Morris, J. Andrew and Daniel C. Feldman (1996), "The Dimensions, Antecedents, and Consequences of Emotional Labor," *Academy of Management Review*, 21, 996-1010.

Neckerman, Kathryn M. and Joleen Kirschenman (1991), "Hiring Strategies, Racial Bias, and Inner-City Workers," *Social Problems*, 38, 433-47.

Olins, Wally (1994), *Corporate Identity*. London: Thames and Hudson.

Petty, Richard E., John T. Cacioppo, and David Schuman (1983), "Central and Peripheral Routes to Advertising Effectiveness: The Moderating Role of Involvement," *Journal of Consumer Research*, 10 (September), 135-46.

Polanyi, Michael (1964), *Science, Faith and Society*. Chicago: University of Chicago Press.

Poole, Gary D. and Kenneth D. Craig (1992), "Judgments of Genuine, Suppressed, and Faked Facial Expressions of Pain," *Journal of Personality and Social Psychology*, 63, 797-805.

Price, Linda, Eric Arnould, and Patrick Tierney (1995), "Going to Extremes: Managing Service Encounters and Assessing Provider Performance," *Journal of Marketing*, 59 (April), 83-97.

Rafaeli, Anat (1989), "When Cashiers Meet Customers: An Analysis of the Role of Supermarket Cashiers," *Academy of Management Journal*, 32, 245-73.

———— and Robert I. Sutton (1987), "Expression of Emotion as Part of the Work Role," *Academy of Management Journal*, 12, 23-37.

———— and ———— (1989), "The Expression of Emotion in Organizational Life," in *Research in Organizational Behavior*, Vol. 11, L. L. Cummings and Barry M. Staw, eds. Greenwich, CT: JAI, 1-42.

———— and ———— (1990), "Busy Stores and Demanding Customers: How Do They Affect the Display of Emotion?" *Academy of Management Journal*, 33, 623-37.

Sarbin, Theodore R. and Vernon L. Allen (1968), "Role Theory," in *The Handbook of Social Psychology*, Gardner Lindzey and Eliot Aronson, eds. Reading, MA: Addison-Wesley, 488-567.

Sartre, Jean-Paul (1956), *Being and Nothingness*. New York: Washington Square Press.

Scheier, Michael F. and Charles S. Carver (1983), "Two Sides of the Self: One for You and One for Me," in *Psychological Perspectives on the Self*, Vol. 2, Jerry Suls and Anthony G. Greenwald, eds. Hillsdale, NJ: Lawrence Erlbaum, 123-57.

Schlenker, Barry R. (1980), *Impression Management: The Self-Concept, Social Identity, and Interpersonal Relations*. Monterey, CA: Brooks/Cole.

Schouten, John (1991), "Selves in Transition: Symbolic Consumption in Personal Rites of Passage and Identity Reconstruction," *Journal of Consumer Research*, 17(4), 412-25.

Schutz, Alfred and Thomas Luckmann (1973), *The Structures of the Life World*. Evanston, IL: Northwestern University Press.

Scott, Marvin B. and Stanford M. Lyman (1968), "Accounts," *American Sociological Review*, 33, 46-62.

Shostack, G. Lynn (1981), "How to Design a Service," in *Marketing of Services*, James H. Donnelly and William R. George, eds. Chicago: American Marketing Association, 34-43.

———— (1987), "Service Positioning Through Structural Change," *Journal of Marketing*, 51 (January), 34-43.

Shulman, David (1994), "Dirty Data and Investigative Methods: Some Lessons from Private Detective Work," *Journal of Contemporary Ethnography*, 23, 214-53.

Silver, Maury and John Sabini (1985), "Sincerity: Feelings and Constructions in Making a Self," in *The Social Construction of the Person*, Kenneth J. Gergen and Keith E. Davis, eds. New York: Springer-Verlag, 191-201.

Solomon, Michael R., Carol Surprenant, John A. Czepiel, and Evelyn G. Gutman (1985), "A Role Theory Perspective on Dyadic Interactions: The Service Encounter," *Journal of Marketing*, 49 (Winter), 99-111.

Staw, Barry M., Pamela I. McKechnie, and Sheila M. Puffer (1983), "The Justification of Organizational Performance," *Administrative Science Quarterly*, 28, 582-600.

————, Robert I. Sutton, and Lisa H. Pelled (1994), "Employee Positive Emotion and Favorable Outcomes at the Workplace," *Organization Science*, 5 (February), 51-71.

Sutton, Robert I. (1991), "Maintaining Norms About Expressed Emotions: The Case of Bill Collectors," *Administrative Science Quarterly*, 36, 245-68.

———— and Anat Rafaeli (1988), "Untangling the Relationship Between Displayed Emotions and Organizational Sales: The Case of Convenience Stores," *Academy of Management Journal*, 31, 461-87.

Sykes, Gresham M. and David Matza (1957), "Techniques of Neutralization: A Theory of Delinquency," *American Sociological Review*, 22, 664-70.

Tedeschi, James T. and Marc Riess (1981), "Identities, the Phenomenal Self, and Laboratory Research," in *Impression Management Theory and Social Psychological Research*, James T. Tedeschi, ed. New York: Academic Press, 3-22.

Thoits, Peggy A. (1983), "Multiple Identities and Psychological Well-Being: A Reformulation and Test of the Social Isolation Hypothesis," *American Sociological Review*, 48 (April), 174-87.

Thomas, W. I. (1937), *The Unadjusted Girl*. Boston: Little, Brown.

Trilling, Lionel (1972), *Sincerity and Authenticity*. Cambridge, MA: Harvard University Press.

Turner, Victor (1988), *The Anthropology of Performance*. New York: PAJ Publications.

Wharton, Amy S. and Rebecca J. Erickson (1993), "Managing Emotions on the Job and at Home: Understanding the Consequences of Multiple Emotional Roles," *Academy of Management Journal*, 18, 457-86.

Williams, Christine L. (1995), *Still a Man's World: Men Who Do "Women's Work."* Berkeley: University of California Press.

Wilshire, Bruce (1982), "The Dramaturgical Metaphor of Behavior: Its Strengths and Weaknesses," *Symbolic Interaction*, 5(2), 287-97.

4

A Model of Aesthetic Value in the Servicescape

JANET WAGNER

Aesthetic value is a pivotal concept in philosophy, the visual arts, and architecture. As competition among corporations intensifies, and as brand differentiation becomes more challenging, aesthetic value is emerging as a major influence on positioning and communication strategy. The term "aesthetics" has historically been associated with the fine arts—painting, sculpture, architecture, and music. In the 20th century, however, aesthetics (meaning style) has also been used to refer to the design of everyday objects, such as cars and appliances, purchased and used by consumers. Recently, the term has become popular in the commercial sphere, where it refers to the design of ads, corporate logos, and business environments, including servicescapes (Schmitt and Simonson 1997). A well-designed servicescape is considered attractive, conveys a unified image to the customer, and differentiates the firm from its competitors.

Bitner (1992) defines the servicescape as the physical (or built) environment in which a service is delivered. The aesthetic value of the service environment is important for three reasons. First, services are intangible products, so customers may depend on the design of the servicescape to provide information on service quality. Second, customers are often on the premises when services are being delivered, so the design of the service environment may be a source of pleasure, in and of itself. Third, aesthetic value may heighten the customer's overall satisfaction with the service experience.

The purpose of this chapter is to present a model of aesthetic value in the servicescape (see Figure 4.1) that integrates concepts from philosophy, design, and marketing. In the model, I focus on visual aspects of the servicescape—its architecture and decor. My objectives are to provide a framework for scholars to use in generating hypotheses on the aesthetic value of the servicescape and to

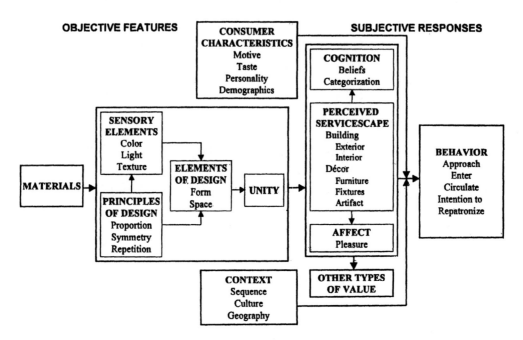

Figure 4.1 Model of Aesthetic Value in the Servicescape

identify conceptual and methodological challenges facing scholars interested in studying aesthetic value.

Holbrook (1994, 1999) developed a typology of consumer value, based on axiology, in which aesthetics is one of eight categories of value derived from the experience of using products.[1] In axiology, value is defined as an experience in which a subject interacts with an object (Frondizi 1971). Objects of value are called "axioforms," and, in a marketing context, can be any product—a good, service, an event, or an idea (Holbrook 1999). Value is the pleasure derived from perceiving, evaluating, and judging a product or some facet of a product. In the proposed model of aesthetic value, the subject is the customer (consumer or business) interacting with the servicescape.

In philosophy, there are two schools of thought on aesthetic value—objectivist and subjectivist. Whereas objectivists (e.g., Kant 1964) view aesthetic value as inherent in the design of the object, subjectivists (e.g., Hume 1963) argue that aesthetic value lies in the subject's response to the design. Marketing models assume a subjectivist stance, focusing on the customer's psychological and behavioral responses to either product form (Bloch 1995) or the servicescape (Bitner 1992). Models of design in the visual arts (Davis 1987; Feldman 1972) and architecture (Ching 1996; Lang 1987), on the other hand, tend to emphasize the objective properties of the aesthetic object. To date, there is no marketing model showing in detail the objective features of design that contribute to aesthetic value.

If service firms are to provide attractive servicescapes, a broader, more detailed understanding of the objective properties of design and what they contribute to judgments of aesthetic value is needed. The proposed model merges objective and subjective perspectives on aesthetic value. Objective concepts from theories of the visual arts and architecture (Ching 1996; Davis 1987; Feldman 1972) are set in a framework of subjective concepts borrowed from philosophy (see Wagner 1999 for a review of these concepts) and marketing (Bitner 1992; Bloch 1995; Holbrook 1994, 1999). It is argued that the objective features of design should be included in the model of aesthetic value because they are the source of the subject's psychological and behavioral responses to the aesthetic object.

Visual aspects of the object—design elements, sensory properties, and design principles—are presented, with a discussion of how they are related and how they affect aesthetic value independently and in interaction with one another. The model includes concepts representing the customer's cognitive, affective, and behavioral responses to the aesthetic object. The model also contains sets of concepts—customer characteristics and contextual effects—thought to moderate the influence of the objective features of design on customer response. The proposed model may be viewed as a generic model of aesthetic value, with concepts that apply to the design of any object. In this chapter, it is applied to the design of the servicescape.

As defined in the model, aesthetic value is an experience derived from perceiving, evaluating, and judging the design of the architecture and decor of the servicescape. Architecture is defined as the design of the built environment, including its exterior and interior. Decor is defined as furniture, fixtures, and artifacts added to enhance the attractiveness of either the exterior or the interior. Aesthetic value may be derived from the overall design of the physical environment or from any of its components. Like other types of value, the aesthetic experience may occur in a single encounter or may accrue in a series of encounters (Mandler 1982). To qualify as aesthetic value, the aesthetic experience should be unified, meaningful, and positive.

In the strictest sense, aesthetics refers to the perception of a stimulus through any of the senses—sight, hearing, touch, smell, or taste. The proposed model of aesthetic value focuses on the visual elements of design, for three reasons. First, although services vary in how much they rely on physical evidence to communicate value (Zeithaml and Bitner 1996), the visual elements are the dominant physical aspect of all servicescapes—lean or elaborate. Lean servicescapes, such as automatic teller machines and drop boxes for overnight delivery, are almost entirely visual. Even elaborate servicescapes, such as amusement parks and themed restaurants, which offer rich and varied sensory experiences, rely heavily on the visual aspects of design (see Bitner 1992). Second, the objective properties of aesthetic value do not generalize across all categories of sensory experience (Whewell 1995). For example, the elements of design in the visual arts differ from the elements of composition in music. Third, it is the visual aspects of the physical environment that have the greatest impact on behavior (Lang 1987) and should be of the most use in developing marketing strategy.

Apart from the work of Holbrook and his colleagues (Holbrook 1981, 1986, 1994; Holbrook and Moore 1981; Huber and Holbrook 1981), marketing scholars have produced very little empirical research on aesthetics. A trickle of research is beginning to emerge, however, on how consumers respond to selected elements of visual design in products (Eckman and Wagner 1994; Veryzer and Hutchinson 1998), brand logos (Henderson and Cote 1998), and advertising (Meyers-Levy and Peracchio 1995). With the exception of Bitner's (1990) study on how office appearance affects customer responses, there is virtually no empirical research on the visual aspects of aesthetic value in the servicescape.

OBJECTIVE FEATURES OF THE SERVICESCAPE

The objective features of the servicescape are important because they represent elements that can be controlled in making decisions about the design of the service environment. To provide customers with attractive servicescapes, marketers need to be familiar with the objective features of design, how they relate to one another, and what they contribute to aesthetic value. In design theory, there are two broad categories of objective features—the visual elements and the principles of design—that provide conceptual and theoretical continuity across the visual arts (Feldman 1972). Design can be defined as a set of visual elements, organized by the principles of design, to create aesthetic value.

The Visual Elements

The visual elements are "constituents of perception" resulting from the designer's manipulation of materials (Feldman 1972). In "generic" design theory, the visual elements are broadly defined to include both two- and three-dimensional properties—line, shape, form, space, color, light, and texture. The servicescape is three-dimensional, so an appropriate system for classifying visual elements is that of architectural theory. In architectural theory, there are two sets of visual elements—the three-dimensional design elements of form and space, and the sensory properties of light, color, and texture. Neither line nor shape is treated as a design element because of its relationship to form. As explained below, line is the source of form, and shape is a property of form (Ching 1996). Both the design elements and the sensory properties can be applied to the design of the building that houses the servicescape, any room within the servicescape, or any three-dimensional element of decor.

The Design Elements: Form and Space

In design theory, form has at least three meanings. First, it is a synonym for the external appearance or visual image of an object (Bloch 1995). Second, form refers to the overall structure of a design—the way in which the visual elements are organized to create unity. Third, in the design of three-dimensional objects, form is a synonym for outline or enclosure (Ching 1996). In the built environment, form is defined by the exterior and interior surfaces—facade, roof, walls, floors, and ceilings—that enclose a space. The form of decorative objects—furniture, fixtures, and artifacts—is also defined by surfaces, which enclose space, mass, or some combination of the two.

In theories of the visual arts (e.g., Ching 1996; Davis 1987; Feldman 1972; Lang 1987), form is derived from line. When line is extended in three dimensions (height, depth, and width), it creates a plane. A form is created when planes are, in turn, juxtaposed to enclose space. Planes have openings—doors, windows, and skylights—that create transitions between the exterior space in which a building is positioned and the interior space in which the servicescape is located. The space occupied by the servicescape is a three-dimensional field in which a service or some aspect of service is performed. For example, in a hotel, lobby space is dedicated to registration, guest room space is assigned to sleeping, and space in the bar is devoted to socializing.

Form and space have physical properties—shape, size, and position—that contribute to the aesthetic value of the servicescape. Shape is outline—the principal feature by which customers categorize buildings (Ching 1996; Lang 1987), the service providers they house, and decorative and functional objects. For example, gas stations and fast food restaurants, stripped of their signage, can be easily recognized by the shape of their exteriors. Similarly, a dentist's chair and an easy chair have distinct shapes. Whereas size refers to the physical dimensions of form (and space), position refers to their location, relative to other objects in the environment. Both size and position facilitate judgments of aesthetic value, because they are criteria used by subjects in judging proportion and scale. From the perspective of consumers, size and position may also enhance judgments of social value. For example, in the design of planes used for transoceanic flights, the seats in first class are larger than those in economy class. In fine restaurants, a table positioned near the kitchen has less aesthetic and social value than one by a window or fireplace. In the conference business, a hotel located near downtown shopping and entertainment is preferred to one on the outskirts of town.

The Sensory Elements: Light, Color, and Texture

The term "aesthetics" is derived from the Greek and means "sense perception" (Hermeren 1988). In architectural theory (and in other theories of the visual arts), light, color, and texture are sensory properties of an object that contribute to perceptions of aesthetic value.

Light, which is electromagnetic energy, is essential to perceptions of aesthetic value because it makes things visible (Feldman 1972). In the servicescape, aesthetic value may be affected by the type of light—radiant (emitted) or ambient (reflected)—and its source—natural or artificial. When reflected by surfaces, light is perceived as color. Sunlight, which is composed of equal parts of all colors of the visible light spectrum, is believed to be best for enhancing the color of the environment and is virtually impossible to duplicate through artificial lighting (Hope and Walch 1990). Artificial light, however, is easier to control, because it isn't subject to the vagaries of time of day or weather. Of the three sensory properties, light may be the most important, because it provides definition for form, space, color, and texture.

Color is the sensation created by wavelengths of visible light reflected from pigment on a surface, such as a wall, floor, or ceiling. The major property of color is hue, which, depending on the color theory, refers to either a particular wavelength in the light spectrum or a particular position on a color wheel. In color theories based on light, the primary hues are red, green, and blue. In pigment-based theories, the principal hues are red, yellow, green, blue, and purple (Davis 1987; Hope and Walch 1990). Either light or pigment may be mixed to create an infinite number of hues, of which people are capable of perceiving relatively few. Hue has attributes of intensity (brightness or dullness) and tone (lightness or darkness). The attributes of color are highly interactive (Albers 1963; Arnheim 1974; Davis 1987). For example, a dull green may be perceived as olive, and a light red may be perceived as pink. Color is also highly interactive with the attributes of other visual elements, particularly form (Ching 1996). To illustrate, a bright red form may appear larger than a dark blue form, and a yellow form may appear closer than a purple form.

Texture is the visible (and tangible) contour of a surface. Unlike light and color, which are sensed exclusively by sight, texture is both seen and felt (Ching 1996; Davis 1987; Feldman 1972). In architecture, texture is imparted by varying the size and shape of the parts of a building. Texture is also created by the materials of which surfaces are constructed. For example, texture may be created by brick on a facade and by tile on a roof. In the interior of a servicescape, texture may be created by carpet on the floor or by skylights in the ceiling.

Principles of Design

The principles of design are guidelines for creating relationships among the visual elements in a design. They are also subjective patterns of relationships among the visual elements that create a sense of order and coherence in the visual image. In the visual arts and architecture, there are three basic principles of design: proportion, rhythm, and symmetry (Ching 1996; Davis 1987; Feldman 1972), which are derived from the gestalt principles of continuity, similarity, and proximity. The purpose of the design principles is to create unity, which is the fundamental quality of aesthetic value.

Proportion is a comparative relationship involving the size of one part and the whole of an object, or one part of an object and another (Feldman 1972). Although proportion may involve any visual element, in architecture, it usually involves form and space. For example, proportion might involve the size of the roof relative to the rest of the building, the size of one room relative to another, or the height of a door relative to its width. "Ideal" proportions are expressed as mathematical systems, derived from proportions of the human body and based on the belief that the resulting numerical relationships are inherently attractive. In Western culture, such systems include the Golden Section (Ching 1996), the Fibonacci series (Feldman 1972), and Le Corbusier's (1954) Modulor. A derivative of proportion is scale—the size of the object relative to other objects in its environment. In the servicescape, scale considerations include the relationship of a building to its site, furniture or fixtures to a room, or a painting to a wall. In the design of a building, proportion enhances aesthetic value by imposing a sense of rhythm among the parts of a building (Lang 1987).

Rhythm is the repetition of any visual element—form, space, color, light, or texture (Feldman 1972)—that creates a sense of continuity and unifies the subject's perception of form. In the design of the servicescape, rhythm contributes to aesthetic value by directing the customer's eye around a space and guiding his or her movement through space. According to Ching (1996), buildings include elements that are by nature repetitive. Spaces are repeated (and grouped) to accommodate functional requirements—patient rooms in hospitals, offices for attorneys in law firms, and waiting areas at airport gates.

Symmetry is equilibrium or balance between design elements, by size or visual weight (Feldman 1972). In designing the built environment, symmetrical forms and spaces are organized around an imaginary "axis." There are two fundamental types of symmetry—bilateral symmetry, in which similar (but not necessarily identical) forms or spaces are arranged on opposite sides of a shared axis, and radial symmetry, in which similar elements extend outward from two or more intersecting axes (Ching 1996). Bilateral symmetry, the simpler of the two, is used in the design of most buildings. Radial symmetry is more common in large, elaborate servicescapes, such as hospitals, airports, and sports stadiums.

Unity in Aesthetic Value

Unity is order or coherence in the design of a visual image. As the definition implies, a unified design is one in which the visual elements are organized according to principles of proportion, rhythm, and symmetry (Davis 1987; Feldman 1972). Gestalt theory suggests that customers have an innate preference for order in visual images (Bloch 1995). In the servicescape, a unified design elicits positive aesthetic responses, delivers a consistent message with respect to the image of the service firm, and directs the customer's behavior in approaching, entering, and circulating through the servicescape.

The "peril" of unity in design is too much sameness (Feldman 1972). Variety can be achieved by manipulating attributes of the visual elements and the relationships among them. For example, variety in form can be created by manipulating shape and size, and variety in color can be introduced by managing tone and intensity. To attract and hold the attention of the customer, there must be enough contrast between the levels at which the attributes are presented. There must also be sufficient complexity (Eibl-Eibesfeldt 1988; Turner and Poppel 1988). In general, consumers have been found to prefer moderate variety and complexity to either high or low levels (Berlyne 1974). Kotler (1973) observed that service environments have strong "wearout" effects that may be exacerbated by servicescape designs that are too extreme. In research on the aesthetic value of architectural facades, consumers reacted negatively to too much complexity (Huber and Holbrook 1981).

Variety and complexity also may be introduced through the principles of design. Variations on rhythm, such as alternation and gradation, may be used to enhance consumer interest (Davis 1987) and direct behavior. For example, alternation in texture is used in the design of the hallways in some hotels: squares of smooth carpeting are alternated with squares of sculptured carpeting to create visual continuity and direct guests from their rooms to the elevator. A well-known application of gradation is the roof of the Sydney Opera House, in which the roof is composed of wavelike shapes that are graduated in size. In servicescapes that depend on natural light, there is gradation in color over the course of the day.

As indicated earlier, a variety of proportional systems is considered attractive in Western culture. With respect to complexity, a more complicated proportion, such as 2:3:5:8, is considered more interesting than one that is less complicated, such as 2:3 or 5:8 (Lang 1987). Although symmetry seems inherently "balanced," variety can be introduced by varying the shape of forms along the axis and by introducing sensory properties, such as color and texture, that vary in visual weight. Variety also may be introduced by manipulating the position of openings such as doors and windows, or by varying the position of forms along the axis (Ching 1996).

In marketing, Veryzer and Hutchinson (1998) explored the contribution of unity to aesthetic value in the design of consumer products, including lamps, refrigerators, and telephones. The results suggest that designs unified by the repetition of visual elements are evaluated more positively than those that are not. To date, there has been no research on the aesthetic value of unity in the servicescape.

CONSUMER RESPONSES TO DESIGN OF THE SERVICESCAPE

Perceptions of design in the servicescape lead to psychological and behavioral responses from the customer. Psychological responses include cognition and affect (Bitner 1992; Bloch 1995). Behavioral responses include approach, entrance, and circulation (Ching 1996; Lang 1987).

Psychological Responses

Cognition

The design of the servicescape is a mode of nonverbal communication (Bitner 1992) that influences the customer's beliefs and facilitates the categorization process. The design elements, the sensory properties, and relationships among them may all affect beliefs about the servicescape. Customers may develop "cognitive maps" composed of the physical layout and other aesthetic attributes of the physical environment (Lang 1987). The design of the servicescape may also influence beliefs about the type and quality of the service provider, the target customer (Fischer, Gainer, and Bristor 1998), and the people providing the service (Bitner 1990).

Bloch (1995) noted that there is a long-standing controversy about the process by which beliefs based on visual cues are formed. The crux of the argument is whether the processing of visual information is linear (the additive effect of processing one element at a time) or holistic (configurational processing of the entire visual image). Theories of the visual arts and architecture (Ching 1996; Davis 1987; Feldman 1972; Lang 1987) suggest that the visual elements are highly interactive, a condition consistent with cue configurality. Bloch speculates that, in aesthetic judgments, both linear and configurational processing may be involved. Support for this position is provided by Eckman and Wagner (1994), who explored the processing of visual images by having consumers evaluate slides of colored line drawings of men's suits, developed from a conjoint model with interaction terms. Numerous main effects were observed for the objective features of the designs; however, judgments of attractiveness were dominated by the interaction of form and color. In recent research on the design of consumer products, Veryzer and Hutchinson (1998) reported a "superadditivity effect" in the processing of visual images, in which the joint effect of unity in two design features is greater than the sum of the individual parts.

In aesthetic value, cognitive responses may also involve categorization of the service provider. Bitner (1992) observes that the design of the servicescape is likely to be associated with a particular category of service. For example, the design of a hospital will have a set of unique features, as will the design of a bank or restaurant. In recent qualitative research, Fischer, Gainer, and Bristor (1998) studied the extent to which consumers categorize servicescapes (beauty salons and barbershops) as gendered, based on objective features of design. The results suggest that categorization by gender is more likely to stem from the perceived gender of the target customer than physical aspects of the environment. The categorization process is based on comparison of the design (or some feature of the design) to some ideal or prototype that is an exemplar of its category. Veryzer and Hutchinson (1998) studied the effect of prototypicality on aesthetic judgments of consumer products. Both prototypicality and "prototype distortion" (change in one or more visual elements) had strong positive effects on aesthetic judgments.

Mandler (1982) argued that value judgments (including judgments of aesthetic value) exist on a cognitive continuum, ranging from "description" to "evaluation." Description depends primarily on objective features of the object, including design and sensory elements, which are the basis of categorization. Evaluation, on the other hand, depends primarily on the relationships among the visual elements, which are determined by the principles of design. Most judgments of aesthetic value, however, are both descriptive and evaluative.

Affect

Bitner (1992) suggests that the design of the servicescape elicits affective responses from customers. According to axiologists, the affective component of any type of value (known as "appreciation") has dimensions of polarity, valence, and immediacy . The polarity of an affective response may be either positive or negative (see Bloch 1995); however, aesthetic value is assumed to be positive—aesthetic objects are "valued" because the consumer derives pleasure from consuming them (Kainz 1962). The valence of the affective response is its intensity and is similar to Mehrabian and Russell's (1974) concept of arousal, which appears in Bitner's (1992) model of the servicescape. Valence varies within and across product categories, and it ranges from moderate to strong (Bloch 1995). Compared to other types of value (particularly utilitarian and social value), aesthetic value is thought to be more intense. It seems likely, however, that the pleasure derived from the design of commercial products and servicescapes is less intense than that derived from other aesthetic products, particularly the fine arts (Bloch 1995). Immediacy is the element of surprise or unexpectedness. Surprise may be an extreme version of disconfirmation that exceeds the customer's "zone of acceptance" for unexpected events (see Oliver, Rust, and Varki 1997). Thus, customers may be surprised by the extent to which the attractiveness of a servicescape exceeds the level expected.

Affective responses to the servicescape are thought to influence the customer's willingness to patronize a service provider (Bitner 1992). Oliver, Rust, and Varki (1997) studied affective responses to two service experiences—an amusement park and a symphony performance. The results confirm that surprise and arousal contribute to positive affect.

Behavioral Responses to Design of the Servicescape

In the built environment, perception is sequential. The aesthetic experience is derived from movement in time, though a sequence of spaces (Ching 1996)—from the exterior to the interior and back again, from one room to another, and from one part of a room to another. Lang (1987) observes that most research on aesthetics focuses on perceptions of two-dimensional design, even though people move through the servicescape in three dimensions. A well-designed servicescape presents a sequence of "vistas" that captures and holds the attention of consumers as they move through it. Interest is created by well-organized spaces (rooms, hallways, stairwells) and attractive surfaces (walls, floors, ceilings) that are easily comprehended and enjoyed.

In the proposed model, aesthetic value is assumed to be a positive experience, in which consumers are disposed to approach, enter, and circulate through the servicescape. Approach is a subjective process triggered by physically viewing, or anticipating viewing, a building or interior space from a distance. In approach, consumers prepare to sense, experience, and use the servicescape (Ching 1996). Expectations are set, not only for aesthetic value but also for other types of value to be delivered by the service provider, based on where the consumer has been and anticipates going.

Entering the servicescape is an act of "penetrating a vertical plane" that divides the exterior and the interior of the building, or one space in a building from another (Ching 1996). The aesthetic value of an entrance is that it represents the physical and psychological transition between spaces. Entrances vary from unexceptional "holes in the wall," which are standard in utilitarian servicescapes, such as those of doctors and dentists, to elaborate, articulated gateways, typical of status-oriented and entertainment-based servicescapes, such as upscale hotels, museums, and symphony halls.

In circulation, consumers move through the servicescape, following a physical and psychological path that passes by and through a series of spaces, terminating at one or more locations. Circulation is the core of the aesthetic experience in the servicescape and "sets the stage" for consumers to experience other types of value (e.g., efficiency, quality, status, entertainment, spirituality) by interacting with the servicescape and the employees delivering the service. Oliver, Rust, and Varki (1997) suggest that a positive experience in the servicescape influences the customer's intentions to repatronize a service provider.

MODERATORS OF AESTHETIC VALUE

Characteristics of the Customer

Both the Bloch (1995) and Bitner (1992) models suggest that certain characteristics of the customer may moderate psychological and behavioral responses to design of the servicescape. Research on moderators of aesthetic value in the servicescape is meager; however, empirical work in other categories of design indicates that aesthetic value is moderated by customer motives, taste, personality, and demographics.

Motives

Philosophers (e.g., Mothersill 1984; Santayana 1955) suggest that the mental processing of attractive visual images is a higher order need, similar to self-actualization or personal enrichment. In processing visual images, consumers are most satisfied by those that are positive and unified, but varied enough to hold their attention (Turner and Poppel 1988). For example, a view of the runway from the window of an airport restaurant, revealing a variety of attractive planes taking off and landing in an orderly manner, may enrich the patron's experience while awaiting a flight.

Taste

The customer's ability to recognize, discern, or appreciate the aesthetic attributes of an object is known as taste (Santayana 1955; Whewell 1995) or aesthetic sensibility (Mothersill 1984). Bloch (1995) argues that taste may be either innate or acquired. Innate taste is the result of design acumen—a type of aesthetic intelligence with which individuals are born—whereas acquired taste is the result of education and experience. Wallendorf, Zinkhan, and Zinkhan (1981) suggest that taste is similar to cognitive complexity—the ability of consumers to understand complex aesthetic stimuli. Good taste may differ from popular taste, in that popular taste is subject to the dictates of fashion (Whewell 1995).

The development of taste requires repeated exposure to, knowledge of, and involvement in a particular category of design (Goldman 1995). Expertise in one aesthetic category does not necessarily translate to others, as demonstrated by the fact that architects and designers often specialize in one type of servicescape, such as hotels, hospitals, airports, sports stadiums, or restaurants. The ability to appreciate good design is based on learning the features of attractive forms and updating standards by which they are evaluated over time (Eibl-Eibesfeldt 1988). As taste is cultivated, an individual can discriminate finer details and more classes of design features.

Consequently, architects and designers may recognize visual relationships that their clients do not (Lang 1987). Although good taste is often equated with the taste of experts, it is not limited to design professionals. Loyal customers who are frequent patrons of a particular service category may learn to recognize good design in the servicescape. Huber and Holbrook (1981) studied the effect of learning on aesthetic value in architecture. In a pre-/posttest experiment, subjects were shown slides of building facades before and after a lecture on architectural design. Preferences for order and symmetry were greater in the posttest condition.

Holt (1998) suggests that service firms may segment their customers by "cultural capital"—taste in a particular category or categories of consumption. Customers with high cultural capital (HCC) prefer a consumption style that is unique and "ideationally difficult." HCCs consider materialism and luxury as crass, favoring services that "deliver experientially," such as ethnic restaurants and travel to exotic locations. Customers with low cultural capital (LCC) are less well off economically. LCCs enjoy status symbols and prefer services such as cruises and expensive restaurants.

Personality

Although research on personality has been in abeyance for 30 years, Bagozzi (1994) proposed that the effect of personality on consumer responses is a topic with potential for growth. One trait that may affect customer response to the servicescape is arousal seeking (see Bitner 1992). Cox and Cox (1994) studied the effect of arousal seeking and complexity on aesthetic preferences for fashion goods. Although arousal seeking had no main effect, it had an interaction effect with complexity, albeit in the direction opposite to that expected; whereas consumers high in arousal seeking preferred designs of low complexity, those who were low in arousal seeking had no preference. Other personality traits, including visual-verbal orientation and romanticism-classicism (Holbrook 1986), have been found to moderate aesthetic responses for fashion objects.

Demographic Variables

Bloch (1995) observed that demographic variables such as age and sex may moderate judgments of product design. There is no research, however, on the effect of either variable on aesthetic value in the servicescape. In other categories of art and design, there is a limited amount of research on the moderating effects of age and gender on judgments of aesthetic value. For example, Holbrook and Schindler (1989) found that consumers favor music popular when they were in their late teens and early twenties. Eckman and Wagner (1994) showed that older men prefer the proportion of longer tailored jackets. Research on the effect of gender on preferences for clothing design has provided mixed results. Whereas Holbrook (1986) observed differences among males and females in their preferences for clothing design features, other researchers (e.g., Eckman and Wagner 1994) report that gender has no effect.

Contextual Effects

In addition to consumer characteristics, certain contextual effects may moderate objective and subjective features of aesthetic value. Contextual effects include sequence, culture, and geography.

Sequence effects are the result of the order in which products are acquired (Bloch 1995), events are experienced, or spaces in a building are encountered (Ching 1996). With respect to acquisition, consumers may collect aesthetic objects, over time, that are similar stylistically. As additional items are acquired, the aesthetic value of each item as well as that of the entire "ensemble" may be enhanced (see Bell, Holbrook, and Solomon 1991). In the consumption of services, consumers may acquire ensembles of experiences in service categories in which they are particularly involved. For example, some consumers may collect, over time, experiences with restaurants that offer "crummy atmosphere" but "good food." Wallendorf, Zinkhan, and Zinkhan (1981) argue that sequence effects are common in aesthetic "events," such as music, dance, and theater performances, that cannot be perceived all at once. Similarly, sequence effects are common in architecture. In the design of buildings, a sequence is a "perceptual thread" linking spaces—foyers, hallways, rooms, stairwells—of a building (Ching 1996). Spaces are perceived relative to where the consumer has been (spaces previously experienced) and where the consumer expects to go. In the servicescape, the sequence of spaces affects the order in which customers experience delivery of the service. For example, in a doctor's office, the customer often moves from the reception area to a hallway, to an examination room, and, finally, to the doctor's consultation area.

Beliefs about what is attractive vary among and within cultures. For example, standards of proportion and the meaning of colors vary between Western and Eastern cultures. Whereas Western consumers prefer proportions based on the human body, the Japanese prefer proportions based on the "ken," a unit derived from the size of floor mats (Ching 1996). In the West, light colors are considered feminine and dark colors masculine. In the East, the opposite is true. Within U.S.

culture, African Americans have been found to prefer more intense colors and "truer" hues than European Americans (Williams, Arbaugh, and Rucker 1980).

Geography may also moderate the effect of design on aesthetic judgments (Ching 1996; Lang 1987). Aesthetic value is enhanced when servicescapes have materials, design elements, and sensory features that are compatible with, or leverage, features of the site, climate, and topography. For example, outdoor restaurants are common in the Virgin Islands, where the weather is balmy, there is little rain, and the land adjacent to beaches is "buildable." In Santa Fe, where the landscape is arid, adobe is the dominant material in all buildings, including those of service providers.

RESEARCH CHALLENGES

In empirical research on aesthetic value in the servicescape, researchers face two major challenges. The first—the complex structure of most visual images—is theoretical. The second—designing empirical stimuli to maximize external validity—is methodological.

As discussed earlier, the visual elements are discrete concepts that have direct effects on aesthetic value. Gestalt theory suggests that, because of the configurational nature of visual images, visual elements also exhibit complex interaction effects (Arnheim 1974; Davis 1987; Feldman 1972). Although there is no research on interaction effects in design of the servicescape, interaction effects have been demonstrated in research involving other aesthetic products (Eckman and Wagner 1994; Holbrook and Moore 1981). Testing for interaction effects in visual images poses a challenge, even in simple, two-dimensional designs, because the sheer number of possible interactions makes direct measurement impossible. Researchers are advised to focus on those that are likely to be of greatest theoretical importance and of the most practical use to designers (Veryzer and Hutchinson 1998).

The validity of visual stimuli has been tested in a long stream of research by Holbrook and his colleagues (Holbrook 1981, 1986; Holbrook and Moore 1981; Huber and Holbrook 1981), with contributions from others (Whisney, Winakor, and Wolins 1979). Clearly, the ideal stimuli are real aesthetic objects (Holbrook 1986); however, procuring real stimuli for experimental work is impractical. In the case of the servicescape, locating or constructing environments with appropriate sets of attributes would be prohibitively expensive. Moreover, securing the cooperation of service firms in such a venture would be highly unlikely because of the potential impact on revenues and customer loyalty. In studies involving other aesthetic categories, researchers have compromised by developing verbal stimuli that describe the aesthetic object or using visual stimuli such as photographs or line drawings.

The main argument against using verbal stimuli to convey aesthetic images is the difficulty of describing visual attributes through verbal protocols. Gestalt principles suggest that because visual attributes are processed configurationally, pictures may be more effective than words in capturing the underlying interaction effects. Holbrook and Moore (1981) compared the processing of information on a fashion object (a sweater), as presented in pictorial and verbal stimuli. Both sets of stimuli were developed using a conjoint model with interaction terms to capture configurational effects. More main effects were captured by the pictorial stimuli; however, numbers of interaction effects captured by the pictorial and verbal stimuli were similar. Nevertheless, the results supported cue configurality, in that the strength of the most powerful interaction effect exceeded that of the most powerful main effect.

Researchers choosing to use pictorial stimuli may use photographs or line drawings. Bitner (1990) used photographs in research on the appearance of the servicescape. Similarly, photographs were used as stimuli in research on the aesthetic value of fashion objects by Morganosky and Postelwait (1989). Although photographs offer the advantage of presenting realistic images, the images must be carefully controlled to avoid confounds. Line drawings offer a high degree of experimental control over manipulation of the design elements and sensory properties (see, for example, Eckman and Wagner 1994; Holbrook 1986; Veryzer and Hutchinson 1998). The disadvantage of line drawings is the difficulty of incorporating color and texture in reproducible instruments, a problem that can be addressed by adding color to line drawings, which can then be photographed and shown to subjects as slides (see Eckman and Wagner 1994).

Research designed to compare the validity of photographs to that of line drawings has yielded conflicting results. Whisney, Winakor, and Wolins (1979) compared evaluations of attractiveness from photographs and line drawings of career attire and found no differences. Huber and Holbrook (1981), on the other hand, compared aesthetic judgments of 20th-century architectural facades, using photographs and line drawings, and found low convergent validity.

The question of the appropriateness of using two-dimensional stimuli to study the aesthetic value of three-dimensional objects remains unresolved. It is of particular concern, however, in studying the design of servicescapes because of the sequential nature of the experience, which may be most easily captured by "being there." The virtues of phenomenological techniques in studying the servicescape are demonstrated by Sherry's (1998) richly detailed account of the consumer experience in Nike Town Chicago. To date, the phenomenological approach has been underutilized in the study of conventional servicescapes, such as doctors' offices, law offices, hotels, and airports. Conventional servicescapes are designed to support intangible products. Unlike retail store environments, in which merchandise is the focus of the aesthetic experience, the physical environment is likely to be the dominant source of aesthetic value in the servicescape.

In the future, computer simulations (see Burke 1994) may be used in research on aesthetic value to blend qualities of both phenomenological and experimental techniques. Simulations of the consumer's experience approaching, entering, and circulating through the servicescape may have more external validity than other types of experimental stimuli. Although limitations imposed by interaction effects may persist, computer simulation will allow controlled manipulation of the visual elements of greatest theoretical importance and practical meaning for managers.

In the meantime, both scholars and practitioners stand to benefit from both phenomenological and experimental research on aesthetic value in the servicescape.

NOTE

1. Other categories include efficiency, quality, status, esteem, play, morality, and spirituality.

REFERENCES

Albers, Josef (1963), *Interaction of Color.* New Haven, CT: Yale University Press.

Arnheim, Rudolf (1974), *Art and Visual Perception.* Berkeley: University of California Press.

Bagozzi, Richard P. (1994), "ACR Fellow Speech," in *Advances in Consumer Research,* Vol. 21, Chris T. Allen and Deborah Roedder John, eds. Provo, UT: Association for Consumer Research, 8-11.

Bell, Stephen S., Morris B. Holbrook, and Michael R. Solomon (1991), "Combining Esthetic and Social Value to Explain Preferences for Product Styles With the Incorporation of Personality Effects," *Journal of Social Behavior and Personality,* 6(6), 243-74.

Berlyne, Daniel E. (1974), "Novelty, Complexity and Interestingness," in *Studies in the New Experimental Aesthetics,* David E. Berlyne, ed. New York: John Wiley & Sons, 175-80.

Bitner, Mary Jo (1990), "Evaluating Service Encounters: The Effects of Physical Surroundings and Employee Responses," *Journal of Marketing,* 54 (April), 69-82.

——— (1992), "Servicescapes: The Impact of Physical Surroundings on Customers and Employees," *Journal of Marketing,* 56 (April), 57-71.

Bloch, Peter H. (1995), "Seeking the Ideal Form: Product Design and Consumer Response," *Journal of Marketing,* 59 (July), 16-29.

Burke, Raymond R. (1994), "The Virtual Store: A New Tool for Consumer Research," *Stores,* 76 (August), RR1-RR3.

Ching, Francis D. K. (1996), *Architecture: Form, Space and Order,* 2nd ed. New York: Van Nostrand Reinhold.

Cox, Dena and Anthony Cox (1994), "The Effect of Arousal Seeking Tendency on Consumer Preferences for Complex Product Designs," in *Advances in Consumer Research,* Vol. 21, Chris T. Allen and Deborah Roedder John, eds. Provo, UT: Association for Consumer Research, 554-59.

Davis, Marian L. (1987), *Visual Design in Dress.* Englewood Cliffs, NJ: Prentice Hall.

Eckman, Molly and Janet Wagner (1994), "Judging the Attractiveness of Product Design: The Effect of Visual Attributes and Consumer Characteristics," in *Advances in Consumer Research,* Vol. 21, Chris T. Allen and Deborah Roedder John, eds. Provo, UT: Association for Consumer Research, 560-64.

Eibl-Eibesfeldt, Irenaus (1988), "The Biological Foundation of Aesthetics," in *Beauty and the Brain,* Ingo Rentschler, Barbara Herzberger, and David Epstein, eds. Boston: Birkauser Verlag, 29-68.

Feldman, Edmund Burke (1972), *Varieties of Visual Experience.* New York: Harry N. Abrams.

Fischer, Eileen, Brenda Gainer, and Julia Bristor (1998), "Beauty Salon and Barbershop: Gendered Servicescapes," in *Servicescapes: The Concept of Place in Contemporary Markets,* John F. Sherry, Jr., ed. Chicago: NTC/Contemporary Publishing Company, 565-90.

Frondizi, R. (1971), *What Is Value?* LaSalle, IL: Open Court.

Goldman, Alan H. (1995), "Aesthetic Properties," in *A Companion to Aesthetics,* David E. Cooper, ed. Malden, MA: Blackwell, 342-47.

Henderson, Pamela W. and Joseph A. Cote (1998), "Guidelines for Selecting or Modifying Logos," *Journal of Marketing,* 62 (April), 14-30.

Hermeren, George (1988), *The Nature of Aesthetic Qualities.* Lund: Lund University Press.

Holbrook, Morris B. (1981), "Integrating Compositional and Decompositional Analyses to Represent the Intervening Role of Perceptions in Evaluative Judgments," *Journal of Marketing Research,* 28 (February), 13-28.

———— (1986), "Aims, Concepts, and Methods for the Representation of Individual Differences in Esthetic Responses to Design Features," *Journal of Consumer Research*, 13 (December), 337-47.

———— (1994), "The Nature of Customer Value: An Axiology of Services in the Consumption Experience," in *Service Quality*, Roland T. Rust and Richard L. Oliver, eds. London: Sage, 21-71.

———— (1999), "Introduction to Consumer Value," in *Consumer Value: A Framework for Analysis and Research*, Morris B. Holbrook, ed. London: Routledge, 1-28.

———— and William B. Moore (1981), "Feature Interactions in Consumer Judgments of Verbal vs. Pictorial Presentations," *Journal of Consumer Research*, 8(2), 103-13.

———— and Robert M. Schindler (1989), "Some Exploratory Findings on the Development of Musical Tastes," *Journal of Consumer Research*, 16 (June), 119-24.

Holt, Douglas B. (1998), "Does Cultural Capital Structure American Consumption?" *Journal of Consumer Research*, 25(1), 1-25.

Hope, Augustine and Margaret Walch (1990), *The Color Compendium*. New York: Van Nostrand Reinhold.

Huber, Joel and Morris B. Holbrook (1981), "The Use of Real Versus Artificial Stimuli in Research on Visual Esthetic Judgments," in *Symbolic Consumer Behavior*, Elizabeth C. Hirschman and Morris B. Holbrook, eds. New York: Association for Consumer Research and the Institute of Retail Management, New York University, 60-68.

Hume, David (1963), *Essays Moral, Political and Literary*. Oxford, UK: Oxford University Press.

Kainz, F. (1962), *Aesthetics the Science*. Detroit: Wayne State University Press.

Kant, Immanuel (1964), *Critique of Judgment*, J. C. Meredith, trans. Oxford, UK: Clarendon.

Kotler, Philip (1973), "Atmospherics as a Marketing Tool," *Journal of Retailing*, 49(4), 48-64.

Lang, Jon (1987), *Creating Architectural Theory*. New York: Van Nostrand Reinhold.

Le Corbusier (1954), *The Modulor*. Cambridge: MIT Press.

Mandler, George (1982), "The Structure of Value: Accounting for Taste," in *Affect and Cognition*, M. S. Clark and S. T. Fisher, eds. New York: Academic Press, 3-36.

Mehrabian, Albert and James A. Russell (1974), *An Approach to Environmental Psychology*. Cambridge: MIT Press.

Meyers-Levy, Joan and Laura A. Peracchio (1995), "Understanding the Effects of Color: How the Correspondence Between Available and Required Resources Affects Attitudes," *Journal of Consumer Research*, 22 (September), 121-38.

Morganosky, Michelle A. and Deborah S. Postelwait (1989), "Consumers' Evaluations of Apparel Form, Expression, and Aesthetic Quality," *Clothing and Textiles Research Journal*, 7(2), 11-15.

Mothersill, Mary (1984), *Beauty Restored*. Oxford, UK: Clarendon.

Oliver, Richard L., Roland T. Rust, and Sajeev Varki (1997), "Customer Delight: Foundations, Findings, and Managerial Insight," *Journal of Retailing*, 73(3), 311-36.

Santayana, George (1955), *The Sense of Beauty*. New York: Dover.

Schmitt, Bernd and Alex Simonson (1997), *Marketing Aesthetics*. New York: Free Press.

Sherry, John F., Jr. (1998), "The Soul of the Company Store: Nike Town Chicago and the Emplaced Brandscape," in *Servicescapes: The Concept of Place in Contemporary Markets*, John F. Sherry, Jr., ed. Chicago: NTC/Contemporary Publishing Company, 109-46.

Turner, Frederick and Ernst Poppel (1988), "Metered Poetry, the Brain, and Time," in *Beauty and the Brain*, Ingo Rentschler, Barbara Herzberger, and David Epstein, eds. Boston: Berkauser Verlag, 71-90.

Veryzer, Robert W., Jr. and J. Wesley Hutchinson (1998), "The Influence of Unity and Prototypicality on Aesthetic Responses to New Product Designs," *Journal of Consumer Research*, 24 (March), 374-94.

Wagner, Janet (1999), "Aesthetic Value: Beauty in Art and Fashion," in *Consumer Value: A Framework for Analysis and Research*, Morris B. Holbrook, ed. London: Routledge, 126-46.

Wallendorf, Melanie, George Zinkhan, and Lydia S. Zinkhan (1981), "Cognitive Complexity and Aesthetic Preference," in *Symbolic Consumer Behavior*, Elizabeth C. Hirschman and Morris N. Holbrook, eds. New York: Association for Consumer Research and Institute for Retail Management, New York University, 52-59.

Whewell, David (1995), "Aestheticism," in *A Companion to Aesthetics*, David Cooper, ed. Malden, MA: Blackwell, 6-9.

Whisney, Anita J., Geitel Winakor, and Leroy Wolins (1979), "Fashion Preference: Drawings Versus Photographs," *Home Economics Research Journal*, 8 (November), 138-50.

Williams, Judy, Joyce Arbaugh, and Margaret Rucker (1980), "Clothing Color Preferences of Adolescent Females," *Home Economics Research Journal*, 9, 57-63.

Zeithaml, Valarie A. and Mary Jo Bitner (1996), *Services Marketing*. New York: McGraw-Hill.

PART 2

Technology/Participation

5

Self-Service and Technology

Unanticipated and Unintended Effects on Customer Relationships

JAMES G. BARNES
PETER A. DUNNE
WILLIAM J. GLYNN

Increasingly, many forms of customer service are being delivered with the help of technology. Virtually everywhere consumers turn today, they will encounter situations where some component of a service they wish to use or access requires interaction with some form of technology. Much of this technology-delivered service is initiated and carried out by the consumer and involves no direct or indirect contact with representatives of the service provider. The customer decides that he or she needs the service, initiates the contact via technology, and completes the interaction, without ever being in face-to-face or voice contact with an employee. These technology-based, self-service interactions are the modern equivalent of routine contacts in which customers interacted with employees on a regular basis only a few short years ago. Over the past 20 years, the modern consumer society has bonded with advancing technologies to enable companies to delegate the provision of such services to customers themselves, in concert with sophisticated technology.

We encounter these situations at every turn. Our daily lives are full of situations where we enter into interactions and complete transactions without ever dealing directly or indirectly with a representative of the service organization. We use e-commerce to order from Internet-based retailers. We do our banking through ATMs, over the telephone, or through the Internet. We access information on airline schedules over the telephone by dealing with interactive voice response (IVR) systems. Students register for university courses and collect their grades on-line. We pay directly at the gasoline pumps using our credit cards. We pay for many retail purchases using a debit card that transfers funds directly from our bank account into the retailer's. The list of examples goes on.

The introduction of technology into the delivery channel for services that once required interaction with employees of the service provider has created a self-service environment in which customers deliver their own services. This has tended to eliminate, and will continue to systematically eliminate, the social or affective component of the encounter. This chapter will examine some of the implications and effects of this self-service environment and will consider the motivation of service providers in introducing such technology-delivered service. We will also examine the nature of the value created for customers through such systems and whether a market segmentation approach to their introduction might be advisable.

Presumably, when managers in service organizations consider the introduction of technology-based, self-service delivery systems for certain components of the service offering, they do so from two perspectives. There are benefits to be created for both the service organization and its customers. Delivering service via technology is generally more cost-effective for the service provider. The technology is reliable and consistent in delivering service, and it provides high levels of efficiency. It is available 24 hours a day, 7 days a week; never calls in sick; and never takes a vacation. It also offers benefits to the service organization that are beyond the view of customers, such as the cash-flow benefits provided by electronic funds transfer systems.

The benefits to customers of such automated service-delivery systems mirror to some extent those to the service firm. Barring problems with the technology, the customer can access the service at any time, from any location, completely at his or her convenience. The level of service provided is consistent from place to place and from occasion to occasion. Having access to such systems gives the customer an ability to control the interaction much more than is the case when the customer has to deal with employees.

CUSTOMER SATISFACTION AND VALUE CREATION

Cumby and Barnes (1996) have suggested that the factors which contribute to customer satisfaction in dealing with service providers may be viewed at five levels:

1. the core service being provided,
2. various support services and systems that contribute to the delivery of the service,
3. the technical accuracy in delivering the core and support services,
4. the interaction that customers have with employees of the firm, and
5. certain affective aspects of the interaction—essentially, how the customer is made to feel.

DRIVERS OF CUSTOMER SATISFACTION

Inverted pyramid showing from top to bottom: Affective Dimensions of the Interaction; Interaction with the Firm and Its Employees; Technical Performance; Processes and Support; Core.

Figure 5.1 Drivers of Customer Satisfaction

It may be argued that the service provider can create value for the customer at each of these stages, and that different forms of value are created in each case (see Figure 5.1).

By introducing technology-based, self-service systems into the interaction between customer and service provider, the firm supposedly is improving the quality of service provided to its customers. Customers (or at least some customers) will perceive additional value to have been created when they can access bank services from their homes at midnight, or when they can register by Internet from their offices for a course at the local community college. It may be suggested, however, that other forms of value creation are being ignored when the sole focus is on efficient service delivery. Marketers may also not be paying sufficient attention to the fact that some customers may want to access different *forms* of value when dealing with the service provider. That is, different clients may desire different forms of service and may resent a forced choice (or no choice at all).

It may be argued that reliance on technology-based, self-service systems to manage interactions with customers focuses on value creation at only three of the levels implicit in the model presented in Figure 5.1. Such systems do enable customers to access the core service that they need: the financial transaction, the course registration, or the airline reservation. They also represent support services in enabling customers to access information or to effect transfers of funds or registering of information. They also tend to carry out such service provision in an efficient and timely fashion, leading to the conclusion that the service is technically accurate. The existence of such systems, however, generally precludes (or may make very difficult) interaction with employees of the firm, and, it is suggested, pays little attention to how the customer is made to feel by the interaction. As well, such systems generally allow for neither customization of service nor the addressing of special needs or circumstances that may arise in an encounter. This type of "support" is difficult to provide via technology.

What, therefore, is the effect of introducing technology into the channel of delivery of a service and of delegating the provision of the service to the customer? It removes human interaction from the provision of the service, and it creates an environment in which the responsibility for service provision rests with the customer, rather than with the service provider. Most often, the firm takes a cost-cutting or efficiency view; there are economies to be realized, and the possibility exists to reduce operating costs. Perhaps, as an aside, there is promise that there will be improved performance for the consumer with regard to consistency and efficiency of delivery. In other words, there is hope of improved technical service—but is that all there is to consider? Should we not also ask whether there is more to the repeated provision of service to a client than its technical characteristics alone?

IMPACT ON AFFECTIVE RESPONSE

In focusing on the provision of service via technology, does the firm lose sight of the affective dimension, or the quality-of-delivery aspects, when there is little or no interpersonal contact? It can be clearly seen that there are variations in the degree of personal contact in our daily service experiences, from face-to-face or even hands-on, to totally technologically driven. This *must* impinge on the nature of these interactions and the resultant affective response of the customer. Perhaps a more salient question is whether the affective component of the experience is less important the farther one moves away from face-to-face contact. Could there be a *qualitative* difference in the nature of affect? If so, what does this mean for the future development and management of client relationships and service-quality initiatives?

It is important to realize that we must broaden the definition of "service encounter" to include *any* interaction with the organization, so as to allow for the future discussion and study of service encounters in this rapidly expanding environment, which is characterized by high levels of technology and a self-service approach to service provision.

Although it appears that short-term financial goals on the part of the firm weigh heavily in decisions to implement technology-based service systems, it may also be that service providers see this as the view of the consumer as well; that is, that the customer's primary concern is also the promise of savings. This is to assume that the viewpoint of the customer, as another stakeholder, is considered during the process of designing alternative delivery channels. The introduction of technology in the self-service context has allowed the service provider to delegate the provision and delivery of service to the customer. How *do* consumers view the introduction, or the increasing presence, of technology in the delivery of the services they utilize—services that were until recently provided through face-to-face contact with employees?

BEHIND THE SCENES OR FULL VIEW

Three forms of technology might be seen to affect the "production" and delivery of goods and services: materials, methods, and information technologies (Lovelock 1995). Alternatively, we may look at the implementation of technology such that it is utilized backstage, quietly improving the process of "production," or in front of the curtain and on the main stage, performing and interacting directly with clients. It is the front stage that is the platform for traditional service delivery, where service providers and clients meet. More directly, it is here the technology upstages or replaces the "roles" of personnel and reduces the requirements for "live" performances. Information technology is the form of technology that most often alters the stage upon which the service provider–client encounter takes place. At the extreme, the effect can be to reduce contact to a "virtual" stage.

Much (possibly most) of the impact of technology on the provision of service to consumers takes place behind the "line of visibility" (Kingman-Brundage 1995). The application of information technology has created situations where considerable information is available to marketers, for example, with the result that direct marketing programs are more efficient and better targeted to reach customers who are likely to be interested. Technology also has made it possible for companies to undertake service beyond the view of customers, as is the case when repairs to a telephone line are made "at the switch" without the need for a visit to the customer's home. In some cases, repairs are made before the customer even realizes there was a problem.

In the case of the application of technology in a self-service context, the interaction becomes displaced to the back stage and the customer is still very aware of the fact that technology is in use. This, in some respect, comes to mean that the technology is no longer behind the scenes. It is up front and "visible." The customer knows he or she is "interacting" with a machine and reacts accordingly. It is this direct contact with the back stage that has the potential to influence customer response to the service provision. Consumers are largely unaware of those advances "behind the scenes" that influence administration and "production" of the service—and as a result do not think of how these have affected the services they receive. Those changes that customers do focus on are those examples that they "see" or access directly. These adaptations to a technology-based encounter must create opinions or views among customers as to what they feel the organization is attempting to achieve.

PERCEPTIONS OF VALUE

Are these technology-based "advances" in the provision of service *perceived* as an increase or decrease in the level of service offered by a service provider? What forms of value are perceived to be added when a service provider moves to the provision of service via technology? How do different market segments react? In some instances the service provider can, in effect, become virtually invisible. More directly, do customers and prospective customers perceive that these "advances" have value? As mentioned, if we assume the consumer viewpoint has already been considered, then this reliance on technology to deliver certain services implies that technical/functional performance is all that is thought by marketers to be important to the consumer. It would seem intuitive that different customers would have different needs and different weighting on the various components of service presented by the service provider as representing or having value. The current trend toward increased provision of service in a technology-based, self-service format appears to downplay or eliminate the possible role that may be played by a relationship/affective component of value.

Although there are services that are highly routinized and transactional in nature, many more of the services that consumers require are specialized, require customization, and are of a personal nature. These more personal encounters traditionally result in a great deal of repeated social interaction and elicit socioemotional responses. Westbrook (1987) recognized that postpurchase evaluation of a product/consumer experience was not exclusively a cognitive process. As well, Barnes (1997) has demonstrated that the degree of "closeness" in a relationship between a service provider and a customer is an important predictor of long-term satisfaction and customer retention. Affective responses were previously given a secondary role in consumer evaluations of experience. The affective aspects of customer interaction have in recent years been receiving recognition as having a major role in human motivation and a major influence on information processing and consumer choice.

EFFECT ON AFFECT

We must determine if and how the application of technology in self-service situations alters the affective component of customer relationships. Cumby and Barnes (1997) have suggested that the affective dimensions of an exchange have an overriding influence on all other elements. The assertion here is that consideration of the feelings that are produced by how the customer is treated by, or interacts with, representatives of the service organization is critical to the effective management of service encounters. This refers to how the customer is made to *feel* during the service encounter. This also implies that it is of consequence to actually *elicit* some affect, but clearly positive affect is desired. This greatly influences satisfaction, thereby coloring the future potential of the relationship.

Implicit in the model presented earlier of the factors that drive customer satisfaction (Cumby and Barnes 1996) is the fact that the *actual* interaction with other people contributes to a customer's level of satisfaction with a service encounter. Although there are feelings elicited by the interaction between the customer and technology, it is suggested that much of the affective component of the customer's reaction to service is attributed to his or her contact with employees of the service organization. The issue, in the context of this discussion, is the effect of the application of technology in self-service situations as it relates to the value that is created for customers in different segments. This value is created by the fact that they now access a particular service by initiating contact with technology, whereas they had in the past obtained the same service by interacting with an employee of the firm. It is suggested that some customers feel that they derive considerable value by having service made available through this technology, whereas others feel that overall value has been diminished.

It is illogical to assume that the affective components of service delivery and the value associated with interaction with employees suddenly become unimportant simply because service providers choose an alternate route of service delivery. Are service providers, by moving to the delivery of service through technology, eliminating a facet that is of great benefit in encouraging customer retention and loyalty? This application of technology may jeopardize the feeling of security that is experienced by consumers by virtue of their having both informal and formal feedback loops that enable the service provider to ensure it is in tune with changing customer needs and demands. The importance of interpersonal contact between customer and service provider cannot be underestimated for its role in providing information concerning what the customer desires and feels with regard to the services that he or she is receiving. This is especially relevant in what is currently a very dynamic environment where the perceptions and needs of customers may change or evolve.

More than a decade ago, Dean and Brass (1985) reported that the perceptions of employees who were more central to communication networks, boundary-spanning employees, and employees close to the organization's boundaries were more similar to the perceptions of the outside observer (i.e., customers and prospective customers). Barnes and Glynn (1995) found that employees who were closest to regular face-to-face contact with customers were more likely to think like the customers in terms of what aspects of service are most important than were employees who work in "back room" settings and who rarely have direct contact with customers. How does an organization develop or maintain loyalty, favorable affective responses, and close relationships in the face of this new technology-based service delivery challenge?

If we recognize that the interpersonal and "feelings" components of service do not lose their importance regardless of how service is delivered, then how does a company manage these when service is delivered through technology? How can we know how we are making customers *feel*? Or are they now left *feeling* nothing because the interpersonal contact has been removed? Is it possible that the introduction of technology has created a situation where the potential exists for the creation of negative feelings such as frustration and neglect, and less of an opportunity for the creation of such positive interpersonal feelings as empathy and understanding? The introduction of self-service, technology-based service may represent a step backward for marketing and a poor gauge for service quality.

Many important services are more than discrete transactions, and thus service organizations are social organizations and experiences. Through the increasing presence of technology in the delivery of services, the "social" component of customer interaction is becoming systematically displaced. This technology-based view of service provision considers service delivery principally from a transactional, as opposed to a relationship, point of view. It suggests that the parties involved are concerned exclusively with the core service. It tends to focus solely on the technical side of service delivery and ignores the consumer's needs or desire for human interaction. It addresses the accuracy and efficiency of service delivery but places no emphasis on the affective dimensions of the interaction with customers. It ignores the considerable value that is added by contact with employees.

CUSTOMER RELATIONSHIPS AND HIGHER ORDER VALUE CREATION

The past several years have witnessed much focus in both services and tangible goods marketing on the concept of the development of relationships with customers. Development and maintenance of a genuine relationship requires some degree of interaction between the service provider and the client, thereby creating a bond between the two parties. Goodwin and Gremler (1996) have reported that the social dimension of the service encounter contributes to customer loyalty—a bond. Loyalty to service firms, identified as a key component of the service-profit chain (Heskett et al. 1994), has been associated with a customer's personal relationship with a service provider. From these experiences, customers develop the *perception* of customization, empathy, appreciation, friendliness, communality, and feelings of trust. "Loyal" customers will often describe the "ambience" of service delivery and their strong feelings toward the service provider, whereas nonloyal customers are generally more influenced by economic and convenience factors.

Can we conclude that there is something in the face-to-face (voice-to-voice) interaction that creates these desired bonds, closeness, or loyalty? It would appear that a mutually beneficial cycle can be achieved—value drives customer satisfaction, customer satisfaction drives customer loyalty, and customer loyalty drives profitability and growth (Heskett et al. 1994). If we look to the model of customer satisfaction cited earlier (Cumby and Barnes 1996), we can see where the greatest potential appears to lie for ultimate consumer satisfaction. The missing link remains in not sufficiently defining value from the consumer perspective. Services marketers must focus on the higher order drivers of customer satisfaction, where there is a link between the satisfaction of the customer and the interpersonal and affective aspects of service provision.

Can we assess the importance of affect and customer relationships when technology-based channels of delivery are employed? Can we determine if their importance has diminished? Is the lack of personal contact in the delivery channel more than made up for by the added convenience it allows? Again, we arrive at the concept of value—from the consumer's perspective. Are the bonds that result from personal contact weakened, or have they evolved into a different perspective? Are we replacing relationships with disaffected bonds of communication through technology? Can a genuine customer relationship flourish in such an impersonal context?

SEGMENTS OF TECHNO-RECEPTIVITY

There are consumers who will accept change and others who immediately resist the intrusion of technological "advances." Researchers have identified a segment of consumers who adapt to technological changes only to return to traditional face-to-face service delivery channels because of dissatisfaction with the innovation (Prendergast and Marr 1994). These issues must be addressed when segmenting and targeting markets to allow for this variability in consumers' receptivity to technology. Furthermore, it cannot be assumed that it is the "seniors" market segment, as may seem intuitive, that represents the last bastion of resistance toward technology. Perhaps the key initiative to be undertaken in services marketing is that of segmentation, with due consideration placed on the increasing role played by technology in delivery. The perceptions of consumers with regard to technology and value will play a key role in effective segmentation.

In the past, many firms appear to have given little consideration to the long-term implications of technology-based delivery channels. This is surprising because these alternate routes of communication and service delivery have altered, and will continue to alter, the essence of the relationship between service provider and client. Because the service organization is a social one, technology can change entirely how business is conducted and the resulting employee-customer relationships. These changes would obviously alter the prevailing culture currently existing within an organization.

It must also be considered that the marketplace is not a vacuum. The mass "technological-ization" and "media-ization" of our environment is having more widespread impact than simply altering the consumer's view of retail relationships. Societal attitudes, as a result, are changing at a pace probably never before experienced. There exists now in the marketplace a segment of consumers who are more educated than ever before as to how business and commerce works and who are skeptical of institutions and authority figures—they demand more information and yet are more distrustful of that which they receive (Barnard and Welsh 1997).

IMPACT ON CUSTOMER RELATIONSHIPS

In the midst of this dynamic context, we are, however, left with one variable that is still seen by many service providers as static and unidimensional—the customer relationship. Previous attempts at "relationship marketing" have yielded fragile insights into a concept (the relationship) that is now experiencing various pressures to change. The one variable that should be of greatest interest to service providers and marketers is left without an on-ramp to the information highway.

In many organizations, it would appear that while technology evolves, the development of customer relationships and service quality initiatives remains slow to respond. Attention that *is* directed toward these areas is prone to an "insider" bias as the physical and psychological distance between the service provider and the customer becomes greater and greater. Boundaries are being erected—a solid wall of technology. As channels become more technology-based, communication through the wall becomes bothersome and unwieldy for the customer. The only aspects of the service that are "visible" to the client are those that he or she performs. The prolonged absence of contact with the service provider that is likely to characterize the relationship when the customer becomes dependent on a technology-based means of accessing service has the potential to erode the emotional attachment that the customer may have felt toward the service provider when customer contact was through employees. The result is likely to be an ongoing relationship that is much more superficial and fleeting. Where contact is only through technology, the customer is much less likely to feel loyalty toward the service provider and is more prone to switching.

Consumer utilization of the technology should not be taken as tacit approval or acceptance. Consumers may use the technology because there is no *perceived* alternative—they may still feel there is the cooling effect of being held at arm's length and may simply accept that this is a logical progression in the gradual decline in relationships with business, the natural result of "progress." Some segments of the market are accustomed to the promise of "new and improved" and are willing to test that promise. There are experience seekers who will try the latest—however, with this segment, often referred to as the "Nexus generation," retention and long-term loyalty are difficult to crack (Barnard and Welsh 1997). This "Nexus generation" expects more than consumers of the past and possesses skeptical attitudes toward what is offered.

The ever-increasing trend of fevered bidding for consumer attention on the part of service providers has evolved into a component of entertainment and amusement for the browsing shopper. This consumer will make decisions based on some combination of objective requirements and subjective, personal measures of value, while all the technological tools and clamor for their attention provide entertainment during the process. Although consumer perceptions of value may still be based on "traditional" measures, could it be that these new "value-added" channels of service distribution are simply seen as extraneous details? The value created for the customer may not be that which was conceived by the service provider. The pursuit by organizations to provide the first and the best is to the marketplace only clamor and entertainment—some consumers are quick and glad to utilize the new technology to see what all the activity, and discussion, is about. This apparent fervor for technology is perhaps interpreted as true value recognition by the service provider, thereby possibly feeding a cycle of misunderstanding. If this is the case, then it is the service provider who is not receiving value for the money spent on the installation of technology-based access to service.

The result of creating arms-length access to service through technology is that relationships which had been established begin to erode as customers no longer have direct contact with the firm or its employees. No longer do they meet tellers in the branch or talk with order takers for the catalog company. For new customers, no opportunity exists in the face of the new channels for genuine, emotive relationships to be established. The relationship between a customer and a bank or telephone company is entirely convenience based, with little or no affective content. Customers see the existence of the new systems as enabling them to take control of service delivery, facilitating access and making it much more convenient to obtain routine services. Many, however, resent the fact that such systems result in an erosion of the relationships that existed in the past. They long for a closer relationship and someone to turn to when they have problems. The result is increased cynicism and a propensity to switch service providers. The challenge that companies face when they launch such systems is to foster closer customer relationships in the face of the technology.

Nobody would argue that technology should not offer value. Should this not be the primary consideration of marketing and information systems managers when deciding on the implementation of new technology? This statement, however, is sufficiently vague that it carries very little meaning. Who benefits? Should all stakeholders benefit, or should certain groups receive preferential consideration? For that matter, what *exactly* is value? How is it measured? How much return is enough to justify implementation? Does the question *imply* a singular meaning of value? What if there are costs for one party involved in creating value for another? What if the introduction of technology adds some forms of value for a group of customers while eroding value for others?

IMPLEMENTING NEW
SERVICE-DELIVERY CHANNELS

The introduction of technology as a means to deliver certain components of service should be taken as a part of long-term strategic planning. How technology will be perceived and accepted must, therefore, be carefully researched. How can the process of introduction be supported and facilitated? Are we forcing the technology on the consumer, or is it at least *perceived* that way? In the rush to innovate through technology, we are standardizing service delivery to a level that often cannot recognize the individual service requirements of clients. The focus should be toward utilization of the potential to create mass customization—to allow greater efficiency, consistency, and value, while allowing a sense of recognition and individuality to the individual. Further, this should be combined with attempts to segment customer groups, allowing them the choice to use a technology-based access channel or not. Otherwise, we may, theoretically, be improving technical customer service (narrowly defined as efficiency or access), but at the cost of customer relationships. This is not beneficial from the organizational or managerial viewpoint. Not only is such an approach focused on short-term benefits for the firm and the customer, but it may also in fact contribute to the creation of more superficial customer relationships in the future.

Relationship distance is a concept that becomes important when viewing delivery channel decisions from a management perspective. First, it is important to realize that, despite all efforts and expense by the organization to develop customer relationships, these relationships do not *actually* exist unless the customer perceives that an ongoing relationship is in place between the two parties. Second, there must be some understanding of how *close* the customer perceives the relationship to be, and what distance he or she feels is appropriate and comfortable (Barnes 1997). This will vary according to the nature of the service (dry cleaner versus financial services versus medical services) as well as by segment. There may well be a "standard" of closeness that is appropriate for an industry, but *within* that industry there will likely be a range that allows for individual comfort and preference based on personality variables. Critical to remember at all times, however, is that the introduction of technology-based channels for self-service will increase the challenge of achieving greater relationship closeness with most segments. This logically follows from the decrease in personal contact that will result from utilizing this "once-removed" channel.

PERSONALIZATION AND PARALLEL SYSTEMS

When deciding to introduce a technology-based service delivery channel, the challenge for management is to design measures of personalization into the channel. These would allow for flexible reactions to individual customer needs and possibly permit the recognition of clients and their particular preferences. Different services would probably receive differential benefits, especially in consideration to the trade-off of decreased customer interaction and relationship development. An issue that should occupy the attention of management in designing self-service systems relates to how personalization and recognition can be designed into the technology-based channel. Such an approach calls for the recognition of clients and for tailored messages to convey the impression that some degree of personal contact is still possible.

It is important for management to recognize that different customers will give a different weighting to various needs such as price and convenience in their interaction with a service provider. As a result, there will be some variation in the meaning of value for different segments. For some consumers, importance will be placed on convenience; others, what they want from a service provider will be skewed toward social bonds and quality of interpersonal contact. Genuine customer relationships and the value that customers associate with them will be more important to some segments of customers than to others. The fundamental premise of market segmentation is that all customers cannot be treated alike. This must be considered when determining the value created by technology. Economies may be possible while closer customer relationships are developed through offering parallel streams of service. While offering its customers the convenience, flexibility, and timely access promised by technology-based self-service systems, firms should also consider developing alternative and parallel systems to deliver the emotive, affective content that characterizes genuine customer relationships.

The creation of a parallel process to deliver the affective side of a relationship in the face of an impersonal technology-based contact system allows compensation for the mechanistic, unfeeling nature of service delivery via technology. A flexible system would allow customers to access either a technology-based or a more conventional, personal delivery option, while also allowing utilization of *both* new and traditional channels. This can be supplemented with such measures as periodic outbound calling, mail-outs, and the provision of designated employees to serve as contact points within the company. Without opportunities for personal contact and the resultant affective component, service providers are leaving themselves vulnerable to being taken for granted by consumers and to the risk of becoming commoditized, as is often seen in the case of utility services such as electricity and telephone services, and increasingly so in the technology-based delivery of certain financial services.

There is a segmentation issue to be addressed as well. Service providers need to know how various segments will respond to the technology-based delivery of service. Customers will differ in terms of how they define service and value. We can, therefore, argue for a segmented approach to the introduction of such services, rather than a universal conversion of all customers to a technology-based system.

REFERENCES

Barnard, R. and J. Welsh (1997), "The Next Shoppers: Marketers Are Doting on the Preferences of 18 to 35 Year Olds," *Financial Post*, (November 8), P8, P12+.

Barnes, James (1997), "Closeness, Strength and Satisfaction: Examining the Nature of Relationships Between Providers of Financial Services and Their Retail Customers," *Psychology and Marketing*, 14(4), 765-90.

———— and W. Glynn (1995), "The Customer Wants Service: Why Technology Is No Longer Enough," *Journal of Marketing Management*, 9(1), 43-53.

Cumby, Judith A. and James G. Barnes (1996), "Relationship Segmentation: The Enhancement of Databases to Support Relationship Marketing," in *Contemporary Knowledge of Relationship Marketing*, Proceedings of the Third Research Conference on Relationship Marketing, Atul Parvatiyar and Jagdish N. Sheth, eds. Atlanta: Roberto C. Goizueta Business School, Emory University, 14-24.

———— and ———— (1997), *How We Make Them Feel: A Discussion of the Reactions of Customers to Affective Dimensions of the Service Encounter*, in *New and Evolving Paradigms: The Emerging Future of Marketing* [CD-ROM], proceedings of three conferences of the American Marketing Association, Dublin, Ireland, June 12-15.

Dean, J. and D. Brass (1985), "Social Interaction and the Perception of Job Characteristics in an Organization," *Human Relations*, 38(6), 571-82.

Goodwin, Cathy and Dwayne Gremler (1996), "Friendship Over the Counter: How Social Aspects of Service Encounters Influence Consumer Service Loyalty," in *Advances in Services Marketing and Management*, Vol. 5, T. A. Swartz, D. E. Bowen, and S. W. Brown, eds. Greenwich, CT: JAI, 247-82.

Heskett, James L., Thomas O. Jones, Gary W. Loveman, W. Earl Sasser, Jr., and Leonard A. Schlesinger (1994), "Putting the Service Profit Chain to Work," *Harvard Business Review*, 72 (March-April), 164-74.

Kingman-Brundage, Jane (1995), "Service Blueprinting," in *Understanding Services Management*, William J. Glynn and James G. Barnes, eds. Chichester, UK: John Wiley and Sons, 119-42.

Lovelock, Christopher (1995), "Technology: Servant or Master in the Delivery of Services?" in *Advances in Services Marketing and Management*, Vol. 4, T. A. Swartz, D. E. Bowen, and S. W. Brown, eds. Greenwich, CT: JAI, 63-90.

Prendergast, G. and N. Marr (1994), "Disenchantment Discontinuance in the Diffusion of Self-Service Technologies in the Services Industry: A Case Study in Retail Banking," *Journal of International Consumer Marketing*, 7(2), 25-40.

Westbrook, R. (1987), "Product/Consumption-Based Affective Responses and Post-Purchase Processes," *Journal of Marketing Research*, 24(8), 258-70.

6

Technology in Service Delivery

Implications for Self-Service and Service Support

PRATIBHA A. DABHOLKAR

Advances in technology have revamped service delivery in recent years, with a tremendous impact both on self-service options and on service support. Today, customers can choose between a variety of technological options to perform services for themselves (Zinn 1993). At the same time, companies employ technology at various stages in the service delivery process and in service support operations to improve the quality and productivity of their service offering (Blumberg 1994). These developments are changing the way service firms and customers interact and have opened up many new research issues for investigation within services marketing (Dabholkar 1994b).

An early, well-known application of a technology-based self-service option was that of the automated teller machine (ATM) in the early 1980s. ATMs were a breakthrough service option at the time and met with some resistance because people were not used to the idea of interacting with a machine instead of a person to conduct their banking. Today, self-service technology is challenging the notion that provider-client interaction is an essential feature of services marketing; for example, in banking, technology-based self-service options now include transactions conducted via telephone, the Internet, and smartcards, and at home via television (Prendergast and Marr 1994a). Other recent applications of technology-based self-service options include automated airline ticketing, postage machines, film development, in-room hotel checkout via television terminals, electronic medical kits for home use, brokerage software, self-scanning at retail stores, and home shopping using interactive television or the Internet (Dabholkar 1994b).

WHAT DO CONSUMERS WANT FROM TECHNOLOGY-BASED SELF-SERVICE OPTIONS?

In implementing self-service technology, many service firms hope to offer faster, better service to customers. Research has shown that technology-based self-service does appear to increase the actual or perceived speed of service and reduce waiting time for customers (Cowles and Crosby 1990; Dabholkar 1991b, 1996; Prendergast and Marr 1994a). If the technology is cumbersome or complex, however, or if the customer is not technologically proficient, this type of option can actually increase the service delivery time. One way to avoid this latter scenario is for firms to target the more complex technologies (e.g., financial or brokerage software) to technologically proficient segments. Another way to avoid it is to simplify the technologies to the extent that anyone can use them (e.g., touch screen technology for retail information and ordering).

But is faster always better? For many convenience-oriented services, speed is closely associated with service quality (Dabholkar 1991b, 1996; Langeard et al. 1981; Lovelock and Young 1979; Sellers 1990). Ledingham (1984) suggests that efficiency and speed are particularly important to people who use technology to serve themselves. Other consumers, however, value human interaction above anything else in service delivery. In a study of retail banking in New Zealand, Prendergast and Marr (1994a) found that three-fourths of the respondents planned to continue using ATMs because of perceived time savings, whereas one-fourth were disenchanted with ATMs, mainly because they preferred the human interaction. The authors also found that half of the respondents planned to continue using telephone banking and electronic fund transfer because of perceived time savings, whereas the other half had decided not to use telephone banking and electronic fund transfer, again because they preferred the human interaction. For the segments that value human contact over technology, service delivery options with human interaction should be available and technology should be used in service support operations to enhance the personal service.

Past research (Dabholkar 1996) has also examined whether technology-based self-service options increase or decrease perceived control for customers, and whether perceived control translates into perceived quality. It is interesting, but perhaps not surprising, that technologically proficient customers perceive a higher sense of control and greater quality, whereas those resistant to new technologies do not. The differences disappear with technologies that are simple enough for anyone to use. Other aspects of control in self-service are unrelated to the technology aspect. Some people feel more in control when they perform the service for themselves, whereas others feel more in control having someone else wait on them (Bateson 1985; Dabholkar 1990; Langeard et al. 1981;

Lovelock and Young 1979), a sense of "behavioral" control. Offering consumers a choice among different service options (including those based on technology) is also likely to increase their "decisional" control. Some technology-based self-service offers the customer not only control but also privacy (e.g., using health monitors in the home). More research is needed to explore all these issues.

ADOPTION OF TECHNOLOGY-BASED SELF-SERVICE OPTIONS

In addition to speed, control, and privacy, what do consumers perceive as relevant attributes for evaluating technology-based service for possible adoption? Previous research on the adoption of computer technology has shown that perceived ease of use and "fun" influence usage intentions (Davis, Bagozzi, and Warshaw 1989, 1992). In a services context, research shows that customers who view technology-based service as easy to use, reliable, and enjoyable also perceive higher service quality in such delivery options (Dabholkar 1991b, 1996). Service firms are starting to incorporate these and similar findings for service design implementation and promotional strategies. For example, National Car Rental emphasizes speed of service delivery and reliability in its ads for automated car rental machines located in airports (Dabholkar 1996). Service firms in the travel industry, such as airlines, hotels, and resorts, are starting to emphasize the consumer's ease of use and enjoyment while browsing through on-line travel options by themselves.

Customers participate in service production in a way that they do not with the production of goods, so acceptance of new technologies is much more critical in service industries. This acceptance includes loss of human interaction as well as the learning of new skills and the assumption of some liability (Fitzsimmons 1985). Factors that are relevant for trial and adoption (Gatignon and Robertson 1985; Rogers 1983) can be conceptualized specifically for a technology-based self-service option in terms of different types of risks (Dabholkar 1991a). One way to reduce these risks and to encourage adoption of technology-based self-service is to offer a variety of options with different combinations of technology and human components (Dabholkar 1994b). Meuter and Bitner (1998) write that self-service can be viewed along a continuum where the customer can perform all, part, or none of the service. This idea can be incorporated into service design so as to accommodate different needs of customers and aid their transition to technology-based self-service, making that transition more gradual.

SITUATIONAL AND INDIVIDUAL DIFFERENCES IN USING TECHNOLOGY-BASED SERVICES

Situational factors can also encourage or discourage trial and adoption of technology-based service delivery. Studies have shown that waiting time can have a strong negative influence even on those with favorable attitudes toward technology-based self-service options (Dabholkar 1991b, 1996). Waiting, therefore, is a big concern for a growing number of services, where technological options are still not quite as fast as they could be. Waiting time, especially in accessing on-line services and downloading information about services, can be a huge deterrent to usage. Research is needed on the design of service operations to reduce waiting time where possible and to develop innovative ways to keep customers occupied while they wait to use technology-based services (Dabholkar 1990).

Consumer familiarity with technology has a direct bearing on strategies for service design and introduction. Greater familiarity with technology results in more favorable attitudes toward using technology-based self-service options (Dabholkar 1992). Furthermore, once consumers become comfortable with a particular technology in one service industry, they more readily adopt similar technologies in other service industries (Dabholkar 1992, 1994b). Also, with increasing familiarity, consumers are likely to use less complex decision-making and choice models for technology-based self-service options (Dabholkar 1994a). Such findings suggest that creating "technologically comfortable" consumers in general would be directly beneficial to service firms considering any form of technology-based service delivery. More research is needed to determine the categories of technology across which the benefits of familiarity may be transferred.

Given the differences among customers in relating to technology, researchers have begun to explore personality and demographic factors related to the acceptance of technology-based service. Dabholkar (1991a, 1992) found that a personality factor, "need for interaction" with a service provider, had a significant negative effect on the acceptance of technology-based service. Similarly, Forman and Sriram (1991) found that some customers resist technology-based self-service because they may be lonely and crave social interaction. As mentioned previously, some banking customers resist technological advances because they prefer human interaction (Prendergast and Marr 1994a). Stevens, Warren, and Martin (1989) found that "nonadopters" of automated teller machines shared certain demographic characteristics, yet many were more concerned about safety issues related to isolated ATMs rather than being reluctant to use technology per se. In fact, Evans and Brown (1988) suggest that safety and convenience are important factors for most consumers in considering whether to use off-site self-service options. Clearly, more research is needed into individual differences related to technology-based self-service so as to develop effective strategies for segmentation.

PRICING, OPERATIONS, AND PRODUCTIVITY ISSUES IN TECHNOLOGY-BASED SERVICE DELIVERY

Other questions related to the acceptance and success of technology-based service delivery also need to be addressed. For example, do consumers use technology-based self-service options only if they perceive a price saving, or might they actually be willing to pay more? Traditional thinking was that consumers would use self-service only if there was a price savings. A higher price for self-service may be justifiable, however, if greater customer involvement increases the perception of quality or value to the customer (Blumberg 1994). For example, market research and database companies often charge customers a higher price for experimenting with customizing databases for themselves, even though the customers' participation actually cuts costs for companies (Dabholkar 1990). On the other hand, brokerage companies charge lower fees for customers who trade stocks on-line without the help of a broker. Not surprisingly, it appears that pricing for technology-based self-service is largely related to industry practice as well as the company's own positioning strategy.

The impact of technology on service support is critical and closely linked to the impact on the customer and ultimately on the business. Traditionally, customer participation in service production has been viewed as nonproductive and inefficient (Chase 1978; Mills and Morris 1986). These views were challenged when researchers (e.g., Langeard et al. 1981; Lovelock and Young 1979) proposed that self-service could be viewed as a means to increase the productivity and effectiveness of service delivery. Basing self-service options on technology has the potential to extract the maximum benefits regarding operational efficiencies (Dabholkar 1990, 1991b; Lovelock 1995). At the same time, other researchers (e.g., Hackett 1992) are wary of potential problems with the growing use of technology in service delivery. The potential for problems is especially apparent if service firms enthusiastically invest in customer support technology without a clear understanding of the critical processes and sequences involved in the operations. Technology should help streamline already known processes instead of becoming a burden to the firm, loaded with expensive and unnecessary options.

Hackett (1992) cautions service firms that technology-based service delivery implies the absence of human intervention in case of service failure, a lack of personal relationships, an overemphasis on cost savings, and reduced opportunities for cross-selling other services. Although these concerns are valid, thoughtful planning can overcome each of the potential problems. Comprehensive and reliable technological support can help service providers offer faster and better service to customers. Systems can be designed so that a service support employee can be contacted easily and quickly in case of service failure. Databases can gather sufficient information about customers that can be used to personalize future offerings for them. Cost savings can be passed on to consumers where possible and certainly should not be overemphasized if they reduce the quality of the service. Finally, it is very simple to offer other services (i.e., cross-sell) through technological media, as is already being done effectively on the Internet.

Several researchers and practitioners feel strongly that technology has a positive impact on service delivery. Blumberg (1994) writes that service firms can increase productivity with technological breakthroughs and reduce costs using alternate delivery systems such as self-service. For example, Cub Foods' high-tech store directories are used by customers (about 60,000 times a week) to find the locations of items in the store; this self-service technology results in substantial cost savings to the store and time savings to the customer (Sellers 1990). Contrary to traditional thinking, technology can make the service more personal if used appropriately. By arming their sales and service staffs with computers and up-to-date information, Frito-Lay and Taco Bell have been able to free their employees from "grunt" work so that they can have more time to attend to customers and access better information to serve them (Sellers 1990).

Databases and technological decision support systems help firms collect, process, and distribute the necessary information for service support (Berkeley and Gupta 1995). For high-contact services, firms need the tools and processes to efficiently collect information on customer expectations and suggestions, and they need to incorporate these into the system to "construct detailed customer profiles, eliminate service-specification errors, speed service, and improve service consistency" (Berkeley and Gupta 1995, p. 33). Quinn (1996) writes that information technology used in service support is boosting firm productivity and providing greater convenience (e.g., store checkout), greater accuracy (e.g., health diagnostics), greater reliability (e.g., bank statements), greater safety (e.g., airline travel), and greater flexibility (e.g., home entertainment) for the consumer.

A variety of operational and financial performance issues still need to be addressed. For example, is there a start-up time before faster service is achieved? Are certain populations so familiar with technology that this start-up time is minimal? What role does ergonomics play in designing technology-based service delivery? Are technology-based self-service options more or less expensive than full service delivery options that may or may not rely on technology? How long is it before cost reductions, if any, are realized? Do full-service options based on technology increase perceived control for employees? Furthermore, what impact does increased perceived control for employees have on perceived quality for customers? Does technology-based service delivery lead to higher customer loyalty and retention? Is there a positive impact on profits, and how long does it take to achieve acceptable financial results? Finally, how can service firms learn to design effective and efficient technology-based self-service options by monitoring competitors as well as firms in other service industries?

FUTURE PROSPECTS FOR TECHNOLOGY-BASED SERVICE DELIVERY AND RELATED RESEARCH

Today, the majority of consumers in advanced economies are "savvy" about technology and quite comfortable using touch screen and other technology-based self-service options (Deutsch 1989). A panel of experts from banking and supplier technologies in New Zealand predict that self-service technologies in banking will continue to increase, freeing up time for bank tellers to offer advice and to cross-sell financial services (Prendergast and Marr 1994b). With emerging technologies, fast food restaurants are in a position to learn about customers on a household-by-household basis rather than in terms of broad demographic segments and to track changes in consumption patterns and loyalty much more closely (Wallace 1995). Interactive television and the Internet are sparking a resurgence in the home delivery of restaurant food as well as groceries. It is an opportune time for service firms to increase their reliance on technology to achieve benefits to themselves and to customers. The health care industry, for example, offers awards to organizations and software vendors who cooperatively and effectively deploy emerging technologies to improve service delivery related to health care as well as to health care plans. A challenge for all service firms is to move forward to meet the expectations of technologically proficient customers without neglecting technology-resistant customers who prefer to use traditional service delivery options (Barrett 1997).

Past research (Dabholkar 1994b) has examined a variety of options for technology-based service design, whether backstage or frontstage, on-site or off-site, and has raised research issues closely related to managerial strategy and implementation. In this chapter, research issues have been raised regarding various aspects of technology-based service delivery. One area of investigation is to determine what consumers want from technology-based self-service options (in terms of attributes) so marketers can design and promote these options accordingly. Another potential research area involves the adoption process related to technology-based service delivery, so marketers can learn how to reduce perceived risks and increase consumer familiarity with technology. A third area for future research is related to the impact of situational and individual influences on choices in technology-based service delivery, with implications for service design and promotion. This last area involves cost, operations, and productivity issues with implications for pricing, service design, and financial performance. As discussed in this chapter, researchers have begun to address many of these issues, yet the future is wide open to investigate the various research questions related to technology in service delivery in an effort to offer service firms clearer guidance on future service design and comprehensive marketing strategies.

REFERENCES

Barrett, Mark (1997), "Alternate Delivery Systems: Supermarkets, ATMs, Telephone Banking, PCs, and On-Line Banking," *Bankers' Magazine*, 180(3), 44-51.

Bateson, John E. G. (1985), "Self-Service Consumer: An Exploratory Study," *Journal of Retailing*, 61(3), 49-76.

Berkeley, Blair J. and Amit Gupta (1995), "Identifying the Information Requirements to Deliver Quality Service," *International Journal of Service Industry Management*, 6(5), 16-35.

Blumberg, Donald F. (1994), "Strategies for Improving Field Service Operations Productivity and Quality," *The Service Industries Journal*, 14(2), 262-77.

Chase, Richard B. (1978), "Where Does the Customer Fit in the Service Operation?" *Harvard Business Review*, 56(6), 137-42.

Cowles, Deborah and Lawrence A. Crosby (1990), "Consumer Acceptance of Interactive Media," *The Service Industries Journal*, 10(3), 521-40.

Dabholkar, Pratibha A. (1990), "How to Improve Perceived Service Quality by Increasing Customer Participation," in *Developments in Marketing Science*, Vol. 13, B. J. Dunlap, ed. Cullowhee, NC: Academy of Marketing Science, 483-87.

———— (1991a), "Decision-Making in Consumer Trial of Technology-Based Self-Service Options: An Attitude-Based Choice Model," doctoral dissertation, Georgia State University.

—— (1991b), "Using Technology-Based Self-Service Options to Improve Perceived Service Quality," in *Enhancing Knowledge Development in Marketing*, Mary Gilly et al., eds. Chicago: American Marketing Association, 534-35.

—— (1992), "The Role of Prior Behavior and Category-Based Affect in On-Site Service Encounters," in *Diversity in Consumer Behavior*, Vol. 19, John F. Sherry and Brian Sternthal, eds. Provo, UT: Association for Consumer Research, 563-69.

—— (1994a), "Incorporating Choice Into an Attitudinal Framework: Analyzing Models of Mental Comparison Processes," *Journal of Consumer Research*, 21 (June), 100-118.

—— (1994b), "Technology-Based Service Delivery: A Classification Scheme for Developing Marketing Strategies," in *Advances in Services Marketing and Management*, Vol. 3, Teresa A. Swartz, David E. Bowen, and Stephen W. Brown, eds. Greenwich, CT: JAI, 241-71.

—— (1996), "Consumer Evaluations of New Technology-Based Self-Service Options: An Investigation of Alternative Models of Service Quality," *International Journal of Research in Marketing*, 13(1), 29-51.

Davis, Fred D., Richard P. Bagozzi, and Paul R. Warshaw (1989), "User Acceptance of Computer Technology: A Comparison of Two Theoretical Models," *Management Science*, 35(8), 982-1003.

——, ——, and —— (1992), "Extrinsic and Intrinsic Motivation to Use Computers in the Workplace," *Journal of Applied Social Psychology*, 22(14), 1109-30.

Deutsch, Claudia H. (1989), "The Powerful Push for Self-Service," *The New York Times*, April 9, S3-1.

Evans, Kenneth and Stephen W. Brown (1988), "Strategic Options for Service Delivery Systems," in *Proceedings of the AMA Summer Educators' Conference*, Charles A. Ingene and Gary L. Frazier, eds. Chicago: American Marketing Association, 207-12.

Fitzsimmons, James A. (1985), "Consumer Participation and Productivity in Service Operations," *Interfaces*, 15(3), 60-67.

Forman, Andrew M. and Ven Sriram (1991), "The Depersonalization of Retailing: Its Impact on the 'Lonely' Consumer," *Journal of Retailing*, 67(2), 226-43.

Gatignon, Hubert and Thomas S. Robertson (1985), "A Propositional Inventory for New Diffusion Research," *Journal of Consumer Research*, 11 (March), 849-67.

Hackett, Gregory P. (1992), "Investment in Technology: The Service Sector Sinkhole?" *Sloan Management Review*, 34 (Winter), 97-103.

Langeard, Eric, John E. G. Bateson, Christopher H. Lovelock, and Pierre Eiglier (1981), *Marketing of Services: New Insights From Consumers and Managers*, Report No. 81-104. Cambridge, MA: Marketing Science Institute.

Ledingham, John A. (1984), "Are Consumers Ready for the Information Age?" *Journal of Advertising Research*, 24(4), 31-37.

Lovelock, Christopher H. (1995), "Technology: Servant or Master in the Delivery of Services?" in *Advances in Services Marketing and Management*, Vol. 4, Teresa A. Swartz, David E. Bowen, and Stephen W. Brown, eds. Greenwich, CT: JAI, 63-90.

—— and Robert F. Young (1979), "Look to Consumers to Increase Productivity," *Harvard Business Review*, 57 (May-June), 168-78.

Meuter, Matthew L. and Mary Jo Bitner (1998), "Self-Service Technologies: Extending Service Frameworks and Identifying Issues for Research," in *Marketing Theory and Applications*, Dhruv Grewal and Connie Pechman, eds. Chicago: American Marketing Association, 12-19.

Mills, Peter K. and James H. Morris (1986), "Clients as 'Partial' Employees of Service Organizations: Role Development in Client Participation," *Academy of Management Review*, 11(4), 726-35.

Prendergast, Gerard P. and Norman E. Marr (1994a), "Disenchantment Discontinuance in the Diffusion of Technologies in the Service Industry: A Case Study in Retail Banking," *Journal of International Consumer Marketing*, 7(2), 25-40.

—— and —— (1994b), "The Future of Self-Service Technologies in Retail Banking," *The Service Industries Journal*, 14(1), 94-114.

Quinn, James B. (1996), "The Productivity Paradox Is False: Information Technology Improves Service Performance," in *Advances in Services Marketing and Management*, Vol. 5, Teresa A. Swartz, David E. Bowen, and Stephen W. Brown, eds. Greenwich, CT: JAI, 71-84.

Rogers, Everett M. (1983), *Diffusion of Innovations*. New York: Free Press.

Sellers, Patricia (1990), "What Customers Really Want," *Fortune* (June 4), 58-68.

Stevens, Robert E., William E. Warren, and Rinne T. Martin (1989), "Nonadopters of Automatic Teller Machines," *ABER*, 20(3), 55-63.

Wallace, Jeffrey H. (1995), "Recipe for Success: Throw Technology Into the QSR Mix," *Nation's Restaurant News* (June 5), 34.

Zinn, Laura (1993), "Retailing Will Never Be the Same," *Business Week,* (July 26), 54-60.

7

Customer Participation in Services Production and Delivery

AMY RISCH RODIE
SUSAN SCHULTZ KLEINE

One of the fundamental characteristics that distinguishes services from goods is the simultaneous production and consumption of service products. The customer is often present in the "service factory" (Lovelock 1981) and therefore has some impact on service quality and his or her own satisfaction. For many services, the customer not only consumes the service but also has a hand in producing and delivering it (e.g., physical therapy, guitar lessons, a cycling expedition). Although the importance and consequences of contact *employees'* attitudes and behaviors have received a great deal of attention, the effects of *customers'* attitudes and behaviors have been overlooked. It behooves services marketers to understand and manage their customers' participation in service production and delivery in order to maximize outcomes for *both* customers and providers.

Our purpose in this chapter is to define and describe customer participation. We review conceptual ideas and empirical evidence regarding the benefits of customer participation for customers and providers. Implications for managers are described. Finally, because so few studies have tackled customer participation empirically, we include ideas for future research.

CUSTOMER PARTICIPATION

Customer participation (CP) is a *behavioral* concept that refers to the actions and resources supplied by customers for service production and/or delivery. CP includes customers' mental, physical, and emotional inputs (Hochschild 1983;

Larsson and Bowen 1989; Silpakit and Fisk 1985). *Mental inputs* include information and mental effort. Information may range from a customer's complex goals for an investment portfolio to the source of a stain on a dry cleanable garment. Mental effort includes cognitive labor, such as preparing to articulate symptoms to a health care provider effectively, or reviewing materials to ask intelligent questions of a Realtor. *Physical inputs* include customers' own tangibles and physical efforts. Tangibles range from the customer's own body (e.g., fingernails to manicure) to customer-owned or -managed tangibles (e.g., yard to landscape) (Lovelock 1983). Physical efforts include labor, such as enacting the steps involved in on-line banking, serving oneself at a salad bar, or following the regime prescribed by a physical therapist. CP may entail customers' *emotional inputs*, such as behaving patiently and pleasantly while interacting with a less-than-competent or unpleasant frontline employee. Emotional labor, like other customer inputs, is expended when customers believe that the benefits outweigh the costs. Of course, many service contexts require multiple forms of customer contributions. For example, both mental and physical inputs are required for investing with a discount brokerage. Mental, physical, and emotional inputs are all needed to successfully complete a smoking cessation program.

CP can be contrasted conceptually with several related concepts. CP is distinguished from *customer contact* (Chase 1978, 1981; Kellogg and Chase 1995). Customer contact, as originally conceptualized, is the percentage of time a customer is present in the service delivery system relative to total service time (Chase 1978); the higher the percentage, the greater the contact. More recently, the construct has been operationalized by duration of employee/customer communication, value of information exchanged, and mutual confiding and trust between employee and customer in an exchange (Kellogg and Chase 1995). Extent of contact is viewed from the perspective of the firm and is a strategic variable in service design and positioning (Chase and Tansik 1983). In contrast, CP is viewed from the customers' perspective; it covers the scope of customers' inputs into service production and delivery and is not constrained to the boundaries of a service encounter (Mills and Moberg 1982).

CP is also distinct from *customer involvement*. Using everyday language, we might describe the participating service customer as being "involved" in co-creating the service. In the marketing and consumer behavior literature, involvement refers to a customer's personal interest in a particular service; it describes a *dispositional* characteristic of a customer. A customer's involvement in a service or in selection of a service provider may be relatively short-lived (e.g., for someone who is thrust into selecting investment services on a one-time inheritance), or involvement can be more enduring (e.g., for someone who seeks investment services for ongoing purposes). Such predispositions come with the customer to the service encounter. In contrast, customer participation is manifested through customers' *behaviors* that unfold as service is co-created. A customer may participate extensively in service delivery and remain relatively uninvolved (e.g., routine grocery shopping). Alternatively, a service may offer few opportunities for participation although the customer may be highly involved in the service product (e.g., opera attendance by an aficionado).

Finally, CP in service production is conceptually distinct from *customer consumption*—the process of experiencing the benefits of service production and delivery. Admittedly, the difference is more apparent in some service contexts than in others. For example, a customer's consumption of the benefits of a haircut, legal defense, or wedding photography is fairly easy to distinguish from customer inputs into producing and delivering those benefits. It is more difficult to distinguish CP from consumption in more experience-based services such as tour-guided mountain climbing. More research is needed to tease out the distinctions among these concepts in contexts where the experience is an end in itself and the service is highly participative.

CUSTOMER PARTICIPATION AS IT RELATES TO CUSTOMER EVALUATIONS

Empirical work about CP has been sparse to date. Findings consistently show that CP is related to customers' perceptions of service quality, satisfaction, and future intentions. The valence of the relationship seems to depend in part, however, on the substantive nature of the customer's inputs.

Customer Perceptions of Service Quality

CP is related to perceptions of service quality (Cermak, File, and Prince 1994; Dabholkar 1996; Kelley, Skinner, and Donnelly 1992; Kellogg, Youngdahl, and Bowen 1997). In one study, banking customers recognized that their inputs of information and labor ("customer technical quality") and their manner during the encounter ("customer functional quality") affected the interaction (Kelley, Skinner, and Donnelly 1992, p. 199). Findings also showed that customers' perceptions of the quality of their own inputs were related to their perceptions of the provider's service orientation. Elsewhere, customers' critical incidents from a wide range of service contexts revealed four types of behaviors customers enact to ensure a high-quality service encounter: (a) preparation before the encounter, (b) relationship building and (c) information exchange during the encounter, and (d) intervention (i.e., customers' own attempts to recover from service failure) (Kellogg, Youngdahl, and Bowen 1997). In another study, subjects imagined ordering fast food via a touch screen or verbally (Dabholkar 1996). Results showed that technological participation corresponded with customers' expectations for enjoyment, perceptions of control, and a positive attitude toward technology; each of these outcomes had a strong positive effect on expected service quality. Empirical evidence to date generally supports a positive relationship between CP and perceived service quality.

Customer Attributions

CP is related to customer attributions because participating customers may take partial responsibility for the caliber of the outcome. Scholars hypothesize that consumers attribute at least some of their dissatisfaction with a negative outcome to their own inability to perform their part of service production (Zeithaml 1981). The more actively a consumer participates, the "more important it becomes to understand his or her perceptions of each party's relative contribution to the outcome" (Andreasen 1983, p. 64). Theoretically, higher levels of customer participation lead to a higher likelihood that consumers will attribute a dissatisfactory outcome to themselves versus the service firm (Silpakit and Fisk 1985). Empirical findings show that in a highly participative service context, consumers did not blame the service provider for a negative outcome (Hubbert 1995). These findings stand in contrast to results showing that customers were more likely to blame the provider for negative outcomes they had no part in producing or delivering (e.g., Folkes 1984; Folkes and Kotsos 1986). Thus, *participating* consumers are expected to be "less of a threat" to the organization (Mills, Chase, and Margulies 1983; Zeithaml 1981). Empirical findings show that customers who blame the service provider for a negative or dissatisfactory experience are angrier (Folkes 1984) and spread more negative word of mouth to others than consumers who blame themselves (Krishnan and Valle 1979; Richins 1983; Valle and Wallendorf 1977).

Customer Satisfaction

CP is related to customer satisfaction (Cermak, File, and Prince 1994; Kelley, Skinner, and Donnelly 1992; Kellogg, Youngdahl, and Bowen 1997; Oliver and DeSarbo 1988). For example, customers' perceptions of their own inputs corresponded positively to their satisfaction with banking services (Kelley, Skinner, and Donnelly 1992). Also, customers' own preparation, relationship building, and information exchange activities were mentioned more frequently when satisfactory versus dissatisfactory incidents were recalled (Kellogg, Youngdahl, and Bowen 1997). In contrast, customers' own intervention activities were more frequently mentioned when *dis*satisfactory incidents were recalled. Interestingly, participants reported higher levels of effort (time, thought, and emotion) for dissatisfactory incidents than for satisfactory ones (Kellogg, Youngdahl, and Bowen 1997). It may be that the higher effort reported after dissatisfactory incidents is related to customers having to invoke more intervention activities than expected. Results from an experiment showed higher customer satisfaction when subjects attributed success to their own inputs versus provider inputs (Oliver and DeSarbo 1988). In general, more customer participation appears to correspond with higher levels of satisfaction except when customers must put forth extra or unexpected effort to prevent or overcome service failure.

Customers' Future Intentions

Initial empirical evidence finds CP related to customers' future intentions (Cermak, File, and Prince 1994; Dabholkar 1996). Empirical findings indicate that customer participation affects service quality expectations, which, in turn, affect customers' intentions to use a technology-based, self-service delivery system (Dabholkar 1996). Other findings show that participation affects intentions to repurchase or to spread word of mouth, but the valence of this effect varies across service types (Cermak, File, and Prince 1994). Additional empirical research is needed to clarify the conditions under which higher levels of customer participation yield stronger, positive future intentions.

CUSTOMER PARTICIPATION PROVIDES BENEFITS TO SERVICE FIRMS

A variety of potential benefits have been identified for firms that include customers in service production and delivery. Evidence that CP positively affects customer evaluations is reviewed in the previous section. Other benefits may include increasing productivity or providing opportunities to add value to the services mix, to fill a market niche, to reach unserved markets, and ultimately to gain greater customer loyalty and retention.

Increasing Productivity

It has long been recognized that resources provided by customers are not unlike those provided by service employees (Barnard 1948) and that it may be beneficial to include customers within the social boundaries of the service firm (Parsons 1956). Many agree that productivity is enhanced when customers are regarded as "partial employees" and their participation is planned and managed (e.g., Bateson and Langeard 1982; Bowen 1986; Bowen and Jones 1986; Gartner and Riessman 1974; Larsson and Bowen 1989; Lovelock and Young 1979; Mills, Chase, and Margulies 1983; Mills and Moberg 1982). Indeed, there are times when customers have the resources (e.g, information, ability, and motivation) to perform even more effectively than service workers (Mills, Chase, and Margulies 1983).

Valued-Added Service

Integrating customer participation may give firms the opportunity to provide value-added services that are too costly to provide otherwise. For example, a motel chain without restaurant facilities may establish a breakfast buffet that requires guests to come to the lobby and prepare their own light breakfast. Although customers do virtually all the work to produce and deliver the service, making the buffet available provides a supplementary, truly value-added benefit (breakfast) to the core service (lodging) where one did not previously exist. Firms that are first-to-market or that offer superior customer-valued, customer-generated supplementary services often gain competitive advantage.

Filling Market Niches

A marketing mix specifically designed to incorporate CP may provide a unique bundle of benefits that fills a heretofore unmet market niche. A classic example is Kinkos, Inc., a very successful business whose service design is built on customer inputs of tangibles, information, and/or physical labor. Another example is MainStay Suites, a relatively new, modestly priced hotel chain that targets longer-stay travelers willing to serve themselves. An interactive kiosk facilitates rapid checkin and -out. A breakfast buffet is available in a dining area adjacent to the lobby. Each room includes a fully equipped kitchen. Guests forgo daily housekeeping and have access to a "supply closet" stocked with towels and linens, kitchen utensils, toiletries, and other supplies. MainStay Suites serves a unique niche through its creative use of customer participation in service design.

Reaching Unserved Markets

A service product redesigned to accommodate more, or different types of, customer participation may appeal to unserved market segments or open up previously inaccessible markets. For example, many online or distance-education college courses provide customers with at least partial control over delivery location and times. This delivery system provides new opportunities to segments unable to attend traditionally scheduled college classes (e.g., residents of rural areas, employees who travel extensively, or busy executives) but that are able to participate as students in nontraditional ways.

Enhancing Customer Loyalty and Retention

Service providers who offer unique benefits via greater customer participation can obtain greater customer loyalty and retention than competitors who do not offer such benefits. Unique benefits increase customers' switching costs to a different provider. For providers of standardized, low-risk services, greater CP often leads to reduced nonmonetary costs for customers via shorter encounters, or greater efficiency and convenience. Examples include drive-in dry cleaners and banks that offer Internet access to bank accounts. Additionally, greater CP can enhance a feeling of connection to the provider for more customized services such as special-occasion catering or interior design services. For these kinds of services, CP is integral to service design and delivery. Empirical findings show that customers in a strong relationship with a provider have more confidence and perceive less risk in the provider, enjoy friendly relationships with employees who are more likely to know them, and believe they receive special treatment or perks

(Gwinner, Gremler, and Bitner 1998). By optimizing CP elements through creative service design, providers encourage greater customer loyalty and retention.

SERVICE MIX AND CUSTOMER DETERMINANTS OF CUSTOMER PARTICIPATION

Role Size Sets Boundaries for Participation

Customer role size is an important determinant of the degree of CP in a service encounter or relationship. Customer role size is the proportion of the service product that is produced and delivered by the consumer him/herself (Bowen 1986). Customer role size varies dramatically across services, ranging from nothing more than showing up to receive the service (e.g., attending a movie) to contributing most of the resources that produce the outcome (e.g., complying fully with a smoking cessation program) (Bitner et al. 1997; Hubbert 1995). Even within a single industry, ideal role size may vary significantly. For example, contrast the ideal role size for customers of a discount brokerage with that of a traditional brokerage firm. Actual levels of customer participation are guided by planned role size but ultimately are determined by customers' ability and willingness to co-produce and deliver the service product.

Customer Ability to Participate

Customer ability refers to customers' possession of the needed resources to participate at the ideal role size, that is, the level specified by the firm for optimal service quality and satisfaction. In the broadest sense, ability includes all pertinent resources such as knowledge, skill, experience, energy, effort, money, or time. The mix of resources that constitutes a customer's ability circumscribes his or her participation options. For example, without basic computer skills and a certain amount of time and effort, a customer does not have the ability to participate in on-line banking. In any given situation, the perceived benefit/cost ratio affects the appeal of participation options.

Role clarity is one aspect of knowledge that contributes to ability. Also known as "motivational direction" (Kelley, Donnelly, and Skinner 1990; Kelley, Skinner, and Donnelly 1992), role clarity means understanding how to perform a role (Bowen 1986). One source of role clarity is a customer's own experience with a particular provider, that is, possessing a "strong script" for co-producing the product with a specific service provider (Abelson 1981; Leigh and McGraw 1989). For example, a longtime patron of a branch bank knows the procedures for accessing his safety deposit box and which tellers are more efficient or friendly. A second source of role clarity is experience in similar service settings. A seasoned traveler staying at a particular hotel for the first time still knows to make a reservation and make arrangements for late check-in. Based on previous experiences elsewhere, he may participate in creating his own positive experience by requesting a nonsmoking room away from vending machines. Third, a customer completely new to a service context relies on experience with similar contexts, and fourth, that customer will use other customers' behavior for guidance. Thus, a first-timer on a cruise draws from her experience at resort hotels and observes the behavior of other passengers as she gains role clarity.

Service firms can enhance customers' role clarity via organizational socialization and "orientation aids" (Bowen 1986, p. 379). Organizational socialization is the process whereby firms communicate with customers regarding the appropriate behaviors for producing and delivering the service (Kelley, Donnelly, and Skinner 1990; Kelley, Skinner, and Donnelly 1992). Organizational socialization can be accomplished in a number of ways, including (a) formal programs such as universities' freshman orientation, (b) realistic service previews as in hospital communications informing arriving patients about the step-by-step process in an upcoming medical procedure (Bowen 1986; Faranda 1994; Mills and Morris 1986), (c) organizational literature such as brochures given to new members of a gym that describe classes and services, and (d) environmental cues such as counters located just inside a bank lobby that are stocked with forms, pens, and calculators (Bitner 1992). Other orientation aids include employees (e.g., doormen), procedures (e.g., queues), and rules (e.g., dress codes) that communicate and clarify appropriate customer role behaviors (Bowen 1986). For example, river rafting guides model behavior and use procedures to socialize customers into contributing participants (Arnould and Price 1993). Thus, understanding, facilitating, and enhancing customers' abilities are key to optimal customer participation.

Customer Willingness to Participate

Ideal levels of CP require customer willingness to participate. Changes in a customer's resource mix (i.e., ability) may change his or her willingness to participate in various aspects of the service. For example, a busy professional may conclude she no longer "has time" to organize tax documents and would rather pay her accountant to provide this additional service. Three types of benefits motivate participation: (a) efficiency in the process, (b) efficacy of the outcome, and (c) hedonic/emotional benefits. These motivations are not mutually exclusive, and different segments may carry out the same actions while seeking different benefits. For example, one airline passenger may hand-carry bags on board because it is more time-efficient, whereas another does so to retain control over her luggage. As in most facets of life, given the opportunity, people/customers participate to the extent that their benefits outweigh their costs.

Customers participate in producing and delivering some services so as to *maximize efficiency*, or minimize total monetary and nonmonetary costs (Bateson 1983; Bateson and Langeard 1982; Dabholkar 1996; Silpakit and Fisk 1985). This may be most applicable to routine and low-risk contexts. For example, nowadays gas station customers not only pump their own gas but also have the option to "pay at the pump." This alternative eliminates the time, effort, and human interaction required to "pay inside." As the gas station example illustrates, adopting technology is often a means for enhancing efficiency. Most consumers find operating an ATM less costly in time and effort than interacting with a teller; indeed, many are willing to pay a service fee for the privilege of ATM usage. The patronage of on-line retailers for services once available only through traditional provider-to-consumer encounters (e.g., registration for college courses) is escalating rapidly. The use of information accessed via touch-tone phone systems and the Internet demonstrates that many consumers are willing to modify the ways in which they participate in order to make the most efficient use of their own time, money, and other resources.

A second motivation to participate is to *maximize the efficacy* of the outcome. Certain services entail higher levels of various risks—social (e.g., haircut), financial (e.g., investment management), functional (e.g., car repair), or technological (e.g., on-line college registration). Optimal outcomes for such services can be achieved only with customers' inputs of tangibles, information about the problem or service-related goals, and/or effective communication. These inputs facilitate the provider's efforts to customize the product to customer specifications. Although many customers are motivated to participate because they enjoy doing so (as discussed in the next section), many others participate solely to reduce the likelihood of substandard outcomes. Levels of CP may increase if customers perceive potential or imminent service failure without increased participation (Kellogg, Youngdahl, and Bowen 1997). For example, a student with a low grade at midterm may begin to attend class more regularly and study more diligently.

A third motivation for CP is to receive *psychological benefits*. That is, customer participation itself can be a benefit of consuming certain services. Novelty or anticipated enjoyment may lead customers to participate (Dabholkar 1996; Holbrook and Hirschman 1982). Customer purchase and/or product involvement may drive participation. Experiential benefits may be most dramatic in highly involving service settings. For example, whereas important outcomes for a river rafting expedition include making it down the river alive, satisfaction and a sense of having an "extraordinary hedonic experience" emerge because of the rafters' participation (Arnould and Price 1993). Experiential benefits include harmony with nature, personal growth, self-renewal, and a sense of camaraderie and community among participants (Arnould and Price 1993; Celsi, Rose, and Leigh 1993). Such emotions are similar to those empirically shown to motivate behavioral loyalty in a highly involving and participative context (Allen, Machleit, and Kleine 1992). Designing a service to facilitate participants' experience of such emotions solidifies provider-customer bonds in contexts where hedonic experiences are among the benefits sought (e.g., sports venue, wedding reception).

Another psychological benefit motivating more active CP is *increased perceived control*. For example, a copy service customer who makes her own photocopies and compiles them into an important document gains an increased sense of control potentially leading to greater personal satisfaction. In one study, participation in routine service contexts such as pumping gas, using an ATM, and carrying bags onto a plane was inherently attractive to certain customers (Bateson 1983). These respondents valued efficiency and "perceived control over the situation" (p. 52). Dabholkar (1996) found the sense of behavioral control resulting from entering one's own order for fast food on a touch screen to be an important feature to customers, apart from its contribution to greater efficiency or effectiveness. Research in health care settings shows that patients' greater sense of cognitive or psychological control leads to improved posttreatment outcomes such as less pain or shorter hospital stays (e.g., Langer, Janis, and Wolfer 1975; Young and Humphrey 1985). Additionally, Dennis (1987) identified three dimensions of cognitive control in health care: knowing and fulfilling the patient role, being involved in making decisions, and directing interpersonal and environmental components. Each of these dimensions involves some kind of additional customer effort, or participation. In the context of mammography screening, Faranda (1994) found that greater perceived control leads to greater satisfaction. Thus, the emerging picture is one of certain customers who seek psychological and/or behavioral control as a benefit of participation. Moreover, as Lasch (1984) argues, people increasingly desire to restore some sense of control in an environment of information overload, bureaucracy, and complex systems that lead to feelings of helplessness and dependency. CP lends itself to obtaining an increased sense of independence, self-efficacy, and self-control. These psychological benefits may be sought as ends in themselves.

To summarize, customers' ability and willingness influence how much they actually participate. Benefits include greater efficiency, greater efficacy, and/or psychological benefits such as hedonic outcomes or perceived control.

IMPLICATIONS FOR MANAGERS

The specifics of CP in a service—that is, how much and what kinds—should stem from the firm's mission and vision statements. As a firm develops service concepts, identifies potential segment(s), selects target market(s), and positions its marketing mix, one of management's strategic decisions is to determine the ideal level of customer participation. Every element of the marketing mix is affected by this decision. For example, after huge success as a direct marketer, Dell Computer Corporation implemented on-line sales to customers via its website. On-line customers participate by doing their own research, making product decisions, accessing the website, specifying the product and attributes desired, and placing the order. By Fall 1998, Dell's on-line sales exceeded $10 million per day—more than 10% of total sales (Gillmore 1998). Dell anticipates that more than half its sales will be via the Internet by the year 2001.

Segmenting the Market and Positioning the Service Product

Firms may choose to segment the market based on customer ability. Dell positions its services toward customers who already know about computers and their own hardware needs. A college may differentiate its degree program by using innovative scheduling targeted to segments unable to attend traditionally scheduled classes. For example, a community college in the resident city of one of the authors offers a graduate degree in 1 year by holding classes on consecutive

Saturdays. Similarly, distance education provides a solution to would-be students who live in remote areas.

An alternative is to segment the market based on customer willingness to participate via a benefits segmentation strategy. A service mix may be targeted to a segment seeking greater efficiency (e.g., ordering postage stamps through the mail). Alternatively, providers may position services based on outcome efficacy. For example, although many customers participate in the prepurchase process by visiting retailers and "trying on" garments to ensure good fit, fine clothiers target narrower segments by offering tailoring. All elements in the service mix support the positioning strategy (e.g., upscale facilities and furnishings, knowledgeable and attentive sales personnel, higher prices, and a more customized prepurchase process). This service requires additional customer participation, including inputs of time, money, effort, knowledge of the look desired, and communication skills. Others retailers may position these services to segments that seek this bundle of benefits only under extraordinary and/or risky circumstances (e.g., brides). Lifestyle, perceived risk, and situational variables are informative when positioning services toward customers seeking service outcome efficacy.

New Products and Product Line Extensions

New service products and product line extensions may emerge from providers' innovative design of customers' roles. Customers are now able to seek the types of distance learning opportunities referred to above because of the development and adoption of technology. Anecdotal evidence shows that motivated students participate even more fully in discussion and assignments than in traditional classrooms (Kunde 1998). Universities' increased use of technology, provision of more on-line options, and enhanced accessibility to the Internet may encourage even greater numbers of students to choose distance learning. Such new products may attract entirely new segments of students to the marketplace.

Managing Customer Role Size

Although the *ideal* customer role size is designed by the service provider via the services mix, in reality, customers' actions determine *actual* role size. A firm's customers are likely to adopt an array of role sizes, from too large (overparticipation) to too small (underparticipation). Customers who underparticipate experience an inferior bundle of benefits (e.g., a dieter loses less weight, a student learns less). Overparticipation demands more time, customization, or costs from the firm than planned (e.g., a client directing his hairstylist too closely, an investment client checking in with her broker too frequently). Thus, managers must socialize new customers and provide orientation aids to communicate the most appropriate role size for optimal outcomes. Given a particular role size, providers must understand the distinguishing characteristics, beliefs, or goals that differentiate various segments' willingness to participate (Bateson 1983). Understanding differences is the first step toward designing service mixes that deliver the set of benefits sought by each segment. This information enables firms to communicate and socialize segments toward ideal levels of customer participation.

FUTURE DIRECTIONS IN RESEARCH ABOUT CUSTOMER PARTICIPATION

Although accorded substantial conceptual importance, CP has received little empirical attention. Numerous opportunities exist to develop our understanding of the pertinent nomological relationships. In this section, we briefly highlight a number of areas needing empirical study.

The role of customer participation in the services mix is often complex, yet it is worthwhile to specify the relationships between customer participation and other variables of interest. Researchers could more fully explore antecedents of CP. For example, does higher involvement lead to more customer participation via a greater willingness to participate? How do other predispositions such as attitude toward participation or toward the service provider affect actual levels of customer participation? How do customer ability and willingness to participate affect actual participation? CP appears to be an individualistic variable—some customers are more likely to participate than others (Bateson 1983; Bowen 1990). How does this "need to participate" affect the actual role size adopted by customers of a service encounter or relationship? Do customers of various participation levels view particular services differently, and if so, how does this affect their perceptions of quality and satisfaction? How can service providers segment their markets using ability, willingness, or actual role size (Bateson 1983)?

A more finely tuned understanding of the effects of customer participation on customer evaluations (e.g., perceived quality, satisfaction, or future intentions) and behaviors requires empirical study. For example, under what conditions does customer participation lead to negative evaluations (e.g., dissatisfaction) instead of the more-often-demonstrated positive evaluations? What is the relative influence of customer participation on evaluations compared to other variables over which the provider has more complete control? For example, how does customer participation interact with degree of customer contact to influence evaluations (Silpakit and Fiske 1985)? In what ways can the interactions between participation, trust, and other variables lead to relationship building for customers and providers? To what extent does customer participation influence word-of-mouth behavior?

The psychological benefits of CP deserve additional empirical attention. How can these benefits be parlayed into achieving goals such as greater satisfaction and/or provider attachment and loyalty? When are psychological outcomes sought as benefits in and of themselves? For example, more extensive levels of participation may lead to customers experiencing higher levels of self-esteem because they perceive themselves to be on equal terms with the provider versus being passive recipients of the service. Higher self-esteem also may result from taking a more responsible role in contributing to quality assurance. When is the need for control likely to emerge as a motive for participation? Is control-seeking a personality or situational variable (Bateson 1983)? How does the relationship among perceived control, perceived service quality, and satisfaction change with varying degrees of involvement and participation?

Individuals are socialized into specific customer roles over time and through experience with a particular provider and/or various types of providers (e.g., Kelley, Donnelly, and Skinner 1990). How does intensity and type of CP change along the path of socialization into an organization? How do more fully socialized customers influence the participation of newcomers? What are appropriate methods for influencing more optimal levels of customer participation?

A benefit to providers is the increased responsibility and blame that participating customers may assume for service failure. Under what circumstances are participating customers more likely to assume blame? Under what circumstances do they blame the provider? When do participating customers take credit for success, and when do they credit the provider? Do customers assume credit or blame that more rightly belongs to the provider, or vice versa? Are attributions to oneself and the provider mutually exclusive? Under what circumstances are situational factors credited or blamed by participating customers?

Ideally, empirical findings will guide when, how, and for which segments a service provider ought to encourage (or discourage) customer participation. Ultimately, predictors, consequences, and the relative influence of role size are important for providers who engage in providing unique and valued bundles of benefits to retain and develop profitable customer relationships.

REFERENCES

Abelson, Robert P. (1981), "Psychological Status of the Script Concept," *American Psychologist*, 36 (July), 715-29.

Allen, Chris T., Karen A. Machleit, and Susan Schultz Kleine (1992), "A Comparison of Attitudes and Emotions as Predictors of Behavior at Diverse Levels of Behavioral Experience," *Journal of Consumer Research*, 18 (March), 493-504.

Andreasen, Alan R. (1983), "Consumer Research in the Service Sector," in *Emerging Perspectives in Services Marketing*, Leonard L. Berry, G. Lynn Shostack, and Gregory D. Upah, eds. Chicago: American Marketing Association, 63-64.

Arnould, Eric J. and Linda L. Price (1993), "River Magic: Extraordinary Experience and the Extended Service Encounter," *Journal of Consumer Research*, 20 (June), 24-45.

Barnard, C. (1948), *Organization and Management*. Cambridge, MA: Harvard University Press.

Bateson, John E. G. (1983), "The Self-Service Customer—Empirical Findings," in *Emerging Perspectives in Services Marketing*, Leonard L. Berry, G. Lynn Shostack, and Gregory D. Upah, eds. Chicago: American Marketing Association, 50-53.

—— and E. Langeard (1982), "Consumer Uses of Common Dimensions," in *Advances in Consumer Research*, Andrew A. Mitchell, ed. Chicago: Association for Consumer Research, 173-76.

Bitner, Mary Jo (1992), "Servicescapes: The Impact of Physical Surroundings on Customers and Employees," *Journal of Marketing*, 56 (April), 57-71.

——, William T. Faranda, Amy R. Hubbert, and Valarie A. Zeithaml (1997), "Customer Contributions and Roles in Service Delivery," *International Journal of Service Industry Management*, 8(3), 193-205.

Bowen, David E. (1986), "Managing Customers as Human Resources in Service Organizations," *Human Resource Management*, 25(3), 371-83.

——— and Gareth R. Jones (1986), "Transaction Cost Analysis of Service Organization-Customer Exchange," *Academy of Management Review*, 11(2), 428-41.

Bowen, John (1990), "Development of a Taxonomy of Services to Gain Strategic Marketing Insights," *Journal of the Academy of Marketing Science*, 18(1), 43-49.

Celsi, Richard L., Randall L. Rose, and Thomas W. Leigh (1993), "An Exploration of High-Risk Leisure Consumption Through Skydiving," *Journal of Consumer Research*, 20 (June), 1-23.

Cermak, Dianne S. P., Karen Maru File, and Russ Alan Prince (1994), "Customer Participation in Service Specification and Delivery," *Journal of Applied Business Research*, 10(2), 90-97.

Chase, Richard B. (1978), "Where Does the Customer Fit in a Service Organization?" *Harvard Business Review*, 56 (November-December), 137-42.

——— (1981), "The Customer Contact Approach to Services: Theoretical Bases and Practical Extensions," *Operations Research*, 24(4), 698-706.

——— and David A. Tansik (1983), "The Customer Contact Model of Organizational Design," *Management Science*, 29, 1037-50.

Dabholkar, Pratibha A. (1996), "Consumer Evaluations of New Technology-Based Self-Service Options: An Investigation of Alternative Models of Service Quality," *International Journal of Research in Marketing*, 13, 29-51.

Dennis, Karen E. (1987), "Patients' Control and the Information Imperative: Clarification and Confirmation," *Nursing Research*, 39 (May-June), 162-66.

Faranda, William T. (1994), "Customer Participation in Service Production: An Empirical Assessment of the Influence of Realistic Service Previews," doctoral dissertation, Arizona State University, Tempe.

Folkes, Valerie S. (1984), "Consumer Reactions to Product Failure: An Attributional Approach," *Journal of Consumer Research*, 10 (March), 398-409.

——— and Barbara Kotsos (1986), "Buyers' and Sellers' Explanations for Product Failure: Who Done It?" *Journal of Marketing*, 50 (April), 74-80.

Gartner, Alan and Frank Riessman (1974), *The Service Society and the Consumer Vanguard*. New York: Harper & Row.

Gillmore, Dan (1998), "Direct Approach Pays Off for Dell," *San Jose Mercury News*, November 13. Retrieved November 12, 1998, from the World Wide Web: www.mercurycenter.com/business/top/006486.html

Gwinner, Kevin P., Dwayne D. Gremler, and Mary Jo Bitner (1998), "Relational Benefits in Services Industries: The Customer's Perspective," *Journal of the Academy of Marketing Science*, 26(2), 101-14.

Hochschild, Arlie Russell (1983), *The Managed Heart: Commercialization of Human Feeling*. Berkeley: University of California Press.

Holbrook, Morris B. and Elizabeth C. Hirschman (1982), "The Experiential Aspects of Consumption: Consumer Fantasies, Feelings, and Fun," *Journal of Consumer Research*, 9 (September), 132-40.

Hubbert, Amy R. (1995), "Customer Co-Creation of Service Outcomes: Effects of Locus of Causality Attributions," doctoral dissertation, Arizona State University, Tempe.

Kelley, Scott W., James H. Donnelly, Jr., and Steven J. Skinner (1990), "Customer Participation in Service Production and Delivery," *Journal of Retailing*, 66(3), 315-35.

———, Steven J. Skinner, and James H. Donnelly, Jr. (1992), "Organizational Socialization of Service Customers," *Journal of Business Research*, 25, 197-214.

Kellogg, Deborah L. and Richard B. Chase (1995), "Constructing an Empirically Derived Measure for Customer Contact," *Management Science*, 41(11), 1734-49.

———, William E. Youngdahl, and David E. Bowen (1997), "On the Relationship Between Customer Participation and Satisfaction: Two Frameworks," *International Journal of Service Industry Management*, 8(3), 206-19.

Krishnan, S. and Valerie A. Valle (1979), "Dissatisfaction Attributions and Consumer Complaint Behavior," in *Advances in Consumer Research*, Vol. 6, William L. Wilke, ed. Chicago: Association for Consumer Research, 445-49.

Kunde, Diana (1998), "Distance Learning Latest Trend in Management Education," *The Dallas Morning News*, (June 24), 1D.

Langer, Ellen J., Irving L. Janis, and John A. Wolfer (1975), "Reduction of Psychological Stress in Surgical Patients," *Journal of Experimental Social Psychology*, 11(2), 156-65.

Larsson, Rikard and David E. Bowen (1989), "Organization and Customer: Managing Design and Coordination of Services," *Academy of Management Review*, 14(2), 213-33.

Lasch, Christopher (1984), *The Minimal Self: Psychic Survival in Troubled Times*. New York: W. W. Norton.

Leigh, Thomas W. and Patrick F. McGraw (1989), "Mapping the Procedural Knowledge of Industrial Sales Personnel: A Script-Theoretic Investigation," *Journal of Marketing*, 53 (January), 16-34.

Lovelock, Christopher H. (1981), "Why Marketing Management Needs to Be Different for Services," in *Marketing of Services*, James H. Donnelly and William R. George, eds. Chicago: American Marketing Association, 5-9.

———— (1983), "Classifying Services to Gain Strategic Marketing Insights," *Journal of Marketing*, 47 (Summer), 9-20.

———— and Robert F. Young (1979), "Look to Consumers to Increase Productivity," *Harvard Business Review*, 59 (May-June), 168-78.

Mills, Peter K., Richard B. Chase, and Newton Margulies (1983), "Motivating the Client Employee System as a Service Production Strategy," *Academy of Management Review*, 8(2), 301-10.

———— and Dennis J. Moberg (1982), "Perspectives on the Technology of Service Organizations," *Academy of Management Review*, 7(3), 467-78.

———— and James H. Morris (1986), "Clients as 'Partial Employees' of Service Organizations: Role Development in Client Participation," *Academy of Management Review*, 11(4), 726-35.

Oliver, Richard L. and Wayne S. DeSarbo (1988), "Response Determinants in Satisfaction Judgments," *Journal of Consumer Research*, 14 (March), 495-507.

Parsons, T. (1956), "Suggestions for a Sociological Approach to the Theory of Organizations," *Administrative Science Quarterly*, 1, 63-85.

Richins, Marsha L. (1983), "Negative Word-of-Mouth by Dissatisfied Consumers: A Pilot Study," *Journal of Marketing*, 47 (Winter), 68-78.

Silpakit, Patriya and Raymond P. Fisk (1985), " 'Participatizing' the Service Encounter," in *Services Marketing in a Changing Environment*, Thomas M. Bloch, Gregory D. Upah, and Valarie A. Zeithaml, eds. Chicago: American Marketing Association, 117-21.

Valle, Valerie and Melanie Wallendorf (1977), "Consumers' Attributions of the Cause of Their Product Satisfaction and Dissatisfaction," in *Consumer Satisfaction, Dissatisfaction, and Complaining Behavior*, Ralph H. Day, ed. Bloomington: Department of Marketing, School of Business, Indiana University, 26-30.

Young, L. and M. Humphrey (1985), "Cognitive Methods of Preparing Women for Hysterectomy: Does a Booklet Help?" *British Journal of Clinical Psychology*, 24 (November), 303-4.

Zeithaml, Valarie A. (1981), "How Consumer Evaluation Processes Differ Between Goods and Services," in *Marketing of Services*, James H. Donnelly and William R. George, eds. Chicago: American Marketing Association, 186-90.

8

Perceived Control and the Service Experience

JOHN E. G. BATESON

The purpose of this chapter is to review the literature which suggests that perceived control is a crucial determinant of how individuals interpret the service encounter—their physical interaction with the service firm—to determine their emotional experience regarding the encounter. The first section of this chapter introduces the idea that the need for control over one's environment is a key driving force in human beings, and it shows how this idea has evolved from the work of White (1959), DeCharms (1968), and Brehm (1966). The second section points out that the inherent nature of the service encounter means that the customer must give up some control; the customer must obey the rules and procedures of the firm providing the service. At the same time, the service provider is also motivated to take control of the encounter. This apparent conflict poses major problems for the management of service firms. Fortunately, control theory is much richer, suggesting that behavioral control is not the only way for individuals to create a sense of perceived control. This expanded model is then applied to the consumer's experience, and I review the impact of perceived control on the consumer's choice process, the consumer's well-being, crowding, and queuing and/or way-finding. Finally, directions for future research are suggested using perceived control as a research paradigm.

CONTROL AS A HUMAN DRIVING FORCE

The study of human motivation started with basic psychological drives such as hunger and sex. Psychologists discovered, however, that with the rapid development of modern society, physiological driving forces were inadequate to explain a large range of human behaviors. As a consequence, new concepts were intro-

127

duced that aimed to explain those behaviors enacted primarily for goals beyond physiological drive reduction. Among these new theories was one which asserted that there exists a human need to demonstrate one's competence, superiority, and mastery over the environment. A considerable number of authors have written explicitly or implicitly on control as a crucial human driving force; among them, White (1959), DeCharms (1968), and Brehm (1966) have attracted the most attention.

White (1959) was one of the pioneers who brought the concept of control into the study of human motivation. He proposed a new construct, "effectance motivation," as the underlying motivating force for a variety of human environmental behaviors, such as exploration and manipulation, that apparently are unrelated to any primary physiological drive. This motive for control was a feeling of efficiency and competence in dealing with one's environment.

In the development of the theory of personal causation, DeCharms (1968) also noted the significance of control as a motivating force. His theory draws heavily from the concept of perceived locus of causality for behavior. "Pawn" and "origin" are the two terms coined by DeCharms for individuals with external and internal locus causality, respectively. In essence, an origin is a person who feels that he or she originates his or her own actions and has control over all salient environmental outcomes. Pawns, on the other hand, are individuals who get the feeling of being pushed around, having no control over their own actions and environmental outcomes. The theory argues that people have the desire to be origins rather than pawns: "man strives to be a causal agent, to be the primary locus of causation for, or the origin of, his behavior; he strives for personal causation" (DeCharms 1968, p. 269).

Brehm's (1966) reactance theory is another widely recognized theory that highlights the motivating role of control. The theory states that whenever an individual's behavioral freedom is threatened, that person will be motivated to reassert control over the environment. For instance, children's attempts to enact behaviors that are disapproved of by their parents can be interpreted as efforts to demonstrate superiority and control over the external constraints. The strength of the motivating force is proposed to be a direct function of (a) one's expectation of freedom, (b) one's attributed importance of freedom, and (c) the intensity of the threat.

THE SERVICE ENCOUNTER: A THREE-CORNERED FIGHT FOR CONTROL?

The production and consumption of services generally involve a series of interactions between consumers and both the contact personnel and the settings that are provided by service organizations (Eiglier and Langeard 1977). From these interpersonal (contact personnel and consumer) and human-environment (consumer and service setting) interactions, consumers attempt to get their needs and wants satisfied. This organization-consumer interface is commonly known as the service encounter (Czepiel, Solomon, and Surprenant 1985). There is a clear distinction between this tangible series of interactions and the service experience, which is defined here as the consumer's emotional feelings during the service encounter.

One of the characteristics that makes services unique is that the customer has a production role as well as a consumption role in the service encounter. This idea has been suggested by writers in many fields of study. In the marketing field, the early work of Langeard et al. (1981) proposes that production and consumption take place simultaneously and that the customer is an integral part of the process. Lovelock and Young (1979) suggest that productivity within the service firm may be increased by getting the customer to do more work.

In the field of organization behavior, Schneider (1980) has suggested an open-systems approach in which the consumer is regarded as part of the service organization. Mills (1983) and Mills and Moberg (1982) have suggested that the customer be regarded as a "partial employee." They even list the kinds of activities that the customer must perform if the service is to be delivered correctly.

In economics, Gartner and Reissman (1974) have suggested that the participation of customers should be recognized by measuring "consumer intensity" in the service sector as well as the more usual capital and labor intensity. In the field of operations management, Chase (1978, 1981) and Chase and Tansik (1982) have suggested that for the efficient operation of the service firm, the customer-contact part of the process must be isolated from the back office. They suggest that operations efficiency is inversely related to the amount of customer contact. Their proposition is based on their assumption that in the consumer-impinging part of the operation, the customer becomes an integral part of the process, with a consequential loss of efficiency.

The customer must, therefore, be viewed as an integral part of the process and is required to perform certain tasks. There is a mutual interdependence between three parties: the customer, the contact personnel, and the firm as embodied in the operating procedures and the environment.

At one level, these three have much to gain by working together. The customer, by working with the service personnel within the framework imposed by the firm, hopes to gain satisfaction and value for money. The contact person, by working with the customer in the way specified by the firm, hopes for job satisfaction, customer satisfaction, and remuneration. The firm can make money in the long run only by satisfying staff and customers in a way that makes economic sense from an operations perspective.

The "need for control," however, is one of the forces that drives these parties apart (Bateson 1985a). The customer desires to demonstrate competence, superiority, and mastery over the environment. That environment, however, consists of contact personnel who themselves want to be in control, and the operations and environment created by the service firm, which in turn serve to supplant the control of both the contact personnel and the customer. Schneider, Partington, and Buxton (1980) performed a number of studies that view the service firm as an "open system" and the server as a boundary-role person. Their framework indicates that the server and the customer both experience the physical environment and procedures of the firm. Under such assumptions, it seems reasonable to suppose that servers' behavior will be influenced by their desire for control of the service encounter.

One very early study (Whyte 1949) clearly illustrates this need for control on the part of the server. Adopting a sociological perspective, Whyte studied the operation of a large restaurant. He was particularly concerned with the ability of waitresses to cope with the stress of the situation. One of his more interesting insights is gained from a study of waitresses who broke down and cried. He studied this group closely and attempted to identify what made them different.

Whyte's finding was that whether a waitress cried or not depended on her ability to operate in a different way. As he expresses it (1949), "Actually, it appeared that the waitress who maintains her own emotional equilibrium plays a very active leadership role with the customer. She does not simply respond to the customer but takes the initiative to control his behavior" (p. 135).

Since that early study, much work has gone into understanding the boundary-spanning role of the service provider. Service providers clearly are subject to potentially conflicting demands from both customers and the organization. This has been shown to lead to both role conflict and ambiguity. Role conflict refers to the perception that any role has within it objectives that are in conflict with one another. Ambiguity refers to roles that are unclear in nature and goals. It would be logical to suggest that both role conflict and ambiguity lead to a serious loss of control.

Sutton and Rafaeli (1988) studied the strategies used by service providers to reduce role conflict and ambiguity. All the strategies mirror the approaches described by Whyte (1949) and can be interpreted as ways to re-establish control. Service providers can refuse to notice a customer who wishes to place an order. An alternative strategy is to move into a people-processing mode (cf. Klaus 1985), where customers are treated as inanimate objects to be processed rather than as individuals. Physical symbols and furniture are often used to boost the service providers' status and, hence, sense of control (Godsell 1977). In the extreme case, the service provider overacts the role and forces the customer into the subservient role.

THE NEED FOR CONTROL AS A MANAGERIAL PROBLEM

Whatever else happens in a service encounter, the customer must give up some personal control. The service firm cannot operate without the customer's input. To offer that input, the customer must give up some control and obey the procedures expected of the service delivery system and the service personnel. If we accept the premise that the loss of control may be viewed negatively by the customer, then we can view the service encounter as a transaction in which the customer exchanges money and control for the benefits obtained.

In the vast majority of cases, the service encounter will also include an employee—the contact person. The loss of control by the customer personnel will have a negative impact on their motivation. This apparently impossible conclusion is, in fact, soluble by considering in more detail both the true nature of the need for control and the separation of perceived and actual control. I describe these issues next.

Perceived and Actual Control

As far as the existing literature is concerned, objective mastery of a situation is unanimously regarded as unnecessary for the perception of control. Rothbaum and his colleagues proposed a distinction between primary and secondary control (Rothbaum, Weisz, and Snyder 1982). They argue that when objective or behavioral control is not available, individuals will employ various cognitive means to fit themselves into the environment with a sense of control.

Averill (1973) has provided a framework to understand these cognitive means for creating perceived control. In a review of the laboratory experimental approach to the study of control, he suggests that there are three forms of control: behavioral, cognitive, and decisional. I describe each in turn.

Behavioral Control

Behavioral control is the "availability of a response which may directly influence or modify the objective characteristics of a threatening event" (Averill 1973, p. 286). Thus, behavioral control is actual, rather than perceived, control. Averill notes that studies have used a number of different ways to operationalize behavioral control. Some studies have been concerned with allowing subjects control over how, when, and by whom the stimulus is administered. Averill calls this subcategory of behavioral control "regulated control." Others have given the subjects the opportunity to modify the stimuli; this is called "stimulus modification" by Averill.

Numerous studies have investigated the impact of control on respondents' reactions to aversive stimuli. These are laboratory studies involving the administration of electric shocks, hurtful noises, or even pictures of dead bodies. The impact of these stimuli on the respondent, often a student, is then measured. The measurement is often physiological—palm sweating, for example—or in terms of some state measure of stress. Other studies measure the impact of these stimuli on respondents' ability to perform tasks such as sorting cards. Control is varied in these kinds of studies by giving respondents a switch with which they can turn off the stimulus (e.g., Straub, Tursky, and Schwartz 1971). All these studies show that the availability of behavioral control ameliorates the negative effects of the stimuli. For example, a study by Sherrod (Sherrod et al. 1977) revealed that subjects who administered the aversive stimuli to themselves exhibited better performance in a proofreading task.

These findings can be related to Seligman's (1975) theory of learned helplessness. According to Seligman, when individuals repeatedly experience an uncontrollable event, they perceive a noncontingency between their personal efforts and the resulting outcomes. The individuals may then generalize the noncontingency to future events of similar or even different nature. Symptoms of helplessness such as passivity, lowered tolerance for frustration, and impaired task performance are the results of such a perceived noncontingency. Therefore, the learned helplessness theory argues that any psychological and behavioral system of control can be explained by one's perceived contingency or noncontingency between action and outcome.

Cognitive Control

Cognitive control refers to the way a potentially harmful event is interpreted. Averill (1973) defines it as "the processing of potentially threatening information in such a manner as to reduce the net long-term stress" (p. 293). He defines cognitive control with two elements: information gain and appraisal. Information gain refers to the predictability of the event and to its anticipation. Appraisal, by comparison, involves the evaluation of events.

In his review, Averill points out that information per se does not ameliorate stress. A number of studies have shown that the presence of information alone may increase rather than decrease stress (Cromwell et al. 1977). Psychologists have advocated that people prefer a congruence between their expected and real experience. According to Abelson (1976), humans are motivated to believe that all environmental events happen in a predictable manner. Within consumer behavior, the satisfaction literature suggests that satisfaction occurs when perceived events are equal to or greater than expectations (Churchill and Surprenant 1982).

A group of theorists have been working on the anxiety-reducing effects of providing information about an impending aversive stimulus (e.g., the procedures and equipment to be used) or the sensation one would usually experience with such a stimulus. Such information is designed to help respondents to appraise the experience in a more positive way (Leventhal and Everhart 1979). For example, Mills and Krantz's (1979, Experiment 1) field experiment demonstrated this effect; in a blood transfusion center, a group of donors were given information about the blood-drawing procedure as well as the normal physiological and psychological reactions to donating blood. Dependent measures included (a) nurse action against faintness and distress and (b) subjects' self-reports of discomfort. One major finding of the study was that informed donors expressed lower levels of distress during the blood withdrawing procedure than uninformed donors.

Decisional Control

Decisional control is defined by Averill (1973) as "choice in the selection of outcomes or goals" (p. 289). Initially, it appears to be the same as behavioral control; the distinction rests on the idea that the availability of alternative goals in complex situations need not be related to the aversive stimulus. Thus, by changing, or having the option of changing, the focus of achievement in a particularly stressful situation, the individual may be able to achieve a sense of control even though no behavioral control over the aversive stimulus is available.

Perhaps the best way of illustrating decisional control is by example. Consider a Christmas shopping trip to a busy department store, under two different conditions. In the first case, it is Christmas Eve, and all the shopping must be completed. In the second, it is a Saturday 2 or 3 weeks before Christmas. In the latter situation, decisional control can be exercised simply by deciding that it does not matter whether the shopping is done. This decision is not whether to be in the potentially stressful situation (behavioral control) but what needs to be done in it. Such a choice is clearly not available on Christmas Eve. The result is that the crowds of shoppers stop being a hindrance to one's own actions and instead become a scene of the Christmas festivities to be enjoyed.

There will be no decision making unless one has two or more options to solve a problem and the freedom to choose any one of the available options. Accordingly, most authors have referred to terms such as "choice" and "freedom of choice" when they write on decisional control. The term "freedom" frequently has been used interchangeably with "choice"; that is, the more limited are the available alternatives, the less freedom or flexibility one will have in a situation.

Averill stresses that these modes of control do not operate alone, but that interactions often occur. Langer and Saegert (1977) and Langer (1983), in their discussion of control models, suggest that behavioral and cognitive control may operate in a hierarchical way. If behavioral control is unavailable, individuals may reduce the aversiveness first by believing that they have control, then by reappraising the threatening event, and finally by having information about what will happen to them as a result of the stimulus.

Attribution and Control

A separate body of research has suggested that the extreme version of cognitive control is the attribution process. The generalized motive to exert control upon one's environment has been hypothesized to affect the way a person interprets any available environmental information and explains the person's own as well as other people's behavior. According to Kelly (1967, 1972), the human attributional process not only contributes to people's understanding of the world but also serves to meet a more important objective—to encourage and maintain a sense of control over the environment. Results from laboratory studies have corroborated the hypothesis that the stronger the control motivation, operationalized through the degree of prior control deprivation, the higher is the tendency of an individual to form attributions (e.g., Pittman and Pittman 1980).

As well as stimulating the attribution process, human desire for control also directs and distorts one's attribution. Three types of attribution bias have been identified by Pittman and Pittman (1980). There is a pervasive tendency for people to (a) accept responsibility for success and reject responsibility for failure, (b) overestimate their ability to cause an outcome that is actually determined by chance, and (c) believe their own behaviors are determined predominantly by situational factors whereas other people's behaviors are caused mainly by stable dispositional variables such as personality traits. All these biases are asserted by a number of authors (Pittman and Pittman 1980; Wortman 1976) to reflect the existence of human control motivation.

THE EXPANDED CONTROL MODEL APPLIED TO THE CONSUMER'S SERVICE EXPERIENCE

The expanded model of perceived control offers the opportunity to resolve the inherent conflict over control within the service encounter. From the manager's point of view, the following questions arise concerning the consumer's need for control:

- Can we increase the perceived control of the customer and thereby increase the perceived value for money from the transaction?
- How does the customer view our encounter in terms of perceived control, and more important, how is it viewed relative to our competitors' encounters?
- Can we educate the customer so that the encounter is at least predictable—that is, use information to increase cognitive control?
- Can we educate the customer so that any negative impact of loss of control is understood in advance—that is, use information about appraisal to increase perceived control?
- Can we disassemble the components of the encounter and understand how each one influences the perceived control of the customer? Can we build perceived control into our encounters?

A number of studies provide insight into the answers to these questions in the context of the service encounter.

Perceived Control as Part of the Choice Process

Langeard et al. (1981) investigated the consumer's decision-making process for services. In particular, they were concerned with the choice between a do-it-yourself option and a more traditional approach to receiving a service. The initial part of their study was qualitative. One of the outputs of this stage was a series of dimensions along which interviewees appeared to be appraising services (Bateson 1983; Bateson and Langeard 1982). These dimensions were

1. the amount of time involved,
2. the individual's control of the situation,
3. the efficiency of the process,
4. the amount of human contact involved,
5. the risk involved,

6. the amount of effort involved, and

7. the individual's need to depend on others.

In trying to separate those consumers who were prepared to "do it themselves" from those who were not, research has found two dimensions to be crucially important: time and control (Bateson 1985b). Those consumers prepared to do it themselves saw clear differences between the two options in the dimension of the individual's control of the situation. They saw the more traditional method of receiving the service as offering less control. This factor was crucial because the respondents who were prepared to do it themselves also rated this dimension as the most important one to them in choosing between the options. This effect was observed across all six service environments studied, ranging from banks to gas stations to hotels and airlines.

Retaining Control in Low-Control Situations

The hospital service encounter constitutes a stressful event in its own right for most people. A number of medical studies have focused on the impact of the medical procedures themselves on the health of patients. Many procedures regarded as routine by medical staff are perceived by the patient as extremely stressful and may indeed have a detrimental effect on health (Cromwell et al. 1977). It has been suggested that much of the stress is caused by the loss of perceived control experienced by many patients. The combination of the administrative needs of the hospital to be efficient and the operational requirements of the medical treatment means that hospitals leave little room for the individual to feel in control.

To test this idea and to try to overcome this problem, a number of researchers have experimented with giving behavioral or cognitive control back to the patients. For example, Langer, Janis, and Wolfer (1975) studied the pre- and postoperative stress of surgical patients under different levels of cognitive control. They manipulated cognitive control by varying the degree of explanation given to the patient about the procedure and the effects the patient was likely to experience before, during, and after the operation. The results showed reduced levels of stress and positive benefits for well-being, including a more speedy recovery, under conditions of high perceived control.

In a separate study of intensive care patients (Langer, Janis, and Wolfer 1975), the authors showed the impact of returning some behavioral control. Intensive care situations remove most perceived control from the patient; however, patients who were allowed to choose when they received visitors, when they ate, and the level of exercise they could undertake all showed lower levels of stress and got better faster.

Krantz and Schultz (1980) conducted a study on the "institutionalization" produced in elderly patients when they enter another extreme encounter, namely, homes for the aged. Institutionalization has been related to the learned helplessness of Seligman (1975, as described previously). Krantz and Schultz (1980) suggest that an individual's response to relocation to a home can be understood in terms of the perceived controllability and predictability of events surrounding the move and how much less control the home for the aged is perceived to provide compared to the previous environment.

Respondents who made a conscious personal decision to enter a home were far more likely to be able to cope with the transition than those for whom the decision was made by others. Within the homes for the aged and nursing homes, Langer and Rodin (1976) showed that enhanced personal responsibility, such as the opportunity to control time of entry and visitors, resulted in happier and more active nursing home residents. In a follow-up study, those residents with higher levels of behavioral control were found to live longer (Rodin and Langer 1977).

Capacity, Crowding, and Control in Service Encounters

One of the key features that separates services from goods is the inability of services to buffer the production process (Chase 1978, 1981). Within companies that produce goods, the use of a raw material inventory and a finished goods inventory enables the manufacturing process to be buffered so as to run at a steady rate. This buffer increases productivity dramatically. The experiential nature of services, however, which stems from the service encounter itself being the "product," makes such an approach impossible.

Service operations have to cope directly with huge variations in demand. Operational efficiency often comes from the ability to cope with peaks of demand without having to increase staff and resources for those levels. Service firms are usually designed to have resources available for the peaks, and as a result, most will lose money most of the time. For retail services, in which the consumer is in the physical environment created by the firm, capacity is often defined by crowding.

Stokols (1972) has asserted that there is a need to distinguish between the terms "density" and "crowding." Density refers to the physical condition, "in terms of spatial parameters" (Stokols 1972, p. 275). On the other hand, perceived crowding is the subjective, unpleasant feeling that is experienced by an individual.

For a service firm, the choice is simple: either increase the physical capacity of the service operation or find ways to have higher levels of "density" without triggering the crowding response. There is a considerable body of literature suggesting that these solutions are possible given that the intervening variable between density and crowding is perceived control (Schmidt and Keating 1979).

Proshansky, Ittelson, and Rivlin (1974) have suggested that density is a key determinant of an individual's perceived control in a particular setting. Density can facilitate or obstruct desired behaviors; the influence it has will then determine the individual's perception of crowding. For example, Rodin, Solomon, and Metcalf (1978) have shown that high perceived crowding results when density reduces an individual's ability to perform a desired action. Nonetheless, there is considerable evidence showing that perceived crowding is also a direct function of density (e.g., Langer and Saegert 1977). This finding is not unexpected, because perceived crowding refers to the "negative subjective experience of certain density levels" (Rapoport 1975, p. 134).

Three studies have attempted to show that it is possible to modify the impact of density on an individual by deliberately changing the level of perceived control. Langer and Saegert (1977) hypothesized that the negative impact of density would be lessened if respondents' perceived cognitive control was increased by giving them information about the likely effects of crowding before being exposed to it. Hence, they manipulated the information gain and appraisal component of cognitive control.

A 2 × 2 factorial design was employed in a real-life setting—a supermarket—where respondents were subject to variation in crowding and cognitive control. Cognitive control was manipulated by a warning about the potential crowding and its likely effects. Respondents were given a long shopping list and told to choose the most economical product for each item from among the various package sizes and brands. They were allowed 30 minutes for the task. Respondents were also given a supermarket survey after completing the task.

The results showed that crowded respondents attempted to find significantly fewer items on the list than uncrowded respondents, and of those items attempted, significantly fewer were correct choices. Across the rest of the items in the supermarket survey, crowded respondents scored significantly lower than uncrowded subjects. Contrary to expectations, the impact of the information was independent of crowding. Those respondents who were able to exercise cognitive control in this way attempted more items on the text and answered more correctly. More important, they were significantly more positive on all items in the questionnaire regarding the shopping experience. This result is contrary to the hypothesis that this information effect would occur only in those respondents suffering crowding.

In the second study, Hui and Bateson (1991) tested the model shown in Figure 8.1. Density is hypothesized to influence perceived crowding both directly and through perceived control. Perceived control is also influenced through consumer choice. Perceived crowding and perceived control are hypothesized to influence emotions, and these in turn influence behaviors. Such a model tests the mediating effects of perceived control directly because it involves a separate manipulation of perceived control.

An experimental study was conducted in which consumer choice in the service encounter and consumer density were manipulated independently, and their effects on the consumer's psychological and behavioral responses to the service encounter were examined. Two service settings, a bank and a bar, were used in the study. Results from a pilot study indicated the people tend to believe that consumer density has less negative impact on the service experience in a bar setting than in a bank setting. Most respondents said they would not mind staying in a high-density bar but that they would definitely try to avoid a high-density bank. In short, a 3 (consumer density: high, medium, and low) × 2 (consumer choice: choice and no choice) × 2 (service setting: bank and bar) experimental factorial design was employed. (Consumer density and consumer choice were between-subjects factors, whereas service setting was a repeated measures factor.)

Consumer density was operationalized through color slides that portrayed three different numbers of consumers in a medium-sized branch of a bank and a

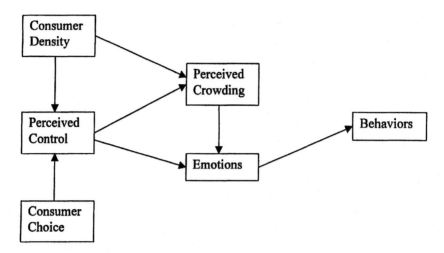

Figure 8.1 Effects of Consumer Density and Consumer Choice on the Service Experience

country bar. Written scenarios were employed to operationalize the choice treatments and to describe the features of the various service situations. Choice was operationalized by giving respondents the opportunity not to perform the service transaction at that time; that is, behavioral control.

The results strongly supported the role of perceived control. The following measures were taken: crowding, perceived control, pleasure (to operationalize emotions), and approach avoidance (to operationalize behaviors). The results were tested using a multisample LISREL (Jöreskog and Sörbom 1989). The model provided an excellent fit, and the only modification that produced a significant improvement in fit was a direct link between consumer choice and pleasure. The manipulation of both crowding and choice provided a powerful test of the role of perceived control. The simple relationship between density and crowding was mediated by the manipulation of choice, and this mediation clearly took place through perceived control.

In a separate third study (Bateson and Hui 1992), these results were replicated in a different setting: a railway station ticket office. The study was performed using slides, a video representation, and a quasi-experimental design to test the validity of these different methodological procedures. As well as showing the validity of the different procedures, the study showed again the crucial intervening effect of perceived control.

These studies suggest that the perceived control concept can contribute in different ways to create a more pleasant service experience. Giving more choice to the consumer in the service encounter is one alternative. For example, drawing heavily from the concepts of control and choice, Mills and Krantz (1979), in the study described earlier, allowed blood donors to choose which arm was used. This manipulation has been found to ameliorate significantly donors' experiences in blood transfusion centers. In fact, greater consumer choice is considered to be one crucial benefit of service customization, a common competitive strategy that is employed by service organizations (Surprenant and Solomon 1987).

These studies also demonstrate that perceived control is a powerful concept in explaining consumers' reactions to consumer density in the service environment. Negative outcomes of high density can be minimized by returning some control to the customer. The Surprenant and Solomon study (1987) did so by increasing perceived choice, but other authors have suggested that similar effects can be obtained from providing situational and emotional information (Baum, Fisher, and Solomon 1981), distraction and attribution (Worchel 1978), and architectural and interior design (Baum and Valins 1977).

Way-Finding and Queuing

A number of other elements of the service encounter have been studied using perceived control. The physical environment sends an explicit and implicit set of signals to customers. Disorientation occurs when consumers are no longer able to derive clear signals. Complex service operations can increase consumer fear of "getting lost," and poor legibility can lead to incomprehension or uncertainty about how a system actually works. These problems can be potentially offset by consumer experience, but in general this problem of "way-finding" is likely to lead to delays, anger, and frustration (Wener 1985). Much of the way-finding literature focuses on perceived control as an intervening variable (Winkel and Sasanoff 1976). For example, Wener and Kaminoff (1983) show that better, informative signs can act to improve perceived control and slow down the onset of perceived crowding in dense situations.

An alternative solution to a crowded retail service environment is a queue. The unpleasantness of the crowding may, however, be replaced by the unsatisfactory waiting experience. The psychology of queuing shows that even an apparently objective waiting time is actually subjective. A number of studies have shown that variables that could be interpreted as influencing perceived control do in fact reduce perceived waiting time. Katz, Larson, and Larson (1991) showed that warning about the likely length of the queues reduced perceived waiting time and increased satisfaction. This finding could be interpreted as increasing cognitive control. Taylor (1995) showed that when delays in queues were perceived to be under the control of the service provider, they received more negative evaluations. Finally, Hui and Tse (1996) showed that being provided information about the waiting duration and where the consumer was in the queue (cognitive perceived control) affected the emotional and cognitive response to the wait. These types of information were chosen explicitly to manipulate control.

PERCEIVED CONTROL AS
A RESEARCH PARADIGM

The perceived control approach as a research paradigm for the study of the service encounter has many advantages. It is a concept that can be understood clearly by managers. Leaving aside the complexities built into the basic idea by later workers, the underlying idea is one that is intuitively attractive. The straightforward nature of the concept must not be underestimated as an advantage because, if the ultimate aim of research is to aid those managers in the design of a service encounter, an easily understood concept is important.

From a research perspective, this approach has the advantage of being rooted in social psychology. Research in the field of service management therefore can be based on theoretical and empirical foundations that already have been laid. Within social psychology there are still unresolved issues, so this managerial research could contribute back to the underlying discipline. The existence of refined concepts, methodological approaches, and a richness of ideas should lead to early results in services marketing.

These very same psychological underpinnings present problems in the context of the service encounter. The first is, of course, the artificiality of much of the work. The controlled administration of electric shocks to psychology students is not directly transferable to services. In the real-world applications of the concept in social psychology, another kind of problem arises. Many of the studies have been performed in what, by service-encounter standards, are extreme situations. Both hospitals and homes for the aged are institutions in which a great deal of control has been wrested from the residents. By comparison, the control withdrawn in the typical service encounter is far less severe. The studies described earlier, however, particularly that of Hui and Bateson (1991), suggest that at least some features of the service encounter are powerful enough to induce changes in perceived control.

Perceived control lends itself to experimental manipulation. Indeed, in many of the psychological studies the high and low conditions were taken as given. The work of Hui and Bateson (1991) on simulation has opened up the opportunity for cost-effective laboratory experiments in perceived control that still have high levels of ecological validity.

Directions for Future Research

There are four broad areas for future research. The first is to extend the areas of application of perceived control. The crowding and choice studies (Bateson and Hui 1987; Hui and Bateson 1991; Langer and Saegert 1977) address a limited but important part of the encounter. As this chapter has pointed out, there seems to be an obvious applicability to the architectural design of the service environment, particularly as it relates to way-finding. Queuing research is an established area in services research, and it would seem to be an easy extension of this research to use perceived control as a paradigm.

The second broad area is methodological. Perceived control needs to be measured more accurately. It can be left as an experimentally manipulated variable, but even then a manipulation check would be useful. The measures of perceived control need to be refined. Hui and Bateson (1991) have developed two scales for perceived control. Mehrabian and Russell's (1974) scale of dominance and Glass and Singer's (1972) scale of helplessness were combined as a seven-point semantic differential scale. Both dominance and helplessness have been considered as an alternative label for perceived control (Russell and Mehrabian 1976; Seligman 1975). Three of the nine items contained in the "dominant" and "helplessness" scales were excluded either because the item was inappropriate to the context or because it had a negative contribution to the reliability (Cronbach's alpha = 0.77). The second perceived control scale (alpha = 0.61) contained three seven-point Likert-type items ("I would feel that everything is under my own control," "I would feel it difficult to get my own way," and "I would feel able to influence the way things were"). Within the context of the analysis, the scales were reliable enough not to threaten the robustness of the model. Further research is clearly needed, however, to develop more refined measures of perceived control.

The third area of research would be to extend the research to encompass the service provider. Managerially, there are two key issues:

1. Can we give more control to contact personnel to allow them to serve the customer better?
2. Can we configure the encounter to increase the level of perceived control of the service providers without necessarily increasing their behavioral control?

The first question relates to the level of behavioral control given to the service provider. In organizational behavior, this area has been explored under the heading of "empowerment" (Kelly 1993; Schlesinger and Heskett 1991). The second question closely mirrors the consumer research and would require looking at everything from crowding to way-finding and the like, but from the perspective of the service provider rather than the consumer.

The final area of research suggested to generalize this conceptualization would be to look at the whole issue of individual variations in the need for control. As stated previously, control has been defined as the human motivation to demonstrate one's competence and mastery of the environment. The strength of such a motivating force, however, is not necessarily identical across individuals. For example, control is likely to be more important for individuals who are described as assertive, decisive, and active. Hence, Burger and Cooper (1979) have developed a Desirability of Control Scale to measure individual variation in the strength of the control driving force. All studies to date have averaged across individuals rather than looking at the potential impact of individual differences.

A survey of 453 university students revealed that the Desirability of Control Scale exhibited discriminant validity from Rotter's Locus of Control Scale (Burger and Cooper 1979). The latter personality construct is only a generalized belief in one's ability to control the environment; it does not carry a good or bad connotation. On the contrary, desirability of control is concerned with individual differences in the evaluation of control.

According to the theoretical framework proposed by Burger and Cooper (1979), individuals with high desire for control will suffer from more deleterious impact when a sense of lack of control is induced by an aversive situation. External types of people (those who have a generalized belief that situational outcomes are out of their objective control) who exhibit incidentally a high desire for control have been shown to be the most depressed group of individuals (Burger 1984).

These personality types would provide fruitful investigation into likely segments for service customers.

Although it is the nature of research that some questions remain unanswered, this chapter was intended to demonstrate the usefulness of perceived control as a paradigmatic approach to issues within services marketing and management.

REFERENCES

Abelson, Robert F. (1976), "Script Processing in Attitude Formation and Decision Making," in *Cognition and Social Behavior*, John S. Caroll and John S. Payne, eds. Hillsdale, NJ: Erlbaum.

Averill, James R. (1973), "Personal Control Over Aversive Stimuli and Its Relationship to Stress," *Psychological Bulletin*, 80(4), 286-303.

Bateson, John E. G. (1983), "The Self-Service Consumer—Empirical Findings," in *Marketing of Services*, Leonard Berry, Lynn Shostack, and G. Upah, eds. Chicago: American Marketing Association.

———— (1985a), "Perceived Control and the Service Encounter," in *The Service Encounter: Managing Employee/Customer Interaction in Service Business*, John A. Czepiel, Michael R. Solomon, and Carol F. Surprenant, eds. Lexington, MA: Lexington Books, 67-82.

———— (1985b), "Self-Service Consumer: An Exploratory Study," *Journal of Retailing*, 61 (Fall), 49-76.

———— and Michael K. Hui (1987), "A Model for Crowding in the Service Experience: Empirical Findings," in *The Service Challenge: Integrating for Competitive Advantage*, John A. Czepiel et al., eds. Chicago: American Marketing Association, 85-90.

———— and ———— (1992), "The Ecological Validity of Photographic Slides and Videotapes in Simulating the Service Setting," *Journal of Consumer Research*, 19 (September), 271-81.

———— and Eric Langeard (1982), "Consumers' Use of Common Dimensions in the Appraisal of Services," in *Advances in Consumer Research*, Vol. 9, Andrew Mitchell, ed. Chicago: American Marketing Association, 173-76.

Baum, Andrew, Jeffrey D. Fisher, and Susan K. Solomon (1981), "Type of Information, Familiarity, and the Reduction of Crowding Stress," *Journal of Personal and Social Psychology*, 40(1), 11-23.

———— and Stuart Valins (1977), *Architecture and Social Behavior: Psychological Studies of Social Density*. Hillsdale, NJ: Erlbaum.

Brehm, J. (1966), *A Theory of Psychological Reactance*. New York: Academic Press.

Burger, J. M. (1984), "Desire for Control, Locus of Control, and Proneness to Depression," *Journal of Personality*, 52(1), 71-89.

———— and H. M. Cooper (1979), "The Desirability of Control," *Motivation and Emotion*, 3, 381-93.

Chase, Richard B. (1978), "Where Does the Customer Fit in the Service Operation?" *Harvard Business Review*, 56, 137-42.

———— (1981), "The Customer Contact Approach to Services: Theoretical Bases and Practical Extensions," *Operations Research*, 29(4), 698-706.

———— and David A. Tansik (1982), "The Customer Contact Model for Organizational Design," *Management Science*, 29(9), 1037-50.

Churchill, Gilbert A. and Carol Surprenant (1982), "An Investigation Into the Determinants of Customer Satisfaction," *Journal of Marketing Research*, 19 (November), 491-504.

Cromwell, R. L., E. C. Butterfield, F. M. Brayfield, and J. J. Curry (1977), *Acute Myocardial Infarction: Reaction and Recovery*. St Louis, MO: C. V. Mosby.

Czepiel, John A., Michael R. Solomon, and Carol F. Surprenant (1985), *The Service Encounter: Managing Employee/Customer Interaction in Service Business*. Lexington, MA: Lexington Books.

DeCharms, R. (1968), *Personal Causation*. New York: Academic Press.

Eiglier, Pierre and Eric Langeard (1977), "Services as Systems: Marketing Implications," in *Marketing Consumer Services: New Insights*, Pierre Eiglier et al., eds. Cambridge, MA: Marketing Science, 83-103.

Gartner, A. and F. Reissman (1974), *The Service Sector and the Consumer Vanguard*. New York: Harper & Row.

Glass, David C. and Jerome E. Singer (1972), *Urban Stress: Experiments on Noise and Social Stressors.* New York: Academic Press.

Godsell, Charles T. (1977), "Bureaucratic Manipulation of Physical Symbols: An Empirical Investigation," *American Journal of Political Science*, 21 (February), 79-91.

Hui, Michael K. and John E. G. Bateson (1991), "Perceived Control and the Effects of Crowding and Consumer Choice on the Service Experience," *Journal of Consumer Research*, 18 (September), 174-84.

—— and David K. Tse (1996), "What to Tell Consumers in Waits of Different Lengths: An Integrative Model of Service Evaluation," *Journal of Marketing*, 54 (April), 81-90.

Jöreskog, Karl G. and Dag Sörbom (1989), *LISREL 7 User's Reference Guide.* Moorsville, IN: Scientific Software.

Katz, Karen, Blair Larson, and Richard Larson (1991), "Prescriptions for the Waiting in Line Blues," *Sloan Management Review*, 32 (Winter), 45-53.

Kelly, N. N. (1967), "Attribution Theory in Social Psychology," in *Nebraska Symposium of Motivation*, Vol. 15, D. Levine, ed. Lincoln: University of Nebraska Press.

—— (1972), "Attribution in Social Interaction," in *Attribution: Perceiving the Causes of Behavior*, E. E. Jones et al., eds. Morriston, NJ: General Learning Press.

Kelly, Scott (1993), "Discretion and the Service Employee," *Journal of Retailing*, 9(1), 104-26.

Klaus, Peter (1985), "The Quality Epiphenomenon," in *The Service Encounter: Managing Employee/Customer Interaction in Service Business*, John A. Czepiel, Michael E. Solomon, and Carol R. Surprenant, eds. Lexington, MA: Lexington Books.

Krantz, D. S. and R. Schultz (1980), "A Model of Life Crisis, Control, and Health Outcomes: Cardiac Rehabilitation and Relocation of the Elderly," in *Advances in Consumer Psychology*, Vol. 2, A. Baum and J. E. Singer, eds. Hillsdale, NJ: Lawrence Erlbaum.

Langeard, Eric, John E. G. Bateson, Christopher H. Lovelock, and Pierre Eiglier (1981), *Marketing of Services: New Insights From Consumers and Managers*, report no. 81-104. Cambridge, MA: Marketing Science Institute.

Langer, Ellen (1983), *The Psychology of Control.* Beverly Hills, CA: Sage.

——, Irving L. Janis, and John A. Wolfer (1975), "Reduction of Psychological Stress in Surgical Patients," *Journal of Experimental Social Psychology*, 11(2), 156-65.

—— and Judith Rodin (1976), "The Effects of Choice and Enhanced Personal Responsibility for the Aged: A Field Experiment in an Institutional Setting," *Journal of Personality and Social Psychology*, 34(2), 191-98.

—— and Susan Saegert (1977), "Crowding and Cognitive Control," *Journal of Personality and Social Psychology*, 35(3), 175-82.

Leventhal, M. and D. Everhart (1979), "Emotion, Pain and Physical Illness," in *Emotions in Personality and Psychopathology*, C. E. Izard, ed. New York: Plenum.

Lovelock, Christopher H. and R. Young (1979), "Look to Consumers to Increase Productivity," *Harvard Business Review*, 47 (May-June), 168-79.

Mehrabian, Albert and James A. Russell (1974), *An Approach to Environmental Psychology.* Cambridge, MA: MIT Press.

Mills, Peter K. (1983), "The Socialization of Clients as Partial Employees of Service Organizations," working paper, University of Santa Clara.

—— and D. J. Moberg (1982), "Perspectives on the Technology of Service Operations," *Academy of Management Review*, 7(3), 467-78.

Mills, Richard T. and David S. Krantz (1979), "Information, Choice and Reactions to Stress: A Field Experiment in a Blood Bank With Laboratory Analogue," *Journal of Personality and Social Psychology*, 37(4), 608-20.

Pittman, T. S. and N. L. Pittman (1980), "Deprivation of Control and the Attention Process," *Journal of Personality and Social Psychology*, 39, 377-89.

Proshansky, Harold M., William H. Ittelson, and Leanne G. Rivlin (1974), "Freedom of Choice and Behavior in a Physical Setting," in *Environmental Psychology*, Harold M. Proshansky et al., eds. New York: Holt, Rinehart & Winston, 170-81.

Rapoport, Amos (1975), "Toward a Redefinition of Density," *Environment and Behavior*, 7(2), 133-58.

Rodin, Judith and Ellen J. Langer (1977), "Long-term Effects of a Control-Relevant Intervention," *Journal of Personality and Social Psychology*, 35(12), 897-902.

——, Susan K. Solomon, and John Metcalf (1978), "Role of Control in Mediating Perceptions of Density," *Journal of Personality and Social Psychology*, 36(9), 988-99.

Rothbaum, F., J. R. Weisz, and S. S. Snyder (1982), "Changing the World and Changing the Self: A Two-Process Model of Perceived Control," *Journal of Personality and Social Psychology*, 42, 5-37.

Russell, James A. and Albert Mehrabian (1976), "Some Behavioral Effects of the Physical Environment," in *Experiencing the Environment*, Saul B. Cohen and Bernard Kaplan, eds. New York: Plenum, 5-18.

Schlesinger, Leonard A. and James L. Heskett (1991), "The Service-Driven Service Company," *Harvard Business Review*, 59 (September-October), 71-81.

Schmidt, Donald E. and John P. Keating (1979), "Human Crowding and Personal Control: An Integration of Research," *Psychological Bulletin*, 86(4), 680-700.

Schneider, Benjamin J. (1980), "The Service Organization: Climate Is Crucial," *Organizational Dynamics*, 8 (Autumn), 52-65.

——, J. J. Partington, and V. M. Buxton (1980), "Employee and Customer Perceptions of Service in Banks," *Administrative Science Quarterly*, 25, 252-67.

Seligman, Martin E. P. (1975), *Helplessness*. San Francisco: Freeman.

Sherrod, Drury R., Jaime N. Hage, Phillip L. Halpern, and Bert S. More (1977), "Effects of Personal Causation and Perceived Control on Responses to an Aversive Environment: The More Control, the Better," *Journal of Experimental Social Psychology*, 13(1), 14-27.

Stokols, Daniel (1972), "On the Distinction Between Density and Crowding: Some Implications for Future Research," *Psychological Review*, 79(3), 275-78.

Straub, Ervin, Bernard Tursky, and Gary E. Schwartz (1971), "Self-Control and Predictability: Their Effects on Reactions to Aversive Stimulation," *Journal of Personality and Social Psychology*, 18(2), 157-62.

Surprenant, Carol F. and Michael R. Solomon (1987), "Predictability and Personalization in the Service Encounter," *Journal of Marketing*, 51 (April), 86-96.

Sutton, Robert I. and Anat Rafaeli (1988), "Untangling the Relationship Between Displayed Emotions and Organizational Sales," *Academy of Management Journal*, 13(3), 461-87.

Taylor, Shirley (1995), "The Effects of Filled Waiting Time and Service Provider Control Over the Delay in Evaluation of Service," *Journal of the Academy of Marketing Science*, 23(1), 38-48.

Wener, Richard E. (1985), "The Environment Psychology of Service Encounters," in *The Service Encounter: Managing Employee/Customer Interaction in Service Business*, John A. Czepiel, Michael R. Solomon, and Carol F. Surprenant, eds. Lexington, MA: Lexington Books.

—— and Robert D. Kaminoff (1983), "Improving Environmental Information: Effects of Signs on Perceived Crowding and Behavior," *Environment and Behavior*, 15(1), 3-20.

White, Robert W. (1959), "Motivation Reconsidered: The Concept of Competence," *Psychological Review*, 66(5), 297-333.

Whyte, W. Foote (1949), *Men at Work*. Homewood, IL: Dorsey/Richard Irwin.

Winkel, Gary H. and Robert Sasanoff (1976), "Analysis of Behaviors in Architectural Space," in *Environmental Psychology: People and Their Physical Settings*, 2nd ed., Harold M. Proshansky et al., eds. New York: Holt, Rinehart & Winston, 351-63.

Worchel, Stephen (1978), "Reducing Crowding Without Increasing Space: Some Applications of an Attributional Theory of Crowding," *Journal of Population*, 1(3), 216-30.

Wortman, Camille B. (1976), "Some Determinants of Perceived Control," *Journal of Personality and Social Psychology*, 31(2), 282-94.

SECTION **II**

Services:
Demand Management

9

Services and Seasonal Demand

STEVEN M. SHUGAN
SONJA RADAS

Seasonality is so prevalent that nearly every service in every country experiences its effect. Although seasonal items such as toys and Christmas trees immediately come to mind, seasonality influences marketing strategies in nearly every industry. For example, annual government actions, such as taxation, have a dramatic effect on accounting services, brokerage services, banking, and even book retailing. Annual sports seasons have a dramatic impact on the marketing strategies of advertisers, the promotional programs of retailers, and the scheduling of competitive entertainment services. The school year affects travel-related service providers such as airlines, hotels, and car rental agencies, as well as retailing and entertainment services.

In many cases, one industry's seasonality causes another industry's seasonality. Christmas, for example, creates seasonal sales for retailers. Sales in retailing, in turn, creates seasonality for services who sell to retailers such as transportation services, credit-checking services, display assembly services, and delivery services. The same effect occurs in other industries; for example, sporting events affect hotels and restaurants, and new auto releases in the autumn may create demand in auto-related industries as well as in companies supplying credit for car buyers.

Manufactured goods often mitigate the impact of seasonality with the use of different inventorying strategies. These inventory strategies help smooth production and labor problems associated with off-peak demand. Service providers, unfortunately, are often not as lucky. Their ability to inventory services is far more limited. That inability leads to both marketing and operational problems associated with seasonal demand (e.g., Lovelock 1984). In this chapter, we focus on the implications of seasonality for marketing decisions. We start by more carefully defining seasonality.

AUTHORS' NOTE: We thank the Russell Berrie Foundation for helping finance the data collection for this article. The authors contributed equally to this article.

SEASONALITY DEFINED

Seasonality involves predictable and uncontrollable variations in demand over time. The predictability usually follows from a recurrent pattern associated with events or activities. The precise pattern and the relevant time interval, however, can vary dramatically from industry to industry. Seasonal patterns can be associated with peak demand that lasts for hours, days, weeks, months, years, or some combination of time periods. These demand peaks can recur following almost any predictable and uncontrollable pattern.

Health clubs, for example, experience hourly seasonal patterns of demand, peaking in the evening and early morning, when many members are not working. Motion picture exhibitors can experience daily seasonal patterns in demand, finding that most moviegoers visit on weekends. Airlines experience monthly seasonality, with demand peaking during the summer season. The Olympic Games cause shifts in demand in sports-related industries every 2 to 4 years. Still another example is restaurants, which experience multiple seasonal patterns in demand. Restaurants experience hourly seasonal patterns reflecting times of meals: breakfast, lunch, and dinner. They experience daily seasonal demand with peaks on weekends, and they also experience annual seasonal patterns associated with holidays such as Mother's Day and Thanksgiving. We now discuss these different aspects of seasonality in turn.

ASPECTS OF SEASONALITY

Predictable Demand Variations

We have defined seasonality as being predictable. In most cases, this predictability is associated with recurring events that are beyond the control of any one firm. We must distinguish these uncontrollable events from usual but unpredictable variations in demand. Unpredictable variations in demand often result from random chance and, by definition, fail to exhibit well-defined cycles. These unpredictable variations in demand may occur when a large number of customers suddenly and simultaneously demand, by chance, the use of a particular service. For example, a large number of customers may suddenly arrive, by chance, at a supermarket or at a bank. Several construction projects may, by chance, begin on the same date, and each project may demand the same services from architects, carpenters, masons, concrete contractors, and other service providers.

The management of unpredictable demand is fundamentally different from the management of predictable demand variations. A service provider anticipating a high season, for example, may raise prices during that high season to benefit from the predictable increase in the demand. With unpredictable variations in demand, a service provider may be unable to find a profitable way to exploit a sudden increase in demand or stimulate demand when few customers arrive. For example, restaurants usually are unable to raise or lower prices instantly when an evening brings unexpectedly high or low demand, respectively.

Moreover, unlike seasonality, unpredictable variations in demand usually are unique to an individual service provider and not common across all service providers. Hence, the management of unpredictable demand is fundamentally different because customers are immediately lost to competitors. A restaurant, for example, that experiences a sudden, unexpected increase in demand may lose customers to a competitive restaurant not experiencing a similar increase in demand. During common peak periods, however, such as weekend evenings, both restaurants are operating at capacity. When at capacity, neither loses demand to the other. This argument suggests that the nature of competition is different when demand variations are predictable. Moreover, the nature of competition may also be different when a service industry is operating at capacity.

Uncontrollable Demand Variations

The second aspect of seasonality is the inability to control seasonal variations in demand. Unlike demand shifts made possible through promotional activities or advertising, seasonal demand changes are beyond the control of any one firm. For example, firms in numerous industries, such as movie exhibitors, amusement parks, and children's camps, experience demand related to the children's school year. For all practical purposes, each service provider must treat seasonal demand as exogenous and beyond its immediate control.

With seasonality, each service provider still retains the ability to influence its own demand using marketing tools such as advertising and pricing. Seasonality, however, will have an uncontrollable impact on the response to most marketing tools. The same price reduction or promotional effort, for example, may generate more demand during a high season than during a low season.

Note that we should distinguish between the impact of seasonality on demand and its impact on sales. We usually observe only the sales of an industry and not its demand. In most cases, observing industry sales patterns may be sufficient for measuring seasonal patterns. For example, the box office sales of all motion pictures should reflect the seasonal demand for motion pictures. By observing sales, however, we are observing the demand curve at only a single point in time. To make accurate comparisons across time, we must assume that marketing practices are roughly constant, but when the seasonal pattern influences the industry's marketing practices, the sales curve may not perfectly reflect the underlying pattern. Were firms to increase their prices during peak seasons, industry sales during peak seasons might underestimate the true seasonal pattern because the increased prices might decrease industry peak sales and produce the appearance of less variation in demand across seasons. The same problem would occur when the industry operates at capacity during the peak season and demand exceeds capacity. Here again, the observed sales may underestimate the impact of seasonality on demand. Hence, observed sales may provide only an approximation for observed seasonal patterns. It might be more accurate to also examine obvious endogenous factors, such as changes in price, to refine the seasonal pattern observed in industry sales. Nevertheless, given the little research done on seasonality, it might be better to use that approximation than to ignore the influence of seasonality.

CAUSES OF SEASONALITY

Natural Causes

The historic cause for seasonality has been the transition between the four divisions of the year: summer, fall, winter, and spring. These seasons were predictable; each begins at an equinox or solstice. The seasons brought specific climatic changes and dramatic effects on industries such as agriculture. Given that many early economies were primarily agricultural, and some continue to be so today, seasonality played and continues to play an important role in many economies.

Seasonality also played an important role in history. Many festivals and holidays revolve around annual seasons. Political and military campaigns were planned around seasons. Many religious events and religious undertakings were also planned around annual seasons. As seasons approach, some products or services may become unavailable or available only at lower quality levels. For example, fruits and vegetables may become unavailable, and the quality of certain fish, lobster, and other seafood may vary from season to season. Moreover, the types of customers may change. A hotel in Orlando, Florida, may be the destination for families with children during the summer and a destination for business travelers or conventions during the winter.

When seasons are related to natural events, they are usually predictable and usually readily observable. For example, the sales of many items related to sports that are dependent on the weather, such as baseballs, gloves, bats, and helmets, parallel the season for the associated sport. Although weather is seldom perfectly predictable, we are usually safe when predicting the impact of weather on many industries. Ski resorts, for example, will experience increased demand in winter.

These effects extend beyond simple increases in sales for different industries. Seasons are also highly correlated with social phenomena. Aggravated assaults peak in the summer season while heart attacks decrease in the summer season. The spring season brings peak numbers of triplet births and suicides. Single births, in contrast, usually have a peak season in the late summer. Half of all adolescents first have intercourse during the months of May, June, July, and August. Stroke deaths for men and women are both highly seasonal; men's peak in the late autumn and women's peak in the winter. The peak period for high blood pressure deaths is from December to April, and the off-peak period is from June to August. Mania or manic episodes increase in frequency during the warmer months. Men tend to grow beards during one season and remove them in another.

Made Causes

Beyond natural changes in weather, there are numerous other causes for seasonality. In some cases, seasons remain annual. For example, the predictable Christmas season brings increased demand for gift items, warehouses, credit card services, travel-related services, and restaurants.

Periodic annual government action, such as taxation, often causes seasonal patterns in demand. Durable goods retailers experience increased demand during periods following tax refunds. Income tax preparation guides and related books hit the best-seller lists in periods when firms and consumers need to prepare tax returns.

Government actions can also change seasonal demand. The government, for example, can change the date when a holiday is celebrated or the deadline of filing required documentation. All these actions can have profound effects on demand in numerous industries.

In some cases, industries themselves create their own seasonal patterns. Periodic trade shows foster seasonal activities, such as new product or service releases. New auto releases create autumn demand in auto-related industries. Although it is often difficult for any one firm to change the industry's seasonal pattern, a group of firms might be able to make permanent season shifts.

Most natural seasonal patterns are annual. Other causes of seasonality, however, can create monthly, weekly, or hourly seasonality. Airlines, amusement parks, beauty salons, restaurants, car rental agencies, cinemas, and employment agencies, as well as firms supplying communications, construction materials, education, public utilities, financial services, and lodging, all experience non-annual seasonal demand, sometimes in addition to seasonal demand. Airlines experience hourly seasonal demand from business travelers in the early mornings and late afternoons. Many amusement parks observe increased demand on weekends. Beauty salons observe increased demand on Friday and Saturday afternoons. Restaurants experience increased demand at mealtimes and on weekends. Cinemas experience increased demand on nearly all holidays.

IMPACT OF SEASONALITY

Concentrated Sales

Many companies face concentrated periods where most of their sales occur. Scotts Company, for example, is the country's leading producer and marketer of consumer turf and lawn care products. Scotts faces 70% of its sales during the March and June quarters. For another example, consider storage batteries in autos. For good reason, batteries are usually replaced in the winter, when they most often fail.

The weather may be the key for many travel-related businesses, such as ski resorts, that depend on either snow or sun-drenched beaches. Cold weather may

Sales

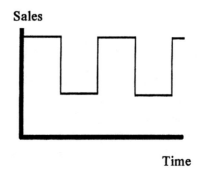

Time

Figure 9.1 Step Function Depicting Peak Season and Off-Peak Season

also increase the demand for chemicals and fuels (e.g., natural gas) whose consumption moderates temperatures or controls growing conditions. Finally, weather traditionally affects agricultural activities and related industries because weather affects which crops should be planted and harvested at what times, as well as crop yield. Tractor Supply Co., for example, experiences peaks in both sales and profits in the second and fourth fiscal quarters. Lighting products are also highly seasonal because the hours and intensity of daylight vary across seasons. For these products, sales peak during the fall and winter months when daylight savings time ends and the days become much shorter. Sales of indoor foliage plants also vary dramatically by season. For these plants, 40% of sales revenues usually come in the spring season, and another 30% of sales revenues come in the summer season. Also related to weather are sales of car care items. These items include waxes, polishes, paint striping, wheel treatments, finish protectors, and wiper blades. The sales of these items are highly seasonal. They usually peak in the spring and are quite low in the winter. Possibly because of weather-related illnesses, sales of various over-the-counter drugs, such as acetyl-salicylic acid (i.e., aspirin) are highly seasonal.

Seasonality becomes so pronounced in some industries that these industries routinely incur losses in the off-season. For example, elementary and secondary textbook businesses often incur operating losses during the off-season (i.e., in the first two fiscal quarters).

The Shape of the Seasonal Pattern

Seasonal patterns can take different shapes. Figures 9.1 and 9.2 show two shapes that seem particularly appropriate for theoretical analysis. The shape in Figure 9.1 is a step function depicting two seasons: a peak season and an off-peak season. Both the peak season and the off-peak season have the same intensity throughout. The shape in Figure 9.2 shows a smooth transition from peak to off-peak sales, with no clearly delineated peak and off-peak season.

Both of the seasonality patterns shown in Figures 9.1 and 9.2 are simple recurring patterns involving only a peak and an off-peak season. Both of these

Sales

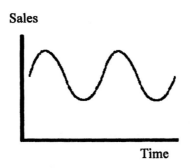

Time

Figure 9.2 Smoother Transition Between Peak and Off-Peak Sales

simple seasonality patterns are convenient patterns for theoretical research. Even these patterns, however, provide complex implications.

For example, suppose we are examining the optimal launch of a new durable. When the life cycle of the durable is extremely short compared to the duration of the peak season, the first sales pattern (Figure 9.1) usually implies either launching when the durable is complete or waiting to the beginning of the next peak. In the second sales pattern (Figure 9.2), intermediate launches are more likely. Moreover, as the life cycle of the durable increases, more complex launching strategies can become profitable. A durable product with a slow growth followed by high peak sales may find it desirable to launch immediately before the peak and use word of mouth to enhance the peak.

Although Figures 9.1 and 9.2 both represent interesting seasonality patterns for theoretical work, real seasonality patterns tend to be far more complex. Figures 9.3 and 9.4 provide examples.

Figure 9.3 shows the actual seasonality pattern for Disney World in Florida, and Figure 9.4 shows the actual seasonality pattern for the motion picture

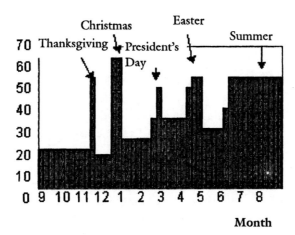

Figure 9.3 Seasonality Pattern for Disney World in Florida

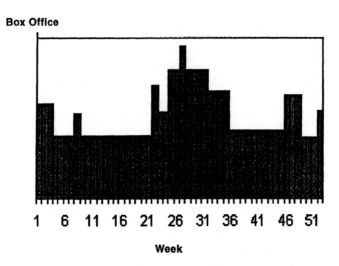

Figure 9.4 Seasonality Pattern for the Motion Picture Industry

industry (domestic sales). The recent literature contains many interesting recent articles on this latter industry (e.g., Sawhney and Eliashberg 1996).

MODELING SEASONALITY

In this section, we describe several views of seasonality and a time transformation model of seasonality.

Different Views of Seasonality

We describe several views of seasonality, including market size, purchase rate, and other interpretations.

Market Size Interpretation

One common view of seasonality is that high seasons merely increase the size of the market. Suppose, for example, that a market consists of 100 buyers during the peak season. During the off-peak season, demand reduces to half of peak demand. Thus, we might say that the off-peak market consists of only 50 buyers.

Although this argument appears reasonable, it requires many additional assumptions before it becomes consistent. For example, suppose we launch a new product or service in the peak period and obtain sales of 60 units. Now consider what our sales should be in the off-peak period.

If our product or service is a nondurable, we might expect 60/2 or 30 units of sales in the off-peak period. That expectation is consistent with a zero-growth assumption. In other words, sales would have continued at a level of 60 units were it not for the decreased demand occurring during the off-peak period. We might say that half of our current buyers are no longer in the market. The buyers who leave are similar in every respect to the buyers who remain. Hence, our sales merely decrease to half of their original levels, or 60/2 or 30 units. Hence, merely changing the market size is consistent with a nondurable product or service with zero growth, assuming that buyers who leave the market are similar to buyers who remain.

Now consider a single-purchase durable product or service. In this scenario, once a buyer purchases our service, he or she leaves the market. For example, once the buyer sees a movie at the theater, the buyer does not return to see it again in the second period.

In such circumstances, merely changing the market size creates conceptual problems. For example, again suppose that 60 buyers purchase the durable during the peak period when the durable is introduced. In that case, these 60 buyers would leave the market. It seems that the 60 buyers leaving the market should have an impact on sales in the off-peak period. Our prior assumption is that the market size in the off-peak period is the same regardless of the number of sales in peak period.

We might think that we should decrease the off-peak period's market by the number of buyers who left the market, that is, 60. Doing that calculation, however, might leave a negative market size in the off-peak period. Obviously, we cannot simply subtract the number of buyers in the first period to obtain the market size in the second period.

We must consider more precisely what is happening in the market. We might say that in the off-peak period, the probability of a purchase by a buyer decreases. For example, in the peak period, the probability of seeing the movie is 60%, so $.6 \times 100 = 60$ buyers see the movie. In the second, off-peak period, the probability of seeing the movie is only 30%, so the market size remains at 100 buyers but buyer probabilities of purchase decrease. In some markets, the probability of purchase may decrease to zero or near zero. In other words, all the buyers remain in the market, but all or many of these buyers have decreases, possibly dramatic, in their purchase probabilities.

When we allow the market size to remain constant, we avoid the conceptual problems associated with both durable services whose sales exhaust their market and nondurables whose growth depends on sales in prior periods. For example, consider the movie example. In the peak period, the purchase probability would be 60% and sales would be $.6 \times 100$ or 60 buyers. In the second period, $100 - 60$ or 40 buyers would remain in the market. In the second, off-peak period, however, the probability of purchase decreases to 30%. With a market of 40 buyers and a purchase probability of 30%, we would expect sales of $.3 \times 40$ or 12 purchases. Hence, adjusting the purchase probability is a more logical approach to modeling seasonality than an adjustment of the market size. By adjusting purchase probabilities, the accounting of the number of buyers who have purchased the service remains uncomplicated by the transitions to different seasons. This argument becomes even more cogent when we introduce marketing mix variables.

Suppose again that we introduce a service in the peak season. In the peak season, we might use marketing mix variables such as advertising and promotions that are discontinued in subsequent periods. Many buyers may become aware of the service in the first period, and those buyers would continue to be aware of the service in subsequent periods regardless of whether the subsequent periods are peak or off-peak periods. For example, advertising might make 90 of 100 potential buyers aware of a new service when that service is introduced in the peak period. Those potential buyers would continue to be aware of the service in all subsequent periods. Entering an off-peak period may diminish sales by decreasing purchase probabilities, but awareness would remain at 90 people. Moreover, were we to enter a high season, the number of aware customers would not increase beyond 90 people merely because purchase probabilities increase. The number aware of the service would remain consistent over time.

Purchase Rate Interpretation

Radas and Shugan (1998b) consider another interpretation of seasonality. They consider seasonality to be a change in the "rate of purchases" or transformed time. In other words, the rate of purchasing increases during the high season and decreases during low seasons. The rate of purchase, for example, may vary from week to week following a weekly seasonal pattern.

Note that the rate of purchase is similar to the concept of a purchase probability; however, it is a more general concept. The rate of purchase can be applied to both models, with and without fixed market sizes. Moreover, when the service is a nondurable exhibiting no growth in sales, the rate of purchasing concept reduces to the market size interpretation of seasonality.

With the Radas and Shugan (1998b) approach, we can interpret seasonal changes as changes in the rate at which time progresses. We understand this interpretation as follows. A service may have a life cycle that would exist without seasonality. This life cycle is a time series of sales. When we lower price, we might change some parameters in that life cycle. When we advertise, we might change other parameters. The life cycle, however, would describe the sales of the service in the absence of seasonality.

When seasonal effects occur, the rate of growth along the life cycle changes. As the season becomes stronger, the growth increases. One month in the peak season may be equivalent to 2 months in the off-peak season. One month of sales in the peak season may generate 2 months of off-peak sales. One month of advertising in the peak season may produce the impact of 2 months of off-peak advertising. In other words, entering a peak season increases the rate at which time progresses.

As the season becomes weaker, the growth along the life cycle decreases. One month in the off-peak season may be equivalent to only a few days in the peak season. One month of sales in the off-peak season may be equivalent to only a few days of sales in the peak season. One month of advertising in the off-peak season may produce the impact of only a few days of advertising in the peak season. In other words, entering off-peak periods decreases the rate at which time progresses.

Other Interpretations

We have focused, and will continue to focus, on the modeling of seasonality and the incorporation of seasonality into decision models. It is, however, possible to take another interpretation of seasonality. It is possible, for example, to consider seasonality to be a contaminant in the data that merely prevents a clean estimation of the model of interest.

This interpretation of seasonality suggests that seasonal influences should be removed from the data before analyzing that data. For example, we might divide our current monthly sales by the sales in the same month during some past base year. By dividing the sales of each month in the current year by the sales in the respective month during the base year, we can "de-seasonalize" the data and examine growth and the impact of management decision variables without observing clear seasonal effects.

There are many possible methods for de-seasonalizing data beyond the method of dividing by some base number. With all these methods, however, we do not avoid the problem of understanding seasonality. When we employ any of these methods, we make an implicit assumption about the way we expect seasonality to affect our data. Moreover, we assume that seasonality has little or no impact on the variables of interest in our model other than sales. This assumption may or may not be consistent with the underlying model.

Consider a simple example. Suppose our underlying model is that everyone who is exposed to an advertisement in one period buys in the next period. If an ad reaches 100 people in April, our unit sales in May are 100. Now suppose that we place 100 ads in April; we would expect unit sales of 100 in May. These 100 unit sales would be predicted based on de-seasonalized data (i.e., sales data from which the impact of seasonality has been removed). The actual sales prediction, therefore, would need to be adjusted for seasonality. If May produces twice the demand of April, we would need to double our forecast of 100 and predict unit sales of 200 units in May. Using this seasonal adjustment may be consistent with the view of seasonality as a contaminant, but it seems inconsistent with the underlying model of how advertising works. Here, 100 people buy the product who did not see the ad in April. Adjusting for seasonality implicitly changes the theory of the underlying model because the model sees only the de-seasonalized data, and all estimates, therefore, are based only on the de-seasonalized data. In this example, removing seasonality makes a strong assumption. It assumes that high seasons produce new buyers who have the same awareness and knowledge as the buyers who were exposed to advertising in the previous period.

A Time Transformation Model of Seasonality

It is beyond the scope of this chapter to present the mathematical details of the seasonality adjustment presented by Radas and Shugan (1998b). Instead, we present a more intuitive interpretation.

Consider a service with a life cycle function. The life cycle function represents sales at each point in time. The function may or may not be dependent on marketing mix variables. The service will follow this life cycle in the absence of seasonality.

Radas and Shugan (1998b) suggest that as the season intensifies (i.e., we enter a high season), the service ages more quickly along its life cycle. Conversely, when we enter a low season, the service ages less quickly along its life cycle. Hence, seasonality merely alters the aging process and can be modeled simply as a transformation of time.

This interpretation of seasonality has the advantage of not altering the assumptions underlying the original life cycle. In other words, if we hypothesize a life cycle with some well-developed theory of diffusion, marketing mix affects, lagged advertising effects, and so on, seasonality has no impact on either our theory or the predicted life cycle. The time transformation, however, allows us to modify our life cycle from what our theory predicts to what we should observe when seasonality is present.

In this chapter, we adopt that theory of seasonality, and some of the subsequent sections discuss the implications of that theory. We should note that for mature services, whose sales no longer exhibit a systematic trend, the transformation of time interpretation provides the same predictions as the changing market size interpretation of seasonality. In other words, the two interpretations of seasonality are indistinguishable when sales are not trending upward or downward.

RECENT FINDINGS ON SEASONALITY

In this section, we discuss the launch of new services and shifting demand.

Launching New Services

In this discussion of launching new services, we consider the launching problem, the service's life, and launching strategies, and we discuss when to wait before launching a new service.

The Launching Problem

Radas and Shugan (1998b) studied the introduction of new durable services and services such as motion pictures. A buyer purchases a durable only once. Hence, durables' sales start at some positive level and eventually decline to zero. In some cases, however, sales decline to a maintenance level consisting of new buyers entering the market and replacement purchases. This maintenance level of sales is generally much smaller than sales during the growth phase of the new service.

A firm can launch a new durable as soon as the durable is developed, regardless of whether development is completed during a high or low season. The firm can, alternatively, wait to launch the durable until the next high season. There are several advantages to waiting until the high season.

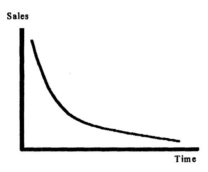

Figure 9.5 Exponential Life Cycle

The high season may bring increased opportunities for distribution. It may be very difficult to obtain distribution for a new service during the off-peak season. A retailer, for example, may be unwilling to carry new winter garments at the end of the winter season. With a decrease in selling effort for the category, it may be very difficult to obtain distribution for a durable in the off-peak season. Increased distribution suggests more rapid growth along the life cycle.

In contrast, consider some single-purchase services and some other services including some motion pictures. In the motion picture industry, theaters or exhibitors sometimes have only limited ability to increase and decrease allocations during different seasons. They may schedule later shows and eliminate discounts during peak periods, but exhibitors of motion pictures may still have an insufficient number of films during the off-peak season. In this case, launching during the off-peak season may provide more distribution for new films with, of course, far fewer people going to the theater each week (Krider and Weinberg 1998).

Another factor is the time value of money. After investing in a new service, the service provider would like to get a return on that investment as soon as possible.

Radas and Shugan (1998b) show that the shape of the new service's sales along its life cycle is very important in determining when to launch a new service. For example, they consider two typical shapes for the sales, the exponential life cycle (shown in Figure 9.5) and the Bass diffusion life cycle (shown in Figure 9.6). In

Figure 9.6 Bass Diffusion Life Cycle

each case, the sales curve shown is the one that would exist in the absence of seasonal changes in demand.

The exponential life cycle corresponds to a durable whose sales slowly exhaust the market. The diffusion life cycle corresponds to a durable whose initial awareness may be low. As initial sales occur, however, word of mouth among prior buyers causes an acceleration in sales. Eventually, as the number of buyers increases, the market becomes saturated and sales peak. As more buyers purchase the durable, the market becomes exhausted and sales decline to zero.

The Service's Life

Suppose that we complete the development of a new product or service during the off-season. We want to know whether we should launch that service now or wait to launch it in the peak season or the next high season. If we launch now, the life cycle of the service will follow an exponential curve. If we wait until the high season, the life cycle will again follow an exponential curve, but the curve will start at a much greater level and we will achieve greater sales.

Radas and Shugan (1998b) study this situation, examining two cases. In the first case, the life span of the product or service is endogenous; the life of the service is determined by the seller or, in the case of motion pictures, the exhibitor. The seller continues to carry the service until the potential discounted sales fall below some critical level. When the seller expects the service's potential sales to be sufficiently small, the seller drops the service. Hence, the life of the service depends on its sales, which, in turn, depend on when the service is launched. The other case involves a service with an exogenous life. The service provider (or in the case of motion pictures, the studio) signs a contract with the distributor (or exhibitor) to carry the service for a fixed length of time. As a result, the service's life is exogenous or predetermined before the launch.

Launching Strategies

Radas and Shugan (1998b) find that when the life of the service is endogenously determined, we should launch the service whenever it is completed. In other words, we should never wait until the high season. The intuition underlying this result suggests that the service enjoys a longer life during the off-peak season because it takes a longer time to exhaust the service's life.

Accordingly, when a service's life cycle exhibits an exponential pattern and the service is discontinued when its sales potential drops below a particular level, the service should be launched when it is completed. The benefits of launching now exceed the benefits of waiting for higher seasonal demand because, when the life is endogenous, the service enjoys a longer life during the off-peak season. The discounted sales during the season quickly drop below the cutoff, so the life is short and the advantage to waiting is small.

Now let us consider the case when the service's life cycle is exogenous or predetermined by contract. There are two possible scenarios. First, the service's life cycle is short compared to the length of time between now and when the high

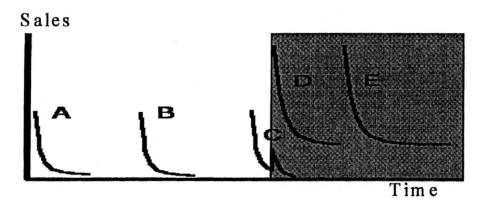

Figure 9.7 Strategies to Consider When Life Cycle Is Short Compared to Season

season begins. Alternatively, the service's life cycle is long compared to the length of time between now and when the high season begins.

Consider the case when the service's life cycle is both exogenous and short compared to the duration of the season. Possible strategies are shown in Figure 9.7.

The shaded area in Figure 9.7 represents the high season. Our choices are as follows. We can launch now, in which case the entire life cycle occurs in the low seasons (see curve A). Alternatively, we can wait a short time, in which case again the life cycle is entirely in the low season (see curve B). We can wait until some of the tail of the life cycle is in the high season (see curve C). We can wait until exactly the beginning of the high season (see curve D). Finally, we can wait until after the beginning of the high season (see curve E).

In this example, the service faces the same life during the peak and off-peak seasons, but far less sales off-season. The launching decision must consider compromising some sales now against greater sales later. For short-lived services, it does not pay to wait if no part of the sales curve enters into peak season. If waiting is at all profitable, the delay will have to be long enough to bring part of the sales tail into the season. Doing so will accelerate the sales and thus increase revenues. Hence, profits are lower for curve B than curve A (in the B scenario, some time has already slipped by, and some sales are forgone, without the launch lasting through high season, whereas in scenario A, the service was made available earlier and thus can be sold over a longer duration). In fact, profits decline as curve B moves to the right.

It is possible to show that curve E provides less profit than curve D. If the peak season is flat, the best delay is exactly to the beginning of the season. Any longer waits will not bring additional increase in sales but will certainly increase losses from discounting. These constraints leave either curve A, C, or D as possible introduction strategies.

Note that the service faces the same life when launching now (curve A), waiting until the tail reaches the high season (curve C), or launching at the beginning of the high season (curve D). The service enjoys the lowest sales, however, in the first strategy (curve A) and the highest sales in the last strategy (curve D), respectively.

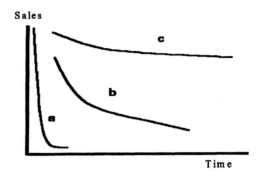

Figure 9.8 Profitable Launching Depends on Curvature

When to Wait

Waiting until the high season (curve D) becomes more profitable, relative to other strategies, when the difference in demand between the high and low season increases—larger differences will bring sharper increases in sales. Waiting until the high season (curve D) also becomes more profitable when the time until the high season decreases—longer waits bring losses incurred from discounting (for the time value of money). Waiting until the high season (curve D) becomes more profitable when demand in the low season decreases because there is less of an opportunity cost. Finally, the advantage of waiting depends positively on the increase in sales that the peak season brings, and negatively on the discount rate (which reflects the time value of money).

If a service's life is sufficiently long, the service will pass through the peak season while still early in its life. Therefore, the benefit of waiting will be smaller than the impact of discounting (i.e., getting the revenue at a later date). If the peak season is far away, the loss incurred by discounting will outweigh the increase in sales brought by waiting until the peak season.

The curvature of the life cycle is also very important (see Figure 9.8). Waiting until the high season becomes more profitable, relative to other strategies, when the curvature is intermediate (curve B in Figure 9.8). Launching now becomes more profitable when the curvature is very large (curve A in Figure 9.8) or very small (curve C in Figure 9.8).

This result suggests that when most of the service's sales are early in its life, the launch should be immediate. When most of the service's sales are late in its life, we should also launch now. Intermediate cases, however, favor waiting for the peak season.

Note that the high season tends to accelerate sales and move these sales forward. When the curvature is very large, there is less advantage to that acceleration because sales are already accelerated in the low season. When the curvature is very small, there is also less advantage to that acceleration because the impact of the acceleration is very small. With intermediate curvature, however, the acceleration can be meaningful and waiting until the high season can increase profits.

Finally, as we have already stated, there are three possible launching strategies. We could launch now (Figure 9.7, curve A), wait until the beginning of the high season (Figure 9.7, curve D), or use some intermediate wait (Figure 9.7, curve C). It can be shown that with an exponential life cycle (Figure 9.5) under very specific conditions, the intermediate wait can produce the highest level of profit, but that such cases are rare. In most cases, the best strategy is either to launch immediately or wait until the high season to launch.

This result is not the case with the Bass diffusion life cycle (Figure 9.6), for which intermediate waits are more likely to provide greater profits than for the exponential function. Intermediate waits can provide greater profits than immediate launches or waiting until the beginning of the next high season. With the diffusion life cycle, there is a period of growth before sales peak and subsequently decline. It is possible that we should delay the introduction so that all or most of the growth period occurs in the low season, while the peak and subsequent decline in sales occur in the high season. Hence, an intermediate wait (Figure 9.7, curve C) is more often a better launching strategy when the sales of the service follow a Bass diffusion life cycle (Figure 9.6).

These intermediate waits can be optimal because diffusion models exhibit an initial period of growth. It is sometimes best to have that growth occur in the low season. In this situation, the service provider should launch shortly before the high season and start the diffusion process so that peak sales occur in the peak season.

The intuition for this result lies in the shape of the sales curve. Consider the shapes of the sales curves in the low and the high seasons. In each period, as we move into the future, incremental seasonal sales continue to decrease with the exponential sales pattern; however, sales increase in the growth phase of the diffusion sales pattern. Of course, sales eventually decrease in both sales patterns.

With an exponential model, therefore, the benefit to waiting continues to decrease until all sales occur in the high season. Waiting to launch by one minute, for example, merely shifts the sales forward by one minute without changing the general shape of the curve. Only the tail of the sales curve shifts upward when that tail enters the high season. If that upward shift in the tail makes it more porfitable to wait than to launch now, then we should move the entire sales curve into the high season: We should wait to launch until the high season begins. If waiting one minute is not more profitable than launching immediately, we should not wait at all: We should launch immediately. Intermediate waits are never best with an exponential sales pattern. Consequently, with an exponential sales pattern, the optimal solution is to either push all sales into the high season or launch immediately.

With a diffusion model, after the peak enters the high season, the incremental benefit to waiting decreases. Although extreme solutions are still common, it is possible that the benefit to waiting exceeds the cost before the entire curve is in the high season.

The Bass diffusion model has parameters representing the rate of diffusion through the population. The findings on these parameters are similar to those for the exponential distribution. As Figure 9.9 indicates, when the parameters are

Sales

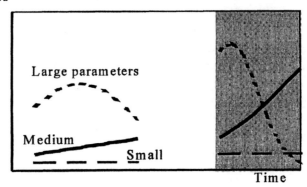

Figure 9.9 Profits for Launching Immediately Are Highest When Parameters Are Large or Small

very large or very small, the relative profits to launching immediately increase. When the parameters take moderate values, a waiting strategy can be more profitable than launching immediately.

Very small parameters (the dashed line in Figure 9.9) yield a very slow growth whenever we launch. Although waiting provides somewhat higher sales, the discount rate favors launching now. Here, the time value of money overwhelms the incremental sales possible during the high season.

With very large parameters (the dotted line in Figure 9.9), growth is so rapid that the service completes much of its life in the low season. Waiting provides some incremental sales at the end of the life cycle. These sales are relatively small. As a result, the time value of money dominates.

With intermediate parameters (the solid line in Figure 9.9), the service is unable to complete the rapid stage of its life cycle during the low season. Waiting so that some sales are in the high season allows accelerated growth, and the service completes this rapid stage. In this situation, waiting for the high season dominates. The incremental high season sales compensate for the time value of money.

Shifting Demand

With regard to shifting demand, we discuss the concept of shifting and its profitability. We also discuss bundling as a strategy and its profitability.

The Concept of Shifting

Many service providers employ a strategy called "demand shifting." This popular strategy attempts to shift demand from high seasons, when demand sometimes exceeds capacity, to low seasons when most service providers are operating well below capacity constraints. There are many examples of demand shifting. One example involves city governments trying to shift automobile traffic from rush hour periods to less crowded times of day. Some cities have attempted to shift demand by encouraging the staggering of employee work hours. Another example is an electrical utility that gives its customers timing devices so that customers can start electrical appliances such as dishwashers during off-peak periods when the customers may not be at home. Still another example of this strategy involves water authorities that restrict lawn watering to times when demand for water is low. Finally, the postal system's campaign "Mail Early for Christmas" is a classic example (Shostack 1977).

The Profitability of Shifting

At first glance, shifting demand appears to be a reasonable strategy. As a service provider, we may have a seasonal time period when we are operating at capacity and we are unable to service additional customers. It seems reasonable to try to shift some of those customers to an off-peak period when we have sufficient capacity to serve them.

Despite the apparent desirability of this strategy, the strategy is wrong (Radas and Shugan 1998a). Not-for-profit services may find that demand shifting strategies are an effective way of achieving social objectives, but shifting strategies offer no more profits and often decrease overall profits. Demand shifting strategies become unprofitable because their costs exceed their benefits. To generate sufficiently high demand during the peak season to allow shifting, we must offer at a sufficiently low price. Associated with that low price is an opportunity cost. We charge all customers who receive the peak season service a slightly lower price than each of them would be willing to pay. The additional profits generated during the off-season, at an even lower price, are insufficient to overcome the opportunity cost of charging that lower price during the peak season. In fact, the best strategy, as we will see, is to enhance peak demand.

Bundling as a Strategy

Let us consider a bundling strategy that enhances peak demand. This strategy offers customers who purchase our service during the peak period free service during the off-peak period. That is, those customers who purchase during the peak period at peak prices also obtain off-peak service for no additional cost. Examples of this type of bundling include frequent flier clubs and cellular telephone companies (e.g., Ameritech Cellular Services offers to new customers free service in off-peak periods, which are from 8 p.m. to 6 a.m. on weekdays and all day on weekends). In other cases, customers buy a package consisting of peak and off-peak units of the service.

Being more precise requires some knowledge about the demand function. For our discussion, let us consider two possible demand functions. The first is the linear demand function shape in Figure 9.10, and the second demand function is the constant elasticity demand function shown in Figure 9.11. Note that the shapes may vary according to the demand function's parameters; however, the following conclusions are valid regardless of the specific shapes.

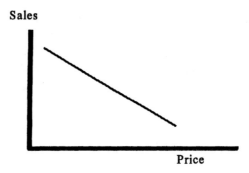

Figure 9.10 Linear Demand Function

It is possible to show that when the demand is linear or constant elasticity, it is never more profitable to shift demand from the peak season to the off-peak season. For a profit-seeking service provider, demand shifting from the high to the low season is never the best strategy. Suppose that, given peak demand, we set our price to maximize our profits and we find that, at that best price, demand exceeds capacity. Rather than trying to shift the excess demand to the off-peak period, we should instead increase our price during the peak season. We should increase our price until the number of customers that we expect to demand our service during the peak period exactly equals our total available capacity. By setting our peak-season price to that level, we discourage customers who seek the service during the peak period and essentially eliminate expected excess peak-season demand. Doing so leaves no demand to shift to the off-peak period.

The Profitability of Bundling

Unlike shifting strategies, bundling can provide greater profits. In effect, bundling works in the reverse direction. Bundling increases peak demand by enhancing the value of buying the service during the peak period. In other words, a bundling strategy is a reverse shifting strategy, shifting demand to the peak period.

Figure 9.11 Constant Elasticity Demand Function

Bundling can be profitable because the service provider makes considerable profits from raising the price during the peak period. During the period of peak demand, the service provider is operating at capacity. During that period, small price changes can have a dramatic impact on profits.

As the service provider (in the simplest case), we face a linear demand function. Defining the market potential as the demand for the service when the price approaches zero, the market potential is then the intercept of the demand function with the x-axis. Of course, we would not choose a price of zero. The intercept (i.e., the quantity demanded at a price of zero) nevertheless is a good measure of the strength of demand because it measures the height of the demand function. For example, when the off-peak market potential is less than twice our capacity, the demand even at a price of zero is insufficient to generate enough customers to fill twice the capacity. This would mean that at usual prices, there would be excess capacity.

In analysis of demand, demand is computed precisely, and the market potential is only one measure of the strength of demand. Now let us consider some findings in the literature.

When we face a linear demand function and when the off-peak market potential is less than twice available capacity, and when bundling expands peak-season market potential—all reasonable conditions—then some bundling increases profits. When the off-season market potential is sufficiently small, then there will be some excess off-peak capacity. This situation occurs whenever the off-peak market potential is less than twice the available off-peak capacity. When we have that excess capacity, it is always beneficial to profits to use that excess capacity during the peak-season to enhance peak-season demand. When we are at capacity during the peak period, bundling allows us to charge a higher price for every unit of that capacity. When we are not at capacity during the peak period, bundling allows us to increase sales during the peak season and, perhaps, increase sales to capacity.

By comparison, consider the case when (a) our peak-season market potential is less than our available capacity, (b) our peak price sensitivity is sufficiently large, and (c) there is a large proportion of customers who have bought the bundle who would not have bought otherwise. When these three conditions are present, it is most profitable to bundle all sales. With a very large capacity, our off-peak service should not be sold separately. We should always bundle it with the peak-season service. One example of this is Ameritech's cellular phone rate system, in which a customer buys peak time together with off-peak time, and the customer never has the opportunity to buy off-peak time alone.

Again, consider the situation when demand is linear in price. We define adjusted market potential as the demand that would result from pricing at cost. When our adjusted peak-season market potential is greater than twice our capacity, then our best strategy depends on our off-peak season market potential. When our adjusted off-peak season market potential is much larger than twice our capacity, we should not bundle any of our peak-season sales. When our adjusted off-peak season market potential is somewhat larger or smaller than twice our capacity, we should bundle some, but not all, of our peak-season sales. When our adjusted off-peak season market potential is very small, we should bundle all of our peak-season sales.

Let us explore the profitability of bundling when our adjusted peak-season market potential is large relative to our capacity (greater than twice our capacity). With only one exception, this statement suggests that the advantage of bundling increases as the adjusted off-peak season market potential becomes smaller. The intuition behind this result is straightforward. When the adjusted off-season market potential diminishes, the value of capacity during the off-peak season also diminishes. With less adjusted off-peak season market potential, maximizing off-peak season profits requires less capacity.

As each unit of off-peak capacity becomes less valuable, the advantage of bundling increases because our cost of bundling is precisely the opportunity cost associated with off-peak capacity. Our cost of bundling is minimized when off-peak capacity has no value to us. Given that intuition, we might wonder why we have one exception when our adjusted off-season market potential is just less than twice our available capacity. In that situation, we still find bundling profitable, but bundling only part of our sales is more profitable than bundling all of our sales. This result has as much to do with price sensitivities as it does with off-peak capacity.

The difference between price sensitivities for the peak season and off-peak season can be an important factor influencing the profitability of bundling. The larger this difference in price sensitivities, the more profitable bundling becomes, and the optimal number of bundled sales increases. Consequently, service providers with little capacity should avoid bundling when peak-season and off-peak price sensitivities are similar. They should use bundling when price sensitivities are very different. When the difference in sensitivities is very large, it becomes optimal to bundle the entire off-peak capacity.

We can conclude that bundling becomes more profitable as the adjusted off-peak season market potential diminishes, except when off-peak sales are close to capacity and our off-peak price sensitivity is small relative to peak-season price sensitivity. When off-peak price sensitivity is low, we are able to charge more for off-peak season capacity by having a higher off-peak price. Charging more for off-peak capacity makes that capacity more valuable because each unit of that capacity now generates more revenue. Bundling may force us, when we are near capacity, to forgo some of that revenue. Hence, we might want to limit the quantity of bundled sales when the off-peak price is high and we are operating at near capacity during the off-peak season. Table 9.1 summarizes these findings.

Finally, we consider the case of the constant elasticity demand function. Consider the case when the peak market potential is larger than capacity. In that case, when the off-peak market potential is sufficiently small relative to capacity, bundling improves profits. When the off-peak market potential is large relative to capacity, then bundling can still improve profits when peak-season market potential is sufficiently large.

When the off-season market potential is sufficiently small, there will be some excess off-peak capacity. This excess capacity can be used during the peak season to enhance peak-season demand. When we are at capacity during the peak period,

TABLE 9.1 Summary of Bundling Results

	Large Peak Demand	*Small Peak Demand*
Bundle all sales when:	Small off-peak demand	Large differences between peak and off-peak price sensitivity; many customers buy bundle who would not have otherwise bought
Bundle some sales when:	Intermediate off-peak demand	Small off-peak demand; bundling expands peak-season demand
Do not bundle when:	Very large off-peak demand	

bundling allows us to charge a higher price for every unit of that capacity. When we are not at capacity during the peak period, bundling allows us to increase sales during the peak season and, perhaps, increase sales to capacity.

CONCLUSIONS

Almost every service displays some seasonality. We discussed one approach that provides a theoretical foundation for modeling seasonality. That approach transforms time so that during high seasons, time moves more quickly than observed time. During the low seasons, transformed time moves more slowly than observed time.

The transformed time approach does more than just adjust sales for seasonal demand. The approach accelerates and decelerates the service's sales and aging along its life cycle. The transformation also provides a way of parsimoniously adding a known seasonal pattern to any dynamic model, without changing the foundation of the original underlying model.

The transformation approach also provides implications for the timing of new service introductions, including whether to launch in a current low season or wait for the next high season. The shape of the life cycle is important. For example, when the sales of the service are continuously decreasing, we should either launch now or wait until the beginning of the next high season. Intermediate waits are less profitable than launching immediately. When the early growth rate is either very rapid or very slow in the off-season, we should launch immediately—waiting until the high season fails to improve profits. When growth is intermediate, we can possibly improve profits by waiting until the next high season.

We also conclude that demand shifting strategies are ineffective for private service providers who seek to improve profits. It is better for these private service providers to eliminate excess demand during peak periods, for example with higher peak prices, than to attempt to shift some of this peak demand to the off-peak period. For-profit service providers should, instead, focus on demand-stimulating strategies. We show, for example, that we can improve profits through bundling, that is, selling services during the peak bundled with free off-peak service. In doing so, we find that service providers should focus on stimulating demand during the peak period, rather than shifting peak demand to the off-peak period.

REFERENCES

Krider, Robert E. and Charles B. Weinberg (1998), "Competitive Dynamics and the Introduction of New Products: The Motion Picture Timing Game," *Journal of Marketing Research*, 35 (February), 1-15.

Lovelock, Christopher (1984), "Strategies for Managing Capacity-Constrained Service Organizations," *Service Industries Journal*, 4 (November), 12-30.

Radas, Sonja and Steven M. Shugan (1998a), "Managing Service Demand: Shifting and Bundling," *Journal of Services Research*, 1(1), 47-64.

——— and ——— (1998b), "Seasonal Marketing and Timing New Product Introductions," *Journal of Marketing Research*, 35(3), 296-315.

Sawhney, Mohanbir S. and Jehoshua Eliashberg (1996), "A Parsimonious Model for Forecasting Gross Box Office Revenues of Motion Pictures," *Marketing Science*, 15(2), 113-31.

Shostack, G. Lynn (1977), "Breaking Free From Product Marketing," *Journal of Marketing*, 41 (April), 73-80.

10

Waiting for Service

Perceptions Management of the Wait Experience

SHIRLEY TAYLOR
GORDON FULLERTON

> I was at the health service. I checked in 5 minutes before my appointment.
> I was told by the receptionist to wait in the waiting room.
> After 50 minutes of waiting, I was furious, angry.
>
> —*Patient at a doctor's office*

It is not uncommon for a wait for service to be an unpleasant experience, and recently empirical evidence of this relationship has been provided in a number of settings (e.g., Chebat, Filiatrault, et al. 1995; Chebat, Gelinas-Chebat, et al. 1995; Coffey and DiGiusto 1983; Folkes, Koletsky, and Graham 1987; Hui and Tse 1996; Taylor 1994).

Service waits can often feel overly long as well, as is captured in the following:

I waited three quarters of an hour. It felt like forever. (delayed restaurant customer)

They were backed up and I was surrounded by sick little kids. It made it feel like forever. (patient who waited 45 minutes for a doctor's appointment)

This intuitive relationship has also been shown to hold in a number of empirical settings (e.g., Chebat, Filiatrault, et al. 1995; Chebat, Gelinas-Chebat, et al.

1995; Hornik 1984). As the following comments from delayed customers illustrate, the wait can have adverse effects on the customer's evaluation of the service:

> My phone call would be put on hold for hours until I finally got through to an operator who would set up a time for the "phone man" to come by the house. I was extremely disappointed with the phone company's service. (customer of phone service trying to get a new line installed)

> The wait affects my evaluation of the service in that I am now in a grumpy mood at the cash register and then become hostile and slightly rude. (customer who waited 10 minutes at a fast food restaurant)

> I didn't feel the service was adequate considering the wait. A 5-minute consult for an hour wait makes you feel like fast food. (patient who waited 60 minutes for a doctor's appointment)

> I was buying a binder. It took half an hour; it should have taken no time since the store was empty. I was extremely angry and vowed I would never return to that store again. (customer who waited 30 minutes at a stationery store)

This adverse impact of delays on service evaluations has also been evidenced in a number of empirical settings (Chebat, Filiatrault, et al. 1995; Davis and Vollman 1990; Dubé-Rioux, Schmitt, and LeClerc 1989; Katz, Larson, and Larson 1991; Taylor 1994, 1995; Taylor and Claxton 1995; Thompson and Yarnould 1995; Tom and Lucey 1995).

Waiting for services is a pervasive element of the shopping experience. Service providers have recognized the deleterious effects of waits; however, despite organizations' efforts to reduce waits through operations management techniques, waits still exist. Thus service providers have turned to perceptions management in an effort to control waiting's adverse effects. If you cannot control the actual waiting time, then control the customer's perception of it. To do this, the variables that influence the wait experience must be identified.

This chapter outlines some of the important variables that have been recognized as influencing how customers react to a service wait. Two key variables have been shown to determine the waiting experience: the perceived duration of the wait and the affective reaction to the wait. These two key variables, along with a number of other antecedent variables, combine to affect the customer's evaluation of the service (see Figure 10.1). After a brief outline of the various types of service waits and the types of services studied, we will discuss each of these variables and how they affect the wait experience. The few models that have attempted to integrate these variables are then presented, and the future of research in this area is discussed.

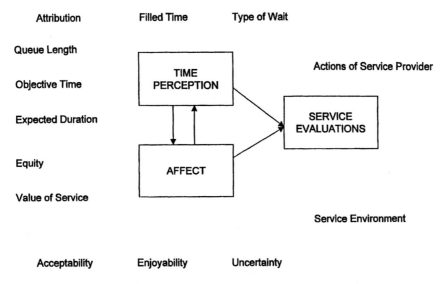

Figure 10.1 Key Variables in the Service Wait Experience

TYPES OF WAIT

The term "wait" can refer to many different types of waiting situations. Service waits can either occur pre-process (before the service begins) or in-process (waits occurring during the service experience) (Dubé, Schmitt, and LeClerc 1991; Dubé-Rioux, Schmitt, and LeClerc 1989; Hui, Thakor, and Gill 1998; Maister 1985). Taylor (1994) identified three different types of pre-process waits: pre-schedule (arriving early for a scheduled starting time), postschedule or delay (having the starting time postponed), and queue waits (which usually operate on a first come, first serve principle). Schwartz (1978) also suggested that waits can be classified as either active (waiting for a short duration) or passive (waiting for a long duration). One other type of wait classification is whether the wait occurs on-site or off-site (Taylor 1994). In addition, Hui, Thakor, and Gill (1998) recognize two types of service waits: procedural (where the customer would expect completion of the service) and correctional (where there is a chance that the service may not be completed).

The distinction between different types of wait is important because it has been shown that customers react differently to different types (e.g., Dubé-Rioux, Schmitt, and LeClerc 1989; Hui, Thakor, and Gill 1998). In addition, some types of wait, such as queue waits, are more conducive than others, such as delays, to operations management intervention. Most of the empirical studies to date have examined on-site pre-process waits, with the majority focusing on queue waits. Thus, there exist extensive opportunities for examining other types of waits and their associated waiting experiences.

SERVICES EXAMINED

Although the type of wait may be important in understanding the wait experience, so may the type of service studied. Services have been categorized in a number of different ways (e.g., Bowen 1990; Iacobucci and Ostrom 1996; Lovelock 1983). Thus far, wait experience research has not applied any of these classifications to examine any differences between types of services.

Wait experience research has been conducted in both field and lab settings. Field settings include banks and financial institutions (Chebat and Filiatrault 1993; Chebat, Gelinas-Chebat, and Filiatrault 1993; Hui, Dubé, and Chebat 1997; Katz, Larson, and Larson 1991), airline travel (Folkes, Koletsky, and Graham 1987; Taylor 1994; Taylor and Claxton 1995), health services (Mowen, Licata, and McPhail 1993; Thompson and Yarnould 1995), dental services (Coffey and DiGiusto 1983), educational services (Dubé, Schmitt, and LeClerc 1991; Hui, Thakor, and Gill 1998; Hui and Tse 1996), art galleries (Meyer 1994), retail stores and supermarkets (Hornik 1984; Tom and Lucey 1995), career counseling services (Taylor 1995), and fast food restaurants (Davis and Maggard 1990). A number of studies have also been completed in laboratory settings involving written, video, or computer-generated scenarios (Chebat and Filiatrault 1993; Chebat, Filiatrault, et al. 1995; Chebat, Gelinas-Chebat, and Filiatrault 1993; Chebat, Gelinas-Chebat, et al. 1995; Dubé, Chebat, and Morin 1995; Dubé-Rioux, Schmitt, and LeClerc 1989; Hui, Dubé, and Chebat 1997; Hui, Thakor, and Gill 1998; Kumar, Kalwani, and Dada 1997). The vast majority of these studies have examined only a single service setting or situation; thus, there exist ample research opportunities to generalize results across service settings.

THE THREE KEY VARIABLES
IN THE WAIT EXPERIENCE

Numerous studies have identified three key variables in the wait experience: perceived duration, affect, and service evaluations. It is clear that all three variables are related; however, different studies have hypothesized and tested different causal orderings—specifically between perceived duration and affect. In Figure 10.1, it is suggested that there are reciprocal relationships between these two variables.

Perceived Duration

Perceived duration of a wait has been one of the key variables studied in waiting research. Perceived duration refers to the consumer's perception of the length of time over which the person is engaged in waiting. It has been suggested that the perceived duration of the delay is a more important variable than objective time of delay because perceptions of delays are likely to be a more proximal cause of service evaluations (Hornik 1984). The perceived duration of the delay may directly affect the consumer's evaluation of the service (Chebat, Gelinas-Chebat, and Filiatrault 1993; Clemmer and Schneider 1993; Hui, Thakor, and Gill 1998; Hui and Tse 1996; Katz, Larson, and Larson 1991). It has also been argued that the perceived duration of the wait may indirectly affect the overall evaluation through such mediating variables as affect (Chebat, Filiatrault, et al. 1995; Chebat, Gelinas-Chebat, et al. 1995; Hui, Thakor, and Gill 1998; Hui and Tse 1996; Taylor 1994).

Affective Reactions

Affect is the second major variable studied in waiting research. Affect is defined as a series of "feelings and emotions that people have in relation to the attitude object" (Eagly and Chaiken 1993, p. 10). In waiting studies, it has been operationalized as uncertainty and anger (Folkes, Koletsky, and Graham 1987; Taylor 1994), pleasure (Chebat, Gelinas-Chebat, et al. 1995), anxiety (Coffey and DiGiusto 1983; Osuna 1985), overall mood (Chebat, Filiatrault, et al. 1995; Meyer 1994), and satisfaction (Hui, Dubé, and Chebat 1997; Hui, Thakor, and Gill 1998). As indicated above, affect has been identified as a variable mediating the relationship between perceived duration and evaluations in many waiting studies (Taylor 1994). Baker and Cameron (1996) hypothesize the reverse effect—perceived duration mediates the relationship between affect and evaluations. The hypothesis that perceived duration mediates the relationship between affect and behavioral intentions was tested by Hui, Dubé, and Chebat (1997) but was not supported.

A number of studies identify affect as a proximal determinant of service evaluations. Taylor (1994) concludes that affect in the form of anger directly affects evaluation. As consumers become more angry, their overall evaluation of the service becomes less favorable. Similarly, Hui and Tse (1996) found a direct path between affect and service evaluation in three wait conditions: short, intermediate, and long duration. Chebat, Gelinas-Chebat, et al. (1995), operationalizing affect as overall mood, find that mood makes a direct impact on service evaluation.

A number of constructs have been identified as proximal determinants of the affective response to delay, including attributions as to the locus and stability of the delay, length of delay, acceptability of the wait, time filled during the wait, uncertainty reduction through the provision of information, and the service environment.

Service Evaluations

The ultimate dependent variable studied in waiting research has been evaluations: evaluations of quality and evaluations of satisfaction. Many researchers have identified service quality as the ultimate dependent variable in the chain of delay-related constructs (Chebat, Filiatrault, et al. 1995; Dubé-Rioux, Schmitt, and LeClerc 1989; Taylor 1994, 1995). Customer satisfaction has also been identified as the ultimate dependent variable in discussions of evaluations in the presence of waits and delays (Katz, Larson, and Larson 1991; Kumar, Kalwani, and Dada 1997; Thompson and Yarnould 1995; Tom and Lucey 1995). Most of the research on waits and delays does not distinguish between evaluations of a quality nature and those of a satisfaction nature despite the argument that satisfaction and service quality are distinct, albeit related, constructs (Gotlieb, Grewal, and Brown 1994; Taylor and Baker 1994).

Researchers have identified a number of constructs as being proximal causes of service evaluation in addition to perceived duration and affect, namely attributions, filled time, perceived and objective waiting time, and perceived wait minus expectations.

DETERMINANTS OF THE WAIT EXPERIENCE

The following list outlines many of the variables researched as determinants of the wait experience (namely, determinants of perceived duration, affect, and evaluations). Studies that have examined the wait experience are presented and summarized in Table 10.1. This table outlines the type of study and the independent and dependent variables examined. By identifying the important independent variables, we can determine perceptual management opportunities to reduce the negative effects of waiting.

Type of Wait

A number of researchers have examined the question of whether the type of wait affects the wait experience (Davis and Maggard 1990; Dubé-Rioux, Schmitt, and LeClerc 1989; Hui, Thakor, and Gill 1998). Davis and Maggard (1990) found that pre-process delays have a more damaging effect on service evaluation than in-process delays. Pre-process waits are suggested to be of longer duration than in-process waits (Haynes 1990; Maister 1985). Delays experienced in the serving process have been found to make a smaller impact on service evaluation than either those at the pre-process or post-process stages (Dubé, Schmitt, and LeClerc 1991; Dubé-Rioux, Schmitt, and LeClerc 1989). Hui, Thakor, and Gill (1998) found that for procedural delays, pre-process waits resulted in more negative affect than in-process delays; the reverse was true for correctional delays.

It has been suggested that if service providers can convey the sense that the service has begun, customers are less averse to waiting; seating customers at the bar while they wait for a table in a restaurant is a common example of this practice. As Maister (1985) suggests, this reduces the "fear of being forgotten" (p. 117).

Objective Time

The objective time of delay or wait is defined as the real time spent by a consumer in a service waiting situation as measured with a standard clock (Hornik

1984). Katz, Larson, and Larson (1991) identified a direct link between the objective time of the delay and the overall evaluation of the service. Empirically, it has been demonstrated that consumers tend to overestimate the perceived time of wait or delay (Hornik 1984). Thus, service providers must be concerned more with perceived duration, not the clock time of the wait.

Perceived Wait Minus Expectations

> I waited roughly 45 minutes. I had expected to wait 10-15 minutes max. It felt like hours were passing. (customer who waited 45 minutes for a dentist)

> It has taken 3 months to get our deck fixed and it is still not done. I expected it to be done in a week. This makes me extremely mad and frustrated. (customer waiting for carpenter)

A number of researchers have found that expectation disconfirmation involved with the wait is a determinant of overall service evaluation—that is, how much longer than expected the wait was (Hui and Tse 1996; Kumar, Kalwani, and Dada 1997; Mowen, Licata, and McPhail 1993; Thompson and Yarnould 1995; Tom and Lucey 1995). Relatedly, Taylor (1994) found that punctuality was a direct determinant of service evaluation. Punctuality may be viewed as another disconfirmation-related construct.

To the service provider, this should indicate that realistic expectations of the delay should be set. Consumers tend to get angry when the service provider makes what is perceived to be a promise about the length of the wait and then violates this psychological contract with the customer. On the other hand, one should also be cautious about promising longer than expected waits in order to impress customers by serving them earlier than promised. There is a chance that the customer will learn this pattern and adjust expectations, or worse, leave the service because the promised time was too long.

Uncertainty

> No one told us what was going on! (comment from an airline passenger delayed 45 minutes)

Uncertainty of waiting time has to do with the absence of expectations or knowledge about when the customer is likely to receive the service for which he is waiting (Haynes 1990). In situations where the consumer has little ability to judge the likely length of a wait or delay, the perceived wait is likely to be longer than when the consumer has knowledge about the objective length of the wait (Haynes 1990; Maister 1985). Uncertainty results in feelings of uneasiness and anxiety (Maister 1985; Taylor 1994).

Providing information about the length of the delay has been shown to reduce the perceived wait by reducing uncertainty (Hui and Tse 1996). Kumar, Kalwani,

TABLE 10.1 Summary of the Literature on Delays and Evaluations

Author(s)	Research Design	Type of Wait	Services Studied	Dependent Variable	Independent Variable(s)
Coffey and DiGiusto (1983)	Field experiment	Pre-process, wait passive, on-site	Dentistry	Affect	Perceived duration, gender
Hornik (1984)	Cross-sectional survey	In-process, queue, passive, on-site	Retail	Perceived duration	Length of queue, objective delay, enjoyability of wait
Maister (1985)	Non-empirical	Queue/delay	—	Perceived duration	Filled time, enjoyability of wait, pre-process vs. in-process, affect, uncertainty, equity, service value
Folkes, Koletsky, and Graham (1987)	Cross-sectional survey	Pre-process, delay passive, on-site	Air travel	Evaluation Affect	Attributions for delay, affect Attributions
Larson (1987)	Non-empirical	Queue, on-site	—	Perceived duration	Filled time, equity, uncertainty reduction
Dubé-Rioux, Schmitt, and LeClerc (1989)	Written vignette experiment	Delay on-site	Restaurant	Evaluation	Pre-process vs. in-process vs. post-process, uncertainty
Davis and Maggard (1990)	Cross-sectional survey	Delay passive, on-site	Restaurant	Evaluation	Pre-process vs. in-process
Haynes (1990)	Non-empirical	Pre-process, queue, on-site	—	Perceived duration	Filled time, equity, pre-process vs. in-process, uncertainty, service value, actions taken by provider, expectations
Dubé, Schmitt, and LeClerc (1991)	Field experiment	Delay, on-site	Educational services	Affect	Pre-process vs. in-process vs. post-process
Katz, Larson, and Larson (1991)	Cross-sectional survey	In-process, queue, on-site	Banks	Perceived duration	Filled time, uncertainty reduction
Chebat and Filiatrault (1993)	Video vignette experiment	On-site, delay	Bank	Perceived duration Acceptability of wait Affect Evaluation	Active vs. passive, in-process vs. none In-process vs. none In-process vs. none Active vs. passive, in-Process vs. none
Chebat, Gelinas-Chebat, and Filiatrault (1993)	Video vignette experiment	On-site, delay	Bank	Perceived duration Affect Attention	Visual stimulation, affect, attention Visual stimulation Affect, visual stimulation

178

Study	Method	Wait type	Service context	Evaluation	Waiting information
Mowen, Licata, and McPhail (1993)	Field experiment	Pre-process	Hospital	Evaluation	Value placed on service, perceived duration
Meyer (1994)	Field experiment	Pre-process, queue, on-site	Art gallery	Expected time to service	
Taylor (1994)	Cross-sectional survey	Pre-process, delay, on-site	Air travel	Evaluation Affect	Perceived duration, filled time, attribution for delay, affect, punctuality Perceived duration, attribution for delay, filled time
Chebat, Filiatrault, et al. (1995)	Video vignette experiment	In-process, delay, on-site	Banks	Evaluation	Affect, attributions for delay
Chebat, Gelinas-Chebat, et al. (1995)	Video vignette experiment	Pre-process, queue, on-site	Bank	Perceived duration Acceptability of wait	Affect Affect, filled time, perceived duration
Taylor (1995)	Experiment	Pre-process, delay, on-site	Career counseling	Evaluation counseling	Attributions for delay, filled time
Taylor and Claxton (1995)	Cross-sectional survey	Pre-process, on-site	Air travel	Evaluation	Punctuality
Thompson and Yarnould (1995)	Cross-sectional survey	Pre-process, delay, on-site, passive	Hospital	Evaluation	Expectation disconfirmation
Tom and Lucey (1995)	Written vignette experiment	In-process, delay passive	Retail	Evaluation	Perceived delay, expectation disconfirmation, attributions for delay
Baker and Cameron (1996)	Non-empirical	On-site, delay/queue, pre-process/in-process	—	Evaluation Perceived duration Affect	Perceived duration, affect, filled time, attributions for delay, service environment Affect, filled time, attributions for delay, service environment Filled time, attributions for delay, service environment
Hui and Tse (1996)	Experiment	In-process, delay/queue, passive, on-site	Course registration	Evaluation Affect	Perceived duration, affect, acceptability of wait Acceptability of wait

(Continued)

TABLE 10.1 *Continued*

Author(s)	*Research Design*	*Type of Wait*	*Services Studied*	*Dependent Variable*	*Independent Variable(s)*
Hui, Dubé, and Chebat (1997)	Video vignette experiment	In-process, delay/ queue	Bank	Perceived duration	Service environment, affect
				Affect	Service environment
				Evaluation	Service environment, affect
				Behavioral intent	Evaluation, affect, perceived duration
Kumar, Kalwani, and Dada (1997)	Experiment	Delay/queue, passive	—[a]	Evaluation	Expectations, disconfirmation, promise
Hui, Thakor, and Gill (1998)	Experiment	In-process, delay, passive	Course registration	Perceived duration	Service stage, delay type
				Affect	Service stage, delay type, perceived duration
				Evaluation	Affect, perceived duration

a. Not explicitly indicated in this experimental design.

180

and Dada (1997) found that providing a waiting time guarantee as a means of reducing uncertainty significantly improved in-process satisfaction scores but made no significant impact on end-of-process evaluations. Thus, service providers can reduce the negative influences of a wait by reducing the uncertainty about the wait duration and the impact that the wait may have on the customer. For example, informing a delayed airline passenger of the duration of the delay and the impact that will have on him or her making a connecting flight will reduce the uncertainty and associated effects. The service provider, however, must be accurate in estimates of the duration. Providing information prior to the wait about the length of the delay may well lead to the creation of annoyance and negative evaluations if the actual or perceived wait exceeds expectations created by providing such information (Katz, Larson, and Larson 1991).

Length of Queue

The length of the waiting line as a spatial stimulus influences the perceived wait duration (Hornik 1984). As the line becomes longer and space becomes more crowded, the length of the perceived wait increases (Hornik 1984). At the same time, length of queue may influence perceived anxiety about the likelihood of being served, thus making the wait seem longer (Maister 1985). Some service providers prefer multiple queues instead of single queues for this reason; however, multiple queues often result in perceived inequities ("the other line always moves faster"), which in turn result in longer perceived duration and more negative affect.

Equity

> When I arrived, I was third in line for help. As I was waiting more people arrived for help and cut in front of me. At the time I was quite angry because I had to wait while everyone else went ahead of me. (student waiting outside a professor's office)

> I was at the grocery store. I was in a hurry so I was in the express lane. The man in front of me had 30+ items. I was furious because I really needed to get on the road. (customer who waited 10 minutes in the grocery checkout line)

Maister (1985), Larson (1987), and Haynes (1990) argue that unfair waits are perceived as being longer than equitable waits. Wait equity is a function of the extent to which there is a correspondence between arrival and exit from the queue such that those who have been waiting longest are served first when a service provider becomes available. Wait equity is rooted in the concept of social justice (Larson 1987). Perception of unfairness also can be influenced by the degree to which the consumer has actively made a choice as to the line in which he or she will stand or the category of service he or she will receive (Haynes 1990). There also may be special circumstances in which customers are willing to accept violations of the "first come, first serve" principle, for example, a hospital emergency room.

This relationship suggests to service providers that they attempt to adhere to a "first come, first serve" system whenever appropriate. Services that utilize a "take a number" process follow this line of reasoning. In addition to equity, the number serves as a source of information about where the customer stands in the queue. To a certain extent, this decreases the amount of uncertainty involved with the wait.

Filled Time

> I was alone and getting more frustrated as time went by. I pretty much just stared at my shoes. (bank customer who waited 10 minutes)

> I waited for 5 minutes. Because I was alone, it felt much longer. (customer waiting for fast food)

> I was alone. I had to buy train tickets. They said it would be just a moment. I started to get tired of standing. So I sat down. I didn't know how to occupy myself. I just stared into space and kept checking my watch. (customer waiting to buy a train ticket)

> I don't mind waiting as long as I have my book. (customer of a hair salon)

It has been suggested that perceived wait duration increases when the wait is "empty"—time is not being "filled" (Haynes 1990; Katz, Larson, and Larson 1991; Larson 1987; Maister 1985). Thus, it is important to distract the consumer's attention from the duration of the wait by providing information or causing the consumer to engage in activities while waiting (Maister 1985). Taylor (1994) found that filling time decreases both boredom and attention to the wait, thereby influencing the affective response to the wait. On the other hand, Chebat and Filiatrault (1993) found that filled time led to longer perceived waits but also led to more positive evaluations of service quality. Baker and Cameron (1996) hypothesize that social interaction or the opportunity to interact with other customers during the wait is a positive influence on the level of affect resulting from the delay. This is similar to Maister's (1985) position that "solo" waits seem to be longer than "group" waits. The presence of filled time during the wait also makes an impact on the consumer's overall evaluation of the service provider (Taylor 1995).

Thus, service providers can alter customers' wait experience and its adverse effects by filling customers' time during the wait. Any filler that takes the customer's attention away from the wait will do, although Taylor (1995) found that fillers related to the service (such as career materials for a career counseling service) resulted in higher service evaluations than unrelated fillers (such as popular magazines). Note, however, that both related and unrelated fillers resulted in higher service evaluations than no fillers at all.

Some providers who deliver part of their service via telephone have adopted the practice of providing taped information as a means of filling time during the wait. Although the provision of relevant information while customers are on hold may be preferable to "elevator music," consumers may respond to what they perceive as repetitive information with a negative response.

> It wouldn't have seemed so long if I was hearing different messages and getting different information. As it was, the repetition made me more aware of the length of the wait. (customer of an airline reservation system)

Value of the Service

> I got mad waiting that long as I was not used to it. But Jamiroqha is a great, innovative band with a good live show. In this case, I believe it was worth the wait. (customer who waited 5 hours for concert tickets)

The value of the service is subjectively determined by the customer. It has been suggested that consumers perceive that waits are shorter when they are purchasing goods or services that are more valuable (Haynes 1990; Maister 1985). Value relates not only to the purchase price of the service being purchased but also its importance to the customer. Thus, a wait in the office of a medical specialist may well seem shorter than an objectively equal wait at the office of a medical general practitioner. This phenomenon may be explainable in part via the principle of scarcity. Because "valuable services" may also be "scarce," consumers may accept that waiting is unavoidable. Although intuitively plausible, this relationship has not been empirically tested; thus, service providers must interpret this relationship with caution.

Actions of the Service Provider

Haynes (1990) puts forward that visible actions of the service provider, undertaken to improve the speed of the serving process, may reduce perceived waiting time. They can also affect the customer's mood, as is illustrated by the following:

> There was a small line up ahead of me at the bank. Only two customer service reps were working. I was slightly annoyed that no one else came to help when the line grew. (customer who waited 20 minutes at the bank)

Despite its intuitive appeal, an empirical examination of this relationship has not been conducted. It is believed, however, that service providers can better manage wait situations by making sure that only customer service personnel are visible to the waiting customers. Katz, Larson, and Larson (1991) suggest that, for example, banks should have support staff hidden from the front of the bank so that waiting customers don't expect these people to get up and help them when customer service is not their job.

One obvious managerial action during the wait is to offer an apology. As one customer put it:

> I have been with this bank for 15 years and use it frequently. I would have been OK if the teller had said sorry but instead my wait wasn't acknowledged at all. (customer who waited at a bank for 20 minutes)

Attribution

> There was only one person working so I had to wait. The fault of the wait was the bagel store as there weren't enough people working. It was my first time at this store and I don't think I'll go back. (customer who waited in line at a bagel store for 5 minutes)

Attribution has to do with consumer assessments as to the reasons why a certain condition exists (Folkes, Koletsky, and Graham 1987). Attributional issues that are important are locus of control, degree of controllability, and stability. Locus of control has to do with whether the perceived reason for the wait or delay lies mainly with the service provider, the customer, or extraneous sources. Controllability has to do with how much control the locus has over the wait. Stability has to do with whether the delay has a stable or unstable cause. A stable cause is one that will likely manifest itself in a delay again in the very near future, whereas with an unstable cause for delay, customers are likely to be uncertain as to the future appearance of this particular cause of delay (Folkes, Koletsky, and Graham 1987). These attributions of the locus and stability of the wait/delay have been hypothesized as leading to the affective reaction brought forward from the service experience (Baker and Cameron 1996). Both the degree of service provider control (Folkes, Koletsky, and Graham 1987; Taylor 1994; Tom and Lucey 1995) over the wait/delay and the stability of the delay (Folkes, Koletsky, and Graham 1987) have been found to be significantly related to the emerging affective response, such as anger.

As attribution for the delay becomes attached to actions of the service provider, the overall evaluation becomes less positive. Attributions as to the controllability of delays have been found to directly influence overall evaluations of service (Taylor 1995). Folkes, Koletsky, and Graham (1987) found that attributions relating locus of control and stability of failure directly affected evaluation in the form of complaining and repurchase intentions. Chebat, Filiatrault, et al. (1995) demonstrated that an overall measure of service provider attribution for the delay significantly affected overall service quality. Thus, there is substantial evidence to support the notion that attributions of control by the service provider over the delay and stability of the delay will directly affect the wait experience.

This result is difficult for the service provider to deal with directly unless the wait is not the service provider's fault. When service providers are at fault for the wait, often other aspects of the wait experience are manipulated to try to alleviate the negative effect of the attribution (such as offering complementary services or offering an apology). It is recommended that customers be told the source of their wait to reduce their uncertainty. Taylor (1994), however, found that delayed airline customers often misattributed the cause of their delays to nonairline sources. This actually benefited the airline.

Service Environment

> The wait at the hair salon was about an hour. But I enjoyed being there since the salon was very sophisticated and elegant. (customer of a hair salon)

Baker and Cameron (1996) hypothesize that the characteristics of the service environment, such as lighting, sound, and temperature, mediate that relationship between delay and affect resulting from a delay. They suggest a number of guidelines for service facility design to minimize the negative effects of a delay. For example, the warmer the color of the service environment, the more negative the affect. Despite the appeal of these principles, Coffey and DiGiusto (1983) found that dental patient anxiety did not differ according to whether patients waited in a sterile hospital hallway environment or a well-lit, comfortable waiting area. It may also be the case that consumers experience longer perceived waits in pleasant environments. Chebat, Gelinas-Chebat, and Filiatrault (1993) found that consumers experienced longer perceived waits in an environment where they were highly visually stimulated. This finding was surprising because it was opposite to their hypothesis, and it is counter to the conventional wisdom that empty waits are longer (Haynes 1990; Maister 1985).

INTEGRATIVE MODELS

Few studies have sought to integrate the many variables discussed previously. The studies from three sets of authors, Taylor (1994), Hui and Tse (1996), and Baker and Cameron (1996), are important to the extent that they identify integrated models of the relationship between delay and service evaluation generated by a wait.

The core of Taylor's (1994) model, shown in Figure 10.2a, is that delay brings forward negative affect, which influences overall service evaluation. In the Taylor model, affect and uncertainty serve as mediators of the relationship between delay and evaluation. Delay also has an effect on evaluation through the construct of punctuality. This model was empirically tested and was shown to be consistent with data collected from delayed airline passengers.

The core elements of the Hui and Tse (1996) model, shown in Figure 10.2b, are that information about the delay brings forward an affective response, perceptions about the duration of the delay, and expectations, which in turn influence evaluations. This model is different from that of Taylor (1994) in that affect is not identified as a mediator of the relationship between perceived delay and evaluation; rather, each construct has distinct nonmediated effects on service evaluation. Hui and Tse's (1996) model was empirically tested with students waiting for a computerized registration system and was shown to be consistent with the data collected.

The core of the Baker and Cameron (1996) model, shown in Figure 10.2c, is that affect is a consequence of the objective duration of the delay, which in turn

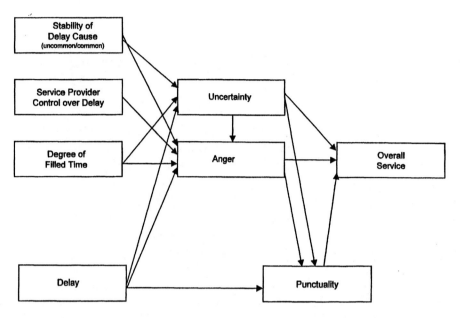

Figure 10.2a Taylor Model

SOURCE: Adapted from "Waiting for Service: The Relationship Between Delays and Evaluations of Service," *Journal of Marketing*, 58(2), p. 58, Taylor, © copyright 1994 by the American Marketing Association. Reprinted with permission.

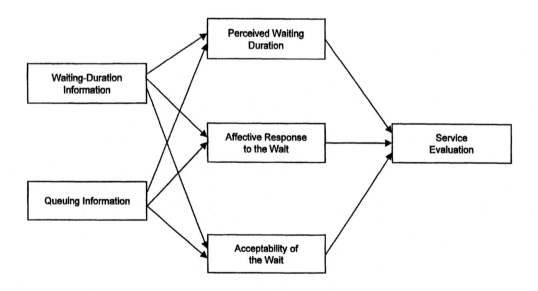

Figure 10.2b Hui and Tse Model

SOURCE: "What to Tell Consumers in Waits of Different Lengths: An Integrative Model of Service Evaluation," *Journal of Marketing*, 60(2), p. 83, Hui and Tse, © copyright 1996 by the American Marketing Association. Reprinted with permission.

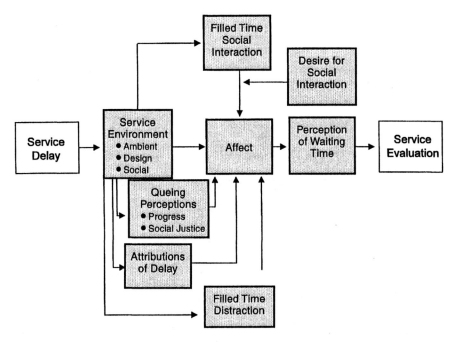

Figure 10.2c Baker and Cameron Model

SOURCE: "The Effects of the Service Environment on Affect and Consumer Perception of Waiting Time: An Integrative Review and Research Propositions," *Journal of the Academy of Marketing Science*, 24(4), p. 339, Baker and Cameron, © copyright 1996 by the *Journal of the Academy of Marketing Science*. Reprinted with permission.

influences perceived waiting time. Perceived duration mediates the relationship between affective response and evaluation; thus, the model is different from those of Taylor (1994) and Hui and Tse (1996) in terms of the hypothesized role of affect in the relationship between perceived delay and evaluation. Baker and Cameron's model has not been empirically tested.

Other studies examine multiple variables, but full models outlining all direct and indirect relationships are limited. It is clear from the long list of independent variables outlined earlier that there is ample opportunity to refine constructs and develop more comprehensive models.

THE ROAD AHEAD

Although there is still much to be learned about the wait experience, we have made a considerable advance in our understanding in the past 10 years. Perceived duration, affect, and evaluations seem to be the core constructs of interest, and we know that perceived duration and affect both influence service evaluations. Numerous research efforts have generated a list of variables that affect these three key variables. As we have seen, though, these constructs have been defined in many different ways and have been measured with a variety of scales and items. This has no doubt contributed to the wide variation in findings.

The field is still rife with opportunities to understand the wait experience. Despite the burgeoning number of studies investigating the wait experience in the past 10 years, there still have not been any studies that have allowed customers to directly identify the key variables (the quotations in this chapter are from a critical incidents study aimed at this objective). Other alternative research methodologies such as ethnographies, depth interviews, and phenomenological studies may also offer insight into the wait experience.

As suggested earlier, refinements to constructs, studies of various types of waits and services, and more integrative models are needed to expand this field of research. As the field expands, and as customers become even more time conscious, these needs will be addressed and service providers will be armed with a set of perception management techniques to address waits and delays.

REFERENCES

Baker, Julie and Michaelle Cameron (1996), "The Effects of the Service Environment on Affect and Consumer Perception of Waiting Time: An Integrative Review and Research Propositions," *Journal of the Academy of Marketing Science*, 24(4), 338-49.

Bowen, John (1990), "Development of a Taxonomy of Services to Gain Strategic Market Insights," *Journal of the Academy of Marketing Science*, 18(1), 43-49.

Chebat, Jean-Charles and Pierre Filiatrault, (1993), "The Impact of Waiting in Line on Consumers," *International Journal of Bank Marketing*, 11(2), 35-40.

——, ——, Claire Gelinas-Chebat, and Alexander Vaninsky (1995), "Impact of Waiting Attribution and Consumer's Mood on Perceived Quality," *Journal of Business Research*, 34, 191-96.

——, Claire Gelinas-Chebat, and Pierre Filiatrault (1993), "Interactive Effects of Music and Visual Cues on Time Perception: An Application to Waiting Lines in Banks," *Perceptual and Motor Skills*, 77, 995-1020.

——, ——, Alexander Vaninsky, and Pierre Filiatrault (1995), "The Impact of Mood on Time Perception, Memorization, and Acceptance of Waiting," *Genetic, Social, and General Psychology Monographs*. Washington, DC: Heldref, 413-24.

Clemmer, Elizabeth and Benjamin Schneider (1993), "Managing Customer Dissatisfaction With Waiting: Applying Social Psychological Theory in a Service Setting," in *Advances in Services Marketing and Management*, Vol. 2, Teresa A. Swartz, David E. Bowen, and Stephen W. Brown, eds. Greenwich, CT: JAI, 213-29.

Coffey, P. A. F. and Janice DiGiusto (1983), "The Effects of Waiting Time and Waiting Room Environment on Dental Patients' Anxiety," *Australian Dental Journal*, 28(3), 139-42.

Davis, Mark and Michael Maggard (1990), "An Analysis of Customer Satisfaction With Waiting Times in a Two-Stage Service," *Journal of Operations Management*, 9(3), 324-34.

—— and Thomas Vollman (1990), "A Framework for Relating Waiting Time and Customer Satisfaction in a Service Operation," *Journal of Services Marketing*, 4(1), 61-71.

Dubé, Laurette, Jean-Charles Chebat, and Sylvie Morin (1995), "The Effects of Background Music on Consumers' Desire to Affiliate in Buyer-Seller Interactions," *Psychology and Marketing*, 12(4), 305-19.

——, Bernd Schmitt, and France LeClerc (1991), "Consumers' Affective Response to Delays at Different Phases of Service Delivery," *Journal of Applied Social Psychology*, 21(10), 810-20.

Dubé-Rioux, Laurette, Bernd Schmitt, and France LeClerc (1989), "Consumers' Reaction to Waiting: When Delays Affect the Perception of Service Quality," in *Advances in Consumer Research*, Vol. 16, Thomas Srull, ed. Provo, UT: Association for Consumer Research, 59-63.

Eagly, Alice and Shelly Chaiken (1993), *The Psychology of Attitudes*. Fort Worth, TX: Harcourt Brace Jovanovich.

Folkes, Valarie, Susan Koletsky, and John Graham (1987), "A Field Study of Causal Inferences and Consumer Reaction: The View From the Airport," *Journal of Consumer Research*, 13 (March), 534-39.

Friedman, Hershey and Linda Friedman (1997), "Reducing the Wait in Waiting-Line Systems: Waiting Line Segmentation," *Business Horizons*, (July-August), 54-58.

Gotlieb, Jerry, Dhruv Grewal, and Stephen Brown (1994), "Consumer Satisfaction and Perceived Quality: Complementary or Divergent Constructs," *Journal of Applied Psychology*, 79(6), 875-85.

Haynes, Paula (1990), "Hating to Wait: Managing the Final Service Encounter," *Journal of Services Marketing*, 4(4), 20-26.

Hornik, Jacob (1984), "Subjective vs. Objective Time Measures: A Note on the Perception of Time in Consumer Behavior," *Journal of Consumer Research*, 11 (June), 615-18.

Hui, Michael, Laurette Dubé, and Jean-Charles Chebat (1997), "The Impact of Music on Consumers' Reactions to Waiting for Services," *Journal of Retailing*, 73(1), 87-104.

———, Mrugank Thakor, and Ravi Gill (1998), "The Effect of Delay Type and Service Stage on Consumers' Reactions to Waiting," *Journal of Consumer Research*, 24(3), 469-80.

——— and David Tse (1996), "What to Tell Consumers in Waits of Different Lengths: An Integrative Model of Service Evaluation," *Journal of Marketing*, 60(2), 81-90.

Iacobucci, Dawn and Amy Ostrom (1996), "Perceptions of Service," *Journal of Retailing and Consumer Services*, 3, 195-212.

Katz, Karen, Blaire Larson, and Richard Larson (1991), "Prescription for the Waiting-in-Line Blues: Entertain, Enlighten, Engage," *Sloan Management Review*, 32 (Winter), 44-53.

Kumar, Piyush, Manohar Kalwani, and Maqbool Dada (1997), "The Impact of Waiting Time Guarantees on Consumers' Waiting Experiences," *Marketing Science*, 16(4), 295-314.

Larson, Richard (1987), "Perspectives on Queues: Social Justice and the Psychology of Queuing," *Operations Research*, 35(6), 895-905.

Lovelock, Christopher (1983), "Classifying Services to Gain Marketing Insights," *Journal of Marketing*, 47 (Summer), 9-20.

Maister, David (1985), "The Psychology of Waiting Lines," in *The Service Encounter*, John Czepiel, Michael Soloman, and Carol Surprenant, eds. Lexington, MA: Lexington Books, 113-23.

Meyer, Thierry (1994), "Subjective Importance of Goal and Reactions to Waiting in Line," *Journal of Social Psychology*, 134(6), 819-27.

Mowen, John, Jane Licata, and Jeannie McPhail (1993), "Waiting in the Emergency Room: How to Improve Patient Satisfaction," *Journal of Health Care Marketing*, 13(2), 26-33.

Osuna, Edgar Elias (1985), "The Psychological Cost of Waiting," *Journal of Mathematical Psychology*, 29, 82-105.

Schwartz, Barry (1978), "Queues, Priorities and Social Process," *Social Psychology*, 41(1), 3-12.

Taylor, Shirley (1994), "Waiting for Service: The Relationship Between Delays and Evaluations of Service," *Journal of Marketing*, 58(2), 55-69.

——— (1995), "The Effects of Filled Waiting Time and Service Provider Control Over the Delay on Evaluations of Service," *Journal of the Academy of Marketing Science*, 23(1), 38-48.

——— and John Claxton (1995), "Delays and the Dynamics of Service Evaluations," *Journal of the Academy of Marketing Science*, 22(3), 254-64.

Taylor, Steven and Thomas Baker (1994), "An Assessment of the Relationship Between Service Quality and the Formation of Consumers' Purchase Intentions," *Journal of Retailing*, 70(2), 163-78.

Thompson, David and Paul Yarnould (1995), "Relating Patient Satisfaction to Waiting Time Perceptions: The Disconfirmation Paradigm," *Academic Emergency Medicine*, 2(12), 1057-62.

Tom, Gail and Scott Lucey (1995), "Waiting Time Delays and Customer Satisfaction in Supermarkets," *Journal of Services Marketing*, 9(5), 20-29.

11

Pricing the Service Offering

An Integrative Perspective

PAUL J. KRAUS

A marketing team at a leading management consulting firm has just received some good news. A large potential client has invited these marketing consultants to submit a proposal for a major new project. The proposal, complete with a full estimate of professional fees, is due in less than a week. The marketing consultants are faced with a critical decision. Clearly, in specifying a price, they must consider the possibility that a competitor will make a lower bid, but the degree to which they should price low is not clear. Should they limit the scope of the proposal to ensure that the project can be completed at low cost? Or should they instead aim to differentiate their firm by opting to compete on quality, offering an expanded set of deliverables at a moderately higher price? How will the client react if they underestimate, pricing significantly lower than competitors—will their firm be seen as offering better value, or will its image as a leading consultancy be tarnished by the impression of cutting corners? In what way will their decisions affect how the firm is positioned in the consulting market and the type of business it is likely to receive in the future?

In addition to client perceptions, there are also considerations internal to the firm. For example, to what degree should the team consider the firm's opportunity costs? Should they price lower if business is slow? Should they underprice the initial work to begin to develop a stronger relationship and then reap the investment later by selling future projects? Which of these factors should take precedence? To what degree do the answers depend on the project, the client, or the competition? More important, how could the team find out?

DECISIONS, DECISIONS, DECISIONS

As this example illustrates, the pricing of services involves a far more complex array of choices than might at first be apparent. Although many existing frameworks can be applied to help managers make sense of these decisions, most were developed in the context of goods pricing and therefore fall short of capturing the scope and complexity of issues frequently encountered in the pricing of many services. The factors that affect optimal pricing in a services context may differ from those involving goods for several reasons. First, the relative intangibility of services compared to goods may lead consumers to place greater emphasis on extrinsic cues rather than the intrinsic attributes of the service itself (Zeithaml 1988). Price may serve as such an extrinsic cue, enabling consumers to draw inferences about the likely quality of the service. Second, the degree of customization and consumer involvement that characterizes many services allows the service product and price to be jointly tailored to suit consumer needs (Lovelock 1996). Third, services are highly perishable, and short-run capacity is often limited by human resource constraints, so demand management issues are of particular importance and price often plays a role in smoothing demand. Finally, the relationship-oriented aspect of many services introduces important temporal pricing and customer retention issues into the pricing decision that often differ from loyalty issues involving goods. Thus, issues in services pricing may require a broader, more flexible framework than those typically applied to the pricing of goods.

The main goal of this chapter is to provide an integrative framework for thinking about the key factors that can influence the pricing of service offerings. To this end, we draw on theory both from the literature on pricing and from services research. In doing so, we also aim to identify areas where prior research has been limited, thus highlighting some key avenues for future study.

APPROACHES TO
THE PRICING OF SERVICES

Insights into the pricing of services emerge from several disciplines, from traditional economic theory to more recent work in marketing, consumer psychology, and behavioral decision theory. Each of these perspectives takes a different set of considerations into account and focuses on unique aspects of the pricing decision. Competition, costs, capacity, and consumer perceptions all play key roles in the development of an optimal long-term pricing strategy. In this section, we address each of these factors in turn, focusing on some of their major contributions and their normative implications for services pricing.

Competition and Pricing:
Implications From Economic Theory

Neoclassical economic theory provides a variety of perspectives for understanding price determination, from models of perfect competition to monopoly models and models in between (i.e., imperfect competition). Each of these models makes certain general assumptions about the nature of consumer preferences and then uses these assumptions to specify demand for the product[1] as a function of price. This demand, in conjunction with supply, is shown to determine the market-clearing equilibrium price for each unit; that is, the price at which demand is equal to supply.

In perfect competition, it can be shown that firms are price takers, meaning they are compelled to price at the market rate at the risk of losing effectively all of their sales (see, e.g., Samuelson 1995). This model assumes, however, that there are many competitors, each providing a commodity product, with all competitors' products viewed by consumers as perfectly interchangeable substitutes. In the case of our consulting scenario, this model implies that to the degree that project tasks are standard, clearly specified, and can be provided by many consulting firms, the team can expect less flexibility in deviating from customary industry rates. Under these conditions, jobs would be expected to go to the lowest bidder.

In reality, in most categories, and especially in services, alternative brands are not viewed as perfect substitutes. Therefore, although the model makes straightforward predictions (that firms will set prices at the competitive rate), its fundamental assumptions often do not hold. Thus, we should consider alternative models.

At the other extreme, models of monopolistic competition allow firms with differentiated brands to set an optimal price that maximizes profit based on the level of demand for the brand as well as the firm's marginal costs of production (Samuelson 1995). This optimal price will depend largely on the characteristics of consumer demand; for example, brands for which consumers are more price sensitive by definition face a higher elasticity of demand and must therefore charge a lower price to retain sufficient sales to maximize profits. On the other hand, brands that attract less price sensitive consumers face lower demand elasticities and can charge a premium without losing profits. Thus, under this class of model, a brand's optimal price is a function of both its costs and the degree to which consumers are willing to pay more for its unique attributes. In the consulting example, this prediction suggests that highly customized, unique skills and deliverables may enable the firm to price higher than bids from other firms that have fewer skills or that propose more standardized work.

Between these two extremes, there are many industries in which competition takes the form of an oligopoly, in which the supply of a fairly standard product is concentrated among a small number of market leaders. Game theoretic models are often used to analyze price setting in these contexts. In "Bertrand equilibrium," each of the two competing firms in a duopoly decides on an optimal price based on the total level of industry demand and the anticipated response it expects from its competitor (Tirol 1988). In "Cournot equilibrium," firms compete by setting output quantity instead of price (Tirol 1988). In each of these models, the optimal price level that results is determined by the mutual balance of competitive responses and is generally the same for each firm. More elaborate models take into account potential asymmetries in market power in the form of price leadership and implicit collusion, allowing firms to price higher than would be possible in a perfectly competitive market. In our consulting scenario, these models would suggest that if only a small number of firms were bidding for the project, the team should price strategically based on their best estimates regarding the likelihood that other firms will underbid them.

Another critical concept that emerges from the economics literature on pricing is that of price discrimination. Different consumers place different value on the same product, so firms can increase profits by finding ways to vary the price they charge to different consumers, as in cases of customer segmentation. There are many ways to achieve different price levels, including offering quantity discounts, running price promotions, offering value-added services, or varying pricing over time (Lilien, Kotler, and Moorthy 1992). Each of these strategies works because it extracts a higher price from those consumers who are willing to pay more to have the product tailored to their needs. The optimal pricing of services should therefore reflect not only competitive forces but also a tailoring of price to capitalize on variations among consumers. Again, in application to the consulting example, this perspective would suggest pricing at different rates to different clients based on the characteristics of the project at hand, for instance offering different fee structures based on the urgency of the work and the time frame involved.

Costs and Capacity in Pricing Decisions

Although economic theory illustrates that optimal pricing is a function of both supply and the elasticity of consumer demand, in practice many firms do not have access to (or do not seek) information that would enable them to accurately anticipate demand. Instead, many traditional approaches to pricing have relied on "cost-plus" methods of price setting in the effort to ensure a certain profit margin without requiring a full analysis of the demand side (Simon 1989). This approach, while common, is likely to be suboptimal for a variety of reasons. First, it tends to ignore consumer responses, thereby neglecting the role of price changes on sales volume. Although it ensures a given contribution to margin on each sale, this approach offers no guidance as to what price level will yield enough sales to maximize total profits. Second, because cost-plus pricing fails to account for competitor responses, it can easily lead firms to price out of the market when their cost levels are uncompetitively high and potentially sacrifice profits when costs are low. Thus, while convenient, simple cost-plus pricing methods are rarely advisable. In the case of our consulting scenario, for example, cost-plus pricing would lead to charging the same standard hourly rate regardless of the degree of competition or the uniqueness of the task, thereby losing bids on easy work and ceding profits in areas for which the firm is known to possess a specialized advantage.

A related strategy for pricing may be performed through the optimization of production capacity (Simon 1989). In industries such as airlines where short-run capacity is largely predetermined, prices may be set to make the "best use" of that capacity, rising when capacity is tight and falling when it is slack (cf. Ehrman and Shugan 1995). This approach is based on an ongoing assessment of price effects on demand levels in the course of operations, so it implicitly takes consumer and competitive responses to price changes into account as the industry evolves through time. However, to the degree that it does so reactively, rather than proactively, it does not provide managers with adequate forecasting tools to match pricing to current conditions in real time or anticipate the effects of future changes in the consumer and competitive environments. Pricing to fill capacity, of course, is optimal only when variable costs are negligible; if they are significant, care must be taken that the price reductions still allow for the recovery of these additional costs. Still, when the costs of unused capacity are high and the service is highly standardized, "yield management" can provide a practical and relatively effective means of pricing to maximize revenues for a preset level of capacity. Returning to the consulting scenario, this approach would suggest that the proposed professional fees be determined based on expected staffing constraints and the availability of human resources at the time of the project. In service contexts where idle resources are particularly costly, these concerns may be especially valid.

Pricing and Consumer Perceptions

The perspectives discussed thus far have focused largely on the role of price as an allocative mechanism that exerts a negative influence on consumer demand. Prices also serve, however, to convey other information to consumers and may in turn influence their perceptions of the service offered. A substantial literature in both economics and consumer psychology has demonstrated a number of ways in which consumer quality perceptions may be highly contingent on a brand's stated price. As Milgrom and Roberts (1986) and other economists have illustrated, a brand's price may serve as a "signal" of product quality. According to the signaling model, price (under certain conditions) can serve as a medium by which firms credibly signal high quality because consumers assume that any attempt by the firm to overprice so as to misrepresent its true product quality would constitute a forfeiture of sales. Research from the behavioral literature also suggests that price may affect consumers' quality perceptions by serving as a heuristic cue (Monroe and Krishnan 1985). In particular, when systematic assessments of brand attributes fail to yield a single clear preference (such as in the consulting example, in which some of the ideal features of the service may be ambiguous), consumers may rely on heuristics to determine their choice (Petty, Cacioppo, and Schumann 1983). One such heuristic might be the assumption that because many high-quality services are more expensive, a more expensive provider is more likely to offer higher quality. The degree to which such heuristics are likely to be used in any specific purchase context may depend on a host of factors; for example, when task complexity is high, consumer involvement is low, or no better basis exists for a more systematic decision, consumers are generally more likely to use heuristics (e.g. Petty, Cacioppo, and Schumann 1983).

Beyond the use of price as a heuristic, some work in the marketing literature has begun to build conceptual models of how price and other cues affect consumer perceptions of brand quality. According to Zeithaml (1988), price cues may play a greater role for credence and experience goods in initial purchase contexts, as well as for many services where intrinsic attributes are frequently less available than extrinsic ones. In this model, "gross value" is viewed as the consumers' appraisal of the overall desirability of the product or service, independent of the perceived sacrifice associated with its cost, whereas "net value" is an appraisal of worth net of costs. Price may thus have opposite effects on perceptions of gross and net value, increasing assessments of gross value while decreasing those of net value. In this model, there is therefore a trade-off between the positive effect of price on brand image and its negative effect on sales volume. The optimal price for a service must balance these considerations. Some recent research has begun to show that in the absence of more objective performance criteria, consumers may rely more on price cues when their perceived risks (e.g., financial, social) are high (Olshavsky, Aylesworth, and Kempf 1995). In the case of our consulting scenario, for example, when the objective monitoring and evaluation of consultant performance is difficult but the outcomes of the project are critical, price cues may take on an especially important role.

The optimal price for a service should also reflect its positioning relative to competitors and the target customer segment it aims to serve. The price of a service aimed at price sensitive buyers will serve as a very different type of cue from the price of a service targeted at upscale buyers. Similarly, managers positioning their brands as the "full-service" option may need to be especially cognizant of the influence of pricing in consumer quality assessments. These effects may be especially important for new brands that have not yet established a reputation in their category. Applied to the consulting example, firms positioned as delivering high-level strategic advice may wish to be especially careful that their fees reflect this strategic focus, in order to distinguish their services from those of firms that perform more standard work at the tactical level, which is generally lower priced.

The Role of Context in Pricing Decisions

Recent evidence from the consumer behavior literature has also illustrated the critical effect of the purchase context on customer attitudes toward a given price. Context can influence consumer responses to price in a variety of ways. First, setting the actual price well below a "reference price" such as a "regular price" can increase consumer preferences for the service. The use of promotional discounts has long been recognized to have a larger impact on sales than changes in regular prices (Blattberg and Neslin 1990). Similarly, differential pricing across a line of services can create context effects. For example, announcing the availability of a higher-priced service option can significantly increase demand for the original, lower-priced alternative (Huber, Payne, and Puto 1982). These effects also imply that the optimal pricing of a service needs to take into account the relative prices of competing brands. For those service sectors in which price cue effects are limited, pricing at a set discount to a rival brand can result in a more substantial response to the discount brand than would be generated in the absence of the more expensive competitor.

WHAT CONSIDERATIONS ARE MOST IMPORTANT AND WHEN?

As this discussion illustrates, research from an array of perspectives contributes unique insights to the services pricing dilemma; however, the key question still remains: What factors influence which of these considerations take precedence? In the consulting example, for instance, how can the team best go about arriving at a single most appropriate price? The answer, not surprisingly, hinges critically on a closer understanding of both the category and the consumer. A critical first step to price setting is to identify the basic forces that influence competition in a given service category. Different services markets vary immensely in the basis on which competition occurs. The discussion here will highlight four such bases and illustrate how each influences the theoretical framework that is likely to be most relevant and helpful in each context.

Competition Centered on Price

For a number of services, consumer preferences and competitive responses hinge almost exclusively on price. In some mature service categories, the provision of services may become highly standardized, especially if consumer needs are homogeneous, products are substitutable, and switching costs are low. In this environment, attempts to differentiate and capture a price premium may meet with failure. Potential examples of this kind of industry setting include the consumer market for discount long-distance phone services and basic Internet access providers. Many consumers do not perceive substantial differences in the quality of the services, so they will switch frequently to obtain better price deals. Accordingly, pricing in this environment may be most fruitfully analyzed in terms of the frameworks from economic theory. The particular economic model that should be applied will depend on other aspects of competition in the category, such as the degree of concentration in the industry. When the number of competitors is high and concentration is low, firms will act largely as price takers in perfect competition models. They will be constrained to set their price close to or at the market rate, or they risk losing substantial sales. On the other hand, if concentration is high and competition occurs largely between a small number of firms, game theoretic models may be more useful tools to analyze mutual strategic response. In a duopoly, for example, prices are likely to be set based on the effects of anticipated responses from the other competitor. Models of tacit collusion and price leadership can be used to analyze the conditions under which a higher than normal price can be maintained.

Competition on Operations

For other services, internal cost considerations will be of relatively high importance relative to other criteria. In the airline and hospitality industries, for example, where fixed costs are high, profitability hinges substantially on the ability to fill plane or room capacity. Although economic models are also useful in analyzing pricing in these contexts, in practice short-term price setting often involves yield-management methods to adjust pricing to match demand with available supply. For example, given a certain level of fixed capacity (and assuming low marginal costs), the optimal short-term price will be determined largely by an assessment of the maximum price that will still make the best use of capacity and cover variable costs. Longer-term price decisions depend on adjustments in capacity levels, which depend in turn on projected demand and industrywide capacity.

Competition on Image

Although the services mentioned thus far reflect fairly standard products for which consumers are less responsive to differentiation, providers of many other services compete actively based on customer perceptions of their image. For many services, the ideal set of offerings and attributes is somewhat ambiguous and depends on consumer preferences. Higher-end consulting and legal services often fit this description, because the work is highly customized and dependent on substantial levels of trust. In such circumstances, the price effects of direct competition are moderated by the uniqueness and lack of substitutability of the individual brands; theory from the consumer behavior literature may provide a more helpful framework for understanding the key issues involved in the pricing decision. As this research has illustrated, consumers are most likely to rely on price cues when more diagnostic means to assess quality are not readily available and the level of perceived risk is high (Olshavsky, Aylesworth, and Kempf 1995). In these cases, consumer inferences about the quality and completeness of the service brought about by a low price level may offset any competitive price advantage.

Price cue effects can also depend on the customer segment targeted by the brand in question. Upscale consumers may perceive a social risk associated with buying at a discount (Olshavsky, Aylesworth, and Kempf 1995), and there is some evidence that discount promotions can tarnish brand image (Dodson, Tybout, and Sternthal 1978). Accordingly, pricing in an image-driven market must reflect both the degree of perceived risks and the desired positioning of the brand.

Competition on Flexibility and Variety

Finally, services may compete on the flexibility and variety of their offerings. In many service contexts, providing a diverse assortment of related services can allow consumers to tailor the purchase to fit their specific needs. Examples of these services abound, from restaurants with unique menus to salons with highly personalized hair stylists and beauticians. In these cases, pricing should reflect an attempt to capture premia for these more "customized" products. If the costs of these services are comparable, the service provider can price discriminate between consumers with differential willingness to pay and thereby increase the profitability of the deal. In markets where consumers have diverse tastes and a high demand for variety, pricing should reflect the low degree of substitutability and higher consumer switching risks implicit in these unique services. If a certain dish, prepared and served in a given way, can be found only at a particular restaurant, consumers will in general be more willing to pay a higher price for it than might otherwise be the case. We pay more for things that are rare. Thus, pricing in these markets should always reflect the specialized nature of the product offered.

Implications of this Framework for Pricing Strategy and Category Competition

As I hope has become clear, the degree to which alternative factors are likely to be at issue in specific pricing contexts depends greatly on the characteristics of the industry or category in question. Moreover, these characteristics may change through time and across markets, so that the factors that were once relevant, in prior competition, may become less relevant as the category evolves, while new considerations may grow in importance. For example, previously standard services may become differentiated and customized, shifting the basis of competition from price to image or flexibility, or vice versa. Thus, marketers need to keep in constant step with important trends in the competitive environment. More important, however, is the implication that there may be strategic ways in which service firms might help influence or change the basis of competition to suit their advantage. By differentiating, expanding, or bundling their service offerings in unique ways, firms may be able to influence consumer perceptions and expectations from the category in ways that set new standards for the rest of the industry and confer advantage on the innovating firm.

CONCLUSIONS AND AREAS FOR FUTURE RESEARCH

Although this integrative approach offers some key suggestions on the role of alternative considerations in service pricing decisions, it also raises many additional questions for future research. Because no single set of pricing rules is likely to suit all contexts, further study is required to understand the specific determinants of consumer reactions to price and why they may evolve differently for different services. This work may in turn allow researchers to begin to answer some central questions in marketing strategy. How, for example, can service firms influence which factors consumers will tend to consider? What firm practices lead consumers to develop service relationships and brand loyalties that enhance retention and a willingness to spend more?

Each of these questions provides a starting point to strengthen our understanding of the services pricing dilemma. By adopting an integrative, contingent approach to pricing, marketers can begin to reconcile the many complex issues that pervade the pricing decision.

NOTE

1. The generic term "product" is used in this chapter to include both goods and services.

REFERENCES

Blattberg, Robert C. and Scott A. Neslin (1990), *Sales Promotion: Concepts, Methods, and Strategies.* Englewood Cliffs, NJ: Prentice Hall.

Dodson, Joe A., Jr., Alice M. Tybout, and Brian Sternthal (1978), "Impact of Deals and Deal Retractions on Brand Switching," *Journal of Marketing Research*, 15(1), 72-81.

Ehrman, Chaim M. and Steven M. Shugan (1995), "The Forecaster's Dilemma," *Marketing Science*, 14(2), 123-47.

Huber, Joel, John W. Payne, and Christopher Puto (1982), "Adding Asymmetrically Dominated Alternatives: Violations of Regularity and the Similarity Hypothesis," *Journal of Consumer Research*, 9, 90-98.

Lilien, Gary L., Philip Kotler, and K. Sridhar Moorthy (1992), *Marketing Models.* Englewood Cliffs, NJ: Prentice Hall.

Lovelock, Christopher H. (1996), *Services Marketing*, 3rd ed. Upper Saddle River, NJ: Prentice Hall.

Milgrom, Paul and John Roberts (1986), "Price and Advertising Signals of Product Quality," *Journal of Political Economy*, 94 (August), 796-821.

Monroe, Kent B. and R. Krishnan (1985), "The Effect of Price on Subjective Product Evaluations," in *Perceived Quality: How Consumers View Stores and Merchandise*, Jacob Jacoby and Jerry C. Olson, eds. Lexington, MA: Lexington Books, 209-32.

Olshavsky, Richard W., Andrew B. Aylesworth, and DeAnna S. Kempf (1995), "The Price-Choice Relationship: A Contingent Processing Approach," *Journal of Business Research*, 33, 207-18.

Petty, Richard E., John T. Cacioppo, and David Schumann (1983), "Central and Peripheral Routes to Advertising Effectiveness: The Moderating Role of Involvement," *Journal of Consumer Research*, 10 (September), 135-46.

Samuelson, Paul A. (1995), *Economics*, 15th ed. New York: McGraw-Hill.

Simon, Hermann (1989), *Price Management.* New York: North-Holland.

Tirol, Jean (1988), *The Theory of Industrial Organization.* Cambridge, MA: MIT Press.

Zeithaml, Valarie A. (1988), "Consumer Perceptions of Price, Quality, and Value: A Means-End Model and Synthesis of Evidence," *Journal of Marketing*, 52, 2-22.

SECTION **III**

Services: Excellence
and Profitability

12

The Service Profit Chain

Intellectual Roots, Current Realities, and Future Prospects

ROGER HALLOWELL
LEONARD A. SCHLESINGER

In the early 1990s, the Service Management faculty at Harvard Business School, led by James L. Heskett, W. Earl Sasser, and Leonard A. Schlesinger, introduced a new framework[1] for understanding the sources of profitability and growth in labor-dominant[2] service firms. Labeled the Service Profit Chain ("the chain") and illustrated in Figure 12.1, the framework illustrates hypothesized sources of growth and profitability as a series of relationships among different elements (the links of the chain), each of which warrants individual close management attention.

The introduction to this chapter discusses the utility of the Service Profit Chain for managers and briefly outlines its theoretical roots. The chapter then describes each link in the chain in detail and discusses some of the empirical work supporting it. These descriptions are followed by an illustration of how one firm, Sears Roebuck and Co., used the chain to create change, measure results, and contribute to the management of both its operations and strategy on an ongoing basis. The chapter concludes with an overview of new directions in related research. These include, first, an examination of "full profit potential," a new analysis technique and management perspective that is designed to help a firm optimize the value of its exchanges with its customers and employees, and thus optimize its profitability. Second, we discuss technology-intermediated services, such as those available through the Internet, in which the human service provider is supported or supplanted by technology. This discussion emphasizes the importance of providing greater customer value through technology intermediation, in lieu of simply offering a technology-intermediated duplication of a service already offered using a traditional human-to-customer approach.

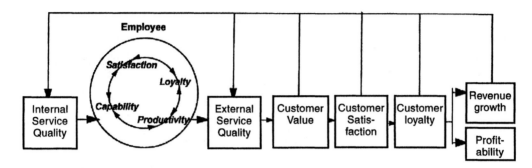

Figure 12.1 The Service Profit Chain

The purpose of the Service Profit Chain is to provide managers with a framework to help them manage and evaluate the management of labor-dominant service firms. The chain is essentially a performance hypothesis that enables managers to focus on (predominantly) quantifiable measures that lead to financial performance outcomes. Thus, the chain provides leading measures, in contrast to financial results that lag actual performance. As a source of leading indicators, the Service Profit Chain is consistent with the advice of Kaplan and Norton (1996) regarding what they call the "Balanced Scorecard."

The Service Profit Chain finds its roots in both inductive and deductive research. Its inductive roots can be found in the work of Heskett, Sasser, Schlesinger, and their colleagues, who completed numerous detailed case studies of service organizations in which they observed the relationships suggested in the chain. Many of these are documented in Heskett, Sasser, and Hart (1990) and Heskett, Schlesinger, and Sasser (1997). They are also available, adapted for teaching purposes, in specific case studies used in the Harvard Business School course "Service Management," some of which are included in Sasser, Hart, and Heskett (1991).

The Service Profit Chain also has deductive roots in several academic research streams, including operations, human resources, strategy, and organizational behavior. At its core, the chain draws from the concept of exchange-relationships (March and Simon 1958) in that each link relates to those before and after it because value is exchanged among the constituents described in the links. For example, customer satisfaction is hypothesized to result in customer loyalty because a customer who perceives that he or she receives more value from a relationship with one firm than from relationships with other firms is more likely to be loyal to that firm. Value is defined as perceived service quality delivered relative to perceived service quality expected, all of which is relative to price (cf. the Servqual work of Zeithaml, Berry, and Parasuraman 1988).

A similar value exchange occurs between a labor-dominant service organization and its employees, including front-line service providers. When an organization provides an employee with the tools needed to serve customers well, and when the employee feels that she or he receives superior value (in monetary or nonmonetary compensation) from the organization, the employee receives what we refer to in the chain as internal service quality. Thus, value is transferred from the firm to the employee. In turn, the employee is expected to be more productive, satisfied, and loyal to the firm, reducing the labor-dominant service firm's costs while improving its service quality. Thus, some part of the value transferred to employees is transferred again to customers and the firm, resulting in another value exchange. This type of value exchange draws on the employee commitment literature, which posits that employee satisfaction is related to operational and financial organizational outcomes (e.g., Mowday, Porter, and Steers 1982).

Other deductive elements in the Service Profit Chain relate to the belief that customer satisfaction is maximized when a service is designed and delivered to meet the specific needs of targeted customers. This belief stems from both (a) the operations research around the focused factory, originating with the work of Skinner (1974), and (b) observations that firms delivering service that is narrow in scope (relative to their competitors) often deliver higher levels of service quality at lower cost.

Strategy theory also contributes to the Service Profit Chain. Firms that organize around the chain must integrate two approaches to strategy: competitive positioning (Porter 1980, 1996) and organizational resources (Prahalad and Hamel 1990; Wernerfelt 1984). The external service value link in the chain relates directly to competitive positioning, in that external service value is the value a firm delivers, as perceived by its customers, relative to its competitors. Thus, external service value is the combination of pricing and differentiation[3] the firm intends to provide, as well as the firm's ability to provide it (i.e., its execution). Intended pricing and differentiation relate to competitive positioning, and the ability to deliver them relates to organizational capabilities in combination with competitive positioning (Heskett 1986; Porter 1996).

Thus, the Service Profit Chain is rooted in diverse and multidisciplinary academic perspectives as well as real-world observations and experiences. These complex origins have served to strengthen the chain. Borrowing a principle from research design, when multiple sources of data lead to a similar conclusion, "triangulation" results, increasing the level of confidence that the conclusion is correct. A similar phenomenon may occur with the Service Profit Chain, as these multiple approaches all contribute to a single, internally consistent framework.

THEORETICAL AND EMPIRICAL EXAMINATION OF LINKS IN THE SERVICE PROFIT CHAIN

In this section, we describe the theoretical links among the elements in the Service Profit Chain, as well as some of the empirical work conducted to date examining those relationships.[4] We begin at the far right of the Service Profit Chain—the relationship of customer loyalty to a firm's revenue growth and profitability—and work back through the chain to its starting point, ultimately illustrating how internal service quality affects employee loyalty, productivity, capability, and satisfaction.

Customer Loyalty and Profitability/Growth

The relationship of customer loyalty to profitability and growth finds its managerial (as opposed to theoretical) origins in the principle of the "lifetime value of a customer," aptly described by car dealership owner Carl Sewell in his book *Customers for Life* (Sewell and Brown 1990). The lifetime value of a customer is the profit contribution a customer will deliver to a service firm over an average customer life.[5] The principle is powerful because it illustrates in a simple and easily communicable way that a customer who may appear to represent a relatively insignificant cash flow (e.g., $10 in the case of a home-delivered pizza) may actually be worth thousands of dollars if he or she remains loyal. When this idea of lifetime value is combined with the managerial adage that "It is less expensive to keep a customer than to get a new one," the relationship of profitability and growth to customer loyalty becomes clear from a managerially intuitive perspective. In fact, the relationship between customer loyalty and a firm's profitability and growth intuitively appeals to many managers in leading service organizations, and those managers' actions reflect and reinforce the relationship.

The empirical validation of these managerial ideas began when Reichheld and Sasser (1990) published a paper on the relationship between customer loyalty and profitability in selected service firms. This research confirmed that such a relationship did exist for their substantial sample and suggested that for many service firms the loyalty/profitability relationship may be stronger than the market share/profitability relationship described by Buzzell, Gale, and Sultan (1975). The theoretical logic supporting Reichheld and Sasser's hypothesis is that generally speaking, loyal customers (a) reduce a firm's marketing costs (including the cost of acquiring a customer) through repeat purchase and word-of-mouth advertising, (b) reduce operating costs through familiarity with the firm's operating system, and (c) increase revenue through reduced price sensitivity.

One of the primary benefits of the customer loyalty/profitability and growth relationship is that it aligns the interests of the firm and the customer. Rather than focusing on which party captures a greater portion of the total value created, the hypothesis that customer loyalty leads to profitability suggests that by focusing instead on creating more value for customers (vis-à-vis competitors), a firm gains their loyalty and ultimately increases its portion of value through profit and growth.

External Service Quality, Customer Value, Customer Satisfaction, and Customer Loyalty

Moving back three links in the chain are the relationships among external service quality and customer value, customer value, and customer satisfaction and between customer satisfaction and customer loyalty. As noted previously, these links derive from the value exchange principle, originally espoused by March and Simon (1958). In short, customers who are satisfied as a result of receiving greater value than that perceived to be available from other sources are loyal because they have optimized their relationship for this service. External service quality is an integral part of these relationships because of the contribution it makes to customer value (again, defining value as expected service relative to actual service, relative to price). The relationships among quality, value, satisfaction, and loyalty are especially strong for services that tend to be high in experience or credence characteristics (Zeithaml 1981).

The definition of customer value used in the Service Profit Chain contains an important strategic positioning element. "Customer value" is defined as value as perceived by the customer (relative to expectations); thus, high customer value as delivered by one service organization could be very different from high customer value delivered by a firm performing a similar service positioned to appeal to a different type of customer (different either demographically or psychographically). The essence of the value exchange concept is discussed by Grant and Schlesinger (1995), who argue that a firm must optimize the value it delivers to groups of customers who are increasingly segmented. The smaller the group served (ultimately becoming a group of one), the less variance will occur among the members' needs, and thus the greater the firm's opportunity to exceed their expectations by delivering exactly what they want. The firm can then either charge a premium for a highly differentiated service product or attempt to increase the volume of service it delivers by reducing costs and prices. In the latter strategy, only what the customer wants is delivered—peripheral service elements not valued by targeted customers are eliminated. This gives the firm the opportunity to create a high-quality service at a relatively low cost, delivering extraordinary value to the customer group.

Clearly, the goal of serving smaller groups better must be weighed against the economies of scale available in some service offerings. Still, as technology enables service firms to achieve economies of scale at lower volumes and to better understand smaller groups of customers' preferences at increasingly lower costs, firms will be able to position their service offering to ever smaller groups, exceed those groups' expectations, and encourage their loyalty.[6]

Numerous researchers have discussed the relationships among quality, value, satisfaction, loyalty, and profitability. Different aspects of these relationships are discussed by (among others) Heskett, Sasser, and Hart (1990); Reichheld and Sasser (1990); Zeithaml, Parasuraman, and Berry (1990); Gummesson (1992); Rust and Zahorik (1993); Anderson and Fornell (1994); Reichheld (1996); Storbacka, Strandvik, and Grönroos (1994); Jones and Sasser (1995); Rust, Zahorik, and Keiningham (1995); and Schneider and Bowen (1995).

Jones and Sasser (1995) delve into the customer satisfaction/customer loyalty relationship, developing a contingent framework illustrating how the relationship differs based on a firm's competitive environment. They posit that firms in a monopoly or oligopoly situation will have high customer loyalty even if satisfaction is mediocre or low, given that there are no, or few, alternative service providers to which customers can defect. Although their case is not as extreme, firms able to deliver highly differentiated service, or substantially increase switching costs, may also see relatively high levels of loyalty at only moderate levels of satisfaction.

In contrast, firms in highly competitive markets will see relatively low levels of loyalty even as customer satisfaction steadily increases. Only when satisfaction is very high will loyalty increase dramatically. Jones and Sasser cite one example of this type of loyalty/satisfaction relationship at Xerox. In this case, managers learned that a customer reporting service satisfaction of five (on a five-point scale, with five indicating highest satisfaction) was six times as likely to repurchase Xerox products than a customer reporting a satisfaction level of four.

Jones and Sasser illustrate, using the title of their article, "why satisfied customers defect." The answer lies in the finding that the satisfaction/loyalty relationship is neither constant nor usually linear, and must be understood on an industry-by-industry, if not firm-by-firm, basis. A corollary issue to emerge from their work is a better understanding of the need to, in the vernacular, "wow" customers. Clearly, in highly competitive industries with low barriers to competition, the ability to consistently exceed expectations (to "wow" customers) can be seen as a source of competitive advantage. In other industries in which competition is limited and will remain so, however, the extent to which a firm must dedicate itself to "wowing" customers may be fundamentally different.

Several empirical studies of the relationships among quality, value, satisfaction, and loyalty have been conducted. Because quality and value are considered implicit in satisfaction, these studies tend to focus on measurements of customer satisfaction, customer loyalty (attitudinal and behavioral), and, in some cases, profitability. These studies include Anderson, Fornell, and Lehmann (1994); Anderson and Sullivan (1993); Boulding et al. (1993); Fornell (1992); Hallowell (1996); Nelson et al. (1992); and Rust and Zahorik (1991).

Employee Capability, Satisfaction, Loyalty, and Productivity and Their Relationship to External Service Value

The idea that employee satisfaction is related to organizational outcomes (customer satisfaction, reduced costs, and eventually superior financial performance) has a long, rich, and controversial history going back to the Hawthorne experiments at the Western Electric Laboratories in the 1930s (Roethlisberger and Dickson 1939). One prominent work on employee commitment acknowledges that although some empirical studies have verified the relationship, other empirical studies have been unable to do the same (Mowday, Porter, and Steers 1982). The relationship is likely highly situational, and thus conditional on elements exogenous to the models developed.

Some service management researchers have accepted the ambiguity of these findings and have begun to explore the relationship between employee satisfaction and customer satisfaction from new perspectives. Schneider and Bowen (1985), replicating and extending work initiated by Schneider, Parkington, and Buxton (1980), illustrated that employees' perceptions of service quality relate strongly to customers' perceptions of service quality. Schlesinger and Zornitsky

(1991) took this work further, showing that employees' perceptions of their ability to deliver high-quality service (called "employee capability") related strongly to customers' perceptions of service quality, in fact more strongly than did employee satisfaction. Hallowell, Schlesinger, and Zornitsky (1996) hypothesize that employee satisfaction may be an outcome of employee capability, which in turn potentially explains the management observation that although satisfied employees do not necessarily create satisfied customers, there are rarely satisfied customers without satisfied employees.

The Service Profit Chain enables better understanding of the employee/customer satisfaction relationship. Specifically, the strength of that relationship may be contingent upon four elements relevant to employees—capability, satisfaction, loyalty, and productivity—that are thought to influence customer satisfaction. The logic behind this hypothesis is simple. Capable employees have the ability to deliver good service (service perceived by customers as having high value). If systems, procedures, lack of tools, or rules impede employees' ability to deliver good service, then it is unlikely that employees will generate customer satisfaction. Employees who are dissatisfied with their jobs are less likely to treat customers as well as do employees who enjoy their work. Loyal employees are more willing to subjugate their short-term interests to the long-term interests of the organization, providing superior service quality to customers. Furthermore, loyal employees also tend to stay with an organization longer, reducing the cost of employee turnover as well as its negative effect on service quality (Heskett, Sasser, and Hart 1990). Finally, employee productivity can have an important effect on the other side of the value equation: cost. External service value can rise even if service quality remains level, if price is reduced. For price to be reduced without a decline in profitability, cost must decline. This reduction in cost (and thus price) can be made possible by improved employee productivity.

Internal Service Quality and Its Relationship to Employee Capability, Satisfaction, Loyalty, and Productivity

The final link in the Service Profit Chain is the relationship between internal service quality and employee capability, satisfaction, loyalty, and productivity. Internal service quality can be defined as the quality of services that employees and managers receive from an organization to enable them to do their jobs. Elements of internal service quality include workplace design, job design, employee selection, reward and recognition systems, training, policies and procedures, management style, goal alignment, and communication and tools (including information technology and automation) for serving internal or external customers. Thus, internal service quality is inherently situational, in that any number of its different elements may be more or less important in different organizations at different times.

Internal service quality has been discussed in both the service management and quality literatures by numerous scholars, including Garvin (1988); Zemke and Bell (1989); Heskett, Sasser, and Hart (1990); Zeithaml, Parasuraman, and Berry

(1990); Hart and Bogan (1992); and Berry (1995).[7] Although these scholars rarely use the term "internal service quality," they illustrate the importance of many of its elements to employee and customer outcomes.

Very little empirical work has been conducted in marketing on internal service quality, possibly because of the lack of organizations currently measuring their performance on it. Two studies (Hallowell, Schlesinger, and Zornitsky 1996; Schlesinger and Zornitsky 1991), however, illustrate a relationship between elements of internal service quality and service capability, as well as a relationship between internal service quality and job satisfaction.

The purpose of this section of the chapter has been to illustrate the relationships in the Service Profit Chain, providing a sample of scholars who have examined them theoretically and empirically. Most of these scholars have examined these relationships independently (the relation of one link to another) or in small groups (e.g., the linkages among satisfaction, loyalty, and profitability). Within the last few years, however, four organizations have begun to measure each of the links in the chain. To our knowledge, none of these organizations has found any of the relationships in the chain to be either absent or so weak as to be insignificant or ineffective. Two of these firms prefer to remain completely anonymous. Another is Sears Roebuck and Co., whose experience is discussed in the next section of this chapter. The fourth firm is a regional bank in the United States which is discussed at length in Loveman (1998).

SEARS AND THE SERVICE PROFIT CHAIN

In 1992, Sears Roebuck and Co. (Sears) incurred a loss of $3.9 billion on sales of $52 billion.[8] What had once been the largest retailing chain in the U.S. trailed behind K-mart and Wal-Mart. In response to this financial loss and related concerns, the board of directors brought in Arthur Martinez to lead Sears Retail Group (and soon thereafter to be named CEO of the entire company). Martinez's efforts to turn around the once great American retailer included selling off non–core retailing operations and revitalizing the core retail operations using a model remarkably similar to the Service Profit Chain. Within 4 years, the consensus in the retail industry suggested that Sears's operations were not only stabilized but improved. This opinion was reflected in Sears's stock price, which increased 274% between September 1992 and June 1997, exceeding the increases in Coca-Cola (which increased 239% in the same period), The Walt Disney Company (140%), and Sears's direct competitor, J. C. Penney (82%).

The turnaround at Sears is attributed by Sears executives in part to the implementation of Service Profit Chain–inspired management. Managers also acknowledge inspiration from Kaplan and Norton's (1996) "Balanced Score-card." Sears's adaptation of the Service Profit Chain was based on the principle that managers knew that they needed to improve financial performance (a lagging indicator) but wanted guidance on what they should do on a day-to-day basis to affect long-term financial improvement. The elements of the Service Profit Chain provided leading indicators that helped to focus managers' attention on what Sears considered the drivers of financial performance, specifically employee and customer measures.

Recognizing that the Service Profit Chain is complex and difficult to communicate easily, Sears executives distilled the chain into what they deemed the three Cs: that Sears needed to be a Compelling place to work, a Compelling place to shop, and a Compelling place to invest. Sears abbreviated the relationships among work, shop, and invest into the following equation:

$$\text{Work} \times \text{Shop} = \text{Invest}.$$

Although formal establishment of causality is not absolute, Sears is comfortable stating that quality of work (defined by measures of employee satisfaction) affects quality of shopping (defined by measures of customer satisfaction), which results in the quality of the organization as an investment. Sears intentionally chose a multiplicative relationship for work and shop because it suggests that if the quality of either component falls below a certain level (one, numerically), the resulting total will be less than the larger of the two measures (i.e., $2 \times 0.8 < 2$). Thus Sears must seek to achieve some degree of balance in its efforts to improve, recognizing that work and shop are inherently related.

Although "work $\times$ shop = invest" is attractively simple, the complete model that Sears uses is more complex and provides more guidance to managers. Sears data[9] suggest that employees' attitudes about their job combine with their attitudes about the company to influence their behavior (including employee retention). These employee behaviors in turn influence customer perceptions of both service quality and merchandise value, which in turn affect customer impression (their term for customer satisfaction), which ultimately affects customer retention and word-of-mouth recommendation. These customer behaviors influence revenue growth and profitability.[10]

Although Sears prefers not to release complete data on these relationships (or the data analysis methodology) for competitive reasons, some information is available. Based on data collected in at least two surveys (conducted with a brief time lag), Sears identified that a 1.3 unit[11] increase in customer impression resulted in a 0.5% increase in revenue growth. Similarly, an increase in employee attitude concerning job and company of 5 units resulted in a 1.3 unit increase in customer impression.

Customer impression at Sears is determined by a complex set of factors, the strongest of which involve employee behaviors and other elements essential to the customer's shopping experience. Customer impression ("shop") was linked most strongly with five components: (a) associate (employee) competency, (b) associate helpfulness, (c) right merchandise in stock, (d) value for price paid, and (e) returning merchandise. Because Sears considers each of these elements as a different dimension of customer value, this finding is consistent with the Service Profit Chain's hypothesis that customer value drives customer satisfaction.

Of the five elements that relate most closely to customer impression, two are employee behaviors—associate competency and associate helpfulness—that Sears has linked to employee attitudes. Sears surveyed its employees on different aspects of their satisfaction with both their job and the company (although some of the questions also loosely relate to employee productivity and capability). The specific statements and questions to which employees responded were the following:

- I like the kind of work I do.
- My work gives me a sense of accomplishment.
- I am proud to say I work at Sears.
- How does the amount of work you are expected to do influence your overall attitude about your job?
- How do your physical working conditions influence your overall attitude about your job?
- How does the way you are treated by those who supervise you influence your overall attitude about the job?
- I feel good about the future of the company.
- Sears is making the changes necessary to compete effectively.
- I understand our business strategy.
- Do you see a connection between the work you do and the company's strategic objectives?

Although Sears has not quantified the relationship between employee attitudes and internal service quality, the company has made significant efforts to improve the level of support given to its front line. In doing so, Sears has improved the tools (tangible and intangible) that employees have for serving customers. For example, to enhance traditional support functions such as training and development, Sears founded a centralized "university" and requires managers to attend classes on a variety of topics. Doing so helped to link training and development activities to behaviors, values, and objectives Sears desired.

Communication was also vastly improved through the development of tools such as Learning Maps™,[12] which are visual "maps" of concepts Sears wanted to share with the front line. Examples of maps include (a) the changes in the retail competitive landscape (a map titled "A New Day on Retail St." outlined new competitors and demographic changes over the last three decades) and (b) the amount of profit Sears earns on a typical dollar of retail sales, which employees had believed to be $0.45 when the actual figure was closer to $0.027 (a map called "The Sears Money Flow"). Use of the maps occurred in a cascade through the organization, with top managers facilitating discussions of the topics with middle managers, who then facilitated discussions with unit and other front-line managers, who in turn facilitated discussions with their front-line and support personnel.

Sears also increased front-line support by reorganizing selling space within the retail units. Furniture was moved to less-expensive, off-mall stores (Sears Home Life stores) to improve return on assets and allow employees to focus on selling higher-turn items. Mall stores were remodeled to modernize the look and feel of selling space. Store managers were given greater latitude, and merchandise was

Figure 12.2 Service Profit Chain Relationships at Sears

updated. In these ways, and numerous others, Sears improved the support it provided to its front-line employees, thus improving internal service quality in an effort to enhance the firm as a compelling place to work. Figure 12.2 presents the Service Profit Chain relationships at Sears.

Implementing the Service Profit Chain at Sears

Understanding relationships such as those in the Service Profit Chain is a strong starting point for an organization, but it is only that: a starting point. The relationships must be accepted by managers and employees, acted on in the day-to-day conduct of business, and integrated into the design of the firm's strategy, structure, and systems.

Sears was fortunate in that many of its top managers intuitively appreciated the relationships illustrated in the Service Profit Chain. According to one top executive, gaining consensus to use a model inspired by the chain was relatively easy, because the group that generated the idea saw it as their own. Disseminating the model within the organization was not as difficult as it might have been in the light of the collective memory of Sears's past, in which employees were knowledgeable and motivated, customers were well served, and loyalty and profits were high. Many individuals in the organization, especially those career managers who had been at Sears in the 1960s and early 1970s, longed for the re-emergence of a similar virtuous cycle.

As open as the firm was to the Service Profit Chain, Sears also took concrete steps to embed the chain into its strategy and systems. For example, one of Arthur Martinez's first tasks was to identify its core customer. Before 1993, Sears had assumed that its core customer was a man interested in items such as tools and appliances. In fact, women with moderate incomes and families emerged as the firm's core decision makers and purchasers. Sears dramatically changed its merchandising and external communications strategy to reflect this new knowledge. The women's clothing department, which had always been somewhat utilitarian, saw an influx of new merchandise buyers, and thus new merchandise. Sears also introduced a cosmetics department. These changes were designed to attract female shoppers into the store to purchase from these areas, as well as from Sears's traditionally strong product lines, such as tools and appliances. A new advertising campaign invited women to "Come see the softer side of Sears." In this effort,

Sears began to hone the customer value element of the Service Profit Chain, which requires an understanding of who the core customer is and how he or she defines value.

Sears also implemented new systems to measure specific elements of the Service Profit Chain, including customer impression and loyalty (the latter tracked through Sears's charge card[13]) as well as employee attitudes about their jobs and the company. In 1998, Sears began testing a system to link an individual customer's service experience with the individual employee(s) who had served that customer. After making a purchase, randomly selected customers received a coupon with their receipt asking them to call a toll-free phone number to activate the coupon and answer a short series of questions about their service encounter. Although the test was still under way at the time of this writing, preliminary results suggest a high response rate and a low incidence of gaming.

Reward systems also were changed. Sears altered its incentive systems to reward all managers above the store-unit level (including top executives) for improving Service Profit Chain measures. At the same time, Martinez announced that he would acquire five times his annual salary in Sears stock, and he set guidelines for similar stock ownership multiples other executives were expected to adopt. A higher percentage of salespeople received performance-rated incentives, and all managers at the store level were included in pay-for-performance programs.

Although the use of Service Profit Chain measures did not extend into the stores themselves, the basis for promotion of operating managers switched from their ability to achieve financial goals to their coaching skills. To advance in the firm, managers had to clearly support their employees, which was determined by measures such as a 360-degree reviewing process (in which managers were reviewed by both superiors and subordinates). This process is one example of a tool that Sears implemented to improve internal service quality, the first element in the Service Profit Chain.

This glimpse into how Sears implemented the Service Profit Chain illustrates several points. First, the managers who will implement the chain must understand and accept the relationships between and among the links in the chain. For Sears, this was relatively easy (and it need not be difficult at other firms). Second, the organization must be willing to measure performance on the elements of the chain. In general, organizations are most effective at measuring lagging indicators such as revenue and profit. They also typically have some experience measuring customer satisfaction, albeit somewhat infrequently and inaccurately (they may not measure the appropriate elements of satisfaction or the appropriate customers). Firms rarely, however, measure employee satisfaction, capability, or (for service firms) productivity, and they almost never examine internal service quality. These latter measurements are essential if a firm is to inspire change and improve profitability using the Service Profit Chain.

Third, firms may benefit (as Sears believes) from linking Service Profit Chain measurements to variable compensation. Although such linked measures represent only a part of total variable compensation for middle managers and executives at Sears, they form a substantial portion of total compensation (Hallowell

1997b). Thus, if managers decide to build their businesses by investing in people and service in a way that does not make financial results immediately apparent, they are rewarded for interim improvements in employee and customer measures, which should ultimately influence financial performance. In this way, Sears accepts the risk of causality in the Service Profit Chain, which encourages managers to focus on the elements of the chain that they can influence directly, knowing that those efforts will be rewarded. In turn, the organization knows that it will be rewarded with greater profit and growth over the long term.

Finally, the importance of an often overlooked element of the Service Profit Chain is well illustrated by the Sears case. As noted previously, the Service Profit Chain has its roots in a view of organizational strategy that integrates the competitive positioning and organizational capabilities perspectives. Observers of the Service Profit Chain often focus on its explicit strategic elements only, believing that the chain is consistent with an organizational capabilities view of strategy exclusively. In fact, implicit in the "external service value" link in the chain is an important dimension of strategy elaborated on in the competitive positioning literature. External service value is value, as perceived by the customer, vis-à-vis the value offerings of competing firms. Thus, a firm may excel on every link in the Service Profit Chain, but if it delivers the same value proposition, in the same quantity, as its competitors, it is unlikely to exhibit unusual growth or profitability.

Sears has recognized the importance of the "external service value" link in two ways. First, by identifying the core customer, learning how she defines value, and changing portions of its merchandise mix and communications strategy, Sears changed its competitive positioning (albeit subtly). Second, Sears executives openly question whether their existing competitive positioning can deliver the growth they will need to remain an attractive investment. There may be excess industry capacity to serve Sears's targeted customer on the dimensions on which Sears currently provides service. The future result of such overcapacity is likely to be price cutting, which will damage Sears as a non–low-cost producer (given that it cannot adopt a truly high-service strategy such as Nordstrom's). Sears acknowledges that it is facing the question, "Will it be enough to do *what* we do and to do it better, or do we need to *do something different*, also doing that well?" Sears thus illustrates the importance of both *what* a firm does and *how well* it does it. Although such a conclusion sounds elementary, it is often overlooked by developers of strategy theory who argue that their single perspective is superior to all others.

NEW DIRECTIONS IN RESEARCH

Where does Service Profit Chain research go from here? Although numerous possibilities exist, two new directions have already emerged. These are known as "full profit potential" and "technology-intermediated services." Both share a common underlying assumption that is integral to the chain itself: that a firm's ability to exceed customer expectations is strategically important because exceeding expectations is at the intersection of the two components of strategy—competitive positioning (having a value proposition higher than that of competitors) and organizational capabilities (being able to deliver that value proposition).[14]

Full Profit Potential

The first of the new directions in which Service Profit Chain research is moving involves a transformation in thinking about the lifetime value of a customer (the value to the firm generated by a loyal customer), referred to as "full profit potential." Analysis of the lifetime value of a customer examines the value of a customer given his or her current buying patterns over an average relationship life span. This remains a relatively radical idea in many organizations where employees and managers see a customer only in terms of the profit he or she will generate as a result of the next transaction. This most typical mind-set is a point in space (in terms of its dimensionality), and looking at the lifetime value of a customer is merely a line—an improvement from one to two dimensions, but still not as multidimensional as the world in which we live.

Increasing the dimensionality of the model requires a new question to be asked: What if the customer's behavioral patterns could be changed? Specifically, what if the customer would buy more? What if the "what is bought" had a higher margin? What if he or she would buy for a longer period? What if the firm could sell to more customers? These questions expand the model to three or more dimensions. Now, instead of a point in space (the value of a customer defined as the value of the next transaction) or a line (the value of a customer defined as the value accruing to the firm over an average buying life span given current behavior), there is a cube (the value of a customer defined as potential profit over time given specific behavioral changes). By looking at existing behavior and the resulting profit, and contrasting it with the profit potential of new behaviors, the tremendous opportunity in customer relationships can be seen and understood. Figure 12.3 illustrates an example for a grocery retailer in which the shaded area represents existing profit per customer and the cube represents potential profit given specific behavioral changes.

The power of this type of analysis is in illustrating the profit potential of a customer whose needs a firm consistently exceeds to the degree that that customer is willing to change behavior. This may involve doing more business with the firm, conducting business in a different way, or engaging in acts such as word-of-mouth advertising that benefit the organization. In the case of the grocery retailer in Figure 12.3, the behavioral change highlighted involves shifting from being one type of customer (e.g., a prospect, a cherry picker, or an occasional shopper) to a new type of customer (e.g., a primary shopper). It is important that the new relationship is mutually beneficial; it is not an attempt to sell something customers do not appreciate. This is a plan to exceed the expectations of consumers so well that they are willing to change their behavior; thus, it is a plan for value exchange, in which each party believes it receives a high level of value in the relationship.

Full profit potential analyses also can be applied to the relationship between employees (the workforce) and the firm. As with customer/firm analyses, the

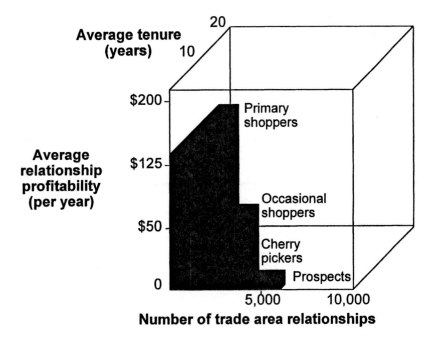

Figure 12.3 Potential Versus Existing Profit per Customer by Type of Customer

purpose of an employee/firm analysis is to explore ways to understand the potential value of an optimized employee/firm relationship and to maximize the value each party receives through their affiliation.

Figure 12.4 illustrates a full profit potential analysis for a workforce/firm relationship considering employee tenure, behavior profile (optimal behavior as opposed to current behavior), and the percentage of a firm's employees having the ability to exhibit optimal behavior.

The notion of value exchange is consistent with the view of the world espoused by the Service Profit Chain in that both approaches view the world as an expanding pie. A focus on the creation of value for employees and customers enables the pie to expand, creating more value for employees, customers, and shareholders.

Technology-Intermediated Services

Another new direction in which Service Profit Chain research is moving explores technology-intermediated services, defined as service encounters in which an employee has been replaced by some form of technology (from automated teller machines to the Internet for some retailers and information providers). Although the right-hand side of the Service Profit Chain remains intact under these new conditions, there is a radical change in the left-hand side because humans are no longer on the front line, interacting with customers. Figure 12.5 illustrates the Technology-Intermediated Service Profit Chain.

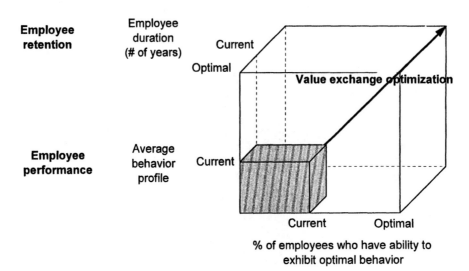

Figure 12.4 Profit Potential Analysis

At this early research stage, interface capability is somewhat of a "black box," although several working hypotheses are developing that may help to elaborate on it in the future. At the heart of this research is the belief that simply changing the interface is not enough for firms exploring new service delivery methods. Instead, these firms need to determine how new interfaces can create more value for both customers and the firm, and implement them in such a way that both parties benefit (Rayport and Sviokla 1994).

Although the substitution of machines for human labor is a practice virtually as old as civilized humanity's existence, this new iteration—in which machines provide service interfaces directly with customers—may ultimately create a new industrial revolution. New interfaces are adding value to some services in completely new ways: encyclopedias can describe what something looks like, but when they are Internet or CD-ROM based, they can show it, and they can say it. Consumers can get vastly more information about a product in a cost-effective manner when shopping on the "net." Costs also can be reduced. Newspapers can distribute their product (information) for a fraction of the cost involved in physical production and distribution. Airlines can provide tickets electronically for considerably less than the cost to issue them on paper.

What do these changes mean? Ultimately, organizations will be able to deliver more value to customers. This could translate into better service at the same cost, the same service at lower cost, or, best of all (from the customer's perspective), better service at lower cost. The captains of industry in the 19th century did this in manufacturing by harnessing scale and scope in industries such as steel and oil. Technology-intermediated service interfaces may ultimately deliver similarly radical productivity improvement in some services in the near future.

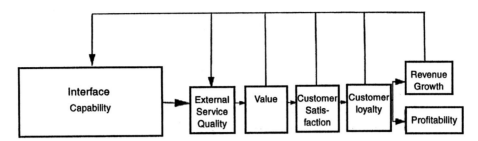

Figure 12.5 Technology-Intermediated Service Profit Chain

NOTES

1. The framework was introduced completely in Heskett et al. (1994).

2. Labor-dominant service firms are defined as those service firms where labor is both an important component of total cost and capable of differentiating the firm's service from that of its competitors.

3. Competitive positioning is generally thought of from the position of the firm, and thus its primary dimensions are cost leadership or differentiation (Porter 1980). When viewed from the customer's perspective, however, competitive positioning relates to price and differentiation. The Service Profit Chain incorporates both perspectives: Customers are interested in relative price while firms are interested in both price and costs.

4. This portion of the chapter draws heavily on Hallowell (1996) and Loveman (1998).

5. Some firms prefer to calculate lifetime value using revenue, rather than profit, figures. Doing so may be helpful for firms in industries characterized by having thin margins because the numbers attached to the value of a customer remain large. In this way, the value of a customer may continue to have a motivational impact on service employees.

6. This concept has elements that are similar to those in "mass customization" as espoused by Pine, Pepper, and Rogers (1995).

7. A more complete discussion of these works can be found in Hallowell, Schlesinger, and Zornitsky (1996).

8. Information in this section, unless otherwise referenced, was derived from Hallowell (1997b) and the underlying research for that case study.

9. Sears worked with Claes Fornell International, which used causal pathway modeling to establish the relationships described (e.g., see Anderson and Fornell, chapter 15, this volume).

10. See Rucci, Kirn, and Quinn (1998) for a diagram of these relationships.

11. "Unit" refers to the unit of measure Sears used to measure work and shop elements.

12. Learning Map[TM] visuals are trademark products created and owned solely by Root Learning, Inc. of Perrysburg, Ohio.

13. Management acknowledged that tracking loyalty through the Sears charge was imperfect, but given the ubiquity of Sears cards (Sears is the largest provider of store credit in the United States) and many customers' use of the card (Sears accepted no other form of credit except its Discover card until 1993), management considered the practice less problematic than it might have been for other department stores.

14. The authors acknowledge that in some cases, competitive positioning can contribute to a firm's ability to deliver its value proposition (Hallowell 1997a; Porter 1996).

REFERENCES

Anderson, Eugene W. and Claes Fornell (1994), "A Customer Satisfaction Research Prospectus," in *Service Quality: New Directions in Theory and Practice*, Roland T. Rust and Richard Oliver, eds. Thousand Oaks, CA: Sage, 241-68.

——, ——, and Donald R. Lehmann (1994), "Customer Satisfaction, Market Share and Profitability: Findings From Sweden," *Journal of Marketing*, 58 (July), 53-66.

—— and Mary Sullivan (1993), "The Antecedents and Consequences of Customer Satisfaction for Firms," *Marketing Science*, 12 (Spring), 125-43.

Berry, Leonard L. (1995), *On Great Service*. New York: Free Press.

Boulding, William, Ajay Kalra, Richard Staelin, and Valarie A. Zeithaml (1993), "A Dynamic Process Model of Service Quality: From Expectations to Behavioral.Intentions," *Journal of Marketing Research*, 30 (February), 7-27.

Buzzell, Robert D., Bradley T. Gale, and Ralph G. M. Sultan (1975), "Market Share—A Key to Profitability," *Harvard Business Review*, 53 (January-February), 97-105.

Fornell, Claes (1992), "A National Customer Satisfaction Barometer: The Swedish Experience," *Journal of Marketing*, 56 (January), 6-21.

Garvin, David A. (1988), *Managing Quality*. New York: Free Press.

Grant, Alan W. H. and Leonard A. Schlesinger (1995), "Realize Your Customers' Full Profit Potential," *Harvard Business Review*, 73 (September-October), 59-72.

Gummesson, Evert (1992), "Quality Dimensions: What to Measure in Service Organizations," in *Advances in Services Marketing and Management*, Vol. 1, Teresa A. Swartz, Stephen W. Brown, and David E. Bowen, eds. Greenwich, CT: JAI, 177-205.

Hallowell, Roger (1996), "The Relationships of Customer Satisfaction, Customer Loyalty, and Profitability: An Empirical Study," *The International Journal of Service Industry Management*, 7(4), 27-42.

—— (1997a), "Dual Competitive Advantage in Labor-Dependent Services: Evidence, Analysis, and Implications," in *Advances in Services Marketing and Management*, Vol. 6, David E. Bowen, Teresa A. Swartz, and Stephen W. Brown, eds. Greenwich, CT: JAI, 23-59.

—— (1997b), *Sears Roebuck and Co. (A) and (B)*, Harvard Business School Cases 9-898-007 and 9-898-008. Boston: Harvard Business School Case Services.

——, Leonard A. Schlesinger, and Jeffrey Zornitsky (1996), "Internal Service Quality, Customer and Job Satisfaction: Linkages and Implications for Managers," *Human Resource Planning*, 19(2), 20-31.

Hart, Christopher W. L. and Christopher E. Bogan (1992), *The Baldrige*. New York: McGraw-Hill.

Heskett, James L. (1986), *Managing in the Service Economy*. Boston: Harvard Business School Press.

——, Thomas O. Jones, Gary W. Loveman, W. Earl Sasser, Jr., and Leonard A. Schlesinger (1994), "Putting the Service Profit Chain to Work," *Harvard Business Review*, 72 (March-April), 164-74.

——, W. Earl Sasser, Jr., and Christopher W. L. Hart (1990), *Breakthrough Service*. New York: Free Press.

——, Leonard A. Schlesinger, and W. Earl Sasser, Jr. (1997), *The Service Profit Chain*. New York: Free Press.

Jones, Thomas O. and W. Earl Sasser, Jr. (1995), "Why Satisfied Customers Defect," *Harvard Business Review*, 73 (November-December), 88-99.

Kaplan, Robert S. and David P. Norton (1996), *The Balanced Scorecard: Translating Strategy Into Action*. Boston: Harvard Business School Press.

Loveman, Gary W. (1998), "Employee Satisfaction, Customer Loyalty, and Financial Performance: An Empirical Examination of the Service Profit Chain in Retail Banking," unpublished paper, Harvard Business School.

March, James and Herbert Simon (1958), *Organizations*. New York: John Wiley and Sons.

Mowday, Richard T., Layman W. Porter, and Richard M. Steers (1982), *Employee Organization Linkages*. New York: Academic Press.

Nelson, Eugene T., Roland T. Rust, Anthony J. Zahorik, Robin L. Rose, Paul Betalden, and Beth A. Siemanski (1992), "Do Patient Perceptions of Quality Relate to Hospital Financial Performance?" *Journal of Health Care Marketing*, 13 (December), 1-13.

Pine, B. Joseph, Don Pepper, and Martha Rogers (1995), "Do You Want to Keep Your Customers Forever?" *Harvard Business Review*, 73 (March-April), 103-8.

Porter, Michael E. (1980), *Competitive Strategy*. New York: Free Press.

—— (1996), "What Is Strategy?" *Harvard Business Review*, 74 (November-December), 61-78.

Prahalad, Coimbatore K. and Gary Hamel (1990), "The Core Competence of the Corporation," *Harvard Business Review*, 68 (May-June), 105-11.

Rayport, Jeffrey F. and John J. Sviokla (1994), "Managing in the Marketspace," *Harvard Business Review*, 72 (November-December), 141-50.

Reichheld, Frederick F. (1996), *The Loyalty Effect*. Boston: Harvard Business School Press.

———— and W. Earl Sasser, Jr. (1990), "Zero Defections: Quality Comes to Services," *Harvard Business Review*, 68 (September-October), 105-11.

Roethlisberger, F. J. and William J. Dickson (1939), *Management and the Worker.* Cambridge, MA: Harvard University Press.

Rucci, Anthony J., Steven P. Kirn, and Richard T. Quinn (1998), "The Employee-Customer-Profit Chain at Sears," *Harvard Business Review*, 76 (January-February), 82-98.

Rust, Roland T. and Anthony J. Zahorik (1991), "The Value of Customer Satisfaction," working paper, Vanderbilt University.

————and———— (1993), "Customer Satisfaction, Customer Retention, and Market Share," *Journal of Retailing*, 69 (Summer), 193-215.

————, ————, and Timothy L. Keiningham (1995), "Return on Quality (ROQ): Making Service Quality Financially Accountable," *Journal of Marketing*, 59 (April), 58-70.

Sasser, W. Earl, Jr., Christopher W. L. Hart, and James L. Heskett (1991), *The Service Management Course: Cases and Readings.* New York: Free Press.

Schlesinger, Leonard A. and Jeffrey Zornitsky (1991), "Job Satisfaction, Service Capability, and Customer Satisfaction: An Examination of Linkages and Management Implications," *Human Resource Planning*, 14(2), 141-49.

Schneider, Benjamin and David E. Bowen (1985), "Employee and Customer Perceptions of Service in Banks: Replication and Extension," *Journal of Applied Psychology*, 70(3), 423-33.

———— and ———— (1995), *Winning the Service Game.* Boston: Harvard Business School Press.

————, John J. Parkington, and Virginia M. Buxton (1980), "Employee and Customer Perceptions of Service in Banks," *Administrative Science Quarterly*, 25, 252-67.

Sewell, Carl and Paul B. Brown (1990), *Customers for Life.* New York: Pocket Books.

Skinner, Wickham (1974), "The Focused Factory," *Harvard Business Review*, 52 (May-June), 113-21.

Storbacka, Kaj, Tore Strandvik, and Christian Grönroos (1994), "Managing Customer Relationships for Profit: The Dynamics of Relationship Quality," *The International Journal of Service Industry Management*, 5(5), 21-38.

Wernerfelt, Birger (1984), "A Resource-Based View of the Firm," *Strategic Management Journal*, 5(2), 171-80.

Zeithaml, Valarie A. (1981), "How Consumer Evaluation Processes Differ Between Goods and Services," in *Marketing of Services*, James H. Donnelly and William R. George, eds. Chicago: American Marketing Association, 186-90.

————, Leonard L. Berry, and A. Parasuraman (1988), "Communication and Control Processes in the Delivery of Service Quality," *Journal of Marketing*, 52 (April), 35-48.

————, A. Parasuraman, and Leonard L. Berry (1990), *Delivering Quality Service.* New York: Free Press.

Zemke, Ron and Chip R. Bell (1989), *Service Wisdom.* Minneapolis, MN: Lakewood Books.

13

Estimating the Return on Quality

Providing Insights Into Profitable Investments in Service Quality

ANTHONY J. ZAHORIK
ROLAND T. RUST
TIMOTHY L. KEININGHAM

WHAT HAPPENED TO THE QUALITY MOVEMENT?

The quality revolution has reached maturity in the United States. The initial euphoria generated by books such as Crosby's *Quality Is Free* (Crosby 1979) and others has met its limitations. The Total Quality Management (TQM) movement that promised that America could indeed compete with the Japanese, whose product quality had become superior during the 1970s and 1980s, has often found mixed results in American companies.

There is no question that the movement served as a wake-up call to many U.S. industries that had begun to take their customers for granted. A "quality revolution" was begun in American industry in both the goods and services sectors, and to meet the business world's demand for advice on how to proceed during the late 1980s and early 1990s, the business press rushed to market a tremendous number of books dealing with quality practices and customer satisfaction. Their content ranged from anecdotes (Zemke and Schaaf 1989) to implementation guides (Deming 1986; Heskett, Sasser, and Hart 1990; Juran and Gryna 1980).

AUTHORS' NOTE: The authors acknowledge the contributions of Stephen Clemens and Daniela Kudernatsch to research discussed in this chapter.

The result of this new obsession was often quite positive. Many slumbering American companies woke up to the new competitive, global realities, and their products and services are once again considered world class.

On the other hand, some of the quality practices that were transplanted from Japan to America, either in whole or in part, were found to be incompatible with American industrial culture (Arnold and Plas 1993; Grant, Shani, and Krishnan 1994). Moreover, many firms became disillusioned when they found themselves in financial difficulty because of the high cost and small returns from many investments in quality improvements.

There are some notable examples of companies that spent lavishly on quality programs and received high ratings for the quality of their products, services, and processes, but found that this spending did not pay off in profits and customer loyalty. For example, in 1990, IBM chairman John Akers put full management support behind a companywide quality improvement program called Market-Driven Quality (Bemowski 1991), the accomplishments of which included a Malcolm Baldrige National Quality Award for its Rochester division in 1990 and NASA's quality and excellence award, the George M. Low Trophy, in 1992. Nevertheless, the company's sales did not improve, and it was forced to lay off tens of thousands of workers, suffered record losses, and pushed Akers into retirement. Another Baldrige winner, the Wallace Company, a Houston pipe distributor to the oil industry, went bankrupt and was liquidated within 2 years of receiving its prize after losing $300,000 per month (Rust, Zahorik, and Keiningham 1994). In another highly publicized case, Florida Power & Light won Japan's coveted Deming prize, but ratepayers refused to bear the extraordinary cost of doing so, and most of the quality programs were dismantled ("The Post-Deming Diet" 1991; Wiesendanger 1993).

That is not to say that the proponents of the Total Quality Movement were wrong. In spite of the aforementioned examples, the relationship between quality and profitability has been documented by many authors. Studies that compare profits and quality ratings across companies have long found that those firms with the highest quality in their industries or with the most satisfied customers tend to be the most profitable (Anderson, Fornell, and Lehmann 1994; Anderson, Fornell, and Rust 1997; Buzzell and Gale 1987; Fornell 1992; Nelson et al. 1992). The relationship was also validated by *Business Week* ("Betting to Win" 1993) when it found that stocks of Baldrige Award winners had outperformed the Standard & Poor's 500 by 33% to 89%.

In general, the problem is not with the objective of improved quality, but in what companies choose to emphasize when they seek to improve quality. Quality is in the eyes of the customer. To remain competitive, companies must invest in aspects of their products that customers value. "High quality" in aspects of the product or service that the customer does not use or appreciate is wasted unless it has other profit-generating effects, such as lower production costs. In short, management must treat spending on quality improvements as an investment, which means that it must determine whether such spending will result in higher profits somehow, or will merely add to costs. We refer to a measure of the return on these investments as "Return on Quality" or ROQ.

The growing importance of ROQ analysis has attracted analysts using several approaches. For example Dillon et al. (1997) describe the use of a structural equations model to predict the profit impacts of service upgrades at a credit card company. (See Zahorik and Rust 1992 for a survey of earlier attempts to understand this issue.) In this chapter, we describe a different method, using data captured in standard customer satisfaction surveys and basic information about market dynamics to predict the effects on market share and profitability of increased quality. Details are available in Rust, Zahorik, and Keiningham (1994).

STRUCTURING THE PROBLEM TO INVEST WISELY IN QUALITY

Quality affects profits in several ways. Costs of production are lower and revenues are increased.

Lower Costs of Production

The premise is that it is cheaper to produce a product or service correctly the first time than it is to absorb the costs of rework, handling customer complaints, and other activities that will be required to "make good" on a defective product (Gryna 1988). This preventive aspect is what Crosby (1979) had in mind when he titled his influential book *Quality Is Free*. These costs can be quite large in the manufacturing of goods, so the philosophy that quality can pay for itself helped win many converts to the quality movement. The cost savings may not be as dramatic in service industries where there is a high degree of customization, but they can still be considerable (Anderson, Fornell, and Rust 1997).

In general, these internal costs are the first place one should look for returns, because the cost savings can be large, the positive impact on customer satisfaction can be immediate, and the diagnosis of causes generally is straightforward. Cost reductions from the elimination of sloppy production practices are the "low hanging fruit" of quality improvement efforts.

On the other hand, the search for these problems is internally focused, rather than customer focused. When improvements greatly reduce the cost of providing the intended product, the value of the effort is clear; however, many "improvements" may not significantly reduce costs and may even increase them. Some improvements are apparent only to the designers or engineers who manage the process and may be invisible to customers; these are the spending efforts that tend to reduce ROQ.

Increased Revenues

Improved quality also increases profits by increasing units sold in three ways: customer retention, attraction of new customers, and increased usage rates. We discuss each in turn.

Increased Retention of Current Customers

Increased retention of its customers increases a firm's market share and can have a significant impact on profits (Reichheld and Sasser 1990). Many customer satisfaction studies have shown a clear relationship between customer satisfaction and retention (Anderson and Sullivan 1993; Boulding et al. 1993; Fornell 1992; Fornell and Wernerfelt 1987; Rust et al. 1999; Rust and Zahorik 1993; Rust, Zahorik, and Keiningham 1994, 1995; Woodside, Frey, and Daly 1989). The relationship between satisfaction and repurchase intention is easy to measure using standard customer satisfaction surveys and is a regularly observed result in proprietary studies.

Attraction of New Customers

Improved quality is likely to be an attraction to new customers as well, both those currently patronizing the competition and newcomers to the market. These newly won customers will have heard about the improved quality through several channels, most notably by word of mouth from the firm's current customers and from advertising in which the firm touts its new standards.

Word of mouth has long been recognized as an important marketing communication (Arndt 1967), and the manner in which product news spreads through populations has been modeled by many scholars from sociology (Rogers 1962) to marketing (Bass 1969; Sultan, Farley, and Lehmann 1990). Most practitioners of customer satisfaction measurement find positive relationships between overall satisfaction and a customer's willingness to recommend the firm to others. Danaher and Rust (1996) found that sales of a cellular telephone service were affected by both advertising and word-of-mouth effects driven by quality improvements. Even though many customer satisfaction questionnaires ask about customer willingness to recommend, however, little research has been done to help marketers to understand how to use the data for practical predictions of future sales. There are several practical problems in using purchase intention data to forecast sales that unfortunately make such analyses impractical for most firms.

Lags. First, whereas repurchase schedules by current customers may follow a regular, or at least predictable, pattern, the effects of word of mouth on sales are much harder to predict. Kordupleski, Rust, and Zahorik (1993) found a lagged correlational relationship between customer satisfaction with an industrial good and sales to other customers that could be interpreted as being due to the spread of word of mouth, and the lag was 4 to 6 months. Service providers such as restaurants or low-cost consumer goods could be expected to have much shorter lag times. Understanding the lag for a given product and relating it to customer satisfaction requires much more data than a customer satisfaction survey typically provides.

Poor measures of word-of-mouth activity. Second, unlike advertising, which is controlled by the firm and can be measured for recall and persuasion, there is really no way to directly measure the amount of word of mouth or to assess its quality. Word of mouth must be treated at the moment as an unmeasurable black box relationship between customer satisfaction and subsequent increases in sales to new customers.

Poor sales data. Third, the final part of the puzzle necessary to measure the impact of word of mouth is data on new and crossover sales. In our experience very few companies keep careful records on whether a given sale is to a current, new, or competitor's customer, so only aggregate sales data are available. Without this information, it is not possible to determine the separate effects of improved retention versus increased capture of new customers.

Increased Usage Rates

A final oft-cited effect of improved quality on profits is the purported heavier usage and therefore greater revenue contribution by longer-term customers. Reichheld and Sasser (1990) found that longer-term holders of credit cards tend to use them more, a result that many managers corroborate. If increased quality improves satisfaction and increased satisfaction improves retention rates, the chain of effects implies yet another benefit of investments in quality. The linkage may not necessarily be due to increased retention, however. Danaher and Rust (1996) found a positive relationship between satisfaction and service usage even in a new cellular phone market. They found evidence for a proposed alternative mechanism to explain this relationship, namely that satisfactory products and services have higher utility and so warrant a higher percentage allocation of the customer's time and resources. Whatever the cause, many companies report positive relationships between customer satisfaction and sales.

The relationships between satisfaction, repurchase intent, and actual purchase volume are evident in Figures 13.1a and 13.1b. These data describe a monthly information subscription service.

This discussion suggests that the most sensible place for organizations to begin to measure the effects of customer-driven quality is on the benefits of increased customer retention. This measure focuses on the most immediate effect of quality improvement—the effect on one's own customers, who will be the first to experience it. Moreover, repurchase intentions can be gathered, along with customer satisfaction data, by standard survey methods. With improved record keeping that allows customers' stated intentions to be calibrated with actual retention rates, these numbers can provide reasonably solid forecasts.

MODELING THE CHAIN OF EFFECTS

Modeling the impact of quality improvements on retention and profits requires a multistage model, as depicted in Figure 13.2. In this model, company performance

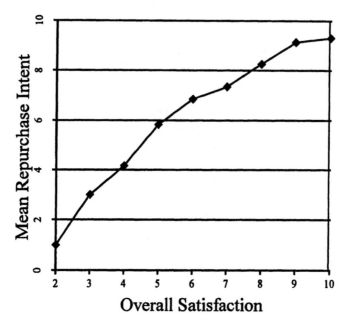

Figure 13.1a Repurchase Intention Increases With Overall Satisfaction

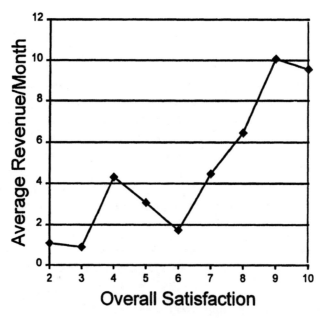

Figure 13.1b Revenues Tend to Be Highest for Highly Satisfied Customers

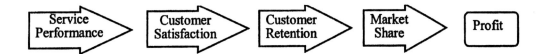

Figure 13.2 The Chain of Effects That Lead to Profit

influences customer satisfaction, which in turn affects customer willingness to remain loyal. Current customer loyalty affects market share and profitability.

We will discuss the process of modeling this chain of events in several stages. (Details are provided in Rust, Zahorik, and Keiningham 1994.) First, one must be able to understand what drives customer satisfaction and the extent to which customer satisfaction drives loyalty. Next, one must translate changes in loyalty into changes in sales volume and market share. Finally, revenue and cost data can be brought in so the analyst can compare the investment in quality with the changes in contribution to be realized from the change in sales volume. These comparisons allow the calculation of ROQ.

The Drivers of Overall Satisfaction

The initial step in an ROQ analysis is to understand what determines customers' overall satisfaction, so that investments can be made in areas truly critical to customers. The relationship among the components of a service and overall satisfaction is often represented as a hierarchy, as in Figure 13.3 (Kudernatsch 1998). This particular example depicts the structure of customer satisfaction with the call center of a telephone/Internet-accessed retail investment bank. In such a hierarchy, overall satisfaction that drives retention is always the root. Overall satisfaction is in turn determined by satisfaction with various components, or "processes," of the service. Satisfaction with the various processes further depends on satisfaction with process details, or "subprocesses." Specific service encounters, often referred to as "moments of truth," could be processes or subprocesses, depending on their complexity or impact on overall satisfaction. Although this dissection process could continue further, the practical limitations on questionnaire length generally require that the firm dig no more deeply than the subprocess level.

Well-established methods exist to help the analyst identify the structure of this tree. Exponents of Quality Function Deployment (QFD) and the House of Quality (Hauser and Clausing 1988) have been developing similar hierarchies, called affinity diagrams, for decades to understand what drives customer perceptions of quality (Nayatani et al. 1994).

The first step is to identify all likely processes and subprocesses using qualitative research sessions with customers and employees, as well as literature searches, sifting of complaint files, and management brainstorming. It is most critical at this stage that no critical "drivers of satisfaction" be overlooked, so the list of candidate "turn-offs" and "turn-ons" can easily consist of several hundred items.

PROCESSES

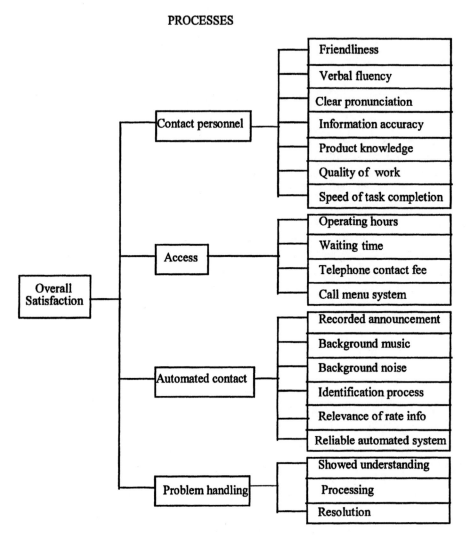

Figure 13.3 A Satisfaction Hierarchy for a Call Center Bank
SOURCE: Based on Kudernatsch (1998).

The second stage requires the analyst to group these individual items into a coherent tree structure. Developing multilevel structures for these hierarchies is important for the subsequent analysis. The authors' experience with numerous field studies suggests that flat hierarchies (i.e., with only two levels)—in which all details are linked directly to overall satisfaction, with no process-level measures taken—often lead to very unsatisfactory and unactionable results. In any event, the structure selected must satisfy several criteria:

1. It must reflect how customers see the service and its components.
2. The processes should be reasonably independent of each another, as should the subprocesses within each process. To make actionable and targeted recommenda-

tions to management regarding quality improvements, the various processes must be defined in such a way that steps to improve one do not necessarily affect others (i.e., they are independent). In particular, satisfaction ratings with the various components of the service should be uncorrelated with one another.

3. Actionability of recommendations also requires that the processes and subprocesses correspond to areas of management responsibility.

Several approaches exist for establishing a hierarchical structure among these items (Griffin and Hauser 1993), including the use of panels of experts to structure items into processes and subprocesses, as well as research tasks in which samples of customers are asked to group related and unrelated items. (Some analysts also use factor analysis to find natural structures based on pilot studies of customer satisfaction ratings on the list of items, but in our experience, this data-driven approach can lead to unactionable structures. Moreover, to derive relative importance scores, it is useful to have an independent satisfaction rating of each process, rather than simply a factor score composed of ratings of related subprocesses.) The final hierarchy then usually reflects a workable compromise among customer perceptions, management areas of responsibility, and the analyst's theory of the chains of influences among the various concepts being measured.

The hierarchy also becomes the backbone of the customer satisfaction questionnaire and the subsequent ROQ analysis. The "nodes" of the hierarchy have been determined to be the issues that most affect customer satisfaction and loyalty and are, therefore, the issues whose performance must be tracked with customers. The questionnaire must ask customers to rate satisfaction with each node of the hierarchy: repurchase intention, overall satisfaction, overall satisfaction with each process, and satisfaction with each subprocess. The analysis of the data will help management set priorities for the issues where improvement is necessary.

COLLECTING AND ANALYZING THE DATA

Management needs two pieces of information from the survey to begin to allocate resources to a quality improvement strategy: (a) how the firm is doing and where improvement is possible, and (b) which of those areas is likely to have large impacts on levels of overall satisfaction and loyalty, and which ones customers do not care about. We describe both streams of requisite information.

Performance Measurement

The first set of information is the basic "report card summary" that most companies extract from their satisfaction survey data: means, top and bottom box scores, and other characterizations of the data that can be used to assess current performance against that of previous periods or against competitors. These data also can be used to compare the firm's performance in various areas.

This information alone is not an adequate indication of where funds can be invested profitably to improve retention. Not all processes and subprocesses have the same impact on overall satisfaction, so a low score in a particular area does not necessarily indicate the need for immediate improvement there. Management must invest the organization's funds only where investment will result in a payout of increased retention. An additional step therefore is necessary—the determination of relative importance.

The hierarchical structure identified earlier can be used to identify processes with the greatest impact, by determining correlational effects between overall satisfaction and satisfaction with each of the processes. Managers will want to invest only in improving process and subprocess areas that will affect overall satisfaction and retention, and, of course, that also need a lot of work. Areas where the firm is doing very well or that have a low impact on retention have no immediate need for increased investment.

Determining Derived Importance

Some analysts ask customers directly about the importance of service attributes (Parasuraman, Zeithaml, and Berry 1988). This method produces individual-level data that can be used for segmentation analysis and other important uses. It also can double the length of a questionnaire, however, and individual-level information may not be relevant to the analysis. If the analyst needs only to determine the aggregate-level importance of processes and subprocesses, these can be derived directly from just the satisfaction scores using correlations. If variation in satisfaction with a process across individual customers is reflected in a similar variation in overall satisfaction scores, then the high correlation is interpreted to mean that the process must be "important" as a "driver" of satisfaction. If variations in satisfaction with the process are only weakly reflected in corresponding variations in overall satisfaction, the low correlation suggests that the process is "unimportant."

In general, it is unwise to infer causality from correlational data; however, doing so has become common practice in customer satisfaction research, possibly for two reasons. First, years of discussions with customers support the notion that overall satisfaction indeed depends on satisfaction with specific aspects of a service, and that they are related. Second, in practice, the correlations with overall satisfaction vary considerably across processes, and in reasonable ways, supporting the notion that satisfaction with processes is not the result of a halo effect emanating from the overall impression but that causality does go from subprocess to process, and from process to overall satisfaction.

The correlational relationships typically are measured using pairwise correlations or multiple regression, in which overall satisfaction is the dependent variable and process-level satisfaction scores are the independent variables. (To understand the drivers of satisfaction with processes at the next level, the process scores become the dependent variables and their respective subprocess scores become the independent variables in turn.) The standardized coefficients of the regression may be compared to determine the relative importance of the processes, provided that the predictors are not correlated with one another. In practice, processes often are highly correlated, making regression a suboptimal tool for this task. Procedures for dealing with multicollinearity abound, including ridge regression (Hoerl and Kennard 1970) or the equity estimator (Krishnamurthy and Rangaswamy 1989, 1994; Rangaswamy and Krishnamurthy 1991), but practitioners often cite unsatisfactory results from using them in this context.

The whole issue of multicollinearity can be sidestepped for the moment by the common practice of comparing the simple pairwise correlations between overall satisfaction and the individual processes (Rust et al. 1996). This practice clearly and unambiguously shows which processes are correlated with overall performance, but there is a trade-off with the ability to predict the effects of quality improvements—it is unclear from the data what will happen if management decides to improve the performance of one of two highly correlated processes. Will satisfaction with the other go up as well, or might the correlation between the two processes have been spurious? Management judgment is useful and necessary to adjust forecasts of the results of quality improvements involving highly correlated processes. It is for this reason that we recommended previously that the analyst seek a structure based on independent processes, if possible.

We also mentioned that results of the analysis are clearer when the questionnaire measures satisfaction at the process level as well as the subprocess level. This recommendation is based on the fact that the correlations between subprocesses and overall satisfaction are typically small and erratic, making them hard to interpret. Results are generally much more interpretable when the process-level measures are used as intermediary variables to determine importance.

Putting Them Together

The report card scores and importance measures are best summarized in the familiar form of a performance-importance diagram, such as that in Figure 13.4. The diagram clearly shows that the process in most dire need of attention is "Access." Being in the upper left-hand corner of the diagram means that it has a low satisfaction score and yet is very important to overall satisfaction and retention. Investing in improvements to other processes may have far less impact on retention, and therefore be poorer investments. For example, "Problem handling" has even lower levels of satisfaction but is far less important, and "Contact personnel" is more important but offers far less opportunity for improvement.

THE CONCEPTS OF SATISFACTION AND DELIGHT

Simply satisfying customers may not be enough to generate increases in loyalty and profits. As Figures 13.1a and 13.1b showed in the case of the information subscription service, loyalty increases as satisfaction increases. Although one

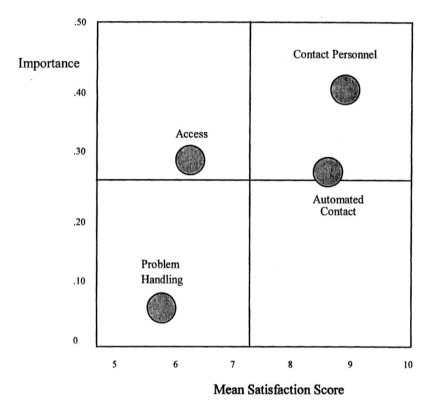

Figure 13.4 A Performance-Importance Diagram Based on Mean Performance Scores Showing the Drivers of Overall Satisfaction for a Call Center Bank

SOURCE: Based on Kudernatsch (1998).

might characterize a score of 6 or 7 on this firm's 10-point scale as moderate satisfaction for the customer, average repurchase intention scores become close to certainty, and the highest level of sales are achieved only when the customer gives the very highest ratings of 9 or 10. Such qualitatively different levels of satisfaction are commonly observed. In particular, although satisfaction is often measured on a 7- or 10-point scale, in fact there are only three levels of satisfaction that customers pass through that are of interest to most managers: dissatisfaction, satisfaction, and delight (Rust, Zahorik, and Keiningham 1994).

The definition of satisfaction generally accepted in the marketing literature is based on "expectancy disconfirmation," or the difference (positive or negative) between what a customer believes he or she actually got and what was expected beforehand (Day 1984; Oliver 1980; Olshavsky and Miller 1972; Olson and Dover 1976). Expectations are themselves the result of customers' knowledge of what other companies are providing, what the company itself has claimed it can do in its advertising, and what word of mouth and past experience have led the customer to expect from this particular provider. If customers believe that performance met or exceeded their expectations, they are by definition *satisfied*;

if not, they are *dissatisfied*. We will also see that performance can greatly exceed expectations; in such cases the customer is said to be *delighted*.

These comparisons are what marketing researchers implicitly assume they are getting when they ask customers about satisfaction. In contrast, the SERVQUAL methodology (Parasuraman, Zeithaml, and Berry 1985, 1988; Zeithaml, Berry, and Parasuraman 1993) attempts to capture disconfirmations directly by asking separate questions about performance and expectations, and determining disconfirmation by computing differences. The reliability of this procedure has been questioned (Brown, Churchill, and Peter 1993; Carman 1990; Cronin and Taylor 1992; Peter, Churchill, and Brown 1993; Teas 1993) due in part to an argument that subjects may have difficulty reconstructing their precise expectations after experiencing a service. Certainly, direct questions regarding importance doubles the length of the questionnaire.

Instead of asking separate performance and expectations questions, many analysts recommend measuring disconfirmation directly by asking subjects to rate their recollections of how they found aspects of the experience from "much worse than expected" to "much better than expected." (Babakus and Boller 1992; Carman 1990; DeSarbo et al. 1994; Devlin, Dong, and Brown 1993; Oliver 1980; Rust, Zahorik, and Keiningham 1994). This disconfirmation approach is also consistent with managers' experience with customer satisfaction and quality assessments. Even when satisfaction is measured on a 10-point scale, managers tend to aggregate the data into three natural categories (DeSarbo et al. 1994):

> *Dissatisfied customers*, who have used one of the categories near the bottom of the scale, say 1-5. Many of these customers probably experienced explicit problems and are upset. For them, perceived performance fell short of expectations, and they are highly likely to switch to another company.
>
> *Just-satisfied customers*, whose expectations have been met, but not exceeded, with ratings of perhaps 6, 7, or even 8. In general, these ratings indicate a parity product, as good as competitive offerings but no better. These customers may be back, but they are vulnerable to competitive marketing.
>
> *Delighted customers*, with extremely high ratings of 9 or 10 (and in some product categories, only the 10s), whose expectations were exceeded by the company's performance.

The organization can increase retention by managing the customers in each group and shepherding them into increasingly positive categories through appropriate quality improvement efforts. The required programs generally differ, however. Turning dissatisfied customers into satisfied customers usually requires a program to seek out and eliminate sources of service breakdowns and problems, whereas turning satisfied customers into delighted ones means finding ever better ways to anticipate customers' needs and surprise them with unexpectedly high-quality service.

Significant increases in retention can be achieved by moving customers from dissatisfied to satisfied, or satisfied to delighted, but real loyalty can be achieved only by maximizing membership in the "delighted" category. The concept of delight (i.e., positive surprise) as a special case of disconfirmation has been the subject of numerous scientific investigations (Chandler 1989; Oliver 1989; Oliver, Rust, and Varki 1997; Westbrook and Oliver 1991; Whittaker 1991), and its effects on building loyalty and increasing spending are well known to marketing managers. In an often-cited example, AT&T found that retention rates among customers rating its products "good" was only 60% compared to a 90% loyalty rate among those giving "excellent" ratings (Gale 1994).

Although any scale can be used to classify customers into these three groups, finding the appropriate division points on a 7- or 10-point satisfaction scale requires empirical investigation. For example, Figure 13.1b strongly suggests that among customers of that firm, a rating of 9 or 10 is qualitatively different from lower ratings, suggesting that a top-2-box measure be used to track delight in that case. Customers of different firms and different product categories may use the same scale differently, so each case must be interpreted for itself.

On the other hand, we have had considerable success with a scale that measures disconfirmation directly using a three-point scale: "worse than expected," "about as expected," and "much better than expected." Note that the two end categories are not symmetrically worded. A problem experienced by many companies with standard satisfaction scales is that of overuse of the top categories by respondents, making it hard to identify truly delighted customers and to track changes in aggregate performance. This asymmetric three-point scale tends to force all but the most enthusiastic responses to the middle category, because of the extreme wording used on the upper end. At the lower end of the scale, dissatisfied customers do not have to have had extremely negative experiences to be at risk of defecting to a competitor.

Diagnosing What Should Be Done

Separating customers into those who are dissatisfied, satisfied, and delighted provides important priorities for management investments in quality. In general, if the number of dissatisfied customers is high, the first priority should be to eliminate the problems that cause dissatisfaction. It may be pointless or even offensive to customers to seek new ways to provide dazzling levels of service while major sources of irritation still persist. Only when the problems have been brought under control and as many customers as is financially feasible have been converted from dissatisfied to satisfied should the firm begin looking for ways to delight the just-satisfied customers.

To see where to invest in these two stages, we recommend developing two sets of performance-importance (PI) diagrams similar to those described earlier, one for drivers of dissatisfaction and one for drivers of delight. Performance can be measured as the percentage of dissatisfied or delighted customers. (Note the reversal of interpretations for high values here.) To measure importance, one can use regression coefficients to be described below or compute pairwise coefficients of association (e.g., ϕ) between overall and process satisfaction or processes and subprocesses. (These would be computed after converting the various measures to dummy variables that indicate whether a person is dissatisfied or not, or

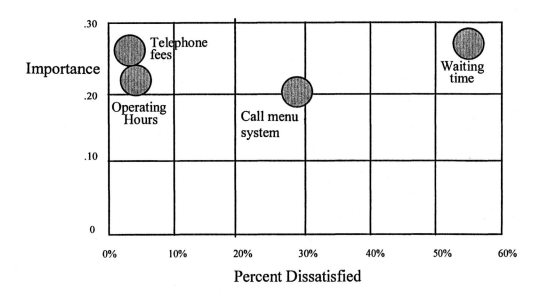

Figure 13.5 A Performance-Importance Diagram Describing Subprocess Drivers of Dissatisfaction for the Process "Access" of the Call Center Bank
SOURCE: Based on Kudernatsch (1998).

delighted or not, as the analysis would warrant.) Figure 13.5 shows such a diagram depicting the status of the four subprocesses of the process "Access" of the call center bank described in Kudernatsch (1998). The bank had found unacceptable levels of overall dissatisfaction with Access that had to be addressed. This PI diagram indicates that waiting time is an important driver of dissatisfaction with access and has a high level of dissatisfaction. It was recommended as the focus of a quality improvement program.

RELATING SATISFACTION LEVELS TO RETENTION

To analytically relate a customer's overall satisfaction to retention, the ROQ model groups customers into the three levels: dissatisfied, satisfied, and delighted. In general, each level has a significantly different mean retention rate, and the firm's overall retention rate is the weighted average of the three values. The percentages of customers in the three groups must add up to 100 percent, so this weighted average can be expressed more efficiently as

$$R = b_0 + b_1 OS + b_2 OD,$$

where R is the overall retention probability, OS is the percentage of satisfied customers (i.e., just satisfied or delighted—or the percentage of customers not dissatisfied), and OD is the percentage of delighted customers. The coefficients of this equation can be estimated by ordinary least squares (OLS) using stated or actual retention measures as the dependent variable and the dummy variables indicating satisfaction and delight as the independent variables. (See Rust, Zahorik, and Keiningham 1995 for details.)

The ROQ model continues the use of the hierarchical structure identified earlier by modeling overall dissatisfaction as the result of dissatisfaction with one or more processes:

$$OS = \beta_0 + \Sigma \beta_i \, PS_i$$

just as overall delight must be the result of delight with one or more processes:

$$OD = \beta_0 + \Sigma \beta_i PD_i.$$

Similarly, positive or negative reactions to each process are modeled as a function of reactions to each of the respective subprocesses.

Because the criterion variables in these equations, when estimated on the individual-level dummy variables, are dichotomous nominal variables, one should properly use logistic regression to analyze these relationships. We have found, however, that OLS provides suitable estimates from a practical standpoint, because changes in the percentage of dissatisfied or delighted customers due to quality improvement efforts are in practice modest. These formulas will be used in the next stage of ROQ analysis to predict changes in retention, share, and profitability resulting from changes in the quality of service provided.

In addition, if multicollinearity among the dummy variables is not severe, the β_is can be used as indicators of the relative importance of the respective processes or subprocesses. As mentioned earlier, however, standard practice is to avoid the issue of multicollinearity by estimating relative importance from the pairwise ϕ coefficients between the relevant satisfaction dummy variables.

ESTIMATING THE RETURN ON QUALITY

Taking Stock

The previous analyses are essential to understand where opportunities for quality improvements might lie. Step 1 is to decide whether the organization must still discover further sources of dissatisfaction, or whether it would be more profitable to find ways to proceed to delight customers. The second stage requires a thorough analysis of the various performance-importance diagrams to identify process- or subprocess-level drivers of dissatisfaction or delight that (a) allow enough room for improvement and (b) will have enough impact on improving retention.

This analysis does not go far enough, however. Seeing an important area in need of improvement is one thing; deciding what to do about it is another. Just because a PI diagram indicates a process with high levels of dissatisfaction and a strong relationship to overall satisfaction does not mean that *any* project designed to address the problem is worthwhile. Some problems are just too expensive to fix. The firm might be better off segmenting its market and concentrating on keeping those customers who are satisfied with what the firm is currently able to provide.

The next stage of the analysis requires management to propose quality improvement projects that are likely to affect satisfaction with the target area. Then ROQ analysis determines whether the projected resulting increase in customer retention and additional profits will cover the cost of implementing the project.

ROQ Analysis

ROQ analysis uses the hierarchical structure determined earlier, and the equations describing the links between nodes of the hierarchy developed in the analysis stage, to predict the financial outcomes of specific quality improvements. For example, in the case of the call center bank, long waiting times were considered a particularly strong determinant of dissatisfaction with access, the process that in turn most determines overall dissatisfaction with the firm. Management might propose an expensive and immediate upgrade of the computerized answering system as well as additional phone personnel to handle the number of incoming calls. Before proceeding with this large expenditure to solve the problem, management should determine if it will be a good investment.

The ROQ model simply estimates the chain of effects from the quality improvement effort to the change in retention (using the equations determined earlier). First of all, the analyst must have some idea of the likely reduction in waiting time dissatisfaction this system upgrade is likely to accomplish. There are several possible ways to determine this likelihood. Initially, the analyst might use management judgment based on past experience, a content analysis of complaints received, or other "soft" types of data. This initial input can be adjusted to worst-case and best-case scenarios to get a feel for the sensitivity of the estimate to the precision of this estimate. If in all cases the resulting impacts on retention and profits are uniformly negative or uniformly positive, a decision to kill or proceed with the project could be made at this stage. If the data suggest possible but uncertain profitability, management might be wise to undertake a pilot project to get a firmer handle on the impact that the proposed project might have on the entire system.

Once a proposed change in subprocess dissatisfaction is provided, an analyst can proceed to use the model to estimate the corresponding chain of effects, described in Figure 13.6. Using the relationships established earlier, a reduction in dissatisfaction with an important subprocess will have a (smaller) effect on reducing dissatisfaction with the entire process of which it is a part. Similarly, the reduction in dissatisfaction with the process will have a (still smaller) effect on reducing overall dissatisfaction. Finally, because some percentage of customers

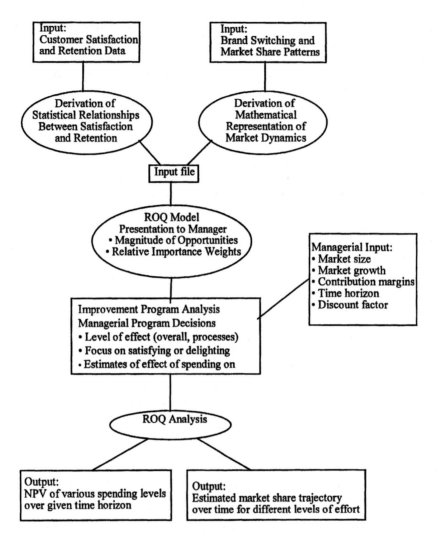

Figure 13.6 Inputs and Outputs of ROQ Analysis

SOURCE: *Return on Quality: Measuring the Financial Impact of Your Company's Quest for Quality*, p. 106, Rust, Zahorik, and Keiningham, © copyright 1994 by Richard D. Irwin. Reprinted with permission.

have been shifted from the ranks of the dissatisfied to the satisfied, the overall retention rate increases, and the firm now keeps customers it would otherwise have lost. This causes an upward change in the firm's market share trajectory over time and increases revenues. This marginal increase in revenues resulting from increased share plus any cost savings from improved work productivity can be compared to the cost of implementing the project (both start-up and ongoing cost requirements) to compute a return on investment, the ROQ.

To implement the analysis, certain measures of the size and switching rates of the market must be established, along with some data on the firm itself:

1. *Retention rates.* The survey asks for stated retention rates. These reported rates need to be reconciled with actual retention rates. For many firms, this number is not well known, but it is essential to calibrate the model.

2. *Attraction percentage.* To understand the switching dynamics of the market, the model requires input of the percentage of new-to-the-market customers who choose the firm's services. Acquiring this number may require a separate survey of top-of-mind awareness or surrogate measures for new customers.

3. *Market size.* The model is expressed in retention rates and market shares, but to convert these numbers to money we need to know how big the game is.

4. *Market share.* Retention rates affect market share. We must know where we are to see where we might go.

5. *Market growth rate.* Most firms have some estimate of this number for general planning. The estimate is critical to predict how large the market will be in subsequent periods.

6. *Average contribution margin per customer.* This number is essential to convert predictions of new customers into marginal revenues. The figure is often expressed as a per-period average. Estimating it requires cooperation with one's cost accounting department.

7. *A time horizon.* Changes in service quality take time to get noticed and to affect retention, so like any investment they take time to pay out. The firm must specify the length of time it will allow the investment to pay for itself. This time allocation will depend on the firm's financial policies and the life cycle of the service improvement under consideration. For example, some moves that provide a temporary competitive advantage may last a very short time as competitors seek to match or better them.

8. *A cost of capital.* There is no reason that investing in quality should not be held to the same standards as other investments the firm might make.

Using this information and assumptions about market dynamics, one can produce payback schedules such as that shown in Figure 13.7. (This chart is based on output from a software program called *nCompass*, described in Keiningham and Clemens 1995.)

In this chart, the financial implications of a program to reduce waiting time are explored for the call center bank we have described. The quality improvement under consideration involved hiring and training enough additional phone agents to increase the capacity of the phone system by four people at all times. An analysis of complaints and load demands led managers to estimate that the percentage of customers dissatisfied with waiting time would drop from 54.3% to 10%. The costs of the program involved an additional investment of $30,000 and ongoing costs of $360,000 per year. If these assumptions are valid, the model predicts that the result would be an increase in the average retention rate from 78% to 79.3% per year. The bank used a 3-year planning horizon and used a 15% discount rate to evaluate the investment.

Figure 13.7 shows that the program may be overpriced (again, given the model assumptions). In particular, although the reduction in dissatisfaction will lead to additional revenues, these increased revenues will not cover the estimated costs of the program within the 3-year horizon. The net present value of cash flows is

Focus of improvement: Waiting time. Currently 54.3% of all customers are dissatisfied with subprocess: waiting time. The proposed improvement will result in 10% being dissatisfied.

Current retention rate: 78%
Proposed retention rate: 79.3%
Discount rate: 15.0%
Projected life (years)   3

Period	0	1	2	3
Market share	.5000	.5046	.5073	.5088
Market size	56,000	78,400	109,760	153,664
Change contribution	$0.00	$136,500.00	$299,250.00	$504,750.00
Expenses	($30,000.00)	($360,000.00)	($360,000.00)	($360,000.00)
Savings	$0.00	$0.00	$0.00	$0.00
Net cash flow	($30,000.00)	($223,500.00)	($60,750.00)	$144,750.00
Net present value	($30,000.00)	($224,347.83)	($270,283.56)	($175,108.08)

Net present value in Period 3: −$175,108.08
Return on quality: −21.3%

Figure 13.7 An ROQ Cash-Flow Forecast Showing a Predicted Negative Rate of Return for a Proposed Quality Improvement Program
SOURCE: Based on Kudernatsch (1998).

−$175,108.08, for a negative return on investment of −21.3%. The bank must find an alternative, more cost-effective way to address waiting times.

CONCLUSION

The scramble to improve quality that began in the 1980s has been tempered by the realities of losses and bankruptcies of companies that did not treat spending on quality as an investment. Spending to improve quality and customer satisfaction can indeed pay handsome dividends, but without an ROQ analysis to guide management, many expenditures fail to pay out. The result is a misguided distrust of all quality and customer satisfaction improvement programs.

ROQ analysis can reverse this trend and put customer satisfaction programs on a sound economic basis. Most of the data necessary to do the computations are already being collected by many firms in their customer satisfaction surveys, internal customer records, competitive market information, and test marketing data. Also, many of the managerial judgments used in the initial estimates of the model are those already made by managers on a regular basis, but their implications are not analytically explored in forecasting models.

By quantifying market share and profit implications of proposed quality improvements, we enable such improvements to compete for funds with other corporate spending programs. Otherwise, quality and satisfaction programs will continue to be regarded as expensive fads that can be slashed in tough times, rather than as critical components of a viable organization's marketing strategy.

REFERENCES

Anderson, Eugene W., Claes Fornell, and Donald R. Lehmann (1994), "Customer Satisfaction, Market Share, and Profitability," *Journal of Marketing*, 58 (July), 53-66.

——, ——, and Roland T. Rust (1997), "Customer Satisfaction, Productivity, and Profitability: Differences Between Goods and Services," *Marketing Science*, 16(2), 129-45.

—— and Mary W. Sullivan (1993), "The Antecedents and Consequences of Customer Satisfaction for Firms," *Marketing Science*, 12 (Spring), 125-43.

Arndt, Johan (1967), "Role of Product-Related Conversations in the Diffusion of New Project," *Journal of Marketing Research*, 4 (August), 291-95.

Arnold, William W. and Jeanne M. Plas (1993), *The Human Touch*. New York: Wiley.

Babakus, Emin and Gregory W. Boller (1992), "An Empirical Assessment of the SERVQUAL Scale," *Journal of Business Research*, 24, 253-68.

Bass, Frank M. (1969), "A New Product Growth Model for Consumer Durables," *Management Science*, 15 (January), 215-27.

Bemowski, Karen (1991), "Big Q at Big Blue," *Quality Progress*, 24 (May), 17-21.

"Betting to Win on the Baldie Winners" (1993), *Business Week*, (October 18), 18.

Boulding, William, Ajay Kalra, Richard Staelin, and Valarie A. Zeithaml (1993), "A Dynamic Process Model of Service Quality," *Journal of Marketing Research*, 30 (February), 7-27.

Brown, Tom J., Gilbert A. Churchill, Jr., and J. Paul Peter (1993), "Improving the Measurement of Service Quality," *Journal of Retailing*, 69 (Spring), 127-39.

Buzzell, Richard and Bradley T. Gale (1987), *The PIMS Principles: Linking Strategy to Performance*. New York: Free Press.

Carman, James M. (1990), "Consumer Perceptions of Service Quality: An Assessment of SERVQUAL Dimensions," *Journal of Retailing*, 66 (Spring), 33-55.

Chandler, Colby H. (1989), "Quality: Beyond Customer Satisfaction," *Quality Progress*, 22 (February), 30-32.

Cronin, J. Joseph and Steven A. Taylor (1992), "Measuring Service Quality: A Reexamination and Extension," *Journal of Marketing*, 56 (July), 55-68.

Crosby, Philip B. (1979), *Quality Is Free*. New York: McGraw-Hill.

Danaher, Peter J. and Roland T. Rust (1996), "Indirect Financial Benefits From Service Quality," *Quality Management Journal*, 3(2), 63-75.

Day, Ralph S. (1984), "Toward a Process Model of Consumer Satisfaction," in *Conceptualization and Measurement of Consumer Satisfaction and Dissatisfaction*, H. Keith Hunt, ed. Cambridge, MA: Marketing Science Institute, 153-83.

Deming, W. Edwards (1986), *Out of the Crisis*. Boston: MIT Center for Advanced Engineering Study.

DeSarbo, Wayne, Leonard Huff, Marcello M. Rolandelli, and Jungwhan Choi (1994), "On Measurement of Perceived Service Quality: A Conjoint Measurement Approach," in *Service Quality*, Roland T. Rust and Richard L. Oliver, eds. Thousand Oaks, CA: Sage, 199-220.

Devlin, Susan, H. K. Dong, and Marbue Brown (1993), "Selecting a Scale for Measuring Quality," *Marketing Research*, 5(3), 12-17.

Dillon, William R., John B. White, Vithala R. Rao, and Doug Filak (1997), " 'Good Science': Use Structural Equation Models to Decipher Complex Customer Relationships," *Marketing Research*, 9 (Winter), 22-31.

Fornell, Claes (1992), "A National Customer Satisfaction Barometer: The Swedish Experience," *Journal of Marketing*, 56 (January), 6-21.

—— and Birger Wernerfelt (1987), "Defensive Marketing Strategy by Customer Complaint Management: A Theoretical Analysis," *Journal of Marketing Research*, 24 (November), 337-46.

Gale, Bradley T. (1994), *Managing Customer Value*. New York: Free Press.

Grant, Robert M., Rami Shani, and R. Krishnan (1994), "TQM's Challenge to Management Theory and Practice," *Sloan Management Review*, 35 (Winter), 25-35.

Griffin, Abbie and John R. Hauser (1993), "The Voice of the Customer," *Marketing Science*, 12 (Winter), 1-25.

Gryna, Frank M. (1988), "Quality Costs," in *Quality Control Handbook*, 4th ed, Joseph M. Juran and Frank M. Gryna, eds. New York: McGraw-Hill, 4.1-4.30.

Hauser, John R. and Don Clausing (1988), "The House of Quality," *Harvard Business Review*, 66 (May-June), 63-73.

Heskett, James L., W. Earl Sasser, Jr., and Christopher W. L. Hart (1990), *Service Breakthroughs*. New York: Free Press.

Hoerl, Arthur E. and Robert W. Kennard (1970), "Ridge Regression: Biased Estimation for Non-Orthogonal Problems," *Technometrics*, 12(1), 55-67.

Juran, Joseph M. and Frank M. Gryna, Jr. (1980), *Quality Planning and Analysis From Product Planning Through Use*. New York: McGraw-Hill.

Keiningham, Timothy L. and Stephen Clemens (1995), *nCompass Users Manual*, unpublished manuscript, Nashville, TN.

Kordupleski, Ray, Roland T. Rust, and Anthony J. Zahorik (1993), "Why Improving Quality Doesn't Improve Quality," *California Management Review*, 35 (Spring), 82-95.

Krishnamurthy, Lakshman and Arvind Rangaswamy (1989), "The Equity Estimator for Marketing Research," *Marketing Science*, 6 (Fall), 336-57.

———— and ———— (1994), "The Statistical Properties of the Equity Estimator: A Reply," *Journal of Business and Economic Statistics*, 12 (April), 149-53.

Kudernatsch, Daniela (1998), *Return on Quality: Ein Ansatz zur monetären Bewertung von Qualitätsverbesserungsmassnahmen—kritische Darstellung und empirische Anwendung im Call Center*. Munich: FGM Verlag.

Nayatani, Yorhinobu, Toru Eiga, R. Futami, and H. Miyagama (1994), *The Seven New QC Tools*. White Plains, NY: Quality Resources.

Nelson, Eugene T., Roland T. Rust, Anthony J. Zahorik, Robin L. Rose, Paul Betalden, and Beth A. Siemanski (1992), "Do Patient Perceptions of Quality Relate to Hospital Financial Performance?" *Journal of Healthcare Marketing*, 13 (December), 1-13.

Oliver, Richard L. (1980), "A Cognitive Model of the Antecedents and Consequences of Satisfaction Decisions," *Journal of Marketing Research*, 42 (November), 460-69.

———— (1989), "Processing of the Satisfaction Response in Consumption: A Suggested Framework and Research Propositions," *Journal of Consumer Satisfaction, Dissatisfaction, and Complaining Behavior*, 2, 1-16.

————, Roland T. Rust, and Sajeev Varki (1997), "Customer Delight: Foundations, Findings, and Managerial Insight," *Journal of Retailing*, 73 (Fall), 311-36.

Olshavsky, Richard and John A. Miller (1972), "Consumer Expectations, Product Performance and Perceived Product Quality," *Journal of Marketing Research*, 9 (February), 19-21.

Olson, Jerry C. and Philip Dover (1976), "Disconfirmation of Consumer Expectations Through Product Trial," *Journal of Applied Psychology*, 64 (April), 179-89.

Parasuraman, A., Valarie A. Zeithaml, and Leonard Berry (1985), "A Conceptual Model of Service Quality and Its Implications for Further Research," *Journal of Marketing*, 48 (Fall), 41-50.

————, ————, and ———— (1988), "SERVQUAL: A Multiple-Item Scale for Measuring Consumer Perceptions of Service Quality," *Journal of Retailing*, 64(1), 12-40.

Peter, J. Paul, Gilbert A. Churchill, Jr., and Tom H. Brown (1993), "Caution in the Use of Difference Scores in Consumer Research," *Journal of Consumer Research*, 19 (March), 655-62.

"The Post-Deming Diet: Dismantling a Quality Bureaucracy" (1991), *Training* 28 (February), 41-43. (Excerpts from two letters sent to employees of Florida Power and Light Co. by James L. Broadhead, FLP's chairman and CEO)

Rangaswamy, Arvind and Lakshman Krishnamurthy (1991), "Response Function Estimation Using the Equity Estimator," *Journal of Marketing Research*, 28 (February), 72-83.

Reichheld, Frederick F. and W. Earl Sasser, Jr. (1990), "Zero Defections: Quality Comes to Services," *Harvard Business Review*, 68 (September-October), 105-11.

Rogers, E. M. (1962), *The Diffusion of Innovation*. New York: Free Press.

Rust, Roland T., Stephen Clemens, John Gregg, Timothy Keiningham, and Anthony Zahorik (1999), "Return on Quality at Chase Manhattan Bank," *Interfaces*, 29(2), 62-72.

————, Greg L. Stewart, Heather Miller, and Debbie Pielack (1996), "The Satisfaction and Retention of Front-Line Employees: A Customer Satisfaction Measurement Approach," working paper, Owen Graduate School of Management, Vanderbilt University.

———— and Anthony J. Zahorik (1993), "Customer Satisfaction, Customer Retention and Market Share," *Journal of Retailing*, 69 (Summer), 193-215.

———, ———, and Timothy L. Keiningham (1994), *Return on Quality: Measuring the Financial Impact of Your Company's Quest for Quality*. Chicago: Richard D. Irwin.

———, ———, and ——— (1995), "Return on Quality (ROQ): Making Service Quality Financially Accountable," *Journal of Marketing*, 59 (April), 58-70.

Sultan, F., John U. Farley, and Donald R. Lehmann (1990), "A Meta-analysis of Applications of Diffusion Models," *Journal of Marketing Research*, 27 (February), 70-77.

Teas, R. Kenneth (1993), "Expectations, Performance Evaluation, and Consumer Perceptions of Quality," *Journal of Marketing*, 57 (October), 18-34.

Westbrook, Robert A. and Richard L. Oliver (1991), "The Dimensionality of Consumption Emotion Patterns and Consumer Satisfaction," *Journal of Consumer Research*, 18 (June), 84-91.

Whittaker, Barrie (1991), "The Path to Excellence," *Canadian Business Review*, 18 (Winter), 18-21.

Wiesendanger, Betsy (1993), "Deming's Luster Dims at Florida Power & Light," *Journal of Business Strategy*, 14 (September-October), 60-61.

Woodside, Arch G., Lisa L. Frey, and Robert Timothy Daly (1989), "Linking Service Quality, Customer Satisfaction and Behavioral Intention," *Journal of Health Care Marketing*, 9 (December), 5-17.

Zahorik, Anthony J. and Roland T. Rust (1992), "Modeling the Impact of Service Quality on Profitability: A Review," in *Advances in Service Marketing and Management*, Vol. 1, Teresa A. Swartz, Stephen W. Brown, and David E. Bowen, eds. Greenwich, CT: JAI, 247-76.

Zeithaml, Valarie A., Leonard Berry, and A. Parasuraman (1993), "The Nature and Determinants of Customer Expectations of Service," *Journal of the Academy of Marketing Science*, 21 (Winter), 1-12.

Zemke, Ron and Dick Schaaf (1989), *The Service Edge: 101 Companies That Profit From Customer Care*. New York: Plume Books.

14

Customer Satisfaction With Service

RICHARD L. OLIVER

Research on the customer satisfaction response is now approaching a mature phase whereby the major antecedents, core mechanisms, and consequences have been identified. As discussed shortly, proposed models of the satisfaction process, including that provided here, detail the many concepts that may be entertained by consumers when forming satisfaction judgments. These concepts—or, more properly, psychological constructs—are generic in nature and pertain to all goods and services. The attributes or features that are unique to the consumable under study are known to operate within a broader consumer psychology and to cause specific satisfaction processes to emerge. The end result of this attribute-process interplay is the familiar satisfaction response.

The purpose of this chapter is to describe a current view of satisfaction mechanisms in the context of service provision. The reader should not expect that these mechanisms will differ qualitatively from those existing in a "product model"; rather, it will be suggested that the nature of service consumption will cause some mechanisms to be more prominent in the final satisfaction judgment and others to be less so. This greater presence of certain mechanisms results from the fact that service provision is much more interpersonal in nature and evocative of affective reactions.

BASIC SATISFACTION MECHANISMS

The origins of satisfaction begin with comparison standards; hence, satisfaction has been referred to as a "comparator" response (Oliver 1997). Beginning with the necessity to fulfill basic needs, individuals have been assessing life outcomes against requirements or desires from the earliest of times. This comparator operation distinguishes satisfaction from other states of affect, such as happiness or pleasure, which can occur without a comparison standard.

Because much of consumption is voluntary, or is undertaken with various substitutable options in advanced economies, these requirements can be translated into expectations. The consumer would be observed to say that a consumable was chosen for purchase because he or she expects that it will fulfill needs, provide pleasure, alleviate pain, or meet other needs or desires. Thus, the expectation becomes the driving force and initial perception for satisfaction responding to occur. Consumers do not necessarily have to process expectations because many exist in passive mode. An example might be the expectation that stores are likely to price their merchandise fairly. Later, the consumer may observe data that falsify this expectation, such as when encountering lower prices elsewhere. This observation now makes the expectation active, resulting in (dis)satisfaction. Thus, passive expectations are as important as active expectations in the satisfaction response.

The previous example illustrates the principle that expectations can be a primary standard against which consumable (e.g., service) performance is compared. The role of performance observation is the second key aspect of satisfaction responses. In fact, all standards used in the satisfaction judgment require that performance be realized in order for that standard to affect satisfaction. Oliver (1997) catalogs a number of these comparators, all of which result in a specific type of cognition recognizable to consumers as influences on satisfaction.

For example, when performance is compared to expectations, a cognition known as expectancy disconfirmation (to be discussed) results. Similarly, performance compared to needs results in need fulfillment, and comparisons to excellence standards result in quality judgments. Comparisons to fairness standards generate perceptions about equity or inequity, those to "what might have been" result in regret, and those to costs and sacrifices yield value. Each of these operations can be couched in terms of whether the expectation is active or passive. Needs, desires for excellence, and costs tend to be active, whereas fairness and the performance of alternatives (the imagined outcome had another option been chosen) tend to be passive.

If one assumes, for the moment, only a single expectation-based comparative operator, the satisfaction process can be viewed in the following manner. Once performance is observed and the comparison to expectations made, a concept known as *expectancy disconfirmation* is realized. Because the disconfirmation can be negative (performance is worse than expected), positive (performance is better than expected), or neutral (performance is as expected), the valence of the disconfirmation (positive, neutral, negative) must be stated. Generally, positive disconfirmation contributes to the positivity of satisfaction, negative disconfirmation contributes to its negativity, and confirmation indeed "confirms" the consumer's expectation.

As noted, standards other than expectations may act as parallel influences on satisfaction through performance comparisons. Often, the difference between what consumers receive and what they hold as a standard is referred to as a discrepancy or congruency/incongruency. The concept of performance comparisons to standards is similar in nature to the disconfirmation concept as previously described.

One such comparison, which will be detailed more closely here, is that of fairness—also known as equity/inequity or justice (see Oliver and Swan 1989). In this particular comparison, consumers harbor passive fairness standards along a number of dimensions pertaining to how they are treated in transactions. The first of these is referred to as distributive justice, whereby the consumer judges his or her outcomes (and inputs) against those of the provider. Examples include fair pricing, the perceived commission of sales agents, and even the tip given a waitperson.

Two other standards are prominent in equity judgments (see Goodwin and Ross 1992). In accord with the notion of procedural justice, consumers are also known to judge the manner by which service is delivered. Data suggest that consumers may prefer that they be given the opportunity to participate in the service process and further may prefer to feel that their participation influenced the eventual outcome of the encounter. Common violations of this occur in monopoly industries such as government and public utilities, as well as in services that are delivered to consumers in mechanical fashion such that personalization is difficult or impossible (e.g., air travel, mass merchandisers).

The last standard is that of interactional fairness. Here, consumers are known to expect that service providers will treat them with respect, politeness, and dignity. Rudeness, discourtesy, condescension, and ignoring or not acknowledging the buyer's self-worth are examples that can occur in service provision that would contradict expected interactional fairness.

THE ROLE OF ATTRIBUTION

Attributions are the assessments of causal responsibility for outcomes deemed relevant in life. When either good or bad service is received, consumers may ask why this particular event occurred. When they reflect on the causes of their perceived service encounter and arrive at an explanation, an attribution has been generated. The complexity of this attribution has been described in terms of the number of defining characteristics or "dimensions" required for its explanation, as discussed next.

In a framework popularized by Weiner (1986), attributions are described in three dimensions. The first is that of causal agency—the entity responsible for the event. The possibilities include an attribution to the self (the individual forming the attribution) or to another individual (or thing). The second dimension is that of controllability. In essence, the causal agent is judged on whether the outcome was subject to control (i.e., could it have been changed or prevented?). The third is that of stability, or the likelihood of similar outcomes if the situation is repeated. Because the present focus is on service provision by others, the relevant attribution dimensions are other causality, controllability, and stability.

TABLE 14.1 The Affect Markers of Disconfirmation and Equity States

Disconfirmation Status	Low Salience Outcomes	High Salience Outcomes
Expected favorable:		
Better than expected	Glee	Delight
As expected	Contentment	Pleasure
Worse than expected	Annoyance	Disappointment
Expected unfavorable:		
Less negative than expected	Mitigation	Relief
As expected	Toleration	Distress
More negative than expected	Dismay	Despair
Expected fair (equitable):		
More fair than expected	An unusual state, perhaps resulting in gratitude or (even) guilt	
As expected	Usually not processed, but appreciated when it is	
Less fair than expected	Resentment	Anger

THE ROLE OF EMOTION

Research shows that emotion also plays a significant role in the satisfaction response (e.g., Oliver 1993, 1997; Westbrook and Oliver 1991). Generally, there appear to be three major sources of satisfaction emotion. The first results from an overall impression that the purchase outcome was favorable or unfavorable (i.e., good for me or bad for me), resulting in general affects such as happiness or sadness. The second results from specific comparisons, such as disconfirmation, inequity, or regret. The third results from the attributions, to be discussed, whereby consumers attribute gratitude or blame for good and bad outcomes. These emotions are more distinct and can be viewed as "markers" of the specific type of outcome received. Oliver (1997) has posited many of these; a brief summary of those resulting from specific comparisons appears in Table 14.1.

In similar manner, Folkes (1988) notes that the nature of the attribution process in consumption, as described by the dimensions, is rife with emotional overtones. Thus, the satisfaction process is now further expanded with regard to yet another sequence of events consisting of service outcomes, attributions for these outcomes, and the emotions generated by the attributions. Some common responses to each of the attribution states (assuming external attributions only for reasons to be discussed) are shown in Table 14.2. These responses, some of which are "quasi-emotions," then become "blended" with those from the disconfirmation and discrepancy states, resulting in a general emotional tenor about the service experience.

Each of these affective markers, evoked by the states of disconfirmation and attribution, becomes a tandem input to the satisfaction response. Thus, satisfaction has both a cognitive character via disconfirmation *and* an affective character similar to the nature of the affective blend. In this sense, satisfaction is a hybrid

TABLE 14.2 Emotional Markers for the Attribution States

	Favorable Outcome	*Unfavorable Outcome*
Controllable outcome	Praise/gratitude	Blame/anger
Uncontrollable outcome	Surprise/delight	Disappointment/tolerance
Expected stable outcome	Confidence	Withdrawal
Expected unstable outcome	Tentativeness	Hesitation

response, carrying both knowledge data and emotional content. A complete graphic of the satisfaction process as described here is shown in Figure 14.1.

The top section of Figure 14.1 shows the expectancy disconfirmation model as outlined in this chapter. In this section, performance—the outcome dimension desired by the consumer—is compared to the consumer's expectations. Services or goods, or both, would be evaluated for the performance received. The bottom section of the figure entertains many nonperformance dimensions and those standards expected as "normal." The equity dimensions discussed previously would be considered at this stage. Note that both expectancy disconfirmation and other discrepancies from "normal" result in specific emotions that are blended into a summary response that affects satisfaction. A net positive blend contributes to satisfaction, while a net negative blend contributes to dissatisfaction. Also shown in Figure 14.1 are direct effects from the disconfirmation/discrepancy responses to satisfaction.

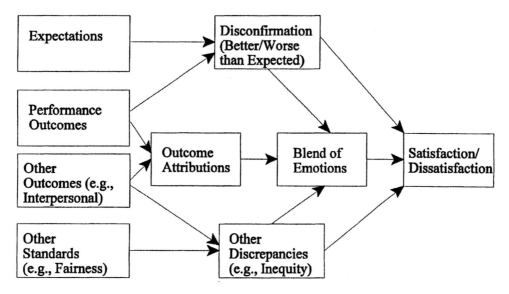

Figure 14.1 An Expectations/Standards Disconfirmation Model of Satisfaction

The middle section of Figure 14.1 contains the attribution sequence. Depending on the particular combination of praise or blame leveled at the service provider, whether the outcome was perceived as controllable or not, and whether it can be expected to continue into the future, the consumer will harbor emotions that are first blended with those from the other mentioned sources, then fed into the satisfaction response.

THE MODEL AS APPLIED TO SERVICE SATISFACTION

As stated previously, the operation of the model components would not be expected to change simply because a service provision rather than a product performance was being assessed. Rather, it would be expected that the human delivery aspect of service would bring forth greater attention to—and processing of—those model components most subject to interpersonal influences. The net result of the human element of service delivery is a greater interplay of emotion in the service satisfaction response, when compared to goods.

Differences between judgments of objects, such as goods, and those of personal performances have been studied intensively under the topic of social cognition (Fiske and Taylor 1991). Generally, social judgments, as opposed to judgments of objects, result in more positive evaluation because the performance of individuals and the role each plays in a complex (service) performance is more ambiguous (Menon and Johar 1997). These observations, however, would seem to be more accurate for generally favorable service encounters.

Positive encounters do have favorable implications for the service provider; as with any other satisfying experience, consumers will respond with higher intentions to repatronize, greater praise, and more favorable recommendations to others. Research shows, however, that individuals' satisfying experiences have less effect on overall satisfaction than negative incidents have on dissatisfaction (e.g., Anderson and Sullivan 1993). One reason for the disproportionate lessened effect on satisfaction is the "fundamental attribution error" whereby individuals are known to prefer to take credit for successes (i.e., good service) and to blame others and other things for failures (i.e., poor service). Another explanation is that people are more sensitive to negative information than its positive counterpart because it is less frequently observed and, therefore, more vivid. For these reasons, it may become more critical to avoid service errors than to "delight" the customer. Unfortunately, the human element of service delivery, as opposed to the goods component, is more prone to "error" because of the idiosyncratic variability in human performance and the high likelihood of a mismatch between provider and client. Thus, it would be instructive to know where these errors are most likely to influence satisfaction adversely.

From the model in Figure 14.1, it is clear that the role of individual service providers touches all major aspects of the satisfaction response as described here through the nexus of the emotion influence. First, the service provider, in many cases, is one and the same with the service performance and, hence, disconfirmation. From Table 14.1, it is clear that disconfirmation states are evocative of corresponding emotions. In the specific case of performance below expectations, the provider will easily be judged as responsible for the actual outcome. This attribution is the second aspect of the problem. It is known from research that, in the case of service failure (poor performance), which itself is distressing, further anger is expressed when the agent is viewed as responsible and that the failure could have been prevented. Moreover, avoidance behavior results when this outcome is expected to persist into the future.

In the event that the provider is only one cog in the machine and not directly responsible for the problem (e.g., a restaurant server bringing poorly prepared food), the situation is lessened only slightly. Although the server is not responsible for the food preparation, the server did deliver the food and is part of the larger restaurant operation. Thus, the controllability dimension of attribution is removed, but the responsibility dimension is not.

Finally, further complications can be expected when the service provision, whether a failure or success, is delivered with fairness violations, particularly those of a procedural or interactive nature. The inequity is easy to envision in this restaurant example. Overpriced entrees (distributive justice), late-arriving patrons served before earlier-arriving patrons (procedural justice), and rude or rushed service on the part of the server (interactional justice) can add to the already tarnished service experience. In fact, it is possible that the various negative experiences will be synergistic in the sense that the aggregate negativity will be greater than the sum of its parts.

SUMMARY

This chapter has attempted to show how service provision is a special case of the popular expectancy/standards disconfirmation model. It is special in the sense that the interpersonal nature of service brings forth those elements of satisfaction that have greater emotional potential, thus enhancing the effect of emotion on satisfaction or dissatisfaction. This greater effect can come about in a number of ways. One is through end-result performance itself. Human providers have more variability in their performance because of personal mood swings and the somewhat unpredictable interactions with diverse customers. Thus, perceived failure is more likely. A second mechanism is through the emotions generated by poor performance in comparison to expectations.

Still a third impact occurs because service must be delivered to the client and is frequently rendered in complex settings with many human interactions (e.g., medical care). This complexity opens up the possibility of unfair treatment in comparison to fairness standards. Such treatment frequently will be attributed to the service provider, with a corresponding emotional response—a fourth mechanism. For all these reasons, the emotional content of the satisfaction response must be more closely monitored in services. The antecedents of such emotional responses must also be measured, resulting in greater requisite attention to the components of the satisfaction model.

REFERENCES

Anderson, Eugene W. and Mary W. Sullivan (1993), "The Antecedents and Consequences of Customer Satisfaction for Firms," *Marketing Science*, 12 (Spring), 125-43.

Fiske, Susan T. and Shelley E. Taylor (1991), *Social Cognition*. New York: McGraw-Hill.

Folkes, Valerie S. (1988), "Recent Attribution Research in Consumer Behavior: A Review and New Directions," *Journal of Consumer Research*, 14 (March), 548-65.

Goodwin, Cathy and Ivan Ross (1992), "Consumer Responses to Service Failures: Influence of Procedural and Interactional Fairness Perceptions," *Journal of Business Research*, 25 (September), 149-63.

Menon, Geeta and Gita Venkataramani Johar (1997), "Antecedents of Positivity Effects in Social Versus Nonsocial Judgments," *Journal of Consumer Psychology*, 6(4), 313-37.

Oliver, Richard L. (1993), "Cognitive, Affective, and Attribute Bases of the Satisfaction Response," *Journal of Consumer Research*, 20 (December), 418-30.

———— (1997), *Satisfaction: A Behavioral Perspective on the Consumer*. New York: Irwin/McGraw-Hill.

———— and John E. Swan (1989), "Equity and Disconfirmation Perceptions as Influences on Merchant and Product Satisfaction," *Journal of Consumer Research*, 16 (December), 372-83.

Weiner, Bernard (1986), *An Attributional Theory of Motivation and Emotion*. New York: Springer-Verlag.

Westbrook, Robert A. and Richard L. Oliver (1991), "The Dimensionality of Consumption Emotion Patterns and Consumer Satisfaction," *Journal of Consumer Research*, 18 (June), 84-91.

15

The Customer Satisfaction Index as a Leading Indicator

EUGENE W. ANDERSON
CLAES FORNELL

Financial and accounting-based measures of performance, such as productivity, sales, and net income, are fundamental to evaluating past activities, but they provide limited information about the future (Kaplan and Norton 1992). An individual business or a national economy cannot manage effectively while relying solely on backward-looking measures. To attempt to do so is tantamount to driving an automobile while looking only in the rearview mirror. Managers and public policymakers also need to know what lies ahead. As predictors of repeat business, customer satisfaction indices provide a leading indicator of financial health that complements traditional measures.

Traditional measures also provide an incomplete picture of the present. Such approaches speak volumes about levels of production but tell us little about the quality of consumption. A large market share or a productive sales force may be a liability if customers are only marginally satisfied. Substantial trade-offs may exist between quantity and quality (Anderson, Fornell, and Rust 1997; Huff, Fornell, and Anderson 1996). Increasing volume (e.g., seats per plane, tables per waiter, children per care provider, students per class, classes per instructor, cases per lawyer) is likely to lead to lower quality and lower customer satisfaction. Firms must strike the right balance between their efforts to compete *efficiently* and *effectively*. By focusing attention on the quality of consumption, customer satisfaction measures can help guide management in doing so.

There is also a need for balance when gauging the health of an economy. Traditional measures that are used to understand the economy provide information about the amount of activity (e.g., GDP per capita, unemployment, growth, coal production) but do not assess adequately the quality of what is produced. For example, if the price index rises because of increased quality, then inflation

255

concerns may be unwarranted. Without a measure of the quality of output, it is difficult to understand the meaning of traditional measures of the quantity of output, such as productivity. In today's modern market economies, where the decisions of buyers are the driving force, it is surely as important to measure the quality of what is produced as it is to measure its amount. Customer satisfaction, especially if measured in a manner that is uniform and systematic, can help complete our picture of the economy.

Our intended message is this: To fully understand today's firms and national economies requires performance measurement that accounts for *both* quality and quantity. In the past, world markets were characterized by mass production and consumption of commodities, relatively low levels of competition, and widespread growth. In such a world, where ensuring supply and growth were paramount, it was sufficient to measure the quantity of output in gauging the health of a particular firm or even a nation's economy as a whole. Today's world is strikingly different. Customers are more sophisticated, their preferences and expectations are constantly changing, and new segments are evolving while old ones disappear. Large numbers of aggressive new competitors are challenging incumbents for market leadership. Technological change is sweeping aside old ways of doing business, creating new means of producing value for customers, new forms of competition, and entire new industries. To compete in such a turbulent world, a more complete understanding of financial and economic performance is required.

In this chapter, we provide an overview of an established measure of performance that complements traditional performance criteria. Customer satisfaction indices (CSIs) provide an important complement to financial measures of performance at the firm level and of economic indicators at the national level. In the discussion that follows, we describe the nature and purpose of CSIs, the methodological developments that have led to their creation, and current research relating CSIs to both financial performance of firms and the economic health of nations.

THE NATURE OF CSIs

A CSI measures the quality of goods and services as experienced by those who consume them. An individual firm's CSI represents its served market's (i.e., its customers') overall evaluation of the total purchase and consumption experience, both actual and anticipated (Anderson, Fornell, and Lehmann 1994; Fornell 1992; Johnson and Fornell 1991). Hence, CSIs represent a cumulative evaluation of a firm's market offering, rather than an individual's evaluation of a specific transaction. Although transaction-specific satisfaction measures may provide specific diagnostic information about a particular product or service encounter, overall customer satisfaction is a more fundamental indicator of the firm's past, current, and future performance (Anderson, Fornell, and Lehmann 1994).

Why Customer Satisfaction?

Customer satisfaction's role as a leading indicator of financial and economic performance is traceable directly to its links to behavioral and economic consequences beneficial to the firm (Anderson, Fornell, and Lehmann 1994). Customer satisfaction leads to greater customer loyalty (Anderson and Sullivan 1993; Bearden and Teel 1983; Bolton and Drew 1991; Boulding et al. 1993; Fornell 1992; LaBarbera and Mazursky 1983; Oliver 1980; Oliver and Swan 1989; Yi 1991). Through increasing loyalty, customer satisfaction secures future revenues (Bolton 1998; Fornell 1992; Rust, Zahorik, and Keiningham 1994, 1995), reduces the cost of future transactions (Reichheld and Sasser 1990), decreases price elasticities (Anderson 1996), and minimizes the likelihood that customers will defect if quality falters (Anderson and Sullivan 1993). Word of mouth from satisfied customers lowers the cost of attracting new customers and enhances the firm's overall reputation, while that of dissatisfied customers naturally has the opposite effect (Anderson 1998; Fornell 1992). For all these reasons, it is not surprising that empirical work indicates that firms providing superior quality enjoy higher economic returns (Aaker and Jacobson 1994; Anderson, Fornell, and Lehmann 1994; Anderson, Fornell, and Rust 1997; Bolton 1998; Capon, Farley, and Hoenig 1990).

A CSI acts as a leading indicator for industries, economic sectors, and national economies, as well as for individual firms. Through aggregating individual firm CSIs, the resulting indices of macroeconomic satisfaction provide valuable information regarding past, current, and future economic performance. Industry, sector, and national CSIs provide information about the quality of the goods and services produced and an important gauge of the future financial prospects of industries and nations. Understanding macroeconomic satisfaction therefore is useful in monitoring and improving national economic performance, global competitiveness, and quality of economic life.

How a CSI Works

The concept of a CSI, a measure of overall customer satisfaction that is uniform and comparable, requires a methodology with two fundamental properties.[1] First, the methodology must recognize that a CSI is a customer evaluation that cannot be measured directly. Second, as an overall measure of customer satisfaction, a CSI must be measured in a way that not only accounts for consumption experience but also is forward-looking.

Accordingly, a CSI must be embedded in a system of cause and effect relationships as shown in Figure 15.1, making a CSI the centerpiece in a chain of relationships running from the antecedents of customer satisfaction—including expectations, perceived quality, and value—to its consequences, such as voice and loyalty. The primary objective in estimating this system or model is to explain customer loyalty. It is through this design that a CSI captures the served market's evaluation of the firm's offering in a manner that is both backward- and forward-looking.

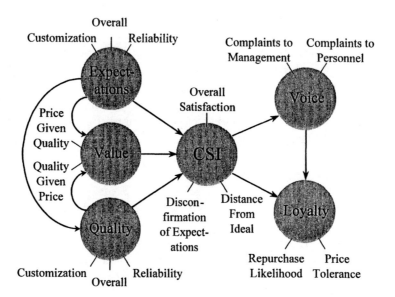

Figure 15.1 A Customer Satisfaction Index (CSI) Model

Customer satisfaction (CS) has three antecedents: perceived quality, perceived value, and customer expectations. Perceived quality or performance, the served market's evaluation of recent consumption experience, is expected to have a direct and positive effect on customer satisfaction. The second determinant of customer satisfaction is perceived value, or the perceived level of product quality relative to the price paid. Adding perceived value incorporates price information into the model and increases the comparability of the results across firms, industries, and sectors. The third determinant, the served market's expectations, represents both the served market's prior consumption experience with the firm's offering, including non-experiential information available through sources such as advertising and word of mouth, and a forecast of the supplier's ability to deliver quality in the future.

Following Hirschman's (1970) exit-voice theory, the immediate consequences of increased customer satisfaction are decreased customer complaints and increased customer loyalty (Fornell and Wernerfelt 1988). When dissatisfied, customers have the option of exiting (e.g., going to a competitor) or voicing their complaints. An increase in satisfaction should decrease the incidence of complaints. Increased satisfaction should also increase customer loyalty. Loyalty is the ultimate dependent variable in the model because of its value as a proxy for profitability (Reichheld and Sasser 1990).

CS and the other constructs in the model are latent variables that cannot be measured directly, so each is assessed by multiple measures as indicated in Figure 15.1. To estimate the model requires data from recent customers on each of these 15 manifest variables (for an extended discussion of the survey design, see Fornell et al. 1996). Based on the survey data, a CSI is estimated using a latent variable econometric technique known as partial least squares (Wold 1989). Partial least squares is an iterative procedure for estimating causal models. Other causal modeling techniques, such as the structural equations models fit via packages such as LISREL, would be inappropriate because estimating a CSI poses problems for such approaches. To estimate a CSI requires a technique that handles skewed and non-normal data, accommodates both continuous and categorical variables, and minimizes bias resulting from multicollinearity. Partial least squares is superior to LISREL in all three of these respects. To calculate a CSI, PLS estimates weights for the survey measures based on their power to explain customer loyalty. The estimated weights are used to construct index values (transformed to a 0-to-100 scale) for the CSI and the other model constructs (Fornell et al. 1996).

National Customer Satisfaction Indices

The National Quality Research Center (NQRC) at the University of Michigan Business School has developed national systems for measuring customer satisfaction in Sweden (1989) and the United States (1994); provided pilot studies in Taiwan, New Zealand, Korea, and Brazil; gained approval to launch national indices in Malaysia, Canada, and Brazil; and currently is working with 15 European Union countries to introduce the European Customer Satisfaction Index in early 1999. Prior to adoption in the United States and the European Union, exhaustive analyses of possible approaches to measuring a CSI identified the methodology underlying the NQRC CSIs as preferable to other potential approaches (European Union 1997; National Economic Research Associates 1993). Attempts to produce a CSI in Germany, Norway, and Switzerland use different methodologies that are not directly comparable to the standardized and uniform NQRC CSIs. As the American, Asian, and European measurement systems are implemented, it will become desirable to make cross-national comparisons of firm, industry, and national CSIs. These countries will be using the same measurement approach, making such comparisons valid and meaningful.

The NQRC CSIs are designed to be representative of a nation's economy as a whole. For example, in selecting the companies to measure for the American Customer Satisfaction Index (ACSI), all seven major economic sectors (one-digit SIC code level) with reachable end-users are included in the design. Within each sector, the major industry groups (two-digit SIC codes) are included on the basis of relative contribution to GDP. Within each industry group, several representative industries (four-digit SIC codes) are included on the basis of total sales. Finally, within each industry the largest companies are selected, so that coverage includes the majority of each selected industry's sales.

The ACSI values for individual industries, sectors, and the overall economy are computed by aggregating firm-level results (Fornell et al. 1996). An industry-level ACSI is an aggregate of firm results weighted by firm sales (e.g., Philip Morris sales for Miller beer only in the beverages/beer industry, excluding other corporate Philip Morris sales). A sector ACSI is an aggregate of industry results weighted by industry sales. The overall ACSI is an average of the sector results, weighted by the sectors' contributions to the Gross Domestic Product (GDP).

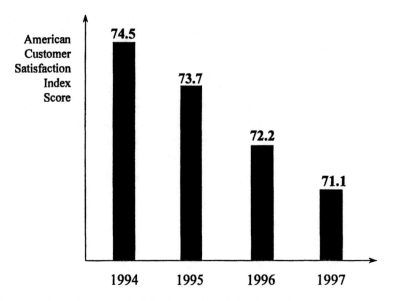

Figure 15.2 American Customer Satisfaction Index (ACSI) Over Time

SUMMARY OF CSI RESEARCH

CSIs and Benchmarking

CSI measures lend themselves well to benchmarking over both time and context (e.g., industry). For example, it is interesting to observe the decline in the American Customer Satisfaction Index (ACSI) shown in Figure 15.2. The ACSI fell from the baseline level of 74.5 in 1994 to 71.1 in 1997. The observed decline is driven by decreasing customer satisfaction in the service sector of the economy. To the extent that long-term profitability depends on customer loyalty and the efficiencies gained from long-term buyer-seller relationships, this drop in satisfaction with services should be seen as a warning signal about the long-term financial prospects for the firms affected. More important, given that services are a large and growing portion of the economy, such a decline may reflect a weakening of the economy in general and lower living standards with regard to consumption quality.

Tracking the ACSI over time also yields interesting insights at the firm level. One of the biggest winners in the first release of the firm-level results of the index was the U.S. Postal Service, which rose 13.0% to 69 in 1995 (Stewart 1995). The postal service is engaged in a massive effort to improve the quality of its services and posted record profits in 1995-1996. Conversely, large declines in the index were seen at companies that subsequently engaged in substantial downsizing, such as GTE (down 5.3% to 72) and K-Mart (down 5.4% to 70).

Firm, industry, sector, and national ACSI scores can also be compared cross-sectionally within a given time period. For example, one can determine how well a particular firm is doing relative to the best firms in its own industry, the best firms in other industries in that sector, or the best firms in the nation as a whole. Industries and sectors can be compared with one another in a similar fashion.

The ACSI can also be compared to extant CSIs of Sweden and Taiwan. For example, the pattern of sector differences found in the ACSI is consistent with that observed in the SCSB and the TCSI. Across these cultures, goods score higher than services, and public administration is always the lowest-scoring sector.

Although it is relatively straightforward to ask which firms, industries, sectors, and nations are relatively more effective at providing satisfying goods and services, it is quite a different question to ask whether a particular firm, industry, sector, or nation is performing well. To do so, it is necessary to put the ACSI index numbers in context; that is, once "structural" differences are taken into account, is a particular ACSI score good or bad? This question pertains to differences in ACSI attributable to *conduct*, as opposed to *structure*, as we shall explain. Such benchmarking judgments are relatively straightforward within a particular industry, where firms can be compared against one another. In such cases, industry structure is held constant, such that differences in firm performance may be attributed to the firm's conduct.

Firms that do particularly well relative to their competition include Southwest Airlines, with an ACSI of 76 relative to an industry average of 67, and BellSouth, with a score of 78 relative to an industry average of 71. Their nearest competitors, Delta and Ameritech, are at 69 and 73, respectively. Both firms have developed strategies that are difficult to imitate, and their resources have put them far ahead of the competition in their respective industries. Firms that trail the competition in their industry include Hyundai, with an ACSI of 68 relative to the automobile industry average of 79, and McDonald's, with a score of 60 relative to the fast food industry's average of 66, making each vulnerable to aggressive competitors.

Although different industries are likely to share some similar characteristics, within a sector benchmarking must be done with regard to differences in industry structure. The ACSI for long-distance service (77) is greater than for local telephone service (71). Consequently, it is possible to say that customer satisfaction with long-distance service is higher. It is more difficult, however, to evaluate the industry performance without first taking into account differences in satisfaction resulting from structural characteristics. In other words, greater competition is likely driving higher ACSI in long-distance service, so it is problematic to evaluate the conduct of the industry without first taking this structural difference into account. For example, a score of 77 for long-distance service may actually be weak given the industry's structural characteristics, and the local telephone industry's score of 71 may be high given its situation. If so, then long-distance services might be encouraged to do better, even in the presence of apparently higher customer satisfaction. At the same time, the performance of local telephone service would be relatively "better" given that the served market is more satisfied than one would expect based on its industry characteristics. Hence, benchmarking requires further adjustments, like golf handicaps, to account for possible structural differences.

Development of a deeper understanding of how to handicap ACSI scores for benchmarking purposes seems like a promising avenue for future research. It will be useful, for example, to determine the relative influence of industry-level versus within-firm effects on the CSI. The result should be a better understanding of the extent to which firms' attempts to improve customer satisfaction are constrained by industry characteristics. Such refinements will allow for more accurate firm and employee benchmarking, suggesting important implications for the development of strategy, the allocation of resources, performance evaluation, and satisfaction-based compensation policies. Furthermore, the ability to understand the unique roles of firm- and industry-level characteristics has important public policy implications, making interindustry comparisons of customer satisfaction scores more meaningful.

Linking Customer Satisfaction to Financial Performance

Anderson, Fornell, and Lehmann (1994) provide a theoretical and empirical investigation of the relationship between customer satisfaction and profitability. Many companies are frustrated that their efforts to improve quality are not translating quickly enough into economic returns; these authors develop a theoretical rationale for why and when such returns should be expected and empirically show that there are strong returns for those firms that increase quality. An annual one-point increase in customer satisfaction has a net present value of $7.48 million over 5 years for a typical firm in Sweden. Given the sample's average net income of $65 million, this represents a cumulative increase of 11.5%. If the impact of customer satisfaction on profitability is similar for firms in the *Business Week* 1000, then an annual one-point increase in the average firm's satisfaction index would be worth $94 million or 11.4% of current return on investment (ROI). Thus, the research provides hope to managers who might otherwise curtail or abandon their efforts in this area.

Anderson, Fornell, and Rust (1997) investigate the links between customer satisfaction, productivity, and profitability. Although there is widespread belief that customer satisfaction and productivity operate in concert, there is reason to doubt whether this is necessarily the case for organizations in which service plays an important role. A model relating customer satisfaction and productivity to profitability is developed and used to generate hypotheses for when we should, and should not, expect synergies, or perhaps trade-offs, between customer satisfaction and productivity. Specifically, there are more likely to be trade-offs between customer satisfaction and productivity when customers' perceptions of quality are more dependent on customization (i.e., whether or not the product fits the customer's requirements) as opposed to standardization (i.e., whether or not the product reliably performs its function). To test the model's propositions, it is argued that customer satisfaction for firms in service industries is relatively dependent on customization, whereas customer satisfaction in goods industries is relatively dependent on standardization. The empirical analysis finds that although improvements in both productivity and customer satisfaction are associated with higher profits for goods manufacturers, higher levels of one or the other, but not both simultaneously, are associated with higher returns for services. The somewhat counterintuitive implications of the study are that such firms should emphasize either productivity or customer satisfaction at any one time, but rarely both, as is commonly observed in practice.

The empirical evidence that the ACSI is a leading indicator of financial performance is becoming increasingly persuasive. This fact is true for accounting profits as well as shareholder value. Specifically, it has been shown that both the ACSI (Ittner and Larcker 1996) and its Swedish counterpart (Anderson, Fornell, and Lehmann 1994) have a positive association with ROI. In terms of market value, Ittner and Larcker (1996) estimate that a one-unit change in ACSI is associated with a $654 million increase in the market value of equity above and beyond the accounting book value of assets and liabilities. Stock trading strategies based on either the ACSI or SCSB have delivered portfolio returns well above market returns (Fornell, Ittner, and Larcker 1995). In addition, recent results suggest that the public release of ACSI scores causes a significant stock market reaction—positive market-adjusted returns for firms with high ACSI scores and negative adjusted returns for low-scoring firms (Fornell, Ittner, and Larcker 1995).

Despite the encouraging evidence regarding the link between a CSI and financial performance, there is ample room for further inquiry. Clearly, there is a need for more sophisticated analyses of the CSI-profit link that adequately controls for factors that may bias estimates of the relationship, such as fixed, random, and time-varying "unobservable" effects. In terms of measurement, a particularly promising approach is Tobin's q, the ratio of market value to book value or replacement cost of the firm's tangible assets (Montgomery and Wernerfelt 1988; Tobin 1969). Tobin's q has the advantage of imputing equilibrium returns based on all information available to the capital market.

Another important direction for future research is to investigate systematic differences in the relationship between customer satisfaction and financial performance. By understanding such differences and identifying factors that moderate the CSI-profit relationship, we can gain a clearer understanding of when customer satisfaction is likely to be most strongly associated with profitability.

Linking Customer Satisfaction to Economic Performance

At the national level, a CSI provides a leading indicator for economic performance. National stock exchange indices, such as the Dow Jones Industrial Average (DJIA), have been shown to be predictive of national economic perfor-

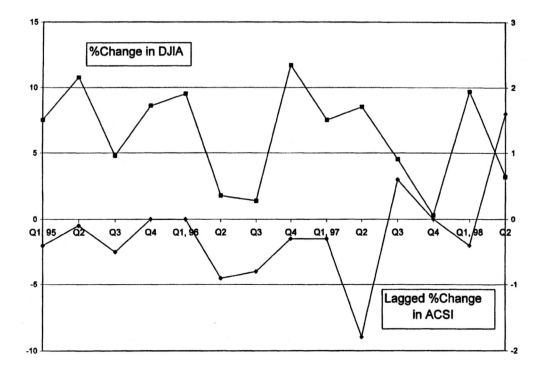

Figure 15.3 Changes in American Customer Satisfaction Index (ACSI) Lagged by One Quarter Against Changes in Dow Jones Industrial Average (DJIA)

mance as measured by GDP (Harvey 1989). Changes in the ACSI appear, in turn, to lead changes in the DJIA, as shown in Figure 15.3. If this relationship is not spurious (and our research is beginning to substantiate that it is not), it provides planners with a new means of evaluating and forecasting economic growth.

In terms of other measures of national economic performance, a national CSI provides complementary information. For example, it is widely accepted that price indices do an inadequate job of capturing quality information. For a measure such as the Consumer Price Index (CPI), the qualities inherent in the bundle of goods and services on which it is based change dramatically over time. Hence, a "true" hedonic price index—a price index adjusted for the level of quality—and a satisfaction index could head in opposite directions.

Today, there is a good deal of bewilderment among economists about the low inflation rate and the high employment level. The ACSI provides an answer to this puzzle: In recent years inflation has shown up not in price but in the deterioration of (service) quality. In other words, the CPI is holding relatively steady, while the national ACSI is declining. Hence, the ACSI suggests that there is actually inflation because a dollar today buys less service than it did a few years ago. Future research may further compare relative price indices for goods and services and their satisfaction scores. One possible alternative is to combine economic welfare and productivity information in a single "value" index. This would entail viewing the level of a hedonic customer satisfaction index as a benefit and price as a cost.

Linking a CSI to Firm Conduct

Although several studies link customer satisfaction to financial performance (e.g., Anderson, Fornell, and Lehmann 1994; Anderson, Fornell, and Rust 1997), none examines the internal processes that create customer satisfaction, translates it into competitive advantage, and drives financial performance. What determines the success of efforts to increase customer satisfaction and, as a result, improve financial performance? An important area for future CSI research is to identify and measure those aspects of firm conduct most vital to customer satisfaction, as well as to determine which are most important in driving customer satisfaction and financial performance. Such an effort would provide valuable guidance from a strategic perspective, as well as a diagnostic tool for firms interested in evaluating and improving their own satisfaction measurement and implementation efforts.

SUMMARY

Customer satisfaction indices provide new and important leading indicators of business and economic performance. The evidence is mounting that CSIs are predictive of financial results and supply a hitherto missing link in interpreting performance indices such as productivity and price. In the coming years, we expect the usefulness of CSIs to rise still further with increased understanding of how CSIs vary across firms, industries, and nations, as well as the links between CSIs, antecedent management activities, and their ultimate financial consequences.

NOTE

1. For a more extensive and detailed description of the ACSI methodology, see the *American Customer Satisfaction Index: Methodology Report*, available from the American Society for Quality Control, Milwaukee, WI.

REFERENCES

Aaker, David A. and Robert Jacobson (1994), "The Financial Information Content of Perceived Quality," *Journal of Marketing Research*, 31 (August), 191-201.

Anderson, Eugene W. (1996), "Customer Satisfaction and Price Tolerance," *Marketing Letters*, 7(3), 19-30.

——— (1998), "Customer Satisfaction and Word-of-Mouth," *Journal of Service Research*, 1(1), 1-14.

———, Claes Fornell, and Donald R. Lehmann (1994), "Customer Satisfaction, Market Share, and Profitability," *Journal of Marketing*, 56 (July), 53-66.

————, ————, and Roland T. Rust (1997), "Customer Satisfaction, Productivity, and Profitability: Differences Between Goods and Services," *Marketing Science*, 16(2), 129-45.

———— and Mary Sullivan (1993), "The Antecedents and Consequences of Customer Satisfaction for Firms," *Marketing Science*, 12(2), 125-43.

Bearden, William O. and Jesse E. Teel (1983), "Selected Determinants of Consumer Satisfaction and Complaint Reports," *Journal of Marketing Research*, 20 (February), 21-28.

Bolton, Ruth N. (1998), "A Dynamic Model of the Duration of the Customer's Relationship With a Continuous Service Provider: The Role of Customer Satisfaction," *Marketing Science*, 17(1), 45-65.

———— and James H. Drew (1991), "A Multistage Model of Customers' Assessments of Service Quality and Value," *Journal of Consumer Research*, 17 (March), 375-84.

Boulding, William, Ajay Kalra, Richard Staelin, and Valarie Zeithaml (1993), "A Dynamic Process Model of Service Quality: From Expectations to Behavioral Intentions," *Journal of Marketing Research*, 30 (February), 7-27.

Capon, Noel, John U. Farley, and Scott Hoenig (1990), "Determinants of Financial Performance: A Meta-Analysis," *Management Science*, 36 (October), 1143-59.

European Union (1997), "European Customer Satisfaction Index Feasibility Study," Research Report, National Quality Research Center, University of Michigan Business School, Ann Arbor, MI.

Fornell, Claes (1992), "A National Customer Satisfaction Barometer: The Swedish Experience," *Journal of Marketing*, 56 (January), 1-21.

————, Christopher D. Ittner, and David F. Larcker (1995), "Understanding and Using the American Customer Satisfaction Index (ACSI): Assessing the Financial Impact of Quality Initiatives," *Proceedings of the Juran Institute's Conference on Managing for Total Quality*. Wilton, CT: Juran Institute, 76-102.

————, Michael D. Johnson, Eugene W. Anderson, Jaesung Cha, and Barbara Bryant (1996), "The American Customer Satisfaction Index: Description, Findings, and Implications," *Journal of Marketing*, 60(4), 7-18.

———— and Birger Wernerfelt (1988), "A Model for Customer Complaint Management," *Marketing Science*, 7 (Summer), 271-86.

Harvey, Campbell R. (1989), "Forecasting Economic Growth With the Bond and Stock Markets," *Financial Analysts' Journal*, (September/October), 38-45.

Hirschman, Albert O. (1970), *Exit, Voice, and Loyalty—Responses to Decline in Firms, Organizations, and States*. Cambridge, MA: Harvard University Press.

Huff, Leonard, Claes Fornell, and Eugene W. Anderson (1996), "Quality and Productivity: Contradictory and Complementary," *Quality Management Journal*, 4(1), 22-39.

Ittner, Christopher D. and David F. Larcker (1996), "Measuring the Impact of Quality Initiatives on Firm Financial Performance," *Advances in the Management of Organizational Quality*, Soumen Ghosh and Donald Fedor, eds. New York: JAI, 1-37.

Johnson, Michael D. and Claes Fornell (1991), "A Framework for Comparing Customer Satisfaction Across Individuals and Product Categories," *Journal of Economic Psychology*, 12(2), 267-86.

Kaplan, Robert S. and David P. Norton (1992), "The Balanced Scorecard—Measures That Drive Performance," *Harvard Business Review*, 70 (January-February), 71-79.

LaBarbera, Priscilla A. and D. Mazursky (1983), "A Longitudinal Assessment of Consumer Satisfaction/Dissatisfaction: The Dynamic Aspect of the Cognitive Standardization," *Journal of Marketing Research*, 20 (November), 393-404.

Montgomery, Cynthia A. and Birger Wernerfelt (1988), "Diversification, Ricardian Rents, and Tobin's q," *RAND Journal of Economics*, 19 (Winter), 623-32.

National Economic Research Associates (1993), "Developing a National Quality Index," Research Report, National Quality Research Center, University of Michigan Business School, Ann Arbor, MI.

Oliver, Richard L. (1980), "A Cognitive Model of the Antecedents and Consequences of Satisfaction Decisions," *Journal of Marketing Research*, 17 (November), 460-69.

———— and John E. Swan (1989), "Consumer Perceptions of Interpersonal Equity and Satisfaction in Transactions: A Field Survey Approach," *Journal of Marketing*, 53 (April), 21-35.

Reichheld, Frederick F. and W. Earl Sasser, Jr. (1990), "Zero Defections: Quality Comes to Services," *Harvard Business Review*, 68 (September-October), 105-11.

Rust, Roland T., Anthony J. Zahorik, and Timothy L. Keiningham (1994), *Return on Quality: Measuring the Financial Impact of Your Company's Quest for Quality*. Chicago: Probus.

———, ———, and ——— (1995), "Return on Quality (ROQ): Making Service Quality Financially Accountable," *Journal of Marketing*, 59 (April), 58-70.

Stewart, Thomas A. (1995), "After All You've Done for Your Customers, Why Are They Still Not Happy?" *Fortune*, (December 11), 178-82.

Tobin, James (1969), "A General Equilibrium Approach to Monetary Theory," *Journal of Money, Credit, and Banking*, 1, 15-29.

Wold, Herman (1989), *Theoretical Empiricism: A General Rationale for Scientific Model Building*. New York: Paragon House.

Yi, Youjae (1991), "A Critical Review of Customer Satisfaction," *Review of Marketing 1989*, Valarie A. Zeithaml, ed. Chicago: American Marketing Association, 112-56.

SECTION **IV**

Service Recovery

16

Service Recovery

Research Insights and Practices

STEPHEN S. TAX
STEPHEN W. BROWN

Service recovery is now recognized as a significant driver of customer satisfaction and loyalty and an important component of a quality management strategy (Fornell and Wernerfelt 1987; Rust, Zahorik, and Keiningham 1996; Smith, Bolton, and Wagner 1998; Tax and Brown 1998). Performing very well in recovery can overcome disappointment and enhance relationships, whereas performing poorly can severely damage satisfaction, trust, and commitment and lead to customers switching service providers (Keaveney 1995; Smith and Bolton 1988; Tax, Brown, and Chandrashekaran 1998). This realization has led some firms (e.g., FedEx, Hampton Inn) to treat service recovery as an investment and deploy considerable resources in programs (e.g., service guarantees, employee training) and assets (e.g., customer call centers) to improve recovery efforts. This contemporary view of service recovery differs dramatically from the perspective held only a short time ago, and still practiced by many firms: that resolving complaints represents a cost to be minimized despite the consequences (Hoffman, Kelley, and Rotalsky 1995).

The purpose of this chapter is to examine fundamental service recovery issues and strategies, including a review and synthesis of relevant literature and the identification of selected managerial practices designed to improve recovery effectiveness. The chapter is organized as follows. We first provide a definition of service recovery that extends the view taken in the contemporary marketing literature. Next, we explore the association between service recovery and customer and employee satisfaction and loyalty. These relationships have raised the profile of service recovery and established its link with relationship management and overall firm success. Third, we examine consumer complaining behavior and link it with strategies that can help firms identify service failures. We then turn to an examination of how customers evaluate responses to complaints, accompanied by approaches firms can take to improve those evaluations. Finally, we consider how firms can learn from service failure, focusing on classifying service failures and integrating the data with intelligence gathered through other mechanisms to inform service redesign decisions.

DEFINING SERVICE RECOVERY

Unfortunately, much of the services literature equates service recovery with complaint handling. Such definitions limit the potential of service recovery as a management tool and, we believe, are partly responsible for the ineffective deployment of recovery strategies. Expanding on Lovelock (1994), we define service recovery as a process that identifies service failures, effectively resolves customer problems, classifies their root cause(s), and yields data that can be integrated with other measures of performance to assess and improve the service system. This process-oriented approach fits with quality management perspectives and is consistent with the Baldrige National Quality Award criteria for earning service recovery points.

SERVICE RECOVERY, SATISFACTION, AND LOYALTY

One of the most significant findings in service research is that customer loyalty drives profitability (Reichheld 1993). Furthermore, there is evidence that as relationships develop over time, effective service recovery is a key determinant of satisfaction, trust, and commitment (e.g., Bolton 1998; Hart, Heskett, and Sasser 1990). In examining the relative impact of service recovery satisfaction and prior experience with the firm on customer trust and commitment, Tax, Brown, and Chandrashekaran (1998) found that specific service recovery experience overwhelmed customers' cumulative prior experiences in forming customer trust and commitment. They also observed, consistent with Smith and Bolton (1998), that relying on service recovery to enhance relationships is extremely risky. Customers tend to have high expectations and a limited zone of tolerance once failures occur (Zeithaml, Berry, and Parasuraman 1993), making successful complaint handling difficult. Tax and his colleagues' results were similar to the findings of Hart, Heskett, and Sasser (1990), indicating that the majority of customers felt worse about the firm after going through the complaint handling process. This challenges prior research (e.g., Technical Assistance Research Program 1986) indicating that just getting customers to complain was worthwhile, even if their problem was not resolved effectively. This leads to the basic conclusion that only very effective service recovery will lead to enhanced customer satisfaction and loyalty.

A second service recovery loyalty issue concerns the question "How does service recovery affect the employees involved?" The cycle of service success/failure implies that being able to deal effectively with customer problems is also closely related to employee satisfaction and loyalty (Schlesinger and Heskett 1991). In our research, we have observed two informative themes related to employees and service recovery. First, customers who found the service recovery handled very well also commented that the employee was (a) concerned about the problem, (b) eager to help, and (c) happy that the complaint was resolved to the customer's satisfaction. Second, when customers indicated that they found the complaint handled poorly, employees were frequently observed to be (a) rude and defensive, (b) indifferent to providing assistance, and (c) angry as the dispute progressed (Tax and Brown 1998).

Research has not specifically examined how service recovery influences the attitude and behavior of employees, with the exception of Bowen and Johnston (forthcoming). They use the term *internal service recovery* in reference to what an organization does to make employees feel whole after dealing with a customer complaint. In exploratory work in a bank setting, they found that handling customer complaints was frequently considered emotionally difficult by employees and that it affected their job satisfaction. Respondent comments about the complaint handling process included the following: "frustrating," "you need to develop a tough skin," "it's a problem for new staff," "leads to a poor working environment," and "a daily challenge." They suggest that front-line employees who handle complaints may develop *learned helplessness*. This means that the work environment causes them to become passive and engage in maladaptive behaviors (e.g., act immaturely or uncreatively). The major causes of this in the service context are the inability to prevent the failure in the first place and not being able to provide a satisfactory response to the complaint.

This implies that individual service recovery incidents affect the satisfaction of not only the customer but also the employees involved. The service profit chain (Heskett et al. 1994) indicates that employees' satisfaction is directly related to their productivity and retention as well as customer satisfaction and loyalty. Complaint episodes that are positive and lead to favorable outcomes for the customer also encourage employee loyalty, while negative service recovery incidents contribute to lowering both customer and employee loyalty. Maintaining employees is particularly critical in industries where customer relationships are more closely associated with the individual service provider than the organization. For example, American Express pays close attention to the satisfaction of its investment advisers because the company estimates that more than 30% of an adviser's clients will defect if the adviser leaves the company.

CONSUMER RESPONSES TO SERVICE FAILURES

A necessary condition for service recovery is identifying when failures occur. One underappreciated opportunity is encouraging customers to complain following a failure. Research, however, indicates that customers rarely choose to inform the firm following a service failure; rather, they frequently engage in activities such as negative word of mouth and brand switching (e.g., Technical Assistance Research Program 1986). Investigations into consumer responses to failure are informative regarding some of the challenges associated with recovery. Considerable research has considered the following questions: What action(s) do consumers take following a dissatisfying experience? What factors influence the selection of these responses?

An initial classification scheme to address the first question was a hierarchical framework proposed by Day and Landon (1977). They suggest that consumers first decide whether to convey an expression of dissatisfaction (action) or take no action. The second-level decision concerns whether the response taken is public or private. Public actions include seeking redress directly from the business, taking legal action, or complaining to public or private agencies. Private actions include boycotting the seller or manufacturer (brand switching) and/or engaging in negative word of mouth.

A second conceptual approach was offered by Day (1984). He examined consumer complaint behavior from the perspective of the goals being sought. Day suggested that the goals of complaining can be classified into three broad themes: redress seeking (complain to firm or take legal action), complaining (in this context referring to negative word of mouth), and personal boycotting (relates to brand switching).

Singh (1988) proposed and tested a third classification system. This scheme identifies three sets of responses once dissatisfaction occurs: voice responses (e.g., seek redress from the seller; no action) private responses (word-of-mouth communication), and third-party responses (e.g., take legal action). Classification is based on identifying the object toward which the consumer complaint behavior (CCB) responses are directed. Three different "types" of objects are proposed. Voice CCB is aimed at objects that are directly involved in the dissatisfying exchange (e.g., retailer, manufacturer). Singh suggests that the no-action responses are included in this category because they appear to reflect feelings toward the seller. In contrast, private responses are directed at objects that are external to the consumer but not directly involved in the dissatisfying experience (e.g., friends, relatives). The final category, third-party CCB, includes actions that are directed at formal external parties, such as the Better Business Bureau or the legal system.

With respect to the second question, considerable research has sought to identify variables that explain the choice of responses to failure. The predictors include demographic and personality variables (e.g., age, income, education, occupation, assertiveness, self-confidence) and problem/situational characteristics (e.g., problem severity, perceived firm responsiveness, cost of complaining, experience with the firm). With respect to the option of complaining to the firm, older, wealthier, and more educated customers are more likely to select that option. Other factors positively associated with this choice are problem severity, price level, whether the firm is held responsible for the failure, whether it is believed the institution will be responsive, and whether the customer has a positive attitude toward complaining. Customers are less likely to complain to the firm when the cost of complaining is high and when they are unsure of their rights and/or the firm's obligations.

More recently, Dubé and Maute (1996) examined how cognitive and emotional responses affected selection of CCB. They found that negative word of mouth was mostly driven by emotional responses (e.g., anger), whereas loyalty was affected by both cognitive and emotional (e.g., calmness) responses. Complaining to the firm was positively influenced by anger emotions and negatively associated with satisfaction with the entire experience (initial transaction and recovery) and the recovery itself.

Another approach to understanding CCB was taken by Singh (1990), who developed a typology of consumer dissatisfaction response styles. Singh empirically derived four clusters of complaint response groups, which he labeled Passives, Voicers, Irates, and Activists. He examined their propensity to engage in voice (actions directed at the seller/producer), private actions (complaints to friends/relatives or switching brands), and third-party actions (talk to lawyers or an agency such as the Better Business Bureau). Passives fall below average on intentions to complain to any source. Voicers actively complain to service providers but show minimal interest in providing negative word of mouth or seeking support from third parties. Irates are consumers who are above average with respect to lodging private responses, are average in their tendency to complain directly to sellers/providers, and are below average with respect to third-party actions. Finally, Activists are dissatisfied patrons who score above average on all complaint dimensions.

The key service recovery insights of CCB research are that a high percentage of dissatisfied customers do not complain and that several barriers help explain this behavior. This implies that either the barriers need to be removed or other means of identifying when failures have occurred need to be utilized. This challenge is addressed in the next section.

IDENTIFYING SERVICE FAILURES

From a managerial standpoint the central question arising from the previous discussion is, "How can we get customers to complain to us rather than complain to their friends and/or switch service providers?" A second, related question is, "Even if customers don't complain, can we identify when failures have occurred and respond to them?" By studying the recovery practices of leading service firms, strategies to increase the percentage of service failures identified and reported can be observed. These strategies include setting performance standards, training customers on how to complain, and using technological support offered through customer call centers and the Internet (Tax and Brown 1998).

Setting Performance Standards

One reason customers choose not to complain about service failures is that they have unclear expectations for performance and, therefore, are not really sure themselves when a service has failed. A strategy that can successfully overcome the problem of unclear expectations is the implementation and communication of service standards, often accomplished through the introduction of service guarantees. By specifying free delivery if a customer does not receive a package by 10 a.m., FedEx makes it clear when the service has failed. A number of restaurant chains have determined that customers value lunch service within 15 minutes of ordering and have established delivery time as the critical service standard.

Training Customers in Complaining

Another barrier to complaining is customers being unclear about how to go about the process. Scotiabank, one of Canada's large chartered banks, has introduced a pamphlet in all of its branches that explains the bank's complaint process. The pamphlet first stresses the importance the bank places on maintaining customer relationships, then promises quick action to resolve problems. This is accomplished by detailing with whom complaints should be initially lodged and then describing the appeals procedure.

Utilizing Technology

To improve overall customer service and to lower the cost and increase the responsiveness of the recovery process, many firms have introduced toll-free telephone call centers. General Electric, for example, uses its Answer Center as the core component of its customer relations and recovery strategy. The Answer Center is open 24 hours a day, 365 days a year to service approximately 3 million annual calls. GE places its 800 number directly on all of its products and encourages customers experiencing problems to contact the firm directly. By maintaining easily accessible and thorough customer and product records, GE service reps are able to diagnose and solve problems quickly, enhancing perceptions of responsiveness and lowering the cost of complaining.

Some firms are now utilizing the Internet in a variety of ways to help customers access service recovery via a website. Cisco Systems has created a searchable database that provides a keyword search of questions and answers provided to other customers. This approach provides the customer a fast, convenient response to the problem. Problems that cannot be handled through on-line technology are referred to the telephone support system.

Although not an exhaustive list, these approaches to generating complaints and identifying service failures are reflective of strategies that can help overcome traditional barriers to recovery. Firms that can increase both the reporting of failures and successful resolution stand to improve profitability.

RESPONDING TO SERVICE FAILURES

Although initial research sought to establish a link between complaint handling satisfaction and subsequent postpurchase behavior, more recent attention has

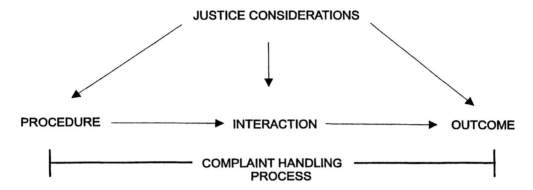

Figure 16.1 The Role of Justice in the Complaint Handling Process

SOURCE: Adapted from Bies and Moag (1986).

NOTE: A complaint resolution is viewed as a sequence of events in which a procedure generates a process of interaction and decision through which an outcome is allocated to someone. Each part of the sequence is subject to fairness considerations and thus, every aspect of a compalint resolution (procedure, interaction, outcome) may create a potential justice episode.

been directed at understanding how customers evaluate recovery experiences. The dominant perspective that has emerged centers on justice theory. Justice, in general, concerns the perceived fairness of decisions. This has evolved over time to include decision outcomes (distributive justice), decision-making procedures (procedural justice), and, more recently, interpersonal behavior in the delivery of outcomes and enactments of procedures (interactional justice). The theory has been applied in a number of conflict resolution contexts (e.g., buyer-seller, employee-management, marriage, legal disputes) and has been shown to be robust in explaining reactions to conflicts, including complaints (e.g., Blodgett, Hill, and Tax 1997; Goodwin and Ross 1992; McCollough 1998; Smith, Bolton, and Wagner 1998; Tax, Brown, and Chandrashekaran 1998). See Figure 16.1 for a description of the application of justice theory to a complaint episode.

Research involving the three justice concepts, developed independently and only recently, has been integrated into service evaluations in general and service recovery contexts specifically. Next, we examine the relationship between each of the three concepts and service recovery.

Distributive Justice

Theories of distributive justice deal with the allocation of benefits and costs. Research in service recovery has found that when services fail, customers expect to be compensated for their loss (e.g., Berry and Parasuraman 1991; Blodgett, Hill, and Tax 1997; Goodwin and Ross 1992). In addition, many customers expect to be compensated for the inconvenience associated with the failure and having to go through the recovery process (Zemke 1995). The typical forms compensation takes are one or some combination of refunds, credits, correction of charges, repairs and replacements, and apologies (e.g., Kelley, Hoffman, and Davis 1993). Distributive justice has been found to influence satisfaction, repurchase intention, and word-of-mouth decisions in a variety of service recovery settings (e.g., retail, hotel, restaurant, airline, auto repair) across a number of research methods (experiments, surveys, critical incidents).

Procedural Justice

Procedural fairness concerns the policies and rules that form the complaint process. Exploratory work in the organizational behavior field identified several possible elements of procedural justice: consistency, bias suppression, accuracy, correctability, representativeness, and ethicality (Leventhal, Karuza, and Fry 1980). Tax, Brown, and Chandrashekaran (1998) used a critical incident–based method to study the core elements of procedural justice in complaint responses and found several important aspects. Among the issues most frequently referred to were the firm assuming responsibility for the failure, the speed and convenience of the process, the firm following up to ensure the situation was resolved, the firm being flexible in applying policies, and the customer having some control over the process.

Organizational research has found relationships between procedural justice and satisfaction with variables such as pay, performance appraisals, layoff policies, and selection procedures. Although some marketing studies have directly supported the impact of procedural justice on customer decision making, considerable research supports the impact of many of the elements on service and recovery evaluations (e.g., Bitner, Booms, and Tetreault 1990; Clemmer 1988; Goodwin and Ross 1992; Smith, Bolton, and Wagner 1998; Tax, Brown, and Chandrashekaran 1998; Taylor 1994).

Interactional Justice

Interactional justice concerns the behavior of firm representatives during the complaint process. The inclusion of interactional matters, such as communication between parties, helps explain why some people feel unfairly treated even though they characterize the decision-making procedure and outcome to be fair (Bies and Shapiro 1987). Research has found that fair interpersonal treatment affects assessments of service encounters (Bitner, Booms, and Tetreault 1990; Clemmer 1988), enhanced evaluations of service quality (Parasuraman, Zeithaml, and Berry 1985), and satisfaction with complaint handling (Blodgett, Hill, and Tax 1997; Tax, Brown, and Chandrashekaran 1998). Key elements of fair interpersonal behavior involve demonstrating politeness, concern, and honesty, as well as providing an explanation for the initial failure and putting effort into resolving the problem (Tax, Brown, and Chandrashekaran 1998).

In summary, the three fairness dimensions each significantly contribute to recovery evaluations and combine to explain a high percentage of variation in satisfaction with complaint handling. Furthermore, significant interactions indicate that performing poorly on even one fairness dimension severely limits the potential for customer satisfaction. This means that firms compensating customers do not get a return on the investment if the restitution is provided by rude, unsympathetic employees or if the process is a hassle for the customer. Next, we consider strategies firms can use to improve all three dimensions of the complaint handling process.

STRATEGIES FOR RECOVERING SUCCESSFULLY

Although several strategies can help achieve success, four practices jointly can dramatically improve service recovery effectiveness: human resource management practices, establishing service recovery guidelines and standards, providing easy access and effective responses through call centers, and maintaining customer and product databases.

Human Resource Management Practices

It is clear that successful service recovery is often highly influenced by the effectiveness of the front-line employee who receives the complaint. Developing hiring criteria and training programs that take into account employees' service recovery role directly affects fairness evaluations. Ford, for example, puts all job candidates through its Assessment Center to evaluate nine skill levels. Areas particularly relevant to service recovery include written and oral communication, listening skills, problem analysis, organization and follow-through, resilience, and stress management. Ford's Assessment Center includes recovery skills—such as knowledge of company policies and warranties, listening skills, diffusion of anger, and interpersonal skills—in the training of employees. To provide new employees with a realistic job preview, they use simulation exercises such as a meeting with an irate customer, a meeting with dealers, and a written report of a dealer meeting.

Providing employees with the authority to respond to service failures substantially affects all three fairness dimensions (Bowen and Lawler 1995). First, employee attitudes and effort improve when they are given the power to resolve problems. Second, the speed and convenience of the process is enhanced when employees can act immediately rather than having to seek out a manager or another department to respond to the problem. Third, outcome fairness improves when employees have the flexibility to provide the appropriate compensation, based on the customer's circumstances and requirements. Empowerment complements the use of service guarantees. Hotels such as Hampton Inn and Holiday Inn rely on employees to deliver on promises and provide restitution if the service fails. At Hampton Inn, any employee, including reservations staff, janitors, and maids, can invoke the guarantee and provide the customer with a complete refund.

Establishing Guidelines and Standards

Developing guidelines for service recovery that focus on achieving fairness and satisfaction represents a direct approach to improving performance. The Ritz

Carlton policies mandate that employees be polite (interactional), take quick action and respond to a problem within 20 minutes (procedural), and correct the problem (outcome). Ford also has developed specific standards related to service recovery responsiveness and accessibility. The metric for responsiveness includes 5-day turnaround on correspondence and 20-day closure on executive complaints; accessibility standards include 95% accessibility to incoming callers and maximum 30-second hold on calls.

Providing Easy Access and Effective Responses

In addition to removing barriers to the customer's decision to complain, call centers contribute to all three fairness dimensions. The hours of operation (24 hours a day, 365 days a year) and up-to-date customer and product information at the GE Answer Center make for convenient access and fast resolution, enhancing procedural fairness. GE follows up with a letter of apology to all callers, which contributes to both procedural and outcome fairness. Customers are provided a goodwill certificate, free home repair, and/or compensation for food spoilage, depending on the nature of the failure. These further contribute to perceptions of fair outcomes. Extensive training of service representatives in recovery practices helps achieve high scores on interactional fairness.

Customer and Product Databases

Using databases in conjunction with call centers and websites helps firms achieve fairness goals. By recording failures, Cisco Systems improves recovery, because identifying systematic problems leads to faster and more accurate diagnoses of customer complaints and the improvement of its website's expert systems. Cisco's approach gives the customer greater control and flexibility in resolving the problem, enhancing service fairness. GE maintains extensive databases on customer purchases and service incidents that help guide recovery decisions. For example, recognizing that customers are particularly upset when products fail just after a warranty expires, they include warranty information in the customer database, and service reps can adjust compensation accordingly (e.g., waive the cost of the repair call). These strategies reflect a comprehensive approach to improving recovery. They require an organization-wide emphasis on customer retention and an investment in the process.

LEARNING FROM FAILURE

Bill Marriott, CEO of Marriott Corp., demands that his firm not only do whatever is necessary to take care of guests but that employees also track, measure, and follow up on how to handle the situation better the next time (Bowen and Lawler 1995). To profit fully from investments in service recovery, firms need to classify the failure and integrate the information gleaned from the failure with information from other sources.

Classification of Service Failures

An important component of learning from service failure is identifying the root cause(s) and the underlying process(es) contributing to the problem. Classifying failures is a key link to understanding both how specific customer problems can be resolved and what process improvements need to be made. Bitner, Booms, and Tetreault (1990) used the critical incident technique to identify a service encounter classification model that has implications for organizing service failures. Based on this research, failures fall into groups including service delivery system failures, failures in response to customer needs and requests, and failures related to unprompted and unsolicited employee actions. Each group comprises multiple categories that further segment types of failures. Employing a similar methodology, Kelley, Hoffman, and Davis (1993) focused on the classification of retail failures. They identified 15 failure categories such as out of stock, improper charges, product defects, bad information, alterations and repairs, slow/unavailable service, and problems with special orders. They also examined how effectively retailers responded to the failure groupings and the subsequent retention rates of customers across categories.

Complaints also can be classified according to the frequency of occurrence and impact on the customer (Rust, Zahorik, and Keiningham 1996). Such data have implications for the amount of resources to employ to fix the service system. FedEx collects daily records of service failures and categorizes and weights failures based on the level of customer dissatisfaction. For example, a package that is 1 hour late is a less significant failure than a package that is lost or sent to the wrong address.

Xerox's "Customer Action Request Form" provides detailed information about customer problems. Complaints are identified as resulting from failures in 1 or more of 13 business areas (e.g., equipment performance, service, mail order/delivery/installation, customer inquiries, sales). Within each category, more detailed coding is provided. For example, customer service problems have 12 possible codes (e.g., difficulty obtaining service, service rep unable to fix problem, service pricing, repair time). Three additional aspects of root causes are identified. The first code deals with whether the problem primarily concerned process, people, product, or policy. Second, the problem is coded as primarily involving one of seven factors: attitude, communication, training, ethics, human error, technical, or invoice. The third code relates to business area (e.g., sales, service, supply and logistics). Information is also kept to track the resolution. This includes who handled the problem, how it was handled, financial implications of the recovery, and details of customer contacts. When completed, the form is delivered to the customer relations administrator, who ensures that the information is provided to all relevant individuals. This comprehensive form contributes to the value of the complaint information for service improvement.

In addition to focusing on the cause of the service problem, classifying complaining customers can help manage long-term satisfaction and loyalty. This is based largely on the damage that cumulative service failures can have on customer retention (Smith and Bolton 1998). The J. Peterman Company, which is in the catalog sales business, places customers who have complained on a VIP list. Each subsequent purchase is given special treatment, including being hand-picked, inspected, and tested.

Customers who complain frequently and/or are rarely satisfied with the resolutions may be the "wrong customer" (Lovelock 1994). Wrong customers may have needs that the organization cannot meet, may require more resources to serve than the revenue that would be generated by their patronage, or may simply be criminals. To manage the potential for customers to take advantage of its service guarantee, Hampton Inn maintains a database of customers who have invoked the guarantee. If the company determines that a customer is violating its trust, rather than booking that customer a room, employees recommend another hotel.

Integrating Recovery and Other Intelligence Data

Complaint data are best deployed in conjunction with other intelligence gathering techniques to determine the importance and pervasiveness of a problem and identify areas for service improvement. The "Service-Quality Information System" developed by Berry and Parasuraman (1997) is a useful model for defining the inputs into the intelligence system. The inputs can include customer, employee, and competitors' customers' surveys, mystery shopping, focus groups, customer and employee advisory panels, and service operating performance data as a comprehensive approach to focus service improvement planning and resource allocation. In Canada, Delta Hotels uses a number of tools in its quest for continual process improvement, including guest comment cards and surveys, employee opinion surveys, mystery shoppers, and quality self-assessments. The multiple methods and sources of data provide a comprehensive view of the quality picture.

Information from call centers and customer databases is also valuable. GE monitors the lifetime performance of every appliance sold as well as the quality of every customer contact. The data collected (requests for servicing, product/service compliments and complaints, (dis)satisfaction with service calls, requests for product information) are integrated into product and service design decisions.

Disseminating the Data

Although data may be collected by various sources within an organization, they must be made available to those responsible for implementing service improvements. Delta Hotels has implemented a number of procedures to ensure that data are effectively disseminated. Departmental meetings are held a minimum of once a month, focusing on the sharing of information, ideas, and plans for process improvement. This includes ensuring that the staff have the tools, training, and resources to impress guests. The company also uses an "Employee Representative Team" that includes one representative from each department and the general manager of a property. This team examines processes that involve more than one department. Delta has focused attention on combining front-line employees with managers at meetings to ensure both the sharing and shared understanding of information. Ford electronically distributes complaint information gathered at its service center directly to the dealerships responsible for settling the dispute. The same information is also sent to marketing research and engineering. These units integrate the complaint data with additional research information.

CONCLUSION

Service recovery is a complex process that can, when done effectively, contribute to customer and employee satisfaction both at the service encounter level and in the development of long-term commitment. Over the lifetime of customer relationships, problems are bound to occur. A growing body of research confirms that, similar to other types of business and personal relationships, how these conflicts are managed is vital to maintaining satisfaction, loyalty, and trust. To be effective, firms need to develop a comprehensive service recovery system that first encourages dissatisfied customers to voice their complaints and, second, provides a "fair" process, interaction, and outcome. To maximize its impact, the recovery system also needs to be integrated into service design and investment decisions contributing to improved performance, customer and employee satisfaction, and firm profitability.

REFERENCES

Berry, Leonard L. and A. Parasuraman (1991), *Marketing Services: Competing Through Quality*. New York: Free Press.

———— and ———— (1997), "Listening to the Customer—The Concept of a Service-Quality Information System," *Sloan Management Review*, 38(3), 65-76.

Bies, Robert J. and J. S. Moag (1986), "Interactional Communication Criteria of Fairness," in *Research in Organizational Behavior*, Vol. 9, R. J. Lewicki, Blair H. Sheppard, and Max H. Bazerman, eds. Greenwich, CT: JAI, 289-319.

———— and Debra L. Shapiro (1987), "Interactional Fairness Judgments: The Influence of Causal Accounts," *Social Justice Research*, 1, 199-218.

Bitner, Mary Jo, Bernard M. Booms, and Mary Stanfield Tetreault (1990), "The Service Encounter: Diagnosing Favorable and Unfavorable Incidents," *Journal of Marketing*, 54 (January), 71-85.

Blodgett, Jeffrey G., Donna J. Hill, and Stephen S. Tax (1997), "The Effects of Distributive, Procedural, and Interactional Justice on Postcomplaint Behavior," *Journal of Retailing*, 73(2), 185-210.

Bolton, Ruth N. (1998), "A Dynamic Model of the Duration of the Customer's Relationship With a Continuous Service Provider: The Role of Satisfaction," *Marketing Science*, 17(1), 45-65.

Bowen, David E. and Robert J. Johnston (forthcoming), "Internal Service Recovery: Initial Conceptualization and Implications," *International Journal of Service Industry Management*.

——— and Edward E. Lawler (1995), "Empowering Service Employees," *Sloan Management Review*, 36 (Summer), 73-84.

Clemmer, Elizabeth C. (1988), "The Role of Fairness in Customer Satisfaction With Services," doctoral dissertation, University of Maryland.

Day, Ralph L. (1984), "Modeling Choices Among Alternative Responses to Dissatisfaction," in *Advances in Consumer Research*, Vol. 11, Thomas C. Kinnear, ed. Ann Arbor, MI: Association for Consumer Research, 496-99.

——— and E. Laird Landon, Jr. (1977), "Toward a Theory of Consumer Complaining Behavior," in *Consumer and Industrial Buying Behavior*, Arch G. Woodside, Ingdish N. Seth, and Peter D. Bennett, eds. New York: Elsevier North-Holland, 425-37.

Dubé, Laurette and Manfred Maute (1996), "The Antecedents of Brand Switching, Brand Loyalty, and Verbal Responses to Service Failures," in *Advances in Services Marketing and Management*, Vol. 5, Teresa Swartz, David Bowen, and Stephen Brown, eds. Greenwich, CT: JAI, 127-51.

Fornell, Claes and Birger Wernerfelt (1987), "Defensive Marketing Strategy by Customer Complaint Management: A Theoretical Analysis," *Journal of Marketing Research*, 24 (November), 337-46.

Goodwin, Cathy and Ivan Ross (1992), "Consumer Responses to Service Failures: Influence of Procedural and Interactional Fairness Perceptions," *Journal of Business Research*, 25, 149-63.

Hart, Christopher W. L., James L. Heskett, and W. Earl Sasser, Jr. (1990), "The Profitable Art of Service Recovery," *Harvard Business Review*, 68 (July-August), 148-56.

Heskett, James L., Thomas O. Jones, Gary W. Loveman, W. Earl Sasser, Jr., and Leonard A. Schlesinger (1994), "Putting the Service Profit Chain to Work," *Harvard Business Review*, 72 (March-April), 164-74.

Hoffman, K. Douglas, Scott W. Kelley, and Holly M. Rotalsky (1995), "Tracking Service Failures and Employee Recovery Efforts," *Journal of Services Marketing*, 9(2), 49-61.

Keaveney, Susan M. (1995), "Customer Switching Behavior in Service Industries: An Exploratory Study," *Journal of Marketing*, 59(2), 71-82.

Kelley, Scott W., K. Douglas Hoffman, and Mark A. Davis (1993), "A Typology of Retail Failures and Recoveries," *Journal of Retailing*, 69(4), 429-52.

Leventhal, Gerald S., J. Karuza, and W. R. Fry (1980), "Beyond Fairness: A Theory of Allocation Preferences," in *Justice and Social Interaction*, G. Mikula, ed. New York: Springer-Verlag, 167-218.

Lovelock, Christopher H. (1994), *Product Plus*. New York: McGraw-Hill.

McCollough, M. A. (1998), "The Effect of Perceived Justice and Attributions Regarding Service Failure and Recovery on Post-Recovery Customer Satisfaction and Service Quality Attitudes" (abstract), in *Enhancing Knowledge Development in Marketing*, Ronald C. Goodstein and Scott B. Mackenzie, eds. Chicago: American Marketing Association, 163.

Parasuraman, A., Valarie A. Zeithaml, and Leonard L. Berry (1985), "A Conceptual Model of Service Quality and Its Implications for Future Research," *Journal of Marketing*, 49 (Fall), 41-50.

Reichheld, Frederick F. (1993), "Loyalty-Based Management," *Harvard Business Review*, 71 (March-April), 64-74.

Rust, Roland T., Anthony J. Zahorik, and Timothy L. Keiningham (1996), *Service Marketing*. New York: HarperCollins.

Schlesinger, Leonard A. and James L. Heskett (1991), "Breaking the Cycle of Failure in Services," *Sloan Management Review*, 32(3), 17-29.

Singh, Jagdip (1988), "Consumer Complaint Intentions and Behavior: Definitional and Taxonomical Issues," *Journal of Marketing*, 52(1), 93-107.

——— (1990), "A Typology of Consumer Dissatisfaction Response Styles," *Journal of Retailing*, 66 (Spring), 57-99.

Smith, Amy K. and Ruth N. Bolton (1998), "An Experimental Investigation of Customer Reactions to Service Failure and Recovery Encounters," *Journal of Service Research*, 1(1), 65-81.

———, ———, and Janet Wagner (1998), "A Model of Customer Satisfaction With Service Encounters Involving Failure and Recovery," working paper No. 98-100, Marketing Science Institute.

Tax, Stephen S. and Stephen W. Brown (1998), "Recovering and Learning From Service Failure," *Sloan Management Review*, 40(1), 75-88.

———, ———, and Murali Chandrashekaran (1998), "Customer Evaluations of Service Complaint Experiences: Implications for Relationship Marketing," *Journal of Marketing*, 62 (April), 60-76.

Taylor, Shirley (1994), "Waiting for Service: The Relationship Between Delays and Evaluations of Service," *Journal of Marketing*, 58 (April), 56-69.

Technical Assistance Research Program (1986), *Consumer Complaint Handling in America: An Update Study*. Washington, DC: Department of Consumer Affairs.

Zeithaml, Valarie A., Leonard L. Berry, and A. Parasuraman (1993), "The Nature and Determinants of Customer Expectations of Service," *Journal of the Academy of Marketing Science*, 21(1), 1-12.

Zemke, Ron (1995), *Service Recovery: Fixing Broken Customers*. Portland, OR: Productivity Press.

17

Complaining

NANCY STEPHENS

Complaints are registered when buyers are unhappy with their purchases. Although traditional views of business suggest that minimizing complaints is a worthy goal, enlightened marketing managers view all feedback—including complaints—as helpful, and they try to encourage it. When customers complain, two potentially positive things happen. First, the company gets the chance to fix the problem and save the customer relationship. Second, customers' dissatisfactions can point to areas of the business that need improvement and perhaps changes in strategy. Clearly, then, complaining is an important postpurchase phenomenon whose value in marketing is increasingly appreciated. It is believed that companies that pay attention to complaints enjoy stronger loyalty from their customers and are more profitable as well.

Complaining became a focus of marketing researchers in the mid-1970s, perhaps as a reflection of the rise in consumerism of that era. Hirschman's (1970) analysis of complaining formed the basis for many early studies, which were concerned with documentation and description of the phenomenon. Researchers busied themselves counting numbers of complaints and classifying them as to type of industry, nature of complaint, and method of complaining.

In addition to documenting the phenomenon of complaining, researchers in the late 1970s and early 1980s also searched for variables to build a model or theory that would explain and predict complaint behavior (e.g., Day and Bodur 1978; Day and Landon 1977; Richins 1983; Warland, Herrmann, and Willits 1975). They wondered if certain market factors would favor or disfavor customer complaining. They tried to identify the characteristics of goods and services that evoked complaints. Some investigations attempted to link complaining to demographic and lifestyle characteristics of consumers. More recent studies, from the late 1980s to the late 1990s, have examined the role of people's emotions in complaining and have looked at complaining in a business-to-business context as well (e.g., Godwin, Patterson, and Johnson 1995; Ping 1997; Westbrook 1987). Managerially oriented research on complaining has identified ways that marketing managers can use complaints as valuable feedback to guide service recovery and marketing strategy. A rich and varied literature of consumer complaining behavior has been developed over the past 25 years.

The purpose of this chapter is to examine the phenomenon of complaining, what is known about it and how that knowledge can be used to help services marketing managers and scholars.

WHERE DOES COMPLAINING FIT IN MODELS OF CONSUMER BEHAVIOR?

Complaining is assumed by most consumer behavior models to occur as a result of dissatisfaction. Dissatisfaction typically has been thought to occur when consumers consider the difference between what was expected and what was actually received in a purchase. If buyers receive much less than they expected, they feel dissatisfaction (Bearden and Teel 1983), and some will voice complaints. Many, however, do not speak up, making dissatisfaction a necessary but not sufficient cause for consumer complaining. In other words, for complaining to occur, a buyer must be dissatisfied, but that alone is not enough. Because some dissatisfied customers do not complain, there are probably additional factors that explain one's propensity to complain in a particular situation. Much of the attention in the complaining literature has been directed toward identifying these other factors.

DOCUMENTING COMPLAINING BEHAVIOR

As is typical with any phenomenon being newly investigated, researchers first performed descriptive studies that counted the numbers of complaints and classified them as to type of industry and nature of complaint (Day and Ash 1979; Day and Bodur 1978; Day and Landon 1977; Diamond, Ward, and Faber 1976). They also analyzed and classified the methods consumers used to complain (Day and Ash 1979; Day and Bodur 1978; Day and Landon 1977; Mason and Himes 1973; Singh 1988, 1990; Technical Assistance Research Program 1979; Warland, Herrmann, and Willits 1975).

How Do Consumers Complain (or Do They)?

An unfortunate finding of virtually every study of consumer complaining is that many dissatisfied buyers do not say anything to the company, the store, or the service provider. Unhappy customers may very well speak up, but only privately, to warn friends and family. At the same time, they frequently resolve not to buy the brand again. A lack of consumer candor is a problem for businesses because they never learn of the problem, get the chance to fix it, or preserve customer loyalty. More important, they do not have the opportunity to diagnose

TABLE 17.1 Percentages of Dissatisfied Consumers Who Complain

	Complained Directly *(company could respond)*	*Complained Indirectly* *or Not at All* *(company could not respond)* [a]
Day and Ash (1979)		
Durables	80	20
Day and Landon (1977)		
Durables	73	27
Services	66	34
Nondurables	52	48
Bolfing (1989)		
Hotel/motel chains	49	51
Andreason (1984)		
Services	48	52
Day and Bodur (1978)		
Services	45	55
Warland, Herrmann, and Willits (1975)	40	60
Richins (1983)	33	67
Moyer (1984)	30	70
Andreason (1985)		
Physician services	8	92
Technical Assistance Research Program (1979)	4	96

a. These dissatisfied consumers may complain to friends and family or even a third party. In the latter case, the company may respond, but its response will not be immediate, which is a condition linked to preserving the customer relationship and loyalty.

the problem to see if it indicates a greater issue that could be solved through better marketing strategy.

Table 17.1 shows the proportion of dissatisfied consumers who complain to companies such that the companies have the opportunity to respond. It ranges from a high of 80% in Day and Ash's (1979) investigation to a somewhat disconcerting low of 4% in a federal government study (Technical Assistance Research Program 1979). People who do not tell the company or an employee when they are disappointed may very well tell friends and family (Day and Ash 1979; Day and Bodur 1978; Day and Landon 1977; Singh 1988; Technical Assistance Research Program 1979; Warland, Herrmann, and Willits 1975; Zaltman, Srivastava, and Deshpande 1978). Fewer than 5-10% will file complaints with third parties such as the Better Business Bureau or a government agency (Day and Ash 1979; Day and Bodur 1978; Day and Landon 1977; Technical Assistance Research Program 1979; Warland, Herrmann, and Willits 1975; Zaltman, Srivastava, and Deshpande 1978). More likely, they will warn others, perhaps causing the business to lose even more customers. In the federal government's study, conducted by the White House Office of Consumer Affairs (Technical Assistance Research Program 1979), consumers who were unhappy, whether or not they complained to the company, typically told 9-10 other people about it.

Clearly, it is in the long-range interest of any organization to hear from its dissatisfied patrons. The consequences of not doing so are that the business potentially suffers a loss of sales, which it may have a difficult time diagnosing (Hirschman 1970). When problems are misdiagnosed, inappropriate marketing strategies may be selected and marketing resources may be wrongly directed. The organization merely compounds its problems unless it can get to the bottom of issues that are causing customers to be unhappy and leave.

What Do People Complain About?

People experience all kinds of problems at each point in the purchase process. For example, before purchasing, people may feel deceived or offended by advertising. As they are ordering, there may be problems concerning delivery or credit. The good or service itself may perform poorly. After purchase, customers may be unhappy with faulty repairs or warranty terms. It is interesting, however, that whether a purchase is a tangible good or an intangible service, at least half of people's complaints involve service issues such as delivery, credit, collections, repairs, and guarantees and warranties (Diamond, Ward, and Faber 1976).

When one looks specifically at complaints in service industries, one finds customers who are unhappy about unprofessional service, work not completed on time, and being overcharged (Bitner, Booms, and Tetreault 1990; Day and Bodur 1978; Day and Landon 1977). Bitner, Booms, and Tetreault (1990) found that the way employees respond to service problems is frequently as important as the problems themselves in creating customer satisfaction or dissatisfaction.

CORRELATES OF COMPLAINING

As marketing scholars documented the phenomenon of complaining, they also tried to explain it in terms of market structure, product characteristics, and consumer traits such as demographics, beliefs and attitudes, personality, and emotion. They searched for variables that would allow them to predict when complaining would occur and when it wouldn't.

Market Factors

Economist Albert Hirschman, in his classic 1970 book *Exit, Voice, and Loyalty*, was one of the first to point out the risk a business takes when it does not hear feedback from customers. He contrasted *monopoly* and *competitive* markets, pointing out that in a competitive market with many sellers, dissatisfied buyers do not necessarily voice their complaints because they can easily exit and go elsewhere. The time and effort it takes someone to speak up is unlikely to pay off, and brand switching is simpler. Businesses in competitive markets that do not make an effort to listen to customers therefore risk losing business without knowing why. A monopoly market, in contrast to a competitive one, may actually increase complaining because customers are captive and exiting to another supplier is not a possibility; complaining is the only chance for improvement. Hirschman's early observations have been borne out in later investigations (Andreason 1984, 1985).

Seller and Service Factors

At least one factor that influences the likelihood of hearing customer feedback is under the organization's control. That is the company's reputation for quality and for being responsive to complaining consumers (Bolfing 1989; Day and Landon 1977; Granbois, Summers, and Frazier 1977). Disgruntled customers are more likely to speak up to companies that care about the quality of their work and try to resolve customer problems. Therefore, it is to the firm's benefit to let customers know that it wants their feedback and cares about their satisfaction.

In contrast, an uncontrollable factor that affects complaining about a good or service is its unique characteristics. If a service is complex, expensive, or considered important, or if the problem with it is serious, consumers will be more likely to voice their complaints (Blodgett and Granbois 1992; Bolfing 1989; Day and Landon 1977; Landon 1977; Lawther, Krishnan, and Valle 1978; Richins 1983). Buyers tend not to complain about low-cost, low-involvement purchases such as nondurables (Day and Landon 1977). Thus, firms that sell simple, inexpensive, everyday services probably need to make a special effort to contact customers for feedback. Examples might be fast food stores, self-service gasoline stations, or grocery stores.

Consumer Factors

Many studies have investigated consumer factors that may enhance or inhibit complaining (Bearden and Teel 1983; Day and Ash 1979; Day and Landon 1977; Fornell and Westbrook 1979; Krishnan and Valle 1979; Mason and Himes 1973; Moyer 1984; Richins 1983; Warland, Herrmann, and Willits 1975; Zaltman, Srivastava, and Deshpande 1978). Several studies have been done in services contexts (Andreason 1985; Day and Bodur 1978; Folkes, Koletsky, and Graham 1987; Singh 1988, 1990).

Demographics and Lifestyle

A fairly consistent finding in the literature is that complainers occupy higher socioeconomic levels in society. Their higher income, education, and social involvement give them the knowledge, confidence, and motivation to speak up when they feel wronged (Day and Landon 1977; Landon 1977; Mason and Himes 1973; Moyer 1984; Singh 1990; Warland, Herrmann, and Moore 1984; Warland, Herrmann, and Willits 1975; Zaltman, Srivastava, and Deshpande 1978). In contrast, customers who do not speak up when they are dissatisfied may be located at lower socioeconomic levels (Kraft 1977; Spalding and Marcus 1981) and may, in fact, be members of particularly vulnerable groups in the marketplace, such as the poor or immigrants (Andreason and Manning 1990).

Beliefs and Attitudes

Consumers' beliefs and attitudes have been associated with their complaining behavior. For example, people who believe that complaining will make a difference are more likely to try it (Blodgett and Granbois 1992; Day and Ash 1979; Day and Bodur 1978). Persons who perceive that many marketing practices are unfair are more likely to complain (Zaltman, Srivastava, and Deshpande 1978). Attributions about who is to blame for a problem also affect people's complaining. Those who believe the problem was caused by someone else and not themselves are more likely to complain (Krishnan and Valle 1979; Richins 1983), particularly if they think the company has control over the situation (Folkes, Koletsky, and Graham 1987). If buyers attribute the problem to themselves, they are less likely to speak up (Godwin, Patterson, and Johnson 1995; Spalding and Marcus 1981; Stephens and Gwinner 1998; Westbrook 1987).

Personality

Personality factors might be involved in consumer complaining, although the literature is sparse on this topic. In general, assertive people are more likely to complain, whereas submissive persons are more likely to keep quiet (Bolfing 1989; Fornell and Westbrook 1979).

Emotions

More recently, people's emotions have been hypothesized to influence their complaining behavior (Bolfing 1989; Godwin, Patterson, and Johnson 1995; Westbrook 1987), especially with regard to noncomplaining (Bolfing 1989; Spalding and Marcus 1981; Stephens and Gwinner 1998). In fact, Westbrook (1987) argued that the emotion that accompanies purchase experience is as important as satisfaction or dissatisfaction, if not more so, in determining people's complaining behavior.

Consumers may feel three different types of negative emotions when they are dissatisfied. The specific feelings are based on their attributions about who is to blame for the problem (Godwin, Patterson, and Johnson 1995; Smith and Ellsworth 1985). Those who blame another party, typically the company or employee, generally feel anger, disgust, or contempt. These negative emotions are the ones most likely to lead to complaining (Folkes, Koletsky, and Graham 1987). They probably lead, as well, to negative word-of-mouth communication to family and friends (Westbrook 1987).

Consumers who see the cause of the problem as situational (i.e., no one is to blame) tend to feel distress or fear. These emotions probably do not result in as much complaining because consumers feel powerless compared to the company, perhaps because of its size or its market position (Stephens and Gwinner 1998). Social fear may also come into play; some dissatisfied buyers keep quiet because they fear being rude, bothering someone, or hurting someone's feelings (Bolfing 1989; Stephens and Gwinner 1998). Stephens and Gwinner (1998) suggested that some consumers may not complain because they empathize with, or feel compassion for, the employee who causes the problem, a finding that may be unique to services because of the face-to-face contact between buyer and seller.

Persons who make internal attributions about the cause of the problem (i.e., they blame themselves) usually experience shame or guilt. These are negative emotions that seem to keep disappointed consumers from speaking up (Godwin, Patterson, and Johnson 1995; Stephens and Gwinner 1998; Westbrook 1987).

Summary

In general, a company can expect to hear from dissatisfied customers if those customers don't have many alternatives in the marketplace. It will get more feedback if its services are complicated or expensive and if it has the reputation of wanting to make customers happy. The people the organization will hear from probably will be upscale individuals who think the company is at fault and who believe that by speaking up they will receive some resolution or satisfaction.

A company probably will not hear from dissatisfied customers if there are many competitors to whom people can easily switch and if the firm sells simple, low-cost services. The disappointed customers who silently depart will most likely be those at lower socioeconomic levels who do not think voicing a complaint will do any good.

COMPLAINING IN A BUSINESS-TO-BUSINESS CONTEXT

Only recently have marketing scholars shown interest in complaining in a business-to-business environment. They have tried to find out if the literature of consumer complaining applies in this new context (Dart and Freeman 1994; Hansen, Swan, and Powers 1996, 1997; Ping 1997). In the few studies published, it generally has fit.

For example, the same set of complaining measures, administered to samples of consumers and to samples of business owners, company managers, and purchasing agents found fairly similar styles of responding to dissatisfaction. Among consumers, people who will talk to the company before switching, warning others, or contacting a third party constitute about a third of customers (Singh 1990). Among owners of businesses, the same proportion, about one third, will voice complaints to a supplier of professional services before changing (Dart and Freeman 1994). Among purchasing agents and company managers, however, a higher proportion (51%) will contact the seller to get their concerns addressed (Hansen, Swan, and Powers 1996) before patronizing another provider. Perhaps purchasing agents and company managers, because they are being paid to act on behalf of others, are more diligent about setting right a troubled supplier relationship before switching.

Business executives who do not speak up when they are dissatisfied with a supplier are similar to silent consumers in that they will engage in negative word-of-mouth communication to others as well as silently switch suppliers without mentioning any dissatisfactions to the offending firm (Dart and Freeman 1994; Hansen, Swan, and Powers 1996). Such behaviors are harmful to the organization and subject it to the same hazards that Hirschman (1970) predicted in consumer markets; that is, slow and silent loss of sales for reasons unknown to the firm. The seller's goal should be to enhance the feedback to the firm, especially complaints, so that a mysterious sales slowdown can be avoided (Hansen, Swan, and Powers 1997; Ping 1997). Methods of getting one's business customers to speak up are to (a) provide expert information that buyers want, (b) communicate important information to customers quickly, (c) avoid encroaching on areas that buyers feel are their responsibility, and (d) try not to make buyers highly dependent (Hansen, Swan, and Powers 1997).

In the business-to-business arena, then, the same set of rules seem to apply as in the consumer arena. Companies should try to listen to customers, find out what dissatisfactions they may have, and resolve those problems.

COMPLAINING: OPPORTUNITY FOR SERVICE RECOVERY AND FUTURE LOYALTY

Customer complaints bring the customer relationship to a crossroads where the company's actions and communications will determine the future. Company policy and/or an employee's decisions typically will decide whether the customer goes or stays.

The wise organization will use *defensive* marketing strategy, trying to save the customer relationship and make it stronger than it was before. Engaging in such a strategy succeeds with most customers (Gilly and Gelb 1982; Kolodinsky 1992) and may ultimately mean that the company can spend less money attracting new customers (Fornell and Wernerfelt 1987). Why? Customers with resolved complaints not only will be loyal themselves but also will tell others about their experience, generating positive word of mouth for the firm. In a federal government study, 95% of complainers continued patronage when their complaints were dealt with quickly, and they told an average of five others about it (Technical Assistance Research Program 1979). Clearly, the strategy of encouraging feedback is the wiser and more profitable choice (Reichheld and Sasser 1990).

Defensive marketing strategy, hanging on to the customers a company has, means regarding complaints as opportunities delivered by customers. When a company is notified, via a complaint, that something has gone wrong in the transaction or relationship, it should do two things: act immediately and analyze the complaint further to see if it indicates a systemic problem.

Acting immediately entails acknowledging the complaint to the customer, taking responsibility, and solving the problem quickly and fairly (Conlon and Murray 1996). A company whose employees can respond quickly and effectively to complaints can turn failures into successes and can create greater loyalty than existed before the problem occurred (Bitner, Booms, and Tetreault 1990; Hart, Heskett, and Sasser 1990). To accomplish this, the company has to understand the customer's point of view and probable expectations (Goodwin and Ross 1990). For example, people who lose money in a transaction may have different ideas of what is fair than people who complain about a dirty restroom in a service facility (Gilly and Gelb 1982). Tax, Brown, and Chandrashekaran (1998) showed that fairness, in the customer's mind, generally consists of three things. First, the company must deliver *distributive* justice by solving the problem. Second, it ought to give the complainer *procedural* justice, fixing things quickly and without hassle. Third, the organization should provide *interactional* justice, treating the complainer with honesty and respect. A final, but important, step in responding successfully to complaints is thanking the complainer and informing him or her of what has been done about the issue (Hart, Heskett, and Sasser 1990).

Analyzing the complaint further to see if it indicates a problem area means formalizing the solicitation and analysis of complaints. The company must find ways for complaints to make it into the marketing intelligence system that informs marketing strategy decisions (Kasouf, Celuch, and Strieter 1995). Too many companies do not take full advantage of the diagnostic potential of complaints. They may respond to the customer but may not have developed a clear way to save, organize, and use complaints.

To improve its solicitation of complaints, the company should encourage customer feedback by making it easy to get in touch and by assuring customers that their opinions are wanted. The company should provide multiple means of contact (Hart, Heskett, and Sasser 1990), such as special telephone numbers, telephone surveys of recent buyers, and website addresses, and it should publicize them constantly. In addition to resolving the problem, the company must enter the information into a database that can be analyzed. The company may find out that particular aspects of the service are causing problems or that certain locations or employees are generating more complaints. For example, Hart, Heskett, and Sasser (1990) observed that new goods and services or new employees often cause problems and should be monitored closely. Each firm will be able to identify its own potential hot spots and plan for service recovery when problems occur.

Organizations that have developed strong systems for soliciting, analyzing, and acting on complaints will find competition easier. They will know what thoughts and feelings their customers are having and will be able to develop more focused and effective strategy for the future.

SUMMARY

Complaining is a postpurchase process that may or may not occur when customers are disappointed. Companies that sell expensive, complex services in less competitive markets to upscale buyers are most likely to hear complaints, whereas companies that sell inexpensive, simple services in more competitive markets to low socioeconomic customers are less likely to hear complaints. The appropriate challenge and goal for any organization selling any service to any type of customer is to get feedback and complaints from its buyers. Research shows that such information, when acted upon, can improve customer relationships and foster greater customer loyalty.

REFERENCES

Andreason, Alan R. (1984), "Consumer Satisfaction in Loose Monopolies: The Case of Medical Care," *Journal of Public Policy and Marketing*, 2, 122-35.

—— (1985), "Consumer Responses to Dissatisfaction in Loose Monopolies," *Journal of Consumer Research*, 12 (September), 135-41.

—— and Jean Manning (1990), "The Dissatisfaction and Complaining Behavior of Vulnerable Consumers," *Journal of Consumer Satisfaction, Dissatisfaction and Complaining*, 3, 12-20.

Bearden, William O. and Jesse E. Teel (1983), "Selected Determinants of Consumer Satisfaction and Complaint Reports," *Journal of Marketing Research*, 20 (February), 21-28.

Bitner, Mary Jo, Bernard M. Booms, and Mary Stanfield Tetreault (1990), "The Service Encounter: Diagnosing Favorable and Unfavorable Incidents," *Journal of Marketing*, 54(1), 71-84.

Blodgett, Jeffrey G. and Donald H. Granbois (1992), "Toward an Integrated Conceptual Model of Consumer Complaining Behavior," *Journal of Consumer Satisfaction, Dissatisfaction and Complaining Behavior*, 5, 93-103.

Bolfing, Claire P. (1989), "How Do Consumers Express Dissatisfaction and What Can Service Marketers Do About It?" *The Journal of Services Marketing*, 3 (Spring), 5-23.

Conlon, Donald E. and Noel M. Murray (1996), "Customer Perceptions of Corporate Responses to Product Complaints: The Role of Explanations," *Academy of Management Journal*, 39(4), 1040-56.

Dart, Jack and Kim Freeman (1994), "Dissatisfaction Response Styles Among Clients of Professional Accounting Firms," *Journal of Business Research*, 29, 75-81.

Day, Ralph L. and Stephen B. Ash (1979), "Consumer Response to Dissatisfaction With Durable Products," in *Advances in Consumer Research*, Vol. 6, William Wilkie, ed. Ann Arbor, MI: Association for Consumer Research, 438-44.

—— and Muzaffer Bodur (1978), "Consumer Response to Dissatisfaction With Services and Intangibles," in *Advances in Consumer Research*, Vol. 5, H. Keith Hunt, ed. Ann Arbor, MI: Association for Consumer Research, 263-72.

—— and E. Laird Landon (1977), "Toward a Theory of Consumer Complaining Behavior," in *Consumer and Industrial Buying Behavior*, Arch G. Woodside, Jagdish N. Sheth, and Peter D. Bennett, eds. New York: North-Holland, 425-37.

Diamond, Steven L., Scott Ward, and Ronald Faber (1976), "Consumer Problems and Consumerism: Analysis of Calls to a Consumer Hot Line," *Journal of Marketing*, 30 (January), 58-62.

Folkes, Valarie, Susan Koletsky, and John L. Graham (1987), "A Field Study of Causal Inferences and Consumer Reaction: The View From the Airport," *Journal of Consumer Research*, 13 (March), 534-39.

Fornell, Claes and Birger Wernerfelt (1987), "Defensive Marketing Strategy by Customer Complaint Management: A Theoretical Analysis," *Journal of Marketing Research*, 24 (November), 337-46.

—— and Robert Westbrook (1979), "An Exploratory Study of Assertiveness, Aggressiveness, and Consumer Complaining Behavior," *Advances in Consumer Research*, Vol. 6, William Wilkie, ed. Ann Arbor, MI: Association for Consumer Research, 105-10.

Gilly, Mary C. and Betsy D. Gelb (1982), "Post-Purchase Consumer Processes and the Complaining Consumer," *Journal of Consumer Research*, 9 (December), 323-28.

Godwin, Beth, Paul G. Patterson, and Lester W. Johnson (1995), "Emotion, Coping and Complaining Propensity Following a Dissatisfactory Service Encounter," *Journal of Satisfaction, Dissatisfaction and Complaining Behavior*, 8, 155-63.

Goodwin, Cathy and Ivan Ross (1990), "Consumer Evaluations of Responses to Complaints: What's Fair and Why," *The Journal of Services Marketing*, 4(3), 53-61.

Granbois, Donald, John O. Summers, and Gary L. Frazier (1977), "Correlates of Consumer Expectation and Complaining Behavior," in *Consumer Satisfaction, Dissatisfaction and Complaining Behavior Proceedings*, Ralph L. Day and H. Keith Hunt, eds. Bloomington: Indiana University, 18-25.

Hansen, Scott W., John E. Swan, and Thomas L. Powers (1996), "Encouraging Friendly Complaint Behavior in Industrial Markets," *Industrial Marketing Management*, 25, 271-81.

————, ————, and ———— (1997), "Vendor Relationships as Predictors of Organizational Buyer Complaint Response Styles," *Journal of Business Research*, 40, 65-77.

Hart, Christopher W. L., James L. Heskett, and W. Earl Sasser, Jr. (1990), "The Profitable Art of Service Recovery," *Harvard Business Review*, 68 (July/August), 148-56.

Hirschman, Albert O. (1970), *Exit, Voice, and Loyalty: Responses to Decline in Firms, Organizations, and States*. Cambridge, MA: Harvard University Press.

Kasouf, Chickery J., Kevin G. Celuch, and Jeffrey C. Strieter (1995), "Consumer Complaints as Market Intelligence: Orienting Context and Conceptual Framework," *Journal of Consumer Satisfaction, Dissatisfaction and Complaining Behavior*, 8, 59-68.

Kolodinsky, Jane (1992), "A System for Estimating Complaints, Complaint Resolution, and Subsequent Purchases of Professional and Personal Services," *Journal of Consumer Satisfaction, Dissatisfaction and Complaining Behavior*, 5, 36-44.

Kraft, Frederic B. (1977), "Characteristics of Consumer Complainers and Complaint Repatronage Behavior," in *Consumer Satisfaction, Dissatisfaction and Complaining Behavior Proceedings*, Ralph L. Day and H. Keith Hunt, eds. Bloomington: Indiana University, 79-84.

Krishnan, S. and Valerie A. Valle (1979), "Dissatisfaction Attributions and Consumer Complaint Behavior," in *Advances in Consumer Research*, Vol. 6, William Wilkie, ed. Ann Arbor, MI: Association for Consumer Research, 445-49.

Landon, E. Laird, Jr. (1977), "A Model of Consumer Complaining Behavior," in *Consumer Satisfaction, Dissatisfaction and Complaining Behavior Proceedings*, Ralph L. Day and H. Keith Hunt, eds. Bloomington: Indiana University, 26-29.

Lawther, Karen L., S. Krishnan, and Valerie A. Valle (1978), "The Consumer Complaint Process: Directions for Theoretical Development," in *New Dimensions in Consumer Satisfaction, Dissatisfaction and Complaining Behavior*, Ralph L. Day and H. Keith Hunt, eds. Bloomington: Indiana University, 10-14.

Mason, J. Barry and Samuel H. Himes, Jr. (1973), "An Exploratory Behavioral and Socio-Economic Profile of Consumer Action About Dissatisfaction With Selected Household Appliances," *Journal of Consumer Affairs*, 7 (Winter), 121-27.

Moyer, Mel S. (1984), "Characteristics of Consumer Complainants: Implications for Marketing and Public Policy," *Journal of Public Policy and Marketing*, 3, 67-84.

Ping, Robert A., Jr. (1997), "Voice in Business-to-Business Relationships: Cost of Exit and Demographic Antecedents," *Journal of Retailing*, 73(2), 261-81.

Reichheld, Frederick F. and W. Earl Sasser, Jr. (1990), "Zero Defections: Quality Comes to Services," *Harvard Business Review*, 68 (September-October), 105-11.

Richins, Marsha L. (1983), "Negative Word-of-Mouth by Dissatisfied Consumers: A Pilot Study," *Journal of Marketing*, 47 (Winter), 68-78.

Singh, Jagdip (1988), "Consumer Complaint Intentions and Behavior: Definitional and Taxonomical Issues," *Journal of Marketing*, 52 (January), 93-107.

———— (1990), "A Typology of Consumer Dissatisfaction Response Styles," *Journal of Retailing*, 66 (Spring), 57-99.

Smith, Craig A. and Phoebe C. Ellsworth (1985), "Patterns of Cognitive Appraisal in Emotion," *Journal of Personality and Social Psychology*, 48(4), 813-18.

Spalding, James B., Jr. and Norman Marcus (1981), "Postal and Telephone Complaint Handling Procedures: A Comparative Study of the U.S. and the U.K.," in *Consumer Satisfaction, Dissatisfaction and Complaining Behavior Proceedings*, Ralph L. Day and H. Keith Hunt, eds. Bloomington: Indiana University, 91-97.

Stephens, Nancy and Kevin P. Gwinner (1998), "Why Don't Some People Complain? A Cognitive-Emotive Process Model of Consumer Complaint Behavior," *Journal of the Academy of Marketing Science*, 26(3), 172-89.

Tax, Stephen S., Stephen W. Brown, and Murali Chandrashekaran (1998), "Customer Evaluations of Service Complaint Experiences: Implications for Relationship Marketing," *Journal of Marketing*, 62(2), 60-76.

Technical Assistance Research Program (1979), *Consumer Complaint Handling in America: A Final Report*. Washington, DC: White House Office of Consumer Affairs.

Warland, Rex H., Robert O. Herrmann, and Dan E. Moore (1984), "Consumer Complaining and Community Involvement: An Exploration of Their Theoretical and Empirical Linkages," *Journal of Consumer Affairs*, 18(1), 64-78.

———, ———, and Jane Willits (1975), "Dissatisfied Consumers: Who Gets Upset and Who Takes Action," *Journal of Consumer Affairs*, 9 (Winter), 148-63.

Westbrook, Robert A. (1987), "Product/Consumption-Based Affective Responses and Postpurchase Behavior," *Journal of Marketing Research*, 24 (August), 258-70.

Zaltman, Gerald, Rajendra K. Srivastava, and Rohit Deshpande (1978), "Perceptions of Unfair Marketing Practices," in *Advances in Consumer Research*, Vol. 5, H. Keith Hunt, ed. Ann Arbor, MI: Association for Consumer Research, 263-68.

18

Service Guarantees

Research and Practice

AMY L. OSTROM
CHRISTOPHER HART

It is said that there are no guarantees in life except death and taxes. Whoever said that has never spent a night at a Hampton Inn, shipped an important letter via Federal Express, or gotten dental insurance through Delta Dental. These three companies are evidence of the power of guarantees and their ability to transform the very essence of an organization, both internally in terms of the *esprit de corps* among employees and externally, transforming customers' perceptions and evaluations. Although the best service organizations have long practiced a policy of attempting to do almost whatever it takes to achieve customer satisfaction (e.g., we expect restaurants to replace food that has not been prepared properly and hotels to give us a new room if the plumbing is faulty), service organizations, in particular, are beginning to recognize that guarantees can serve not only as a marketing tool but also as a means for defining, cultivating, and maintaining quality throughout an organization.

The idea of offering a guarantee is not new. The advent of modern-day guarantees can be traced to Cyrus McCormick, who in 1855 began to provide a written money-back guarantee with his mechanical reapers, and to John Wanamaker, who a few years later began offering to guarantee customer satisfaction with every item sold in his department stores. Although their guarantees were first denounced as financial folly, McCormick and Wanamaker quickly gained customers and profits that made them then among the richest people in the United States. These offers introduced the public to the idea that a guarantee could be much more than just a means for undoing a faulty commercial transaction; a guarantee could be a powerful statement about the way a company did business.

WHY OFFER A SERVICE GUARANTEE?

From an organizational perspective, offering a guarantee can provide considerable benefits.[1] First, implementing a guarantee forces a company to focus on its customers. Figuring out what to guarantee requires a detailed understanding of the target customers' expectations about aspects of the service being provided. A guarantee also sets clear standards for employees and the organization. Schneider and Bowen, in their book *Winning the Service Game* (1995), argue that one of the most effective ways to bring about strong service performances on the part of employees is by providing them with a goal to achieve. Accomplishing important goals serves as a reward in and of itself for employees, and it can also be used as a basis to dole out other rewards such as feedback, recognition, or bonuses (Schneider and Bowen 1995). Offering a guarantee instantly provides employees with a service-related goal that can quickly and effectively achieve goal congruence between employees and the organization.

Another important benefit a guarantee offers is that it generates feedback from customers: It encourages customers to complain. Research suggests that only a small percentage of dissatisfied customers actually put forth the effort to complain to the company (Heskett, Sasser, and Schlesinger 1997; Technical Assistance Research Programs Institute 1986). A well-implemented guarantee increases customer complaints for several reasons. First, the guarantee promise helps to clarify the criteria that customers should use to judge the service. Second, it also communicates to customers that they have a right to complain—that indeed the service provider wants to know if they feel they have not received what the company promises. Finally, the guarantee payout provides an incentive for them to complain.

Customer complaints generated by a guarantee are a source of feedback that can have both short-run and long-run implications for a firm. In the short run, the instant when the customer invokes a guarantee is a "moment of truth" for the company. Each time a customer complains, rather than walking out the door never to return, represents the opportunity for a company to engage in service recovery. The importance of service recovery cannot be overstated. It is the firm's opportunity to turn things around for the customer and, if handled well, can result in highly satisfied customers (Bitner, Booms, and Tetreault 1990). In this regard, service recovery is creating an opportunity out of a situation a business wishes never occurred. In the long run, looking across customers, the information collected about why guarantees were invoked can pinpoint the causes of customer dissatisfaction, providing critical information about what systemic improvements need to be made.

Promus Hotel Corporation has reaped substantial internal benefits from the implementation of its 100% Satisfaction Guarantee at the Hampton Inn chain (and, subsequently, its other brands: Embassy Suites and Homewood Suites). Studies of the guarantee's impact show increases in employee morale attributable to their being given the ability and motivation to act on behalf of guests and by generating employee pride in delivering outstanding service. Not surprisingly, this in turn has led to reductions in employee turnover. Operationally, the guarantee continues to uncover opportunities for service improvements as well as to attract high-caliber franchisees to the Promus System. Potential franchisees for whom Promus's 100% Satisfaction Guarantee is unpalatable simply do not apply.

Overall, by translating each element of customer dissatisfaction into financial pain for the company, a powerful service guarantee that is designed and implemented well cuts through bureaucracy, topples barriers, creates a sense of shared mission, and refocuses the company on service elements that need improvement. By providing an often daunting but achievable goal, it energizes managers and employees and creates enthusiasm within the organization. Equally important, a guarantee creates a feedback link between customers and operations that enables the company to identify what customers want and need and, simultaneously, results in painful consequences if the company does not pay attention or if it loses sight of the customer.

Although a guarantee's internal benefits can be substantial, its effect on consumers is what is discussed most often and studied in the academic literature. The interest in understanding the impact of company promises on consumer perceptions started with investigation into the impact of warranties for goods on consumer evaluations.[2] Several marketing studies have investigated warranties for durable goods in terms of (a) the importance of warranty information to consumers (Lehmann and Ostlund 1972; Olson and Jacoby 1972), (b) how product warranties affect consumers' risk perceptions (Bearden and Shimp 1982; Erevelles 1993; Shimp and Bearden 1982), and (c) how they affect consumers' attitude toward the product and perceptions of product quality (Boulding and Kirmani 1993; Erevelles 1993; Innis and Unnava 1991). The results from these studies suggest that warranties for durables can reduce consumers' perceptions of risk and, under some conditions, such as when there are few other cues for consumers to use to judge quality, can lead to more positive consumer evaluations of the product, especially prepurchase.

It is likely that as the nature of the promise shifts from a warranty against product failure to a guarantee emphasizing customer satisfaction, the impact of such a promise on customer perceptions should be even greater. For example, for most manufacturing companies, customer satisfaction depends primarily on product functionality and reliability. These qualities are relatively easy to measure and are required in standard product warranties. If the product does what it is supposed to do, most customers will be satisfied and not invoke the warranty; therefore, the benefit to a customer of an unconditional product guarantee is the customer's ability to return the product in instances when he or she is dissatisfied with a product even if it is functioning properly and reliably. For example, a customer might want to return a product because the instruction manual is confusing, a competitor introduces a better product, the product becomes dirty or scratched, or the color loses its appeal.

Research focusing specifically on satisfaction guarantees for services suggests that offering a guarantee can reduce consumers' risk perceptions of purchasing the service and that it can enhance customers' prepurchase evaluations of the firm, especially when consumers perceive there to be a high level of variability in the service quality offered in the industry (Ostrom and Iacobucci 1998). Along those same lines, research by Promus Hotel Corp. indicates that its 100% Satisfaction Guarantee continues to attract new guests to its hotels, which has direct implications for the bottom line.

Ultimately, the impetus for offering a guarantee is that it will positively affect profitability. Although quantifying a guarantee's contribution to company profits can be difficult, companies that have done so have evidence of the impressive results that can be obtained when a strong guarantee is well implemented. Promus meticulously tracks the costs and benefits of its guarantee. For example, in 1990, the first year of the guarantee program, the company found that roughly 2% of its guests chose to stay at the hotel because of the guarantee, increasing revenue by $7 million. More than 3,300 guests who had invoked the guarantee returned to a Hampton Inn that same year, with 61% of these people saying they returned specifically because of the guarantee. The repeat business from these guests brought in an extra $1 million that year. Hence, the guarantee contributed an extra $8 million to the Hampton Inn top line, while the company paid only $350,000 in guarantee invocations. This figure is somewhat conservative in that it does not include the nearly half of all guests who did not invoke the guarantee but who indicated that the guarantee made them more likely to stay at a Hampton Inn in the future. The results for 1991 were even more dramatic, with the estimated incremental revenue resulting from the guarantee jumping to $18 million, while the level of payouts remained flat.

Another example of the financial impact of a guarantee comes from the Robert Wood Johnson University Hospital, a teaching hospital and trauma center located in New Brunswick, New Jersey. The hospital's emergency department guarantees that patients will be seen in 15 minutes by a nurse and within 30 minutes by a physician—or the hospital pays the bill (Pallarito 1995). Financial benefits that the hospital's management attribute to the guarantee include additional revenues of $150,000 a month—$1.8 million a year—that previously had been lost because of the 50 would-have-been patients who left the emergency department each month without being seen by medical personnel or receiving treatment.

The results from these companies suggest that extraordinary guarantees can give a significant lift to the bottom line of service firms that provide a service level sufficiently high that guarantee invocations are modest. In general, cost/benefit calculations do not take into account less tangible benefits that accrue from a well-designed and -implemented guarantee, such as improved employee morale (e.g., 85% of Hampton Inn employees said the guarantee motivates them to do a better job), better management decision making, improved quality processes, and improved long-term customer loyalty. These "softer" benefits, though difficult to quantify, are cited by firms that have successfully implemented strong service guarantees as being important elements in building customer-centric organizational cultures.

In addition to the aforementioned benefits, other important reasons exist for service firms to consider offering a powerful service guarantee. First, service firms have a greater opportunity than manufacturers to differentiate themselves through a guarantee, because service firms are not mandated to do so by law. (The Uniform Commercial Code in the United States requires that warranties be offered for every "tangible, movable good"; tangibility excludes services and movable excludes real estate.) Consequently, outside of retailing and overnight package delivery, the percentage of service firms offering strong guarantees is relatively low. Besides the legal aspect, the low prevalence is likely attributable to the fact that the root of dissatisfaction for many services is vague in comparison to the clear-cut sources of problems with durables, which typically involve demonstrable defects or lack of functionality.

Wirtz (1998), in his exploratory study of guarantees offered by several service firms in Singapore, found that companies that were the only competitor offering a guarantee in their industry attributed more of their success to the guarantee in comparison to firms in industries where offering a guarantee was more common. With competition growing increasingly fierce and customers becoming more demanding, companies are eager to find ways to differentiate themselves from a host of competitors and to address customer concerns about obtaining the greatest value possible. Although most service companies are continually trying to convey to customers that satisfying them is a primary goal, few efforts communicate this commitment more powerfully than a guarantee.

Guarantees also might be especially useful for service firms because of customers' elevated risk perceptions. The heterogeneity in service-delivery quality in labor-intensive services and the simultaneous production and consumption nature of services often make them unpredictable and inconsistent. In addition it is harder to control and to correct errors before the services are delivered to customers. These elements are likely to increase consumers' perceptions of the riskiness of services relative to goods (Guseman 1981; Murray and Schlacter 1990). These risk-producing characteristics of services, however, can be viewed as challenges that create an opportunity for service companies to employ a strong guarantee to reduce customers' prepurchase risk perceptions. For professional services, the impact might even be greater, given the further elevated risk perceptions resulting from high prices, the serious adverse consequences of poor performance, and the tendency for these services to be customized, which reduces the usefulness of past performance as a reliable indicator of quality.

Guarantees also can be helpful for many services such as restaurants, auto repair shops, advertising agencies, and other businesses that depend on referrals and are particularly vulnerable to negative word of mouth. If dissatisfied customers are more likely to complain when a guarantee is offered, guarantees for these types of services can provide businesses with an opportunity to make things right, reducing negative word of mouth and potentially turning the tide to create a future referral source—as opposed to a "terrorist."

To many service firms, offering a powerful guarantee might not appear to be a gigantic leap. Some firms might have already incorporated the goal of complete customer satisfaction into their corporate philosophies. When customer problems occur, these firms do whatever is necessary to solve the problem. In such instances, offering a guarantee might simply be a matter of formalizing the concept to further increase market share and customer loyalty, ingrain the concept of absolute

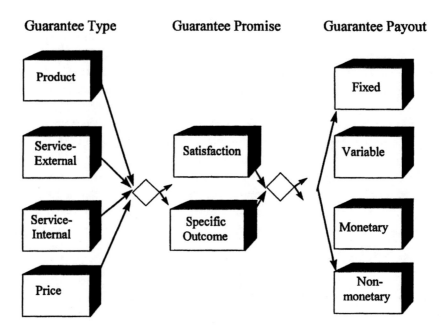

Guarantee Type   **Guarantee Promise**   **Guarantee Payout**

Figure 18.1 Guarantee Design Options

customer satisfaction more deeply into the organization, and, ideally, improve profit margins. Doing so also might force service organizations to deal with common services issues that traditionally have been the cause of lowered service quality, such as inconsistency of service in the case of multisite service firms and the temptation to provide service in excess of capacity constraints.

TYPES AND ELEMENTS OF GUARANTEES

Designing a guarantee offers a number of options. Figure 18.1 shows the different guarantee design elements. Our focus will be on service guarantees, specifically external and internal service guarantees.

External guarantees are offered by a company to its external customers. Internal guarantees are offered by one group in a company to other people or groups within that same company. Although internal guarantees can look and function exactly like external guarantees, their immediate focus is on internal customers, with the goal of raising quality in a specific area. We will talk about each in turn.

External guarantees can be implicit or explicit. Many companies operate successfully with an implicit guarantee, which is a guarantee that is not expressly stated but that customers feel they can count on anyway. For example, Nordstrom department stores are well-known for their willingness to compensate dissatisfied customers even without an explicit promise being made. The same can be said for many fine restaurants and hotels (and even some inexpensive ones); customers who complain generally are given replacements or refunds, despite the lack of any explicit promise to do so. Companies whose customers feel that an implicit guarantee of satisfaction is in place are in an enviable position. Unfortunately, implicit guarantees cannot simply be created overnight. They have to be earned through instance after instance of demonstrating both superior service quality and service recovery in response to service-delivery failures and customer complaints over time. This is something that start-up companies or, especially, companies with unimpressive performance histories might find exceedingly difficult to do. Therefore, "offering" an implicit guarantee generally should be thought of as part of a later stage in a firm's quality evolution. Deploying a strong explicit service guarantee early on is a good approach for enabling a firm to reach this stage.

Although a firm offering an implicit guarantee might leave unstated its guarantee promise and what it will do if it fails to keep that promise (i.e., the guarantee "payout"), a company offering an explicit guarantee clearly states both. There are two main types of explicit guarantees: unconditional satisfaction guarantees and specific-outcome guarantees.

Unconditional Satisfaction Guarantees

Of all the messages that a company can deliver to its customers, an unconditional guarantee of satisfaction is the most powerful. The phrase itself communicates the key points of the message: "Unconditional" means no excuses, no explanations, no fine print; and "satisfaction" means that the customer is the final arbiter of what a company has done right and what it has not. An unconditional guarantee is a company's promise to meet all of its customers' expectations. It makes absolute customer satisfaction a mission statement for how a firm does business. Indeed, First Image, a company that converts computer tapes into microfiche, did exactly that: It created a powerful service guarantee that also served as the company's mission statement. An unconditional guarantee also is the form of guarantee to which managers appear to be naturally drawn, probably reflecting their preferences as consumers. In one consulting firm, groups of executives were asked to draft proposed guarantees. Although the exact wording varied, all the guarantees developed by the executives were essentially unconditional guarantees.

Even though they are powerful, unconditional guarantees usually are the simplest to state. One environmental consulting firm (that chooses to remain confidential) places the following sentence in the cover letter it sends with its proposals: "The firm unconditionally guarantees customer satisfaction or its fees need not be paid." Lands' End, an apparel catalog retailer, has even abbreviated its unconditional guarantee in its advertising to "Guaranteed. Period." Companies operating under these sorts of statements are holding themselves to the highest possible standards: the customer's.

Retailers have long been leaders in offering unconditional satisfaction guarantees; however, recently other types of companies have become bolder in their guarantee efforts, with service firms being among the most adventurous. As mentioned earlier, Promus Hotel brands guarantee guests' hotel stays. Guests who are not satisfied receive a complete refund. Bain & Company, a management consulting firm, has offered some clients an unconditional guarantee for its services. One client was quoted in the *New York Times* as giving this reason for his continuing to do business with Bain: "If they fall short of performance, they don't get paid. Period."[3]

Even services that traditionally have not offered any sort of guarantee are experimenting with unconditional guarantees. For example, a business professor at the University of Southern California offers to refund tuition and textbook costs to any student of his course who is not completely satisfied (as long as he or she invokes the guarantee before final grades are posted). Banc One Corporation offers an unconditional guarantee that it will return fees to any client who is dissatisfied with the quality of its trust service, which can amount to a payout of $10,000 or more. Guaranteeing satisfaction makes sense for many of these service companies where satisfaction *is* the product. With services, objective standards are often hard to define—how do you measure defects in a haircut?—and therefore, customer satisfaction is the most important, if not the only, reliable quality yardstick.

Specific-Outcome Guarantees

Fortunately, a guarantee does not have to unconditionally promise satisfaction to be effective and profitable for a company. "Specific" guarantees allow a company to spell out exactly which elements of the product or service it wants to stand behind. If some other element fails, the company is not obligated to compensate customers, no matter how great their dissatisfaction.

Although such a guarantee might be smaller in scope than an unconditional guarantee of satisfaction, it need not be perceived as inadequate by customers. In fact, specific-outcome guarantees can be quite powerful and, in some situations, might have effects on customer evaluations similar to their unconditional counterparts (Wirtz 1997). Furthermore, in addition to reducing or even eliminating unreasonable payout requests that might occur with an unconditional guarantee, a specific-outcome guarantee has the added advantage of focusing the customer's attention on that aspect of the product or service that the company would most like to emphasize, either because it is important to the customer or because the company believes it has a quality advantage in that area. One classic example is Federal Express, whose overnight delivery guarantee (to most locations) continues to inspire confidence on the part of its customers. (United Parcel Service has been very aggressive in responding to FedEx's guarantee, however, at one point beating FedEx to the punch with an "8 a.m. guaranteed" offer.) A number of other guarantees offered by companies also focus on time, including the Robert Wood Johnson University Hospital Emergency Department guarantee mentioned earlier and General Stair Corporation. General Stair Corp.,[4] a maker of prefabricated stairs and railings, guarantees that it will pay $50 a day if the company is late with either the delivery or the installation of stairs or railings. Since implementing the guarantee, productivity has increased threefold, absenteeism is down 20%, and while area housing starts were down 5%, General Stair's work orders went up 20%.

Delta Dental Plan[5] guarantees several aspects of its service, including no-hassle customer relations (i.e., "Delta Dental Plan will either resolve your question immediately over the phone or we guarantee you an initial update within one business day and continuous follow-up through resolution"—or it will refund $50 per occurrence) and accurate and quick turnaround of ID cards (i.e., "A complete and accurate identification card for each subscriber will be mailed to the group within fifteen calendar days" or $25 is paid to the group per ID card). Internet service providers are also beginning to recognize the potential benefit of offering a guarantee that addresses the common problem of connection shortages. Sprint's Flat Rate Internet Service[6] guarantees that if you ever fail to get a net connection due to a busy signal, you will receive a week's free service ("ISP Guarantee Has Fine Print" 1997). Similarly, AT&T has offered a guarantee for its WorldNet Virtual Private Network Service. If a customer reports that his or her service is down for 10 minutes or more in one day, AT&T will refund 5% of the company's monthly connection charge up to a maximum of 25% in one month (Guy 1997).

Internal Guarantees

Just as an external guarantee can greatly improve a company's standing with external customers, an internal guarantee, which is a guarantee made by one group of employees to another in the same company, can provide a dramatic solution to persistent internal quality problems (which, of course, also ultimately enhances the quality of service delivery to external customers). The basic form and concept of internal guarantees are similar to those of external guarantees, with only a few minor differences. The most obvious difference is that whereas an external guarantee is a promise made by a firm to its customers, an internal guarantee is a promise of superior service (timeliness, accuracy, feedback, courtesy, or whatever is at issue) made by a department to its internal customers, the people to whom work is delivered or whom the department serves in a support function. In a service company, a department might have one internal customer (engineering, for example, serving product development) or several (e.g., the printing department might serve the entire organization).

The other major difference between internal and external guarantees is that although an external guarantee might not be appropriate for all companies, an internal one usually is, whatever the current level of internal or external service quality attained by the firm. Offering an internal guarantee develops partnerships between different parts of the organization, a culture is created that encourages problem solving, and dialogue and feedback processes are established, all of which can lead to large-scale performance improvements for the organization. Examples of such internal guarantees include an arrive-on-time guarantee at a manufacturing company where executives agree to arrive at meetings on time or pay $100 to every other attendee, and Embassy Suites' housekeeping guarantee, in which the supply department pays $5 to any housekeeper who cannot get supplies on the day they are needed. There is an internal guarantee in effect at Creative

TABLE 18.1 Questions to Consider in Guarantee Design and Implementation

I. Deciding who decides
    Is there a guarantee champion in the company?
    Is senior management committed to a guarantee?
    Is the guarantee design a team effort?
    Are customers providing input?

II. When does a guarantee make sense?
    How high are quality standards?
    Can we afford a guarantee?
    How high is customer risk?
    Are competitors offering a guarantee?
    Is the company's culture compatible with a guarantee?

III. What type of guarantee should we offer?
    Should we offer an unconditional guarantee or a specific-outcome one?
    Is our service measurable?
    What should our specific guarantee be about?
    What are the uncontrollable factors?
    Is the company particularly susceptible to unreasonable triggering events?
    What should the payout be?
    Will a refund send the wrong message?
    Could a full refund make customers feel guilty?
    Is the guarantee easy to invoke?

Professional Services, a direct-mail firm, where members of the sales force guarantee to give the production department all the specifications required to provide service to its external customers or the offending salesperson will take the production department to lunch, sing a song at their next department meeting, or input all the specs into the computer himself or herself.

Regardless of the type of explicit guarantee (internal or external), there is consensus on the characteristics that are optimal. First, it should be unconditional in that it is free from restrictions or other qualifiers that limit for whom or when the guarantee applies. Second, it should be easy to understand and communicate. Customers should have no difficulty comprehending the promise being made. Third, the guarantee needs to be meaningful to customers in that what is guaranteed is important to them and the payout is perceived as worthwhile. Finally, it should be easy to invoke as well as quick and easy to collect on. No one wants to jump through hoops to invoke the guarantee, complete a mountain of paperwork, or spend time waiting to get the payout after a failure has occurred. The guarantees that have had the most dramatic, positive impact on the organizations offering them have been those that have met these criteria.

DESIGNING AND IMPLEMENTING THE GUARANTEE

Many questions should be addressed when considering developing a guarantee. Table 18.1 highlights some of the key questions that should be examined.

Deciding Who Decides

First, the likelihood of the success of any guarantee program depends on the extent of management commitment and participation in the guarantee's design and implementation. A guarantee champion can be instrumental in getting the guarantee program off the ground, but commitment by senior management is an absolute necessity given that they control the resources that will be required to implement the guarantee. With senior management's support in place, a decision-making team, preferably one that is cross-functional in nature, should be created to evaluate the pros and cons of offering a guarantee, then guide the design and implementation process in the organization. A team consisting of individuals from different units within the organization will bring a diverse set of perspectives and knowledge to the evaluation process as well as lead to greater buy-in throughout the organization if a "go" decision is made on guarantee implementation. Finally, because the guarantee's role is to make profound promises to customers, customer input is crucial to guarantee design, in terms of what is guaranteed, what payouts are meaningful, and what constitutes the payout process.

When Does a Guarantee Make Sense?

Once the decision-making team is in place, the first task is to determine whether or not a guarantee makes sense for the firm, given its strengths and weaknesses as well as the nature of its industry and the market. There are a number of important considerations. First, the company's current quality standards and performance levels must be evaluated. When firms have established a positive reputation for quality and recovery over time, thereby creating an implicit guarantee in customers' minds, they might get little benefit in terms of attracting new customers by offering an explicit guarantee. It also may be incongruent with the company's established high-quality image (e.g., in making people wonder why a guarantee would be needed at such an outstanding company).

Second, related to the issue of quality standards is the question of whether or not the company can afford to offer a guarantee. The two main cost drivers of guarantee implementation are costs associated with making needed quality improvements and the payouts made to customers. There is an inherent trade-off between the two costs. In theory, a company could invest so heavily in operational improvements that no payouts end up being made, or it could make few or no improvements and assume that it will make a substantial number of payouts. Companies that historically have suffered from low quality performances might find themselves in a truly painful situation after offering a guarantee—especially if necessary improvements have not been made.

Third, one needs to consider customers' risk perceptions. The risk-reducing capabilities of guarantees have been well demonstrated (Bearden and Shimp 1982; Erevelles 1993; Ostrom and Iacobucci 1998; Shimp and Bearden 1982). A guarantee's impact should be most pronounced in purchase situations characterized by higher risk. Elements feeding into higher perceived risk include higher price, high negative consequences of service failure (for the customer or the customer's customers), high customer ego involvement, and low customer knowledge of the service.

A fourth important consideration for any organization is whether or not competitors are offering a guarantee. If guarantees are being offered by competitors, there is a possibility that a guarantee might become a "hygiene" attribute for the industry in that customers simply expect one. In this case, offering a guarantee is necessary to keep up with the competition, the only differentiation potential stemming from designing and offering an *extraordinary* guarantee that goes far beyond competitors'. In industries where guarantees have not been offered, a guarantee has the potential to be an important differentiator.

Finally, whether or not the company's culture is compatible with a guarantee must be examined. Companies that already have a strong commitment to quality and customer satisfaction would likely find the transition to having an explicit guarantee to be relatively straightforward. Companies that have not had this emphasis undoubtedly will face some intense challenges, especially convincing front-line employees that management is serious about the guarantee and will not punish them for invoking it. It takes only a few such punitive instances for a guarantee to lose favor with employees within the organization and drastically reduce the benefits that can accrue from guarantee implementation.

What Type of Guarantee Should We Offer?

If the decision is made to offer an explicit guarantee, the next step is to decide what qualities are going to be guaranteed. The main choice is to determine whether to offer an unconditional satisfaction guarantee or to guarantee specific aspect(s) of the service. Besides being viewed as one of the strongest forms of a guarantee, unconditional guarantees make sense when it is difficult to measure the elements of customer satisfaction (e.g., "courteous" service or "useful" financial advice). Potential drawbacks of offering an unconditional satisfaction guarantee should be considered, for example the uncontrollable factors (e.g., air traffic control problems for airlines) that might affect service delivery and the extent to which the firm would likely be open to unfair guarantee triggerings. The impact of uncontrollable factors often can be reduced by restricting the guarantee to more predictable services. Moreover, the benefits from an unconditional guarantee might still far outweigh the negatives that occur because of unfair triggering. For example, a professional service firm that relies on a few large clients made payouts to clients even for what it considered to be unfair guarantee triggerings. It was painful in the short run, but the clients returned with additional business, making it a worthwhile investment for the company. Companies that could not survive past the short term should think twice (at least) before implementing an unconditional guarantee beyond a pilot test.

For specific-outcome guarantees, the main objective is to determine what aspects of the service are most important to customers and what the company is good at delivering. Examining both can help management decide what should be guaranteed. A major mistake that can occur with a specific-outcome guarantee is that the guarantee could call attention to an otherwise little-considered potential problem, thereby hurting the chances of making a sale. In such cases, the guarantee will die a quick and certain death.

For both unconditional and specific-outcome guarantees, the nature of the payout needs to be specified. As shown in Figure 18.1, a guarantee's payout can be fixed or variable (i.e., all who invoke the guarantee may receive the same payout, or the payout may vary in that the invokee may get to select among several potential payouts), and it can be monetary or nonmonetary. Input from customers at this point is critical. What do customers perceive as fair? Are there types of refunds that might negatively affect customers? A money-back guarantee might conflict with the sophisticated, upscale image that, for example, a high-priced restaurant or a consulting firm wants to project. Also, when a money-back guarantee is in force, customers may feel unmotivated to invoke the guarantee unless their dissatisfaction is considerable—commensurate with the payout. This reluctance may be especially true for customers of service companies, particularly professional service firms. For example, customers who have a strong interest in maintaining their relationship with a service provider may not complain and invoke the guarantee even when they are unhappy with certain aspects of a firm's service. In effect, the guarantee has motivated the customer to not complain, a result that is opposite to the desired goal of obtaining valuable information about a company's flaws for the purpose of improving service quality. Ordinarily this will occur only when customers have not had the nature and purpose of the guarantee made very clear and been provided with numerous opportunities to voice their views pertaining to the quality of the service being delivered.

Finally, once the decision is made about the nature of the guarantee promise, both what is being guaranteed and the payout, the process by which the guarantee will be invoked and the payout distributed needs to be developed. The key characteristic of these processes should be that they are hassle free for customers. Employees must feel empowered to proactively invoke the guarantee—a huge barrier to overcome when a guarantee is launched. In some cases, companies actually reward employees for invoking the guarantee when it is first being implemented to send a clear signal to the organization that management is totally behind the guarantee.

KEY ISSUES IN GUARANTEE RESEARCH

The ability of guarantees to transform organizations internally as well as increase sales and customer retention has been demonstrated vividly through case studies of a number of organizations. There is still much to learn, however, about the specifics of how a guarantee can affect customers throughout the buying process. For example, how much impact does offering a guarantee have on customers' prepurchase perceptions? How is the effect influenced by other quality information or knowledge that the customer has about the firm and whether or not competitors offer a guarantee? How does the timing of guarantee implementation, in terms of the organization's life cycle (i.e., a guarantee being offered by a start-up firm versus being introduced by an established company), influence its effectiveness?

Another important research issue that has yet to be explored fully involves guarantee invocation. Although people may be more likely to complain when a guarantee is offered, does everyone who is dissatisfied invoke a guarantee when it is available? The answer clearly is "no," particularly in face-to-face situations where aggrieved-but-less-than-aggressive customers are forced to ask for guarantee invocations from the very individuals who have offended them in some way. Little research has been done examining factors that may affect whether or not a customer will invoke a guarantee (for an exception see Bolton and Drew 1995). Such research should focus on factors that are likely to play a role in determining whether or not invocation occurs, including attributions for service delivery failure, perceived fairness of the payout in relation to the service failure, and the nature of the relationship between the customer and the service provider.

The potential for a guarantee to positively influence customers' evaluations and repeat purchase has been illustrated by several successful guarantee introductions (e.g., Promus). There is still much to be learned, however, about how guarantee design, the competitive environment at the time of guarantee introduction, customer knowledge, and the process of guarantee invocation affect customers' overall evaluation of the encounter and the firm, as well as their future purchasing behavior.

NOTES

1. This chapter relies heavily on earlier work by Hart (Hart 1988, 1993a, 1993b, 1995; Hart, Schlesinger, and Maher 1992).

2. A warranty is the written form of a company's guarantee.

3. Quote presented in Hart (1993a), originally from "Counselor to the King," *The New York Times*, September 24, 1989, sec. 6, part 2, p. 8.

4. For a detailed account of the design and implementation of its guarantee, see Hyatt (1995).

5. For a more detailed description of Delta Dental's guarantee implementation, see Raffio (1992).

6. Sprint's guarantee does have some fine print. If you get a busy signal, you call customer service, where you will get a reserve access number to try. If that does not work, you have to call customer service back to get the refund of 1 week's service (i.e., $5; "ISP Guarantee Has Fine Print" 1997).

REFERENCES

Bearden, William O. and Terence A. Shimp (1982), "The Use of Extrinsic Cues to Facilitate Product Adoption," *Journal of Marketing Research*, 19 (May), 229-39.

Bitner, Mary Jo, Bernard H. Booms, and Mary S. Tetreault (1990), "The Service Encounter: Diagnosing Favorable and Unfavorable Incidents," *Journal of Marketing*, 54 (January), 1-84.

Bolton, Ruth N. and James H. Drew (1995), "Factors Influencing Customers Assessments of Service Quality and Their Invocation of a Service Warranty," in *Advances in Services Marketing and Management: Research and Practice*, Vol. 4, Teresa A. Swartz, David E. Bowen, and Stephen W. Brown, eds. Greenwich, CT: JAI, 1-23.

Boulding, William and Amna Kirmani (1993), "A Consumer-Side Experimental Examination of Signaling Theory: Do Consumers Perceive Warranties as Signals of Quality?" *Journal of Consumer Research*, 20 (June), 111-23.

Erevelles, Suni (1993), "The Price-Warranty Contract and Product Attitudes," *Journal of Business Research*, 27, 171-81.

Guseman, Dennis S. (1981), "Risk Perception and Risk Reduction in Consumer Services," in *Marketing of Services*, James H. Donnelly and William R. George, eds. Chicago: American Marketing Association, 200-204.

Guy, Sandra (1997), "Guarantees Get Real," *Telephony*, 233(21), 14.

Hart, Christopher W. L. (1988), "The Power of Unconditional Guarantees," *Harvard Business Review*, 66 (July-August), 54-62.

———— (1993a), *Extraordinary Guarantees*. New York: AMACOM.

———— (1993b), "Using Service Guarantees," in *The Service Quality Handbook*, Eberhard E. Scheuing and William F. Christopher, eds. New York: AMACOM.

———— (1995), "The Power of Internal Guarantees," *Harvard Business Review*, 73 (January-February), 64-73.

————, Leonard A. Schlesinger, and Dan Maher (1992), "Guarantees Come to Professional Service Firms," *Sloan Management Review*, 34 (Spring), 19-29.

Heskett, James L., W. Earl Sasser, and Leonard A. Schlesinger (1997), *The Service Profit Chain*. New York: Free Press.

Hyatt, Joshua (1995), "Guaranteed Growth," *INC.*, (September), 69-78.

Innis, Daniel E. and H. Rao Unnava (1991), "The Usefulness of Product Warranties for Reputable and New Brands," in *Advances in Consumer Research*, Vol. 18, Rebecca H. Holman and Michael R. Solomon, eds. Provo, UT: Association for Consumer Research, 317-22.

"ISP Guarantee Has Fine Print" (1997), *PC World*, (December), 63.

Lehmann, Donald R. and Lyman E. Ostlund (1972), "Consumer Perceptions of Product Warranties: An Exploratory Study," in *Proceedings of the Third Annual Conference of the Association for Consumer Research*, M. Venkatesan, ed. Chicago: Association for Consumer Research, 51-65.

Murray, Keith B. and John L. Schlacter (1990), "The Impact of Services Versus Goods on Consumers' Assessment of Perceived Risk and Variability," *Journal of the Academy of Marketing Science*, 18(1), 51-65.

Olson, Jerry and Jacob Jacoby (1972), "Cue Utilization in the Quality Perception Process," in *Proceedings of the Third Annual Conference of the Association for Consumer Research*, M. Venkatesan, ed. Chicago: Association for Consumer Research, 167-79.

Ostrom, Amy L. and Dawn Iacobucci (1998), "The Effect of Guarantees on Consumers' Evaluation of Services," *Journal of Services Marketing*, 12(6), 362-78.

Pallarito, Karen (1995), "Hospital Stands Behind Promise of Fast Service," *Modern Healthcare*, 63.

Raffio, Thomas (1992), "Quality and Delta Dental Plan of Massachusetts," *Sloan Management Review*, 34 (Fall), 101-10.

Schneider, Benjamin and David E. Bowen (1995), *Winning the Service Game*. Boston: Harvard Business School Press.

Shimp, Terence and William Bearden (1982), "Warranty and Other Extrinsic Cue Effects on Consumers' Risk Perceptions," *Journal of Consumer Research*, 9 (June), 38-46.

Technical Assistance Research Programs Institute (1986), *Consumer Complaint Handling in America: An Update Study Part II*. Washington, DC: U.S. Office of Consumer Affairs.

Wirtz, Jochen (1997), "Is Full Satisfaction the Best You Can Guarantee: An Empirical Investigation of the Impact of Guarantee Scope on Consumer Perceptions," in *Proceedings of the Eighth Biennial World Marketing Congress*, Vol. 8. Kuala Lumpur, Malaysia: Academy of Marketing Science, 416-18.

———— (1998), "Development of a Service Guarantee Model," *Asia-Pacific Journal of Management*, 15(1), 51-75.

SECTION V

Service Relationships

19

Relationship Marketing and Management

PAUL G. PATTERSON
TONY WARD

Since Len Berry's (1983) pioneering article on relationship marketing suggested that the development and nurturing of relationships with customers represented a business strategy with considerable potential for long-term success, the concept has been enthusiastically embraced by marketing practitioners and scholars alike. Nevertheless, there is much we don't know, as rigorous research is this area is still in its infancy.

As markets become increasingly competitive, developing relationships that can be maintained in the face of the many inducements to switch service suppliers is seen as a way of creating a sustainable competitive advantage. This is even more so in service industries, where competitive moves are often quickly followed by competitors. Of course the idea of an organization developing a relationship with its customers is not new; in fact, it has been the cornerstone of many successful enterprises in times past. Berry (1995) described it as an "old-new" concept, and reinforcing this view, Grönroos (1994) related relationship marketing approaches of the ancient Chinese and Middle Eastern empires. Indeed, Grönroos cited the proverb "As a merchant, you'd better have a friend in every town." In the business-to-business literature, Levitt (1993) noted that in industrial marketing contexts, the real value to the customer occurs after the sale. He argued that the supplier's focus should shift from simply achieving a sale to delivering superior service (i.e., added value) and thus satisfaction over the lifetime of the relationship (Payne 1997).

The notion of marketing an intangible performance or experience rather than a physical object introduces an extra dimension to a marketing plan. The reality of many services being delivered on a continuous basis, coupled with the fact that

AUTHORS' NOTE: Authors' names appear in alphabetical order.

customers may form relationships with individual service employees (as well as a brand and/or organization), sets the scene for a fresh look at relationship marketing. The creation of a sound conceptual framework for understanding its theoretical foundations, properties, and antecedents has been elevated to new levels in recent times, as a result of the rigorous research effort devoted to studying the concept.

Four factors have influenced the current focus on relationship marketing and customer loyalty: the concept of a customer having a lifetime value, the sophistication of database systems, the rationale that loyalty equals an increase in profits, and the increasingly competitive nature of service markets.

Today, relationship marketing is at the forefront of marketing practice and academic research. The idea of marketing to existing customers to attract their continued patronage and, indeed, loyalty has become well integrated into the various subdisciplines of marketing. Although research in the United States has blossomed in recent years with institutions such as the Center for Relationship Marketing at Emory University, many of the earlier works emanated from Europe. Scandinavian researchers (the "Nordic school of thought" of relationship marketing) at the Swedish School of Economics and others were pioneers in the area (Grönroos 1989; Gummesson 1987), focusing on the interactive network theory in industrial marketing and services. The IMP group (Industrial Marketing and Purchasing) has also been highly influential with its research concentrating on networks, interactions, and relationships in industrial markets (see, for example, Ford 1990; Hakansson 1982; Turnbull and Cunningham 1981), while more recently, the work of Christopher, Payne, and Ballantyne (1991) has approached relationships by integrating the concepts of quality, customer satisfaction, and the marketing function. Clearly, there is only so much one can include in one chapter. Furthermore, because business-to-business services marketing will be explicitly dealt with in the following chapter, the primary focus of this chapter will be *consumer services* (i.e., consumer-producer interactions). Specifically, this chapter addresses the following issues:

- A brief history of the emergence of relationship marketing
- Defining what relationship marketing is and is not
- Benefits and limitations
- The antecedents and dimensions of successful long-term relationships with customer groups
- Customer retention strategies
- How relationship marketing can be integrated with other marketing functions
- Under what conditions a relationship marketing approach is appropriate
- Future directions

PATHWAYS TO GROWTH

Service businesses can grow in one or more ways:

- Attract new customers
- Encourage existing customers to purchase more units of service
- Encourage existing customers to purchase higher-value services (for instance, travel first class rather than economy)
- Reduce the extent of turnover—or "churn"—resulting from desirable customers who defect to a competing service supplier (a particular problem in service providers with low switching costs such as travel agents, taxi companies, or management consultants)
- Terminate unprofitable, stagnant, or otherwise unsatisfactory relationships and replace them with new customers who better match the firm's profit, growth, and positioning goals

Four of these five pathways involve some form of relationship management.

Maintaining and nurturing existing customer relationships is a very different mind-set that requires a different set of marketing activities. In *Serving Them Right*, Laura Liswood (1990) traces the somewhat "abnormal" evolution of marketing:

> In the past, acquisition and retention marketing went hand in hand. Selling and service were part of the same ongoing company-customer relationship. . . . However, as we matured into a more mobile, industrialized, technocratic society, a distinction arose between selling and everything that came after the sale. . . . We relegated the second half of the sale to "customer complaint departments," "service departments," and "warranty departments." This mentality has been reflected for years in the formal structures, hierarchies, and budgeting philosophies of companies. Acquisition marketing and promotion continue to dominate, while customer-service activities are typically underbudgeted, understaffed, viewed strictly as cost centers and assigned to the periphery of a company's competitive strategy. (n.p.)

Traditionally, however, marketing has tended to overemphasize the attraction of new customers—so-called "offensive marketing"—using the 4Ps marketing mix as the tools of the trade. Some argue that marketing in practice has to a large extent been turned into managing this toolbox instead of truly exploring the nature of the firm's market relationships. A well-managed organization, however, will work hard to retain and increase its existing customer base by carefully managing its valued customer relationships—"defensive or relationship marketing."

DEFINING RELATIONSHIP MARKETING

The term *relationship* has many connotations. Many definitions of relationship marketing are provided in a business-to-business context (e.g., Gummesson 1994; Iacobucci 1994). For this chapter, definitions in a consumer context were required. Shani and Chalasani (1993) linked relationship building with products and services, rather viewing it as occurring between the customer and the supplier company: "Relationship marketing centers on developing a continuous relationship with consumers across a family of related products and services" (p. 59). Grönroos (1990) viewed relationship marketing from an overall company perspective: "Marketing is to establish, maintain, enhance and commercialize customer relationships (often, but not necessarily always, long term relationships) so that the objectives of the parties involved are met" (p. 5). In contrast, Morgan and Hunt (1994) concentrated on relational exchanges, stating, "Relationship marketing refers to all marketing activities directed toward establishing, developing, and maintaining successful relational exchanges" (p. 22), while Peelan, Ekelmans, and Vijn (1989) emphasized the mutual influence that the parties exerted upon each other in a relationship: "The term 'relationship' indicates that two persons mutually influence each other's behavior over a long period. The behavior of one provokes behavior from the other" (p. 8).

For the purposes of discussing relationship marketing in the context of consumer service products, the following definition is adopted: Relationship marketing is the establishment of a long-term relationship between the service supplier and customer to their mutual benefit.

There are a number of important parts to this definition:

- A relationship has to be *established* and worked on; that is, it does not usually happen by chance.
- Relationships need to be *long-term* to be most fruitful, inferring that short-term considerations should always be weighed against long-term benefits.
- The relationship is *between* the providing organization (the entity of the organization and/or individual staff) and the customer, implying that the customer acknowledges and wants a relationship.
- The relationship should be to the *mutual benefit* of both parties—a win-win scenario.

It also needs to be pointed out, as Barnes (1995) noted, that not all customers want a relationship.

DATABASE MARKETING

Having an accurate, current database of customer profiles, including information on purchasing, sociodemographics, and brand preferences, allows the astute marketer to target particular customers with a service bundle customized to their particular preferences. Singapore Airlines, for example, knows the drink and food preferences as well as the reading and movie viewing habits of its regular business and first-class travelers. Such information is downloaded on each flight, and upon boarding, a customer is often surprised to find a "Singapore Girl" greet him or her by name and say "Here is your favorite gin and tonic." There is no doubt that a well-conceived and up-to-date database is an indispensable tool in nurturing long-term customer relations.

That's all it is, however: a *tool*.

A relationship implies *mutual* benefits as well as *special status and recognition* between the parties. In this regard, database marketing (as it has become known) is one-sided, with real benefits accruing only to the seller. Database marketing violates one of the basic tenets of a genuine relationship, namely the concept of mutuality. If this is the case, then the process cannot be true relationship marketing. All the activity and focus is from the firm's position, that is, the firm "doing something to" customers, such as "targeting" them or allowing them "membership." It tends to be the case of what the firm can get from the customer. The relationship perspective demands that the customer perspective be taken into consideration: There also has to be something of value in the relationship for the customer, such as some type of benefit or reward (Blois 1995). Barnes (1995) offered the following insightful comment supporting customer involvement: "For no relationship will exist unless the customer feels that one exists" (p. 133). This aspect seems to have been ignored in many current database marketing schemes.

LOYALTY PROGRAMS

A relationship is more than one or two encounters. It implies a number of successive interactions on a continuous basis. Barnes (1995), however, makes the important point that "a succession of interactions does not necessarily lead to a 'relationship' any more than repeat purchasing constitutes loyalty" (p. 1397). Loyalty or relationship commitment implies both emotional and psychological commitment, as well as repeat purchasing behavior. In this sense, many of the so-called "loyalty programs" are one-sided, with the customer staying in the "relationship" only because he or she is locked in by some membership arrangement (e.g., frequent flyer programs). So-called loyalty programs offer incentives to alter consumers' choice behavior. This then effectively makes the consumer a "hostage" of the firm, or at least that is what airlines, retailers, and banks would like to believe. As Dowling and Uncles (1997) pointed out, heavy users are not necessarily committed or exclusively loyal to one seller—what they term *polyga-mous loyalty*. For example, the present data show that, among European business air travelers, 80% are members of more than one airline's frequent flyer program, and in the United Kingdom, the heavy business traveler (the very segment all airlines want a relationship with) are in, on average, 3.1 programs.

RELATIONSHIP MARKETING

True relationship marketing, on the other hand, exists only when the customer wants it to exist, acknowledges that a relationship exists, perceives that it is mutually beneficial, receives special status and recognition, and is prepared to stay with a service provider even in the face of attractive, viable, and available alternatives. In the data reported by Patterson (1998), the following percentages of customers in the sample reported that they were certain to continue dealing with their current service supplier in the foreseeable future: hairdresser services 85%, family doctor 77%, auto service center 77%, and travel agency 69%.

Several reasons explain this result. With the exception of the auto service center, the services mentioned involve people delivering the service face to face. It is known that in some long-term relationships a service provider may actually become part of the customer's social support network (Adelman, Ahuvia, and Goodwin 1994). For example, hairdressers and family doctors often serve as personal confidants. Such social support benefits are important to the consumer's quality of life above and beyond the technical or core service offered. Other reasons for loyalty include reduced risk or uncertainty associated with changing service providers. Such long-term relationships are thought to contribute to a sense of well-being and quality of life (Zeithaml and Bitner 1996); trust is built up, and the consumer can count on a consistent level of service. Furthermore, once a service provider gets to know a customer's preferences and tailors services to suit that person's needs over time, then switching means going through the trouble of educating a new service provider. Finally, many consumers in the late 1990s are "time poor" (especially professionals and dual-career families) and have competing demands on their most precious resource—their time. As a result, they are continually searching for ways to simplify decision making to enhance the quality of their lives. Maintaining a stable relationship with one travel agent, auto repair center, or doctor frees up time for other priorities—in other words, there are several switching costs that a consumer may simply not be prepared to bear.

RELATIONSHIP MARKETING VERSUS RELATIONSHIP MANAGEMENT

Establishing a relationship with a customer may be conceived as comprising two stages: first attracting the customer and then building and managing the relationship over time so that the economic (and sometimes social) objectives of both parties are achieved.

As Christopher, Payne, and Ballantyne (1991) pointed out, too many companies, having achieved a sale, then turn most of their attention and marketing resources to seeking out new customers without appreciating the importance of maintaining and enhancing relationships with existing customers. Figure 19.1 depicts what has become known as the ladder of customer loyalty. The aim is, first, to attract new prospects using marketing mix tools and to begin creating a relationship (we refer to this attract/establish/create phase as *relationship marketing*) over time. Then the objective should be to move customers up the loyalty ladder to the point where they become "clients," "advocates," and finally "evangelists" who not only spread positive word of mouth but also have emotional equity—they are passionate about their service provider. The role of the organization in these latter stages moves from offensive marketing to defensive—*relationship management* if you like—maintaining and enhancing the relationship and

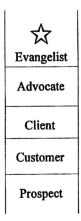

Figure 19.1 Customer Ladder

retaining customers through value-added service and development of trust, satisfaction, and stronger social bonds.

Levitt (1993) had this to say about relationship management in professional service firms:

> It is not surprising that in professional partnerships, such as law, medicine, architecture, consulting, investment banking and advertising, individuals are rated and rewarded by the client relationships they control. These relationships, like other assets, can appreciate or depreciate. . . . Relationship management requires companywide programs for maintenance, investment, improvement and even for replacement. (p. 88)

THE NATURE OF RELATIONSHIPS

The nature of relationships that companies have with customers is quite different in consumer services and business-to-business service environments—as in most areas of service product marketing. Although the definition above can be used for both types of market, the application of relationship marketing techniques usually is quite different.

In a consumer service (retail) situation (e.g., retail banking, hairdressing, financial planning, and medical services), the provider and customer usually meet face to face, unlike retail goods situations where the manufacturer and customer seldom meet. Thus, in consumer service situations there is an ideal opportunity for provider personnel to build long-term relationships directly with their customers. In these situations relationships can be formed on a personal basis between two people, or between two or more providers and the customer(s). These relationships are relatively easy to identify but can be complicated by the customer also identifying with the provider company. For example, a customer may develop a relationship with two or more hairdressers in a salon. If one of these providers leaves, the customer may move to that hairdresser's new salon (if local) or may identify his or her relationship as being stronger with the remaining staff or with the salon itself.

These examples raise a key aspect: *With whom (provider or providers) or what (business or brand) do customers perceive they have the principal relationship?* Research to date clearly shows that there is no correct answer to this question—it will depend on many variables, such as the customer, provider staff, type of service product, strength of various relationships, duration of these relationships, and perceived relationship with the company or the brand image of the company or product.

Customers can have a number of types of relationship with suppliers. These have been described as social, company/brand, virtual, and internal marketing. Each will be discussed briefly.

Social Relationships

Social relationships are interpersonal relationships between provider staff and customers. They could be one-on-one, two-on-one, or more complex. These are social relationships and reflect how two or more individuals interrelate with one another. FedEx recognizes the importance of personal relationships—even if only via the telephone. Using calling line identification technology, all incoming calls from a regular customer are automatically routed to a particular CSO (customer service officer) so that, over time, a relationship is developed between customer and CSO.

Company/Brand Relationships

Company/brand relationships occur in situations where the customer perceives that he or she has a principal relationship with a company or brand, rather than with a person (typical examples would be with a bank or insurance company). We know much less about such relationships because they are more difficult to research: Customers do not seem to be able to articulate their perceptions very clearly. In many cases it appears that people do not evaluate these relationships as much as those that are interpersonal in nature.

Virtual Relationships

A new domain of marketing has emerged in the last few years, marketing on the World Wide Web. This "virtual" domain excludes direct interpersonal contact between the parties and presents a number of challenges to marketers. A similar situation exists in direct marketing, where interpersonal contact is often excluded. There is limited relationship research in these areas, but there is evidence that some customers do perceive a form of relationship with the "virtual" providers (take, for example, the success of the Web bookseller Amazon.com) that are supporting these marketing practices. This may, however, be an example where the return to marketers attempting to build relationships is limited.

Internal Relationship Marketing

Internal relationship marketing is fundamentally different from that described above because it deals with the internal relationships between people (or indeed functional groups) within provider organizations. Such relationships could encompass providers working together, such as on the front desk of a hotel, or people in different departments with one group supporting the activities of front-line staff, as when automobile cleaning and preparation staff in a hire car company make vehicles ready for counter staff to allocate to customers. In this case the support staff (providers) supply a service for the front-line staff (who act as customers in this relationship). The importance of these relationships is well recognized from an operational perspective, but they also have an impact on marketing that is often not realized until something goes wrong.

An important aspect of building relationships is that every employee in an organization (and in particular front-line staff) must appreciate that every contact or action performed (whether visible to the customer or not) has the potential to either improve or damage a relationship with a customer. Gummesson (1992) referred to employees as "part-time marketers." Contact and action have three forms and are defined here as

- Direct personal contact—a personal interaction; that is, a direct interaction, such as a teller serving a customer in a bank or contacting a customer by telephone
- Indirect personal contact—a nonpersonal interaction, such as a bank manager writing to a customer
- Nonvisible activity, such as services delivered by various forms of information technology (e.g., telephone services, Internet commerce)

Because a number of people in an organization may come into contact with an individual customer over a period of time, it is tempting for each staff member to look at each of these contacts as an individual transaction. Likewise, staff who are not visible to the customer may not readily relate their own activities as forming a part of the customer's perception of the organization. From the customer's perspective, however, each individual staff member represents the organization, and *the sum of all interactions* (direct, indirect, and/or nonvisible) with such staff is used by the customer to form an opinion and perception of an organization and an opinion of the strength of his or her personal relationship with that organization.

THE CONTEXT OF RELATIONSHIPS

Before proceeding, we should point out that relationship management occurs in a range of contexts or markets, not only consumer markets. Gummesson (1994) provided an insight as to how wide-ranging and complex the issue is when he said, "It is also imperative to specify which relationships companies should address. I have found thirty relationships, referred to as The 30Rs of Marketing" (p. 10).

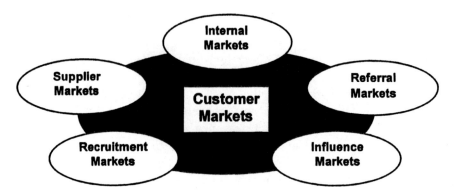

Figure 19.2 The Six Markets Framework
SOURCE: Adapted from Christopher, Payne, and Ballantyne (1991).

An alternative approach is offered by Christopher, Payne, and Ballantyne (1991), who suggest that the relationship contexts may be viewed as types of markets. Their six markets framework is shown in Figure 19.2.

The point is simply that to succeed in today's competitive environment, organizations must develop relationships not only with customer markets but also with a number of key stakeholder groups. Markets are identified as (a) customer markets (new and existing), (b) supplier markets (traditional suppliers), (c) referral markets (existing customers who recommend their service supplier to others and "multipliers" such as a legal firm that may refer work to a financial planner), (d) employee or recruitment markets (concerned with attracting/recruiting the right employees), (e) influencer markets (which might embrace consumer groups, journalists, financial analysts, government bodies, and, of course, shareholders), and (f) internal markets (staff). The cycle of success suggests that highly satisfied staff are motivated to deliver excellent service, and the resultant happy customers also act as a stimulus to staff to continue. This is especially so in service organizations characterized by a medium to high degree of interpersonal contact during service delivery (medical, physiotherapy, personal trainer, education, airlines), where the "moments of truth" are crucial to achieving service quality.

RELATIONSHIPS—
BENEFITS TO THE ORGANIZATION

What is a valued relationship? It is one in which the customer finds value because the benefits received from the service significantly exceed the associated costs of obtaining such benefits. For the firm, it is a relationship that is financially profitable over time. Having a good working relationship between two parties implies that they relate positively to one another, as opposed to just conducting a series of almost anonymous transactions. In a healthy and mutually profitable relationship, both parties have an incentive to ensure that it extends for many years. The seller, in particular, recognizes that it pays to take a long-term perspective, justifying the up-front costs of acquiring new customers and learning about their needs—which may even make the account unprofitable in its first year—by an expectation of future profits. A number of potential benefits to the firm have been identified (for example, see Reichheld and Sasser 1990; Zeithaml and Bitner 1996):

- Opportunities to cross-sell other company services
- Higher customer retention rates (and higher market share)
- Reduced operating costs because the customer is familiar
- Long-term customers often buying greater quantities than first-time customers do
- Such customers invariably are happy to spread positive word of mouth

RELATIONSHIPS—BENEFITS TO THE CONSUMER

Much of the recent published work expounds clearly the benefits to the *firm* of establishing long-term loyal customers (e.g., Morgan and Hunt 1994; Reichheld 1996). Successful, genuine relationships, however, involve a *mutual* fulfillment of promises, with benefits flowing to both parties—that is, a "win-win" situation. There is, however, a paucity of work that has seriously examined benefits flowing to the buyer from staying loyal to a service provider (exceptions include the recent work of Bitner [1995] and Gwinner, Gremler, and Bitner [1998]). To be successful in forging and maintaining long-term relationships requires a clear understanding of *customer* motivations and perceived benefits of staying in a relationship (Barnes 1995).

First-time customers, as well as those who have developed a relationship with a service supplier, fully expect to receive satisfactory delivery of the core service. Customers of an auto service center fully expect their cars will be serviced (or repaired) dependably, those engaging the services of a financial planner each expect to receive a financial plan that will produce the required rate of return at a specified level of risk, and a hairdresser is expected to provide professional hairstyling and a color tint that is consistent with the customer's instructions. This core service or technical benefit (Grönroos 1983) is almost a "given" that any service firm must deliver with consistency if it wishes to stay in business. Mere fault-free provision of the core service, however, is unlikely to be sufficient to encourage customers to engage in a long-term relationship. Other benefits that relate to processes or *how* the service is delivered are necessary. Such benefits include social benefits that encompass the comfortable and friendly relationship that is built up in some service relationships (Goodwin 1994) as well as the extra things ("going the extra mile") that a service provider might do for a long-term, loyal customer. Such benefits, labeled relational benefits, have only recently been the focus of study.

Following this line of thinking, the results of two recent studies suggest that perhaps customers are far more economically rational in their approach to relationship development than previously thought. Studies by Gwinner, Gremler, and Bitner (1998) and Patterson (1998) indicate that customers in fact do consciously seek a series of relational benefits from staying with the one supplier. It appears that not only does the travel agency or auto repair service center seek customers who will be loyal, but customers also want to find a travel agent or auto center that evokes their loyalty (Berry 1995).

Gwinner, Gremler, and Bitner (1998) found three categories of relational benefits that are strongly associated with staying in a relationship with one service provider. In their study of a range of U.S. service providers, they found these benefits to be

- *Confidence benefits*, psychological benefits such as feeling they can trust the service provider, experience less anxiety when they purchase, and have more confidence the service will be done correctly
- *Social benefits* such as being recognized by certain employees, developing friendships with employees, having their name remembered
- *Special treatment benefits* such as being placed on a priority list or getting special deals that most customers don't get

Patterson (1998), in studying Australian clients of medical services, hairdressers, travel agencies, and auto service centers, also found that customers placed a high value on social and special treatment benefits (he did not test for confidence benefits). In both his study and that of Gwinner, Gremler, and Bitner (1998), correlation analysis showed that perceived benefits of staying in a relationship explained a significant amount of the strength of the relationship.

It is also known that some services are far from homogeneous. Theory suggests that relational benefits may vary by service type (Lovelock 1983). For example, we might expect social benefits to be more important in service settings where there is a high degree of interpersonal contact and the service is highly customized (such as hairdressing, physiotherapy, personal fitness training) versus a situation of low contact and standardized service (retail banking). Indeed, services could be classified along numerous dimensions.

Figure 19.3 considers two important service dimensions: (a) the degree of interpersonal contact and (b) credence versus search or experience properties. Both dimensions are likely to affect the nature and importance of benefits received. For example, in services high in credence properties (medical services and other professional services), it is intrinsically difficult for customers to confidently evaluate technical outcomes even after purchase and consumption. Hence, the issue is related to trust and social benefits (how the service is delivered, including the interpersonal skills of the doctor, the comfortable and friendly relationship built up, customer recognition, and so forth). As argued earlier, for high-contact services, social benefits might be expected to be more important than in a low-contact situation. In the medium- or low-contact cell, special treatment benefits are likely to be valued more highly than social benefits.

Although not all customers want a relationship, the findings suggest that for continuously or periodically provided services that are of personal significance,

	Evaluation Properties	
	Credence	Experience
High	Medical Services (GP only)	Hairdressing
Low	Car Servicing	Travel Agency

(vertical axis label: Degree of Interpersonal Contact)

Figure 19.3 Classification of Service Firms With Low Economic Switching Barriers

variable in quality, high in involvement, and/or possessing credence or experience qualities, many customers seek the benefits that flow from dealing with one service supplier. Medical services, hairdressing, travel agency services, retail banking, and car servicing all illustrate the perceived benefits that motivate many customers to desire continuity with the same service firm.

In summary, it is clear that using relationship marketing techniques has the potential to be of significant benefit to both the customers and the firm, the very win-win situation of which successful relationships are made.

ANTECEDENTS OF RELATIONSHIP MARKETING

The antecedents of a relationship are sometimes difficult to identify because every person has a different perspective on life in general and relationships in particular, and will thus develop his or her own set of criteria. There is much we do not know about the antecedents of relationship marketing, but it would appear that two aspects need to be considered: the conditions that are required for a relationship to develop and the dimensions that customers use to evaluate a relationship with a supplier.

Conditions for a Relationship to Develop

It is evident that certain conditions need to be present for customers to develop and maintain a relationship, specifically individual need (for the relationship), value, customer satisfaction, effective communications, and mutuality.

Individual need. It is clear that some customers do not wish to form relationships with suppliers (Barnes 1995; Ward and Smith 1998). If this is the case, then pushing the formation of a relationship is likely to do more harm (to a company's marketing efforts) than good.

Value. It is clear that customers need to perceive that they are receiving value if a relationship is to develop (Lovelock, Patterson, and Walker 1998); that is, the perceived benefits must outweigh the sum of the sacrifices, including forsaking attractive alternatives. It is also clear that if a customer perceives that poor value is being delivered, then a previously good relationship can be damaged very quickly (Ward, Frew, and Caldow 1997).

Customer satisfaction. If customers are not satisfied, there is overwhelming evidence that they will take their custom elsewhere.

Effective communications. The effective and efficient two-way exchange of information using common semantics is necessary and assists with resolving differences (Ward, Frew, and Caldow 1997).

Mutuality. By definition, both parties must want a relationship. If only one party perceives that a relationship exists and is desirable, then it is unlikely that either will benefit.

Dimensions of a Relationship

A number of authors have identified specific dimensions (otherwise referred to in the literature as elements or criteria), such as bonding, empathy, reciprocity, trust, commitment, loyalty, understanding, and shared values (Callaghan 1993; Crosby, Evans, and Cowles 1990; Evans and Laskin 1994; Ford 1980; Morgan and Hunt 1994; Storbacka, Strandvik, and Grönroos 1994). Recent research has identified up to 45 dimensions of relationships used by customers in a retail service environment (Ward, Frew, and Caldow 1997). These results indicate the complex nature of the way in which customers perceive the construct of relationship between themselves and suppliers, and it is clear that each individual has a particular set of dimensions and different perceptions for what he or she means by each of these dimensions.

It is thus not yet possible to state positively that there are a certain number of dimensions of relationship marketing, or how to define each precisely. The research to date has, however, identified a number of dimensions that are repeatedly and commonly found, namely (in no particular order) trust, bonding, empathy, reciprocity, and loyalty.

Trust. Trust can be considered as the essence of a relationship (Morgan and Hunt 1994) and can be defined as having confidence in the dependability of one party to act in the long-term best interests of the other party (Ward, Frew, and Caldow 1997). In particular, customers need to trust a supplier in terms of advice, product quality, reliability of delivery, and postpurchase support. It is difficult to envisage a productive and beneficial relationship between supplier and customer if this dimension is not present.

Bonding. Bonding is a mutual state where the two parties act in such a way that a bond is developed between them.

Empathy. Empathy exists when two parties have an appreciation of, and concern for, each other. Each party will consider the other's perspective in their interactions and dealings.

Reciprocity. A state of reciprocity exists when the two parties operate in such a way that they both gain a benefit from the relationship.

Loyalty. Loyalty (as described earlier) implies both an emotional and a psychological commitment. There are clearly differing levels of loyalty, ranging from an initial shallow state to a deep and sustained level of commitment.

In summary, there is much about relationships in a buyer/seller context that we do not yet fully understand. Furthermore, for both parties to benefit from a relationship, these (and other) dimensions need to be mutually exhibited; that is, relationships need to be balanced for the maximum benefits to accrue. Finally, we must always keep in mind the complex nature of the way in which customers perceive their relationships with suppliers, and vice versa.

CUSTOMER RETENTION

There has been much focus in the last few years, by academics and practitioners alike, on the retention of customers. Retention has always been an important part of marketing and business because almost all businesses rely on repeat purchase of products by existing customers to survive—let alone thrive. It has, for example, been known for centuries that it is easier and cheaper to sell the same or a different product to an existing customer than to acquire a new customer, and that most businesses rely heavily on repeat purchasing by existing customers. In fact, of course, retention is often strongly interrelated with building a relationship with customers, and vice versa.

To establish how to retain customers, it is important to understand why customers are lost. Keaveney (1995) found eight main categories of reasons for customers switching to another supplier: pricing, inconvenience, core service failure, service encounter failure, response to service failure, competition, ethical problems, and involuntary switching.

Pricing. Keaveney (1995) found that pricing was the third-highest reason for switching. Among pricing problems were high prices, unfair pricing, and deceptive pricing. Other research (e.g., Ward, Frew, and Caldow 1997) clearly indicates that the concept of value is also critical in forming relationships, and when absent, it is a major cause of switching behavior. It appears that once a customer perceives that he or she is not receiving good value (this is difficult to define but easy to recognize in a customer's behavior), the relationship has been seriously damaged and the customer prone to switch suppliers.

Inconvenience. In selecting a service supplier, many customers use convenience as a factor, evaluating such dimensions as location, short queues, and opening times (Keaveney 1995).

Core service failure. Keaveney found this to be the most common reason for switching. There is little that can be done in the long term to mitigate the effects of a core service failure (e.g., the plane landed an hour late and the airlines lost my bags; the bank's systems were down and it couldn't provide me with a statement for 3 days; the travel agent simply couldn't get accurate flight information; the mechanic failed to fix the problem). Even the strongest relationships with customers will be strained by poor service design and quality of delivery. With the continuous increase in competition that we see in business today, consistent core service failures will not be tolerated.

Service encounter failures. These are failures in the interpersonal interactions between server and customer, and in particular the behavior of the server. Customers usually establish a level of expectation for the delivery of a service, and if this expectation is not met, they become dissatisfied. Each customer will have a different expectation in terms of both the level of attention required and the nature that such attention takes. One concern is the human element associated with staff providing appropriate behavior in a reasonably consistent manner throughout operating hours, each day of the week, and each week of the year. All these factors make the matching of sought behavior and delivered attention very difficult to balance for all customers, all the time. If, over the long term, a specific customer perceives that he or she is not being looked after in an appropriate manner, then that customer will become prone to look for an alternate supplier. Identifying customers in this state before they defect to a competitor is not easy and rests almost exclusively on the perceptiveness and abilities of front-line staff.

Response to service failure. It is clear that customers who complain or question service suppliers do not respond well when faced with a negative or reluctant response. An inappropriate response, as perceived by a customer, tends to result in switching. This issue needs to be addressed in terms of company attitude toward both customers and staff, as well as through staff training.

Attraction by competitors. Business worldwide is becoming more competitive every year. As a consequence, marketing becomes more competitive every year. Marketplaces are dynamic in nature, and almost every business spends a significant amount of time and energy looking for new customers by luring customers from other suppliers. This is a particular area where building a relationship of loyalty with a customer is a very powerful strategy; loyalty will provide some resistance within customers to being lured away by the advances of competitors.

Ethical problems. This category includes illegal, immoral, unsafe, unhealthy, and other behaviors (Keaveney 1995) that cause customers to feel uncomfortable. These behaviors often result in switching.

Involuntary switching and other factors. This category includes companies closing, customers changing location, and other factors that make continuation of the relationship difficult even if continuance is desirable.

TABLE 19.1 Three Levels of Customer Retention Strategy

Level	Bond Type	Marketing Orientation	Customization	Main Marketing Mix Element	Competitive Advantage Potential
1	Financial	Customer	Low	Price	Low
2	Financial and social	Client	Medium	Personal communications	Medium
3	Financial, social, and structural	Client	Medium to high	Service delivery	High

SOURCE: Adapted from Berry and Parasuraman (1991).

CUSTOMER RETENTION STRATEGIES

Berry and Parasuraman (1991) developed a framework for understanding categories of retention strategies. Their framework proposes that retention marketing (i.e., managing the relationship) occurs at three levels and that each successive level of strategy requires greater customization or individualized service but results in bonds being formed that tie the customer a little closer to the firm (see also the loyalty ladder concept previously presented). As Zeithaml and Bitner (1996) suggest, at each level the potential for sustainable competitive advantage is also enhanced. The three levels of strategy are depicted in Table 19.1.

Level 1

At Level 1, the customer is linked to the firm through various financial or other incentives such as price discounts for volume purchases, free airline miles (e.g., frequent flyer programs), or discounts in exit fees if customers refrain from switching superannuation funds in the first several years of a relationship. Effectively, the aim is to lock in customers for a period of time. The economic incentives make the customer a "hostage" of the firm at this level. These incentive schemes are relatively easy for competitors to imitate, so in the medium term no sustainable competitive advantage is gained. They do, however, give the firm some breathing space to attempt to form a genuine relationship and move customers to the next level.

Level 2

Although economic incentives are important, a longer-term relationship is developed via stronger social bonds at Level 2. Customers are recognized and viewed as individuals. As noted earlier in this chapter, social benefits have value to most clients—they like being recognized and having their name instantly known, or even developing friendships with individual personnel in the service firm, and generally being treated as someone with special status. For example, Crosby, Evans, and Cowles (1990), in a study of business-to-business markets (business clients of an insurance company), found that simple things like staying in touch on a regular basis, providing personal touches such as cards and small gifts on special occasions, sharing personal information (such as is done between friends), and developing rapport at a personal level all enhanced the likelihood of client retention.

Level 3

Strategies at Level 3 are the most difficult for competitors to imitate. This level involves developing structural bonds as well as economic and social ones. Structural bonds involve providing highly customized services to individual clients; these services are designed into the service delivery system and are increasingly technology based. Examples include giving valued clients a special access phone number for bookings (banking or airlines).

In summary, it is clear that relationship marketing has a key role to play in retaining customers and is complemented by the ability to recover customers after a bad experience.

SERVICE RECOVERY

However hard one tries, occasionally something will go wrong with the delivery of a service product. It may not be the provider's fault, as is the case when bad weather prevents an airline flying, but how a firm deals with the crisis and its effects on customers will largely determine whether or not it can retain customers in the future. *The emphasis is on the service provider to sort out the difficulty and look after its precious customers.*

Unfortunately, it is all too common for companies to take the "legal" way out of a difficult situation and to let the customers sort out the bad experience for themselves (and we have all seen this happen when the problem clearly was the company's fault). Think of how much you can build a relationship by helping your customers when something goes wrong and how those very same customers will react to your considerate action. The goal of service recovery, therefore, is not merely to "survive" a bad customer experience by not losing the customer, but to take the opportunity to show customers just how important they are and how much you value their patronage.

Finally, it is important to identify to all staff the importance to them as individuals, and to the organization as a whole, of the real benefits of forming relationships with customers. Experience has shown that unless this happens, the majority of staff will not make the necessary effort to continually work toward building and maintaining relationships with customers. A majority of service providers do not fully appreciate how important this factor is to many customers.

With the time pressures placed on so many people at work, there is an ever present danger of allowing ourselves to descend to the level of the lowest common denominator of service. It is also necessary for providers to show customers how much their relationship and loyalty mean, both to the individual and to the company. There are many ways in which this can be done, such as through loyalty programs, cumulative discounts, simply telling customers (but make sure you really mean it and are seen to really mean it!), and "club" memberships.

THE CUSTOMER VALUE APPROACH TO SEGMENTATION

The fact is that not all customer relationships are worth keeping. Some customers no longer fit the firm's mission or positioning strategy, either because that strategy has changed or because the nature of the customer's behavior or needs has changed. Careful analysis may show that many relationships are no longer profitable for the firm: They cost more to maintain than the revenues they generate. Just as investors need to dispose of poor investments and banks may have to write off bad loans, so each service firm needs to regularly evaluate its customer portfolio and to consider terminating some relationships. To illustrate, one medium-sized financial planning firm interviewed by the authors consciously reduced its customer base by more than 25% over a 1-year period; after 2 years not only had net profit returned to normal, but it had increased by some 50%. This was due to the fact that staff could now devote more time to servicing key accounts and thus sell on a wider array of its services (interview conducted with Scott Financial Services by Patterson in 1997).

What type of customers should we seek to serve? How do we create lasting relationships with them? Market segmentation is at the heart of this question, but unfortunately all too few service businesses respond to the question with the precision that it merits. Segmentation analysis helps in resolving such questions as the following:

- In what ways can the market for our service be segmented?
- What are the needs of the specific segments that we have identified? What is their profile?
- Which of these segments best fits our business mission and capabilities? Which are profitable to serve?
- What do customers in each segment see as our competitive advantages and disadvantages? Are the latter correctable?
- In the light of this analysis, which specific segment(s) should we target?
- How should we differentiate our marketing efforts from those of the competition?
- How should our firm build long-term relationships with customers from the target segments in ways that create mutual value?

Market segmentation is, of course, central to a well-planned and -executed marketing strategy.

THE CONCEPT OF A PORTFOLIO

The term *portfolio* is often used to describe the collection of financial instruments held by an investor or the array of loans advanced by a bank. In financial services, the goal of portfolio analysis is to determine the mix of investments (or loans) that is appropriate to one's needs, resources, and risk preference. In an investment portfolio, the contents should change over time in response to the performance of individual portfolio elements, as well as to reflect changes in the investor's situation or preferences.

We can apply the concept of portfolio to service businesses with an established base of customers. If managers know the annual value of each category of customers (revenues received minus the associated costs of serving them) as well as the proportions represented by each category within the customer base, they can project the ongoing value of all these customers in terms of future revenue streams. Models exist for projecting the future value of the customer portfolio, based on historical data concerning customer acquisitions, classes of service purchased, service upgrades and downgrades, and terminations (Weinberg and Lovelock 1986). These historical data can be adapted to reflect pricing and cost changes as well as the anticipated impact of new marketing efforts.

It is, however, worth being cautious before ignoring a particular market segment because its individual customers are small and do not generate much revenue. When the segment itself is huge, then the collective value of all the customers may be substantial. British Telecom made the mistake of ignoring the needs of its hundreds of thousands of small business customers, focusing its sales efforts on larger customers. When a new account management program was instituted for the small business market, with contact delivered through inexpensive telephone channels rather than through expensive field visits, satisfied customers responded by sharply increasing their purchases of telecommunications services and equipment. In talking about customer portfolios, it is important to distinguish between existing relationships—all the customers with whom the firm does business—and the mix of customers being served at any given point in time. The former determines valuation, based on current and future earnings potential; the latter is central to decisions on how to optimize use of available capacity over time.

DEVELOPMENT OF A RELATIONSHIP

One area of research that is now attracting attention is how the strength of relationships develops. We currently know very little about the way in which such relationships develop, the strength of such relationships, or the variables that

Exchange Transaction	Relational Exchanges
• Discrete	• High Trust
• Short term	• Ongoing
• Little commitment	• Highly personal
	• Highly valued
	• Cooperative
	• Loyal

Figure 19.4 Relationship Continuum

determine how a relationship grows. Limited research to date (Ward and Smith 1998) indicates the following.

- Relationships do strengthen with time for high- (but not for low-) involvement services.
- Older consumers appear to form relationships with service providers more readily than younger consumers.
- Gender generally does not appear to affect the propensity to form relationships.
- The frequency of interpersonal contact appears to have a positive effect for some services.
- About 30% of consumers do not appear to form strong relationships at all.

Application of the above findings without regard to the nature of the service product could lead to firms attempting to build relationships in situations that are not conducive to relationship development, the result being wasted resources. Additionally, one should not overlook the strategic implications of relationship marketing or increasing relationship strength in terms of competitive advantage, differentiation, core competency, key industry success factors, market share, and increased profitability. Understanding the nature of the relationship marketing construct is essential if marketers are to implement effective relationship marketing programs.

UNDER WHAT CONDITIONS IS RELATIONSHIP MARKETING AN APPROPRIATE STRATEGY?

It is insightful to view the relational process on a continuum (Barnes 1995; Congram 1991; Dwyer, Schurr, and Oh 1987), with the endpoints generally being described as in Figure 19.4. Under what conditions is it appropriate for a service firm to embark on such a strategy to achieve the outcome at the far right-hand side of the continuum in Figure 19.4? First, a firm would want to be serious about such a strategy only if it was in its own best interests to do so—that is, *profitable in the long run* (or achieving other key organizational goals such as donations or patronage in the case of a not-for-profit firm). The first thing to note at the outset is that it is not an all-or-nothing strategy—a firm may desire to adopt a relational strategy with only some of its customer segments. In some cases, a firm may want to develop a relationship strategy only with customers in the "high-value" segment.

Take, for example, the case of a hardware store that has two fundamental segments—business accounts (tradespeople and businesses who are large volume users of many building products) and domestic do-it-yourself customers who frequent the store for only relatively small purchases on an infrequent basis. Here an analysis of customer billing shows the 80/20 or Pareto law in action. (The law states that 80% of profits are generated from 20% of customers.) In one case, a hardware store found that the largest 13% of its customer base (i.e., builders and tradespeople) accounted for some 82% of its annual sales revenue (Gordon 1998). In this situation, it makes sense to develop a relationship strategy for this high-value segment, but not with the small domestic user who visits the store only once or twice a year.

Second, customers who have regular and medium-high frequency contact with the firm tend to lend themselves more to relational development. Customers of banks, telecommunications companies, family medical practices, travel agencies, preschool day care centers, hairdressers, and auto service centers, for example, are all potentially long-term loyal customers. Because of the frequency with which they interact with the service organization, the firm can assess this segment's needs and buying behavior, and thus has an opportunity to forge strong social bonds, deliver service customization, develop trust, and demonstrate that it cares about the relationship with the customer. On the other hand, these opportunities are not afforded with infrequent customers (such as those who use a veterinary surgeon only once every 2 years or so, or a specialist doctor or travel agent once a year). Furthermore, on a cost-benefit basis it is probably not worth the firm's effort to do so.

Third, medium-high contact services are more amenable to relationship development than low-contact ones (Ward and Smith 1998). Where the customer must be physically present for an extended period of time for the service delivery to take place, the opportunity exists to strengthen social bonds. This would partly explain the relatively high propensities—77% and 85% of customers, respectively—to be loyal to their hairdresser and family doctor (shown earlier in this chapter). As Czepiel (1990) noted, "The essential social nature of service encounters, a short run phenomenon, provides the occasions in which the buyer and seller negotiate the terms of their exchange relationship—a long-term phenomenon" (p. 13). Because many services appear to be heading down an electronic delivery path (e.g., banking via telephone or Internet, using integrated response systems where only a series of recorded responses is received instead of personal contact) and in doing so are shifting from high-medium contact service delivery to low-contact service, they risk severing existing social bonds and making it almost impossible to develop new bonds, thus condemning the otherwise intangible, ephemeral service experience to the commodity category—and as a consequence making it increasingly difficult to achieve a competitive advantage.

Fourth, services where the *customer is highly involved* (seeing the service as of high personal importance) lend themselves to relationship development. Regular customers of a family doctor, accountant, financial planner, hairdresser, auto service mechanic, day care center, or fitness club are highly involved in the service experience and invest considerable emotional and cognitive energy in the relationship. Such customers are likely to stay in the relationship as long as they see value and trust is not severed.

Perceived risk is the fifth contingency condition. Many services are highly variable and difficult to standardize. Services that are high in credence properties are especially high in perceived risk, precisely because the customer has difficulty confidently evaluating the quality of the service received even after purchase and consumption. Hence, in situations where a customer perceives high risk or uncertainty in the outcome, one risk-reduction strategy is that once having found a firm (e.g., financial planner, accountant, doctor, hairdresser, travel agent), the customer will stay with that service provider. This view is supported in the Gwinner, Gremler, and Bitner study (1998) findings of a benefit category they labeled "confidence benefits" ("I believe there is less risk something will go wrong," "I have more confidence the service will be performed correctly," and "I have less anxiety when I purchase the service").

Finally, when a service provider has what Lovelock (1991) calls a "membership relationship" with a customer, then opportunities for strengthening the relationship are increased. Banks, superannuation and insurance funds, book clubs, and telecommunications companies, for example, have a range of personal customer information as well as the opportunity to capture buying behavior patterns. This allows the potential to segment and customize service offerings to different groups. Furthermore, it makes it time-consuming to switch suppliers.

FUTURE DIRECTIONS

As Leonard Berry (1995) so succinctly put it, "relationship marketing's time has come" (p. 243). Although there is no doubt that managers and researchers have wholeheartedly embraced the concept, there is still much we don't understand, including the following.

- How will information technology (IT) delivery systems affect customer relationships? Specifically, will they sever social bonds, making true relationship development more difficult to achieve, or will a first mover advantage apply and the first to introduce enhanced value via IT delivery capture and retain customers (e.g., the bookseller Amazon.com or on-line travel agency services)?
- What types of customers are most receptive to relationship development, and which are not suited?
- How do relationships develop?
- What weights do various customer segments attach to individual benefits of staying in a relationship?

- What are the key drivers of relationship commitment across different service types?
- What role does value play in relationship development?
- What are the implications for relationship development for organization structure?

It is clear that relationship marketing is a powerful marketing tool, but only for certain products and certain people, and only when applied in such a way that both parties benefit. It is also clear that there is much that we have yet to learn about relationships and how to successfully integrate marketing relationship techniques into marketing plans.

REFERENCES

Adelman, M. B., A. Ahuvia, and C. Goodwin (1994), "Beyond Smiling: Social Support and Service Quality," in *Service Quality: New Directions in Theory and Practice*, R. T. Rust and R. L. Oliver, eds. Thousand Oaks, CA: Sage, 139-72.

Barnes, James B. (1995), "The Quality and Depth of Customer Relationships," in *Proceedings of the 24th European Marketing Academy Conference*, Michelle Bergadaa, ed., Cergy-Fontoise, France, May 10-16, 1997, 1393-1402.

Berry, Leonard (1983), "Relationship Marketing," in *Emerging Perspectives on Services Marketing*, Leonard L. Berry, G. Lynn Shostack, and Gregory Upah, eds. Chicago: American Marketing Association, 25-28.

——— (1995), "Relationship Marketing of Services—Growing Interest, Emerging Perspectives," *Journal of the Academy of Marketing Science*, 23(4), 236-45.

——— and A. Parasuraman (1991), *Marketing Services: Competing Through Quality*. New York: Free Press.

Bitner, Mary Jo (1995), "Building Service Relationships: It's All About Promises," *Journal of the Academy of Marketing Science*, 23 (Fall), 246-51.

Blois, K. J. (1995), "Relationship Marketing in Organisational Markets—What Is the Customer?" *Proceedings of the 24th European Marketing Academy Conference*, Michelle Bergadaa, ed., Cergy-Fontoise, France, May 10-16, 1997, 131-47.

Callaghan, M. B. (1993), *The Development and Application of a Test Instrument for Relationship Marketing Orientation Within Australian Businesses*, Honours Thesis, Faculty of Business, University of Southern Queensland, Australia.

Christopher, M. G., A. F. Payne, and D. Ballantyne (1991), *Relationship Marketing: Bringing Quality, Customer Service and Marketing Together*. Oxford, UK: Butterworth-Heinemann.

Congram, Carole A. (1991), "Building Relationships That Last," in *The AMA Handbook for Marketing for the Services Industries*, C. A. Congram and M. L. Friedman, eds. New York: American Management Association, 263-79.

Crosby, Lawrence A., Kenneth R. Evans, and Deborah Cowles (1990), "Relationship Quality in Services Selling: An Interpersonal Influence Perspective," *Journal of Marketing*, 54 (July), 68-81.

Czepiel, J. A. (1990), "Service Encounters and Service Relationships: Implications for Research," *Journal of Business Research*, 20, 13-21.

Dowling, Grahame and Mark D. Uncles (1997), "Do Customer Loyalty Programs Really Work?" *Sloan Management Review*, 38 (Summer), 71-82.

Dwyer, F. R., P. H. Schurr, and S. Oh (1987), "Developing Buyer-Seller Trust," *Journal of Marketing*, 51(2), 11-27.

Evans, J. R. and R. I. Laskin (1994), "The Relationship Marketing Process: A Conceptualisation and Application," *Industrial Marketing Management*, 25(5), 439-52.

Ford, D. (1980), "The Development of Buyer-Seller Relationships in Industrial Markets," *European Journal of Marketing*, 58 (April), 339-53.

———, ed. (1990), *Understanding Business Markets: Interaction, Relationships, Networks*. London: Academic Press.

Goodwin, Cathy (1994), "Between Friendship and Business: Communal Relationships in Service Exchanges," working paper, University of Manitoba.

Gordon, Mary Ellen (1998), "Relationship Marketing—Is It Black or White?" in *Services Marketing*, C. P. Lovelock, P. Patterson, and R. Walker, eds. Sydney: Prentice-Hall, 213-19.

Grönroos, Christian (1983), *Strategic Management and Marketing in the Service Sector*. Boston: Marketing Science Institute.

———— (1989), "Defining Marketing: A Market-Oriented Approach," *European Journal of Marketing*, 23(1), 52-60.

———— (1990), "Relationship Approach to Marketing in Service Contexts: The Marketing and Organizational Interface," *Journal of Business Research*, 20 (January), 3-11.

———— (1994), "From Marketing Mix to Relationship Marketing: Toward a Paradigm Shift in Marketing," *Management Decision*, 32(2), 4-20.

Gummesson, Evert (1987), "The New Marketing—Developing Long-Term Interactive Relationships," *Long Range Planning*, 20, 10-20.

———— (1992), "Marketing-Orientation Revisited: The Crucial Role of the Part-Time Marketer," *European Journal of Marketing*, 25(2), 60.

———— (1994), "Making Relationship Marketing Operational," *International Journal of Service Industry Management*, 5(5), 5-20.

Gwinner, Kevin, Dwayne Gremler, and Mary Jo Bitner (1998), "Relational Benefits in Service Industries: The Customer's Perspective," *Journal of the Academy of Marketing Science*, 26(2), 101-14.

Hakansson, H., ed. (1982), *International Marketing and Purchasing of Industrial Goods*. Chichester, UK: John Wiley and Sons.

Iacobucci, Dawn I. (1994), "Toward Defining Relationship Marketing," *Relationship Marketing: Theory, Methods and Applications*, proceedings of a research conference at Goizueta Business School, Emory University, 1-10.

Keaveney, Susan M. (1995), "Customer Switching in Service Industries: An Exploratory Study," *Journal of Marketing*, 59, 71-82.

Levitt, Theodore (1993), "After the Sale Is Over," *Harvard Business Review*, (September), 87-93.

Liswood, Laura (1990), *Serving Them Right*. New York: HarperCollins.

Lovelock, Christopher H. (1983), "Classifying Services to Gain Strategic Marketing Insights," *Journal of Marketing*, 47(3), 9-20.

———— (1991), *Services Marketing: Text Cases and Readings*. Englewood Cliffs, NJ: Prentice-Hall.

————, Paul G. Patterson, and R. H. Walker (1998), *Services Marketing—Australia and New Zealand*. Sydney: Prentice Hall Australia.

Morgan, R. and S. D. Hunt (1994), "The Commitment Trust Theory of Relationship Marketing," *Journal of Marketing*, 58 (July), 20-38.

Patterson, Paul G. (1998), "Customer Perceptions of Relationship Benefits Across Service Types," *Australian and New Zealand Marketing Academy Proceedings*, Brendan J. Gray and Kenneth Deans, eds., University of Otago, Dunedin, New Zealand, December.

Payne, Adrian (1997), "Relationship Marketing: The UK Perspective," *Proceedings of Australian and New Zealand Marketing Educators' Conference*, Peter Reed, Sandra Luxton, and Michael Shaw, eds., Melbourne, December 1-3.

Peelan, E., C. F. W. Ekelmans, and P. Vijn (1989), "Direct Marketing for Establishing the Relationships Between Buyers and Sellers," *Journal of Direct Marketing*, 3(1), 7-14.

Reichheld, Frederick F. (1996), *The Loyalty Effect: The Hidden Force Behind Growth, Profits and Lasting Value*. Boston: Harvard Business School Press.

———— and W. Earl Sasser (1990), "Zero Defections: Quality Comes to Services," *Harvard Business Review*, (September-October), 105-11.

Shani, D. and S. Chalasani (1993), "Exploiting Niches Using Relationship Marketing," *Journal of Business and Industrial Marketing*, 8(4), 58-66.

Storbacka, K., Tore Strandvik, and Christian Grönroos (1994), "Managing Customer Relationships for Profit: The Dynamics of Relationship Quality," *International Journal of Service Industry Management*, 5(5), 21-38.

Turnbull, P. W. and M. T. Cunningham (1981), *International Marketing and Purchasing*. London: Macmillan.

Ward, A., E. Frew, and D. Caldow (1997), "An Extended List of the Dimensions of 'Relationship' in Consumer Service Product Marketing: A Pilot Study," *American Marketing Association Conference*, 6, 531-44.

———— and T. Smith (1998), "Relationship Marketing: Strength of Relationship Time Versus Duration," *European Marketing Academy Conference Proceedings*, Per Andersson, ed., Stockholm, May, 569-88.

Weinberg, C. B. and C. H. Lovelock (1986), "Pricing and Profits in Subscription Service Marketing: An Analytical Approach to Customer Valuation," in *Creativity in Services Marketing*, M. Venkatesan, D. Schmalensee, and C. Marshall, eds. Chicago: American Marketing Association.

Zeithaml, Valarie A. and Mary Jo Bitner (1996), *Services Marketing*. Singapore: McGraw-Hill.

20

Antecedents and Consequences of Service Quality in Business-to-Business Services

MARTIN WETZELS
KO DE RUYTER
JOS LEMMINK

In the services marketing literature, the main focus has been on consumer services, leaving business-to-business services as a relatively unexplored area of research. Industrial services can be divided into two broad groups (Boyt and Harvey 1997): (a) maintenance and repair services and (b) business advisory services or professional services. This dichotomy essentially is related to the difference between goods-related or customer services and "pure" services. Professional services are related to core business elements of service providers and as such seem to be important. At the same time, it has been argued that customer services may be the single most important competitive factor in business-to-business environments (Clark 1993). Both types of business services, therefore, seem to be important and will be taken into account in this chapter.

One of the key issues in services marketing research to date has been the search for an in-depth understanding of the measurement and management of service quality. Here, the dominant point of view on quality has been customer perceptions of service provider performance. Although a relatively large body of knowledge has accumulated with regard to consumer services, only a few studies have taken the specific characteristics shared by business-to-business services into account. It seems relevant, therefore, to discuss the point of reference that customers take in their quality assessment of business services. A second key issue in the research literature is the contribution of service quality to the establishment and maintenance of long-term relationships. The exact nature of the (positive) impact of service quality on customer loyalty has remained somewhat equivocal.

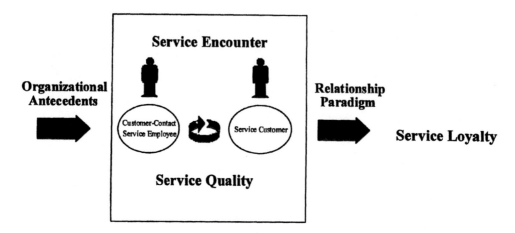

Figure 20.1 Overview of the Structure of This Chapter

With the emergence of the relationship paradigm in services marketing, a number of other factors or "relationship building blocks" have been advanced that may account for the development and maintenance of customer loyalty. Central to both issues is the role of the customer service employee. Because relationships are established between people and because customer perceptions of employee attitudes and behavior in service encounters are the basis of service quality measurement systems, it has been concluded that customer-contact service personnel are essential to the ultimate economic success of the service organization (Hartline and Ferrell 1996). Determinants of the performance of service employees therefore may be considered a third key issue.

In this chapter we propose to discuss the aforementioned issues from the perspective of business-to-business services. First of all, we discuss the focal construct of service quality in business services. Second, we examine a number of factors that may affect the ability of service employees to deliver service quality. Finally, we explore the relative impact of service quality on long-term relationships in business-to-business markets, taking into account relationship as well as business market characteristics. Figure 20.1 provides an overview of the structure of this chapter, linking organizational antecedents to customer relationships in business-to-business services via the central role of the customer-contact employee.

SERVICES QUALITY IN BUSINESS-TO-BUSINESS SERVICES

The most widely used approach to measuring service quality is that of a customer's overall judgment of the service experience, based on a number of dimensions. The SERVQUAL instrument, which identifies five service quality dimensions, is the most widely used exponent of such an approach, particularly in relation to consumer services. Although several successful applications of the SERVQUAL model have been reported in relation to business services, a number of authors have presented alternative, customer-based service quality models that have been developed specifically for the evaluation of business services. The point taken is that in relation to consumer services, business services are characterized by relatively high degrees of intangibility, customization, and customer participation.

Szmigin (1993), for instance, proposes a three-dimensional service quality model for business services that makes a distinction between "hard quality," "soft quality," and "outcome quality." The hard quality dimension refers to what is actually received by the customer from the service provider (e.g., a concept commercial, a market research report). It is related to the technical aspects of the services, which in most cases can be objectively measured. The soft quality dimension is related to the way in which the service is delivered by the employee(s) of the service provider (e.g., the after-sales technician). It is strongly related to the attitude and behavior of service employees. Both dimensions pertain to the quality of the service delivery process in contrast with the outcome quality dimension, which refers to the question whether the outcome of the service process is in line with the objectives of the customer. Szmigin (1993) argues that outcome quality is different because it is susceptible to matters that are beyond the service provider's control. For instance, a business consultant may come up with a report that meets both hard and soft quality standards, but the actual implementation may not always result in the desired results.

Other authors have suggested further nuances in the outcome quality concept (e.g., Halinen 1994), making a distinction between immediate and ultimate outcomes based on an inherent time perspective. The former reflects the fact that a solution to a client-specific problem is offered, whereas the latter is concerned with the consequences of the solution after it has been implemented. The business consultant's advice may provide the right solution to a firm's problem but it may not necessarily result in expected turnover. In the literature on business services quality, the element of the outcome is more emphasized. This seems consistent with the alleged importance of long-term relationships in business markets. Central to the process dimensions, however, is the performance of the service employee. This is an issue to which we turn in the next section.

ROLE STRESS AND SERVICE QUALITY

Service employees fulfill a boundary spanning role and form the continuous link between the organization and the customer. Furthermore, the performance of the customer-contact service employees is essential to the economic success of the organization. In many business-to-business settings, customer-contact service employees are called on to perform innovative and creative activities to solve customers' problems and deliver service quality. Again, this is due to the relatively high degrees of intangibility, customization, and customer participation in business-to-business services. These characteristics may be in sharp contrast with rules, regulations, and targets that have been designed by the service company. As a result, service employees (particularly in business-to-business settings) are prone to role stress, which may in turn affect their ability to deliver service quality. This is an aspect that we will discuss in some detail by developing a conceptual framework of antecedents and consequences of service employee role stress.

Classical role theory posits that each individual performs a certain role in an organization. This role cannot be seen in isolation but is related to other roles in the organization. Other individuals, organizational policies, and the demands and needs of customers attempt to exert influences on employees by communicating role pressures or role expectations. This may result in role conflict and role ambiguity. Role conflict has been defined as "the simultaneous occurrence of two (or more) sets of pressures such that compliance with one would make more difficult compliance with the other" (Kahn et al. 1964, p. 19). For service employees, expectations of the organization, managers, or coworkers stressing operational efficiency may clash with the demands of customers who want problem resolution and/or satisfaction. Role ambiguity occurs when a person does not have access to sufficient and useful information to perform his or her role as a service employee adequately. Role ambiguity may result from the fact that the service employee is uncertain about supervisory expectations or from the fact that he or she does not know how performance will be evaluated and rewarded. We will now examine a number of antecedents and consequences of service employee role stress and develop a conceptual framework.

In many organizations, rules and regulations or formalization is used to govern employee attitudes and behavior. For instance, in an after-sales setting it is frequently specified how many customers should be served within a certain time frame. We assume that formalization will negatively affect role ambiguity and positively affect role conflict. Formalization will create clarity regarding what the organization, management, and colleagues expect from the service employee and thus reduce role ambiguity. Role conflict, on the other hand, may be increased by limiting the discretionary power of the service employee. The service employee is required to work "by the rules," and the rules might not necessarily reflect the customer's point of view.

In contrast, many service organizations nowadays are experimenting with the concept of empowerment. Empowerment reflects providing the service employee with both competence and autonomy in delivering service quality. In relation to role stress, it seems plausible that both employee competence and autonomy will reduce role stress.

In addition to formalization and empowerment, which are often specified in terms of organizational policies, it can be argued that management behavior may also affect role stress experienced by service providers. We argue that leadership behavior, in terms of both initiating structure and leader consideration, will decrease employee role stress. Leader initiating structure pertains to the way in which a manager guides employees, provides explanations, monitors efficiency, and stimulates employees to perform better. This dimension explicitly focuses on goal/task-specific issues. Leadership consideration is how management supports

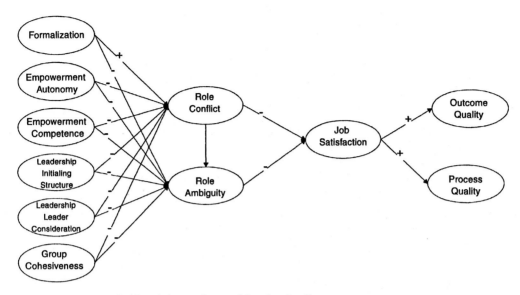

Figure 20.2 Organizational Antecedents of Service Quality

the social and interpersonal relationships of workers (Jackson and Schuler 1985). Leadership consideration is thus primarily oriented toward creating good relationships with employees.

Finally, a supportive working environment depends not only on the behavior and attitude of supervisors but also on the concern and dedication of coworkers. A group-level attribute that has been identified as an antecedent of role stress in organizations in the literature is group cohesiveness (Griffith 1988). Group cohesiveness has been defined as "the desire of individuals to maintain their membership in a group" (Lott and Lott 1965, p. 260). As Kahn and Quinn (1970) argue, the psychological support of direct colleagues may help to decrease the strain of occupational roles. The underlying assumption here is that groups in which close ties between group members exist are more supportive of individual employees than noncohesive groups. Employees in cohesive groups are more likely to communicate with coworkers about problems they experience with respect to role ambiguity and role conflict.

In addition to the aforementioned antecedents, a number of consequences of service employee role stress have been identified. Job satisfaction has often been associated with lower levels of role stress (Babin and Boles 1996). Job satisfaction represents the attitude or knowledge structure that encapsulates workers' feelings and beliefs about the nature of their job and the organization (George and Jones 1996). The higher the level of role stress, the less satisfied a service employee will be. Furthermore, it seems unlikely that unhappy employees will be able or motivated to make customers happy. Alternatively, several authors have suggested that there is a positive relationship between job satisfaction and job performance of service employees in terms of service quality, in terms of both outcome and process quality. An overview of the relationships between role stress (conflict and ambiguity) and its antecedents and consequences is given in Figure 20.2.

Wetzels (1998) has empirically tested the model in the context of an after-sales organization for office equipment, using structural equation modeling. Participants in the study were 256 service engineers, and the study was based on employee perceptions of customer evaluations of service quality. We will briefly summarize the results. It was found that the empowerment autonomy component exerted a strong negative influence on both role ambiguity and role conflict. In addition, it was also found that giving employees a higher degree of autonomy leads to higher job satisfaction levels. In contrast, neither formalization nor empowerment competence had a significant impact on the two role stressors. In an after-sales service organization, therefore, it seems advisable not to rely on mechanistic control systems and to allow employees to customize the service the way they think fit. With regard to the two leadership dimensions, it was found that initiating structure had a negative influence on role ambiguity, whereas leader consideration did not seem to affect either role stressor. Initiating structure seems to be able to clarify role requirements and expectations. Service managers may need to clarify their goals and expectations with regard to their customer-contact service employees. This might be even more important if empowerment is introduced, using self-directed work teams (Barry and Stewart 1997). Group cohesiveness decreases role conflict. In terms of role stress consequences, a negative relationship between role ambiguity and job satisfaction was found. In particular, lack of clarity seems to be responsible for decreasing job satisfaction of service employees. Finally, evidence was found for relatively strong positive relationships between job satisfaction and both process and outcome quality. The satisfaction of service employees seems a necessary condition for delivering excellence in service quality. Service quality, however, is not an end in itself; it is a means to an end. Now that we have discussed the terms and conditions for service quality in a business-to-business setting, we will take a closer look at the impact of service quality on customer loyalty in the next section.

SERVICE QUALITY, RELATIONSHIPS, AND CUSTOMER LOYALTY

Ultimately, customer loyalty in business services is considered the key factor for the development of a sustainable competitive edge (Gremler and Brown 1996). During past decades, customer evaluative judgments (i.e., service quality, satisfaction, and value) have been advanced to account for customer loyalty (Dick and Basu 1994). Here, the implicit theme is that positive evaluations of service quality instigate customers to favor service providers with their patronage. The direct relationship between customer evaluations of services and loyalty in business markets, however, remained somewhat equivocal. First, Wetzels (1998) demonstrates that the service quality–loyalty relationship in business markets is often not simple and straightforward because affective commitment on the part of the customer may act as a moderator. Second, it could be argued that the relationship between satisfaction and loyalty is nonlinear, leading to the fact that loyalty remains unaffected over a relatively large range of satisfaction levels that fall below the critical threshold. Third, in many business markets there is a tendency to develop relationships with single-source suppliers, leading to increased levels of interdependence and switching costs (Wilson 1995). Finally, business service encounters are often characterized by multiple interactions, what has been called the multiheaded customer and seller (Gummesson 1987) in which communication and cooperation play important roles. The direct relationship between customer evaluations and loyalty in business services may be filtered, therefore, by a number of factors. The relationship paradigm suggests a number of these.

Commitment and trust are two "relationship building blocks" that have been suggested frequently. Trust has been conceptualized as the confidence that relationship partners have in the reliability and integrity of each other (Morgan and Hunt 1994). Commitment refers to the motivation to stay with a supplier or, as Moorman, Zaltman, and Deshpande (1992) state, to an enduring desire to maintain a valued relationship. Kumar, Hibbard, and Stern (1994) distinguish two different types of commitment: affective and calculative. Affective commitment expresses the extent to which customers like to maintain their relationship with their supplier. Affective commitment is based on a general positive feeling toward the exchange partner. Calculative commitment refers to a firm's motivation to continue the relationship because it cannot easily replace its current partner and because it cannot obtain the same resources and outcomes outside its current relationship. This dimension posits commitment as a calculative act in which costs and benefits are traded off.

Because commitment entails vulnerability, parties will seek only trustworthy partners (Morgan and Hunt 1994). Trust leads to a high level of affective commitment or, in other words, a strong desire to maintain a relationship. Empirical support for this argument is given by Morgan and Hunt (1994) and Geyskens et al. (1996). Trust may lead customers to focus more on the positive motivation because of a sense of affiliation and identification with the supplier, and this may be a stimulus to focus less on calculative reasons for attachment to a supplier firm. In addition, Geyskens et al. (1996) report a negative relation between trust and calculative commitment. When a firm's trust in a partner increases, there will be less reason to continue the relationship because it feels it needs to on the basis of cost-benefit analyses.

In the complex setting of business services, market and relationship characteristics may determine commitment and trust, in addition to service quality characteristics. Furthermore, commitment and trust may in turn affect loyalty in service relationships. Figure 20.3 represents a framework of business-to-business service relationships.

Service quality characteristics are a decisive factor in determining customer trust and commitment. MacKenzie (1992) demonstrated that customer trust in the office equipment market is influenced positively by customer perceptions of the service offering. Likewise, Venetis (1997) found empirical evidence for a positive relationship between service quality and relationship commitment in

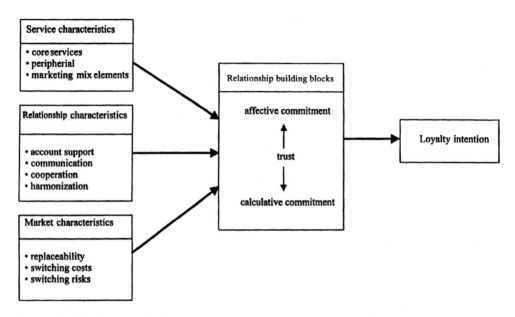

Figure 20.3 A Framework of Business-to-Business Service Relationships

advertising agency–client relationships. In addition to service quality, however, services suppliers are increasingly focusing on relational exchange activities. These comprise the relationship characteristics.

The importance of relationships with customers in business markets as part of companies' operating strategies has been widely acknowledged (Morgan and Hunt 1994). As relationship management becomes institutionalized in firms and emphasis is placed on integrated networks between suppliers and customers, relationship promoters or account managers are appointed and formal transactions reflect informal and interpersonal agreements and commitments (Gemunden and Walter 1994; Ring and Van de Ven 1994). In business service markets, personal contact between supplier and customer is viewed as the most important source of information. Larson (1992), for instance, reports that personal relationship management by boundary spanners leads to a reduction of perceived risk and uncertainty and that personal trust is a major consideration for supplier selection. Furthermore, through personal contacts affective commitment can be established. Account support seems to be an important relationship management variable. In addition, communication, the formal as well as informal sharing of information through frequent two-way dyadic interchanges, also plays an important role in realizing the benefits from a relationship (Anderson and Weitz 1992). As Mac-Kenzie (1992) contends, communication is an aspect that will be considered when relationships are evaluated by customers. Dwyer, Schurr, and Oh (1987) argue that communication is an important input to customer commitment. Anderson, Gerbing, and Hunter's (1987) argument that communication is positively associated with customer trust has been empirically verified by Anderson and Narus

(1990). Moreover, cooperation is another antecedent of trust. Cooperation is a frequent phenomenon in business markets. For instance, CPA firms and their clients may develop joint information systems to facilitate the exchange of information and reduce information asymmetry. Finally, in business relationships, conflict may occur as a result of disagreement or perceived impediments to the attainment of mutual goals and objectives (Dwyer, Schurr, and Oh 1987). Although conflict can have a negative effect on relationships (Anderson and Weitz 1992), solving conflicts constructively may actually strengthen interorganizational relationships and lead to greater trust and affective commitment (Weitz and Jap 1995). It is aimed at reaching mutually acceptable compromises without having to resort to formal procedures and as such is an important input to customer commitment (Gundlach, Achrol, and Mentzer 1995). Harmonization or conflict solving therefore is another relationship management variable.

It has been pointed out that supplier-customer relationships in business are multifaceted phenomena (Heide and John 1988). Whether other suppliers in the market form real alternatives, customer commitment is based not only on the service or relationship offering but also on the costs and risks associated with switching suppliers. We propose, therefore, to take a number of market variables into account. We distinguish three variables: replaceability, perceived switching costs, and perceived switching risks. The replaceability variable refers to the difficulty of replacing one's partner because of the lack of alternative partners (Heide and John 1988). Switching costs and switching risk refer to the costs expressed as time, effort, money, and financial risk involved in switching suppliers. Suppliers may influence perceptions of replaceability and of the costs and risks of switching not only through incompatibility of services but also by developing specific relationship routines and procedures and "vendor-specific learning" (Heide and Weiss 1995). Furthermore, developing supplier-related quality standards has been advocated as an important instrument for lowering switching behavior (Meldrum 1995). Finally, communicating the rapidity of technological developments enables suppliers to close customer consideration sets to competitors (Heide and Weiss 1995). It has been argued that the more dependent a customer is on its supplier, the more motivated the customer will be to develop a strong, cooperative, long-term relationship with its supplier (cf. Ganesan 1994). Kumar, Scheer, and Steenkamp (1995) and Geyskens et al. (1996) provide empirical evidence for a positive relationship between dependence and relationship commitment. Likewise, it has been shown that a positive relationship between perceived switching costs and risk, on one hand, and commitment, on the other, exists in business relationships (Venetis 1997). The more a customer experiences difficulties with switching, the more he or she feels the need to continue working with the supplier.

Commitment indicates the motivation to maintain a relationship. Commitment also has been conceptualized in terms of a temporal dimension, focusing on the fact that commitment becomes meaningful only when it develops consistently over time (Moorman, Zaltman, and Deshpande 1992). As a result of continuity, customer turnover may be reduced and partners will be more inclined

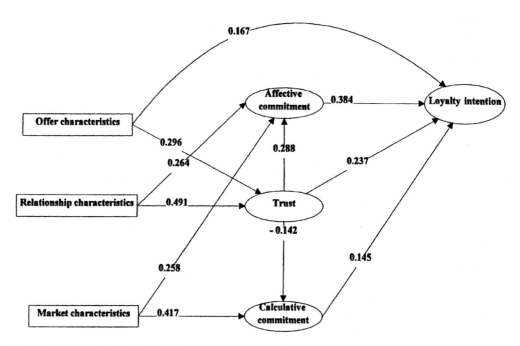

Figure 20.4 Results of Empirical Study

NOTE: Standardized path coefficients vary between 1 and –1 and indicate direction and magnitude of the relationship.

to work together to achieve mutual goals (Anderson and Narus 1990). Through long-term commitment and trust relationship, consequences such as decreased opportunism can be realized (Morgan and Hunt 1994). Kumar, Hibbard, and Stern (1994) use intention to stay in the relationship as an important desirable consequence of commitment that has a direct impact on supplier-customer relationships. Intention to stay reflects the customer's motivation to continue the relationship.

The conceptual framework presented in Figure 20.3 has been empirically tested in the context of high-technology office systems. A sample of 491 customers was used to test the conceptual framework. In Figure 20.4, an overview of the results obtained via structural equation modeling is rendered.

We find that affective commitment is positively influenced by relationship characteristics. This means that activities aimed at managing the relationship with customers contribute to a perception of an enjoyable relationship. Similarly, trust has a positive impact on affective commitment in supplier-customer relationships in business markets. Trust pertains to a customer's confidence and faith that the supplier will be reliable and willing to listen to the customer's wishes and act in his or her best interests. We also find a positive relationship between market characteristics and affective commitment. This may seem counterintuitive but may be explained as follows. It may be indicative of the fact that because of the limited number of suppliers, a high degree of dependence, and high switching costs and risks, suppliers of high-technology products and services may have a relatively powerful position in the market, often as a single-source supplier. Frazier, Gill, and Kale (1989) contend that in such situations the powerful party does not have to resort to coercive measures to ensure well-functioning relationships, but instead can use noncoercive strategies that result in an exchange atmosphere that is perceived as positive and agreeable by the more dependent partner in the relationship. With respect to trust, we find that both offer characteristics and relationship characteristics have a positive impact. Service as well as account support are often cited as major reasons for choosing a supplier in high-technology markets. Furthermore, relationship managing activities by suppliers are often geared toward achieving the customer's confidence by information sharing, cooperative synergy, and lowering levels of perceived risk. For instance, an open information exchange in which proprietary data is shared will instigate customers to work more closely with their supplier and to share their own information. Finally, we find that calculative commitment is relatively strongly determined by market characteristics. Because a relatively large degree of dependence exists in high-technology markets, the motivation to protect idiosyncratic investments in the relationship with a supplier would be in the interest of the customer. The relative impact of market conditions can also be accounted for by the fact that there are likely to be few alternatives that can replace the current supplier in the market. On the other hand, we find a negative relationship between trust and calculative commitment. The less trust a customer has in the supplier, the more the motivation will be based on a calculation of costs and benefits.

In terms of customer loyalty intentions, we find support for the positive impact of the three variables on the intention to remain in the relationship. Our study provides evidence for the relatively important role of affective commitment in business relationships. Because of the complexity of relationships (relatively high uncertainty as well as large investments), all three variables play a role of some importance. The decision to remain in the relationship with the supplier will be based on affective as well as cognitive motivations. We also encounter a direct effect of offer characteristics on the intention to continue the relationship. The centrality of service quality seems to underline the relative importance of this construct.

CONCLUSION AND MANAGERIAL IMPLICATIONS

This chapter focuses on three important issues in business-to-business services. First, the nature of business-to-business service quality was discussed. In contrast to consumer services, we find that in business-to-business services there is more emphasis on the outcome component of service quality. Second, the service employee in business-to-business services plays a pivotal role. It is the performance of the service employee that is equated with service quality. We presented a model that introduced several factors affecting performance of the service employee in terms of service quality. The autonomy component of empowerment is shown to have comprehensive effects throughout the model; it reduces role stress and increases job satisfaction. Finally, we introduced the relationship paradigm to shed some light on the relationships between service quality and customer loyalty. Trust in the company and commitment appear to be important intermediate variables. Apart from the important role of service quality, other factors such as relationship characteristics and market characteristics play an important role.

In sum, these conclusions provide management with ample opportunities to actually manage the relationship with customers. First, changing the control system in the organization so as to empower employees may have a positive impact. Second, communication and cooperation as well as introducing customer-oriented account systems can shape customer relationships. Third, management may change market characteristics by introducing new factors (e.g., long-term contracts to increase switching costs). Although the role of marketing management may be an important one, implementing these organizational changes certainly is not a task for marketing management alone. It requires inherent cooperation with other functional areas within the company to empower employees and to establish customer-oriented account management.

REFERENCES

Anderson, Eugene W. and Barton Weitz (1992), "The Use of Pledges to Build and Sustain Commitment in Distribution Channels," *Journal of Marketing Research*, 29 (February), 18-34.

Anderson, James C., David W. Gerbing, and John E. Hunter (1987), "On the Assessment of Unidimensionality Measurement: Internal and External Consistency Criteria," *Journal of Marketing Research*, 24 (November), 432-37.

——— and James A. Narus (1990), "A Model of Distributor Firm and Manufacturer Firm Working Partnerships," *Journal of Marketing*, 54 (January), 42-58.

Babin, Barry J. and James S. Boles (1996), "The Effects of Perceived Co-Worker Involvement and Supervisor Support on Service Provider Role Stress, Performance and Job Satisfaction," *Journal of Retailing*, 72(1), 57-75.

Barry, Bruce and Greg L. Stewart (1997), "Composition Process and Performance in Self-Managed Groups: The Role of Personality," *Journal of Applied Psychology*, 82(1), 62-78.

Boyt, Thomas and Michael Harvey (1997), "Classification of Industrial Services," *Industrial Marketing Management*, 26, 291-300.

Clark, T. (1993), "Survey Underscores Importance of Customer Service," *Business Marketing*, 78, 41.

Dick, Alan S. and Kunal Basu (1994), "Customer Loyalty: Toward an Integrated Conceptual Framework," *Journal of the Academy of Marketing Science*, 22 (Spring), 99-113.

Dwyer, F. Robert, Paul H. Schurr, and Sejo Oh (1987), "Developing Buyer-Seller Relationships," *Journal of Marketing*, 51 (April), 11-27.

Frazier, Gary, James D. Gill, and Sudhir H. Kale (1989), "Dealer Dependence Levels and Reciprocal Actions in a Channel of Distribution in a Developing Country," *Journal of Marketing*, 53 (January), 50-69.

Ganesan, Shankar (1994), "Determinants of Long-Term Orientation in Buyer-Seller Relationships," *Journal of Marketing*, 58 (April), 1-19.

Gemunden, Hans G. and Achim Walter (1994), "The Relationship-Promoter: Key Person for Interorganizational Innovation Co-operation," in *Relationship Marketing: Theory, Methods and*

Applications, Jagdish N. Sheth and Atul Parvatiyar, eds., proceedings of the 2nd Research Conference on Relationship Marketing, Roberto C. Goizueta Business School, Center for Relationship Marketing, Atlanta.

George, Jennifer M. and Gareth R. Jones (1996), "The Experience of Work and Turnover Intentions: Interactive Effects of Value Attainment, Job Satisfaction and Positive Mood," *Journal of Applied Psychology*, 81(3), 318-25.

Geyskens, Inge, Jan-Benedict E. M. Steenkamp, Lisa K. Scheer, and Nirmalya Kumar (1996), "The Effects of Trust and Interdependence on Relationship Commitment: A Trans-Atlantic Study," *International Journal of Research in Marketing*, 13(4), 303-18.

Gremler, Dwayne D. and Stephen W. Brown (1996), "Service Loyalty: Its Nature, Its Importance and Implications," in *QUIS V: Advancing Service Quality: A Global Perspective*, Bo Edvardsson, Stephen W. Brown, R. Johnston, and E. Scheuing, eds. New York: ISQA, 171-81.

Griffith, James (1988), "Measurement of Group Cohesion in U.S. Army Units," *Basic and Applied Psychology*, 9(2), 149-71.

Gummesson, Evert (1987), "The New Marketing—Developing Long-Term Interactive Relationships," *Long Range Planning*, 20, 10-20.

Gundlach, Gregory T., Ravi S. Achrol, and John T. Mentzer (1995), "The Structure of Commitment in Exchange," *Journal of Marketing*, 59 (January), 79-92.

Halinen, Aino (1994), *Exchange Relationships in Professional Services: A Study of Relationship Development in the Advertising Sector.* Published Dissertation Project, Sarja/Series A-6, Turku School of Economics and Business Administration, Finland.

Hartline, Michael D. and O. C. Ferrell (1996), "The Management of Customer-Contact Service Employees," *Journal of Marketing*, 60 (October), 52-70.

Heide, Jan B. and George John (1988), "The Role of Dependence Balancing in Safeguarding Transaction-Specific Assets in Conventional Channels," *Journal of Marketing*, 52(1), 20-35.

—— and Allen M. Weiss (1995), "Vendor Consideration and Switching Behavior for Buyers in High-Technology Markets," *Journal of Marketing*, 59 (July), 30-43.

Jackson, Susan E. and Randall S. Schuler (1985), "A Meta-Analysis and Conceptual Critique of Research on Role Ambiguity and Role Conflict in Work Settings," *Organizational Behavior and Human Performance*, 36, 16-78.

Kahn, Robert L. and Robert P. Quinn (1970), "Role Stress: A Framework for Analysis," in *Occupational Mental Health*, Alister McLean, ed. New York: Rand-McNally, 161-68.

——, Donald M. Wolfe, Robert P. Quinn, J. Diedrick Snoek, and Robert A. Rosenthal (1964), *Organizational Stress: Studies in Role Conflict and Ambiguity.* New York: John Wiley & Sons.

Kumar, Nirmalya, J. D. Hibbard, and Louis W. Stern (1994), "The Nature and Consequences of Marketing Channel Intermediary Commitment," report No. 94-115. Cambridge, MA: Marketing Science Institute.

——, Lisa K. Scheer, and Jan-Benedict E. M. Steenkamp (1995), "The Effects of Perceived Interdependence on Dealer Attitudes," *Journal of Marketing*, 32 (August), 348-56.

Larson, Andrea (1992), "Network Dyads in Entrepreneurial Settings: A Study of the Governance of Exchange Relationships," *Administrative Science Quarterly*, 37 (March), 76-104.

Lott, Albert J. and Bernice E. Lott (1965), "Group Cohesiveness as Interpersonal Attraction: A Review of Relationships With Antecedent and Consequent Variables," *Psychological Bulletin*, 64(4), 259-309.

MacKenzie, Herbert F. (1992), "Partnering Attractiveness in Buyer-Seller Relationships," doctoral dissertation, University of Western Ontario, Canada.

Meldrum, Mike J. (1995), "Marketing High-Tech Products: The Emerging Themes," *European Journal of Marketing*, 29, 45-58.

Moorman, Christine, Gerald Zaltman, and Rohit Deshpande (1992), "Relationships Between Providers and Users of Marketing Research: The Dynamics of Trust Within and Between Organizations," *Journal of Marketing Research,* 29 (August), 314-29.

Morgan, Robert M. and Shelby D. Hunt (1994), "The Commitment-Trust Theory of Relationship Marketing," *Journal of Marketing*, 58 (July), 20-38.

Ring, Peter S. and Andrew H. Van de Ven (1994), "Developmental Processes of Cooperative Interorganizational Relationships," *Academy of Management Review*, 19 (January), 90-118.

Szmigin, Isabel T. D. (1993), "Managing Quality in Business-to-Business Services," *European Journal of Marketing*, 27(1), 5-21.

Venetis, Karin A. (1997), "Service Quality and Customer Loyalty in Professional Business Service Relationships: An Empirical Investigation Into the Customer-Based Quality Concept in the Dutch Advertising Industry," doctoral dissertation, Maastricht University, Maastricht.

Weitz, Barton A. and Sandy D. Jap (1995), "Relationship Marketing and Distribution Channels," *Journal of the Academy of Marketing Science*, 23 (Fall), 305-20.

Wetzels, Martin G. M. (1998), "Service Quality in Customer-Employee Relationships: An Empirical Study in the After-Sales Services Context," doctoral dissertation, Maastricht University, Maastricht.

Wilson, David T. (1995), "An Integrated Model of Buyer-Seller Relationships," *Journal of the Academy of Marketing Science*, 23(4), 335-45.

21

Sources and Dimensions of Trust in Service Relationships

DEVON S. JOHNSON
KENT GRAYSON

Ever since Dwyer, Schurr, and Oh (1987) emphasized the importance of trust in marketing relationships, it has been a central construct in research on business-to-business sales and service relationships, as well as consumer service relationships. Marketing researchers have highlighted the antecedents and consequences of trust in dyadic relationships, usually predicated on the notion that trust emerges only from factors specific to the interaction. In examining consumers' trust in service firms, this chapter takes a broader view by exploring both relationship-specific and environmental sources of trust, such as personality variables and social norms. We also emphasize the multidimensionality of trust and examine the managerial implications of our framework.

THE RELEVANCE OF TRUST TO SERVICE RELATIONSHIPS

Differences between the consumption of services and goods have been well documented (e.g., Murray 1991). In this section, we show that service consumption is more risky than the consumption of goods and that trust is therefore particularly relevant to service consumers and marketers.

All market offerings are made up of characteristics that are more or less difficult to evaluate (e.g., Darby and Karni 1973; Nelson 1970). "Search" attributes are easiest to evaluate because they can be assessed prior to purchase. For example, the color, styling, and size of an automobile are all search attributes. "Experienced" attributes can be evaluated only while consuming the market offering, and therefore usually can be assessed only after purchase and some trial. The plot, characters, and production values of a film are examples of experience attributes. "Credenced" attributes are difficult to evaluate even after purchase and consumption. The skill, speed, and precision of a surgeon's work are evidenced when the patient is not conscious, and the results of the work are hidden from sight once it is accomplished.

In general, services are more likely than goods to comprise credence attributes, whereas goods are more likely to comprise search attributes (Shapiro 1987; Zeithaml 1991). Because of this, service purchase and consumption often involves more risk. With services, the buyer is more vulnerable to opportunistic behavior from the seller, who may misrepresent the nature of the service offering in advance and who may keep negative aspects of the service hidden from the consumer. Economists refer to this as the "problem of agency," whereby principals are incapable of evaluating their agents (e.g., Bergen, Dutla, and Walker 1992; Eisenhardt 1989). The central problem of agency is the management of risk.

Risk taking and trust are two sides of the same coin (Deutsch 1958, p. 266). Often when we take risks, however large or small, we are also engaging in trusting behavior. For example, we do not "trust" that the blue car we bought yesterday will still be blue tomorrow, or that the compact microwave oven we see in a store will still be the same size when we bring it home. These are certainties that therefore present no risk, so trust is not an issue. On the other hand, we do trust that our baby-sitter will care for our children, our taxi driver has not been drinking, and our plumber has used the right piping. Because services are riskier than goods, issues of trust are more relevant, and the consumption and management of services can be facilitated or hindered significantly by the existence or lack of trust.

SOURCES OF TRUST

Many scholars, practitioners, and consumers use the word "trust," but what, exactly, is it? Among the many definitions of trust is a generally shared view that trust involves one person's expectation that another will behave in a certain way (e.g., Deutsch 1973; Scanzoni 1979; Schurr and Ozanne 1985). Trust also requires that, if the other does not behave as expected, the trusting party will experience more negative outcomes than if the other does behave as expected (Deutsch 1958). Building from this definition (and from other conceptualizations of trust), we argue in this chapter that consumers' trust expectations are developed from different sources, resulting in four types of trust: generalized, system, process-based, and personality-based (cf. Burchell and Wilkinson 1997; Kirchler, Fehr, and Evans 1996; Lane and Bachmann 1996). We also argue that the relevance of these levels of trust varies as the relationship progresses from exploration to commitment (Dwyer, Schurr, and Oh 1987). These dimensions are illustrated in Figure 21.1, and we examine each in the following sections.

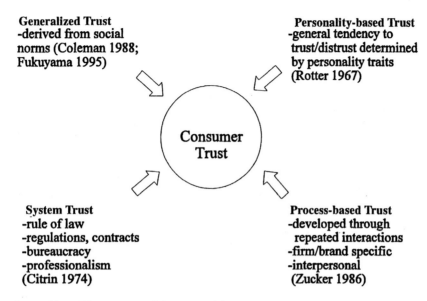

Generalized Trust
-derived from social
norms (Coleman 1988;
Fukuyama 1995)

Personality-based Trust
-general tendency to
trust/distrust determined
by personality traits
(Rotter 1967)

System Trust
-rule of law
-regulations, contracts
-bureaucracy
-professionalism
(Citrin 1974)

Process-based Trust
-developed through
 repeated interactions
-firm/brand specific
-interpersonal
(Zucker 1986)

Figure 21.1 The Sources of Consumer Trust

Generalized Trust

Sometimes we trust without making a conscious decision to do so. On the basis of seeing only a yellow pages advertisement, we hand over our automobiles and household appliances to strangers to repair them. When traveling in an unfamiliar town or city, we purchase and eat the food provided to us on the sole basis of seeing a restaurant sign and a menu. This is the nature of generalized trust, which is the general level of confidence we maintain in the absence of reason to doubt. Members of society will operate under an assumption of generalized trust unless they are given reason to do otherwise. Generalized trust is a collective attribute existing among members of society, dictated by general shared norms of behavior (Lewis and Weigert 1985a). Social norms are enforced not by rules or law but by social mechanisms such as peer pressure and threat of ostracism.

Sociologists have referred to this kind of trust in different ways, but each recognizes its importance for societal welfare. Granovetter (1985) refers to it as trust based on "generalized morality." Coleman (1988) refers to trust between members of a society as "social capital" that is a factor of production much like labor or financial capital. Zucker (1986) refers to it as "background expectations," which are not specific to any situation but serve as a general framework for behavior.

Fukuyama (1995) proposes that different levels of economic development and performance between countries can be attributed to their respective levels of generalized trust. He argues that greater generalized trust fosters greater "spontaneous sociability" between individuals, which translates to their willingness to work together on new business ventures. It is important to note that even an extremely individualistic society characterized by little mutual dependence (such as the Ik in Northern Uganda) has its norms of generalized trust—although the trusting behavior encouraged by these norms is more limited than in other societies (Handelman 1990, pp. 72-76).

System Trust

Sometimes our expectations for others' behaviors are based on rules dictated by legislative and regulatory institutions. Consumers rely on state institutions such as the Federal Trade Commission in the United States or the European Advertising Standards Alliance in Europe to ensure that marketers are bona fide, that their products are safe, and that communication about their products is not misleading. Trust in these institutions depends on the public's satisfaction with the performance of the system. Political officers and institutions are motivated to produce system trust because their legitimacy can be maintained only through public trust (Citrin 1974).

Expectations for system trust are based on a community's written rules and on the effectiveness of regulatory institutions in enforcing these rules. For example, some countries afford greater protection than others in terms of banking, contract law, and advertising regulation.

Process-Based Trust

Borrowing from Zucker (1986), processed-based trust is defined as that which is developed through repeated interaction in a specific dyadic relationship. The source of process-based trust expectations is neither general social norms nor the rule of law, but rather the individual expectations developed by the two (or more) particular parties in the transaction.

Process-based trust is contingent—it depends on the behavior of each party involved in the interactions as well as the history of interactions among the parties. Zand (1972) refers to the process of trust building through repeated interactions as a process of "spiral reinforcement," in which initial levels of trust encourage information flow, which reduces uncertainty and further fosters trust. This in turn leads to more open acceptance of influence between parties, increased interdependence, and increased vulnerability. This process is similar to the contention of Dwyer, Schurr, and Oh (1987) that marketing relationships develop along a trajectory that involves increasing trust based on fulfillment of trust at each stage. Similarly, Bitner (1995) points out that the service firm gains the trust of its customers by keeping its promise at each service encounter.

The general consensus among researchers is that process-based trust is at first fragile and then resilient. A service firm's initial encounter is critically important in creating a first impression (cf. Bitner 1995), without which the consumer will not proceed to the next step in the relationship. Through successive encounters, social bonds are established (Turnbull and Wilson 1989) and the relationship becomes resistant—although not invulnerable—to dissatisfying events. Marketing researchers have focused almost exclusively on process-based trust. Trust has been presented as a quality that is developed between two parties (e.g., a supplier and a manufacturer or a market researcher and a marketing manager) based on their mutual behaviors. This research has produced considerable evidence in support of the contention that process-based trust has a positive influence on marketing relationships. For example, in symmetric marketing relationships (i.e., wherein parties operate with similar amounts of power), trust reduces the propensity of a partner to react negatively to inflexible and unfair behavior (Schurr and Ozanne 1985). Where previous interactions have established trust, conflict is more likely to result in functional outcomes (Morgan and Hunt 1994). Although relationships with asymmetric power are less likely to be trusting ones (Anderson and Weitz 1989; Kumar, Scheer, and Steenkamp 1995a), those that are more trusting are less likely to witness the exercise of power of the stronger party over the weaker (Andaleeb 1995).

Even though a link between trust and economic success may be theoretically defensible and intuitively appealing, there is mixed empirical support for such a relationship. Several studies have indeed confirmed the positive effect of trust on anticipated future interactions (e.g., Crosby, Evans, and Cowles 1990; Doney and Cannon 1997; Ramsey and Sohi 1997), but the lack of support for the direct impact of trust on sales is equally convincing. Data collected by Crosby, Evans, and Cowles (1990) could not support a link between relationship quality (trust and satisfaction) and sales effectiveness. Doney and Cannon (1997) also found that neither trust in a supplier firm nor trust in a salesperson influences a buyer's choice of supplier. Moorman, Zaltman, and Deshpande (1992) found trust in marketing researchers to be unrelated to clients' use of marketing services.

On the face of it, these results suggest that although relationship marketing may have a positive influence on a number of important marketing constructs, it does not directly improve the bottom line. This lack of evidence could be attributed to lack of researcher consideration for the influence of the other types of trust that we describe in this chapter or to the likelihood that different types of trust will have different influences at different points in a relationship. For example, Grayson and Ambler (1997) replicated the Moorman, Zaltman, and Deshpande (1992) results and, after accounting for length of the relationship, found trust to be a significant predictor of service use in short, but not long, relationships. We will return to this general point shortly.

Personality-Based Trust

Considerable research, particularly in social psychology, has supported the view that trust between individuals is a function of an individual's propensity to trust, determined by one's personality traits. Much of this research builds upon work by Rotter (1967), who developed an Interpersonal Trust Scale (ITS) to measure an individual's inherent propensity to trust. Rotter (1967) defines trust as a generalized expectancy held by an individual that the word, promise, or oral or written statement of another individual or group can be relied on. Individuals hold generalized expectancy to trust others, which determines their willingness to trust a partner in specific circumstances. In our framework, a "generalized expectancy" is based not on social norms but rather on personality traits. An individual's propensity to trust is a product of the social learning process that shapes one's personality, especially early behaviors reinforced by parents and peers. In essence, propensity to trust holds trust to be a function of the qualities of the trusting and not the trusted. Taken to the extreme, it implies that a reliance solely on one's propensity to trust may lead to a state of blind trust whereby a party is trusted without an assessment of his or her trustworthiness.

Compared to situational determinants of trust germane to the specific context of the interaction (e.g., an actor's credibility or expertise), personality traits have been demonstrated to have only a moderately significant effect on an individual's level of trust (Schlenker, Helm, and Tedeschi 1973). It has been suggested that propensity to trust is most influential in ambiguous circumstances, devoid of context-specific cues (Martin 1991; Schlenker, Helm, and Tedeschi 1973). Thus, propensity to trust should be a more influential determinant of trust in the initial transaction stage of a relationship, when specific interaction-based cues are not available.

SERVICE RELATIONSHIPS AND THE FOUR TYPES OF TRUST

The four types of trust are not always easily distinguished. For example, an individual's propensity to trust may result as much from having lived in a society with high generalized trust as from being an inherently trusting person. Similarly, the process-based trust built up between two individuals may be strongly influenced by the system-trust mechanisms that support their interactions. We believe it is useful, however, to distinguish between the four types for two reasons. First, the distinction highlights the fact that there are many different sources of trust and that these sources go beyond the process-based trust that has been the primary focus of marketing researchers. This explication should alert both managers and researchers to a number of additional strategic variables that are important to consider when examining the influence of trust.

Second, as we have suggested earlier, the relative influence exerted by these four types of trust is likely to vary as buyer-seller interactions move from discrete transactions to relational exchanges. In the initial stages of a relationship, the buyer has no choice but to rely on both generalized and system trust, especially for market offerings with high credence qualities. For example, when a consumer first approaches an independent financial adviser, he or she relies on the generalized expectation that such advisers operate ethically and on the system-based expectation that unscrupulous advisers will lose their licenses. Without these assurances, the consumer's decision to use a financial adviser involves more uncertainty. In societies high in generalized or system trust, consumers are therefore more likely to enter into relationships with new service providers and are also more likely to engage spontaneously in risky purchasing behavior (Fukuyama 1995).

The purchase decision may also be influenced initially by personality-based trust. A consumer who has a natural predilection toward trusting behavior will (other factors being equal) be more willing to engage in risky purchase behaviors than one who has less personality-based trust.

A customer's first encounter with a service firm is his or her first "moment of truth" and is a potential first step on a road leading away from reliance on generalized, system, and personality-based trust toward a reliance on process-based trust. Because system and generalized trust are held in common by members of society and are equally available to all firms, they offer less potential for competitive advantage. By building process-based trust, however, service firms can encourage customer retention and gain competitive advantage (Barney and Hansen 1994).

Marketing researchers have identified the drivers of process-based trust by proposing and empirically testing several models of trust (see Table 21.1). Marketing channels researchers have identified shared values, goal congruence, perception of transaction-specific investments, cooperation, and age of relationship, among other factors, to be antecedents of process-based trust (e.g., Anderson and Weitz 1989; Anderson and Narus 1990; Morgan and Hunt 1994). Within the services marketing environment, researchers have identified service domain expertise, relational selling behavior, and interpersonal characteristics to be antecedents of process-based trust (e.g., Crosby, Evans, and Cowles 1990; Moorman, Deshpande, and Zaltman 1993).

THE DIMENSIONS OF CONSUMER TRUST

In addition to being influenced by different sources, trust may comprise different dimensions (for an analysis of the dimensions of trust, see Hwang and Burgess 1997). In marketing research, trust has been defined as being composed of such elements as credibility, benevolence, and honesty (e.g., Doney and Cannon 1997, p. 36; Ganesan 1994, p. 3; Kumar, Scheer, and Steenkamp 1995b, p. 58). A buyer who believes that the supplier is credible and honest is one who believes that the supplier will live up to his or her word and has the expertise required to perform the job effectively and reliably. A benevolent supplier is one who is perceived to be positively disposed toward the buyer and willing to make short-term sacrifices with a balanced understanding of unforeseen circumstances. Although these dimensions of trust have been useful in understanding the dynamics of some marketing relationships, research in sociology and social psychology has shown that an examination of additional dimensions of trust may be equally fruitful (cf. Lyons and Mehta 1997; Nooteboom, Berger, and Noorderhaven 1997).

For many years sociologists and social psychologists (e.g., Barber 1983; Lewis and Weigert 1985b; Luhmann 1979) have argued that trust is a multidimensional construct with cognitive, affective, and behavioral dimensions, and recent em-

TABLE 21.1 Models of Antecedents and Consequences of Trust

Researchers	Context	Antecedents	Trust Construct and Definition	Consequences
Doney and Cannon (1997)	Trust of a supplier firm and salesperson	Characteristics of supplier firm and relationship, salesperson and relation	Perceived credibility and benevolence of target of trust	Choice of supplier firm, anticipated future interaction
Morgan and Hunt (1994)	Commitment, trust in marketing channels	Shared values, communication, opportunistic behavior	Confidence in partner's reliability and integrity	Commitment, acquiescence, likelihood of leaving, cooperation, functional conflict, uncertainty
Ganesan (1994)	Trust and dependence in retail buyer/vendor relationships	Specific investments, reputation, experience, satisfaction with previous outcomes	Credibility and benevolence	Retailer's long-term orientation
Moorman, Deshpande, and Zaltman (1993); Moorman, Zaltman, and Deshpande (1992)	Trust in market research provider-user relationship	Individual user characteristics, perceived researcher interpersonal characteristics, perceived user organizational characteristics, perceived interorganizational/ interdepartmental characteristics	User trust in researcher: willing to rely on exchange partner in whom one has confidence	Use market research information, quality interactions, researcher involved in research activities, commitment to relationship
Anderson and Narus (1990)	Manufacturer-distributor firm working partnership	Communication, outcome given comparison levels	Believe another firm will take actions that result in good outcomes	Cooperation, functional conflict, conflict, satisfaction
Crosby, Evans, and Cowles (1990)	Relationship quality (trust, satisfaction) in service selling life insurance	Similarity, service domain expertise, relational selling behavior	Consumers trust in sales context, confidence that salesperson will serve long-term interest of customer	Sales effectiveness, anticipation of future interactions
Anderson and Weitz (1989)	Continuity between manufacturers, sales agents	Support, goal congruence, cultural similarity, age of relationship, communication	Belief that one's needs will be fulfilled by actions of other party	Negative reputation, power imbalance, perceived continuity of relationship
Dwyer and Lagace (1986)	Buyer-seller trust conceptual model	Perception of sellers (honesty, fairness, cooperative intent), experience with buyer/seller, personality		

pirical investigations (e.g., Cummings and Bromiley 1996; McAllister 1995) have supported this theorizing. In relationships, individuals trust cognitively based on their knowledge of their partner's character; they trust affectively based on their emotions toward their partners; and they trust behaviorally by taking actions that display trust in their partners. In essence, cognitive trust involves a conscious decision to trust a partner based on assessments of competence, reliability, and dependability (Butler 1991; Johnson-George and Swap 1982; McAllister 1995; Rempel, Holmes, and Zana 1985). Affective trust relies on the notion that emotional ties developed between individuals can become the basis for trust.

The third component of trust—behavioral trust—results from cognitive and affective trust. Behavioral trust involves the undertaking of a risky course of action based on the confident expectation that all persons involved in the action will act competently and dutifully (Barber 1983). It goes beyond mere execution, in that when we see others taking actions that imply trust, we become more disposed to reciprocate by trusting them (Luhmann 1979). Hence, behavioral trust begets trust. These three dimensions are interdependent and mutually supportive aspects of the trust construct.

Previous conceptualizations of trust in marketing research have tended to emphasize the cognitive dimension. Honesty, credibility, and even benevolence as it has been defined and operationalized tend to be measured based on knowledge of the trusted party (such as whether or not they keep their promises or possess a level of expertise). The affective dimension of trust has been largely ignored in the literature. This bias toward the cognitive dimension is probably appropriate, given the business-to-business environments in which a number of trust studies have been implemented. Although affective dimensions are certainly influential in business-to-business relationships, it is likely that cognitive issues (such as expertise and credibility) will dominate. Consumer relationships with firms and service providers, however, involve risks of specific personal relevance to the individuals involved. Thus, it is more reasonable, and perhaps essential, to include consideration of the affective dimension in the study and management of consumer-level marketing relationships.

At first it may seem inappropriate to speak of affective trust in consumer-service provider relationships because commercial relationships are unlikely to achieve the intensity cited as a requirement for developing affective trust. For example, affective trust has been linked with behavior that is motivated intrinsically, say by the inherent joy of spending time with a close friend (Rempel, Holmes, and Zana 1985). It could be argued that behaviors in commercial relationships are unlikely to be perceived as intrinsically motivated because, ultimately, all actions directed at a buyer are motivated by extrinsic rewards.

It is important, however, not to ignore the social dimensions of service experiences. The influence of interpersonal interactions in creating satisfied customers is well documented throughout the services literature (e.g., Crosby, Evans, and Cowles 1990; Crosby and Stephens 1987; Parasuraman, Zeithaml, and Berry 1985; Solomon et al. 1985). For example, service personalization involves embellishing routine service delivery actions with personal references and gestures that convey a feeling of individuation to the customer (cf. Surprenant and Solomon 1987). These actions include friendly conversation and special favors that transform a dyad from a series of transactions to a relationship. By managing social aspects of dyadic interactions, firms develop social bonds with their customers (Turnbull and Wilson 1989). Within a nexus of good quality in core aspects of the service, the care and concern displayed for the customer may be perceived as intrinsically motivated. Johnson and Grayson (1998) found empirical support for the multidimensionality of trust in relationships between customers and their financial advisers. Cognitive and affective trust were found to be separate dimensions of trust with unique antecedents and consequences for these relationships.

More recently, marketing researchers have examined social support behavior in service relationships (e.g., Adelman and Ahuvia 1995; Adelman, Ahuvia, and Goodwin 1993). Social support occurs when a service provider's verbal or nonverbal communication increases a client's self-esteem or sense of social connection to others (Adelman, Ahuvia, and Goodwin 1993). These researchers have highlighted the importance of non–core-related benefits in attracting and retaining customers. For example, frequency of visits and length of stay at a restaurant or hairdresser may be a function of a customer's need for a sense of identity and social integration. By making friendly conversation and providing a listening ear, service professionals build social connection and a sense of community that engender affective trust.

The magnitude and importance of affective trust is dependent on structural aspects of the service delivery process. Affective trust is more likely to develop in relationships involving frequent and extended interactions with the same service provider. For example, one would expect affective trust to be less relevant to telephone banking because the customer interacts with varying attendants and service encounters are usually brief. Visits to a hairdresser, however, involve repeated and extended service encounters through which social bonding is likely to develop. The development of affective interpersonal trust in service relationships is perhaps best observed in extended service encounters, especially those involving considerable risk to the customer, for example, white-water rafting, climbing, or hiking expeditions. These encounters have been referred to as "extraordinary service experiences" because they are personally challenging and imbued with emotional intensity, dynamic interaction, and spontaneity (Arnould and Price 1993).

Once again, the early phase of an extended service encounter is critical. A trail guide must establish his or her trustworthiness early in the encounter by demonstrating the knowledge and experience required to lead the venture. At this stage, trust is primarily cognitive, because emotional bonds are yet to be established. As the encounter progresses, however, it becomes boundary-open, with both customer and service provider becoming actively involved in sharing their feelings and reacting to each other's emotional behavior (Arnould and Price 1993;

Sutton and Rafaeli 1988). Gradually, trust assumes interpersonal dimensions as social bonds develop.

MANAGERIAL IMPLICATIONS

Trust is widely accepted as an important element of consumer perceptions of brands and companies (e.g., Aaker 1997; Bainbridge 1997), so understanding its different aspects has clear managerial implications. One important managerial conclusion from our framework is that when one source of trust is not available, companies can and should draw from different sources. For example, when the British government's ability to protect its citizens from contaminated beef fell into question during the "BSE scare" (Bentley 1997), food companies could not rely on the government's system trust in fostering general comfort with food quality. Thus, companies like Burger King, McDonald's, and Bird's Eye turned instead to process trust—that is, the trust that each brand had built with its customer base. To capitalize on this trust, all three of these companies (and many others) began to do their own safety labeling (Bentley 1996; Rogers 1997).

Furthermore, companies unaware of the potential impact of generalized and system trust are likely to be missing strategically relevant information. For example, the *Economist* ("In Greed We Trust" 1997) recently reported that Americans' trust in "Wall Street" has been accompanied by falling trust in other institutions such as "the media." Companies in industries where system trust is declining will need to rely more strongly on other forms of trust for building their business. Those where system trust is increasing will need to protect themselves from firms that free ride on customer confidence and thus steal business without having to develop process-based trust with consumers. As we have emphasized, the role of different kinds of trust is likely to change as a relationship progresses from awareness through exploration to commitment.

Currently, a particularly interesting arena for understanding and exploring trust is the Internet. Observers disagree about the degree of trust (or lack thereof) that consumers hold regarding the Internet, but there is little disagreement that this new aspect of social life will require businesses to think differently about trust development (e.g., Babcock 1997; Cairncross 1997; Dyson 1997; Fukuyama 1996; Keen 1997). Today, many aspects of interaction on the Internet do not benefit from strong system trust; therefore, much of the trust that is built on the Internet is process based. As new systems for supporting trust (e.g., digital signatures) become commonplace, the recommended strategies for success on the Internet are likely to change.

In sum, the main point of our chapter is this: There are a number of potential sources of trust, and trust comprises a number of dimensions. For a full understanding of its impact, managers and researchers must take account of these nuances. Although research on trust to date has begun to shed light on our understanding of its influence in marketing relationships, considerable additional work is still required before trust's changing and multidimensional influence will be understood fully.

REFERENCES

Aaker, Jennifer L. (1997), "Dimensions of Brand Personality," *Journal of Marketing Research* 34 (August), 347-56.

Adelman, Mara B. and Aaron C. Ahuvia (1995), "Social Support in the Service Sector: The Antecedents, Process, and Outcomes of Social Support in an Introductory Service," *Journal of Business Research*, 32, 273-82.

——, ——, and Cathy Goodwin (1993), "Beyond Smiling, Social Support and Service Quality," in *Service Quality: New Directions in Theory and Practice*, Roland T. Rust and Richard L. Oliver, eds. Newbury Park, CA: Sage, 139-72.

Andaleeb, Syed Saad (1995), "Dependence Relations and the Moderating Role of Trust: Implications for Behavioural Intentions in Marketing Channels," *International Journal of Research in Marketing*, 12, 157-72.

Anderson, Erin and Barton Weitz (1989), "Determinants of Continuity in Conventional Industrial Channel Dyads," *Marketing Science*, 8(4), 310-23.

Anderson, James C. and James A. Narus (1990), "A Model of Distributor Firm and Manufacturer Firm Working Partnerships," *Journal of Marketing*, 54 (January), 42-58.

Arnould, Eric J. and Linda L. Price (1993), "River Magic: Extraordinary Experience and the Extended Service Encounter," *Journal of Consumer Research*, 20 (June), 24-45.

Babcock, Charles (1997), "Too Much Trust Is a Bad Thing," *Computerworld*, 31 (January 6), 97.

Bainbridge, Jane (1997), "Who Wins the National Trust?" *Marketing*, (October 23), 21-23.

Barber, Bernard (1983), *The Logic and Limits of Trust*. New Brunswick, NJ: Rutgers University Press.

Barney, Jay B. and Mark H. Hansen (1994), "Trustworthiness as a Source of Competitive Advantage," *Structure Management Journal*, 15, 175-90.

Bentley, Stephanie (1996), "Birds Eye Starts 'BSE' Labelling," *Marketing Week*, 19 (April 5), 11.

—— (1997), "A Grubby Business," *Marketing Week*, 20 (May 22), 38.

Bergen, Mark, Shantanu Dutla, and Orville C. Walker, Jr. (1992), "Agency Relationships in Marketing: A Review of the Implications and Applications of Agency and Related Theories," *Journal of Marketing*, 56 (July), 1-24.

Bitner, Mary Jo (1995), "Building Service Relationships: It's All About Promises," *Journal of the Academy of Marketing Science*, 24(4), 246-51.

Burchell, Brendan and Frank Wilkinson (1997), "Trust, Business Relationships and the Contractual Environment," *Cambridge Journal of Economics*, 21, 217-37.

Butler, John K., Jr. (1991), "Toward Understanding and Measuring Conditions of Trust: Evolution of a Conditions of Trust Inventory," *Journal of Management*, 117(3), 643-63.

Cairncross, Frances (1997), *The Death of Distance*. London: Orion.

Citrin, Jack (1974), "Comment: The Political Relevance of Trust in Government," *American Political Science Review*, 68 (April), 973-88.

Coleman, James S. (1988), "Social Capital in the Creation of Human Capital," *American Journal of Sociology*, 94 (Supplement), S95-S120.

Crosby, Lawrence A., Kenneth R. Evans, and Deborah Cowles (1990), "Relationship Quality in Services Selling: An Interpersonal Influence Perspective," *Journal of Marketing*, 54 (July), 68-81.

—— and Nancy Stephens (1987), "Effects of Relationship Marketing on Satisfaction Retention, and Prices in the Life Insurance Industry," *Journal of Marketing Research*, 24, 404-11.

Cummings, Larry L. and Philip Bromiley (1996), "The Organizational Trust Inventory (OTI): Development and Validation," in *Trust in Organizations: Frontiers of Theory and Research*, Roderick M. Kramer and Tom R. Tyler, eds. Thousand Oaks, CA: Sage, 302-30.

Darby, Michael R. and Edi Karni (1973), "Free Competition and the Optimal Amount of Fraud," *Journal of Law and Economics*, 16 (April), 67-86.

Deutsch, Morton (1958), "Trust and Suspicion," *Journal of Conflict Resolution*, 2, 265-79.

—— (1973), *The Resolution of Conflict: Constructive and Destructive Processes*. New Haven, CT: Yale University Press.

Doney, Patricia M. and Joseph P. Cannon (1997), "An Examination of the Nature of Trust in Buyer-Seller Relationships," *Journal of Marketing,* 61 (April), 35-51.

Dwyer, Robert F. and Rosemary R. Lagace (1986), "On the Nature and Role of Buyer-Seller Trust," in *AMA Educators Conference Proceedings,* Terrence A. Shimp et al., eds. Chicago: American Marketing Association, 40-45.

———, Paul H. Schurr, and Seho Oh (1987), "Developing Buyer-Seller Relationships," *Journal of Marketing,* 51 (April), 11-27.

Dyson, Esther (1997), *Release 2.0: A Design for Living in a Digital Age.* New York: Broadway Books.

Eisenhardt, Kathleen M. (1989), "Agency Theory: An Assessment and Review," *Academy of Management Review,* 14, 57-74.

Fukuyama, Francis (1995), *Trust: The Social Virtues and the Creation of Prosperity.* London: Hamish Hamilton.

——— (1996), "Trust Still Counts in a Virtual World," *Forbes,* (December 2), 33, 69.

Ganesan, Shankar (1994), "Determinants of Long-Term Orientation in Buyer-Seller Relationships," *Journal of Marketing,* 58 (April), 1-19.

Granovetter, Mark (1985), "Economic Action and Social Structure: The Problem of Embeddedness," *American Journal of Sociology,* 91, 481-510.

Grayson, Kent and Tim Ambler (1997), "The Dark Side of Long-Term Relationships in Marketing Services," working paper 97-502, London Business School Centre for Marketing.

Handelman, Don (1990), *Models and Mirrors: Towards an Anthropology of Public Events.* Cambridge, UK: Cambridge University Press.

Hwang, Peter and Willem P. Burgess (1997), "Properties of Trust: An Analytical View," *Organisational Behaviour and Human Decision Processes,* 69 (January), 67-73.

"In Greed We Trust: Views of Wall Street" (1997), *Economist,* 345 (November 1), 27.

Johnson, Devon S. and Kent Grayson (1998), "Cognitive and Affective Trust in Service Relationships," working paper 99-501, London Business School Centre for Marketing.

Johnson-George, Cynthia and Walter C. Swap (1982), "Measurement of Specific Interpersonal Trust: Construction and Validation of a Scale to Assess Trust in a Specific Other," *Journal of Personality and Social Psychology,* 43(6), 1306-17.

Keen, Peter G. W. (1997), "Are You Ready for the 'Trust' Economy?" *Computerworld,* 31 (April 21), 80.

Kirchler, Erich, Ernst Fehr, and Robert Evans (1996), "Social Exchange in the Labor Market: Reciprocity and Trust Versus Egoist Money Maximization," *Journal of Economic Psychology,* 17 (June), 313-41.

Kumar, Nirmalya, Lisa K. Scheer, and Jan-Benedict E. M. Steenkamp (1995a), "The Effects of Perceived Interdependence on Dealer Attitudes," *Journal of Marketing Research,* (August), 348-56.

———, ———, and ——— (1995b), "The Effects of Supplier Fairness on Vulnerable Resellers," *Journal of Marketing Research,* 32 (February), 54-65.

Lane, Christel and Reinhard Bachmann (1996), "The Social Construction of Trust: Supplier Relations in Britain and Germany," *Organizational Studies,* 17, 365-95.

Lewis, J. David and Andrew J. Weigert (1985a), "Social Atomism, Holism, and Trust," *Sociological Quarterly,* 26(4), 455-71.

——— and ——— (1985b), "Trust as a Social Reality," *Social Forces,* 63(4), 967-85.

Luhmann, Niklas (1979), *Trust and Power.* Chichester, UK: Wiley.

Lyons, Bruce and Judith Mehta (1997), "Contracts, Opportunism and Trust: Self, Interest and Social Orientation," *Cambridge Journal of Economics,* 21, 239-57.

Martin, Greg S. (1991), "The Concept of Trust in Marketing Channel Relationships: A Review and Synthesis," in *American Marketing Association Educators' Conference Proceedings: Enhancing Knowledge Development in Marketing,* Series 2, Mary C. Gilley and F. Robert Dwyer, eds. Chicago: American Marketing Association, 251-59.

McAllister, Daniel J. (1995), "Affect and Cognition-Based Trust as Foundations for Interpersonal Co-operation in Organizations," *Academy of Management Journal,* 38(1), 24-59.

Moorman, Christine, Rohit Deshpande, and Gerald Zaltman (1993), "Factors Affecting Trust in Market Research Relationships," *Journal of Marketing,* 57 (January), 81-101.

———, Gerald Zaltman, and Rohit Deshpande (1992), "Relationship Between Providers and Users of Marketing Research: The Dynamics of Trust Within and Between Organizations," *Journal of Marketing Research,* 29 (August), 314-28.

Morgan, Robert M. and Shelby D. Hunt (1994), "The Commitment-Trust Theory of Relationship Marketing," *Journal of Marketing,* 58 (July), 20-38.

Murray, Keith B. (1991), "A Test of Services Marketing Theory: Consumer Information Acquisition Activities," *Journal of Marketing*, 55 (January), 10-25.

Nelson, Philip (1970), "Advertising as Information," *Journal of Political Economy*, 81 (July-August), 729-54.

Nooteboom, Bart, Hans Berger, and Niels G. Noorderhaven (1997), "Effects of Trust and Governance on Relational Risk," *Academy of Management Journal*, 40, 308-38.

Parasuraman, A., Valarie A. Zeithaml, and Leonard L. Berry (1985), "A Conceptual Model of Service Quality and Its Implications for Future Research," *Journal of Marketing*, 49 (Fall), 41-50.

Ramsey, Rosemary P. and Ravipreet S. Sohi (1997), "Listening to Your Customers: The Impact of Perceived Salesperson Listening Behavior on Relationship Outcomes," *Journal of the Academy of Marketing Science*, 25(2), 127-37.

Rempel, John K., John G. Holmes, and Mark P. Zana (1985), "Trust in Close Relationships," *Journal of Personality and Social Psychology*, 49(1), 95-112.

Rogers, Danny (1997), "Burger King Lifts British Beef Ban," *Marketing*, (July 3), 2.

Rotter, Julian B. (1967), "A New Scale for the Measurement of Interpersonal Trust," *Journal of Personality*, 35, 651-55.

Scanzoni, John (1979), *Social Exchange in Developing Relationships*. New York: Academic Press.

Schlenker, Barry, Bob Helm, and James T. Tedeschi (1973), "The Effects of Personality and Situational Variables on Behavioral Trust," *Journal of Personality and Social Psychology*, 25(3), 419-27.

Schurr, Paul H. and Julie L. Ozanne (1985), "Influence on Exchange Processes: Buyers' Preconceptions of a Seller's Trustworthiness and Bargaining Toughness," *Journal of Consumer Research*, 11 (March), 939-53.

Shapiro, Susan (1987), "The Social Control of Impersonal Trust," *American Journal of Sociology*, 93(3), 623-58.

Solomon, Michael R., Carol Surprenant, John A. Czepiel, and Evelyn G. Gutman (1985), "A Role Theory Perspective on Dyadic Interactions: The Service Encounter," *Journal of Marketing*, 49 (Winter), 99-111.

Surprenant, Carol F. and Michael R. Solomon (1987), "Predictability and Personalization in the Service Encounter," *Journal of Marketing*, 51 (April), 86-96.

Sutton, Robert and Anat Rafaeli (1988), "Untangling the Relationship Between Displayed Emotions and Organizational Sales: The Case of Convenience Stores," *Academy of Management Journal*, 31(3), 461-87.

Turnbull, Peter W. and David T. Wilson (1989), "Developing and Protecting Profitable Customer Relationships," *Journal of Industrial Marketing Management*, 18, 233-38.

Zand, Dale E. (1972), "Trust and Managerial Problem Solving," *Administrative Science Quarterly*, 117(2), 229-39.

Zeithaml, Valarie A. (1991), "How Consumer Evaluation Processes Differ Between Goods and Services," in *Services Marketing*, Christopher Lovelock, ed. Englewood Cliffs, NJ: Prentice Hall, 39-47.

Zucker, Lynn G. (1986), "Production of Trust: Institutional Sources of Economic Structure, 1840-1920," *Research in Organizational Behavior*, 8, 53-111.

22

Service Relationships, Pseudo-Relationships, and Encounters

BARBARA GUTEK

It is well known that the U.S. economy is now based on services and about 75% of the labor force works in services; manufacturing, following the pattern of farming, consists of an ever smaller share of the labor force. The service economy today is experiencing its own "industrial revolution"; that is, the delivery of services to customers is undergoing a fundamental change that is analogous to the change from custom-made goods to mass-produced goods. In services, this change is reflected in a shift from delivering services in "relationships" to delivering them in "encounters" (Gutek 1995, 1997).

In a *service relationship* a customer and provider expect to have repeated contact in the future. Customer and provider can get to know each other as role occupants, and sometimes as acquaintances or even friends. Over time they develop a history of shared interaction that they can draw on whenever they interact to complete some transaction. Service relationships bear some resemblance to repeated-play prisoner's dilemma games in that customer and provider are interdependent in the same way that the players in a prisoner's dilemma game are interdependent. Both will benefit if both cooperate with each other; that is, the provider gives good service and the customer behaves appropriately (e.g., by paying on time) in the case of service relationships. Expecting to interact in the future an infinite number of times (or at least not knowing when the last interaction will occur) is what induces both players to cooperate to their mutual gain, a phenomenon Axelrod (1984) called "the shadow of the future." If the future casts a sufficiently long shadow, no oversight is required to maintain a

---

AUTHOR'S NOTE: I would like to thank Ben Cherry and Theresa Welsh for their ideas that contributed to this chapter.

relationship; high-quality delivery of service can be maintained simply by the dynamics of the relationship. Thus, it is the anticipation of an indefinite number of future interactions that ultimately defines a service relationship.

Encounters, on the other hand, typically consist of a single interaction between a particular customer and provider (Gutek 1995). Over time, the customer's successive contacts involve different providers rather than the same provider. Each provider is expected to be functionally equivalent. Neither the provider nor the customer expects to interact with the other party in the future. Furthermore, there is no reason why the self-interested service provider should give good service when the customer is not expected to return (although, of course, many do give good service based on other motives such as pride in their work, sense of duty, and the like).

If relationships are like repeated-play prisoner's dilemma games, encounters are like single-play games. Because there is no expectation of future interaction, there is no reason intrinsic to the interaction between the two role players to cooperate with each other. In a single-episode game, mutual cooperation will not develop without some central authority to police the actions of the players (Axelrod 1984). In service delivery, that central authority is management. Management designs a service delivery system that includes structuring the job of service provider and also the role of the customer—as much as possible—so as to deliver service to meet management's requirements. One of the roles of the manager is to monitor the service provider's behavior, and to reward providers when they cooperate and punish them when they defect, thereby attempting to align the provider's self-interest with cooperative behavior (i.e., good service), even though the provider does not expect to interact again with the same customer.

Today service encounters are common: buying a hamburger at a fast food restaurant, getting a driver's license, ordering airline tickets from an airline's reservation center, buying stocks from a discount brokerage. Each time the customer gets a different service provider, but in principle, it does not make any difference which provider the customer gets because management has trained the providers and monitors their behavior to ensure that they deliver good service. Many of the organizations that have created encounter service delivery systems are well known to customers. Rather than the individual service provider, it is the embedding service organization (e.g., McDonald's, SuperCuts, Jiffy Lube, H&R Block, Twentieth Century Insurance, Cigna) that customers identify when they are seeking service, and many choose to go back to the same company each time they need service.

I refer to these kinds of interactions as pseudo-relationships. A *pseudo-relationship* is repeated contact between a customer and a provider-organization. In this case, the customer does not get to know any individual service provider but does become acquainted with the service, products, and procedures of the organization. Customers do not anticipate any future interaction with a particular provider but expect to interact with the firm in the future. The term *pseudo-relationship* is meant to be not pejorative but descriptive. These interactions are essentially encounters because interaction takes place between strangers, but by having

TABLE 22.1 Types of Service Interactions: The Customer's Perspective

	Relationships	*Pseudo-Relationships*	*Encounters*
Reciprocal?	Yes, with provider	With company, not individual	No
Expect future?	Yes, with provider	With company, not individual	No
Shared interaction?	Yes, with provider	With company, not individual	No

repeated contact with the same company and its products and procedures, they provide customers with some of the familiarity of a relationship.

Table 22.1 summarizes these differences among relationships, pseudo-relationships, and encounters. It also suggests some differences in how service providers, customers, and organizations experience these three types of interactions. From the customer's point of view, encounters and pseudo-relationships are different, as they are from the organization's point of view. In the latter, customers represent repeat business and brand loyalty, and the organization may have a record of their experience with the repeat customer. From the perspective of the provider, however, pseudo-relationships and encounters are not different. In both cases, providers interact with strangers with whom they do not expect to interact in the future. They may, however, have some information about a customer identifying that person as a regular customer (via frequent flyer number or client record) and thus be expected to treat some customers differently from others.

In sum, relationships and encounters are conceptually distinct mechanisms for delivering service resembling repeated-play and single-episode games, respectively. In a service relationship, a customer can identify a particular person as his or her service provider. They may not know the person's last name or be able to recollect their name without help, but there is an identifiable person they would see when or if they needed a particular kind of service, and they would expect to go back to that same person if they needed service in the future. Having a service relationship is not dependent on having a choice of providers. Some HMOs, for example, assign physicians to patients, but as long as patients can identify the physician they would see when or if they needed medical care, those patients have a service relationship. Thus, one could have a service relationship (as I have defined it here) without ever having seen their provider, if there is a named person they would see if they needed service. By comparison, customers who receive service in encounters cannot name a particular person they would see for service. Those who receive service in pseudo-relationships would identify a particular firm where they go to receive service, for example Kaiser-Permanente, but not a particular individual service provider because they do not have a regular provider.

Organizations typically have a strong interest in developing pseudo-relationships with customers, and many are looking for ways to convince encounter customers to develop a pseudo-relationship with them. That is, firms would like customers to develop a "relationship" with them the same way customers develop a relationship with an individual provider. From the organization's point of view, pseudo-relationships are more desirable than relationships for at least three reasons. First, although I know of no research that compares the cost of providing service in relationships versus encounters, it would appear that encounters are less expensive. Just as goods typically can be mass-produced at less cost than custom-made, so it would appear to be true of mass-produced services (delivered in encounters). Second, in relationships customers are loyal to individual providers, and given a choice between provider and firm, many might choose the provider. Indeed, "star" providers, those whose own name draws customers more than the name of the firm (Gutek 1995), can often leave a firm and take their customers along. Third, some firms (and their managers) may not have thought about the difference between a customer's loyalty to a particular provider and to a provider firm. Nevertheless, I believe it is not possible to have the same kind of relationship with a firm as with a person because the two are fundamentally different. Based on the differences between relationships and encounters, I believe that firms will achieve better outcomes if they recognize the differences rather than trying to act as if encounters were relationships. Instead they might capitalize on the advantages of encounters. In short, firms might develop greater brand loyalty among customers by developing satisfying encounters instead of modeling encounter interactions after relationship interactions.

MODELS OF SERVICE

The distinction between relationships and encounters provides a somewhat different perspective on the common model of service showing the three key actors in service: the organization, the customer, and the provider. As depicted in Table 22.2, what differentiates a relationship from an encounter is the link between the customer and provider, which is strong in the case of relationships and weak in the case of encounters. What differentiates a pseudo-relationship from other encounters is the link between the customer and the organization, strong in the case of a pseudo-relationship but weak in the case of other encounters. With the exception of an individual provider business, all service operations should fit one of these models.

CHARACTERISTICS OF RELATIONSHIPS AND ENCOUNTERS

Empirical Findings

We have begun a program of research on service relationships and encounters at the University of Arizona. We developed measures of relationships, pseudo-relationships, and encounters and examined their effects. So far, we have conducted four surveys, and two other studies are under way, one in Australia (personal communication, Sherry Schneider 1998). Our first goal was to examine potential differences in important outcomes, namely customer satisfaction and use of

TABLE 22.2 A Model of Relationships and Encounters as a Function of the Strengths of Relationships Among Customers, Organizations, and Providers

	Relationships (customer-provider link is strong)		Encounters (customer-provider link is weak)	
	Customer-Organization Link Is Strong	Customer-Organization Link Is Weak	Customer-Organization Link Is Strong	Customer-Organization Link Is Weak
Organization-provider link is strong	This could be a high-prestige firm, such as a well-known consulting firm or a high-priced law firm where providers are fulfilled and well paid; blue chip customers seek out their services. Probably describes a very small number of businesses because it might be an unstable model, where the provider and organization vie for the customer's loyalty.	In this model, the provider may be a "star" with unique skills who runs his own firm, perhaps in architecture or consulting, as the "X" in "X and Associates." It could also be a direct sales firm such as Amway or Tupperware where the provider is committed to the firm and customers are committed to the provider, often through friendship or kinship.	*Pseudo-relationship: an enhanced encounter.* This describes a pseudo-relationship or enhanced encounter where the customer knows and trusts the organization, which also keeps the loyalty of its employees. The organization must provide well-designed processes for interacting with the customer in this model.	This describes a company that has done a good job of hiring and training employees who like their work but has not built a strong image with customers. This could describe a start-up company, or it could be a company selling something like long-distance phone services, where customers are confused about the many companies and similar offers.
Organization-provider link is weak	This is a relationship business where the customer has a tradition with the organization and also is committed to the provider. An example might be a customer who wants his financial adviser to purchase stock and bond funds from a favorite firm regardless of the affiliation of the financial adviser, or a customer who goes to a nearby hair salon who chooses a "regular" stylist for as long as that stylist stays in that salon.	This describes a relationship business in which the organization serves only as a means to bring together customers and providers. This is good for providers but not for the organization, which risks losing both its providers and its customers. Beauty salons where providers rent space from the salon would fit this model, along with some small consulting firms or traditional medical, therapy, and dental practices where many professionals share space and other resources.	*Pseudo-relationship: an enhanced encounter.* This describes a pseudo-relationship or enhanced encounter where the organization offers good value to the customer and enjoys repeat business but has a high turnover of employees. The organization must keep customer loyalty through competitive pricing and procedures that can be taught quickly to new employees. McDonald's would fit here.	This is an encounter business that does little to gain repeat customers and has high employee turnover. This model might be found in a service that is quick and low cost, perhaps where customers are transient, like a newsstand at an airport.

375

services. These studies showed consistently that customers having a service relationship with a specific provider had more service interactions within a 12-month period and were more satisfied than those who did not have one. Although satisfaction levels were high in service encounters, they were even higher in service relationships. In most cases, however, those customers who had a relationship with a service provider also received some service from someone other than their regular provider, suggesting that encounters play an important supplementary role for customers who have a regular provider. These results held across seven different service areas, three diverse samples, and two different ways of measuring a service relationship (see Gutek et al. 1999).

We have also begun to explore the characteristics of relationships and encounters, focusing on possible differences such as trust, willingness to refer the provider, responses of dissatisfied customers, customized vs. standardized treatment, and amounts of expected and actual wait time. We examined three different service areas—interactions with physicians, hairstylists, and auto mechanics—and found a number of differences among service relationships, pseudo-relationships, and encounters (Gutek, Cherry, and Bhappu 1998). In general, as we hypothesized, customers who receive service in relationships reported greater trust and knowledge, were more likely to complain directly to the service provider when they were dissatisfied, and reported that service was more personalized. Contrary to our hypothesis, they did not report waiting longer to see their service provider. Although customers respond particularly well to service relationships, based on our results for auto mechanics, it appears that it is possible for firms to design pseudo-relationships that also are relatively high in trust and willingness to refer the provider to others.

Hypothesized Differences

A number of characteristics of relationships and encounters have been hypothesized (Gutek 1995), most of which have not yet been explored. Table 22.3 summarizes some of these, focusing on potential differences.

Because many of the hypothesized differences are self-explanatory, I will elaborate on only three of the areas summarized in Table 22.3: attributions, stereotyping, and emotional labor (Gutek 1995).

Attributions

In relationships, customer and provider share a history of interaction that they can draw on to interpret each new interaction. Each knows the other well enough to make accurate attributions (e.g., "because she is usually on time, there must be some external factor that delayed her this morning"). In encounters, where two strangers interact, they will usually make the "fundamental attribution error"; that is, they will make internal attributions (e.g., "she was rude because she is a rude person"). Providers in encounters, however, face special hurdles. Although

TABLE 22.3 Some Characteristics of Relationships and Encounters

Relationships	*Encounters*
No infrastructure necessary	Embedded in infrastructure
Inherent feedback loop	Feedback through management
Based on trust	Based on rules and/or scripts
Customized service	Standardized service
Provider selected on basis of expertise	Provider selected for convenience
Elitist: customers treated differently	Egalitarian: Customers treated the same
May expect a wait for a specific provider, one's "own" provider	Expect a shorter wait for first available provider
May require preplanning or appointments	Encourages spontaneity of use; no appointment necessary
Difficult to start and end (sense of loyalty may interfere with self-interest)	Easy to enter; no obligation to repeat
Works for "credence" service; that is, it is difficult to evaluate quality	Works for "experience" service; that is, it is easy to evaluate
Creates weak ties and networks	Does not foster networks; may preserve anonymity
Fosters emotional involvement	Fosters emotional labor
Fosters knowledge of the other	Fosters stereotyping of the other
Relatively easy to discriminate among customers/providers	Discourages discriminatory behavior by customers/providers
Encourages internal and external attributions of providers and customers	Fosters internal attributions for negative behavior but external attributions for positive behavior of providers

their mistakes may be attributed to them, their successes may be attributed to the organization if the organization has a reputation for success in that area. Just as customers may attribute the taste of a McDonald's hamburger to McDonald's standards for hamburgers (rather than the skill of the burger flipper), the hamburger server's pleasant behavior may be attributed to McDonald's standards for server behavior. Facing a situation where negative behavior and mistakes might be attributed to oneself whereas positive behavior might be attributed to the high standards of the firm contributes to the lack of appeal of the encounter provider job.

Stereotyping and Discrimination

Because provider and customer have no prior basis for judging each other in encounters, it is easy to stereotype the other, or to fit a person to a preconceived notion based on social characteristics. I would, therefore, expect to see more stereotyping (by both customer and provider) in encounters than in relationships. In contrast, in relationships the history of interaction that the two share should foster an accurate image of the other. Differential treatment is, however, another matter. I would expect to find more differential treatment, matching on social characteristics, and discrimination in relationships than in encounters. That is because encounters are universalistic and egalitarian in that everyone is expected to be treated the same. In practice, providers are not supposed to discriminate against any class of customers. Even a relatively biased customer is likely to accept service one time from someone they might not otherwise associate with on a long-term basis, particularly if that person is behaving within the standards set by a firm they trust. Relationships, however, take time to develop, and customers typically can select someone on the basis of sex, race, or age if they so choose. Customers might engage in gender matching, for example, or select a provider who they believe is appropriate to the position (Gutek, Cherry, and Groth 1999). Similarly, faced with customers who are undesirable to them, providers can claim to be fully booked or assert they are unable to accept new customers. Friendships and romances are probably more likely to develop out of relationships than encounters in part because relationship customers and providers may have more in common (as well as more experience together) than encounter providers and customers.

Emotional Labor

In encounters, providers are often expected to behave as if they cared about customers, expending effort called "emotional labor" by Hochschild (1983). A number of studies have focused on the extent to which customer-contact workers are expected to display feelings that they do not actually feel (e.g., Rafaeli 1989a, 1989b; Rafaeli and Sutton 1990). In relationships, in contrast, continuing interaction fosters real emotional involvement. In therapy, for example, the provider (therapist) can become the most important person in the life of the customer. Providers also can develop strong positive or negative feelings about their customers, feelings they must hide rather than display. In sum, in relationships, provider and customer may have to hide their feelings, whereas in encounters, providers especially are often expected to display feelings they do not have. From a sense of reciprocity or obligation, customers, too, may act friendly even when they do not feel that way.

PRACTICAL IMPLICATIONS

Our studies to date suggest that service relationships can work. Given that they are associated with relatively high utilization rates and high satisfaction rates, more service firms might consider them. On the downside, the development and maintenance of relationships may be prohibitively expensive or expose firms to potential threats from strong ties between the individual provider and customer. It is clear from our data, however, that service encounters, including pseudo-relationships, do not engender the same levels of satisfaction that service relationships do. In addition, there are other data, both anecdotal (cf. Koepp 1987) and quantitative, suggesting that Americans are not particularly satisfied with service delivery and showing that Americans are more satisfied with products than with the services they receive ("Are We Happy Yet?," 1997). Perhaps that is because offering service in encounters and pseudo-relationships is still a developing process. Customer satisfaction surveys are a relatively recent phenomenon, so we do not know whether customers are more satisfied today with service encounters than they were in the distant past, but it is probably true that service firms have dramatically improved the minimum standards for service. Service firms probably should be pleased that they are able to offer such satisfying service encounters. On the other hand, there is probably also room for improvement.

The failure to differentiate service relationships from pseudo-relationships perhaps has led firms to try tactics that are not successful in raising customer satisfaction. Firms offering service encounters may not really understand how to deliver service encounters that are satisfying to customers. They might consider focusing less on "personalizing" service and otherwise trying to make encounters feel like relationships. Some customers are put off by strangers acting as if they were close friends when they are providing a service (e.g., Catto 1997; Raspberry 1993). Instead, service firms might concentrate on the potential advantages of service encounters such as speed, reliability, egalitarianism, convenience, predictability, and efficiency.

REFERENCES

"Are We Happy Yet?" (1997), *USA Today*, (special supplement for the American Society for Quality, October 9), 14B.

Axelrod, Robert (1984), *The Evolution of Cooperation*. New York: Basic Books.

Catto, Henry (1997), "Don't Call Me Henry," *Newsweek*, (February 3), 12-13.

Gutek, Barbara A. (1995), *The Dynamics of Service: Reflections on the Changing Nature of Customer/Provider Interactions*. San Francisco: Jossey-Bass.

——— (1997), "Dyadic Interaction in Organizations," in *Creating Tomorrow's Organizations: A Handbook for Future Research in Organizational Behavior*, Cary L. Cooper and Susan E. Jackson, eds. Chichester, UK: John Wiley and Sons, 139-56.

———, Anita D. Bhappu, Matthew Liao-Troth, and Bennett Cherry (1999), "Distinguishing Between Service Relationships and Encounters," *Journal of Applied Psychology*, 84(2), 218-33.

———, Bennett Cherry, and Anita D. Bhappu (1998), "Features of Service Relationships and Encounters," paper presented at the conference "Understanding the Service Workplace," The Wharton School, University of Pennsylvania, October 16-17.

———, ———, and Markus Groth (1999), "Gender and Service Delivery," in *Handbook of Gender and Organizations*, Gary Powell, ed. Newbury Park, CA: Sage, 47-68.

Hochschild, Arlie (1983), *The Managed Heart: Commercialization of Human Feeling*. Berkeley: University of California Press.

Koepp, S. (1987), "Why Is Service So Bad? Pul-eez! Will Somebody Help Me?" *Time*, (February 2), 1.

Rafaeli, Anat (1989a), "When Cashiers Meet Customers: An Analysis of the Role of Supermarket Cashiers," *Academy of Management Journal*, 32(2), 245-73.

——— (1989b), "When Clerks Meet Customers: A Test of Variables Related to Emotional Expressions on the Job," *Journal of Applied Psychology*, 74, 385-93.

——— and Robert Sutton (1990), "Busy Stores and Demanding Customers: How Do They Affect the Display of Positive Emotion?" *Academy of Management Journal*, 33, 623-37.

Raspberry, William (1993), "Call Me MISTER Raspberry," *Cincinnati Inquirer*, (December 3), A10.

23

Brand Switching and Loyalty for Services

LAURETTE DUBÉ
STOWE SHOEMAKER

Brand switching and loyalty have become particularly poignant topics for research and practice in services over the last few decades. In the face of overpopulated and hypercompetitive markets, service providers have shifted the emphasis in marketing strategies from customer acquisition to customer retention in many industries. In fact, in the airline industry, the cost of frequent flyer programs may even be higher than advertising spending (about 3% of revenue for advertising and between 3% and 6% for frequent flyer programs; "Extra Life for Airlines" 1993).

Not surprisingly, a variety of defensive strategies have gradually gained broad acceptance. Defensive marketing strategies such as frequent user programs, service guarantees, and complaint management programs (see Dwyer, Schurr, and Oh 1987; Grönroos 1994; Gummesson 1987; Hu, Toh, and Strand 1988) seek to improve relationships with current customers by focusing on satisfaction and loyalty. In addition, they seek to prevent customers from leaving the firm's franchise, even in the wake of service failure.

If defensive strategies designed to retain current customers appear to be profitable in highly competitive environments (Fornell and Wernerfelt 1987; Hart, Heskett, and Sasser 1990; Reichheld and Sasser 1990; Rust, Zahorik, and Keiningham 1995), our conceptual and empirical knowledge of these strategies, the nature and magnitude of their effects, and the antecedents and moderating conditions of consumer switching/loyalty remain very limited in the context of service industries. This comes in sharp contrast to the abundant stream of research conducted for brand switching and loyalty for manufactured goods industries.

In fact, in the search of the marketing, consumer, and service industry literature performed in preparing for this review, we found an extremely limited number of citations referring specifically to brand switching/loyalty for services. The most directly related line of research that can provide significant insight on brand switching and loyalty for services pertains to the study of service failure, loyalty programs, and other defensive strategies.

In this chapter, we first define brand switching and loyalty in the context of the service industries. Second, we propose a framework for examining how defensive strategies attempt to ultimately shape brand switching and loyalty by influencing the structural parameters of the customer-provider exchange as well as customers' satisfaction and commitment to their relationship to a service brand. Third, we review empirical evidence of the actual effectiveness of defensive strategies in managing customers' switching and loyalty decisions. Fourth, we present possible moderators of the effectiveness of defensive strategies in influencing customers' decision to remain loyal to their service provider or to switch to a competitor. Finally, we discuss challenges for researchers and practitioners involved in the study and development of defensive strategies that can successfully influence customers' switching and loyalty decisions.

DEFINING BRAND SWITCHING
AND LOYALTY FOR SERVICES

Jacoby and Chestnut (1978) have defined brand loyalty as "biased behavioral responses expressed over time by some decision-making unit with respect to one or more alternative brands out of a set of such brands" (p. 80), most often conceptualized as proportions or sequences of purchases of a given brand. The various forms and shades taken by the concepts of loyalty have evolved from this original focus on repeat, sometimes exclusive purchase of a brand, to the cognitive and attitudinal antecedents of such loyalty behaviors. More recently, the concepts of loyalty have evolved further, encompassing a rich diversity of dimensions underlying the relationship that a customer may entertain with a brand (Fournier and Yao 1997).

In the service literature, Bendapudi and Berry (1997) have presented the most comprehensive definition we found for customer loyalty in a service context, as being a response closely tied to the pledge of relational continuity underlying commitment, and generally reflected as continued patronage of the same provider based on dedication or pragmatic constraints. In the words of Rob Smith, president of Focal Point Marketing, a consulting firm specializing in loyalty management (Smith 1998), you can talk about loyalty "when the customers feel so strongly that you can best meet his or her relevant needs, your competition is virtually excluded from his or her consideration set, and he or she buys almost exclusively from you—referring to you as 'her airline,' 'her hotel,' or 'her rental car company.' " It is important, however, to note that in some service industries such as utilities, public services, and health care, loyalty may not necessarily be based on the customers' conviction of the superiority of a provider's offering but instead be tied to constraints such as the high structural cost of switching provider, the lack of alternatives, and regulation.

Services Versus Goods

Thus, brand switching and loyalty in the context of service industries, in addition to fulfilling its basic purpose of building up repeat purchase from one transaction to the next as for manufacturing goods, present unique characteristics that have to be understood if one is to develop defensive strategies to manage them effectively. Two key features differentiate brand loyalty and switching in the context of the services industries in comparison to that of manufacturing goods.

The first relates to the purchase process of services, which precludes the simultaneous offering of alternative brands at the point of purchase decision, for instance the way multiple brands of toothpaste are available on supermarket shelves. Much of managing brand loyalty and switching for manufacturing goods, in addition to building long-term brand equity (Keller 1998), consists primarily of setting conditions favorable to repeat purchase and loyalty at the point of purchase. Such favorable conditions may consist of making sure that the brand is in stock, positioned advantageously on the shelf, and possibly has a price discount. In a service context, because choice decisions are already made when one gets to the point of purchase, loyalty may be as much tied to accrued value for future transactions built into a present purchase as it is to accrued value of present purchase or favorable point-of-purchase conditions. Thus, there is a need for conceptualizing brand switching/loyalty at both the relationship and transaction levels and to consider defensive strategies that add value to both current and future transactions. Consistently, many of the defensive strategies for services, such as loyalty, frequent users, and club programs, are designed precisely for the purpose of providing accrued benefits for both current and future transactions. For instance, a goal of frequent flyer programs is to attract full-fare customers and reward them with free or reduced-price tickets for future trips, possibly personal trips that otherwise would not be taken (Stephenson and Fox 1987).

The second characteristic of services that has a bearing on brand switching and loyalty pertains to the fact that in many industries in this sector, firms are responsible for designing and managing most of consumption, whereas for manufacturing, except for after-sales services, consumption occurs outside the firm's facilities and responsibility. The fact that most of service consumption occurs in the firm's facility translates into numerous opportunities for failures to deliver on the brand promises and, by extension, many opportunities to justify brand switching. Not surprisingly, if for physical goods brand switching is primarily tied to transaction-specific factors relating to in-store promotion, stock availability, and mere variety seeking (Kahn, Kalwani, and Morrisson 1986), product failure appears to be a key driver in service industries. Based on the review of an inventory of 800 service switching behaviors collected from a large sample of adult American consumers of more than 40 different services, Keaveney (1995) observed that service failure was the primary cause of brand switching. The service failures related, in decreasing order of importance, to core service failures, failed service encounters, and inadequate handling of the service failure. Similar results pertaining to the nature of service failures have been reported by Bitner, Booms, and Tetreault (1990), Edvardsson (1992), and Kelley, Hoffman, and Davis (1993).

At the same time, with the customer in the company's facilities during much, if not all, of the consumption process, service firms also enjoy the capacity to intervene during a service failure to prevent deleterious effects. Therefore, finding innovative ways to manage consumers' responses so as to minimize the adverse consequences of service failure may have a high return on investment in the current market conditions. The portfolio of defensive strategies in the service industries therefore must include a set of value-recovery strategies designed to prevent brand switching and reinforce loyalty at the level of the immediate response to the service failure in the current transaction (i.e., preventing the customer from not completing the service transaction), as well as for the maintenance of the long-term relationship with the firm. Dubé and Maute (1998) suggest differentiating customer loyalty in terms of situational or transaction-specific and enduring or relationship-based types. Situational or transaction-specific loyalty is viewed as the immediate, passive, and accommodating response to dissatisfaction in the context of a service failure. Enduring or relationship-based loyalty consists of a longer-term, active response to dissatisfaction in the wake of service failure, one that involves the decision not to terminate the relationship. Roos and Strandvik (1996) have proposed a similar distinction on the brand switching side. They distinguish between the immediate, short-term reaction to a dissatisfying transaction and the long-term termination process in the case of relationship breakup. Corner (1996) recently emphasized the need for marketers to use both value-added (i.e, designed to manage brand switching and loyalty in the context of normal service transaction) and value-recovery (i.e., designed to manage brand switching and loyalty in the context of transactions with service failure) strategies if a service provider is to manage customer switching and loyalty decisions effectively in the service industries.

In Figure 23.1, we summarize the types of defensive strategies that have evolved over time to effectively manage brand switching and loyalty in the service industries, shifting away from an exclusive focus on managing brand switching and loyalty by adding value or reducing cost at the transaction, toward a much more comprehensive portfolio of strategies designed to add and recover value both in current transactions and in the future relationship. In the next section, we provide a conceptual framework accounting for ways in which value-added and value-recovery defensive strategies can accomplish the functions positioned along this continuum.

UNDERSTANDING DEFENSIVE STRATEGIES' EFFECTS ON CUSTOMER SWITCHING AND LOYALTY

Inspired by a framework from interpersonal theory (specifically, the investment model; Rusbult 1980), Dubé and Maute (1998) proposed to conceptualize how defensive strategies may ultimately modulate consumer switching/loyalty by first shaping the structural parameters of the customer-provider exchange in a way

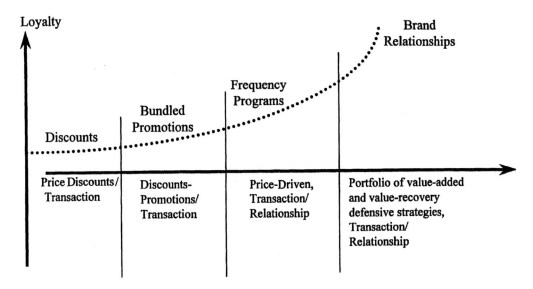

Figure 23.1 Defensive Strategies to Manage Brand Switching and Loyalty in the Service Industries

that influences satisfaction with and commitment to the relationship. The investment model (Rusbult 1980; Rusbult, Zembrodt, and Gunn 1982) makes use of social exchange concepts to predict the evolution of long-term relationships from their values on a series of structural parameters, with the objective of maximizing one's relationship outcomes such as satisfaction and commitment, or their behavioral correlates, loyalty to or exit from the relationship (or, in our context, brand switching and loyalty). This framework is illustrated in Figure 23.2.

In this view, brand switching and loyalty (situational/transaction-specific and enduring/relationship-based) and their immediate antecedents of satisfaction and commitment are seen as outcomes that depend on (a) the *perceived value* of the customer-provider exchange (i.e., the rewards minus the costs associated with the exchange), (b) the *investment size* (i.e., the magnitude of the investment that would be lost if one terminates the relationship; for example, think about how one feels on the verge of finally being able to redeem frequent flyer mileage), and (c) the perceived value of *competitive offering* (i.e., the rewards minus the costs—the perceived value—associated with competitive offerings).

Dubé and Maute (1998) have recently used this framework to derive and test a set of hypotheses on the effect of value-added and value-recovery strategies in different competitive environments as a function of the effect of these strategies on the structural parameters of customer-provider exchange. Neither these authors nor any other published studies have specifically measured whether and how defensive strategies influence these various parameters of the consumer-provider exchange and, in turn, how these structural changes mediate the strategies' effectiveness in terms of managing customer retention. Because practice sometimes precedes science, we have chosen to palliate the absence of such information in the literature by undertaking in-depth interviews with managers responsible

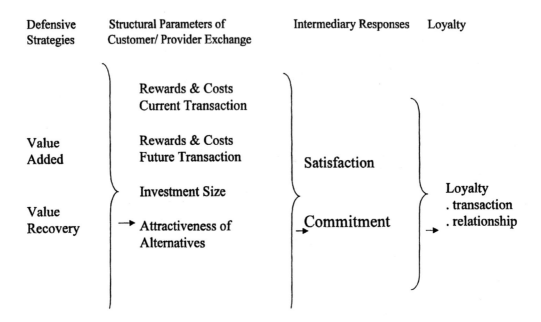

Figure 23.2 The Influence of Defensive Strategies on Brand Switching and Loyalty

for defensive strategies in a service industry; specifically, we looked at the hotel industry. We interviewed managers in eight leading American hotel companies to inventory their value-added and value-recovery strategies and to analyze their various features. These exploratory results are summarized in Table 23.1.

Rewards and Costs Associated With the Brand

According to the model presented in Figure 23.2, the value of a customer-provider exchange is determined by the difference between the rewards and costs associated with service transactions. Value-added and value-recovery strategies are designed specifically to exploit customer perceptions of the rewards and costs associated with present and future service transactions. Beyond the added value derived from increased reward or lower cost derived from specific transactions, value-added strategies permit customers to acquire additional rewards that accumulate for future transactions as long as they maintain their relationship with the brand, or to reduce the costs. Most value-added strategies increase relationship rewards while relationship costs remain unaffected. Airline customers, for example, can obtain additional privileges in the present transaction, such as access to airport lounges, and cross-promotions with complementary services such as hotels and car rentals on a given transaction in addition to future products/services free of charge or at a minimal cost (Barlow 1992).

In general, value-added and value-recovery strategies both affect the value of the buyer-provider exchange, but this influence is exerted in different ways. As mentioned above, value-added strategies increase the rewards associated with the current relationship, whereas value-recovery strategies reduce or eliminate the costs associated with service failure. Value-recovery strategies, however, generally do not affect relationship rewards or investment size because the core offer of the brand is unchanged and customers are compelled neither to purchase additional services nor to maintain the relationship to qualify for redress.

Consider now the sources of value added (or recovered) in current and future transactions in the defensive strategies in place in the hotel industry (see Table 23.1). Features are of various kinds: They relate to financial (e.g., saving money on future transactions, complete reimbursement in the case of service failure, discounts at the gift shop), temporal (e.g., saving time by priority check-in), functional (e.g., check cashing, website available), experiential (e.g., upgrades or turndown services), emotional (e.g., more recognition and/or more pleasurable service experience), or social (e.g., interpersonal link with a service provider) components of the customer/provider exchange. In fact, the companies we studied all had developed defensive strategies that presented a relatively broad portfolio of these various sources of value. Most of them had created, for each member in a value-added defensive program, a preference profile that allows the hotel to "customize" the stay for each guest, adding as much value as possible to each transaction as well as to the long-term relationship.

In fact, the combination of sources of value of different types and tied to current and future transactions may very well be necessary for the effectiveness of defensive strategies in influencing customer switching and loyalty decisions. Service guarantees, for example, are designed to reduce both the financial cost and the psychological uncertainty associated with a service failure. In the limited number of studies that have simultaneously considered the predictive power of both functional and emotional costs on customer responses to defensive strategies in the context of service failure, the effects of the latter have generally surpassed those of the former. For instance, Dubé and Maute (1996) found that when both sets of predictors were included in the same regression models, the power of emotional cost consistently surpassed that of functional cost. Folkes, Koletsky, and Graham (1987) showed that the anger aroused by a service failure in airline services mediated consumer complaining and repurchase intentions. Similarly, Taylor (1994) showed that the overall service evaluation after a service failure (delayed flight) was affected directly by the level of anger and uncertainty it induced.

Service providers have to be careful in choosing the appropriate features to include in shaping customers' perceptions of the value of their relationship with the brand, as well as the appropriate level for each feature. Research (Dowling and Uncles 1997; O'Brien and Jones 1995) suggests that customers may be sensitive to the quality of these strategies. As a first case in point, the cash value of the redemption reward and/or of the compensation for service failure has to be perceived as significant. For instance, members of one hotel's frequency program can earn one free weekend room night with the redemption of 20,000

TABLE 23.1 Features of Value-Added and Value-Recovery Strategies in Eight Leading Hotel Companies

Benefits	Regular Tier Member	Middle Tier Member	Upper Tier Member
Financial rewards (value added: current)	Either 1, 5, or 10 points per dollar spent with no bonus on base points earned	Bonus points earned on regular tier points; bonus can be 10%, 15%, or 20%	Bonus points earned on regular tier points; bonus can be 10%, 25%, or 30%
Financial rewards (value added: future)	Either not available or can combine points with spouse	Either not available or can combine points with spouse	Either not available or can combine points with spouse
Financial rewards (value added: future)	Either no upgrades available or automatic upgrade if room available	Either automatic upgrade if available or one confirmable upgrade every 5 qualifying stays	One confirmable upgrade every 5 qualifying stays + automatic upgrade available whenever paying minimum published room rate, based on availability; or automatic upgrade available whenever available
Financial rewards (value added: future)	150 points for getting friend to join the program or no bonus threshold awards	Bonus points earned on regular tier points; bonus can be 0%, 10%, 15%, or 20%, or 5,000 bonus points after 7 paid VIP stays within calendar quarter	Bonus points earned on regular tier points; bonus can be 0%, 10%, 25%, or 30%, or 5,000 bonus points after 7 paid VIP stays within calendar quarter
Financial rewards (value added: current)	500 points for government or commercial rate, 1,000 points for others; get 20% when presenting rental agreement at check-in; or earn 25% bonus with car rental agreement; earn 250-500 points per Hertz rental; 100 points per car rental partner	500 points for government or commercial rate, 1,000 points for others; get 20% when presenting rental agreement at check-in; or earn 25% bonus with car rental agreement; earn 500 points per Hertz rental	500 points for government or commercial rate, 1,000 points for others; get 20% when presenting rental agreement at check-in; or earn 25% bonus with car rental agreement; earn 500 points per Hertz rental
Financial rewards (value added: current)	Earn hotel points or airline miles; one chain lets you earn both hotel points and airline points; airline miles for stay instead of hotel points; some hotels only hotel points	Earn hotel points or airline miles; one chain lets you earn both hotel points and airline points; airline miles for stay instead of hotel points; some hotels only hotel points	Earn hotel points or airline miles; one chain lets you earn both hotel points and airline points; airline miles for stay instead of hotel points; some hotels only hotel points
Financial rewards (value added: future)	Affinity card where you earn hotel points for credit card spending; earn 2,000 credit card points for 150 hotel points, 330 hotel points, or 1,000 hotel points	Affinity card where you earn hotel points for credit card spending; earn 2,000 credit card points for 150 hotel points, 330 hotel points, or 1,000 hotel points	Affinity card where you earn hotel points for credit card spending; earn 2,000 credit card points for 150 hotel points, 330 hotel points, or 1,000 hotel points
Financial rewards (value added: current)	No discount in gift shop	No discount in gift shop	10% discount in gift shop

Financial rewards (value added: current and future)	Exchange points for free rooms: 8,000 points = one free weekend night, 15,000 points = two free weekend nights; 20,000 points = one night; 12,500 hotel points = 1 free night for mid-scale brand	Exchange points for free rooms: 8,000 points = one free weekend night, 15,000 points = two free weekend nights; 20,000 points = one night; 12,500 hotel points = 1 free night for mid-scale brand	Exchange points for free rooms: 8,000 points = one free weekend night, 15,000 points = two free weekend nights; 20,000 points = one night; 12,500 hotel points = 1 free night for mid-scale brand
Financial rewards (value added: current and future)	Exchange hotel points for airline miles: Some, no change available; others 10,000 points = 2,500 airline miles; 10,000 points = 5,000 miles; some require minimum 9,000 points per exchange	Exchange hotel points for airline miles: Some, no change available; others 10,000 points = 2,500 airline miles; 10,000 points = 5,000 miles; some require minimum 9,000 points per exchange	Exchange hotel points for airline miles: Some, no change available; others 10,000 points = 2,500 airline miles; 10,000 points = 5,000 miles; some require minimum 9,000 points per exchange
Functional/temporal (value added)	Point statement sent every other month with activity; statement sent monthly; statement sent quarterly	Point statement sent every other month with activity; statement sent monthly; statement sent quarterly	Point statement sent every other month with activity; statement sent monthly; statement sent quarterly
Functional/temporal (value added: current and future)	Some hotels offer members-only reservation phone numbers at this level, while others have no members-only reservation phone numbers at this level	Some hotels offer members-only reservation phone numbers at this level, while others have no members-only reservation phone numbers at this level	Some hotels offer members-only reservation phone numbers at this level, while others have no members-only reservation phone numbers at this level
Functional/temporal (value added: current)	No turndown service; availability of service varies by owner of brand	No turndown service; availability of service varies by owner of brand	Turndown service normal at this level; availability of service varies by owner of brand
Functional/temporal (value added: current)	No separate check-in; separate lines; priority check-in; rooms assigned and room key waiting at check-in desk; zip-in, check-in	No separate check-in; separate lines; priority check-in; rooms assigned and room key waiting at check-in desk; zip-in, check-in	No separate check-in; separate lines; priority check-in; rooms assigned and room key waiting at check-in desk; zip-in, check-in
Functional/temporal (value added: current)	No check cashing for member at this level; check cashing up to $250 per stay; no check cashing at all	Check cashing up to $250 per stay, up to $200 per day; no check cashing at all	Check cashing up to $500 per stay; up to $200 per day; no check cashing at all
Functional/temporal (value added: future)	No website available; website available where guests can redeem awards, change addresses, and conduct various transactions	No website available; website available where guests can redeem awards, change addresses, and conduct various transactions	No website available; website available where guests can redeem awards, change addresses, and conduct various transactions
Functional/temporal (value added: current)	No direct billing through individual at this level; no direct billing at all	Direct billing through individual; no direct billing at all	Direct billing through individual; no direct billing at all

(Continued)

TABLE 23.1 Continued

Benefits	Regular Tier Member	Middle Tier Member	Upper Tier Member
Functional/temporal (value added: current)	Not available at all; not available at this level; 7 a.m. check-in; 9-5 check-in, check-out	Available at 10 a.m.; 7 a.m. check-in; 9-5 check-in, check-out	Available at 10 a.m.; 7 a.m. check-in; 9-5 check-in, check-out
Functional/temporal (value added: future)	No priority waiting list during busy times	No priority waiting list during busy times	Priority waiting list during busy times
Psychological/emotional (value added: future)			Attend the Academy Awards as guest of hotel company
Psychological/emotional (value added: current and future)	Customer profiling so hotel knows your wants and needs	Customer profiling so hotel knows your wants and needs	Customer profiling so hotel knows your wants and needs
Psychological/emotional (value added: future)	At least one hotel stay in past 12 months to be a member	Must have at least 4 qualifying stays during calendar year; can pay to join this level or can be earned; 20+ nights; must stay 20 nights in 10 stays	Must have at least 15 qualifying stays or 4 stays and 30 nights; invitation only; 60+ nights; must stay 50 nights in 25 stays
Psychological/emotional (value recovery: current and future)	Customer service centers that can help when problems occur that are not taken care of at hotel level; some hotels have international call centers; some call centers open 24 hours	Customer service centers that can help when problems occur that are not taken care of at hotel level; some hotels have international call centers; some call centers open 24 hours	Customer service centers that can help when problems occur that are not taken care of at hotel level; some hotels have international call centers; some call centers open 24 hours
Psychological/emotional (value recovery: current and future)	Perfect stay programs where all problems guaranteed to be resolved; if not send copy of folio and letter to specific address and get free guaranteed upgrade	Perfect stay programs where all problems guaranteed to be resolved; if not send copy of folio and letter to specific address and get free guaranteed upgrade	Perfect stay programs where all problems guaranteed to be resolved; if not send copy of folio and letter to specific address and get free guaranteed upgrade
Psychological/emotional (value recovery: current)	100% Satisfaction Guarantee (note, hotel with this program does not offer any type of frequency program)	100% Satisfaction Guarantee (note, hotel with this program does not offer any type of frequency program)	100% Satisfaction Guarantee (note, hotel with this program does not offer any type of frequency program)

points. Because $1 equals 10 points, the redemption value is $2,000. In the context of value-recovery strategy, research has shown that the magnitude of monetary compensation offered and the effectiveness of the recovery (Goodwin and Ross 1992; Webster and Sundaram 1998) affect future loyalty and satisfaction. One hotel chain we talked with offers a 100% satisfaction guarantee. If anything goes wrong with the hotel stay, the stay is free. Another chain offers a free guaranteed upgrade certificate on the next stay for problems with the current stay.

Another parameter to set with caution pertains to the range of choice of these rewards and the degree of flexibility in their redemption format. For instance, as mentioned earlier, many hotel chains allow customers to earn either airline miles or hotel points, which enables the guest to choose the reward that he or she wants. As stated, one chain allows for "double-dipping," which means the guest gets both miles and points. The aspirational value of the rewards for specific market segments also has to be assessed. That is, various benefits offered to elite members—for instance, systematic upgrade—may be highly sought, beyond their monetary or functional value, because of the social image attached to them.

The perceived likelihood of achieving the rewards is another aspect of defensive strategies that has to be set at the appropriate level. As one of the hotel frequency program managers mentioned in our interview, "if the goal, i.e., a free hotel room or a free airline flight, is unobtainable then the customer will find no value. That is why we have formed alliances with the airlines, credit card companies, and rental car companies. It is all about giving customers many chances to earn points or miles." The program's ease of use is also critical to a defensive strategy's ability to increase customers' positive perceptions of their relationship with a service provider. One of the problems encountered by certain frequency programs such as AirMiles, a program for multistore retail purchases, is that responsibility originally was given to customers for collecting and keeping track of their frequency points, with insufficient support to do so. Many companies in the hotel industry now provide customers with the ability to keep track of their points/miles via the Internet. Finally, the immediacy with which the rewards or compensations are available is another parameter of defensive strategies that may affect customers' perception of value. Many of the hotel companies we talked to have policies that allow guests to redeem their points anytime; that is, there are no blackout dates.

Investment Size

The most important way in which service providers, and not just those in the hotel industry, attempt to make it more costly for customers to quit the relationship is by differentiating the nature and magnitude of value being created at different membership tiers. In most companies, value-added defensive strategies are differentiated in two to three tiers, corresponding to increasing amounts of purchase as qualifying conditions for service levels. By increasing the "added value per unit of purchase" as one moves from one tier to the next, the provider makes it more costly for the guest not only to switch to a competitor but also to divide his or her share of purchases among various providers. For instance, as one moves up the tier level (e.g., from regular to middle to upper), the points earned for dollars spent increases. This can be seen in Table 23.1, which reveals that middle tier members can earn up to a 20% bonus on points, whereas upper tier members can earn a 30% bonus.

Rewards and Costs Associated With Competitive Offerings

As can be seen in Table 23.1, there is little evidence that either value-added or value-recovery strategies attempt to change directly consumers' perceptions of the rewards and costs associated with competition, as is done with offensive strategies such as comparative advertising. Instead, the various providers attempt to differentiate their offering from the competitors' by multiple variations in the various features of their value-added and value-recovery strategies. For instance, a hotel chain may offer 250 points toward a free stay if one rents a car with a particular rental car company, and another hotel chain may offer 500 points for the same. One needs to be careful when comparing such programs because the rate at which one earns points can vary. Although the business class chains (i.e., Sheraton, Hyatt, and Hilton) generally offer 10 points for each $1 spent, mid-scale properties (i.e., Holiday Inn and Best Western) generally offer fewer points. There is still variability between programs, however. For instance, the bonus points a customer can earn by moving to higher tiers (such tiers are based on stay frequency in a given time period) can range from 10% to 20% at the middle tier and 10% to 30% at the upper tier. Similarly, the availability of upgrades, shown by Bowen and Shoemaker (1997) to be very important to frequent business travelers who stay in luxury properties, can vary by program both within and between tiers. For instance, in the regular tier some chains allow no upgrades whereas others provide an automatic upgrade if a room is available. In the middle tier, there can be automatic upgrades depending on availability, or one can earn an upgrade every five qualifying stays. Finally, program variability also can be seen in the way in which customers can earn points (one hotel chain allows the customer to earn both hotel points and airline miles, whereas other chains make the customer choose one or the other), the redemption of points for a free room (cost varies, between 8,000 points and 12,500 points), and the conversion of affinity card points to hotel points (2,000 points earned on a credit card can be worth either 150, 330, or 1,000 hotel points).

Influence on Satisfaction and Commitment

According to the model presented in Figure 23.2, the impact of defensive strategies on the structural characteristics of the customer-provider exchange ultimately influences brand switching and loyalty by first altering the degree of satisfaction with and commitment to this exchange. Research conducted in the domain of interpersonal and organizational relationships has shown that satisfaction predicts relationship commitment (Rusbult et al. 1988; Rusbult, Zembrodt, and Gunn 1982) even though the two are not isomorphic. As recently demonstrated by Fournier and Yao (1997), in the absence of better alternatives, one's relationship with a brand may be one of "enslavement," with the "involuntary," committed relationship governed exclusively by the lack of alternatives.

In a study using scenarios of airline transactions, Dubé and Maute (1996) found that the postconsumption level of satisfaction depended on functional and emotional residual costs associated with the service failure. Research conducted in the domain of interpersonal and organizational relationships (Rusbult et al. 1988; Rusbult, Zembrodt, and Gunn 1982) suggests that, much like satisfaction, commitment to a customer-provider relationship will be affected by current relationship value, with high rewards and low costs engendering greater commitment. Unlike satisfaction, however, investment size and alternative relationship attractiveness will also affect commitment. Consistently, Bowen and Shoemaker (1997) found that the higher the perceived costs associated with brand switching, the more customers were committed to their current hotel provider.

Link Between Satisfaction/Commitment and Customer Loyalty

Both satisfaction and commitment influence switching/loyalty behaviors. Dubé and Maute (1998) found that satisfaction mediates much of the effect of defensive strategies—in particular for value-recovery strategies—on brand loyalty. In other words, the capacity of value-recovery strategies to sustain customer loyalty—either by inducing calm, patient responses to service failure or preventing relationship termination—is due in large part to the effect that these strategies have on customer satisfaction. For value-added strategies, satisfaction strongly mediated only situational loyalty, explaining most of the variation in immediate responses to service failure. In contrast, the effect on enduring loyalty remained significant, albeit diminished, even after satisfaction had been partialed out.

Turning to the relationship between commitment and loyalty, previous research in the interpersonal and organizational domain (Rusbult et al. 1988; Rusbult, Zembrodt, and Gunn 1982) found that committed subjects reacted to relationship decline calmly, confident that things would improve (situational loyalty), and were less likely to terminate the relationship (enduring loyalty). Bowen and Shoemaker (1997) found that the more committed respondents admitted to be to their current favored hotel provider, the more likely they were to make most of their future purchases from this provider.

Relevant evidence on the relationship between commitment and loyalty in response to value-recovery strategies comes from research on the effect of length of the customer-provider relationship (Ganesan 1994; Hess, Ganesan, and Klein 1998) and on the degree of customers' closeness to the relationships (Goodman et al. 1995; Kelley and Davis 1994) on response to service failure. As for consumers' response to service failure, in general it is found that longer, higher-quality past performance and more committed and closer provider-customer relationships are associated with customers being more tolerant of service failure and more willing to attribute causes of failure to temporary factors—and therefore being more likely to remain loyal—while at the same time having higher expectations for the firm being able to develop successful recovery strategies that can prevent the recurrence of the failure (see Hess, Ganesan, and Klein 1998).

EMPIRICAL EVIDENCE FOR THE EFFECT OF DEFENSIVE STRATEGIES ON BRAND SWITCHING AND LOYALTY

In the previous sections, we provided a conceptual framework to understand better how defensive strategies may operate in influencing customers' switching and loyalty decisions in the context of the service industries. Empirical evidence was presented to support various links along the proposed path between features of value-added and value-recovery strategies and their ultimate impact on switching and loyalty behavior. A complete test of the proposed model still awaits empirical validation. In fact, in our review of the literature, the empirical support for any significant and reliable effect of defensive strategies on loyalty and actual purchase behavior has been remarkably scant.

Consider the most often cited study in papers about or arguing for defensive strategies. Reichheld and Sasser's (1990) article showed, on the basis of data collected in many service industries, that a 5% decrease in customer attrition can increase profits from 25% to 85%. It is noteworthy, however, that these results are about the impact of actual retention and do not say anything about the effectiveness of defensive strategies as long as it is not known how effective a defensive strategy has been in retaining customers. Bowen and Shoemaker (1997), in their study of business customers in luxury hotels, found that only 27.8% of the respondents stated that a frequency program would definitely make them more loyal to a particular hotel. On a positive note, however, they also found that frequency-program members, once in the hotel, will spend more money than nonmember guests.

In fact, the few studies that have attempted to empirically and directly test the effect of defensive strategies on consumer switching/loyalty per se reveal results that are far from being convincing concerning the effectiveness of current defensive strategies in actually retaining customers. Sharp and Sharp (1997), in a study of change of repeat-purchase patterns resulting from a large-scale store loyalty program, found no convincing support for the effectiveness of such defensive strategies. Assessing "excess loyalty," as defined by positive divergence from Dirichlet predictions, they observed excess loyalty in only two out of six stores participating in the program. In addition, within the two stores in which excess loyalty was observed, the excess was observed among those individuals who were not in the program as well as among those who were. Similar results were obtained by Dubé and Maute (1998) in the context of airline services. The positive effect of a value-added strategy (specifically, frequent flyer program) had a positive effect on enduring loyalty in the wake of a service failure only under conditions of low competition. In this simulation, the effect of value-added loyalty on enduring loyalty vanished as soon as a competitor with a similar strategy appeared.

The previous results showing the elusiveness of value-added strategies' ability to maintain their positive impact on customer loyalty/switching in the face of competition are puzzling. Is the historical pattern of evolution of these strategies in service industry a mere bandwagon effect or the reflection of rational decision making based on the return on investment in various defensive strategies? For instance, only 6 months elapsed between the moment American Airlines' Advantage program was launched in May 1991 and the time it was matched by the closest competitors on domestic and transnational carriers (Mowlana and Smith 1993). By the end of 1986, 24 out of the 27 U.S. carriers had designed comparable loyalty programs to attract and retain frequent travelers (Gilbert 1996). An early study (data collected in 1983; Morrisson and Winston 1989) conducted before the industrywide bandwagon reaction occurred showed that frequent flyer programs overall influenced airline/route choice. A later study, however, revealed that even though an overall frequent flyer program effect on airline/route choice persisted, this effect varied across airlines, depending on convenience of locations and routes as well as performance of other service components (Gilbert 1996).

In fact, to understand better the relationship between defensive strategies and their actual impact on brand switching and exclusive loyalty to a service provider, it may be more useful to focus on what Dowling and Uncles (1997) have called "polygamous" loyalty; that is, sharing one's purchases among a limited set of favored providers. In an international study of customer loyalty for brands of a diversity of products, including both manufacturing goods and services, Ehrenberg (1988) found that only a very small percentage of buyers are 100% loyal to a particular brand. Instead, as shown in a later study by Ehrenberg and his collaborators (Uncles, Ehrenberg, and Hammond 1995), it appears that when markets reach equilibrium, consumers tend to share their purchases across three or four brands. Such polygamous loyalty may in fact be most representative of service industries. For instance, a study of European business airline travelers found that on average, a customer was a member of 3.1 programs (OAG business travelers lifestyle survey 1993, cited in Dowling and Uncles 1997). Other sources report that 72% of business travelers participated in one or more frequent flyer programs (Stephenson and Fox 1987). Similar patterns of behavior have been observed in the lodging industry. Bowen and Shoemaker (1997) found that 32.2% of customers belonged to one or two programs. More than 20% (21.1%) belonged to three or less, and 10.7% belonged to at least four programs.

As for value-added strategies, the empirical evidence for the impact of value-recovery strategies on actual brand switching/loyalty behavior also has to be considered with caution. For instance, it has been suggested that effective recovery in the wake of a service failure may enhance consumer satisfaction beyond its expected level in the absence of failure (Bitner, Booms, and Tetrault 1990; Goodwin and Ross 1992; Hart, Heskett, and Sasser 1990). This is consistent with common belief among service managers. According to a manager from a hotel chain that offers a 100% guarantee, recovery in the wake of a service failure enhances consumer satisfaction beyond its expected level in the absence of failure. A convincing empirical test of such a proposition is still pending. What has been shown with reliability across a diversity of industries and using different methodologies is that the presence (compared to the absence) of good value-recovery strategies can reduce the detrimental impact of service failures on satisfaction judgments and brand loyalty/switching decisions (Dubé and Maute 1998; Fornell and Wernerfelt 1987; Hess, Ganesan, and Klein 1998). Moreover, Dubé and Maute (1998) found that such effects of recovery prevailed regardless of the presence of a value-added strategy and the intensity of competitive environment.

EFFECTIVENESS PARAMETERS

What customer or market-level factors moderate a defensive strategy's ability to shape customers' purchases in an effective way? The existing literature on defensive strategies has been relatively silent on this issue. Not surprisingly, most of the defensive strategies currently in place in many service industries still lag in advertising and other offensive strategies in terms of their ability to carve the market from various angles and fine-tune their propositions to customers accordingly. Insights on what may be segmentation variables of interest can be found in the abundant literature on moderators of how consumers react to dissatisfaction. Even though these will be relevant primarily in considering value-recovery strategies, many shed light on variations in the effectiveness of value-added strategies as well.

Individual Characteristics

Research on consumer dissatisfaction and complaining behavior has identified a series of individual characteristics associated with active responses to dissatisfaction and, by extension, may also moderate customer responses to defensive strategies designed to manage brand switching and loyalty. These are higher income and education (e.g., Bearden, Teel, and Crockett 1980; Warland, Herrmann, and Willits 1975), professional jobs (e.g., Andreasen 1985), younger age (e.g., Morganosky and Buckley 1986; Moyer 1984), high self-confidence (e.g., Gronhaug and Zaltman 1981), low sense of alienation (e.g., Bearden and Mason 1984), high assertiveness/aggressiveness (e.g., Richins 1983), high level of knowledge (Andreasen 1985), and experience with the firm (Singh 1990). By extension, individuals presenting higher values on these parameters should be more receptive to the influence of value-recovery strategies.

Beyond the single effects of these personal characteristics, various groupings have been proposed for ways in which they would respond to dissatisfaction (Maute and Dubé forthcoming; Singh 1990). Based on multivariate analyses, Singh (1990) proposed a segmentation scheme based on the type and degree of efforts invested in response to dissatisfaction (segments were voicer, activist, irrate, passive). Maute and Dubé (forthcoming) proposed a segmentation based on how much emotion customers would respond with in cases of service failure (their categories were unemotional, calm, anxious, and angry).

Market-Related Characteristics

The likelihood of brand switching versus alternative responses to service failure is also a function of product- and market-related characteristics (Best and Andreasen 1977; Fornell and Robinson 1983; Technical Assistance Research Programs 1978). Significant variations across product categories in perceived problem severity, blame attribution, amount of effort (Richins 1983), consequences of behavioral responses (Bearden and Oliver 1985; Singh 1990), and market structure (Fornell and Wernerfelt 1987; Singh 1990) have been identified as important moderators of consumers' choice among alternative behavioral responses to dissatisfaction. More specifically, Webster and Sundaram (1998) found that for services that present high criticality for consumers—as operationalized by perceived importance of timely delivery—it is harder for value-recovery strategies to influence consumer satisfaction and loyalty in the wake of a service failure, compared to other services presenting lower criticality. In addition, Bolfing (1989) reports that consumers' responses to service failures and recovery strategies may be a function of their general perceptions of the redress environment.

Another condition that may vary across markets is the mixture of value-added and value-recovery strategies chosen by the provider to manage customers' switching and loyalty decisions. Dubé and Maute (1998) have shown that the positive effects of a value-added strategy providing accrued rewards had a positive effect on customer satisfaction and loyalty only when a value-recovery strategy alleviating cost of a service failure already was present. Their results suggest that a value-recovery strategy may be a necessary prerequisite for some of the value-added effects to emerge. When only a value-added strategy was offered, satisfaction remained at the same level as in the absence of either strategy, while reaching its maximal value when both strategies were present. As for enduring loyalty, the unique presence of a value-added strategy increased enduring loyalty at the standard level of statistical significance; however, when a value-recovery strategy also was present, this effect was magnified.

CONCLUSION

Significant theoretical and methodological development is urgently required to understand, measure, and model consumers' responses to defensive strategies in the context of service industries with the same depth and breadth of knowledge that have developed over the last decades in the domain of customers' responses to offensive strategies such as advertising for manufacturing goods. Research should attempt to identify more precisely, test empirically, and map the underlying mechanisms of those parameters of defensive strategies that are most critical in their ability to influence customer switching and loyalty behaviors. On the managerial side, there is an urgent need to design defensive strategies that offer the right features (i.e., excuse, compensation, or other) at the right moment so that the service experience remains conducive to positive memories, high satisfaction, and brand loyalty, regardless of the possible presence of service failure. Moreover, a more precise market segmentation of these defensive strategies should also improve their effectiveness. In conclusion, we hope that further conceptual and empirical development will enrich research and practice concerned with brand switching and loyalty in the service industries.

REFERENCES

Andreasen, Alan R. (1985), "Consumer Responses to Dissatisfaction in Loose Monopolies," *Journal of Consumer Research*, 12 (September), 135-41.

Barlow, Richard (1992), "Relationship Marketing: The Ultimate in Customer Services," *Retail Control*, 60 (March), 29-37.

Bearden, William and J. Mason (1984), "An Investigation of Influences on Customer Compliant Reports," in *Advances in Consumer Research*, Vol. 11, T. Kinnear, ed. Ann Arbor, MI: Association for Consumer Research, 490-95.

———— and Richard L. Oliver (1985), "The Role of Public and Private Complaining in Satisfaction With Problem Resolution," *The Journal of Consumer Affairs*, 19(2), 222-40.

————, J. Teel, and M. Crockett (1980), "A Path Model of Consumer Complaint Behaviour," in *Marketing in the 80s*, Richard Baggozzi et al., eds. Chicago: American Marketing Association, 101-4.

Bendapudi, N. and Leonard L. Berry (1997), "Customers' Motivations for Maintaining Relationships With Service Providers," *Journal of Retailing*, 73, 15-37.

Best, Arthur and A. R. Andreasen (1977), "Customer Response to Unsatisfactory Purchase: A Survey of Perceiving Defect, Voicing Complaints and Obtaining Redress," *Law and Society*, 11, 701-42.

Bitner, Mary Jo, Bernard H. Booms, and Mary S. Tetreault (1990), "The Service Encounter: Diagnosing Favorable and Unfavorable Incidents," *Journal of Marketing*, 54, 71-84.

Bolfing, Claire P. (1989), "How Do Customers Express Dissatisfaction and What Can Service Marketers Do About It?" *Journal of Service Marketing*, 3 (Spring), 5-23.

Bowen, John and Stowe Shoemaker (1997), "Relationship in the Luxury Hotel Segment: A Strategic Perspective," research report, The Palace Hotel Competition, Center for Hospitality Research, The School of Hotel Administration, Cornell University, Ithaca, NY.

Corner, Bruce A. (1996), "Helping Business Fight Lost-Customer Syndrome," *Marketing News*, 30(1), 4.

Dowling, Grahame R. and Mark Uncles (1997), "Do Customer Loyalty Programs Really Work?" *Sloan Management Review*, 38 (Summer), 71-82.

Dubé, Laurette and Manfred F. Maute (1996), "The Antecedents of Brand Switching, Brand Loyalty and Verbal Responses to Service Failure," *Advances in Services Marketing and Management*, 5, 127-51.

———— and ———— (1998), "Defensive Strategies for Managing Satisfaction and Loyalty in the Service Industry," *Psychology and Marketing*, 15, 775-91.

Dwyer, F. Robert, P. H. Schurr, and Sejo Oh (1987), "Developing Buyer-Seller Relationships," *Journal of Marketing*, 51 (April), 11-27.

Edvardsson, Bo (1992), "Service Breakdowns: A Study of Critical Incidents in an Airline," *International Journal of Service Industry Management*, 3, 417-29.

Ehrenberg, Andrew S. C. (1988), *Repeat Buying: Facts, Theory, and Applications*, 2nd ed. New York: Oxford University Press.

"Extra Life for Airlines" (1993), *Asian Business*, (August), 44-66.

Folkes, Valerie S., Susan Koletsky, and John L. Graham (1987), "A Field Study of Causal Inference and Consumer Reaction: The View From the Airport," *Journal of Consumer Research*, 13 (March), 534-39.

Fornell, Claes and W. T. Robinson (1983), "Industrial Organization and Consumer Satisfaction/Dissatisfaction," *Journal of Consumer Research*, 9, 403-12.

———— and Birger Wernerfelt (1987), "Defensive Marketing Strategy by Customer Complaint Management: A Theoretical Analysis," *Journal of Marketing Research*, 24 (November), 337-46.

Fournier, Susan, and Julie L. Yao (1997), "Reviving Brand Loyalty: A Reconceptualization Within the Framework of Consumer-Brand Relationships," *International Journal of Research in Marketing*, 14 (December), 451-72.

Ganesan, Shankar (1994), "Determinants of Long-Term Orientation in Buyer-Seller Relationships," *Journal of Marketing*, 58 (April), 1-19.

Gilbert, D. C. (1996), "Relationship Marketing and Airline Loyalty Schemes," *Tourism Management*, 17(8), 575-82.

Goodman, Paul S., Mark Fichman, F. Javier Lerch, and Pamela R. Snyder (1995), "Customer-Firm Relationships, Involvement, and Customer Satisfaction," *Academy of Management Journal*, 38(5), 1310-24.

Goodwin, Cathy and Ivan Ross (1992), "Consumer Responses to Service Failures: Influence of Procedural and Interactional Fairness Perceptions," *Journal of Business Research*, 25 (September), 149-63.

Gronhaug, Kjell and G. Zaltman (1981), "Complaint and Non-Complainers Revisited: Another Look at the Data," in *Advances in Consumer Research*, Vol. 8, Kent Monroe, ed. Ann Arbor, MI: Association for Consumer Research, 83-87.

Grönroos, Christian (1994), "From Marketing Mix to Relationship Marketing: Toward a Paradigm Shift in Marketing," *Management Decision*, 32(2), 4-20.

Gummesson, Evert (1987), "The New Marketing—Developing Long-Term Interactive Relationships," *Long Range Planning*, 20 (August), 10-20.

Hart, Christopher W. L., James L. Heskett, and Earl Sasser, Jr. (1990), "The Profitable Art of Service Recovery," *Harvard Business Review*, 68 (July-August), 148-56.

Hess, Ron, Shankar Ganesan, and Noreen Klein (1998), "Service Failures and Recovery: The Impact of Relationship Factors and Attributions on Customer Satisfaction," working paper, Pamplin School of Business, Virginia Tech, Blacksburg, VA.

Hu, Michael Y., Rex S. Toh, and Stephen Strand (1988), "Frequent-Flier Programs: Problems and Pitfalls," *Business Horizons*, 31 (July-August), 52-57.

Jacoby, Jacob and Robert W. Chestnut (1978), *Brand Loyalty: Measurement and Management*. New York: Wiley.

Kahn, Barbara E., Manohar U. Kalwani, and Donald G. Morrisson (1986), "Measuring Variety-Seeking and Reinforcement Behaviors Using Panel Data," *Journal of Marketing Research*, 23 (May), 89-100.

Keaveney, Susan M. (1995), "Customer Switching Behavior in Service Industries: An Exploratory Study," *Journal of Marketing*, 59 (April), 71-82.

Keller, Kevin Lane (1998), *Strategic Brand Management: Building, Measuring, and Managing Brand Equity*. Upper Saddle River, NJ: Prentice Hall.

Kelley, Scott W. and Mark A. Davis (1994), "Antecedents to Customer Expectations for Service Recovery," *Journal of the Academy of Marketing Science*, 22(1), 52-61.

————, K. Douglas Hoffman, and Mark A. Davis (1993), "A Typology of Retail Failures and Recoveries," *Journal of Retailing*, 69 (Winter), 429-52.

Maute, F. Manfred and Laurette Dubé (forthcoming), "Patterns of Emotional Responses and Behavioral Consequences of Dissatisfaction," *Journal of Applied Psychology*.

Morganosky, M. and M. Buckley (1986), "Complaint Behavior: Analysis by Demographics, Lifestyle and Consumer Values," in *Advances in Consumer Research*, Vol. 14, M. Wallendorf and J. Anderson, eds. Ann Arbor, MI: Association for Consumer Research, 223-26.

Morrisson, Steven A. and Clifford Winston (1989), "Enhancing the Performance of Deregulated Air Transportation System," *Brookings Papers on Economic Activity in Microeconomics*, 1, 66-112.

Mowlana, Hamid and Ginger Smith (1993), "Tourism in a Global Context: The Case of Frequent Traveler Programs," *Journal of Travel Research*, 31 (Winter), 20-27.

Moyer, M. (1984), "Characteristics of Consumer Complaints: Implications for Marketing and Public Policy," *Journal of Public Policy and Marketing*, 3, 67-84.

O'Brien, L. and C. Jones (1995), "Do Rewards Really Create Loyalty," *Harvard Business Review*, 73 (May-June), 75-82.

Reichheld, Frederick and W. E. Sasser, Jr. (1990), "Zero Defections: Quality Comes to Services," *Harvard Business Review*, 68 (September-October), 105-11.

Richins, Marsha L. (1983), "Negative Word-of-Mouth by Dissatisfied Customers: A Pilot Study," *Journal of Marketing*, 47 (Winter), 68-78.

Roos, Inger and Tore Strandvik (1996), "Diagnosing the Termination of Customer Relationships," working paper #335, Swedish School of Economics and Business Administration, Helsinki, Finland.

Rusbult, C. E. (1980), "Commitment and Satisfaction in Romantic Associations: A Test of the Investment Model," *Journal of Experimental Social Psychology*, 16, 172-86.

———, D. Ferrel, G. Rogers, and A. G. Mainous III (1988), "Impact of Exchange Variables on Exit, Voice, Loyalty and Neglect: An Integrative Model of Responses to Declining Job Satisfaction," *Academy of Management Journal*, 31, 599-627.

———, M. I. Zembrodt, and L. K. Gunn (1982), "Exit, Voice, Loyalty, and Neglect: Responses to Dissatisfaction in Romantic Involvement," *Journal of Personality and Social Psychology*, 43, 1230-42.

Rust, Roland T., Anthony J. Zahorik, and Timothy L. Keiningham (1995), "Return on Quality (ROQ): Making Service Quality Financially Accountable," *Journal of Marketing*, 59 (April), 58-70.

Sharp, Byron, and Anne Sharp (1997), "Loyalty Programs and Their Impact on Repeat-Purchase Loyalty Patterns," *International Journal of Research in Marketing*, 14 (December), 473-86.

Singh, Jagdip (1990), "A Typology of Consumer Dissatisfaction Response Styles," *Journal of Retailing*, 66(1), 57-99.

Smith, Rob (1998), "Can You Bribe Your Way to Customer Loyalty? Frequency Markting Strategies," presentation at the Strategic Research Institute Seminar on Relationship Marketing, New York, December.

Stephenson, Frederick J. and Richard J. Fox (1987), "Corporate Attitudes Toward Frequent-Flier Programs," *Transportation Journal*, 32 (Fall), 10-22.

Taylor, Shirley (1994), "Waiting for Service: The Relationship Between Delays and Evaluations of Service," *Journal of Marketing*, 58(2), 56-69.

Technical Assistance Research Programs (1978), *Consumer Problems, Consumer Complaints, and the Salience of Consumers' Advocacy Organizations: A Review of the Literature and Results of a National Survey.* Washington, DC: National Science Foundation.

Uncles, Mark, Andrew Ehrenberg, and Kathy Hammond (1995), "Patterns of Buyer Behavior: Regularities, Models, and Extensions," *Marketing Science*, 14 (Summer), 71-78.

Warland, Rex, R. Herrmann, and J. Willits (1975), "Dissatisfied Customers: Who Gets Upset and Who Takes Action," *Journal of Consumer Affairs*, 9 (Winter), 148-63.

Webster, Cynthia and D. S. Sundaram (1998), "Service Consumption Criticality in Failure Recovery," *Journal of Business Research*, 41 (February), 153-59.

24

Frequency Programs in Service Industries

JOHN DEIGHTON

Incentives for patronage have a long history in consumer service industries, dating back at least to stamp programs of the 18th century (Vredenburg 1956), but the development in the 1990s of technology to recognize individual customers and remember their transaction histories at the point of transaction has given them new importance. It may not be an exaggeration to describe loyalty programs as the linchpin of customer management in modern large-scale service providers. Certainly the number and variety have increased rapidly in recent years. A frequency marketing agency, in a listing that is by no means exhaustive, found 121 programs operating in the United States in such service industries as airlines, car rental agencies, catalog retailers, cruise lines, department stores, fitness clubs, gambling enterprises, grocery stores, hotels and resorts, restaurants, shopping malls, specialty retailers, telecommunications providers, and multisponsored programs (Barlow 1998).

Despite their widespread adoption, deficiencies and limitations are often observed (Dowling and Uncles 1997; East, Hogg, and Lomax 1998; Sharp and Sharp 1997). If implemented without subtlety, loyalty programs may raise the cost of doing business for all competitors in an industry, without commensurate benefit. They can create a weighty contingent liability. They are sometimes fairly accused of training customers to expect bribes in exchange for patronage. This chapter proposes a typology that clarifies why some programs are unsuccessful and others are very successful, indeed central to customer management.

TABLE 24.1 A Typology of Loyalty Program Types

	Benefits Are Fungible	Benefits Are Specific to the Relationship
Seller does not know buyer's identity	Trading stamp programs	Quantity discounts
Seller knows buyer's identity	Money-back programs	Privileges programs

WHAT IS A FREQUENCY PROGRAM, WHAT ARE ITS AIMS, AND HOW CAN IT WORK?

Terms like *relationship marketing programs*, *loyalty programs*, *continuity programs*, *frequency programs*, and *points programs* are often used interchangeably to mark out a set of marketing practices that are, with varying degrees of typicality, the topic of this chapter. I define the topic as contracting between buyers and sellers in which the buyer is offered incentives to give the seller more business over time than would have occurred without the contract; that is, to instill a patronage bias.

Absent such a bias, a seller of a frequently consumed service faces a probability on each transaction occasion that the buyer will patronize a competitor. The product of that probability and the total value of the patronage over some time horizon is the prize the buyer seeks. The seller designs and offers a contract that will increase the seller's share of the buyer's category requirements over the term of the contract, at a cost lower than the value of the share won. Practically, the increase shows up in one of only the following two ways:

- More is spent on each purchase occasion covered by the contract.
- Customers otherwise unserved are attracted by the contract.

How can such contracts possibly work? What contract can compensate the buyer for loss of freedom to transact in the marketplace while making the seller better off? That is the topic of this chapter. To address it I shall distinguish among programs on two dimensions, making use of the typology and representative program types shown in Table 24.1, differentiating programs by whether benefits are fungible or specific to the relationship, and whether the seller does or does not know the buyer's identity.

As Klemperer (1987) makes clear, one of a set of *ex ante* homogeneous services may, after the buyer chooses it, be rationally preferred if the seller introduces a frequency program that imposes a switching cost on the buyer by rewarding repeat purchases. What his argument does not explain is why all sellers do not introduce such programs *ex ante*, and, if they do, why the benefits are not thereby competed away. The argument here is that when the seller knows the identity of buyers, programs can be differentiated *ex ante* to retain the most valued customers by offering relationship-specific benefits.

FUNGIBLE BENEFITS WITHOUT IDENTITY

The most primitive kind of frequency program is one that rewards patronage with some cashlike fungible benefit, such as trading stamps, that can be exchanged for merchandise. Such a program is distinguished from a simple cash discount by only one feature—the discount has to be saved up until it reaches a threshold amount. It is during the saving period only that buyers may feel a patronage bias.

Trading stamp programs are essentially price-based, and ultimately zero-sum competitive. In both of the waves of popularity that they experienced in the United States, in the first and then in the fifth decades of the 20th century, it was the very success of the programs that ensured their abandonment (Fox 1968). Trading stamps, small gummed stickers given by retailers to shoppers as a reward for their patronage and issued in amounts in direct proportion to the value of a purchase, were saved to be redeemed for merchandise or cash at stores or redemption centers operated by the company that issued the stamps. It sold green stamps to retailers, who in turn gave them to customers, who could redeem them from the issuing company for merchandise advertised in catalogs. The cost of merchandise and program administration was recovered from payments by retailers, who expected that the price that they paid for the stamps would be returned to them in incremental business. Although trading stamp programs are currently out of vogue in the United States, the Air Miles program in Canada and the Fly Buys program in Australia, as well as ClickRewards on the Internet, are contemporary instances.

Such programs pay out for the consumer as long as the price premium (the price that the consumer pays to patronize a stamp-issuing service provider less the price of an identical service without the stamp), ΔP, is less than the sum of the exchange value of the trading stamp and the monetary value of any psychic reward obtained from collecting the stamps. For the service provider, payout is different depending on whether the customer would have transacted without the stamp or whether the stamp attracts incremental revenue. For the former, the program pays out if the margin "m" on the price premium, ΔP, is less than the cost of administering a stamp to the stamp issuer, C_t, which comprises mainly the purchase price of the stamp from the stamp vendor and the service provider's administration cost. For incremental business, the program pays out if the margin on the premium price, $m(P + \Delta P)$, exceeds C_t. Thus, if the proportion of incremental sales is η, the program survives if

$$C_t < m(\eta P + \Delta P).$$

No program with this structure has survived for long. For the participating vendors, incremental business and price premium both shrink as new vendors enter the program. For the buyer, the psychic rewards of collecting, which depend on network externalities that attend on the collecting buzz, begin to pale over time.

RELATIONSHIP-SPECIFIC BENEFITS
WITHOUT IDENTITY

A simple twist can transform the trading stamp principle into a scheme with the possibility of inducing a more durable patronage bias. The twist is to make the benefits redeemable only from the seller. Whereas stamps are a currency, a *general* asset, credits in a proprietary program are a *specific* asset having value only in the relationship. This property allows them to transform the industries in which they are employed by supplying a basis for building relationships.

An elementary example is a "fifth shoeshine free" offer. Before the first transaction, such a program induces no purchase bias over another vendor offering the same deal, nor over an offer at 20% lower price, which is the same price per shine. Once the buyer accepts the first shoeshine, lock-in occurs (Shapiro and Varian 1999). The buyer faces a switching cost in moving to another vendor because the free shine is a relationship-specific asset.

Why should buyers enter the lock-in trap? The answer may be that they have no choice; all firms of comparable service quality or scope may decline to offer single-serving products at the same per-serving price as the bundle. In the shoeshine example, firms must choose whether to sell shoeshines in bundles of five or compete for individual shoeshines at the lower per-shine price and the nonzero probability of defection on each purchase occasion. High-quality sellers favor bundles, and only low-quality vendors compete for customers with single servings at lower rates.

This equilibrium is the one observed in the airline, hotel, supermarket, and car rental industries.[1] All large airlines offer frequent flyer programs that are roughly equivalent to 20 flights for the price of 19, and they give no discount to buyers who elect not to accumulate toward the bundle. Small airlines offer lower prices. (They also offer frequent flyer programs, but claims on these programs are predictably low.) In the hotel, food retailing, and auto leasing industries, the same separation on quality and national scope is seen.

FUNGIBLE BENEFITS WITH IDENTITY

When a customer carries an identifier (a membership card, a driver's license, or even a thumbprint) and the service provider has a transaction database that can match the identity to personal history, programs can be designed that can confer an advantage on one or more service providers that cannot be competed away by emulation. How can this be?

When customers are anonymous, vendors must make the same offer (or menu of offers) to all comers, so they reveal their offers to competitors, who can copy or undercut. When customers have identity, then by their responses to the vendor's offers they give evidence of their value to the vendor. The vendor is then able to select customers whose distinctive needs so align with the offering of the service provider that both customer and vendor can do business on more attractive terms with each other than they can with other potential marketplace partners. Furthermore, the offers need not be visible to competitors, making possible what some vendors call "stealth marketing."

Woolf (1996) catalogs the kinds of customized offers that have become routine in the frequent shopper programs of U.S. supermarkets. First, these programs use a "special price for members" offer, posted on store shelves and in flyers, to give a broadly visible incentive to shoppers to join the programs and reveal their identities to the stores. Armed with shopper identities and purchase histories, program administrators then identify the top 30% of shoppers in a month and target incremental benefits of membership to this group. For example, stretch goals can be set, based on the previous month's spending, to reward shoppers for increasing their spending per visit or per month. Points can be awarded, in the manner of trading stamps but with the differential feature that specific kinds of shoppers receive incentives for specific changes in shopping behavior. Dreze and Hoch (1998) describe the profitable operation of a retail program that rewarded patrons of its baby care aisles for increased share of requirements.

Do identity programs cover their costs? They have a source of revenue not available to programs in which members are anonymous. Because shoppers using particular brands can be defined, access to these names can be sold to manufacturers of competing brands who can use the programs to deliver invitations to try the competitor. This use of the programs as communication media is so lucrative to the retailers that it is often the source of the funds to run the component of the programs that benefits the stores.

These programs raise the cost of promiscuity for buyers. A traveler who patronizes several airlines or a shopper who uses several food stores forgoes the top tier of program benefits. Although this "reward for loyalty" feature is also a property of programs without identity, the identity programs have one advantage. As we have noted, a consumer can make a rational choice whether to lock in to a "fifth shoeshine free" program or preserve options by patronizing a cheaper supplier. The terms of the trade are manifest. The rewards of an identity program are seldom clear in advance. A customer must reveal his or her value to the vendor before the vendor constructs a particular set of benefits of membership.

RELATIONSHIP-SPECIFIC BENEFITS WITH IDENTITY

Sellers whose identity programs allow them to identify high-value customers can offer a range of nonprice benefits. The general characteristic of these benefits is that they improve the quality of the service experience, rather than lowering its cost. They operate like fungible benefits to create specific assets that deter switching, but they can be designed to have two additional properties.

First, they can be designed to be more attractive to heavy users of the service than light users. For example, airline upgrades and access to private lounges can be more attractive to those who fly often, by interrupting the compounding effects of fatigue and supporting the formation of on-the-road work habits. Heavy users of some credit cards (Diners Club and American Express are examples) receive annual analyses of their expenditures. Such benefits make frequency programs self-segmenting: They are attractive to heavy or exclusive users of the service without being resented by light or non-exclusive users.

Second, many nonprice benefits can be offered without cost to the seller. They can be created from service elements that would otherwise go wasted, and therefore have negligible incremental cost to the seller but significant value to the buyer. Thus, top-tier hotel and car rental customers get upgrades, subject to availability. Cruise ship patrons dine at the captain's table. Airline program members are allowed to board planes earlier.

Another benefit of membership in an identity program, whether intended by the seller or not, is that the buyer has bargaining power in the relationship. The seller knows the value of the buyer, and the buyer knows that the seller knows it. This empowerment of buyers, however, appears not to deter sellers from offering identity programs. Indeed, sellers can preempt the sense of entitlement that a buyer feels when the buyer's value in the relationship is an acknowledged fact of the relationship, by offering differentiated complaint handling procedures or more generous warranties. In general, a little identity in a mass-marketed service encounter seems to benefit both parties.

CONCLUSION

This chapter set out to review designs for programs that create incentives for patronage and answer the question of whether such programs are merely transitory promotional novelties or can be sustainable features of a service industry structure. Four kinds of program are distinguished. Only one, the "trading stamp" program, is unsustainable. It confers an advantage to early adopters, provided that it invests in self-promotion to induce a collecting fad, but the advantages are easily competed away by later entrants.

When the rewards for patronage are paid out in a manner that creates a specific asset in the relationship, then the program induces a sustainable, cost-effective bias toward patronage of the offering firm, one that survives in the face of emulation. This patronage bias is stronger if the buyer of the service has identity in the relationship and if the rewards for patronage take the form not of price reductions but of service enhancements that are valued more highly by heavy users of the service and take the form of service elements that have zero (or low) marginal cost to the seller.

NOTE

1. All these industries in fact offer programs that fall into the next category: relationship-specific benefits with identity. The contention is, however, that the same separation of sellers into high- and low-quality tiers would occur if the benefits were price discounts for quantity purchases.

REFERENCES

Barlow, Richard (1998), "From Evolution to Revolution: The Roots of Fequency Marketing," *Colloquy*, 6(4).

Dowling, Grahame R. and Mark Uncles (1997), "Do Customer Loyalty Programs Really Work?" *Sloan Management Review*, 38 (Summer), 71-82.

Dreze, Xavier and Stephen J. Hoch (1998), "Exploiting the Installed Base Using Cross-Merchandising and Category Destination Programs," *International Journal of Research in Marketing*, 15, 1-13.

East, Robert, Annik Hogg, and Wendy Lomax (1998), "The Future of Loyalty Schemes," *Journal of Targeting, Measurement and Analysis for Marketing*, 7(1), 11-21.

Fox, Harold W. (1968), *The Economics of Trading Stamps*. Washington, DC: Public Affairs Press.

Klemperer, Paul (1987), "Markets With Consumer Switching Costs," *The Quarterly Journal of Economics*, 102 (May), 375-94.

Shapiro, Carl and Hal R. Varian (1998), *Information Rules*. Boston: Harvard Business School Press.

Sharp, Byron and Anne Sharp (1997), "Loyalty Programs and Their Impact on Repeat Purchase Loyalty Patterns," *International Journal of Research in Marketing*, 14, 473-86.

Vredenburg, Harvey L. (1956), "Trading Stamps," Indiana Business Report Number 21, Indiana University.

Woolf, Brian P. (1996), *Customer Specific Marketing*. Greenville, SC: Teal Books.

25

Smart Services

Competitive Advantage Through Information-Intensive Strategies

RASHI GLAZER

It is now quite clear that the long-awaited, but often postponed, "information age" is now a reality. Among the most profound implications of the information revolution for business is the emergence of smart markets, that is, markets defined by frequent turnover in the general stock of knowledge or information embodied in products or services and possessed by competitors and consumers. In contrast to traditional "dumb" markets, which are static, fixed, and basically information poor, smart markets are dynamic, turbulent, and information rich. Smart markets are based on

1. "smart products," on one hand, products and services that have intelligence or computational ability built into them (an obvious example being microprocessors), but, more generally and more important, any offering that adapts or responds to changes in the environment as it interacts with (or is used by) consumers;

2. "smart competitors," competitors who, from the standpoint of the firm, are either changing or about whom the firm continually needs to update its information; and

3. "smart customers," customers who, from the standpoint of the firm, are either changing or about whom the firm continually needs to update its information.

"Smart firms," organizations that have tried to sustain a competitive advantage in the face of the challenges raised by smart markets, have done so largely through their information technology (IT) infrastructure, and it is by now taken for granted that IT is transforming the nature of business practice. The experiences of firms as diverse as American Airlines, USAA Insurance, Federal Express, and pharmaceutical wholesaler McKesson—each of which has altered the dynamics of its industry and changed the requirements for competitive success—are among the most notable and well-publicized business stories in recent years.

In almost all cases, the firms involved, like most organizations, first put in place an IT infrastructure to solve the "bandwidth problem," thus enabling dramatic increases in channel capacity (the speed with which information is transmitted and the amount of information that can be processed). What has distinguished those firms that have gained a significant competitive advantage is that, once having introduced an IT infrastructure, they have then gone beyond the technology to view the information itself as the core asset or carrier of value and the management of information as the primary focus of their attention. In so doing, they have been pioneers in the development and execution of what have come to be called *smart services*, rooted in "information-intensive" strategies (Blattberg, Glazer, and Little 1994; Glazer 1991, 1993; Porter and Millar 1985).

Information-intensive strategies represent an appropriate evolutionary response to the emergence of information-intensive or "smart" markets. Although all individual business functions and the discipline of strategy itself are being reshaped by both the need and the ability to incorporate higher levels of information processing into their activities, many of the most important developments are in the area of marketing—typically the activity (if not formal organizational function) charged with managing the relationships between the firm and its customers. This chapter briefly outlines some of the implications for service firms competing in smart markets with respect to an emerging reconceptualization of corporate assets and performance measures, strategic and tactical/programmatic decision making, and organizational structure.

To begin, we can identify two key consequences of the "information-intensive" environment in which the firm of the future will compete. First is the appearance of what may be accurately described as a new stage in the history of market development—that of "differentiated offerings in decentralized markets" (Blattberg, Glazer, and Little 1994). This is replacing the current era—that of "differentiated offerings in centralized markets"—in which the identification of differences in buyers' tastes gave rise to "brand" competition and target marketing based on segmentation and positioning. By contrast, the new phase is characterized by the abilities to identify individual buyers (who continually provide information about their preferences) and then develop and deliver specific products and services to them.

Second is the widespread breaking down of boundaries where there once were well-defined roles or discrete categories. Boundaries between products are breaking down, in particular, the boundary between products and services. The boundaries between the firm and the external world are breaking down: between the firm and its customers, as customers participate in the design of their own products and communications becomes more interactive and two-way; and between the firm and its competitors, as firms realize they need to form partnerships to put in place the infrastructure necessary for the sale of their own products. Within the firm, boundaries between departments are breaking down, because no department or area has all the information necessary (and the flow of information between departments is not fast enough) to respond to customer requests before the competition does.

In such an environment, there are four defining characteristics of the service business:

1. The *firm itself is information intensive*. This claim means that the firm's offerings are based on the information collected and processed as part of exchanges along the value chain. Whereas traditional products are static, information-intensive services and their associated operations change as new data from the environment becomes incorporated into them. In such a world, information—particularly customer or market information—is seen as the key corporate asset.

2. The firm operates in what might be called a *sense and respond* (as opposed to "make and sell"; Haeckel 1994) mode; that is, it views its mission as the ability to identify and ultimately anticipate customer needs and satisfy customer requests as quickly as possible.

3. The firm focuses on—and believes its value added resides in—processes and people ("the way we do things around here") as opposed to things.

4. The firm sees itself, and not its specific services, as the real carrier of value. As technology becomes the great neutralizer and as life cycles shrink, customer buying behavior evolves from being based on the product/service, through the expanded "offering" (i.e., the rest of the marketing mix), and ultimately on the firm itself.

THE NEW CORPORATE ASSETS: CUSTOMERS AND CUSTOMER INFORMATION

Customers as corporate assets: This is not as obvious as it seems on the surface and has a number of important implications. Most service firms traditionally have paid lip service to the notion that "customers are our most important asset." A careful analysis of the actual businesses of these organizations, however, would reveal that they have done everything possible to avoid having to deal with customers! Indeed, the "holy grail" of service industries in the 20th century has been the standardization of the service offering in the pursuit of economies of scale and more general cost-saving efficiencies.

Identifying the customer as an asset means that the focus of attention shifts away from offerings per se and that the customer, and not the product, is viewed as the real generator of wealth for the company. The source of competitive advantage is seen less in terms of having unique or superior products and more with respect to having special *relationships* with customers. Consequently, both performance measures and organizational structure become aligned around customers as opposed to particular products or services.

Customer information is collected and processed as part of every customer transaction and stored in the customer information file (CIF). In many respects, as a practical matter, this is what it means for the customer to be the asset, because

Low .... Transaction Dependent .... High

Customer Characteristics				Response to Firm Decisions				Purchase History				
C_{11}	C_{12}	C_{13}	...	R_{11}	R_{12}	R_{13}	...	P_{11}	P_{12}	P_{13}	...	$P_{1t}{}^*$
C_{21}	C_{22}	C_{23}	...	R_{21}	R_{22}	R_{23}	...	P_{21}	P_{22}	P_{23}	...	$P_{2t}{}^*$
C_{31}	C_{32}	C_{33}	...	R_{31}	R_{32}	R_{33}	...	P_{31}	P_{32}	P_{33}	...	$P_{3t}{}^*$
...				...				...				
Who they are				What, when, where, how, and why they buy				What they bought, cost of products sold, profit				
C_{i1}	C_{i2}	C_{i3}		R_{i1}	R_{i2}	R_{i3}		P_{i1}	P_{i2}	P_{i3}		$P_{it}{}^*$
												$\Sigma P_{it}{}^*$

Figure 25.1 The Customer Information File

the foundation of "relationship marketing" is continual communication, and therefore information exchanged, between the firm and its customers.

The CIF can be thought of as a single "virtual" database that captures all relevant information about a firm's customers. The database is described as "virtual" because, although operating as though it were an integrated single source housed in one location, it may in reality comprise several isolated databases stored in separate places throughout an organization.

As noted in Figure 25.1, the rows (or records) of the CIF are individual customers—both actual and potential—and not segments. The columns are data that have been collected about customers. At least conceptually, these can be organized into three categories:

C: *Customer characteristics:* typically (though not exclusively) composed of "demographic" data, this is information about customers ("who they are") that is independent of the firm's relationship with the customer.

R: *Response to firm decisions:* perception and preference (e.g., product attribute importance weights) and other marketing-mix response data (price sensitivity, sources of information, channel shopping behavior); this is information about customers ("what, when, where, how, and why they buy") that is based on some (perhaps limited) level of interaction between the firm and its customers.

P: *Purchase history:* data on what products customers have purchased, as well as the revenues and costs, and thus profits, associated with these purchases; this is information that is based on the firm's actual transactions with its customers.

Performance Measures

Figure 25.1 contains one additional column of information in the CIF (at the far right), labeled as P^*. If P_{it} is the actual profit realized from customer i in period t, then P^*_{it} is the potential profit that could have been realized from customer i had the firm made the optimum use of its information assets. $P^* - P$ thus represents forgone or unrealized profits. The new objective function of the firm is to minimize $(P^* - P)$ across all customers in all periods, or, equivalently, to maximize ΣP^*_{it}—the value of the CIF. (If one is serious about the CIF's role as the key corporate asset, then this may also be a measure of the value of the firm!)

Suggesting that the firm sets as its overall performance objective maximizing the returns to the CIF means that notions such as profitability or market share per product are being replaced with concepts such as profitability per customer, increasingly referred to LTV ("Lifetime Value of Customer"; that is, total profits generated from a given customer over his or her "life") or "Customer Share" (the total share of a customer's purchases in a broadly defined product category, such as VISA's "share of wallet" or "share of personal consumption expenditures"). To the degree that LTV or "Customer Share" measures are inherently difficult to operationalize, "intermediate" metrics such as customer satisfaction are emerging as important surrogates or leading indicators, in the sense that they are predictive.

Perhaps one of the most challenging tasks facing the information-intensive service firm, and proof of the extent to which it is serious about the required transformation in perspective, is the integration of these new measures of performance into the organization's traditional accounting system. At one level, for example, few organizations actually know the costs associated with having sold a service to an *individual customer* and thus are unable in practice to identify the respective profits. More generally, because the typical firm's real assets are still seen to be its products or services and the facilities and operations used to support them, this is reflected in the product (or brand) management organizational structure; that is, where profit and loss responsibility is defined with respect to a set of products.

Information-Intensive Strategies

Observations of the activities of firms that have taken the lead in trying to exploit the information in the CIF for competitive advantage have resulted in an emergent picture of information-intensive decision making at both the strategic and tactical or marketing-mix programmatic levels. The goal is to develop a "taxonomy" or categorization scheme of "generic" strategies (notable because of the degree to which they have been replicated across a variety of seemingly different situations) that can be used to compare and contrast them. The result is a preliminary "theory" of information-intensive strategy, paralleling the more traditional strategic framework that has guided management practice in typical "dumb" markets (Glazer 1999):

1. "Mass customization" (Pine 1992): being able to tailor individual offerings to customers without additional costs (getting the best of both worlds between the traditional generic strategies of mass production and niche or target marketing). Mass customization takes advantage of developments in both flexible operations and flexible marketing methods.

2. "Yield management": maximizing the total return to a fixed asset through price discrimination by capitalizing on differential customer price sensitivity (particularly with respect to time). Yield management is used primarily in industries where there are high initial fixed costs but very low variable costs.

3. "Capture the customer": also known as one-to-one marketing, affinity marketing, customer intimacy, event-oriented prospecting, and cross-selling. The ultimate objective is to realize as high a share as possible of a customer's total (lifetime) purchases in a given (often expanding) set of categories.

4. "Virtual company/extended organization": taking on the value-added activities of a firm's partners in the supply chain through integrated database management, in effect dissolving the functional boundaries between the two (technically distinct) organizations.

5. "Manage by wire" (Haeckel and Nolan 1993): developing an "informational representation" of the way the firm makes decisions (of "how we do things around here"), thus allowing the organization to automate the increasing level of interactions with customers that are the keys to competitive success. "Manage by wire" strategies draw on the CIF and other databases, as well as a set of appropriate "expert systems" and other decision tools, with the goal of modeling the enterprise and "committing to code" as much as possible the procedures that form the basis of managerial decision making.

Above and beyond the implementation of any (or several) specific information-intensive strategies, smart service organizations are beginning to recognize that the process of strategic planning itself is undergoing a profound transformation. As the service company of the future begins to operate in the sense-and-respond mode described above, the traditional activities associated with the preparation of market plans (identification of customer needs, design of marketing strategies, etc.) should assume even more importance. At the same time, in keeping with the sense-and-respond mode of operation, market planning and the resulting strategies must be increasingly flexible and adaptable. A plan must be seen less as an exercise in constructing a blueprint or road map (in which every possible future outcome is listed and prepared for in detail) and more as an exercise in pattern recognition, in which general outlines or contingencies are identified and appropriate response mechanisms are put in place. The notion of being able to anticipate customer requirements and respond before the competition replaces "strategic focus" as the guiding principle in the service company of the future.

Furthermore, because information-intensive markets are increasingly turbulent and dynamic, the "shelf life" of any particular market plan is getting shorter and shorter. This does not mean that the planning process is less important (in fact, the converse is true), but it does require that planning become a "real-time" process and that the output—the plan itself—become a living document that can be updated continually as new information is made available. The incorporation of information technology into the market planning process and the creation of "electronic plans" can play an important role in this regard.

Information-Intensive Programs and Tactics

Product decisions, given mass customization, will increasingly involve "systems integration." Systems integrators are firms with the ability to help customers design the best offering for their particular needs from a wide range of technically feasible options that may be provided by suppliers from different organizations (including a firm's competitors). Systems integration is based on the assembly of "modular" components into the best-fitting package for a customer.

Pricing, which is increasingly value based (as opposed to being based on cost or rate of return), will require more precise understanding of customer preferences, particularly regarding preferences for flat-rate vs. usage-sensitive offerings. Furthermore, smart pricing strategies are likely to include "yield management" techniques, such as flexible pricing schedules, which are based on customizing prices in response to heterogeneous customer needs while maximizing the total return to a service "network" at a given point in time. The use of negotiations and auctions (particularly for services with high-fixed-cost infrastructures that have capacity constraints at given points in time) is also likely to be a prominent feature of the pricing environment.

Advertising and promotion will be affected as qualities of interactivity, addressability, and two-way communications replace one-way mass "broadcasting" as the key attributes. On one hand, for the smart service company of the future, communications activities and expenditures are likely to increase if the company is serious about the notion of the customer as an asset and relationship marketing; on the other, efficiencies through target advertising and one-to-one promotions should be realized. Branding should move increasingly to the product family and corporate levels, which is where equity with customers will be established. Beyond this, however, there is a need for strong integration across the communications mix and the different communications activities, particularly coordination so that the company presents a coherent voice and position to its constituencies.

Distribution, or more accurately, channels of distribution, will require greater flexibility with respect to the use of channels. On one hand, there is potential for an expanded role for outside channels; on the other, there is potential for disintermediation (elimination of current channels) as a result of electronic business. At the same time, the key challenges will be how to minimize channel conflicts and how to stay close to the customer and maintain the relationship with the customer even though the outside channel is physically closer to the customer. Information-intensive strategies call attention to the key question of who, along the value-chain, "controls the customer."

Customer service is emerging as one of the most important marketing-mix elements and perhaps the only one that can be the basis for a sustainable competitive advantage. For the service company of the future, it is critical that customer service be tightly integrated with other product management functions.

THE NEW "4 Cs" OF MARKETING

For at least a generation, strategy, once formulated, has been implemented through a set of marketing-mix decisions characteristically described as the "4 Ps": product, price, place (channels of distribution), and promotion. As service companies become more information intensive along the lines discussed above, the "product" component of the marketing mix becomes less a source of differentiation and competitive advantage. The other marketing-mix elements become more important, and managers will have more discretion with respect to the nonproduct marketing-mix elements. Beyond this, however, one of the implications of the emerging information-intensive strategic framework is that the boundaries between these decisions are rapidly dissolving (Glazer 1991), and it is no longer clear where, say, the product "begins" and its "place" or "promotion" ends. Increasingly, what is being "offered" to customers is a set of integrated "bundled" marketing-mix components.

At the same time, it is important to recognize that the traditional strategies and the associated "4 Ps" tend to be functionally oriented and oriented to output. In contrast, information-intensive strategies and their associated decisions are process oriented. In this respect, it may be useful to characterize the set of information-intensive strategies and tactics (when taken as a group) by what may be termed the "new 4 Cs" of marketing:

1. communication: a continual series of dialogues or "conversations" with customers, the goal of which is to get the customer to see the firm as a partner for the particular aspects of his or her life represented by the firm's products and services;

2. customization: tailoring individual offerings (both products and communications messages) from a generic "platform" based on an understanding of the customer's particular needs or behaviors, the goal of which is to create the perception (if not the reality) on the part of the customer that the firm sees him or her as a unique and therefore valued individual;

3. collaboration: an extension of customization that engages the customer in the actual design and delivery of a product offering (e.g., by giving a menu of options from which the customer chooses), the goal of which is to enlist the customer's *participation* in the production process, thus breaking down the boundary between firm and consumer; and

4. clairvoyance: "reading the customer's mind" or *anticipating* his or her needs regarding the firm's product and services, (e.g., by being proactive with certain offerings and communication interventions based on understanding the customer's lifestyle and behaviors), the goal of which is to conserve perhaps the most valuable of all customer resources in the information age: attention (Simon 1972).

SMART SERVICES
ORGANIZATIONAL STRUCTURE

Although it is difficult to predict exactly what the structure of the smart service organization will look like, it is becoming clear that departments (and the company as a whole) will be less hierarchical and more decentralized, with fewer layers coming between customers and the places in the organization where decisions actually are made. It is also clear that the primary goals of any new structure will be to ensure that information flows quickly and effortlessly to where it is needed and that individual managers will be empowered to act on the information quickly and effortlessly; that is, to make decisions. With these goals in mind, it is quite likely that the structure ultimately will revolve around three key components: customer managers, customer teams, and a market learning center.

Customer Managers

In keeping with a shift in focus away from the product and toward the customer as the key asset or source of wealth generation, the service company of the future is likely to be organized around customer managers rather than product managers. The customer manager (CM) will have bottom-line profit and loss responsibility for a set of customer targets; that is, he or she will be charged with developing and delivering a set of offerings to chosen customers. Consistent with this responsibility, the CM will develop "customer plans" that specify the specific strategic objectives to be achieved with respect to designated customer targets and will act as a team leader who coordinates the activities of a variety of marketing-mix professionals or "specialists" (in pricing, advertising, forecasting, etc.) that will be necessary to implement the customer plans.

Customer Teams

Customer teams will be task focused and "fluid"; that is, they will come together on an as-needed basis long enough to accomplish the specific task at hand and then disband (the members will go on to join other teams). Among the most important characteristics of the teams and their information-processing style will be that all members will have access to all information; that is, the current structure whereby information/knowledge is "stored" in separate locations (and therefore "owned" by different functions) will be replaced by "distributed" storage. Information processing will be conducted "in parallel" rather than in the linear sequential form (R&D to Operations to Marketing to Sales) that it is today.

Market Learning Center

The market learning center (MLC) represents the evolution of the traditional marketing research/information and competitive analysis functions. The use of the word "learning" is designed to highlight the fact that, ultimately, the defining characteristic of the information-intensive service company of the future is its capacity for continual learning about its environment. This means that the organization takes in new information and adapts its behavior quickly in response to that new information. Although the MLC will carry out the typical tasks associated with marketing research and competitive intelligence, it differs from the current structure in that it is organized around learning processes, such as information acquisition (through subprocesses such as active scanning, continuous experimentation, and guided inquiries); information distribution, and accessing institutional memories. To the extent that there are separate "departments" or groups within the MLC, they are based on these processes (e.g., a "department" of information acquisition).

Consistent with their role in the service company of the future, managers will need an expanded set of skills beyond the traditional ones associated with being able to develop and execute business. Of course, these "technical" competencies will continue to grow in importance, and individuals will need to update their skills in these areas periodically as new concepts and specific tools are developed. More than anything else, however, just as the defining characteristic of the company as a whole will be its capacity for continuous learning, so too will each manager's job be defined in terms of his or her role as a learner, constantly acquiring new knowledge and changing behavior as a result of what has been acquired. In this sense, the real skill that must be learned is how to be a lifelong learner.

REFERENCES

Blattberg, Robert C. and John Deighton (1991), "Interactive Marketing: Exploiting the Age of Addressability," *Sloan Management Review*, 5-14.

————— and Rashi Glazer (1994), "Marketing in the Information Revolution," in *The Marketing Information Revolution*, Robert C. Blattberg, Rashi Glazer, and John D.C. Little, eds. Boston: Harvard Business School Press, 1-20.

—————, Rashi Glazer, and John D. C. Little, eds. (1994), *The Marketing Information Revolution*. Boston: Harvard Business School Press.

Glazer, Rashi (1991), "Marketing in Information-Intensive Environments: Strategic Implications of Knowledge as an Asset," *Journal of Marketing*, 55, 1-19.

————— (1993), "Measuring the Value of Information: The Information-Intensive Organization," *IBM Systems Journal*, 32, 99-110.

————— (1999), "Winning in Smart Markets," *Sloan Management Review*, 40(4), 59-69.

Haeckel, Stephan (1994), "Managing the Information-Intensive Firm of 2001," in *The Marketing Information Revolution*, Robert C. Blattberg, Rashi Glazer, and John D. C. Little, eds. Boston: Harvard Business School Press, 3-12.

————— and Richard L. Nolan (1993), "Managing by Wire," *Harvard Business Review*, 71(5), 122-32.

Pine, Joseph B., II (1992), *Mass Customization*. Boston: Harvard Business School Press.

Porter, Michael E. and Victor E. Millar (1985), "How Information Technology Gives You Competitive Advantage," *Harvard Business Review*, 85(4), 149-60.

Simon, Herbert A. (1972), "Theories of Bounded Rationality," in *Decision and Organization*, C. B. Radner and R. Radner, eds. Amsterdam: North-Holland, 20-40.

SECTION **VI**

Services: The Firm

26

Functional Integration in Services

Understanding the Links Between Marketing, Operations, and Human Resources

CHRISTOPHER LOVELOCK

What are the keys to success in service businesses, especially for those operating in highly competitive environments? A number of themes run through service management, including the following:

1. the notion of service as time-bound—often with real-time performance—comprising both a core product and an array of supplementary services, many of which are delivered to the customer by service personnel;

2. the importance of understanding, coordinating, and managing the often complex operational processes that underlie creation and delivery of different types of services;

3. the need to ensure that customers understand the roles that they must play in participating in these service processes (roles that vary according to the degree of contact involved and range from active coproduction of the service to passive receipt);

4. recognition of the contribution made to customer satisfaction and relationship building by competent, personable service employees, especially in high-contact service environments;

5. the desirability of managing contacts between employees and customers so that they may be mutually satisfying for both parties;

6. the need for organizations to balance corporate concerns relating to operational productivity against those relating to high service quality, as perceived and desired by customers; and

7. the burgeoning role of technology as a factor in reshaping both the nature of services and the manner and speed with which they are delivered to customers.

Taken jointly, these themes indicate that customers are closely involved in the creation and delivery of many services, sometimes to the extent of actually participating in production. Customers' satisfaction with a service may be conditioned as much by the processes in which they are involved—including interactions with operating systems, service employees, and even other customers—as by the outcome of those processes. This means that unlike the situation that often prevails in manufacturing (especially in the production of consumer packaged goods), the marketing function in services cannot easily be separated from other management activities without damage to the latter's effectiveness. After all, any action involving or affecting customers has marketing implications.

Evert Gummesson (1979) has long emphasized that the work of the traditional marketing department embraces only a small portion of the overall marketing function in a service business—a point also stressed by Christian Grönroos (1990, pp. 175-78). More recently, Gummesson (1994) notes the move to *network organizations* and what is sometimes called the *virtual corporation*, in which functional boundaries are fuzzy around a core competence and relationships are highly flexible.

CHANGING RELATIONSHIPS AMONG MARKETING, OPERATIONS, AND HUMAN RESOURCES

One of the challenges facing senior managers in any type of organization is to avoid what are sometimes referred to as "functional silos" in which each function exists in isolation from the others, jealously guarding its independence. Functionalism based on specialization in specific task areas represents a long tradition in business. As the list of service management challenges presented earlier suggests, however, the three functions of marketing, operations, and human resources need to work closely together if a service organization is to be responsive to its different stakeholders. In short, compartmentalizing management functions or subjugating one function to another is not an appropriate way to organize a modern service firm.

Using the concept of what they call the service profit chain, Heskett et al. (1994) lay out a series of causal links in achieving success in service businesses. These links are summarized in Table 26.1.

In a subsequent book, Heskett, Sasser, and Schlesinger (1997, pp. 236-51) cite several leadership behaviors that are critical to managing the different links in the service profit chain. Some behaviors relate to employees (links 4-7) and include spending time on the front line, investing in the development of promising

TABLE 26.1 Causal Links in the Service Profit Chain

1. Customer loyalty drives profitability and growth
2. Customer satisfaction drives customer loyalty
3. Value drives customer satisfaction
4. Employee productivity drives value
5. Employee loyalty drives productivity
6. Employee satisfaction drives loyalty
7. Internal quality drives employee satisfaction
8. Top management leadership underlies the chain's success

Source: Heskett et al. (1994).

managers, and supporting the design of jobs that offer greater latitude for employees; also included in this category is promoting the notion that paying higher wages actually reduces labor costs after reduced turnover, higher productivity, and higher quality are taken into account. Another set of service leadership behaviors focuses on customers (links 1-3) and includes an emphasis on identifying and understanding customer needs, investments to ensure customer retention, and a commitment to adopting new performance measures that track such variables as satisfaction and loyalty among both customers and employees.

These themes and relationships illustrate the mutual dependency that exists among marketing, operations, and human resources (see Figure 26.1). Although managers within each function may have specific responsibilities, strategic planning and the execution of specific tasks must be well coordinated. Responsibility for the tasks assigned to each function may be present entirely within one firm or distributed between the originating service organization and its subcontractors, who must work in close partnership if the desired results are to be achieved. Although other functions, such as accounting or finance, are central to the effective functioning of a service business, they present less need for close integration because of their lesser involvement in the ongoing processes of service creation and delivery. Now, let's review the role of marketing, operations, and human resources to see how each relates to broader strategic concerns.

The Marketing Function

Production and consumption are usually clearly separated in manufacturing firms. In most instances, a physical good is produced in a factory in one geographic location, shipped to a retailer or other intermediary for sale in a different location, and consumed or used by the customer in a third location. As a result, it is not normally necessary for production personnel to have direct involvement with customers, especially for consumer goods. In such firms, marketing acts to link producers and consumers, providing the manufacturing division with guidelines for product specifications that reflect consumer needs, as well as projections of market demand, information on competitive activity, and feedback on performance in the marketplace. In this linking role, marketing also

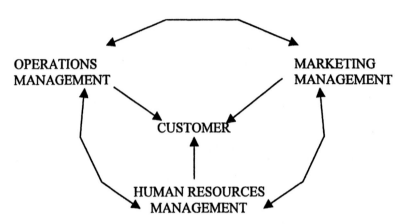

Figure 26.1 The Service Management Trinity

works with logistics and transportation specialists to develop strategies for distributing the product to prospective purchasers.

In service firms, things are different. Many service operations—especially those involved in delivering services that require the customer's presence throughout service delivery—are literally "factories in the field," which customers enter at the specific time that they need the service. In a large chain (such as hotels, fast food restaurants, or car rental agencies), the company's service delivery sites may be located across a country, a continent, or even the entire world. When customers are actively involved in production and the service output is consumed as it is produced, there has to be direct contact between production (operations) and consumers. This contact can take place in either a physical location or through telecommunications. In some instances, there is no contact with personnel, because customers are expected to serve themselves independently or communicate through more impersonal media such as mail, fax, or websites.

How should marketing relate to operations and human resources in those service environments where production and consumption take place simultaneously? In manufacturing firms, marketers assume full responsibility for the product once it leaves the production line, but in services, contact between operations personnel and customers is the rule rather than the exception, although the extent of this contact varies according to the nature of the service. In many instances, operations management is responsible for running service distribution systems, including retail outlets. None of this reduces the need for a strong, efficient marketing organization to perform the following tasks:

1. evaluate and select the market segments to serve;
2. research customer needs and preferences within each segment;
3. monitor competitive offerings, identifying their principal characteristics, their quality levels, and the strategies used to bring them to market;
4. design the core product, tailor its characteristics to the needs of chosen market segments, and ensure that they match or exceed those of competitive offerings;

5. select and establish service levels for supplementary elements needed to enhance the value and appeal of the core product or to facilitate its purchase and use;

6. participate in designing the entire service process to ensure that it is "user friendly" and reflects customer needs and preferences;

7. set prices that reflect costs, competitive strategies, and consumer sensitivity to different price levels;

8. tailor location and scheduling of service availability to customers' needs and preferences;

9. develop communications strategies, using appropriate media to transmit messages informing prospective customers about the service and promoting its advantages;

10. develop performance standards for establishing and measuring service quality levels;

11. create programs for rewarding and reinforcing customer loyalty; and

12. conduct research to evaluate customer satisfaction following service delivery and identify any aspects requiring changes or improvements.

The net result of these requirements is that the marketing function in service businesses is closely interrelated with, and dependent upon, the procedures, personnel, and facilities managed by the operations function. To a greater degree than in manufacturing, marketing, operations, and human resources must work together on a day-to-day basis. Although initially seen as a poor sister by many operations managers, marketing has now acquired significant management clout in many service businesses, with important implications for organizational design and assignment of responsibilities.

The Operations Function

Although the profile of marketing has risen, the operations function still dominates line management in most service businesses. This is hardly surprising, because operations—typically the largest department—creates and delivers the service product. Operations managers are responsible not only for equipment and backstage procedures but also for company-owned retail outlets and other customer facilities. In high-contact services, operations managers may direct the work of large numbers of employees, including many who serve customers directly. In technology-driven firms, operations managers take primary responsibility for the technological infrastructure and interface with research and development specialists to design and introduce innovative delivery systems.

In many firms, most operations managers have been with the organization longer than their marketing colleagues and believe that they understand it better. There is growing recognition, however, of the contributions that marketers can make, not least in understanding customer motivations and habits, identifying opportunities for new product development and entry into new markets, telling customers and prospects about the product, and creating strategies to build customer loyalty in highly competitive environments. Even operations managers who feel that marketing should not become directly involved in line management recognize that marketing specialists can provide useful inputs to service design.

The Human Resources Function

Few service organizations are so technologically advanced that they can be operated without employees. Indeed, many service industries remain highly labor intensive. People are needed for operational tasks (either frontstage or backstage), to perform a wide array of marketing tasks, and for administrative support.

Human resources emerged as a coherent management function during the 1980s. Historically, responsibility for matters relating to employees was often divided among a number of different departments, such as personnel, compensation, industrial relations, and organization development (or training). In their daily work, many employees report to operations departments. As defined by academic specialists, "Human resource management (HRM) involves all managerial decisions and actions that affect the nature of the relationship between the organization and its employees—its human resources" (Beer et al. 1985, p. 236).

Just as some forward-looking service businesses have developed an expanded vision of marketing, viewing it from a strategic perspective rather than a narrow functional and tactical one, so is HRM coming to be seen as a key element in business strategy. Personnel-related activities in a modern service corporation can be subsumed under four broad policy areas (Beer et al. 1985):

1. *Human resource flow* is concerned with ensuring that the right number of people and mix of competencies is available to meet the firm's long-term strategic requirements. Issues include recruitment, training, career development, and promotions.

2. *Work systems* involve all tasks associated with arranging people, information, facilities, and technology to create (or support) the services produced by the organization.

3. *Reward systems* send powerful messages to all employees as to what kind of organization management seeks to create and maintain, especially as to desired attitudes and behavior. Not all rewards are financial in nature; recognition may be a powerful motivator.

4. *Employee influence* relates to employee inputs concerning business goals, pay, working conditions, career progression, employment security, and the design and implementation of work tasks. The movement toward greater empowerment of employees represents a shift in the nature and extent of employee influence (Bowen and Lawler 1992).

In many service businesses, the caliber and commitment of the labor force have become major sources of competitive advantage (Pfeffer 1994), especially in high-contact services where customers can discern differences between the employees of competing firms. A strong commitment by top management to human resources is a feature of many successful service firms (cf. Berry 1995, chaps. 8-10; Schneider and Bowen 1995). To the extent that employees understand and support the goals of their organization, have the skills and training needed to succeed in their jobs, and recognize the importance of creating and maintaining customer satisfaction, both marketing and operations should be easier to manage.

INTERFUNCTIONAL CONFLICT

As service firms place more emphasis on marketing, there is increased potential for conflict among the three functions, especially between marketing and operations. Marketing managers are likely to see the operations perspective as narrow and one-sided. Similarly, they may get frustrated by employee resistance to change or labor agreements that constrain the firm's ability to introduce new services and innovative delivery systems.

How comfortably can the three functions coexist in a service business, and how are their relative roles perceived? Sandra Vandermerwe (1993, p. 82) makes the point that high-value-creating enterprises think in term of activities, not functions, yet in many firms, we still find marketing and operations at loggerheads. For instance, marketers may see their role as one of constantly adding superiority to the product offering to enhance its appeal to customers and thereby increase sales. Operations, by contrast, often takes the view that its role is to pare back these elements to reflect the reality of service constraints—staff, equipment, and so forth—and the accompanying need for cost containment. Conflicts may also occur between human resources and the other two functions, especially where employees are in so-called boundary-spanning roles that require them to serve the seemingly conflicting needs of two masters.

Boundary Spanning

The problem of boundary-spanning jobs is that employees find themselves caught in the middle. For instance, operations may demand that customer-contact personnel focus on speed and efficiency, dealing with each customer as quickly as possible so as to improve productivity and reduce costs. Marketing, in contrast, may insist that employees should spend more time with customers, treat each one as an individual, display appropriate emotions, and try to sell additional services. Conflicting demands such as these are a recipe for stress and burnout. Instead, all three functions need to work together to come up with compatible goals for employee performance, clarify the skills and personal traits needed among employees in particular positions, and provide the necessary support and motivational structure.

Revenue Versus Cost Orientation

Operations managers tend to focus on improving efficiency and keeping down costs, whereas marketers look for opportunities to increase sales and build customer loyalty. Although a proposed marketing innovation may have the potential to attract customers and offer the likelihood of increased sales, the financial and opportunity costs may sometimes be too high to permit its profitable introduction. Marketers who take the trouble to understand the nature and limitations of the existing operation are less likely to fall into the trap of pushing a new service that represents a poor fit with existing facilities, skills, and procedures. Moreover, marketers who have earned credibility with their colleagues in operations and human resources may be able to make the case for investment in new facilities and equipment, changes in labor agreements, retraining of current personnel in new procedures, or even new hires.

Different Time Horizons

Marketing and operations often have different viewpoints concerning the need to expedite a new service. Marketers may be oriented to current customer concerns and eager to achieve an early competitive advantage (or to regain competitive parity) by introducing a new product. The operations division may prefer to adopt a longer time horizon to develop a new technology or to refine new operating procedures. Similarly, human resource managers may caution against rushing to change the nature of employees' jobs, especially in situations where it may take time to obtain acceptance and commitment from employee associations or union leaders.

Perceived Fit of New Products
With Existing Operations

Another problem relates to compatibility. How well does a new product, which may be very appealing to existing and prospective customers, fit into the operation? A classic example of incompatibility comes from an executive in a fast food restaurant chain who related the operational problems attending the introduction of a new menu item.

> It was a big mistake. Our stores are small. They didn't have space for the new equipment that was needed. It really didn't fit with our existing business and was just a square peg in a round hole. Of course, just because it wasn't right for us doesn't mean it wouldn't have been a great success in another quick service restaurant company. It was really popular with our customers, but it started to mess up the rest of our operation.

If a new product is incompatible with existing production facilities, expertise, and employee skills, it follows that good-quality execution may be infeasible. There is, of course, a difference between a permanently bad fit and short-term start-up problems. Resistance by operating personnel is one such start-up problem. There is often a natural tendency to want to make the job as easy as possible, and first-line supervisors may be reluctant to disturb existing patterns by imposing new procedures on employees.

The Three Imperatives

Changing traditional organizational perspectives does not come readily to managers who have been comfortable with established approaches. It is easy for them to become obsessed with their own function, forgetting that all areas of the company must pull together to create a customer-driven organization. Achieving the necessary coordination and synergy requires that top management establish clear imperatives for each function.

Each imperative should relate to customers and define how the function in question contributes to the overall mission. Although a firm will need to phrase each imperative in ways that are specific to its own business, we can express them generically as follows.

1. *The marketing imperative.* The firm will target specific types of customers whom it is well equipped to serve, then create ongoing relationships with them by delivering a carefully defined product package of "all actions and reactions" that they desire to purchase. Customers will recognize this package as being one of consistent quality that delivers solutions to their needs and offers superior value to competing alternatives.

2. *The operations imperative.* To create and deliver the specified service package to targeted customers, the firm will select those operational techniques that allow it to consistently meet customer-driven cost, schedule, and quality goals, and also enable the business to reduce its costs through continuing improvements in productivity. The chosen operational methods will match skills that employees or contractors currently possess or can be trained to develop. The firm will have the resources not only to support these operations with the necessary facilities, equipment, and technology but also to avoid negative impacts on employees and the broader community.

3. *The human resources imperative.* The firm will recruit, train, and motivate managers, supervisors, and employees who can work well together for a realistic compensation package to balance the twin goals of customer satisfaction and operational effectiveness. People will want to stay with the firm and to enhance their own skills because they value the working environment, appreciate the opportunities that it presents, and take pride in the services they help to create and deliver.

Part of the challenge of service management is to ensure that each of these three functional imperatives is compatible with the others and that all are mutually reinforcing.

Improving Intra-Organizational Coordination

The responsibility of top management is to develop structures and procedures that harness the energy of managers in different departments, rather than allowing it to be dissipated in interfunctional disputes or permitting one department to dominate (and thereby frustrate) the others. There are a number of ways in which service firms seek to improve interfunctional coordination and reduce tension.

Transfers and Cross-Training

One approach is to transfer managers from one functional department to another to ensure better understanding of differing perspectives. By working in another department, the transferred manager learns the language and concepts of the other function, understands its opportunities and constraints, and recognizes how its priorities are established. A related approach is to cross-train managers and employers to perform a broader variety of tasks, rather than remaining narrow specialists.

Creating Cross-Functional Task Forces

Another approach is to create a task force for a specific project, such as planning the introduction of a new service, improving quality, or enhancing productivity. Such groups are normally formed on a temporary basis with a defined time deadline for completing a specific task. Ideally, groups should be composed of individuals from each functional area who are well attuned to the others' viewpoints. In operations, this means looking for what one manager has termed "field hands"— personnel who are practical and understand how to deal with people, rather than being totally systems and technology oriented. For marketers, task force membership requires an orientation toward operating systems and what is involved in making them work from both a staffing and a technical perspective; it does not necessarily require detailed technical training or an understanding of the inner workings of technology.

Task force participants should represent a microcosm of the organization yet be insulated from the pressures and distractions of day-to-day management activities. Properly planned and managed, the team environment provides a forum for discussion and resolution of many of the problems likely to occur during, say, the development and commercialization of an innovative service. There needs to be an external mechanism for settling any disputes that task force members cannot resolve among themselves. When a marketing manager is assigned the leadership role, top management's commitment to this individual must be explicit, because it flies in the face of the traditional seniority of operations.

New Tasks and New People

Organizational change requires that new relationships be developed, jobs redefined, priorities restructured, and existing patterns of thought and behavior modified—often sharply. There are two schools of thought here. One involves taking the existing players and redirecting them. The other calls for replacing these people with new ones. The extent to which replacement is feasible depends not only on organizational policies and procedures but also on the availability of suitable new people—either outside or inside the firm. Larger firms obviously have a bigger pool of people on whom to draw; they have managers and specialists in other divisions or regions who have not been "contaminated" by close exposure to the activity in question, yet are sufficiently knowledgeable about the organization that they can become productive quickly in a new project.

Process Management Teams

A more permanent form of team is that which is organized around a specific process. In a marketing context, this approach may include brand management organizations created to plan and coordinate the design and delivery of all frontstage elements for a particular product. One example is found in the brand management teams that are responsible for planning and managing each of British Airways's different classes of service (Torin 1988). Another example is found in the executive operating committees that manage individual hotel units in a chain.

Integrating the Firm's Personnel With the Customer's Organization

Some business-to-business service firms maintain ongoing relationships with customers by locating their own personnel at the customer's site or by bringing customers into their own organization. Taking operations and human resource managers on sales calls or service follow-ups is a related approach. Such activities serve to highlight customer needs and concerns, thus driving home the notion that marketing is everybody's business.

Instituting Gain-Sharing Programs

These programs allow employees to share in improved profits (or in the cost savings achieved at a nonprofit organization). The most significant form of sharing in the fortunes of a business comes through employee stock ownership programs (ESOPs), especially when participation is broadly based and employees own a substantial share of the equity.

ENSURING THAT SERVICE ENCOUNTERS ARE CUSTOMER ORIENTED

One reason why a customer orientation has to extend well beyond the marketing function in a service business concerns service encounters between customers and service employees. A fundamental aspect of service operations is the distinction between the "front stage" and the "back stage." Frontstage procedures are those experienced by the consumer. In the case of low-contact services, such procedures represent a very small proportion of the service firm's total activities. For instance, the extent of personal contact between customers and credit card companies is limited to receiving and paying a monthly statement, and perhaps an occasional letter or telephone call if problems arise. Tasks such as review of credit card applications, credit checks, and processing of credit card slips all take place behind the scenes, yet these brief encounters must be handled well, because they can leave a lasting impression.

By contrast, in a high-contact service such as a hotel, the customer is exposed to the physical facilities and is likely to have service encounters with numerous hotel personnel, ranging from telephone reservation agent to doorman, from bellhop to receptionist, and from restaurant server to housekeeper. Whatever the nature of service encounters, they should be designed and executed with customer needs in mind.

Improving Customer Service in Response to Competitive Pressures

As business in general, and the service sector in particular, becomes more competitive, the need for meaningful competitive differentiation is sharpened. Increasingly, this differentiation includes a search for superior performance not only on the core product but also on each of the supplementary service elements. Achieving such differentiation requires a commitment to formalize standards for all service encounters that might reasonably be anticipated, in ways that reflect the nature of the industry, the culture of the organization, and its desired position in the market. The necessary management tasks will require coordination between managers from different functional backgrounds. These tasks will include

1. conducting ongoing research to determine customer needs, wants, and satisfaction levels concerning each of their service encounters;
2. identifying the key sources of customer satisfaction (or dissatisfaction) and relating them to current service elements;
3. setting customer-based service-level standards for different operational tasks;
4. designing jobs and technological systems to meet these standards; and
5. periodically revising standards and delivery systems in the light of changing customer preferences, technological innovation, and competitive activities.

The human side of quality also is important. Poor performance may include bad manners as well as substandard operational execution. In this instance, the responsibility of an expanded human resources function includes training in human relations skills as part of developing a stronger customer perspective on the part of all contact personnel.

HOW TECHNOLOGY CHANGES ORGANIZATIONS AND CUSTOMER RELATIONSHIPS

One of the driving forces for organizational change is technology, with its dramatic potential for rearranging traditional notions of space and time through the integration of computers and telecommunications, including the many evolving applications of the Internet (e.g., Cairncross 1997; Downes and Mui 1998;

Hagel and Armstrong 1997). Technology changes not only the nature of the operation and, in particular, service delivery processes but also the extent and nature of personal contacts between customers and staff. Even more significantly, it requires a rethinking of market parameters (not least geographic) and market segmentation variables.

Consider the impact of eliminating the traditional branch system in retail banking. This strategy was first adopted in Great Britain by First Direct, the world's first 24-hour, all-telephone bank, which has no branches and never sees its customers, who are located across the United Kingdom and may choose to contact the bank from wherever their travels may take them (Larréché, Lovelock, and Parmenter 1997; Lovelock and Wright 1999, chap. 3). In contrast to traditional banks, with their rigid hierarchical structures—often comprising multiple layers of management, both functional and geographic divisions, and a strong need for control procedures to oversee widely scattered branches—First Direct has a very flat organization, with minimal social or physical distance between the chief executive and the teams of telephone-based banking representatives who serve the bank's customers. All managers and employees are located in a few industrial parks, far from most of the bank's customers, yet thanks to careful recruitment of staff and exhaustive training, backed by good system design, the quality of voice telephone contact with banking representatives is highly rated by customers. The style inside each of the bank's several large, open-plan back offices is professional—everyone is neatly dressed—but also informal in that everyone is on first-name terms, there is just a single cafeteria, and the floor layout is open plan. Not even the chief executive has a private office.

Technology's Role in Integrating Management Functions

Another example of technology's power to reshape service organizations comes from Singapore's World of Sports (WOS) retail chain. The firm's stores are, of necessity, dispersed geographically, separated from one another and from the head office and its adjoining warehouse. The firm's goals of "Speed, Simplicity and Service" are achieved not only through a carefully selected, well-trained, and enthusiastic staff but also through information technology. The latter consists of systems for monitoring all sales and all inventories in real time.

Intelligent terminals at the point of sale capture every sales transaction. Instant information is available on each transaction as it occurs, categorized by the specific item of merchandise (technically known as a stock-keeping unit, or SKU), time of sale, store, and identify of salesperson. Store managers have more time available for coaching and customer relations instead of exercising control. Computerization has revolutionized physical logistics, enabling WOS to create a "virtual warehouse" that consolidates the firm's entire inventory and can be searched for individual SKUs with great speed. If one store does not have a desired item in stock, a sales clerk can immediately search the warehouse inventory and that of other stores. This facility allows the firm to supply a broader range of

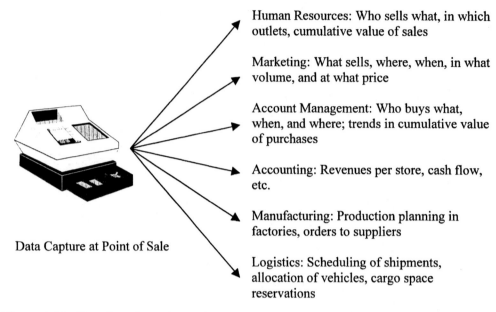

Human Resources: Who sells what, in which outlets, cumulative value of sales

Marketing: What sells, where, when, in what volume, and at what price

Account Management: Who buys what, when, and where; trends in cumulative value of purchases

Accounting: Revenues per store, cash flow, etc.

Manufacturing: Production planning in factories, orders to suppliers

Logistics: Scheduling of shipments, allocation of vehicles, cargo space reservations

Data Capture at Point of Sale

Figure 26.2 How the Information Technology Revolution in Logistics Affects Other Management Functions

items without the expense of large in-store inventories. Information about merchandise and where it is located has become as important as the merchandise itself.

Like WOS, many retailers have moved to install intelligent terminals that can communicate directly with a central computer. Traditional cash registers are out. The data collected by these terminals can be consolidated and analyzed in many ways to meet the needs of different management functions. Figure 26.2 offers a generic representation of how the IT revolution in logistics affects marketing, operations, human resources, and other management functions. Data collected at the point of sale not only provide a control tool to managers in many different functions but also can serve to integrate their activities in ways that enhance mutual cooperation.

How Technology Is Leveraging Customer Service

Regis McKenna, a consultant to numerous high-tech firms, has declared, "I believe that technology is creating a marketplace where everything is going to become service-like" (McKenna 1995a, p. 1). As service firms grow larger and extend their operations across broader geographic areas, corporate managers may become even further removed from the day-to-day operations of the business, and thus from their customers. This development requires new efforts to achieve service consistency across time and geography. Information technology often can help provide the solution.

Service firms with multisite operations are trying to develop programs for building closer ties with customers by centralizing certain functions that don't require face-to-face contact. Computer technology and telecommunications make it possible to provide national (or even global) on-line service out of a central location to serve customers who require information, wish to place orders, or seek to resolve problems. At the same time, technology is creating opportunities for real-time feedback from the marketplace.

McKenna (1995b) makes the point that marketing's traditional, research-based connections to customers are no longer sufficient in a real-time world:

> More continuous connections with customers can provide information that focus groups and surveys cannot. . . . The knowledge of individual customer needs that companies can capture through technology harkens back to the days when the butcher, baker and candlestick maker knew their clientele personally. . . . In that setting, customer service relationships were built-in, face-to-face transactions. . . . Today's technology can recreate the conversation between the shopkeeper and the customer. (p. 88)

Among the procedures that companies are adopting to obtain information from their customers are toll-free numbers to call with questions and complaints, corporate websites that offer information and the opportunity to communicate with the organization by e-mail, and electronic self-service systems (as in electronic banking) that enable the firm to monitor customers' use of its services on a real-time basis.

Part of the attraction of technology for managers who wish to demolish the walls of narrow functionalism is that exploiting new developments to best advantage requires significant reevaluation of existing structures and procedures. Properly implemented, reengineering of existing processes involves creating new organizational approaches of a more flexible and integrative nature.

The Need for Leadership

As was shown in Table 26.1, the final link in the service profit chain is that top management leadership underlies the chain's success. Berry (1995) argues that service leadership requires a special perspective: "Regardless of the target markets, the specific services, or the pricing strategy, service leaders visualize quality of service as the foundation for competing" (p. 9). Recognizing the key role of employees in delivering service, he emphasizes that service leaders need to believe in the people who work for them and make communicating with employees a priority. Love of the business is another service leadership characteristic he highlights, to the extent that it combines natural enthusiasm with the right setting in which to express it. Such enthusiasm motivates individuals to teach the business to others and to pass on to them the nuances, secrets, and craft of operating it. Berry (1999) stresses the importance for leaders of being driven by a set of core values that they infuse into the organization, arguing that "a critical role of values-driven leaders is cultivating the leadership qualities of others in the organization" (p. 44). Among these values, of course, is the way in which the firm chooses to treat its customers and its employees. Berry (1999) also notes that "values-driven leaders rely on their values to navigate their companies through difficult periods" (p. 47).

In hierarchical organizations, structured on a military model, it is often assumed that leadership at the top is sufficient. As Vandermerwe (1993) points out, however, forward-looking service businesses need to be more flexible. Today's greater emphasis on using teams within service businesses means that

> leaders are everywhere, disseminated throughout the teams. They are found especially in the customer facing and interfacing jobs in order that decision-making will lead to long-lasting relationships with customers. . . . [L]eaders are customer and project champions who energize the group by virtue of their enthusiasm, interest and know-how. (p. 129)

CONCLUSION

Within any given service organization, marketing has to coexist with operations, traditionally the dominant function, whose concerns center on cost and efficiency rather than customers. Marketing must also coexist with human resource management, which usually recruits and trains service personnel, including those who have direct contact with customers. An ongoing challenge is to balance the concerns of each function, not only at the head office but also in the field. To a growing degree, information technology is serving to knit together units that were once geographically separated. Leadership at all levels is needed to ensure that new procedures work well and that the firm retains and enhances its market and customer orientation.

REFERENCES

Beer, M., B. Spector, P. R. Lawrence, D. Q. Mills, and R. E. Walton (1985), *Human Resource Management: A General Manager's Perspective*. New York: Free Press.

Berry, Leonard L. (1995), *On Great Service: A Framework for Action*. New York: Free Press.

———— (1999), *Discovering the Soul of Service*. New York: Free Press.

Bowen, David E. and Edward T. Lawler III (1992), "The Empowerment of Service Workers: What, Why, How and When," *Sloan Management Review*, 34 (Spring), 31-39.

Cairncross, Frances (1997), *The Death of Distance*. Boston: Harvard Business School Press.

Downes, Larry and Chunka Mui (1998), *Unleashing the Killer App*. Boston: Harvard Business School Press.

Grönroos, Christian (1990), *Service Management and Marketing*. Lexington, MA: Lexington Books.

Gummesson, Evert (1979), "The Marketing of Professional Services: An Organizational Dilemma," *European Journal of Marketing*, 13(5), 308-18.

———— (1994), "Service Management: An Evaluation and the Future," *International Journal of Service Industry Management*, 5(1), 77-96.

Hagel, John, III and Arthur G. Armstrong (1997), *Net Gain*. Boston: Harvard Business School Press.

Heskett, James L., Thomas O. Jones, Gary W. Loveman, W. Earl Sasser, Jr., and Leonard A. Schlesinger (1994), "Putting the Service Profit Chain to Work," *Harvard Business Review*, 72 (March-April), 164-74.

————, W. Earl Sasser, Jr., and Leonard A. Schlesinger (1997), *The Service Profit Chain: How Leading Companies Link Profit and Growth to Loyalty, Satisfaction, and Value*. New York: Free Press.

Larréché, Jean-Claude, Christopher Lovelock, and Delphine Parmenter (1997), *First Direct: Branchless Banking*. Fontainebleau, France: INSEAD. (Distributed by European Case Clearing House)

Lovelock, Christopher and Lauren Wright (1999), *Principles of Service Marketing and Management*. Upper Saddle River, NJ: Prentice Hall.

McKenna, Regis (1995a), "Everything Will Become a Service and How to Be Successful When It Does," *ITSMA Insight*, (Spring), 1.

———— (1995b), "Real-Time Marketing," *Harvard Business Review*, (July-August), 87-98.

Pfeffer, Jeffrey (1994), *Competitive Advantage Through People*. Boston: Harvard Business School Press.

Schneider, Benjamin and David E. Bowen (1995), *Winning the Service Game*. Boston: Harvard Business School Press.

Torin, Douglas (1988), "The Power of Branding," *Business Life*, (April-May), 56-60.

Vandermerwe, Sandra (1993), *From Tin Soldiers to Russian Dolls*. Oxford, UK: Butterworth-Heinemann.

27

Shaping Service Cultures Through Strategic Human Resource Management

DAVID E. BOWEN
BENJAMIN SCHNEIDER
SANDRA S. KIM

Any proffered explanation of the success of such service role models as Disney, Southwest Airlines, Singapore Airlines, IKEA, Nordstrom, or Shouldice Hospital would invariably mention the role played by these firms' cultures. In addition, there would most likely be favorable comments made about how these organizations manage their people. These variables—*culture* and *human resource management*—seem to hold some keys to an understanding of service organization effectiveness, especially for customer satisfaction.

Moreover, the management literature of the last decade has emphasized the *strategic* role of both culture and human resource management (HRM). Culture has been developed as a potential basis of competitive advantage (Barney 1986). Cultures that are valued by customers and are unique and tough to copy can offer firms a sustainable competitive advantage over their competitors. As for HRM, the thinking has been that the design of the HRM mix (e.g., selection and training) must be driven by the firm's strategy, as fitted to the external environmental context and organizational resources (Fombrun, Tichy, and Devanna 1984). Linking HRM practices to strategy is in contrast to a history of designing HRM practices around issues of legal exposure, financial costs, and so on. Only if HRM practices are tied to strategy can they help deliver the value proposition that the firm hopes will attract and retain customers.

In this chapter we explore in some detail the "lessons learned" about managing culture through strategic human resources management, lessons from our own research and consulting efforts as well as the review of others' work. We will discuss three summary, overarching lessons learned:

1. *The climates and cultures for service excellence experienced by employees in service businesses are related to organizational effectiveness as indicated by customer satisfaction.* In this chapter we will review several research studies that reveal this relationship between employee and customer experiences (e.g., Schneider, White, and Paul 1998). We will argue that although climate and culture issues are important in all organizations, in service businesses how the internal world of those businesses is experienced by employees can become more immediately visible to customers than is true in nonservice businesses. This would be especially true for service businesses with considerable customer contact and on-site customer presence (Chase 1978).

2. *Human resource management (HRM) practices (e.g., selection, training, reward systems, and so on) are a central means by which a firm can manage its service culture and shape it to "fit" its own strategically defined market segments.* To do so, the firm's HRM practices must indeed be *service-focused*. By this we mean that selection must focus on hiring service-oriented employees (Frei and McDaniel 1998); training must emphasize the acquisition of knowledge, skills, abilities, and attitudes about and toward service excellence (Heskett, Sasser, and Schlesinger 1997), including issues of emotional labor (Hochschild 1983); and reward systems must emphasize the achievement of service excellence goals (Schneider and Bowen 1995). In addition to being service-oriented, HRM practices must also be *market-segment relevant*. Service excellence is not obtained through the implementation of a generic set of service-focused HRM practices. Real effectiveness is obtained by matching a firm's HRM mix and HRM emphases to its own particular mix of customers. The firm's strategic focus defines the bridge between these two, and this is where firm market strategy and HRM intersect (Chung 1997).

3. *Tight integration of HRM with other organizational functions is the key to having the desired effect on customer satisfaction.* Schneider and Bowen (1995) have referred to this as "avoiding the HRM trap." All functions, including HRM, marketing, and operations, must reinforce the same service excellence strategy. There must be a *seamless service system* in which all elements are internally consistent in their approach to the customer.

In sum, we will overview how HRM practices influence the service climate and culture of the service delivery system that employees experience and in which they behave and how these, in turn, get reflected in the service quality delivered to customers. We will present both a descriptive focus on how HRM practices shape climate and culture and a prescriptive focus on how a firm's strategy should shape the design of its HRM practices to create the climate and culture appropriate for the type of customers the firm wants to both attract and retain. Finally, we will discuss how an organization's HRM practices must be tightly integrated with other organizational functions to achieve the goal of service excellence that will provide the desired outcomes of profit and customer retention.

SERVICE CLIMATE AND CULTURE

It is useful to first define what we mean by the terms *climate* and *culture* because they mean so many different things to both researchers and executives. Both involve and reflect how employees "make sense" of their work environments, and they represent two facets of a complex psychosocial phenomenon. An organization's climate is the summary sense employees have about what is important in the organization (Schneider and Bowen 1995). More specifically, this sense includes employees' inferences about what the organization is like relative to two generic issues: (a) how the organization goes about its daily business and (b) what goals the organization pursues (Schneider, Brief, and Guzzo 1996). This sense emerges from the "messages" sent by the HRM, marketing, and operations management practices under which employees work and their perceptions of the kinds of behaviors management rewards, expects, and supports.

The study of organizational climate over the years has increasingly assumed a strategic focus, linking climate perceptions to a specific criterion of interest, such as service or innovation (Schneider 1990). This strategic focus yields an interest in the specification of the policies, practices, and procedures that employees experience and the kinds of behaviors employees report being rewarded, supported, and expected. A "climate for service" would exist in the eyes of employees if they perceived that the many messages given by organizational practices and organizational reward systems indicate that service is important and that there are specific ways that it should be delivered.

Climate can be viewed as the more immediately tangible layer on top of the organization's underlying culture. This more immediately tangible layer of the organization that employees immediately experience would be directly related to managerial policies and procedures in general, and human resources management practices and emphases in particular. Where these tangibles come from and why they exist resides in the set of values and beliefs shared by members of an organization, the organization's culture (Kotter and Heskett 1992; Schein 1992). Culture is thought of as residing deeper in the psychosocial life of organizational members than perceptions of the tangibles of the organization; culture connotes a sharing of basic values about what is right and wrong, what works and what does not work; these are values that evolve as the business copes effectively with the ongoing problems of the maintenance and survival of the organization. These basic values that guide the development of organizational structures, policies, and practices are learned over time, and they come to be valued by organizational members precisely because of their relationship to survival. Schein (1992) puts it this way: "Culture ultimately reflects the group's efforts to cope and learn and is the residue of the learning process. Culture thus fulfills not only the function of providing stability, meaning and predictability in the present but is the result of functionally effective decisions in the past" (p. 68).

These values and beliefs are not easily accessed by members; they concern deep feelings, thinking, and emotion more than they do straightforward perceptions of easily observable behavior (Schein 1992). Schein (1992) has written that culture is created by leaders and that newcomers, as leaders to the organization, must be aware of the culture or they will be led by it: "The bottom line for leaders is that if they do not become conscious of the cultures in which they are embedded, those cultures will manage them" (p. 15).

We agree with Schein's emphasis on the leader and suggest further that, because leaders shape the practices and rewards of the organization, the strategic goals at which those practices and rewards are directed signify the strategic imperatives of management to employees. When employees experience many cues as indicating a genuine focus on service, they may infer that management believes in and values service quality and customer satisfaction. At a minimum they will experience the organization as one that emphasizes—creates a climate for—service quality.

Some writers on organizational culture include employee experiences of the more tangible and immediate features of organizational practices and rewards, what we call organizational climate, as part of the organization's culture (Schein 1992; Schneider and Bowen 1985). We will adopt that convention here, with the understanding that other writers on organizational culture explicitly deny any connection whatsoever between the two (Ott 1989; Trice and Beyer 1993).

For simplicity, we will use the word "culture" in this chapter to include research on "climate" as well. Thus, research on climate (Schneider, White, and Paul 1998) and research on culture (Schein 1992) both suggest that the practices and rewards that characterize organizations emerge from the values of management; these practices and rewards serve to signal to employees the strategic imperatives of the organization. In turn, the strategic imperatives both provide a frame of reference for and guide behavior.

THE RELATIONSHIP BETWEEN EMPLOYEE EXPERIENCES OF CULTURE AND ORGANIZATIONAL EFFECTIVENESS

We have done considerable research over the years to identify the various dimensions of practices and rewards that define the elements of service culture and the relationship between service culture and employee outcomes, customer outcomes, and the profitability of the firm. Very early work on customer experiences of bank branch service culture (Schneider 1973) was followed by a pair of later studies that specified dimensions of both customer and employee experiences of the service culture of branch banks (Schneider 1980; Schneider and Bowen 1985; Schneider, Parkington, and Buxton 1980). These dimensions for employees include (a) *managerial behavior* that rewards, supports, plans for, and expects service excellence; (b) *systems support* of service from marketing, personnel, and operations functions (e.g., providing adequate staffing and advertising deliverables); (c) *customer attention/retention* behaviors that demonstrate the importance of customers; and (d) *logistics support* for the tools, equipment, supplies, and facilities needed to deliver service. For customers, the dimensions were quite similar to those that have emerged from the research on SERVQUAL (cf. Zeithaml, Parasuraman, and Berry 1990).

These service culture dimensions have been shown to relate to both employee and customer outcomes. When employees perceive a strong service culture and are provided with the support necessary to provide customer service, they experience more positive consequences at work, less stress, and more job satisfaction (Schneider 1980). In addition, when employees perceive a strong service culture, customers report receiving superior service quality. In other words, the way employees experience the service culture of their work organizations is reflected in the perceptions customers have of the service quality they receive (Schneider and Bowen 1985). These results have been replicated in numerous studies published in the professional journal research literature and books (e.g., Heskett, Sasser, and Schlesinger 1997; Wiley 1996). Furthermore, when employees report that they work in a strong service culture, customers report that they are more likely to retain their business with the organization (Schneider and Bowen 1985).

In addition to this relationship between employee experiences of service culture and customer satisfaction, there is also a strong belief, moderately supported by evidence, that there is a significant relationship between service culture and other organizational effectiveness indicators, including financial performance. The basic culture-performance linkage has been claimed for some 15 years by those associated with the study of corporate culture (e.g., Deal and Kennedy 1984; Peters and Waterman 1982). Case examples such as Federal Express (Lovelock 1994), Disney (Berry 1995), and others (cf. Heskett, Sasser, and Schlesinger 1997) are often mentioned to support the claim, but hard evidence is difficult to find and it is difficult to untangle whether it is service culture or other factors (competitor incompetence or product-service bundling, for example) that are at work.

Some thoughtful reviews of the presumed relationship between culture and financial performance have been critical of even the potential for culture to be reflected in financial performance (Siehl and Martin 1990). So many variables that may be related to financial performance of the firm (market readiness, geography, access to capital) are outside the control of the organization that it may be almost impossible to find such a relationship.

Indeed, there are studies both supportive of the relationship and supportive of a *negative* relationship between service culture and organizational performance. For example, Wiley (1996) reports a study of branch banks in both urban and suburban settings, all under the banner of a single bank. Wiley collected data on service culture and then correlated the data with customer satisfaction and found a positive relationship. When he explored the relationship between customer satisfaction and firm performance, however, he found a positive relationship in the urban branches but a negative relationship in the suburban branches. Wiley's definition of branch performance was based on speed of transactions with customers. In suburban branches, with less traffic, speed of transaction was low, yielding the negative relationship. That is, the more time tellers spent with customers, the more satisfied customers were and the slower the speed of transactions!

Sutton and Rafaeli (1989) showed a similar finding in convenience stores. They found that the higher the customer satisfaction, the lower was store profitability. Like Wiley, they explained their results in terms of transaction speed. That is, in stores where transaction speed demands were high, there was more traffic and more profits; where staff could spend time with customers, the customers were more satisfied but the stores were less profitable. The findings of Wiley (1996) and Sutton and Rafaeli (1989) support the argument of Siehl and Martin (1990) and suggest that there may be numerous contingencies on the degree to which a service culture will be directly translated into firm performance.

Other findings do show that service quality pays off financially for businesses. For example, writing about what they call "the service profit chain," Heskett, Sasser, and Schlesinger (1997) marshal considerable evidence to show that firms such as American Express, BancOne, Southwest Airlines, and Wal-Mart achieve greater profits on equity than their competitors because they manage the service culture of the business. In addition, the massive undertaking known as PIMS (Profit Impact of Market Strategy; Buzzell and Gale 1987) showed that businesses that produce and deliver superior quality generally experience superior profitability. The problem is that it is not always so clear that the route to profits is through service quality: Sometimes it is through price, sometimes through innovation, and sometimes through value (Deshpande, Farley, and Webster 1993; Narver and Slater 1990; Schneider 1991).

Regardless of the study and regardless of the relationship between culture and profits, it is certain and replicable that how employees experience their organization is related to customer experiences. Heskett, Sasser, and Schlesinger (1997, p. 99) call the relationship between employees and customer experiences the "satisfaction mirror," and they report a series of studies at such diverse businesses as MCI, Merry Maids, and Xerox supporting this relationship. These findings, in combination with the studies reviewed by Wiley (1996) and summarized in Schneider (1990), provide ample evidence of the durability of the relationship. In the remainder of this chapter, we will develop the role of HRM much more fully, but at the same time it is important to remember that *all* organizational subsystems contribute to the service culture of a setting.

THE ROLE OF HRM IN THE SERVICE CULTURE

The very broad role played by HRM in shaping the service culture can be summarized relative to four overarching contributions:

Symbolic: HRM sends signals to employees about what the values of the business truly are and what behaviors are expected to make them real. This provides direction and, in the best of cases, inspiration.

HRM practices such as selection, training, and reward systems can send strong messages to employees about management's values and strategic priorities. HRM practices offer employees critical pieces of evidence as to whether the values management espouses are the same values that are enacted in actual practices and what actually gets rewarded. HRM practices can create shared perceptions across individuals as to the firm's strategic goals and means for accomplishing them (Ostroff and Bowen forthcoming). If management claims that customer service is important, does it also utilize validated selection tools for hiring service-oriented employees, factor customer service into pay-for-performance plans, and so on? A strong service culture may emerge if the firm has an internally consistent mix of service-oriented HRM practices that reinforce espoused service values. Alternatively, when HRM practices are at odds with espoused values, then the firm suffers from what has been termed "cultural schizophrenia" (Schneider and Bowen 1995).

> *Substantive:* HRM can ensure that employees have the ability and motivation necessary to perform consistently with the values and norms emphasized in the culture.

HRM plays an important role in shaping any organizational culture, but its role may be further accentuated in service organizations. Many service businesses are labor intensive, making HRM practices a particularly important factor of production. Additionally, in many services, the employee is the service in the eyes of the customer (Normann 1991). Because of this, the HRM practices that select and train the service provider are essentially the core quality-control functions within the firm. HRM practices ensure that employees have the *motivation* and *ability* required to perform the service behaviors expected of them (Schneider and Bowen 1995).

> *Strategic:* HRM practices can be a key ingredient in implementing a formulated service strategy. Generic business strategies are coarsely categorized as being either cost leadership or differentiation (Porter 1980). Service delivered under one strategy clearly requires an HRM mix and service culture different from service delivered under the other.

The HRM practices that exist in a setting create the foundation for particular types of cultures to develop (Schneider 1990). Organizational effectiveness requires that the type of culture (e.g., for service) and the system of HRM practices must be aligned with each other as well as with key organizational context variables, such as business strategy (Ostroff and Bowen forthcoming). Business strategy has been defined by Pfeffer (1998) as the value proposition that a firm offers the marketplace in the hope that it will lead customers to choose it over its competitors. HRM practices are key to delivering the underlying value proposition.

> *Sustainable competitive advantage:* HRM practices and the cultures they help shape can be the basis of competitive advantage even more so than traditional bases such as cost, technological superiority, or differentiated output attributes.

An effective, internally consistent, and innovative set of HRM practices and the service culture that they create can act as a competitive advantage that is difficult for others to copy and thus is quite sustainable (Heskett, Sasser, and Schlesinger 1997). The idea that culture, a mix of employees, and organizational capability can be a source of sustainable competitive advantage has been expressed frequently in recent years (Barney 1986; Lawler 1992; Pfeffer 1998; Ulrich and Lake 1990). As stated in our opening, it is these factors that are often mentioned as responsible for the long-term success of companies such as Nordstrom, Disney, Federal Express, BancOne, and Southwest Airlines.

It is through these four contributions that HRM can strongly affect service organizational culture and effectiveness. To do so requires designing an appropriate service-oriented HRM mix.

Designing a Service-Oriented HRM Mix

The last 15 years have witnessed an explosion of articles and books that address how service organizations differ from product organizations and how, as a consequence, HRM practices have to differ between the two (e.g., Bowen 1996; Bowen and Schneider 1988; Bowen and Waldman 1999; Fromm and Schlesinger 1993; Heskett, Sasser, and Schlesinger 1997; Jackson and Schuler 1992; Schneider 1994; Schneider and Bowen 1992, 1993, 1995). This is not the place to review that lengthy literature. What is useful is to describe what we think are two fundamental truths surrounding the role of HRM in service that we feel underscore the criticality of HRM to organizational effectiveness in services. After overviewing these, we will address how to tailor the HRM mix to "fit" a specific, strategically defined market segment.

First, HRM has a unique role to play in service because service employees, unlike their manufacturing counterparts, are part of both the process *and outcome* of service production. HRM practices have an effect on both technical (what is delivered) and functional (how it is delivered) quality (Grönroos 1990). When service is created in the presence of the customer, employees are shaping customer perceptions of both the "what" and the "how" of service. Consequently, the role that HRM can play in the realm of process perceptions is clear in the SERVQUAL dimensions of empathy, responsiveness, and assurance (Zeithaml, Parasuraman, and Berry 1990). This unique role explains the emphasis on specific HRM recommendations, such as hiring on the basis of personality in customer-contact positions (Frei and McDaniel 1998) and ensuring that performance appraisal and training practices emphasize service delivery (Schneider 1991). HRM practices also seem to create "substitutes for intangibility" in that they shape the employee behaviors that are visible to customers, who then use them as tangible cues in assessing what often are intangible services; the employee as service deliverer becomes both the service and the organization delivering it. Particularly in high-contact, intangible services, quality control becomes an HRM function.

Second, HRM practices in service seem to be correlated with both employee outcomes and customer outcomes; that is, the effects of HRM appear to "spill over" onto customers. As noted earlier, Heskett, Sasser, and Schlesinger (1997) call this the customer-employee satisfaction mirror. This mirror has the very interesting idea behind it that employee satisfaction influences customer satisfaction and vice versa. Heskett, Sasser, and Schlesinger (1997), for example, present the idea that at organizations oriented to high-quality service, such as Nordstrom, customer satisfaction produces a "mirror" effect, further enhancing the potential for future customer satisfaction. Subsequent to the writing of their book, in which they explained that the direction of the relationship was not clear, they wrote and used the term "mirror" as if it went both ways. Schneider, White, and Paul (1998) in fact demonstrated that the relationship over time clearly appears to be reciprocal.

To us this suggests that HRM practices established for customer-contact employees in service organizations have unintentional consequences because they cannot be hidden from the consumer; the service culture "shows" to those who are served. This relationship grew clear in a study by Schneider and Bowen (1985). In their study of bank employees and customers, they found that organizational practices apparently were a source of cues visible to customers and were used by them to evaluate service quality. Moreover, customer reports on apparent employee morale were also strongly related to customer satisfaction; when customers report that employees appear happy with their work, those customers also report that they are satisfied with the service they receive.

Another manifestation of the spillover effect can be found in the argument that when front-line employees feel that they have been treated fairly, they are more likely to treat customers fairly in a manner that favorably influences customers' perceptions of service quality (Bowen, Gilliland, and Folger 1999). Central to employees' perceptions of their own fair treatment is whether or not they feel they have been treated fairly by their firm's HRM practices, such as performance appraisal and reward allocations. In turn, considerable research has documented the relationship between employees feeling fairly treated by HRM practices and their emotional state and attachment to the firm (e.g., Folger and Copranzano 1998).

These HRM-related fairness perceptions are suggested to spill over onto customers in the form of employees engaging in organizational citizenship behaviors (OCBs) that are directed toward customers. OCBs consist of employee actions that are outside formal role requirements and consist of acts of extraordinary conscientiousness, altruism, sportsmanship, civic virtue, and courtesy (Organ 1988). OCBs have been established empirically as a consequence of employee fairness perceptions (Moorman 1991, 1993). OCBs also have been developed as prosocial service behaviors that may favorably affect customer satisfaction (Bettencourt and Brown 1997). These relationships are the basis for the spillover argument that fair HRM can lead to more fair service (Bowen, Gilliland, and Folger 1999).

We believe that these two points, taken together, indicate that the design of the HRM mix should be customer-driven. HRM, however, traditionally has been focused on meeting the needs of the internal world of an organization. Indeed, it has been said that "market-focused human resource management" may sound like an oxymoron to both researchers and practitioners (Bowen 1996). The prevailing internal focus has meant that HRM is deemed to be effective when internally defined standards of employee effectiveness are enhanced by HRM practices (Schneider 1994). Typically this internal focus has been on sales, accuracy, attendance, and other tangible, more easily countable behaviors. With respect to HRM practices and service quality, however, it is important to have an external criterion as well because service excellence is oriented to customers, who are outside the internal domain of the organization itself. Thus, it is useful to consider the customer as a legitimate external standard for evaluating the effectiveness of HRM practices and procedures. That is, customer service quality can be an external criterion to assess the effectiveness of service-oriented HRM practices in an organization.

This perspective of an external focus amounts to an advocacy of what has been termed "customer-driven employee performance" (Bowen and Waldman 1999). It maintains that customer expectations should be the standard by which employee role requirements and desired behaviors should be defined. The authors draw on Lawler's (1996) assertion that a new logic has to be applied to the basic issue of how control is exercised in contemporary organizations. Lawler argues that it is better to have the external market and customers controlling an individual's performance than to rely on rules, procedures, and supervisors. The customer is the ultimate judge of success and the one most likely to guide employees in the proper direction and to prompt change in response to changing customer expectations. In the following section, we describe how to design an HRM mix to be responsive to the market.

Gaining Strategic Focus: Market-Segmented HRM

The assumption of market-segmented HRM is that there is not one "generic" set of HRM practices that will be universally effective. Instead, service managers need to know *which* HRM practices will yield the greatest return to customer satisfaction on *different* dimensions of service quality. Insight on how to address that issue is found in a study by Schneider, Wheeler, and Cox (1992) that explored which HRM practices employees report as symbolizing a culture in which there is a "service passion." Through their content analyses of almost 100 focus groups conducted with employees of financial services organizations, the authors defined service passion as follows. Interviews in which employees spoke both frequently and favorably about service were said to represent a positive service passion. Relating HRM practices to a passion for service, in this study the authors found that positive perceptions of HRM issues such as performance feedback, internal equity of compensation, training, staff quality, and hiring procedures were all positively correlated with the service passion index. Thus, it appears that many facets of an organization's HRM practices contribute to its overall passion for service.

Although a number of HRM practices were significantly correlated with service passion, it is important to note that there were also a number of practices that were not (i.e., staffing levels, career development opportunities, job security, equipment, and external equity of compensation). It is quite likely that in a

TABLE 27.1 Customer Expectations of Service Delivery

Service Segment	Customer Expectations for		
	Speed	*TLC*	*Customization*
Adequate service	0	0	0
Speedy service	+	0	0
Friendly service	0	+	0
Fancy service	0	0	+
Good service	+	+	0
Cold service	+	0	+
Warm service	0	+	+
Terrific service	+	+	+

NOTE: Average = 0; excellent = +.

different industry or company, a different pattern of correlations would emerge. This indicates that there is no one "universal" set of service-oriented HRM practices that will be effective in all settings. What, then, are the contingencies or variables that should guide a particular firm's design of its HRM mix?

HRM practices need to be designed to support a service-delivery strategy consistent with the overall business strategy (e.g., cost leadership or differentiation). More fully, HRM practices need to create a culture not simply for service but for a particular *type* of service. Because strategy is essentially the issue of how the firm can acquire a competitive advantage in the marketplace, it follows that both the business and service delivery strategy must take into account customers' expectations. In effect, through its *substantive* and *symbolic* contributions, HRM can then create the service culture that "fits" customer expectations. It will thereby also realize its *strategic* and *sustainable competitive advantage* contributions as well.

Table 27.1 displays alternative ways of focusing on customer expectations of service delivery. The table shows eight different potential market segments, which result from combining three kinds of customer expectations:

Expectations for *speed:* service that is responsive, reliable, and quick as well as meeting promised deadlines;

Expectations for *tender loving care (TLC):* service that is courteous, understanding, empathetic, friendly, and interpersonal; and

Expectations for *customization* of service: the service offering related to various dimensions of the core service, including issues such as the dress and appearance of personnel, the physical facility in which the service is delivered, and the degree to which customers can choose the attributes of the core service itself.

According to Schneider and Bowen (1995), any service organization could decide to be average (0) or excellent (+) on any one or all of these service attributes, depending on the service segment it is targeting. (Note that there are no minus signs in this table, for service organizations must be at least adequate on each of these three dimensions to survive.) A fast food restaurant may offer speedy service that is excellent with respect to the speed dimension but only average on TLC or customization, while an expensive four-star restaurant may offer terrific service on all three dimensions of service. The types of service such businesses deliver depends on the market segment they are targeting, and their respective customers consequently expect a certain combination of services. Thus, businesses in the "same" service field (e.g., restaurants) that appeal to different market segments must go about their service delivery in different ways. The design of HRM practices such as selection, training, and rewards must focus employee behavior to fit the targeted market segment.

Another application of market-segmented HRM is Bowen and Lawler's (1992, 1995) development of a contingency approach to employee empowerment. They maintain that the degree to which front-line service employees are empowered should depend on the firm's basic business strategy. When a firm competes on low-cost, high-volume service offerings, it needs to question whether there is any value added from spending additional resources on the more complicated selection, training, and even higher compensation that might be necessary to support empowerment. If the targeted market segment values inexpensive, speedy service—not TLC—then Levitt's (1972, 1976) production-line approach of procedurally driven, low-employee-discretion jobs might be the best fit. Alternatively, if the strategy is to compete on the provision of differentiated, TLC service, then designing an HRM mix to empower employees to provide customized service to customers would be appropriate.

In sum, HRM practices that are carefully targeted to meet the needs of specific market segments send messages about who the organization is as a business, who its markets are, what the expectations of those markets are, and what the organization has to do to meet those expectations. Implementing an HRM strategy that targets a particular market segment communicates to everyone why they are there and what must be done to ensure the success of the organization (Schneider 1994).

HRM practices are a key lever in shaping the service culture of a firm. These practices must be tailored to the unique characteristics of service in general and, more specifically, to the expectations of the customers whom the firm's strategy is seeking to attract and retain. Moreover, it is important for the HRM practices of an organization to adapt to meet any changing needs of the market and service segment. If the organization's strategy or customer expectations change, then the culture may need to change as well to emphasize revised goals and means of achieving them. Once again, HRM practices will need to substantively influence the types of skills and motivation of employees and symbolically signal the change in values necessary to remain competitive.

HRM AS PART OF A SEAMLESS SYSTEM

The need for a seamless organization is an inevitable consequence of the truism that no one function alone can satisfy a customer; it takes the entire organization. The implications of this for the HRM function itself is that it must view its *organizational* mission not from the conventional industrial/organizational psychology perspective of equipping employees to perform to meet the requirements of a job, but instead as ensuring that they are capable of doing their part to meet the expectations of customers.

Relatedly, in services, the focus of HRM has to be the *organization* rather than the *job* (Schneider and Bowen 1992). All employees, whether they work in marketing, operations, or finance, must be recruited, trained, and rewarded so that they share the firm's strategic service emphases on what service means in their setting and how it is to be delivered. The goal of HRM is to shape an *organizational* climate for service.

This focus on the role of HRM, or more precisely strategic HRM, should not obscure the recognition that *all* functions of the organization must work together seamlessly in pursuit of customer satisfaction. Even competent, motivated, strategically focused employees cannot produce satisfied customers if information systems are frequently down, facilities are poorly maintained, pricing is not competitive, and so on. When service firms place excess reliance on their employees as the means to customer satisfaction, they fall into what has been called the "HRM trap" (Schneider and Bowen 1995). Ironically, the seductiveness of that trap is partly due to those authors' own research (Schneider and Bowen 1985) that indicated that when employees were satisfied with HRM practices, customers were satisfied with the quality of service received. This finding came to mean to many that if you satisfy your employees, they, in turn, will satisfy your customers. That is by no means the whole truth. The whole truth is that such employees need to be surrounded by a well-designed, well-coordinated *system* if the customer is to be satisfied, and all elements of this service system must act in a coordinated way to produce service excellence.

All organizational departments must be driven by a shared service *logic* if a seamless effort on behalf of the customer is to be accomplished (Kingman-Brundage, George, and Bowen 1995). "Logic" refers to the implicit and explicit principles that drive organizational performance. The challenge for seamlessness is that different departments tend to be driven by competing logics. For example, marketing focuses on the management of demand and strives for effectiveness (e.g., sales), whereas operations management focuses on the management of supply and strives for efficiency (e.g., low costs). Customers may find their pursuit of satisfaction compromised by the competitive, rather than collaborative, nature of these two very different logics.

HRM and the role it plays in shaping a service culture can help smooth the seams across the logics of different departments. Through the HRM mix, the firm can send signals and develop employee competencies and routines that reinforce a shared service logic. As Kingman-Brundage, George, and Bowen (1995) state, "Service logic seeks synergies—collaborative interactions between individuals or groups of people—to create outcomes that customers value as 'seamless service' and that ultimately result in company profitability" (p. 21). Guided by a strategic understanding of what *their* customers value, service firms can use their HRM practices to shape cultures, with an organizationwide shared service logic, that lead to sustained competitive advantage.

REFERENCES

Barney, Jay (1986), "Organizational Culture: Can It Be a Source of Sustained Competitive Advantage?" *Academy of Management Review*, 11(3), 656-66.

Berry, Leonard L. (1995), "Relationship Marketing of Services—Growing Interest, Emerging Perspectives," *Journal of the Academy of Marketing Science*, 23, 236-45.

Bettencourt, Lance A. and Stephen W. Brown (1997), "Contact Employees: Relationships Among Workplace Fairness, Job Satisfaction, and Prosocial Behaviors," *Journal of Retailing*, 73(1), 39-62.

Bowen, David E. (1996), "Market-Focused HRM in Service Organizations: Satisfying Internal and External Customers," *Journal of Market-Focused Management*, 1(1), 31-48.

———, Stephen Gilliland, and Robert Folger (1999), "HRM and Service Fairness: How Being Fair With Employees Spills Over to Customers," *Organizational Dynamics*, 27 (Winter), 7-23.

——— and Edward E. Lawler (1992), "The Empowerment of Service Workers: What, Why, How, and When," *Sloan Management Review*, 33(3), 31-39.

——— and ——— (1995), "Empowerment of Service Employees," *Sloan Management Review*, 36 (Summer), 73-84.

——— and Benjamin Schneider (1988), "Services Marketing and Management: Implications for Organizational Behavior," *Research in Organizational Behavior*, 10, 43-80.

——— and David A. Waldman (1999), "Customer-Driven Employee Performance," in *The Changing Nature of Performance: Implications for Staffing, Motivation, and Development*, Daniel R. Ilgen and Elaine A. Pulakos, eds. San Francisco: Jossey-Bass, 154-91.

Buzzell, Robert D. and Bradley T. Gale (1987), *The PIMS Principle: Linking Strategy to Performance*. New York: Free Press.

Chase, Richard B. (1978), "Where Does the Customer Fit in a Service Operation?" *Harvard Business Review*, 56, 137-42.

Chung, Beth (1997), "Focusing HRM Strategies Toward Service Market Segments: Three Factor Model," doctoral dissertation, University of Maryland at College Park.

Deal, Terence E. and Allan A. Kennedy (1984), "Culture: A New Look Through Old Lenses," *Journal of Applied Behavioral Sciences*, 19(4), 498-505.

Deshpande, Rohit, John U. Farley, and Frederick Webster (1993), "Corporate Culture, Customer Orientation, and Innovativeness in Japanese Firms: A Quadrad Analysis," *Journal of Marketing*, 57, 23-27.

Folger, Robert and R. Copranzano (1998), *Organizational Justice and Human Resource Management*. Newbury Park, CA: Sage.

Fombrun, Charles, Noel M. Tichy, and Mary Anne Devanna (1984), *Strategic Human Resource Management*. New York: John Wiley.

Frei, R. L. and M. A. McDaniel (1998), "Validity of Customer Service Measures in Personnel Selection Measures: A Review of Criterion and Construct Evidence," *Human Performance*, 11(1), 1-27.

Fromm, Bill and Leonard A. Schlesinger (1993), *The Real Heroes of Business and Not a CEO Among Them: How to Find, Train, Manage, and Retain World-Class Service Workers*. New York: Doubleday.

Grönroos, Christian (1990), *Service Management and Strategy: Marketing the Moments of Truth in Service Competition*. Lexington, MA: Lexington Books.

Heskett, James L., W. Earl Sasser, Jr., and Leonard A. Schlesinger (1997), *The Service Profit Chain*. New York: Free Press.

Hochschild, Arlie R. (1983), *The Managed Heart: Commercialization of Human Feeling*. Berkeley: University of California Press.

Jackson, Susan E. and Randall S. Schuler (1992), "HRM Practices in Service-Based Organizations," in *Advances in Service Marketing and Management: Research and Practice*, Vol. 1, Teresa A. Swartz, David E. Bowen, and Stephen W. Brown, eds. Greenwich, CT: JAI, 123-58.

Kingman-Brundage, Jane, William R. George, and David E. Bowen (1995), " 'Service Logic': Achieving Service System Integration," *International Journal of Service Industry Management*, 6(4), 20-39.

Kotter, John P. and James L. Heskett (1992), *Corporate Culture and Performance*. New York: Free Press.

Lawler, Edward E. (1992), *The Ultimate Advantage*. San Francisco: Jossey-Bass.

——— (1996), *From the Ground Up: Six Principles for Building the New Logic Corporation*. San Francisco: Jossey-Bass.

Levitt, Theodore (1972), "Production-Line Approach to Service," *Harvard Business Review*, (September-October), 41-52.

——— (1976), "Industrialization of Service," *Harvard Business Review*, (September-October), 63-74.

Lovelock, Christopher (1994), *Product Plus: How Product + Service = Competitive Advantage*. New York: McGraw-Hill.

Moorman, Robert H. (1991), "Relationship Between Organizational Justice and Organizational Citizenship Behavior: Do Fairness Perceptions Influence Employee Citizenship?" *Journal of Applied Psychology*, 76(6), 845-55.

——— (1993), "The Influence of Cognitive and Affective Based Job Satisfaction Measures on the Relationship Between Satisfaction and Organizational Citizenship Behavior," *Human Relations*, 46(6), 759-76.

Narver, John C. and Stanley F. Slater (1990), "The Effect of a Market Orientation on Business Profitability," *Journal of Marketing*, 54, 20-35.

Normann, Richard (1991), *Service Management: Strategy and Leadership in Services Businesses*, 2nd ed. Chichester, UK: John Wiley and Sons.

Organ, Dennis W. (1988), *Organizational Citizenship Behavior*. Lexington, MA: Lexington Books.

Ostroff, Cheri and David E. Bowen (forthcoming), "Moving Human Resources to a Higher Level: Human Resource Practices and Organizational Effectiveness," in *Multilevel Theory, Research and Methods in Organizations*, K. Klein and S. W. Koslowski, eds. San Francisco: Jossey-Bass.

Ott, J. S. (1989), *The Organizational Culture Perspective*. Pacific Grove, CA: Brooks/Cole.

Peters, Thomas J. and Robert H. Waterman (1982), *In Search of Excellence: Lessons From America's Best Run Companies*. New York: Warner Books.

Pfeffer, Jeffrey (1998), *The Human Equation: Building Profits by Putting People First*. Boston: Harvard Business School Press.

Porter, Michael E. (1980), *Competitive Strategy*. New York: Free Press.

Schein, Edgar H. (1992), *Organizational Culture and Leadership*, 2nd ed. San Francisco: Jossey-Bass.

Schneider, Benjamin (1973), "The Perception of Organizational Climate: The Customer's View," *Journal of Applied Psychology*, 57, 248-56.

——— (1980), "The Service Organization: Climate Is Crucial," *Organizational Dynamics*, 8 (Autumn), 52-65.

——— (1990), "The Climate for Service: An Application of the Climate Construct," in *Organizational Climate and Culture*, Benjamin Schneider, ed. San Francisco: Jossey-Bass, 383-412.

——— (1991), "Service Quality and Profits: Can You Have Your Cake and Eat It, Too?" *Human Resources Planning*, 14(2), 151-57.

——— (1994), "HRM—A Service Perspective: Towards a Customer-Focused HRM," *International Journal of Service Industry Management*, 5(1), 64-76.

——— and David E. Bowen (1985), "Employee and Customer Perceptions of Service in Banks: Replication and Extension," *Journal of Applied Psychology*, 70, 423-33.

——— and ——— (1992), "Personnel/Human Resources Management in the Service Sector," *Research in Personnel and Human Resources Management*, 10, 1-30.

——— and ——— (1993), "The Service Organization: Human Resources Management Is Crucial," *Organizational Dynamics*, 21, 39-52.

——— and ——— (1995), *Winning the Service Game*. Boston: Harvard Business School Press.

———, Arthur P. Brief, and Richard A. Guzzo (1996), "Creating a Climate and Culture for Sustainable Organizational Change," *Organizational Dynamics*, 24(4), 7-19.

———, John J. Parkington, and Virginia M. Buxton (1980), "Employee and Customer Perceptions of Service in Banks," *Administrative Sciences Quarterly*, 25, 252-67.

———, J. K. Wheeler, and J. F. Cox (1992), "A Passion for Service: Using Content Analysis to Explicate Service Climate Themes," *Journal of Applied Psychology*, 77(5), 705-16.

———, Susan White, and Michelle C. Paul (1998), "Linking Service Climate and Customer Perceptions of Service Quality: Test of a Causal Model," *Journal of Applied Psychology*, 83(2), 150-63.

Siehl, Caren and Joanne Martin (1990), "Organization Culture: A Key to Financial Performance?" in *Organizational Climate and Culture*, Benjamin Schneider, ed. San Francisco: Jossey-Bass, 241-81.

Sutton, Robert I. and Anat Rafaeli (1989), "Untangling the Relationship Between Displayed Emotion and Organizational Sales: The Case of Convenience Stores," *Academy of Management Journal*, 31(3), 461-87.

Trice, Harrison M. and Janice M. Beyer (1993), *The Cultures of Work Organizations*. Englewood Cliffs, NJ: Prentice Hall.

Ulrich, David and Dale Lake (1990), *Organizational Capability: Competing From the Inside Out*. New York: John Wiley.

Wiley, John (1996), "Linking Survey Results to Customer Satisfaction and Business Performance," in *Organizational Surveys: Tools for Assessment and Change*, A. I. Kraut, ed. San Francisco: Jossey-Bass, 88-116.

Zeithaml, Valarie A., A. Parasuraman, and Leonard L. Berry (1990), *Delivering Quality Service: Balancing Customer Perceptions and Expectations*. New York: Free Press.

28

Service Operations Management

A Field Guide

RICHARD B. CHASE
RAY M. HAYNES

Service operations management (SOM) existed from the first time that an enterprising caveman offered to skin a dinosaur for his neighbor in return for part of the meat. A more defined service sector began in earnest during the 1950s, driven by the postindustrial economy. Traditionally, SOM is considered to have evolved from the marketing and production operations fields. Beginning in the 1970s, the academic community began to recognize SOM as a potentially separate discipline area, as evidenced by a variety of papers devoted to the importance of services in core typologies (Mills and Margulies 1980), application and research (Mabert 1982), the need for SOM research (Sullivan 1982), and perspectives on service technologies (Mills and Moberg 1982).

Perhaps one of the earliest and most referenced "services" touchstones is the article by Theodore Levitt (1972) that explored the implications of treating services as "manufacturing in the field." Using McDonald's fast food restaurants as an archetype, this article showed the benefits of redefining the service worker's oft-denigrated role of a servant to one of a production worker using technology and systems to provide a high-quality "product," and hence deliver "service without servitude." Legend has it that John Reed (now chairman of Citicorp) had seen a draft of Levitt's article, which resulted in the massive move by First National City Bank to treat the back-office operations like a factory in the early 1970s. These efforts were treated in detail with two Harvard Business School cases (Seeger 1975a, 1975b). Chase (1978) later suggested that the presence of the customer created inherent variability in front-office work and thereby ultimately limited the extent to which front-office work could be rationalized, relative to that of the back office. (For example, the front office must be laid out to accommodate the customer's physical presence, whereas the back office can be laid out to achieve the best process flow for working on the physical inventories that support the front-office service.) In the 1980s, writings explored how service concepts could be used by manufacturers to gain competitive advantage. Chase and Garvin (1989) suggested how manufacturers could, under certain circum-. stances, link the factory (the back office of the manufacturing firm) with the end customer to provide value-added services. Examples were provided showing how shop-floor personnel communicated directly with the customer to aid in troubleshooting and how the factory could work as a sales unit, as a type of showroom demonstrating its workers' skills as well as the firm's technology. More recent writings tie operations to broader corporate performance. Heskett et al. (1994) showed how good human resource management practices foster good service operations performance, and hence profitability—a linkage they termed the "service profit chain." Roth and Jackson (1995) proposed the capabilities-service quality-performance (C-SQ-P) triad. This empirically developed model links service strategy to the key notion of resource-based competitiveness of contemporary organization theory.

Universities soon began teaching classes on services management, most using the first dedicated textbook, developed by Sasser, Olsen, and Wyckoff (1978). This textbook featured traditional content, readings, and a total of 37 cases for discussion of service topics. Today, a good selection of SOM-specific texts is available (e.g., Fitzsimmons and Fitzsimmons 1997; Haywood-Farmer and Nollet 1991; Schmenner 1995). Crossover texts are useful to understand the integrated linkages to marketing (Lovelock 1992; Swartz, Bowen, and Brown 1992) and manufacturing (Chase, Aquilano, and Jacobs 1998).

Today, the service sector is the primary creator of job opportunities and a primary contributor to the economy. By the year 2000, between 75% and 90% of all U.S. jobs were predicted to be in the service sector, and contributions to GNP were expected to be in the same range (Schmenner 1995). The academy, industry, and Wall Street, however, continue to wrestle with exact definitions of a "service," and many pundits tend to make fuzzy explanations.

Jim and Mona Fitzsimmons (1997) propose seven distinctive characteristics of services that are most widely accepted and that have universal application. These attributes include that

1. the customer is a participant in the service process;
2. there is simultaneous production and consumption of service, with delivery in real time;
3. the service deliverable is intangible (but may include supporting goods);
4. services have no inventory because capacity is time perishable;
5. service output (quality and productivity) is difficult to measure;
6. the service location is dictated by proximity to customers; and
7. services tend to be labor intensive.

Using these criteria, the most common service operations include government, banking and finance, health care, transportation, education, travel and tourism, hospitality, utilities, telecommunications, consulting, and retailing. A more detailed look at several of these common services is provided by Haywood-Farmer and Nollet (1991). The very nature of services that are created to serve the public good has driven the government's regulatory policies that define operations in an effort to provide equal access, pricing, and service levels for a wide spectrum of users.

The history of regulation can be traced back to the beginning of the United States; however, active deregulation policy began in the 1960s during the Kennedy administration. The operational efforts at deregulation are time coincident with the emergence of SOM as a field of study (Sampson, Farris, and Shrock 1985). Beginning in the 1970s and until the present, the deregulation of businesses in the service sector has created widespread shifts in the fundamental scope and scale of SOM, as evidenced by activities in the airline, banking, health care, insurance, and telecommunications industries.

Today, the fastest growing "sector" is business services, which has climbed from less than $50 billion in 1985 to more than $300 billion in revenues by 1997 (Melenovsky 1998). At the same time, technology growth has enabled market innovations in the area of electronic commerce, resulting in fundamental shifts in how many traditional services will do business (Cortese and Stepanek 1998). This is somewhat of a dichotomy, with high growth in both people-intensive and technology-intensive service delivery, but it serves to confirm the richness for both opportunities and challenges in the service sector.

- Consider priceline.com as an Internet alternative to visiting your local travel agent and getting the best available prices on tickets directly from the airlines on a bid basis. As a nascent service, the process is certainly not perfected, but it offers promise for significant SOM restructuring in a variety of industries (Leonhardt 1998).

- The book retailing business has been altered dramatically by amazon.com, and the exponential growth of the World Wide Web is daily providing alternate channels for customers in the service chain. Technology is allowing for a blending between service marketing and SOM roles, with the customer actively participating in the entire process.

- In the mid-1990s, the most active recruiters on college campuses nationwide were consulting companies such as Andersen, EDS, Deloitte-Touche, and American Management Systems. Most are recruiting primarily to meet the demands of the implementation of new hardware and software to support the evolving "enterprise resource planning" systems being created by firms such as SAP, Bann, and Oracle. The SOM role is to provide the design, development, implementation, and maintenance of these highly integrated operations.

VALUE AND PERFORMANCE DEFINED

Both providers and customers are seeking increased value from their service encounters, and the balanced use of people and technology is required to meet these needs. The concept of value has driven SOM from the beginning. Although many definitions for value exist, consider a functional equation that can be derived from the basics of the production function and the definition of productivity (Chase, Aquilano, and Jacobs 1998; Heskett, Sasser, and Hart 1990). Productivity (a recognized value metric) is the ratio of output to input, with output defined as performance and all inputs having cost characteristics. Expanding the numerator into key components yields factors of quality, time, and flexibility, with some scalar weighting possible depending on the exact service encounter. (Note that this may also include the quality that comes from making the service-selling environment more entertaining; Pine and Gilmore 1998.) This concept of a value equation was proposed by Edwin Artzt (1992), CEO of Procter & Gamble, and will anchor this chapter and support us on our journey into the magical realm of SOM.

$$Value = Performance/Cost$$

where

$$Performance = \beta_1 \times Quality + \beta_2 \times Speed + \beta_3 \times Flexibility.$$

Each of the four functional factors of quality, time, flexibility, and cost will be explored in more detail with respect to several of the more fundamental concepts and premises that are associated with understanding SOM from a broad perspective. We begin with some basic assumptions that have general acceptance both in the academic literature and among practicing service managers.

FUNDAMENTAL LAWS, MYTHS, AND COMMANDMENTS

Although we intuitively know that the customer is indeed *not* always right, most managers consider that service delivery is an art form blending marketing, operations, and human behavior (Lovelock 1992). Functionally, marketing creates the customer expectation, operations delivers a customer experience, and the nature of customer human behavior molds a perception of the service. Accepting this as a starting point, Maister (1985) proposed two "laws" that create an excellent beginning.

First Law: Satisfaction equals perception minus expectation.

Both SOM and the service marketing fields have leveraged this relationship into much of the work on service quality, including the SERVQUAL model (Berry, Zeithaml, and Parasuraman 1985) and related work by the trio and others.

Second Law: It is hard to play catch-up.

Fixing the situation once the first law has been violated is possible, but like rework in manufacturing, there is often significant cost. This proposition has led to studies and literature in service failure (Schlesinger and Heskett 1991) and fail-safing services (Chase and Stewart 1994). This topic will be covered later in this chapter in the discussion on quality.

Myths

Managing in the service economy (Heskett 1986) is often inherently fuzzy and/or misunderstood. Preconceptions of SOM create a certain amount of folklore that bears careful consideration and rethinking of perspectives. Lovelock (1992) proposed six common myths associated with the service sector.

1. The service economy produces at the expense of other sectors.
2. Service jobs are low paying and menial.
3. All services are labor intensive and have low productivity.
4. Government growth has been the primary driver of the service sector.
5. Services constitute marginal demands after primary needs are satisfied.
6. Service providers are primarily small, cottage, or mom-and-pop operations.

A wealth of examples can be offered to "debunk" the listed myths; we note a few that are thought provoking, one for each of the six myths.

1. General Motors's corporate performance is greatly enhanced by the contribution of its GMAC financial services operation.
2. Physicians' earnings are significantly above average.
3. Banks using ATMs have experienced gains in the use of human resources and overall productivity.
4. Government is currently downsizing while service-related employment and GNP is increasing.
5. Critical services like electric utilities and education are considered primary needs.
6. Many services are extremely large, such as Citibank, the U.S. military forces, and the California State University system, with 23 campuses.

Even allowing for some context specificity, the six items of the list generally are accepted to be myths.

Thou Shalts

Finally, commonsense insight into effective service delivery can often be traced to some fundamental "do's and don'ts." Chase (1985) presented some of these truisms as commandments.

1. Thou shalt make transparent all stages of thy process.

2. Thou shalt challenge every sign and dispatch with extreme prejudice those that are schlocky.

3. Thou shalt maintain at least normal, if not extensive, business hours.

4. Thou shalt honor thy customer's privacy.

5. Thou shalt adhere to the law of the queue.

6. Thou shalt affirm that not all thy customers are created equal.

7. Thou shalt affirm that the only reason for having thy customer on thy premises is to sell him some more of thy services.

8. Thou shalt divide thy workers into people and paper people and assign them tasks accordingly.

9. Thou shalt forbid thy servers to take breaks, eat hero sandwiches, or talk to their boy or girl friends on the phone in thy customer's presence.

10. Thou shalt place thy best people on the firing line.

11. Thou shalt forswear thy stopwatch and rethink thy design specs.

Having set the stage with a brief history of SOM, illuminating examples, and provocative (we hope) lists, we will now begin to consider several of the more "universal" models associated with services. One of the unique features of services is that virtually all people are customers in one manner or another and have had experience in dealing with SOM. Although the actual service encounter or transaction may not be thought of from the perspective of Maister's "laws," most readers can relate a variety of "war stories" in dealing with service providers. Current attention to various aspects of service-sector business has created almost an overload of articles, books, and seminars. Selecting one single source or primer is difficult, but recommended reading for those interested in the dynamics of SOM is "The Mall Is My Factory: Reflections of a Service Junkie" (Chase 1996).

SERVICE MODELS

One definition of a "model" is that it is a small representation of an existing or planned object. This is the context that we often think of when considering model trains, airplanes, or cars. To the economist, a model serves to establish the interrelationships among parameters that can be used to define the dynamics of an economy. To a fashion magazine, the model serves to display goods offered to the public. In SOM, there are many models of how services "work" or operate. After presenting some basic classifications and structural concepts, we will consider the elements from the value equation as operationalized in an SOM environment and then summarize using a "grand model" to create a systemic view of service operations.

Degree of Interaction and Customization

	Low	High
Low	Service factory • Airlines • Trucking • Hotels • Resorts and recreation	Service shop • Hospitals • Auto repair • Other repair services
High	Mass service • Retailing • Wholesaling • Schools • Retail aspects of commercial banking	Professional service • Doctors • Lawyers • Accountants • Architects

(Vertical axis label: Degree of Labor Intensity)

Figure 28.1 The Service Process Matrix
SOURCE: Schmenner (1995).

Classifications

A number of researchers have tackled the task of classifying services. For example, Sasser, Olsen, and Wyckoff (1978) presented a basic scheme in the first SOM textbook, which listed goods and services on a continuum and served to "place" various services into a relative typical purchase bundle. Another viewpoint is presented by Schmenner (1986) in the service process matrix, with two axes featuring degree of interaction and customization versus degree of labor intensity. This model was extended by leveraging each quadrant to include key points offering challenges to service managers (Schmenner 1995) (see Figure 28.1).

The 2 × 2 matrix offers a simple framework for categorizing and comparing various elements associated with services. Lovelock (1983) presents a summary of five matrices, primarily from a marketing perspective but also useful for SOM consideration:

1. Understanding the nature of the service act (tangible/intangible actions vs. recipient people or things),

2. Relationships with customers (formal/informal relationships vs. nature of service delivery),

3. Customization and judgment in service delivery (high/low customization vs. personnel judgment),

4. Nature of demand relative to supply (wide/narrow demand fluctuation vs. supply capacity), and

5. Method of service delivery (single/multiple site vs. nature of interactions; actually a 2 × 3 matrix).

Regardless of the focus of any comparison, the primary goal is to help understand how services may be similar and/or different relative to certain characteristics. This knowledge can then be used to potentially reposition a service for increased performance by transitioning from one quadrant to another. For example, current distance education paradigms using asynchronous learning methodology (ALM) champions the replacement of teacher-student direct contact with technology creating virtual contact. The result is a significant gain in efficiency (a single instructor can now teach an almost unlimited number of students) as well as in effectiveness (students are no longer constrained by physical location).

Structure and Flow

Fundamental to beginning an analysis of any service is the understanding of what the service is delivering and the flow of the delivery process. The work done by Lynn Shostack (1984, 1987) on service blueprinting is generally considered of a seminal nature. The SOM blueprint essentially leverages the concept of a procedural or operational flow diagram, with origins in the data processing field, to establish the structure of a service and be able to analyze it from a systems perspective. The service blueprint for a typical banking transaction presented in Figure 28.2 illustrates the concept.

The same framework is used in the SERVQUAL model, which presents management an opportunity to do gap analysis when there is some discontinuity in the service delivery process (Parasuraman, Zeithaml, and Berry 1988). The flow modeling constructs are also useful for training service employees and providing them a systems-level perspective of the SOM rather than one derived from their own localized functional area. For example, America West Airlines has successfully created both job enlargement and enrichment by cross-training service employees to handle a variety of positions such as reservations and ticket counter agent, customer service representative, flight attendant, and baggage handler.

Time

For most services, time is critical for both provider and customer. Indeed, the user often chooses a service for convenience and to save time compared to an alternative solution, for instance, fast food from a drive-through window versus a home-cooked meal. Chase (1981) offers the underlying theory for an efficiency model of the customer-contact relationship focused on time. This normative model is expanded for organizational design considerations in later work (Chase and Tansik 1983):

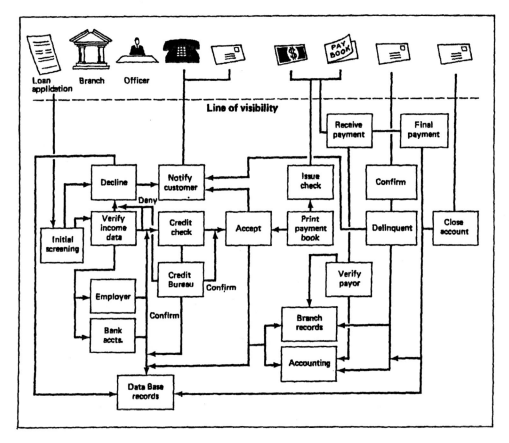

Figure 28.2 Blueprint for Bank Lending Operation
SOURCE: Shostack (1987).

Potential Operating Efficiency =
$\int (1 - [\text{customer contact time/service creation time}])$.

Although this model offers a baseline for considering time efficiency, neither customer utility nor organizationwide production or marketing performance is considered. This model is most useful for analyzing a single transaction. For example, a bank teller cashing a customer check averages 2.1 minutes contact time with the customer, with a service creation time (account balance verification, paper processing, and file updating) of 3.4 minutes. The Potential Operating Efficiency (also called the Potential Facility Efficiency; PFE) equates to approximately 0.38. Now consider an ATM delivering the same cash withdrawal service. The contact time reduces to an average of 1.0 minutes, with creation time held constant at 3.4 minutes. The PFE almost doubles to 0.71. Regardless of the exact numbers, customers appreciate reduced contact time, and the provider gains by being able to service more customers in the same time block, potentially increasing overall productivity. From a more formal perspective, Chase and Stewart

(1994) discussed the time implications of high-contact applications in a study of the savings and loan environment.

Quality

The customer expects quality service, and the provider wants to deliver quality service, but neither may truly know what quality means to the other or how to measure this elusive dimension of service. (More thorough discussions of service quality and customer satisfaction are presented elsewhere in this volume. For initial background, the reader is referred to Berry, Zeithaml, and Parasuraman 1985.)

The underlying critical component necessary to deliver quality service is communication. First, marketing and operations must communicate and agree on the nature and specifics of the service to be delivered. Operations must communicate these specifics and train the employees providing the service in a manner that supports the original expectation. Finally, even though Maister's Second Law exists, the knowledgeable and empowered employee may be able to correct or "fix" the customer perception on a real-time basis. For this to happen, the customer must be able to—and feel encouraged to—communicate dissatisfaction in such a manner as to enable the employee to alter the experience.

Although most services cannot select their customers, management can proactively choose employees in such a manner as to enhance the service encounter (Schlesinger and Heskett 1991). Poorly selected and trained employees often result in high turnover and customer dissatisfaction, creating an ongoing cycle of failure. This cycle can be changed using some of the winning strategies proposed below.

1. Careful selection of employees for both skill and attitude
2. Realistic previews of the job and organization to prospective employees
3. A focus on the nature and quality of early job experience
4. Employee empowerment and latitude, broadly defined
5. Employees' awareness of their roles in customer satisfaction and economic success
6. Scorekeeping and feedback on employee performance
7. Integration of employees into a winning team
8. A focus on aggregate labor costs instead of individual wage levels
9. Concentration on quality at the service core using local definitions

Total quality management (TQM) has become accepted practice in services. Concepts from TQM in manufacturing (benchmarking, control charts, etc.) have been combined with those in services such as guarantees and recovery to enhance the effectiveness of service delivery. The Japanese concept of *poka yokes* or foolproofing has been elaborated on for SOM applications in the context of making service delivery fail-safe (Chase and Stewart 1994). The goal is simply to make the service encounter "error free" through the analysis of the nature of the front-office tasks and transactions that involve the customer. Note that back-office

SOM also can benefit from "fail-safing," but because the customer is not in this part of the process, often tools and techniques from manufacturing can be more readily utilized. There are two categories that must be treated.

First, the server/employee must be fail-safed using *poka yokes* for the task (correctness of operation), treatment (customer courtesy and attention), and tangibles (facility hygiene and appearance). Second, the customer must be fail-safed using *poka yokes* for preparation (role anticipation and correct service selection), encounter (follow system flow instructions and specify requirements adequately), and resolution (signal service failure, learn and adjust expectations). Designing *poka yokes* is part art and part science. Because SOM processes are often unique to the given business, there is no magic formula other than to study the flow for possible fail-safe opportunities.

Flexibility

Although blueprinting may create the structure for a well-defined and consistent process flow, the nature of having the customer directly involved in the delivery mechanism often leads to uncertainties. In general, the more flexibility in routine services, the higher the cost, directly related to longer contact time. The service provider must ascertain the level of contact necessary for the particular "bundle" to be delivered and manage accordingly based on where the customer "fits" in the operation (Chase 1978). Flexibility may also be increased by getting customers to participate more actively in the service, with their discretionary needs more fully addressed by their self-selection of certain service elements (Fitzsimmons and Sullivan 1982). The current trend for employee "empowerment" has an effect on service flexibility but must be tempered with an emphasis on employee selection, skill set recognition, and training. Disney is an oft-cited example of an organization that spends significant amounts of money up front to identify the right person for the job and supplement the natural fit with extensive training and development.

Costs

As the denominator in the value equation, costs are generally considered the purview of the provider and functionally a measure of efficiency of the service delivery. In the sense that hard costs often translate into the price experienced by the customer, "cost" must be considered from that perspective as well. In a technology-driven service process/facility, the capital costs often define the pricing strategy. An ATM has well-defined purchase, maintenance, and service costs that allow for an exact calculation of per-transaction costs at the terminal level. Conversely, in a labor-intensive service, pricing may be derived from perceived costs. A person choosing a plastic surgeon may elect to go to an office staffed by graduates of major U.S. medical schools rather than by "Caribbean Island MD Diploma Mill" graduates, even though both may be board certified and equally capable. In this case, the former may charge a higher price for their services even though the underlying costs are similar for either physician.

Another cost often associated with SOM is not specific but attributable to the fact that people typically wait or "queue up" for service delivery. Chase (1985) alludes to this in his Commandment #5, primarily from the accepted servicing rule of "first come, first served" (FCFS). Quantitatively, queue management can be modeled well with a variety of techniques including software tools simulating calling population, arrival process, configuration, discipline, costs of waiting, costs of serving, service time, and number of servers (Fitzsimmons and Fitzsimmons 1997). More qualitatively, Maister (1985) develops a conception describing the wait in psychological terms, proposing eight ideas that must be addressed by service managers to alter a customer's perception of the wait and related costs.

1. Unoccupied time feels longer than occupied time.
2. Pre-process waits feel longer than in-process waits.
3. Anxiety makes waits feel longer.
4. Uncertain waits feel longer than known, finite waits.
5. Unexplained waits feel longer than explained waits.
6. Unfair waits feel longer than equitable waits.
7. The more valuable the service, the longer the customer will wait.
8. Solo waits feel longer than group waits.

Disney has been acclaimed as mastering the queue challenge in its theme parks, such as Disneyland and Disney World. Far from waits being a secret, Disney makes an effort to communicate so well with the customer that any wait can be perceived as less "costly" with respect to expectations and experiences.

Productivity and Performance

We now consolidate the individual factors associated with the value equation into a macro perspective of the service system. Definitions and semantics may often confuse both the customer and provider in SOM; however, if we go back to the basics previously discussed, we can begin to derive an analogy. Output metrics in services are defined as the customer satisfaction or the perceived effectiveness of the deliverable. Input by definition is a factor most often associated with the service provider, and an efficiency metric is related to delivery costs. (Note that the customer may be concerned with "price," but this is a derivative of actual cost integrated with perceived performance.) These relationships suggest that productivity can now be considered the ratio of effectiveness to efficiency.

A model for service productivity can be established using a 2×2 matrix with the axes of effectiveness and efficiency (Haynes and DuVall 1992) and is presented in Figure 28.3. The premise is that the customer wants high levels of effectiveness with little regard to provider efficiency (unless it translates into hard pricing) and conversely, the provider, while concerned with customer effectiveness, really wants to make a profit and may focus on cost reduction. Use of this model allows the service manager to consider how to balance effectiveness with efficiency and

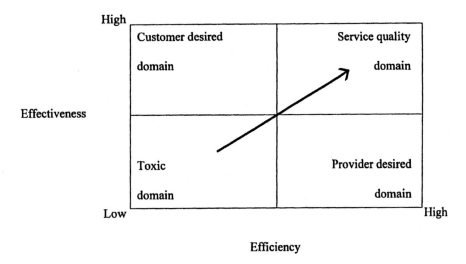

Figure 28.3 The Homeostatic Model

ideally move into a domain of high service quality and productivity. For instance, the toxic quadrant implies both low effectiveness (customer unhappy with service) and high costs (provider margin less than desired) and suggests that the service manager should move into another quadrant quickly for business survival.

Others have studied the balancing of SOM from an organizational effectiveness perspective (Bowen, Chase, and Cummings 1990; Roth and Jackson 1995) and productivity enhancement (Fitzsimmons and Sullivan 1982). Efforts in motivating the customer/provider participants for productivity gain have been discussed by Mills, Chase, and Margulies (1983). In general, the literature suggests that within the same definitional construct of productivity, SOM may benefit from three changes.

1. Transfer to SOM of appropriate technology developed in manufacturing. (Fail-safing/ *poka yoke* is an example of this technology transfer, as previously discussed.)

2. Innovative use of computer-based information systems. (Web enterprise activities are an example, and the Service Operations Management Association website SOMA.BYU, maintained by Scott Sampson, offers a wealth of additional information on SOM.)

3. Recognizing the customer as a productive resource in the service process. (Automated gas pumps are an example of self-service in a retail environment.)

There is tremendous potential for synergy when balancing or incorporating all three of these recommended productivity-related treatments. One primer on technology use and service automation is offered by Collier (1985). An article by Haynes and Thies (1991) provides specific results from studies of automated teller machines and automated gas pumps, where effectiveness is enhanced and efficiency is increased.

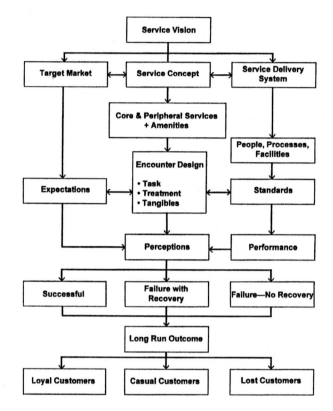

Figure 28.4 Grand Model: Service Design and Service Outcomes

Grand Model Concept

The seven elements of SOM presented at the beginning of this chapter are not meant to be comprehensive but certainly touch on most of the core realities and reference a substantial literature for further study. Success in services can never be assured, but avoiding the obvious pitfalls has been highlighted by two prominent authors in the field from the perspectives of future survival (Schmenner 1986) and lessons to be learned (Heskett 1987). As with any operation, a service must be conceived, designed, developed, and managed realizing that at the end of the day, there will be only three possible outcomes. First, customers who are highly satisfied (or hopefully delighted) will be forever loyal. Second, customers who are relatively satisfied can be considered casual. Finally, customers who perceived their service as being less than satisfactory may well be lost.

Using this rationale, the "Grand Model" is provided in Figure 28.4 to graphically enable a better understanding of the service design and service outcome flow from the initial vision to final outcomes.

The Grand Model links the critical success factors as previously discussed with respect to the micro models presented. The initial service ideas (vision) are operationalized (concept) to both customer requirements and system processes.

The service bundle (core and peripherals) is matched to the actual delivery (encounter) resulting in customer satisfaction (perception) levels. Depending on the management of the satisfaction (failure/recovery) attributes, specific customer classifications can be derived. For most service managers, the goal would be to secure repeat business (loyal customers). Any lesser outcome (casual or lost customers) requires focused reexamination of the Grand Model modules for the particular service. Most services have some feedback structure suggesting a continuous "loop" that incorporates information from both the internal/provider and external/customer sides of the service encounter. Such a mechanism provides the input to fine-tune and integrate the system processes for maximum performance.

FINAL THOUGHTS AND FUTURES

Businesses in the service sector will continue to experience significant issues and opportunities, from active deregulation to waves of mergers/consolidations on an unprecedented scale. Technology in both broad and local terms will push the service frontiers, offering customers and providers increased efficiencies and higher perceived value. Because of the high levels of familiarity that customers have with services, there is often a tendency to trivialize service excellence, writing it off to "good luck" or "charm" or "opportunity," but reality has consistently demonstrated that long-term success can be attributed to truly managing the service-delivery process using many of the tools and techniques described in this chapter. We recommend the article by Chase and Hayes (1991), which suggests that most services can benefit from a return to the concepts presented in Operations Management 101 and a focus on the control of the service encounter from a strategic perspective.

REFERENCES

Artzt, Edwin L. (1992), "Value Model Presentation," Quality Forum VIII, Washington, DC, October.

Berry, Leonard L., Valarie A. Zeithaml, and A. Parasuraman (1985), "Quality Counts in Services, Too," *Business Horizons*, 63 (May-June), 44-52.

Bowen, David E., Richard B. Chase, and Thomas G. Cummings (1990), *Service Management Effectiveness*. San Francisco: Jossey-Bass.

Chase, Richard B. (1978), "Where Does a Customer Fit in a Services Operation?" *Harvard Business Review*, 56 (November-December), 137-42.

——— (1981), "The Customer Contact Approach in Services: Theoretical Bases and Practical Extensions," *Operations Research*, (July-August), 599-606.

——— (1985), "The 10 Commandments of Service Systems Management," *Interfaces*, (May-June), 68-72.

——— (1996), "The Mall Is My Factory: Reflections of a Service Junkie," *Production and Operations Management*, 3(4), 298-308.

———, N. J. Aquilano, and F. R. Jacobs (1998), *Production and Operations Management: Manufacturing and Services*, 8th ed. San Francisco: Irwin/McGraw-Hill.

———— and David Garvin (1989), "The Service Factory," *Harvard Business Review*, 67 (July-August), 61-69.

———— and Ray M. Hayes (1991), "Beefing up Operations in Service Firms," *Sloan Management Review*, 33 (Fall), 15-26.

———— and David M. Stewart (1994), "Make Your Service Fail-Safe," *Sloan Management Review*, 36 (Spring), 35-44.

———— and David A. Tansik (1983), "The Customer Contact Model for Organizational Design," *Management Science*, 29(9), 1037-50.

Collier, David A. (1985), *Service Management: The Automation of Services*. Reston, VA: Reston/Prentice Hall.

Cortese, A. E. and M. Stepanek (1998), "Good-Bye to Fixed Pricing?" *Business Week*, (May 4), 71-84.

Fitzsimmons, James A. and Mona J. Fitzsimmons (1997), *Service Management*. San Francisco: McGraw-Hill.

———— and Robert S. Sullivan (1982), *Service Operations Management*. San Francisco: McGraw-Hill.

Haynes, Ray M. and P. K. DuVall (1992), "Service Quality Management: A Process Control Approach," *International Journal of Service Industry Management*, 3(1), 14-24.

———— and E. A. Thies (1991), "Management of Technology in Service Firms," *Journal of Operations Management*, 10(3), 388-97.

Haywood-Farmer, John and Jean Nollet (1991), *Services Plus*. Quebec: G. Morin.

Heskett, James L. (1986), *Managing in the Service Economy*. Boston: Harvard Business School Press.

————, Thomas O. Jones, Gary W. Loveman, W. Earl Sasser, Jr., and Leonard A. Schlesinger (1994), "Putting the Service Profit Chain to Work," *Harvard Business Review*, 72 (March-April), 164-74.

———— (1987), "Lessons in the Service Sector," *Harvard Business Review*, 65 (March-April), 67-77.

————, W. Earl Sasser, and Christopher W. L. Hart (1990), *Service Breakthroughs: Changing the Rules of the Game*. New York: Free Press.

Leonhardt, D. (1998), "Make a Bid, But Don't Pack Your Bags," *Business Week*, (June 1), 164.

Levitt, Theodore (1972), "Production Approach to Services," *Harvard Business Review*, 50 (September-October), 41-52.

Lovelock, Christopher H. (1983), "Classifying Services to Gain Strategic Marketing Insights," *Journal of Marketing*, 47 (Summer), 9-20.

———— (1992), *Managing Services*, 2nd ed. Englewood Cliffs, NJ: Prentice Hall.

Mabert, V. A. (1982), "Service Operations Management: Research and Application," *Journal of Operations Management*, 2, 203-8.

Maister, David H. (1985), "The Psychology of Waiting Lines," in *The Service Encounter*, John Czepiel, Michael Solomon, and Carol Surprenant, eds. Lexington, MA: Lexington Books, 113-23.

Melenovsky, M. (1998), "Profiting From the Identity Crisis in Service," from presentation by IDC Services Research, San Francisco.

Mills, Peter K., Richard B. Chase, and Newton Margulies (1983), "Motivating the Client/Employee System as a Service Production Strategy," *Academy of Management Review*, 8, 301-10.

———— and Newton Margulies (1980), "Toward a Core Typology of Service Organizations," *Academy of Management Review*, 5, 255-65.

———— and David J. Moberg (1982), "Perspectives on the Technology of Service Operations," *Academy of Management Review*, 7, 467-78.

Parasuraman, A., Valarie A. Zeithaml, and Leonard Berry (1988), "SERVQUAL: A Multiple-Item Scale for Measuring Consumer Perceptions of Service Quality," *Journal of Retailing*, 64(1), 12-40.

Pine, Joseph and James Gilmore (1998), "Welcome to the Experience Economy," *Harvard Business Review*, 76 (July-August), 97-109.

Roth, Aleda V. and W. E. Jackson (1995), "Strategic Determinants of Service Quality and Performance: Evidence From the Banking Industry," *Management Science*, 41(11), 1721-33.

Sampson, R. J., Martin T. Farris, and David L. Shrock (1985), *Domestic Transportation: Practice, Theory, and Policy*. Boston: Houghton Mifflin.

Sasser, W. Earl, R. Paul Olsen, and Darrel D. Wyckoff (1978), *Management of Service Operations*. Boston: Allyn & Bacon.

Schlesinger, Leonard A. and James L. Heskett (1991), "Breaking the Cycle of Failure in Services," *Sloan Management Review*, 32 (Spring), 17-28.

Schmenner, Roger W. (1986), "How Can Service Businesses Survive and Prosper?" *Sloan Management Review*, 27 (Spring), 21-32.

———— (1995), *Service Operations Management*. Englewood Cliffs, NJ: Prentice Hall.

—— (1995), *Service Operations Management*. Englewood Cliffs, NJ: Prentice Hall.

Seeger, J. A. (1975a), "First National City Bank Operating Group A," Harvard Business School Case #474-165. Boston: Harvard Business School.

—— (1975b), "First National City Bank Operating Group B," Harvard Business School Case #474-166. Boston: Harvard Business School.

Shostack, G. Lynn (1984), "Designing Services That Deliver," *Harvard Business Review*, 62 (January-February), 133-39.

—— (1987), "Service Positioning Through Structural Change," *Journal of Marketing*, 51, 34-43.

Sullivan, Robert S. (1982), "The Service Sector: Challenges and Imperatives for Research in Operations Management," *Journal of Operations Management*, 2 (August), 211-14.

Swartz, Teresa A., David E. Bowen, and Stephen W. Brown, eds. (1992), *Advances in Services Marketing and Management*. Greenwich, CT: JAI.

29

Addressing Services Marketing
Challenges Through Franchising

JAMES CROSS
BRUCE J. WALKER

The growth of services in the U.S. economy has been impressive. Services now constitute more than one-half of the gross domestic product and three-quarters of employment in the United States. Furthermore, services account for about 25% of world trade (Coalition of Service Industries Reports 1996). The United States has a large trade surplus in services and a large trade deficit in goods. Stories about the growth of services often lament the demise of certain types of manufacturing, suggesting that service jobs are somehow inferior.

Of course, services have some significant characteristics that affect their marketing and operations. Various authors describe these in terms of the "4 I's" (intangibility, inseparability, inconsistency, and lack of inventory) or some other classification. Cross and Walker (1987) focused on intangibility, the discretionary nature of service purchases, labor intensity, quality control problems, an operations focus, and the small size of many service businesses.

Franchising also receives ample attention in the popular media. Most of the reports chronicle the growth of franchising or the entrepreneurial opportunities associated with franchising (Whittemore 1993). Not all the articles are favorable, however. For example, occasionally an article reports on franchisees' claims that the relationship is weighted in favor of franchisors (Behar 1998; Harris 1997). Other articles focus on alleged "cannibalization," which refers to new franchised units, new company-owned units, or new distribution channels (e.g., supermarkets) taking business away from existing franchisees (Garee and Schori 1998; Morse 1998).

The link between the growth of services and franchising is less well covered. Many franchised businesses are obviously in the service sector. In fact, 22 of the 30 product categories in a recent statistical profile of franchising entailed—in

473

whole or in part—the marketing of services (*The Profile of Franchising* 1998). Furthermore, franchising seems to be a primary method of expanding service businesses. This relationship, however, is generally not explicitly explained in the business media.

This chapter will attempt to illuminate the complementary relationship between services and franchising. What is it about franchising that lends itself to service businesses? Is the growth "parallel" as some have claimed? Could the service sector have grown so quickly without the existence of franchising? This chapter will unfold as follows. Franchising as a method of doing business will be examined in a more technical sense. Then the distinctive attributes (some would say advantages) of franchising will be related to the challenges posed by service businesses. Finally, a look to the future will explore possible trends and what might occur in the next millennium with regard to the complementary relationship between franchising and services marketing.

AN OVERVIEW OF FRANCHISING

Franchising is a type of contractual vertical marketing system. For a firm that seeks to build a network of business units under a common brand name, it is an alternative to a corporate (or vertically integrated) system in which the corporation owns entities, usually retailers, at another level of the channel (Allbery 1997; Maynard 1997). For an individual who desires to open a single business unit (perhaps with intentions to own multiple units), franchising is an alternative to independent operation.

A legally enforceable document governs the relationship of all parties in the franchise arrangement, so fairly precise roles and performance standards usually are present in franchising, with the contract stipulating the details of how the business will be run. Franchising offers a high degree of channel control without some of the costs and limitations of a corporate system.

The most obvious appeals of franchising, to both franchisee and franchisor, are the possible reduction of business risk and potential financial advantages (Justis and Judd 1998). The franchisee gains access to a (supposedly) proven method of doing business that the franchisor has developed. Alternatively, an individual could simply start a similar business as an independent operator, although this can be riskier. From the franchisor's perspective, risk is reduced by developing and adhering to a systematic, stringent approach to screening owners of the business units composing the franchise system. Whether franchising is actually a less risky method of running a business has been vigorously debated (Cross 1998); however, that is typically one of its stated advantages.

With regard to financial advantages, the sponsor or originator of the franchise system (the franchisor) grants rights or privileges to franchisees. The franchisee agrees to do business in a specified manner and to pay fees to the franchisor in exchange for these privileges. The fees usually consist of both an initial franchise fee, an ongoing royalty, and perhaps an ongoing advertising or promotion fee as well. These revenues essentially provide the franchisor with funds for expansion of the system. Without such revenues, the franchisor would have to fund expansion in some other manner, such as issuing stock or taking on debt. Furthermore, these revenues help to underwrite operations, including ongoing business support for franchisees in the system. From the franchisee's perspective, participation in a franchise system should provide the benefits of scale economies (e.g., volume purchasing power for supplies) and access to marketing materials (e.g., professionally prepared ads) that are not cost feasible for an independent operator.

The sizes of the fees charged by the franchisor are determined by how lucrative the business could be, as determined by the market. Obviously, a more successful franchising concept can command higher fees. Different franchise systems structure these fees in various ways; some have higher initial fees, others have lower initial fees and higher ongoing royalties.

Franchising creates trade-offs for both parties to the agreement. A franchisor is essentially sharing expertise—in some cases, trade secrets—with business partners. Moreover, a franchisor's success is also determined, to a large degree, by the efforts of franchisees. A franchisee sacrifices substantial independence as part of a franchise system. Basically, a franchisee has to implement strategic decisions made by the franchisor and abide by various standardized policies and practices. Some franchisees chafe at this loss of independence or, stated conversely, need for conformance.

Franchising represents a distinctive form of partnership. The initial financial payments and the contract act as a "bond" to the franchise system (Mathewson and Winter 1985). Furthermore, a common brand name creates a degree of mutual dependence. The partnership is between franchisor and franchisee, but in addition, in a very real sense, all the franchisees in the system are partners with one another. The success of individual franchisees depends not only on the soundness of the franchisor's business plan and the franchisees' own skills and efforts but also on the diligence and effectiveness of other franchisees in implementing the business plan.

Given the mutual dependence, franchise systems ordinarily conduct a rigorous screening of potential franchisees (Love 1998; Whittemore 1991). The screening revolves mainly around financial stability, with added consideration of business aptitude and experience. In effect, the franchisors act as gatekeepers and keep out undercapitalized operators. Once in business, a franchisee is likely to be a highly motivated operator. To protect what is sometimes a substantial investment, a franchisee typically is willing to work much harder than a regular manager in a corporate vertical marketing system.

Reputable franchise systems provide extensive initial training and ongoing support for franchisees. Along with a well-known brand name, this package of assistance is one of the major appeals of joining a franchise system versus being independent. Various types of control systems and standardized methods are integral to franchising. Standardization is necessary to achieve the high level of consistency across locations that most franchisors consider imperative for successful geographic expansion. Franchisees also generally make contributions to a fund with which the system prepares promotional materials and buys advertising on a large scale. The franchisee thereby gains access to advertising and other forms of promotion that would be beyond the means of most independent businesses.

WHY FRANCHISING WORKS FOR SERVICES

Service businesses have to address the challenges presented by the distinctive nature of their primary offering, namely a service as contrasted with a good. The defining attributes of services have been enumerated as intangibility, inseparability, inconsistency, and lack of inventory (Assael 1985). Other factors also affect service businesses. These attributes will be reviewed briefly in this section, after which the ways in which franchising can help to address the resulting challenges will be discussed.

How Services Are Different

Intangibility refers to a service's lack of physical features. A service itself cannot be held or smelled. In contrast, goods can be examined and tested before purchase. As a result, one of the thrusts of services marketing is to add tangibility via some form of marketing symbolism such as color, uniforms, slogans, or associations.

Inseparability means that production and consumption occur together. Hair cutting and styling is a good example. The cut and styling are created with the help of the consumer. The stylist acts as a direct salesperson, solicits information from the customer, and performs the work. When the consumer leaves the chair, the process is complete. Of course, it could be argued that consumption occurs over the useful life (a few weeks or more) of the cut or styling.

Inconsistency refers to the fact that services are often not of uniform quality. Inconsistency results from the heavy labor component in the production of services. It is often difficult to fully or even partially mechanize the process. People, as contrasted with machines, perform slightly differently across time. The element of variability is not evident, at least not to the same degree, in the typically automated production of goods.

Inventory generally is not present in service businesses. Inventory will exist to the extent that goods are required in producing the service; thus, the amount of inventory found in service businesses spans a continuum. Some service firms (e.g., hotels) have a fair amount of equipment and supplies on hand to do business; in contrast, some service providers (e.g., a tutoring service) might require virtually no equipment or supplies. Of course, it is likely that all service businesses will rely on at least some equipment and supplies (e.g., a laptop computer and diskettes containing educational content for a tutoring service).

Because the product is intangible, a service cannot be produced and stored for future sale. Employees may, in fact, be "inventory" because of the heavy demand on labor in service businesses. For example, service firms add extra workers at

TABLE 29.1 How Franchising Addresses Services Marketing Challenges

Services Marketing Challenge	*Addressed by Franchising Attribute*
Intangibility	Marketing programs (e.g., logos, uniforms) to add tangibility, standardized systemwide promotion
Inseparability	Advertising to stimulate demand in slack periods
Inconsistency	Training programs, monitoring of standards, control systems, systemwide promotion to influence customer expectations
Lack of inventory	Assistance in demand forecasting
Small size of firm	Training programs, ongoing managerial assistance, professionally prepared promotional materials, scale economies as part of system
Focus on production and operations	Training programs, system-level strategic planning, marketing support
Many forms of competition	Multiple locations
Undercapitalized owners	Financing programs, rigorous screening of prospective owners
High failure rates	Tested business concept, initial and ongoing assistance

peak periods such as lunchtime in restaurants. Consequently, accurate demand forecasting is especially critical for service businesses.

Cross and Walker (1987) enumerate other distinctive features of service businesses. Service purchases are probably more discretionary than goods purchases. This is a result of the wider range of substitutes for services. These include other services, goods, doing it yourself (e.g., lawn care), or postponement of the purchase. The small size of many service firms creates problems common to all small businesses. For instance, operators may not be highly skilled in accounting and various management tools. In addition, they may focus their daily activities on operations issues, with an orientation more on production rather than on strategic planning and marketing.

Franchising's Distinctive Attributes

Some of the defining attributes of franchising can address the challenges of service businesses that were outlined previously. For this reason, franchising and services seem to coincide quite often. Cross and Walker (1987) refer to this as a "business marriage." The joint growth of service industries and franchising is not coincidental; they are made for each other.

Exactly why do franchising and service businesses mesh so well? As stated earlier, the attributes of franchising help resolve the problems unique to service industries. How this happens is covered next and also summarized in Table 29.1.

Intangibility is reduced via standardized systemwide promotion. Franchisees contribute to advertising funds. These monies are used for various types of advertising and promotion. Scale economies are present; individual operators would not be able to afford such creative activity or the media costs. Group purchasing power allows the promotions to be economical. Systemwide promotions develop somewhat common expectations in the minds of consumers.

Tangibility is added via logos, spokespersons, and standard layout of facilities and decor that consumers come to associate with the brand. Common pricing policies are also featured across locations.

Various types of standard operations and training attack the problems of inconsistency and inseparability. A problem with service businesses is that the high degree of labor involvement with production of services creates variability in product quality. In some service industries, heavy use is made of unskilled labor. Franchise systems create standard methods of operations. In well-conceived systems, nothing is left to chance; all aspects of running the business are planned. Both managers and employees are trained in these methods. Then vigorous control systems, including on-site inspections by a representative of the franchisor, ensure that standards are being met.

There is no way to automate completely the creation of services, but these approaches reduce the variability considerably. Additionally, standard promotional themes are congruent with these delivery systems. Consumers are conditioned to expect a certain level of product quality and customer service; standard operations allow these expectations to be met.

Problems arising within small firms often relate to a lack of planning and specific expertise. Operations dominate daily activities, and longer-run projects get delayed. Franchising helps address these issues via franchisor-designed training programs and marketing support. In addition to training specific to the service being provided, many systems offer training related to accounting, human resources, sales skills, and purchasing. This comprehensive training and support is another reason franchising is attractive as opposed to running an independent small business.

Franchising also addresses, at least indirectly, the challenge of there being many forms of competition for service businesses. In retail services, this translates into convenience and location. With increased mobility in society, more locations are necessary to provide convenience; otherwise, consumers might postpone the service or perform it themselves. Franchising is used to establish an extensive network of relatively standardized units. Locations could be established within a corporate system, but that would be expensive.

The financing arrangements provided by franchising allow quicker system expansion. The franchisee puts up a good part of the needed funds. Of course, as part of establishing a network of units, a franchisor has to recruit and screen franchisees and set up training and monitoring programs, so there are many other costs involved.

A LOOK AHEAD

What trends will affect franchising in the next decade? Will services and franchising continue to grow in concert? Several categories of changes, some of which are already under way, are discussed next.

New Types of Businesses

The original kind of franchising, referred to as "product and trade name" franchising, is in decline in terms of the number of locations but not in total sales volume. Auto dealers, soft drink bottlers, and gas stations—the predominant businesses in this category—are not service businesses, although they may provide some services. Total sales volume generated by product and trade name franchisors continues to increase, however, because the products distributed through this kind of franchising are essential, or at least highly desired, for virtually every household.

The growth of franchising has been fueled by a new kind of franchising, called "business format" franchising. Most business format franchisors offer a service as their primary product. This kind of franchising covers an entire method (or format) for operating a business. Whereas the focus in product and trade name franchising is on what is sold, the focus in business format franchising is on how the business is run.

Home-based businesses are likely to be another fertile area for franchising growth in the coming years. Telecommuting is now widely practiced; a home-based business is just a different version of this phenomenon. The growth in both telecommuting and home-based businesses can be found in common factors, most notably changes in workers' attitudes toward family, child care, and commuting time and cost. The widespread adoption of personal computing and fax machines as well as advances in telecommunications enable both telecommuting and home-based businesses.

Likewise, the dramatic growth in usage of the Internet has set the stage for a boom in electronic commerce (Green 1999). It is reasonable to expect that franchising will be involved in the surge of both home-based businesses and electronic commerce, providing the same methods as it has in other forms of business—common branding, start-up assistance, standardized operations, and ongoing support (Alexander 1991; Marsh 1990; Plave and Dombek 1998).

New Franchise Locations

It might appear that every intersection in the United States is—or soon will be—the home for four franchised businesses, typically offering various services. Although that is an exaggeration, of course, it is true that prime locations for franchises catering to convenience-oriented consumers are relatively scarce. As a result, franchisors are searching for alternative sites where they can achieve satisfactory levels of sales.

Nontraditional franchise locations in the United States include university campuses, airports, zoos, sports arenas, casinos, and the stores of large retailers such as Wal-Mart. These sites typically offer large amounts of consumer traffic, much of it "captive" to the circumstances (e.g., airports). Pricing flexibility is enhanced to the degree to which consumers are indeed captive—that is, have limited alternatives. Although there are now many franchised units in nontraditional sites, those sites still are a fertile area for growth.

Another way to add locations, while controlling the amount of dollars tied up in facilities, is "co-branding," also called "piggybacking." This practice involves putting multiple franchises within the same facility (Beresford 1995; Scott 1998). For example, a hamburger chain could also sell Mexican food. A lodging chain could offer travelers other desired products, such as business services (e.g., mailing, computers). The twofold rationale for co-branding is to appeal to an additional market segment and to get better asset utilization of the facility. This strategy would be especially appropriate for businesses (e.g., ice cream parlors) that are in heavy demand during certain seasons or times of the day but struggle for customers in other seasons or at other times. For this reason, Baskin-Robbins and Dunkin' Donuts have a co-branding agreement, and Blimpie Subs and Salads are colocated with Pasta Central franchises—a new Blimpie brand (Solomon 1998). Co-branding is also a way in which an operator can spread risk.

A different approach is to forgo a fixed location and rely on a mobile unit. In this approach, the business goes to the customer, rather than the other way around. There are many examples of mobile businesses, offering services such as glass repair, pet grooming, plumbing, various types of auto cleaning and repairs, and home maintenance. These are all service businesses in which consumer convenience is the key attribute. They could be independent or franchised. Again, franchising brings standard methods, equipment, promotion, and training. Mobile units are feasible if any equipment necessary to provide the service can be moved around economically and, of course, if consumers prefer or accept this approach.

A much different alternative is to expand into foreign countries. According to a 1995 survey, 44% of U.S.-based franchisors have franchises in other countries. Furthermore, of those that do not, 55% plan to establish foreign franchises (*International Expansion by U.S. Franchisors* 1996). For many prominent franchise systems, international franchising is increasingly important. For example, McDonald's currently derives a majority of its profits from international locations, although only about 30% of its stores are outside the United States (Leonhardt 1998).

As in any other international venture, a host of new challenges must be addressed. Examples include governmental restrictions and regulations in the host country, income levels, consumer behavior, media availability, currency fluctuations, and expatriation of profits. Some issues especially pertinent to franchising are legal and ownership constraints, minimum wage laws, pricing flexibility relative to income levels, and demand for the product in the context of the culture of the host nation (McLean 1990).

New Sources of Franchisees

A currently popular profile of the "new franchisee" includes "outplaced" business executives. With the restructuring of corporate America, including extensive downsizing of middle management in many large firms, there is a large pool of recently unemployed executives and managers. Franchising is attractive because it allows them to remain in a business situation, yet their destiny is controlled to a large extent by themselves rather than by a corporation. Franchisees are actually semi-independent businesspeople, but they appear to have a great deal of freedom compared to corporate employees. Franchise systems often seek outplaced corporate executives as franchisees for two primary reasons. First, they already have some business expertise. Second, and more important, they likely have received a severance package that provides the financial resources with which to buy the franchise. Some corporate executives who buy franchises, however, become frustrated by the long hours and the lack of amenities they enjoyed in their former roles (Selz 1992).

The majority of corporate restructuring and downsizing in the United States may have already occurred, but that is debatable because the pace of large-scale mergers does not seem to have abated. Europe is some years behind the United States in this trend, so fairly soon there may be a large group of restructured managers in Europe who might be interested in owning and operating a franchised business in their home country.

Another, more subtle market may be developing as a result of the wave of restructuring and downsizing. Younger workers—members of the so-called Generation X—may be taking note of what is happening and having doubts about careers with large corporations. Instead, they may be inclined to establish their own business at a relatively early age. Owning a franchised business may be an attractive option for disaffected members of Generation X. They would be wise to avoid that option, however, if they would be uncomfortable with the standardized policies and practices associated with franchising (Love 1998).

Women and minorities represent two additional pools of prospective franchisees (Whittemore 1990). Many systems have programs in place to help these groups of prospective franchisees acquire financing to purchase and operate a franchised unit. The results, with respect to actual numbers of women and minorities in various franchise systems, have been mixed ("Inroads" 1990; Tannenbaum 1990).

Changed System Structures

There are also noteworthy developments with respect to how franchise systems are structured. One is called ownership redirection (Dant, Kaufmann, and Paswan 1992). Essentially, this means that franchise systems are buying back franchised units and converting them to corporate units. Most large systems always have some sort of blend between franchised and corporate locations; some even have percentage targets for each. Different systems have contrasting philosophies on this issue. With increased redirection, there is a tacit admission that these locations are lucrative and should not have been franchised in the first place, although doing so may have been the only feasible way to expand.

Critics of franchising point to this movement as just another way that franchisees get hurt, namely that the franchisor takes the best locations. There is, however, a financial payoff for the franchisee. A good example of a large-scale redirection program is Supercuts, a chain offering value-priced hair care. Entire metropolitan areas with many franchisees were "redirected" by the franchisor, using stock as currency. It was called the "Stocks for Stores" program. Burger King is currently rumored to be looking at such a plan as well ("Burger King" 1998).

Another interesting development is called "chains within chains" (Bradach 1994; Tannenbaum 1996; Whittemore 1994). Essentially this involves large franchisees playing a much bigger role in their franchise system. Instead of many franchisees owning one or a few locations, these operators will own upwards of 25, even hundreds of, units. In some cases (e.g., Applebee's), the franchisee becomes larger than the franchisor. It also seems to bring the industry full circle back to a corporate model.

One of the stated advantages of franchising is increased motivation on the part of a franchisee who owns a single unit or, at most, several units and personally oversees them. In contrast, "chains within chains" have their own bureaucracies and corporate managers. As such, a franchisor that allows or encourages large-scale owners loses the benefit of added motivation by individual franchisees. Offsetting this loss for a franchisor, the financial advantages of franchising stay intact, and the franchisor deals with fewer, more sophisticated franchisees who have financial staying power and a track record.

CONCLUSION

The growth in franchising is likely to continue, with service businesses being the main applications. What probably will vary, because of sociocultural and techno-logical changes, is the way in which franchise systems are structured. What will not vary is franchising's relevance to services marketing. Franchising, because of its primary attributes, will still be an effective means of addressing some of the key challenges associated with the marketing of services.

Franchising has been part of the U.S. economy for more than 100 years. The early applications, shortly after the start of the 20th century, were in emerging product categories, namely goods such as automobiles and petroleum. The surge in growth since around 1960 has been fueled by other emerging products, primarily various types of services. During this same period, services have become dominant within the domestic economy; thus, it is reasonable to expect that the growth areas for the early 21st century will be other emerging services, some of which surely will be associated with electronic commerce. For the reasons discussed in this chapter, the marketing of these new services as well as more mature services can be enhanced by franchising.

REFERENCES

Alexander, Suzanne (1991), "More Working Mothers Opt for Flexibility of Operating a Franchise From Home," *The Wall Street Journal*, (January 31), B1, B2.

Allbery, John L. (1997), "Franchising: An Alternate Route to Market Expansion," *Retail Insights*, 6(2), 1-3.

Assael, Henry (1985), *Marketing Management: Strategy and Action.* Boston: Kent.

Behar, Richard (1998), "Why Subway Is 'The Biggest Problem in Franchising,' " *Fortune*, (March 16), 126-34.

Beresford, Lynn (1995), "Seeing Double," *Entrepreneur*, (October), 164-67.

Bradach, Jeff (1994), "Chains Within Chains: The Role of Multi-Unit Franchises," in *Proceedings of the Society of Franchising*, Skip Swerdlow, ed., Las Vegas, February 13-14.

"Burger King Adds to Menu Seven Items Under a Dollar" (1998), *The Wall Street Journal*, (March 17), B10.

Coalition of Service Industries Reports (1996), "The Service Economy," 10 (June), 1-20.

Cross, James (1998), "Improving the Relevance of Franchise Failure Studies," in *Proceedings of the Society of Franchising*, Francine Lafontaine, ed., Las Vegas, March 7-8.

———— and Bruce J. Walker (1987), "Service Marketing and Franchising: A Practical Business Marriage," *Business Horizons*, 30 (November-December), 10-20.

Dant, Rajiv P., Patrick J. Kaufmann, and Audesh K. Paswan (1992), "Ownership Redirection in Franchised Channels," *Journal of Public Policy and Marketing*, 11 (Spring), 33-44.

Garee, Michael L. and Thomas R. Schori (1998), "Modeling Can Help Predict Franchise 'Cannibalization,' " *Marketing News*, (November 23), 4.

Green, Heather (1999), "'Twas the Season for E-Splurging," *Business Week*, (January 18), 40, 42.

Harris, Nicole (1997), "Franchisees Get Feisty," *Business Week*, (February 24), 65-66.

"Inroads Into Franchises by Minorities Are Uneven" (1990), *The Wall Street Journal*, (October 8), B1.

International Expansion by U.S. Franchisors (1996). Washington, DC: International Franchise Association Educational Foundation.

Justis, Robert T. and Richard J. Judd (1998), *Franchising.* Houston: Dame.

Leonhardt, David (1998), "McDonald's: Can It Regain Its Golden Touch?" *Business Week*, (March 9), 70-77.

Love, Thomas (1998), "The Perfect Franchisee," *Nation's Business*, (April), 59-65.

Marsh, Barbara (1990), "Franchisees See Home as Place to Set Up Shop," *The Wall Street Journal*, (February 12), B1.

Mathewson, G. Frank and Ralph A. Winter (1985), "The Economics of Franchise Contracts," *Journal of Law and Economics*, 28 (October), 503-26.

Maynard, Roberta (1997), "The Decision to Franchise," *Nation's Business*, (January), 49-53.

McLean, Ernest C., III (1990), "Franchising as an Entry Strategy to the EEC," *The Journal of European Business* (January/February), 19-24.

Morse, Dan (1998), "Franchise Showcase to Close; Two Security Firms Debut," *The Wall Street Journal*, (June 23), B2.

Plave, Lee J. and Brooke Dombek (1998), "What You Should Know About Franchising and the Internet," *Franchising World*, (July/August), 27-32.

The Profile of Franchising (1998). Washington, DC: International Franchise Association Educational Foundation.

Scott, Nancy Rathbun (1998), "Co-Branding Synergizes Franchise Sales," *The Wall Street Journal*, (November 27), B8.

Selz, Michael (1992), "Many Ex-Executives Turn to Franchising, Often Find Frustration," *The Wall Street Journal*, (October 14), A1, A4.

Solomon, Gabrielle (1998), "Co-Branding Alliances: Arranged Marriages Made by Marketers," *Fortune*, (October 12), 188.

Tannenbaum, Jeffrey A. (1990), "Franchisers See a Future in East Bloc," *The Wall Street Journal*, (June 5), B1.

———— (1996), "Chicken and Burgers Create Hot New Class: Powerful Franchisees," *The Wall Street Journal*, (May 21), A1.

Whittemore, Meg (1990), "Expanding Opportunities for Minorities and Women," *Nation's Business*, (December), 58.

———— (1991), "An Inexact Science," *Nation's Business*, (February), 65.

———— (1993), "An Upbeat Forecast for Franchising," *Nation's Business*, (January), 50-55.

———— (1994), "Succeeding With Multiple Locations," *Nation's Business*, (October), 66-74.

Closing Observations

DAWN IACOBUCCI
TERESA A. SWARTZ

These chapters have demonstrated the diversity of perspectives that can be brought to bear on issues of services marketing and management. Our collective understanding of services will benefit from these variant points of view, because as the contributors have illustrated, and as any practitioner managing in a service sector can attest, services and their management are often quite complex systems—a translation of management strategic vision to frontline operational and tactical execution interfacing with customers and technology. Services marketing executives with whom we interact almost sheepishly complain, "It seems like it's harder to market and manage services than, say, consumer packaged goods!" Without undermining the importance of marketing in traditional contexts, we'd like to assure those execs: "It is!"

Books like these by academics usually close with a few words devoted to "future directions"; that is, a consideration of where our field of research might turn next. Ideas for future research can come from several sources: creative insight, deductions from current research, and dialogues and interactions with practitioners, one of the constituencies we purport to serve. We have had the good fortune of obtaining interviews with a couple of stellar marketing professionals—one in a law firm and one a consultant to the health care industry—who are dealing with issues of services marketing. We wanted to get a sense of the problems they face in their sectors.

OBSERVATIONS WITH MS. BARB SESSIONS, OF WINSTON AND STRAWN

Ms. Barb Sessions is Director of Business Development at Winston and Strawn, a superb law firm in Chicago. Her firm is progressive in accepting marketing as a beneficial arm in business. It probably helps that Ms. Sessions is also a lawyer, so that her colleagues cannot assert, "marketing won't work here; you don't understand what we do for a living."

The firm's business environment has become increasingly competitive (and where is this not true?), with the usual result that top management seeks strategies to develop competitive advantages in the eyes of customers. Given that marketing is focused on the customer, it is not long before professionals can see there exist sound strategies from the marketing tradition, and that marketing is not the "smoke and mirrors" that outside critics might envision.

One trend that Ms. Sessions sees clearly in her industry is that more and more, business clients seek law firms with demonstrable experience in their particular industry. Even though Winston and Strawn will clearly know the law better than its clients, it is apparently not convincing to simply claim, "we're a good law firm"; it is better to add, "and we know the intricacies of your business." Accordingly, clientele are being segmented on the basis of industry, and although large firms like Winston and Strawn can serve multiple industry segments, smaller competitors are forced to choose and specialize. Breadth and depth each have their advantages, of course, but the big, good firms like Winston and Strawn can offer both.

Another trend that Ms. Sessions points to as shaping the services that the firm can provide is technology. The form of technological challenges is different across different service sectors; the specific issue facing the law firm is the design of software that can provide integrating capabilities for nationwide cases. For example, in processing a national products liabilities case, knowledge by the left hand (Chicago office) of what the right hand (New York) is doing is invaluable to providing smooth, seamless service. The software is a component of technology that serves the frontline professional services providers, so that they may provide consistently high quality service at their multisite service operations (i.e., offices) to their business clients (somewhat like franchising). Although professional firms usually address service excellence by "hiring the best people," as does Winston and Strawn, the technology serves as a means to optimal service execution in each office and the continuity of service excellence integrated across offices. Furthermore, addressing these consistency and integration issues nationally is just a precursor of the firm's needs, given its increased global presence, as clients take on more multinational flavor.

OBSERVATIONS WITH MR. JOHN PRINCE OF ARTHUR ANDERSEN

Mr. John Prince is Senior Manager at Arthur Andersen, the world-renowned accounting consultancy. Mr. Prince focuses on the health care industry, which has its own challenges of integrating information technologies, specifically patient records and payments systems across physician offices, hospitals, pharmacies, home care providers, sports health care centers, other in- and outpatient facilities, insurance and payer companies, patient employer records, and so forth. Smoothing communications across the players in such broad and idiosyncratic networks will require a herculean effort, one that perhaps only Arthur Andersen, leveraging its tremendous information systems experiences, is positioned to provide.

The fierceness of the competition and cost-cutting measures in the health care industry has motivated an embrace of marketing concepts as a means of attracting and retaining customers (patients and payers). For example, Arthur Andersen advises that health care network managers begin to work with concepts like lifetime customer value, recognizing the opportunities of familiar providers like hospitals, in positive contexts like baby deliveries, as an entrée into its umbrella health care network system—families experience a happy service and keep that hospital and its network partners top-of-mind for subsequent health interventions. Similarly, a network that provides, say, wellness workshops achieves two goals: the initial consumption trial of potential new network patient-members as well as good public relations and heightened awareness in the surrounding community.

Even classic marketing ideas present new challenges to health care systems. For example, Arthur Andersen is helping its health care clients approach advertising in two ways: first, with regard to how to do it, given the relative inexperience of advertising in that industry; and second, with how exactly to finance the extraordinary new expenditures in the very presence of cost-containment measures.

Mr. Prince also speaks of the issues that must be addressed in the confluence of traditional marketing variables (e.g., channels) with contemporary issues (e.g., technology). Specifically, the Internet is providing a heretofore unseen opportunity for patients to obtain technical information about their health situation or that of a loved one. Occasionally, a patient may be better equipped with information than the busy and overburdened physician (e.g., "Hey, doc, what do you think about the findings from the experimental trials of this new drug that they've run in Australia?"), but perhaps more often, the patient either misunderstands the Web-posted information because of a lack of technical training or is misled by a Website that posts poor quality information (for whatever reasons).

Of great interest currently is the assessment of the effectiveness of advertising directly to patients (in traditional media or on the Internet), for example, the "pull" of ads and branding of pharmaceuticals (such as Prozac or Viagra) on behalf of the patient, in a patient-as-customer model, compared with the traditional "push" of the prescribing physician as the authoritative member of the channel. Pharmaceuticals manufacturers are appealing directly to the patients, bypassing the physicians, reducing the effective power of the latter as channel members.

Mr. Prince also had observations about how he and his colleagues have found their roles as consultants changing. He remarked particularly about the structuring of the working relations with their clients. Specifically, the involvement from within Arthur Andersen is expected to be more extensive, both in terms of fronting a multidisciplinary team to anticipate and be flexible in responding to whatever the client's needs might be, and with regard to the duration of the project, noting that a more integrated involvement between client and consultant throughout the process allows for clearer communication and the management of expectations on both sides.

CONCLUSIONS

One trend to which both of these practitioners pointed was that of integration, in one form or another. For all our acknowledgment of the importance of interdisciplinary views, we academics tend to operate functionally independently. Services marketers might be better than most, because we have long addressed, for service delivery compared with managing goods, the greater coordination requirements across marketing, human resources, and operations. We academics behave, and are expected to behave, as "experts," with depth but not necessarily breadth, so when broad perspectives are represented, they often appear, as in this *Handbook*, as depth within chapters and breadth across. Many of our contributors were successful in offering both, but presumably, we could do more to address this issue directly.

Technology was also a theme common to both practitioners' tales. Indeed, can we not predict with utter confidence that technological revolutions will only continue, probably at an ever-increasing pace? Again, the topic of technology, and the extent to which the human-machine interface can enhance or detract from the customer or frontline employee's experience, was key to several of the chapters in this *Handbook*, and at least considered peripherally in others. Perhaps we can aim to focus on the implications of technology for services more centrally in our future research.

We do not know the extent to which the statistics we cited in our introductory chapter are stable, but even if the services sectors continue to comprise "only" 67 to 80% of our economic figures, these numbers suggest the vast opportunities of the services manager armed with services marketing skills. The sky is the limit! Go forth and market your services!

Name Index

Subject Index

About the Editors

Dawn Iacobucci is Professor of Marketing at the Kellogg Graduate School of Management at Northwestern University. She joined Kellogg in 1987 upon receiving her Ph.D. in quantitative psychology from the University of Illinois in Urbana-Champaign. Her research interests include services marketing and customer satisfaction, nonprofits and social marketing, and the development of multivariate statistical analysis models for social network and dyadic interactions data. She has published in such journals as *Harvard Business Review*, *Journal of Consumer Psychology*, *Journal of Marketing*, *Journal of Marketing Research*, *Psychological Bulletin*, and *Psychometrika*. She was recently appointed editor of the *Journal of Consumer Psychology*. She teaches services marketing and marketing research to MBA students and multivariate statistics to doctoral students at Kellogg.

Teresa A. Swartz is Professor of Marketing at California Polytechnic State University in San Luis Obispo, California. Prior to joining the faculty at Cal Poly, she was on the faculty of Arizona State University for 11 years, where she was actively involved with The First Interstate Center for Services Marketing (now The Center for Services Marketing and Management). In addition, she has twice served on the International Board of Directors of the American Marketing Association and was Vice President of the Services Marketing Division. Her international experience includes teaching in Lesotho, Southern Africa, and Toulouse, France, as well as serving as a marketing consultant and expert on services marketing for the Private Services Development Project in the Hashemite Kingdom of Jordan. Her research interests focus on various behavioral issues related to the services sector, including a special emphasis on professional services, identifying ways service principles and concepts can be applied in the public sector, and understanding various factors that influence the customer's evaluation of the service experience. She has published numerous articles, and her work has appeared in a number of outlets, including the *Journal of Marketing*, *Journal of the Academy of Marketing Science*, *Journal of Advertising*, and *Journal of Advertising Research*. In addition, she was guest editor of a special issue of the *Journal of Marketing Education* devoted to services. She was also the lead editor of the annual research volume *Advances in Services Marketing and Management*. Currently, she is a member of the editorial board of the *Journal of Service Research*. She earned her Ph.D. in Business at The Ohio State University.

About the Contributors

Eugene W. Anderson is Associate Professor of Marketing at the University of Michigan Business School. He holds a Ph.D. from the University of Chicago's Graduate School of Business. His research focuses on how individuals evaluate past consumption experience, the behavioral consequences of such evaluations, and the economic and strategic consequences for the firm. His publications have appeared in a variety of outlets, including the *Journal of Consumer Research*, the *Journal of Marketing*, *Marketing Science*, *Marketing Letters*, and *Management Science*. He is a past winner of the American Marketing Association's Best Services Article Award. He is a member of the review boards of the *Journal of Marketing Research* and the *Journal of Service Research*. He sometimes wonders whether anyone actually reads these bios.

James G. Barnes is Professor of Marketing and former Dean of Business Administration at Memorial University of Newfoundland. He holds a Ph.D. from the University of Toronto. He has presented more than 50 papers at national and international conferences and has more than 30 papers in refereed journals, including the *Journal of Consumer Research*, the *Journal of Advertising Research*, the *Services Industries Journal*, and *Psychology and Marketing*. He serves on the Editorial Review Boards of the *Journal of International Bank Marketing* and the *International Journal of Customer Relationship Management*. He has published six books, including *Fundamentals of Marketing*, now in its eighth edition, and *Understanding Services Management*. He regularly delivers management seminars in Canada, Europe, and Australia. His research focuses on services marketing, service quality, and customer relationships. He is also Executive Chairman of The Bristol Group, an integrated marketing communications and information consultancy in Canada.

John E. G. Bateson is a Senior Vice President with Gemini Consulting, which he joined as an officer in 1989. He is global head of the consumer, retail, and distribution practice. He holds a BSc from Imperial College of Science and Technology, an MBA from the London Business School, and a doctorate in business administration from the Harvard Business School. Prior to joining

Gemini, he spent 10 years as a Professor of Marketing at London Business School and Stanford's business school and was a brand manager at Lever Brothers and a marketing manager at Phillips. He has written and consulted extensively in the areas of marketing, channels of distribution, service business, and retailing. He is the author of numerous articles and three books: *Managing Services and Marketing*, *Principles of Services Marketing*, and *Marketing Urban Mass Transportation*. He has given numerous keynote speeches on the emergence of the service economy.

Mary Jo Bitner is the AT&T Professor of Services Marketing and Management at Arizona State University and Research Director of the Center for Services Marketing and Management. She is faculty coordinator for the MBA Services Marketing and Management Concentration. With Valarie Zeithaml, she wrote *Services Marketing* (1996; 2nd ed. forthcoming), a leading text used around the world. She has consulted with numerous businesses on service quality and customer satisfaction and is a frequent presenter on these topics at conferences and executive education programs. Her research focuses on how customers evaluate service encounters and the role of self-service technologies and front-line employee behaviors in determining customer satisfaction with services. Her research has been published in leading marketing journals, including the *Journal of Marketing*, *Journal of the Academy of Marketing Science*, *Journal of Retailing*, and *International Journal of Service Industry Management*. She served as special issue editor of two volumes of the *Journal of Retailing* focusing on service excellence in 1997.

David E. Bowen is Professor of Management, World Business Department, at Thunderbird, the American Graduate School of International Management. He was previously on the faculty of Arizona State University West and the University of Southern California. He received his Ph.D. in business administration from Michigan State University in 1983. His research, teaching, and consulting interests focus on the organizational dynamics of delivering service quality and the effectiveness of human resources management departments. His articles have appeared in *Academy of Management Review*, *Academy of Management Journal*, *Sloan Management Review*, *Journal of Applied Psychology*, *Organizational Science*, *Organizational Dynamics*, and *Human Resource Management*. He coedited the *Academy of Management Review*'s 1994 special issue on total quality management. He has published six books on services management, including *Winning the Service Game* (with Ben Schneider).

Stephen W. Brown, who holds the endowed Edward M. Carson Chair in Services Marketing, is Professor of Marketing and the Director of the Center for Services Marketing and Management at Arizona State University in Tempe. His current work focuses on service loyalty and on manufacturers marketing services and recovering from service failures. He is coauthor of more than 100 articles and 15 books, and coeditor of the annual volume *Advances in Services Marketing and Management*. He is cofounder of the biennial International Quality in Services (QUIS) Conference series, cochairing the 1988, 1994, 1996 and 1998 events in

Sweden and the United States. He is a past winner of the American Marketing Association's annual Career Contributions Award in Services Marketing. An adviser, researcher, and board member of several firms and organizations, he is also a past president of the American Marketing Association.

Richard B. Chase is Justin B. Dart Professor of Operations Management at the Marshall School of Business, University of Southern California. He received his B.S., MBA, and Ph.D., all in operations management, from UCLA. His research focuses on service design and service quality. Recent publications include articles in *Journal of Service Research* (with S. Kimes), *Journal of Operations Management* (with A. Soteriou), and *Production and Operations Management Journal* (with D. Stewart). He is coauthor of *Operations Management: Manufacturing and Services* (8th ed.) and *Fundamentals of Operations Management* (3rd ed.). He is on the editorial boards of a number of journals, including the *Journal of Service Research*. He was listed as one of the leading contributors to the field of services marketing in a *Journal of Retailing* survey and as one of the major contributors in the history of operations management in an *International Journal of Operations Management* survey. His money-back teaching guarantee for his course in service operations management was widely reported in the business press.

James Cross is an Associate Professor of Marketing at the University of Nevada, Las Vegas. He formerly served as department chair and MBA Director at UNLV. He received his Ph.D. from the University of Minnesota and has been on the faculties of Arizona State University and the University of Minnesota. His research interests lie in the area of channels of distribution, including franchising. He has published in outlets such as the *Transportation Journal*, the *Journal of Public Policy and Marketing*, *Business Horizons*, and the *Society of Franchising Proceedings*.

Pratibha A. Dabholkar (Ph.D., Georgia State University, 1991) is Associate Professor and Director of the Marketing Ph.D. program at the University of Tennessee. Her research interests include technology in service delivery; attitude, choice, and means-end models; service quality and customer satisfaction; and business-to-business relationships. Her teaching interests center on services marketing, consumer behavior, and marketing research. Her research has appeared in numerous leading business and marketing publications and national conference proceedings. She is a member of the Editorial Review Boards for the *Journal of the Academy of Marketing Science* and the *Journal of Marketing* as well as Vice President, Membership—U.S.A. for the Academy of Marketing Science and that organization's past Vice President, Academic Affairs. She has received awards for several of her papers as well as her dissertation, and she is the recipient of the 1997–1999 Alma and Hal Reagan College Scholar Award at the University of Tennessee in recognition of an outstanding contribution to the scholarly climate of the college.

Ko de Ruyter is currently Associate Professor of Marketing and Marketing Research at Maastricht University, the Netherlands, and director of the Maastricht

Academic Center for research in Services (MAXX). He has been a visiting professor at Purdue University. He holds master's degrees from the Free University Amsterdam and the University of Amsterdam. He received his Ph.D. in management science from the University of Twente. He has published five books and more than 130 refereed articles in such publications as the *Journal of Economic Psychology*, *International Journal of Research in Marketing*, *International Journal of Service Industry Management*, *Journal of Business Research*, *European Journal of Marketing*, *Information*, and *Management and Accounting, Organisations and Society*. His research interests concern international service management, call centers, relationship marketing, and customer satisfaction and dissatisfaction.

John Deighton is Professor of Business Administration at the Harvard Business School. He heads the Fall first-year marketing course in the MBA program, teaches a second-year elective course titled Interactive Marketing, and teaches a number of the school's executive courses related to marketing, information technology, and service management. His current research investigates the impact of the World Wide Web on the practice of marketing and the management of customer relationships in information-intensive environments. His research has been published in the *Journal of Consumer Research*, the *Journal of Marketing*, the *Journal of Market Research*, and the *Harvard Business Review*. He is Co-Editor of the *Journal of Interactive Marketing*. His Ph.D. is in marketing from the Wharton School, University of Pennsylvania. Prior to joining Harvard in 1994, he was on the faculties of the University of Chicago and Dartmouth College.

Laurette Dubé is an Associate Professor of Marketing at the Faculty of Management, McGill University, Montreal, Canada. She received her Ph.D. from Cornell University. Her work focuses on diverse aspects of consumer behavior in the specific context of services, namely consumption emotions, reactions to waiting and to service environments in general, and satisfaction and loyalty. She is interested in the link between such consumer responses and strategic and operation management practices. She has published more than 30 research articles in top academic journals including *Journal of Consumer Research*, *Journal of Marketing Research*, *Journal of Personality and Social Psychology*, *Marketing Letters*, *Psychology & Marketing*, and *Operations and Production and Operation Management*. She teaches services marketing and management from a multidisciplinary perspective at the undergraduate, MBA, and Ph.D. levels.

Peter A. Dunne is a student in the MBA program at Memorial University of Newfoundland. He holds an Honours Bachelor of Science degree in psychology from Memorial University. He has worked for several years in management positions with a large Canadian bank. His research interests lie generally in services marketing, with a particular emphasis on the impact of technology on customers' perception of service quality.

Pierre Eiglier (Ph.D. in economics, Aix en Provence, 1970) is Professor at the Université de Droit, d'Economie et des Sciences d'Aix-Marseille at the Institut d'Administration des Entreprises, where he was Dean from 1977 to 1981. He was research fellow at Northwestern University in 1972. He has published and taught in the field of the marketing of service businesses and served as a consultant in that area. With Eric Langeard, he cofounded a postgraduate program titled Management of Service Activities. His book *Services Strategy* was scheduled for publication at the end of 1999.

Raymond P. Fisk is Professor and Chair of the Department of Marketing at the University of New Orleans. He earned his B.S., MBA, and Ph.D. from Arizona State University. Previously, he served as Interim Chair and Associate Professor, Department of Marketing, University of Central Florida and Interim Head and Associate Professor, Department of Marketing, Oklahoma State University. He was a Fulbright Scholar in Austria and has taught courses in Ireland, Finland, Portugal, and Sweden. His research interests are in the history, metaphors, and technology of services. He has published in the *Journal of Marketing, Journal of Retailing, Journal of the Academy of Marketing Science, European Journal of Marketing, Service Industries Journal, International Journal of Service Industry Management, Journal of Health Care Marketing, Journal of Professional Services Marketing, Journal of Marketing Education*, and *Marketing Education Review*.

Claes Fornell is the Donald C. Cook Professor of Business Administration at the University of Michigan Business School and the Director of the National Quality Research Center. He received his Ph.D. in economics from the University of Lund in Sweden. As a doctoral student, he was also a Fulbright Fellow at the University of California, Berkeley. His research centers on the relationships among the quality of economic output, customer satisfaction, and financial results. He has written more than 50 published articles and two books. He has served on the editorial board of all the major journals in the field. He is currently engaged in developing a worldwide network of national customer satisfaction indices.

Gordon Fullerton is a Ph.D. candidate in marketing at the Queen's Business School in Kingston, Ontario. He holds a B.Comm. from Mount Allison University and an MBA from Dalhousie University. His research is in the area of service relationships. He has presented his work at a number of scholarly conferences including those held by the Administrative Sciences Association of Canada and the American Marketing Association.

Rashi Glazer is Professor at the Walter A. Haas School of Business, University of California, Berkeley; Co-Director of the Berkeley Center for Marketing and Technology; and Director of the Berkeley Portfolio of Marketing Management Executive Education Programs. He has an MBA (1979) and a Ph.D. (1982) from Stanford University's Graduate School of Business. His teaching and research interests are in the areas of competitive marketing strategy, technology and information-technology strategy, interactive and database marketing, and consumer and managerial decision making. He is the Co-Editor of the new *Journal of Interactive Marketing* (formerly *Journal of Direct Marketing*) and an Associate

Editor of *Management Science*. His articles have appeared in leading publications, and he is the coauthor of three books, *The Marketing Information Revolution*, *Readings on Market-Driving Strategies*, and *Cable TV Advertising*. He is the developer of the INFOVALUE program for measuring the value of a firm's information and SUITS, an interactive computer simulation teaching strategy regarding use of information and information technology.

William J. Glynn is a lecturer in services marketing at the University College Dublin Graduate School of Business. He holds B.Comm., MBS, and Ph.D. degrees from University College Dublin and is a member of the Marketing Institute of Ireland. He was appointed as Director of the B.Comm. (International) Degree (1992-1995) and as the first Director of the University College Dublin Centre for Quality & Services Management in 1994. His previous employment includes work at Dublin City University, Groupe ESSEC (France), Swedish Match, and Abbott Laboratories. He has published services marketing articles in France, Ireland, Italy, the United Kingdom, and the United States. He is the coeditor of *Understanding Services Management* (1995). He is a member of the editorial board of the *International Journal of Service Industry Management* and of the steering committee of the *Prometeo* technical-scientific series (Italy). He has given invited presentations on services marketing at the Academy of Consumer Research—Europe, the American Marketing Association Special Interest Group in Services Marketing, the FAS/EURES conference, the Universities Personnel Association, and the Portuguese Professional Marketing Congress.

Kent Grayson is Assistant Professor of Marketing at the London Business School. His research focuses on two areas. The first centers on issues of truth and deception in consumer behavior, including a focus on symbols and representation. His second research interest is network marketing organizations, which are sometimes called pyramid selling organizations or multilevel marketing organizations. His articles have appeared in the *Journal of Consumer Research*, the *Journal of Marketing Research*, and the *International Journal of Research in Marketing*.

Christian Grönroos, Dr. Econ., is Professor of service and relationship marketing and chairman of the board of the Center for Relationship Marketing and Service Management, a research and knowledge center at Hanken Swedish School of Economics, Finland. His research interests include service marketing and management, service quality, and relationship marketing in both consumer and business-to-business environments. His book *Service Management and Marketing* (1990) has been published in eight languages. His work has appeared in the *Journal of Business Research, Journal of the Academy of Marketing Science, Journal of Marketing Management, European Journal of Marketing, International Journal of Service Industry Management, Journal of Business & Industrial Marketing, Journal of Service Marketing, Integrated Marketing Communications Research Journal*, and *Australasian Journal of Marketing*.

Stephen J. Grove is Professor of Marketing at Clemson University. He earned his B.A. and M.A. at Texas Christian University and his Ph.D. from Oklahoma State University, all in sociology. In addition, he spent 2 years in postdoctorate education in marketing at Oklahoma State University. Previously, he taught on the faculties of the University of Mississippi and Missouri Southern State College. His research interests include impression management in service settings, the application of metaphors in marketing, and environmental marketing issues. His research has appeared in the *Journal of Retailing*, *Journal of Advertising*, *Journal of the Academy of Marketing Science*, *Journal of Public Policy and Marketing*, *Journal of Macromarketing*, *Journal of Health Care Marketing*, *Journal of Business Research*, *Journal of Personal Selling and Sales Management*, *European Journal of Marketing*, *Journal of Services Marketing*, *Services Industries Journal*, and several other academic journals.

Barbara Gutek (Ph.D., University of Michigan, 1975) is McClelland Professor of Management and Policy at the University of Arizona. She is the author or editor of 10 books and more than 80 articles, including *The Dynamics of Service* (1995), *Women's Career Development* (1987, with Laurie Larwood), *Sex and the Workplace* (1985), and *Women and Work: A Psychological Perspective* (1981, with Veronica Nieva). She was President of the Society for the Psychological Study of Social Issues in 1997-1998 and served on the Board of Governors of the Academy of Management from 1995 to 1998. She has been on the editorial boards of numerous journals, including *Academy of Management Journal* and *Journal of Personality and Social Psychology*. In 1994, she received two awards from the APA. Her research currently focuses on two areas: the changing nature of service delivery and the efficacy of the reasonable woman standard in hostile environment cases of sexual harassment.

Roger Hallowell is Assistant Professor at Harvard Business School, where he teaches the second-year elective course "Service Management." His research examines strategy for service firms, focusing on companies with dual competitive advantage (firms delivering cost leadership and differentiated service). He also studies service firms growing through numerous small acquisitions ("consolidations"). His recent work has appeared in *Human Resource Management*, *Human Resource Planning*, and *The International Journal of Service Industry Management*. He earned an AB from Harvard College and an MBA and DBA from Harvard Business School. He has worked on Wall Street and for small businesses in the service sector.

Christopher Hart (Ph.D., Cornell University) is an adjunct professor on the executive-education faculty at the University of Michigan Business School and is president of Spire Group, a management consulting and executive-education firm based in Brookline, Massachusetts, that specializes in helping clients strengthen and expand customer relationships. Previously, he was a professor in the marketing department at Cornell and in the operations management department at Harvard Business School. He is a prolific author, having written six books, including the definitive *Extraordinary Guarantees: A New Way to Build Quality Throughout Your Company and Ensure Satisfaction for Your Customers* and *Service Breakthroughs: Changing the Rules of the Game* (with James Heskett and W. Earl Sasser, Jr.). In addition, he has written more than 40 articles for academic, management, and popular publications, and he won a McKinsey ("Article of the Year") Award for his Harvard Business Review article, "The Power of Unconditional Service Guarantees." He served for 3 years as an examiner for the Malcolm Baldrige National Quality Award.

Ray M. Haynes holds a Ph.D. in supply chain management (Arizona State University, 1988), an M.S. in systems engineering (RCA Institute, 1971), an MBA in marketing (University of Arizona, 1970), and a B.S. in aerospace engineering (University of Arizona, 1967). He is currently Professor of Management at California Polytechnic State University in San Luis Obispo. His 10 years of teaching include courses in services, operations, quality, management of technology, and engineering management. He is the author of more than 100 papers dealing primarily with quality and productivity in service management areas. He has 20 years of experience in industry at such companies as RCA, Allied-Signal, Citicorp, and TRW in engineering management and business development areas, primarily focused in service sector applications such as systems integration, banking, and retail stores. He is an active consultant with high-technology clients such as Hewlett Packard, TRW, the U.S. Navy, and IBM.

Joby John is Professor and Chair of Marketing at Bentley College. He earned his B.S. from Birla Institute of Technology and Science, India; MBA from Madras University, India; and Ph.D. from Oklahoma State University, Stillwater. He is a former marketing officer at Pfizer (India) and ITC, the BAT subsidiary in India. He has taught or guest lectured in several countries, including Australia, Chile, Colombia, Estonia, Finland, India, Spain, and Sweden. His primary teaching, research, and consulting are in the areas of services marketing and cross-cultural issues. He has published in the *European Journal of Marketing, International Marketing Review, Psychological Reports, Journal of Health Care Marketing*, and several other journals. He serves on the Editorial Review Board of the *International Journal of Service Industries Management*. He has conducted executive management workshops on topics such as service quality, customer service, customer equity, and brand loyalty.

Devon S. Johnson is Assistant Professor of Marketing at Goizueta Business School, Emory University. He holds a Ph.D. in marketing from the London Business School (1998). His research interests are consumer-level relationship marketing, customer dissatisfaction, service recovery, and marketing strategy.

Timothy L. Keiningham is Senior Vice President of Marketing Metrics Inc., a marketing consulting and customer retention firm based in Paramus, New Jersey. He is the author of two books, *Return on Quality: Measuring the Financial Impact of Your Company's Quest for Quality* and *Service Marketing* (both books coauthored by Roland T. Rust and Anthony J. Zahorik). In addition, he has written numerous articles for academic, management, and popular publications. He received the Alpha Kappa Psi Foundation Award (with Rust and Zahorik) for the *Journal of Marketing* article "Return on Quality: Making Service Quality Financially Accountable," judged by the editorial review board as representing the most significant contribution to the advancement of the practice of marketing. He also serves on the Editorial Review Board of the *Journal of Service Research*. He received his MBA from Vanderbilt University and his B.A. from Kentucky Wesleyan College.

Sandra S. Kim is a doctoral student in industrial/organizational psychology at the University of Maryland at College Park. She received her B.A. in psychology from the University of California, Berkeley. Her research interests include strategic human resource management, organizational change and innovation, and managing diversity.

Susan Schultz Kleine (Ph.D., University of Cincinnati) is Assistant Professor of Marketing at Bowling Green State University. Her research interests include the role of emotions and symbolic use of goods and services in consumer socialization. She has published articles in the *Journal of Consumer Research* and the *Journal of Consumer Psychology* as well as other consumer research publications.

Paul J. Kraus is a researcher, lecturer, and doctoral candidate in marketing at the J. L. Kellogg School of Management at Northwestern University. Prior to pursuing his graduate work, he was a research analyst and consultant with Mercer Management Consulting, where he assisted *Fortune* 500 clients in the design and implementation of effective market strategies and processes, both domestically and abroad. He holds a master's degree in marketing from Kellogg and a bachelor's degree in economics from Yale University. His research interests focus on the pricing and positioning of new products and services.

Eric Langeard was a faculty member of the business school at the Institut d'Administration des Entreprises at the University of Aix-Marseilles and former president of the European Academy of Marketing. He served as visiting professor at the University of Texas at Austin; the University of California, Berkeley; the University of Michigan; and several European universities. He organized, with Pierre Eiglier, the International Research Seminar in Service Management, held every 2 years. His extensive research encompassed services marketing, particularly the marketing problems of international and domestic service networks, including restaurants, banks, hotels, insurance companies, and hospital management organizations. He was a consultant to several multinational service companies and Marketing Vice President at CPR, a French corporate bank. He was the coauthor, with Pierre Eiglier, of *SERVUCTION, Le marketing des Services*. He died suddenly in November 1998.

Jos Lemmink is Professor of Marketing and Chairman of the Department of Marketing and Market Research, Faculty of Economics and Business Administration, Maastricht University. He was a Visiting Professor at the University of Southern Queensland, Australia, and at Limburg University Center, Belgium. He has published several books and articles in international journals on topics including service marketing and management, satisfaction, and quality management. His work has been published in the *International Journal of Research in Marketing*, *European Journal of Marketing*, and *Journal of Economic Psychology*, among other journals. In 1995, he received the Hans B. Thorelli Best Paper Award from the *European Journal of Marketing*.

Christopher Lovelock is principal of Lovelock Associates. Specializing in the management of services, he gives seminars and workshops around the world. His past academic career includes 11 years on the faculty of the Harvard Business School, 2 years as a visiting professor at the International Institute for Management Development (IMD) in Switzerland, and short-term appointments at Berkeley, Stanford, MIT, Theseus Institute, INSEAD, and the University of Queensland. He is the author of 60 articles, more than 100 teaching cases, and 25 books, most recently *Principles of Service Marketing and Management*, coauthored with Lauren Wright (Prentice Hall, 1999). He is a recipient of the *Journal of Marketing*'s Alpha Kappa Psi Award, the American Marketing Association's Award for Career Contributions to the Services Discipline, and many awards for outstanding cases. He holds M.A. and BCom degrees from the University of Edinburgh, an MBA from Harvard, and a Ph.D. from Stanford.

Richard L. Oliver is the Valere Blair Potter Professor of Management at the Owen Graduate School of Management, Vanderbilt University. He researches consumer psychology with a special focus on customer satisfaction and postpurchase processes. He holds the position of Fellow of the American Psychological Association for his extensive writings on the psychology of the satisfaction response. He has authored *Satisfaction: A Behavioral Perspective on the Consumer* and coedited *Service Quality: New Directions in Theory and Practice*. His articles have appeared in numerous journals, including the *Journal of Consumer Research*, *Journal of Marketing Research*, *Journal of Marketing*, *Journal of Applied Psychology*, *Psychology & Marketing*, *Journal of Consumer Satisfaction/Dissatisfaction & Complaining Behavior*, *Behavioral Science*, *Journal of Economic Psychology*, *Applied Psychological Measurement*, *Psychometrika*, and *Organizational Behavior and Human Decision Processes*.

Amy L. Ostrom is Assistant Professor of Marketing at Arizona State University. She received her Ph.D. from Northwestern University in 1996. Her research focuses on issues related to services marketing, including customers' evaluation of services, service guarantees, customers' role in creating service outcomes, and customers' adoption and evaluation of self-service technologies. Her work has appeared in several journals, including the *Journal of Marketing* and the *Journal* *of Consumer Psychology*, as well as in the Advances in Services Marketing and Management series.

Paul G. Patterson, Ph.D., is Associate Professor in the School of Marketing at The University of New South Wales, Sydney, Australia, as well as Director of the Centre for Applied Marketing. He holds marketing, economics, and management degrees from the University of Wollongong, the University of Technology—Sydney, and The University of New South Wales. Prior to joining the teaching profession, he held management and marketing positions in the banking, telecommunications, marketing research, and public sectors, and later with an international management consultancy firm. He has taught at the universities of Wollongong and Sydney in Australia, Michigan State University in the United States, and more recently Assumption University (ABAC) Graduate School and Thammasat Universities in Thailand. His current research and consulting interests include modeling customer satisfaction and service quality, services marketing especially in a business-to-business environment, relationship marketing, complaining behavior, and the internationalization of service firms. His research has appeared in numerous leading marketing journals, and he is the author of Services Marketing in Australia and New Zealand, a book of text, readings, and cases.

Sonja Radas is Assistant Professor of Marketing at the Olin School of Business, Washington University in St. Louis. She holds a Ph.D. in business administration (marketing) and a Ph.D. in mathematics, both from the University of Florida. Her research interests include services marketing, entertainment marketing, and new product development, in particular timing new product introductions.

Amy Risch Rodie (Ph.D., Arizona State University), formerly Amy R. Hubbert, is Assistant Professor of Marketing at the University of Nebraska at Omaha. Her research interests include customer participation, attributions, and satisfaction in complex service contexts and during the process of service delivery. She has published articles about the customer's perspective in the *International Journal of Service Industry Management*. She teaches consumer behavior, principles of marketing, and marketing management, and she has developed and taught courses on services marketing at both the undergraduate and MBA levels. She frequently presents services marketing workshops for executive education programs.

Roland T. Rust is the Madison S. Wigginton Professor of Management and Director of the Center for Services Marketing at Vanderbilt University. He has published more than 60 refereed journal articles and five books in the areas of service marketing, advertising media, and marketing research methodology and has received best article awards for articles in *Marketing Science*, the *Journal of Marketing*, *Journal of Advertising*, and *Journal of Retailing*. He has received career achievement awards from the American Statistical Association and the American Academy of Advertising, as well as the Henry Latane Distinguished Doctoral Alumnus award from the University of North Carolina at Chapel Hill.

Leonard A. Schlesinger was recently named Senior Vice President, Counselor to the President, and Professor of Sociology and Public Policy at Brown University. Until October 1998, he was the George F. Baker, Jr., Professor of Business Administration at the Harvard Business School; he has been a member of the Harvard Business School faculty from 1978 to 1985 and since 1988. He received his bachelor's degree from Brown University, his master's degree from Columbia University, and a doctorate from the Harvard Business School. He has taught in both MBA and executive programs in the areas of service management, general management, and organizational behavior and human resources management. His research and consulting have focused broadly on the areas of service management and organizational change. Over the past decade, he has lectured and consulted around the world with service and industrial firms as well as governments and international leadership organizations.

Benjamin Schneider is Professor of Psychology and Chair of the Industrial and Organizational Psychology Program at the University of Maryland. He has also taught at Michigan State University and Yale University as well as, for shorter periods of time, at Bar-Ilan University (Israel, on a Fulbright award), the University of Aix-Marseille (France), and Peking University. He holds a Ph.D. in psychology (University of Maryland, 1967) and an MBA (City University of New York, 1964). His academic accomplishments include more than 85 journal articles and book chapters, six books, and appointment to the editorial review boards of the *Journal of Applied Psychology* and other journals. His interests concern service quality, organizational climate and culture, staffing issues, and person-organization fit. Professional recognition for his accomplishments includes election as President of the Organizational Behavior Division of the Academy of Management and of the Society for Industrial and Organizational Psychology. In addition to his academic work, he is Vice President of Organizational and Personnel Research, Inc.

Stowe Shoemaker is Assistant Professor of Marketing in the William F. Harrah College of Hotel Administration at the University of Nevada, Las Vegas. He holds a Ph.D. from Cornell University in the School of Hotel Administration and an M.S. from the University of Massachusetts. His research interests include the antecedents and consequences of customer loyalty, loyalty programs, the psychology of gamblers, pricing, and alternative payment methods. His research has appeared in the *Journal of Travel Research, Cornell Hotel and Restaurant Administrative Quarterly, International Journal of Hospitality Management*, and other publications. He is a regular speaker at the Frequent Travel Marketing Association, an organization of high-level representatives of major hotel companies, rental car companies, and airline companies. He teaches a course on loyalty marketing at Cornell University's Professional Development Program in the School of Hotel Administration.

Steven M. Shugan, the Russell Berrie Foundation Eminent Scholar and Professor of Marketing at the University of Florida Warrington School of Business, received his Ph.D. in managerial economics and decision sciences from Northwestern University. He has taught at the University of Rochester, the University of Chicago, and the University of Florida. He serves on the editorial boards of the *Journal of Marketing Research*, *Journal of Marketing*, *Journal of Services Research*, and *Marketing Science*, and he has consulted for numerous companies in the business service and health care sectors as well as the U.S. Postal Service and the government of Cyprus. He enjoys scuba diving and playing on the Internet.

David Shulman is Assistant Professor of Anthropology and Sociology at Lafayette College. His areas of research are organizations/occupations, research methodology, and deviance, with a specific focus on studying deception and impression management in everyday organizational activity. His articles have appeared in the *Journal of Contemporary Ethnography* and *Sosiologi Idag*. He is currently working on a book-length manuscript titled *Clothing Naked Emperors: Deception and Occupational Culture* that analyzes the ubiquity of deceptive behaviors in the workplace.

Nancy Stephens is Associate Professor of Marketing at Arizona State University. Her research interests center on buyer behavior, marketing promotion, and marketing to senior citizens. Her research has appeared in such publications as the *Journal of the Academy of Marketing Science*, *Journal of Advertising*, *Journal of Advertising Research*, and *Journal of Marketing Research*, as well as numerous conference proceedings. She serves as the Program Director of the Services Marketing and Management Institute held annually at Arizona State University. She received her Ph.D. from the University of Texas at Austin and her M.S. and B.S. (with Honors) from the University of Illinois at Urbana.

Stephen S. Tax is Associate Professor of Marketing at the University of Victoria in Canada. He received his Ph.D. in marketing from Arizona State University. His research interests center on interdisciplinary issues in services management, notably service recovery, marketing communication, and service design. This research has generated publications in the *Journal of Marketing*, *Journal of Retailing*, *Sloan Management Review*, *International Journal of Service Industry Management*, and several other academic and managerial journals. He is highly involved in the Services Marketing Special Interest Group (SERVSIG) of the American Marketing Association (AMA). He has served on the advisory board, co-organized a preconference session for the 1996 AMA Summer Educator's Conference, was cochair of the services marketing track of the 1998 AMA Summer Educator's Conference, and was chair of the theory and management track of the 1999 SERVSIG conference.

Shirley Taylor is Associate Professor at the Queen's School of Business in Kingston, Ontario. Her research is primarily in the area of services marketing, with a special emphasis on managing the wait experience. She has published in numerous marketing journals, including the *Journal of Marketing*, *Journal of the*

Academy of Marketing Science, International Journal of Research in Marketing, and *Journal of Public Policy and Marketing*.

Janet Wagner is Associate Professor at the Robert H. Smith School of Business, the University of Maryland. She holds a B.S. and M.S. from Cornell University and a Ph.D. from Kansas State University. Her areas of research interest include retail buyer decision making, retailer-vendor relationships (including service retailers), and aesthetic aspects of consumer decision making. Her professional experience includes retail buying with Federated Department Stores, and her consulting experience includes work with retailers, retail trade associations, and service firms. She has served on the editorial board of the *Journal of Consumer Research* and is currently on the editorial board of the *Journal of Retailing*. Her research has been published in the *Journal of Marketing Research*, *Journal of Consumer Research*, and *Journal of Retailing*.

Bruce J. Walker is Professor of Marketing and Dean at the College of Business at the University of Missouri—Columbia. Previously, he was Professor of Marketing and Department Chair at Arizona State University. He received his undergraduate degree from Seattle University and his master's and doctorate from the University of Colorado. His research, focusing on franchising, marketing channels, and survey methods, has been published in the *Journal of Marketing*, *Business Horizons*, and other academic and trade journals. Walker is the coauthor of *Marketing*, a textbook used at universities around the world. He is a member of the Board of Trustees for the International Franchise Association's Educational Foundation and the Board of Advisors for the Center for Services Marketing and Management at Arizona State University. He has been active in both the American Marketing Association, as Vice President, and the Western Marketing Educators Association, as President.

Tony Ward is a Senior Lecturer in Marketing and Strategic Management in the Faculty of Business and Law at Central Queensland University, where his main interests are teaching and researching in relationship and services marketing, as well as the supervision of higher degree candidates. He holds a BTech (honors) from Loughborough and a Ph.D. (Marketing) from Queensland University of Technology, AFAMI, EAMA. He teaches primarily marketing of service products, marketing management, and international marketing. He heads a large research group, Human Interactions in Marketing, that is studying both consumer relationship marketing and business-to-business networking. He has published worldwide in relationship marketing and frequently delivers research seminars in Europe and North America. He was employed for 23 years in the aerospace industry in Europe before emigrating to Australia to become an academic.

Martin Wetzels is Assistant Professor with the Department of Marketing and Marketing Research in the Faculty of Economics and Business Administration, Maastricht University, and Secretary and Senior Research Fellow of the Maastricht Academic Center of Research in Services. His primary research interests are service quality, customer satisfaction/dissatisfaction, customer value, quality management in service organizations, services marketing, marketing research, cross-functional cooperation, and relationship marketing. His work has been published in numerous leading research journals, and he has contributed more than 30 papers to conference proceedings.

Anthony J. Zahorik is a vice president of ACNielsen Burke Institute and is coauthor of *Return on Quality: Measuring the Financial Impact of Your Company's Quest for Quality* and *Service Marketing*. He is also a coauthor of numerous articles on customer satisfaction and service quality. Recognition for this work includes an award for the best article in the *Journal of Retailing* and the Alpha Kappa Sigma award for an article in the *Journal of Marketing*.

Printed in the United Kingdom
by Lightning Source UK Ltd.
106641UKS00001B/5-12

9 780761 916123